Lecture Notes of the Institute for Computer Sciences, Social Informatics and Telecommunications Engineering 387

More information about this series at http://www.springer.com/series/8197

Weina Fu · Yuan Xu · Shui-Hua Wang ·
Yudong Zhang (Eds.)

Multimedia Technology and Enhanced Learning

Third EAI International Conference, ICMTEL 2021
Virtual Event, April 8–9, 2021
Proceedings, Part I

 Springer

Editors
Weina Fu 🆔
Hunan Normal University
Changsha, China

Shui-Hua Wang 🆔
University of Leicester
Leicester, UK

Yuan Xu 🆔
University of Jinan
Jinan, China

Yudong Zhang 🆔
University of Leicester
Leicester, UK

ISSN 1867-8211 ISSN 1867-822X (electronic)
Lecture Notes of the Institute for Computer Sciences, Social Informatics
and Telecommunications Engineering
ISBN 978-3-030-82561-4 ISBN 978-3-030-82562-1 (eBook)
https://doi.org/10.1007/978-3-030-82562-1

This Springer imprint is published by the registered company Springer Nature Switzerland AG
The registered company address is: Gewerbestrasse 11, 6330 Cham, Switzerland

Preface

We are delighted to introduce the proceedings of the Third European Alliance for Innovation (EAI) International Conference on Multimedia Technology and Enhanced Learning (ICMTEL 2021). This conference has brought together researchers, developers, and practitioners from around the world who are leveraging and developing multimedia technologies and related enhanced learning methods. The theme of ICMTEL 2021 was "the state of the art and future perspectives of multimedia technologies and enhanced learning".

The technical program of ICMTEL 2021 consisted of 97 full papers, including 2 invited papers, in oral presentation sessions at the main conference tracks. Track 1 – state-of-the-art techniques for multimedia and Track 2 – multimedia-based applications with machine learning methods. The technical program also featured three keynote speeches and four technical workshops. The three keynote speeches were given by Manu Malek from Stevens Institute of Technology, USA, Ng Yin Kwee from Nanyang Technological University, Singapore, and Shuai Liu from Hunan Normal University, China. The five workshops organized were "Deep Learning Techniques for Online Social Network Analysis", which aimed to present novel solutions for problems of online social networks with deep learning methods; "Networking Representations of Data, Images, and Systems", which aimed to provide structure, thinking, and technologies of networking representations for image-based systems; "Intelligent Application in Education", which aimed to focus on the intelligent educational system with multimedia analysis; "Information Fusion and Their Applications", which aimed to analyze how to construct the information fusion system for multimodal multimedia data and the industrial application of the multimodal systems; and "AI-based Data Processing, Intelligent Control, and Their Applications", which aimed to discuss research on the dynamic system of multimedia data processing.

Coordination with the steering chairs, Imrich Chlamtac, Deshuang Huang and Chunming Li, was essential for the success of the conference. We sincerely appreciate their constant support and guidance. It was also a great pleasure to work with such an excellent Organizing Committee team for their hard work in organizing and supporting the conference. In particular, we are grateful to the Technical Program Committee, led by our TPC chair, Shi-Hua Wang, who completed the peer-review process of technical papers and put together a high-quality technical program. We are also grateful to the conference manager, Natasha Onofrei, for her support and all the authors who submitted their papers to the ICMTEL 2021 conference and workshops.

We strongly believe that ICMTEL provides a good forum for all researchers, developers, and practitioners to discuss all science and technology aspects that are relevant to multimedia and enhanced learning. We also expect that future ICMTEL conferences will be as successful and stimulating as ICMTEL 2021, as indicated by the contributions presented in this volume.

Shuai Liu

Conference Organization

Steering Committee

Chair

Imrich Chlamtac   University of Trento, Italy

Co-chairs

Deshuang Huang   Tongji University, China
Chunming Li   University of Electronic Science and Technology
of China, China

Organizing Committee

General Chair

Yu-Dong Zhang   University of Leicester, UK

General Co-chair

Shuai Liu   Hunan Normal University, China

Technical Program Committee Chairs

Shui-Hua Wang   Loughborough University, UK
Ruidan Su   Shanghai Advanced Research Institute, China

Technical Program Committee Co-chairs

Vishnu Varthanan
Govindaraj   Kalasalingam Academy of Research and Education,
India
Xianwei Jiang   Nanjing Normal University of Special Education,
China
Zhuqing Jiao   Changzhou University, China
Siamak Khatibi   Blekinge Institute of Technology, Sweden
Raymond F. Muzic, Jr.   Case Western Reserve University, USA
Pengjiqng Qian   Jiangnan University, China
Yuan Xu   University of Jinan, China

Special Issue Chair

Zheng Zhang   Harbin Institute of Technology, China

Workshops Chair and Co-chairs

Zhuqing Jiao	Changzhou University, China
Xinhua Mao	Nanjing University of Aeronautics and Astronautics, China
Shuhui Bi	University of Jinan, China

Panel Chairs

Arun Kumar Sangaiah	Vellore Institute of Technology, India
Yin Zhang	University of Electronic Science and Technology of China, China
T. S. Pradeep Kumar	Vellore Institute of Technology, India

Session Chairs

Xujing Yao	University of Leicester, UK
Yan Yan	University of Leicester, UK
Wei Wang	University of Leicester, UK
Xinyu Liu	Hunan Normal University, China

Publications Chair

Shuai Liu	Hunan Normal University, China

Tutorials Chair

Zhengchao Dong	Columbia University, USA

Web Chair

Lijia Deng	University of Leicester, UK

Publicity and Social Media Chair

Qinghua Zhou	University of Leicester, UK

Local Chair

Yu Xiang	University of Leicester, UK

Technical Program

Ali Saberi	Iranian Researchers Network, Iran
Aijun Liu	Xidian University, China
Amin Taheri-Garavand	Lorestan University, Iran
Chenxi Huang	Xiamen University, China
Dang Thanh	Hue Industrial College, Vietnam
David Guttery	University of Leicester, UK
Jun Dai	California State University, USA
Kaijian Xia	Soochow University, China

Contents – Part I

Information Techniques for Social/Natural Application

Information Fusion and Their Applications

Contents – Part II

Intelligent Application in Education

Human/Medical Based Data Processing and Systems

AI-based Data Processing, Intelligent Control and Their Applications

Research on Multithreaded Data Scheduling Control Method for Power Communication Based on Wireless Sensor

Zhou Qian[1][(⊠)] and Zhao Bing[2]

[1] Guizhou Power Grid Corporation, Guiyang 550002, China
[2] Elites Partners Corporation, Beijing 100027, China

Abstract. The traditional power communication scheduling control method has the problem of low utilization of network bandwidth. Therefore, a multi thread data scheduling control method of power communication based on wireless sensor is proposed. According to the path of multiple nodes in the communication system, a multi-threaded scheduler is designed to realize the network bandwidth prediction of the power communication system; the parameters of the controlled object are taken as the input variables of the controller, and the power communication dispatching control is realized through the Ryu controller to realize the feedback control and multi-threaded data dispatching control. The results show that the designed data scheduling control method has high utilization rate of network bandwidth and can adapt to the environment with different interference. The control method effectively improves the security of power communication data.

Keywords: Wireless sensor · Power communication · Multithreading · Data scheduling

1 Introduction

With the continuous progress of modern science and the rapid development of economy, smart distribution networks are getting more and more attention, and smart distribution networks are the development trend of future power grids. The intelligent distribution network integrates a variety of advanced technologies, such as data communication technology, new energy technology, sensor technology, power system technology etc. [1]. In this way, the self-healing, interactivity and security of intelligent distribution network can be improved. In order to improve the reliability, real-time performance of the power supply system, the efficiency of power energy utilization and reduce the impact on the environment, the mutual flow of information flow and power flow between power supply and power consumption equipment can be realized [2]. The power grid in the traditional sense refers to the one-way power distribution system, which cannot meet the needs of distributed power in the power grid, while the smart distribution network can meet and apply to various new energy sources. Therefore, the research of smart distribution network has become a hot topic in today's society [3].

© ICST Institute for Computer Sciences, Social Informatics and Telecommunications Engineering 2021
Published by Springer Nature Switzerland AG 2021. All Rights Reserved
W. Fu et al. (Eds.): ICMTEL 2021, LNICST 387, pp. 3–13, 2021.
https://doi.org/10.1007/978-3-030-82562-1_1

WSNs has become an important development direction in the field of intelligent distribution network data communication. At home and abroad, the research on the operational reliability, accuracy, integrity and maximum delay time of WSNs data transmission in intelligent distribution network is in the initial stage. The key point is to ensure the reliability and real-time performance of WSNs data transmission, meet the requirements of power industry distribution network data communication specification, with guaranteed QoS index, which is the practical application of intelligent distribution network data transmission WSNs One of the basic research problems [4].

At present, many algorithms and corresponding improvement measures have been proposed for WSNs to achieve high-efficiency power communication under the condition of limited network resources. A neural network dynamic model for detecting links between nodes is studied. The model uses the nonlinear model and state of the network topology as the input of the neuron network to realize multi-threaded data scheduling control and improve the reliability of power communication. In addition, a data-driven dynamic algorithm is proposed. According to the historical information of mobile nodes, the algorithm dynamically predicts the location of mobile nodes, and uses the routing decision-making method based on geographic information to realize the control optimization of multi-threaded data scheduling. In the above methods, different methods are used to study multi-threaded data scheduling control, but there is nothing to do with a large number of network interference nodes in power communication. These interference nodes occupy too much network bandwidth resources in the scheduling, and compete with many thread characters for network resources. A serious threat to the security of power communication. Relevant scholars have made some progress in this field. Liu Wenjing et al. Proposed the optimal dispatching method of hydro thermal power system based on super efficiency DEA benefit evaluation [5]. The particle swarm optimization algorithm was used for multi-objective optimization of power system data dispatching, the data envelopment analysis algorithm was used for data dispatching classification of power system, and the decision-making unit and benefit evaluation method were designed. This method can effectively improve the system security, but the network bandwidth utilization is not high. Duan yanru et al. Proposed the power dispatching automation and control method based on Smart Grid [6], constructed the optimal control model of power dispatching, estimated the state of power dispatching system, and adjusted it into the optimal load. This method can effectively improve the data regulation time, but the utilization rate of network bandwidth is poor.

Therefore, a multi-threaded data scheduling control method based on wireless sensor for power communication is proposed. According to the path of multiple nodes in the communication system, a multi-threaded scheduler is designed to realize the network bandwidth prediction of power communication system; the power communication scheduling control is realized through Ryu controller to realize feedback control and multi-threaded data scheduling control. The effectiveness of this method is verified by experiments, and the security of power communication data is effectively improved.

2 Wireless Sensor-Based Power Communication Multithread Data Scheduling Control Method

2.1 Multithreading Data Design

In the power communication using wireless sensor network, due to the deployment of wireless sensors, there are multiple network nodes with different functions in the network. These network nodes will generate multiple scheduling tasks at the same time during data scheduling, showing multi-threaded The task mode seriously affects work efficiency and safety [7–9]. Therefore, before control, a data scheduler for multi-threading is designed as an aid to the controller.

A scheduler is introduced into the original data scheduling control structure, which is used to adjust the sampling period of each control loop in real time, so as to ensure the smooth transmission and timely update of the data information of each loop [10, 11]. Among them, the measured bandwidth value, the bandwidth setting value and the error of each loop are all working parameters required when the node is scheduled for real-time operation in the sampling period. The basic structure diagram of the scheduler is shown in Fig. 1.

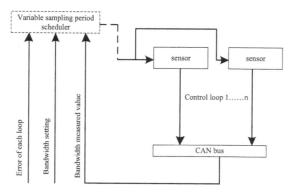

Fig. 1. Scheduler structure diagram

The workflow of scheduling design is mainly divided into three parts: network bandwidth prediction, network bandwidth configuration and sampling period calculation. In the first part, network bandwidth prediction is based on the difference between the current measured network bandwidth value and the original network bandwidth setting value, and then through proportional control to re predict the next network bandwidth value. Here, the predicted new network bandwidth value is the total bandwidth value; In the second part, the network bandwidth configuration is based on the new network bandwidth value predicted in the previous step and the data transmission error value of each loop, and at the same time, according to the importance of each control loop established long ago (weight coefficient value), to configure each in real time The network bandwidth value of the loop; In the last part, the sampling period of each task loop is calculated by the ratio of the data transmission time of the loop network to the network bandwidth allocation value. The calculation of the sampling period needs to be based on the network bandwidth value and the data transmission time of each loop, so as to realize the real-time and effective adjustment of the multi-path sampling period.

It should be explained here that the network used in the variable sampling cycle scheduling design is the CAN bus. The CAN bus is different from other methods in that each message has a priority, that is, it has a priority nature. When multiple nodes access the network at the same time It can be used to judge the order of nodes visiting the communication network. Moreover, the data transmission of sampling can bus has many advantages, such as strong real-time, high reliability and strong anti-interference. When the network load increases, the priority control provided by the CAN bus will significantly improve the working efficiency of the network nodes.

2.2 Forecast Network Bandwidth

The prediction of network bandwidth reflects whether the limited capacity provided by communication network is effectively utilized. The concept of network bandwidth is similar to that of drainage pipeline. The larger the bandwidth is, the greater the cross-sectional area of drainage pipeline is, and the drainage capacity per unit time is stronger. In the power communication multi-threaded data scheduling control method, the network bandwidth prediction process adopts a proportional control method to predict the new network bandwidth value at the next moment. Suppose that the preset value of network bandwidth is R_1 and the real-time measurement value of network bandwidth is R_2, the difference between the actual value and the preset value of network bandwidth can be obtained:

$$E_0 = R_1 - R_2 \tag{1}$$

Calculate the adjustment increment of network bandwidth through proportional control strategy:

$$\Delta \hat{R}(k+1) = \mu(E_0) \tag{2}$$

Formula: E_0 is the difference between the actual value of network bandwidth and the preset value, μ is the proportional adjustment gain, k is the time, and $\Delta \hat{R}(k+1)$ is the proportional adjustment amount of network bandwidth. The predicted network bandwidth is as follows:

$$\hat{R}(k+1) = R(k) + \Delta \hat{R}(k+1) \tag{3}$$

There is a difference between the measured network bandwidth and the predicted network bandwidth. Suppose the ratio between the two is $\bar{w}(k+1)$, Then there is:

$$\bar{w}(k+1) = \frac{\Delta R(k+1)}{\Delta \hat{R}(k+1)} \tag{4}$$

among: $\bar{w}(k+1) \in (0, \bar{w}_{max}]$. The measured network bandwidth is:

$$R(k+1) = R(k) + \Delta R(k+1) \tag{5}$$

By substituting formula 4 into formula 5, the following results are obtained:

$$R(k+1) = R(k) + \bar{w}(k+1)\Delta\hat{R}(k+1) \tag{6}$$

Use the set value R_2 to subtract the left and right sides at the same time, then:

$$R_1 - R(k+1) = R_2 - R(k) - \bar{w}(k+1)\Delta\hat{R}(k+1) \tag{7}$$

Substituting Formula 1 into formula 7, we get the following results:

$$E(k+1) = E(k) - \bar{w}(k+1)\mu E(k) \tag{8}$$

Simplify to get:

$$E(k+1) = E(k)[1 - \bar{w}(k+1)\mu] \tag{9}$$

Record it as:

$$\varphi(k+1) = 1 - \bar{w}(k+1)\mu \tag{10}$$

Then there are:

$$E(k+1) = \varphi(k+1)E(k) \tag{11}$$

For the designed controller, if the proportional gain satisfies:

$$0 < \mu < \frac{2}{\bar{w}_{\max}} \tag{12}$$

Then the feedback control described in formula 10 is exponentially convergent, that is, the network bandwidth can make the exponential convergence reach the desired value, so the feedback scheduler is schedulable. Expand formula 11 to get:

$$E(k+1) = \varphi(k+1)\varphi(k)\ldots\ldots\varphi(1)E(0) \tag{13}$$

According to the matrix theory, we can see that:

$$\begin{cases} |E(k+1)| = |\varphi(k+1)\varphi(k)\ldots\ldots\varphi(1)E(0)| \\ |E(k+1)| \le |\varphi(k+1) \times \varphi(k) \times \ldots\ldots \times \varphi(1) \times E(0)| \end{cases} \tag{14}$$

Given $|1 - \bar{w}_{\max}\mu| < 1$, we can know from Eq. 10:

$$|\varphi(k+1)| \ge |1 - \bar{w}_{\max}\mu| \tag{15}$$

Combining formula 14 and formula 15, we can get the following results

$$|1 - \bar{w}_{\max}\mu| \le |\varphi(k+1)| \le 1 \tag{16}$$

For any value of k, there is always a scalar χ, $0 < \chi < 1$ that makes $|\varphi(k+1)| \le \chi$ true. Substituting it into Eq. 14, there are:

$$|E(k+1)| \le \chi^k|E(0)| < |E(0)| \tag{17}$$

Therefore, once the schedulability lemma is satisfied, the network bandwidth value can gradually converge to the desired target ideal value. Under the condition of satisfying the expected objective ideal value, the control strategy is optimized to realize the multi-threaded data scheduling control of power communication.

2.3 Controller Design

According to the predicted network bandwidth, the range of controlled value variable is set. Communication rate: Divide the communication rate from 10 kbps to 250 kbps into 5 levels, respectively: low: 10 kbps–20 kbps, low: 20 kbps–40 kbps, medium: 40 kbps–80 kbps, high: 80 kbps–160 kbps, high: 160 kbps–240 kbps. Transmission power: the transmission power is divided into 5 levels from 10db to 22 dB, which are low, low, medium, high and high from low to high. Backoff strategy: the backoff strategy is divided into two aspects: the backoff time from 10 to 30 symbols is divided into 5 levels, from low to high are low, low, medium, high and high; the maximum number of backoff is divided into 5 levels from 5 to 15 times, and from low to high are low, low, medium, high and high. After setting the value range of the parameter controlled value variable, design the controller.

In the control method, the Ryu controller is used as the nerve center. The basic components of Ryu controller are the basis of its development and application. Ryu controller contains many components and libraries. It uses python programming language to develop applications. Users can develop their own applications by modifying the functions of each component.

Among the many components, the app component is used to manage the written application; the base component is used to load the application, which contains an app_manager.py file, which is one of the necessary import files when developing an application One; The controller component contains a series of important files that handle switch connections, such as events.py, of p_handle.py, controller.py These are the key documents; The lib component defines many basic data structures and some commonly used network protocols; the of proto component contains files that support various versions of the OpenFlow protocol. It mainly contains two types of files, one is the data structure definition of the protocol, and the other is the protocol analysis. The above components are the key parts of the development controller. In addition, other components also play different roles. In general, Ryu is rich in component types, which is enough to construct multi-threaded data scheduling controller in wireless sensor networks.

The natural advantage of this controller is the separation of control and forwarding, and centralized control is realized by the control plane. Therefore, it is essential for each controller to have a data flow monitoring function. In addition to physical resource information, the network information that can be counted by data flow monitoring also includes information such as logical links, and the same is true for flow information. In the actual monitoring process, the main statistics are the switch port rate information, the number of flows, etc., and the remaining bandwidth of the link and the size of the flow can be calculated based on the statistics of the port information. Using the obtained statistical information enables the controller to better perform data scheduling.

In the process of traffic monitoring, Ryu completes the statistics of port information and flow information through two important messages: of port state request and offpflowstaterequest. This is the request sent by the controller to obtain the information of the switch. In addition, the controller establishes an event handle of the event handling type on the response information of the switch to receive statistics messages of the flow or port that the switch responds. In a complete topology, the statistical information of switch port mainly includes the number of received packets, the number of received bytes, the number of received errors and so on. Similarly, the statistical information of convection also includes various information, such as the length and duration of the flow. After mastering the multi thread data of power communication and matching with the predicted network bandwidth data, the multi thread data scheduling control of power communication can be realized.

3   Experimental Research on Multithreaded Data Scheduling Control Method for Power Communication

3.1   Experiment Setup

In the experiment, the simulation model required for the experiment is built, and the content of the construction is consistent with the general framework established by the original variable sampling cycle scheduling system. The internal transmission dead zone of the sensor and the controller is set up, as shown in Fig. 2.

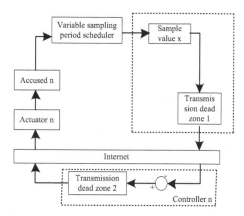

Fig. 2. Structure diagram based on dead time scheduling

Among them: x is the sampling value of the sensor node, r is the given input value of the controller node, and the deviation value e is the difference between the sensor sampling value and the reference input value, that is, the deviation signal of the system in the controller node. The transmission dead zone 1 is set in the sensor node and 2 is set in the controller node. The sensor node is time driven, and the controller node and actuator node are event driven. When the sensor node does not send packets, the controller node and actuator node will not be triggered to execute.

Two new dead zone scheduling strategies are adopted, and the dead zone is set in the sensor node and the controller node at the same time to realize the two-way setting of the forward path and the feedback channel. In the sensor node, compare the difference between the previous sampled signal value and the current sampled signal with the set dead zone threshold, and determine whether the sensor node sends a data packet according to the comparison result; In the controller node, combined with the idea of human simulated intelligent control, the network is scheduled according to the system deviation value. The human simulated intelligent control can maximize the intuitive reasoning of all parameters and feature information in the control process, and implement effective control effect. The six schemes are shown in Table 1.

Table 1. Parameters setting of dead time implementation

Programme	Sensor node	Controller node	Probability value
	Parameter setting of deadband threshold	The output value is in the steady-state range	
One	0.045	($\pm5\%-\pm10\%$)	0.85
Two	0.045		0.75
Three	0.035		0.85
Four	0.055		0.85
Five	0.035		0.90
Six	0.035		0.75

The implementation parameters of six different schemes are fine tuned in different directions. Two points should be noted here. First of all, the increase of dead time threshold in sensor node will limit the node packet, and the difference between the sample values before and after the sensor node is maintained at a small value, which is often not very large. Due to the use of unit step signal, the increase of dead time threshold of sensor node will compress the packet space; at the same time, the probability of controller node is reduced It is also equivalent to restraining the contract to a certain extent. In general, the simulation experiments of the six different schemes are essentially to verify the effectiveness of fine-tuning parameters under different restrictions on outsourcing.

3.2 Adaptability Experiment and Analysis

On the basis of verifying the effectiveness of the control method, the above experimental plan refers to the traditional neural network-based control method and the data-driven control method, and conducts adaptive experiments under the same experimental conditions to verify that the control method faces data flow. Whether real-time changes can ensure a high level of network bandwidth utilization. Use third-party software to monitor data scheduling control and output experimental results. The specific content is shown in Fig. 3.

Compare and observe the results in the figure, the solid line in the figure represents the input value, and the dashed line represents the response curve under different scenarios. From the experimental results, it can be seen that the difference between the neural network control method and the input value is relatively large, and the overshoot of the response curve increases obviously, and then decreases gradually; the overshoot of the

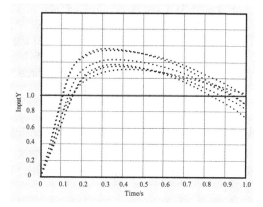

(a) Experimental results of control method based on Neural Network

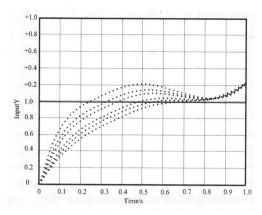

(b) Experimental results of data driven control method

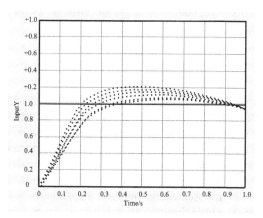

(c) Experimental results of control method based on wireless sensing

Fig. 3. Adaptability test results of different control methods

response curve of the control method based on data-driven increases obviously, and it is always in the state of increase in the follow-up; the response curve of the control method based on wireless sensor is more close to the input value, and the response curve is more close to the input value The increase of overshoot is not obvious. In summary, the designed wireless sensing-based power communication multi-threaded data scheduling control method is more adaptable under different conditions.

3.3 Experiment and Analysis of Network Bandwidth Utilization

Based on the above experimental results, the network bandwidth utilization rates of different control methods under different schemes are calculated, and the calculation results are shown in Table 2.

Table 2. Calculation results of network bandwidth utilization of different control methods

	Control method based on neural network	Data-driven control method	Control method based on wireless sensor
Option 1	54.6%	42.8%	85.2%
Option 2	52.3%	59.6%	89.6%
Option 3	49.2%	57.2%	87.2%
Option 4	48.5%	47.6%	86.4%
Option 5	51.6%	43.2%	90.6%
Option 6	49.7%	41.3%	88.4%

It can be seen from the data in the table that compared with the traditional two control methods, the designed control method based on wireless sensing has higher network bandwidth utilization. Combining the above-mentioned adaptability experiment results, it can be seen that the designed power based on wireless sensing The communication multi-threaded data scheduling control method has stronger performance and better security.

4   Conclusion

In recent years, the application of wireless sensor network technology to power grid communication has attracted the attention of the industry. This article takes the power communication multi-threaded data as the research goal, and based on relevant literature materials, designs the power communication multi-threaded data scheduling control based on wireless sensing Methods, and after the control method design is completed, design a number of comparative experiments. The experimental results verify the effectiveness and safety of the proposed control method. However, only the stability of the controlled object is considered in the study. For dynamic changes, how to adapt to the drastic changes of the environment and have high-throughput is worth further study.

References

1. Yang, L., Haibo, J., Zheng, W., et al.: Access Control and routing optimization strategy for energy-saving aware wireless sensor network. Comput. Eng. **46**(05), 230–239 (2020)
2. Liu, S., Liu, D., Srivastava, G., et al.: Overview and methods of correlation filter algorithms in object tracking. Complex Intell. Syst. (2020). https://doi.org/10.1007/s40747-020-00161-4
3. Chao, M., Long, J., Zhixin, S.: Optimization algorithm for data transmission based on wireless sensor network. J. Nanjing Univ. Posts Telecommun. (Natural Science) **38**(03), 65–71 (2018)
4. Yong, W.U.: Study on delay elimination of wireless sensor network communication. Comput. Simul. **35**(03), 145–148 (2018)
5. Wenjing, L., Xianlan, F., Jiekang, W., Na, S.: Study of hydro-thermal electrical power system optimization scheduling based on super efficiency DEA efficiency evaluation. Water Power 45(02), 98–100,105 (2019)
6. Yanru, D.: Realization of power dispatching automation and control system based on smart grid. Electron. Des. Eng. **28**(04), 189–193 (2020)
7. Fu, W., Liu, S., Srivastava, G.: Optimization of big data scheduling in social networks. Entropy **21**(9), 902 (2019)
8. Zhiguo, C., Guifa, T.: Data transmission algorithm in wireless sensor networks based on cross-layer design and optimization. Sci. Technol. Eng. **19**(16), 245–250 (2019)
9. Liu, S., Bai, W., Zeng, N., et al.: A fast fractal based compression for MRI images. IEEE Access **7**, 62412–62420 (2019)
10. Tianyi, Z., Fengqing, L.: Traffic scheduling method in hybrid optical-electronical data centers based on SDN. Opt. Commun. Technol. **42**(04), 25–28 (2018)

Recognition Method of Metal Material Pitting Defect Based on Visual Signal Processing

Ying Zhao[✉] and Li Zhang

Nanchang Institute of Technology, Nanchang 330108, Jiangxi, China

Abstract. Aiming at the problem of large recognition errors in traditional metal material pitting defect recognition methods, this research aims to improve the recognition performance of metal material pitting defects, and proposes a metal material pitting defect recognition method based on visual signal processing. The rail material parameters are set according to the schematic diagram of the U71Mn rail imitation, and the defective metal material imitation model is constructed according to the distribution position of each crack of the U71Mn rail, and then the optical signal of the metal material pitting defect is collected according to the geometric model imaged by the camera. The image of metal material pitting defects undergoes visual signal processing to extract the details of the image in different directions and scales. Based on this, the Mallet algorithm is used to decompose the image of metal material pitting corrosion defects, and the low-frequency components and high-dimensional components of multiple resolutions and multiple features are obtained, and specific fusion rules are selected to select the components of each layer obtained by decomposition, and then wavelet Inverse transformation, complete the fusion and analysis of visual signals of pitting defects in metal materials. Experimental results show that the recognition method of metal material pitting defects based on visual signal processing has high recognition performance.

Keywords: Visual signal processing · Metal materials · Pitting defect recognition · High dimensional component

1 Introduction

Pitting defects will directly affect the service performance and service life of metal materials. It is of great significance to carry out effective non-destructive testing and evaluation to provide data support for fatigue life prediction [1]. Metal material structure changes state and forms new phase under the action of medium, which leads to corrosion damage. Corrosion damage is very serious to national economy and national defense construction. It will not only lead to production stoppage, material structure failure, resource loss, hazardous material leakage, but also lead to significant economic losses and even catastrophic consequences. According to statistics, the amount of metal scrapped due to corrosion is equivalent to 20%–40% of the annual metal production in the world. The annual average cost of solving corrosion damage in developed countries accounts

© ICST Institute for Computer Sciences, Social Informatics and Telecommunications Engineering 2021
Published by Springer Nature Switzerland AG 2021. All Rights Reserved
W. Fu et al. (Eds.): ICMTEL 2021, LNICST 387, pp. 14–26, 2021.
https://doi.org/10.1007/978-3-030-82562-1_2

for 2%–4% of the national economy, and is increasing year by year. Every year, many countries in the world have to invest a lot of manpower and material resources for corrosion detection and protection. Corrosion detection has become one of the important fields of modern science and technology research. It is of great significance for the safety and economy of metal materials and structures to find and evaluate the corrosion damage timely and accurately.

Pitting corrosion is the initial stage of corrosion damage. Because the metal surface is under tensile stress or chemical substances, the protective layer is damaged and local penetration occurs, so that the metal matrix is directly exposed to the corrosive environment to form local corrosion pores. A form of corrosion damage developed in depth. The occurrence and expansion of pitting corrosion can be divided into two stages, namely pitting nucleation and growth [2, 3]. There are two theories about the causes of pitting corrosion: one is that pitting occurs when the oxygen adsorption point on the metal surface is replaced by chloride ions; the other is that the radius of chloride ions is small and can pass through the passivation film and enter the film. The generated conductive induced ions cause the membrane to maintain a high current density at a specific point, causing the cations to move randomly. When the electric field at the membrane-solution interface reaches a certain critical value, pitting corrosion occurs. After the pitting nucleus is formed, it will continue to grow, and when it reaches a critical size, macroscopic pits will appear. There are many theories about the expansion mechanism of pits, and a well-recognized theory is that the process of autocatalytic occlusion of batteries occurs in pits.

The location of pitting corrosion has strong randomness, and it is easy to form fatigue source in pitting area. Pitting corrosion forms corrosion pits on the surface of the structure, which changes the surface state of the structure, and then leads to local or comprehensive damage. It depends on the comprehensive influence of pitting pit depth, stress level and material fatigue crack. In the interaction between pitting and fatigue, pitting is generally regarded as a surface crack, and the crack growth rate is controlled by the pitting kinetics. When the pitting corrosion grows to the critical size or the fatigue crack growth rate exceeds the pitting corrosion growth rate, fatigue cracks will be initiated at the pitting pit. The fatigue crack nucleates at the pitting pit, then goes through the pitting growth, the transition stage from pitting to fatigue crack formation, the short crack propagation, the long crack propagation and the metal structure damage. Sun Mingjian [4] et al. proposed a non-destructive detection method for metal material defects based on multi-modal signals in view of the single modal signal mode and limited detection range of the existing non-destructive testing technology. This method is based on the photoacoustic nondestructive testing method. First, the finite element method is used to analyze the effect of defects on the laser energy absorption and photoacoustic surface wave propagation, and a defect detection method based on the laser absorption and photoacoustic surface wave is proposed; The multi-modal signal detection platform collects the optical, photoacoustic and ultrasonic signals of the defect, and detects the width and distribution information of the crack, as well as the depth and internal extension; In order to improve the recognition rate of packaging printing defects, Liyan S [5] designed a printing defect detection method based on machine vision. Based on the analysis of common defect types, a detection system is built by using digital signal processor

TMS320DM642, and the process of packaging defect detection is discussed. Based on this, the traditional wavelet transform is improved, which can enhance the image feature information and improve the recognition rate. At the same time, several defect feature extraction methods, including roundness, aspect ratio and gray standard deviation, are presented. Yang Chenlong [6] and others used the recursive analysis method to analyze the detection signal in order to effectively identify the micro defect echo in the ultrasonic testing signal of metal materials. By modeling the ultrasonic backscattering signal. In the ultrasonic testing signal, the echo signal of defect will affect the recursive characteristic of the system. The backscatter signal and defect free backscatter signal of 120 mm diameter low carbon steel bar with 0.8 mm flat bottom hole artificial simulated defects were studied by using recursive analysis. The part of backscattered signal in the test signal of the test block is intercepted, and the recursive analysis is carried out through reasonable parameter selection, and the recursive diagram is drawn. Compared with the recursive image of defect free signal collected by experiment, it is found that the defect signal will produce obvious white cross stripe in the recursive image. Recursive quantitative analysis is used to further study the recursive characteristics of the backscattered signal with defects. The results show that the acquisition time (TT), determination rate (DET) and recursive entropy (entr) are sensitive to the defect signal, and there are obvious peaks at the defect position.

Based on the above background, this paper applies visual signal processing to metal material pitting defect identification, and designs a metal material pitting defect identification method based on visual signal processing. Based on the distribution location of rail cracks, the model of metal material with defects was constructed. Then, the optical signals of metal material pitting defects were collected, and the details of images in different directions and scales were extracted through the signal processing process. Based on this, Mallet algorithm is used to decompose the image of metal material pitting defects, and specific fusion rules are selected to select each layer component obtained by decomposition. Then, through inverse wavelet transformation, the fusion and analysis of visual signals of metal material pitting defects are completed, so as to improve the performance of metal material pitting defect identification. The experimental results show that this method has high recognition performance.

2   Design of Metal Material Pitting Defect Identification Method

2.1   Construction of Metal Model with Defects

A section of U71Mn rail as shown in Fig. 1 was selected as the imitation body. This type of rail is widely used in my country's railway tracks at present, and it is of great significance to use it as an imitation body for research. The material parameters of this type of rail are shown in Table 1. Seven longitudinal cracks were processed on the rail head. The distribution position of each crack is shown in Fig. 2, and the size is shown in Table 2. The shallower rail head cracks 1, 2, 3, and 7 are used to represent defects in the superficial layer, while the deeper cracks 4, 5, and 6 represent defects that penetrate the surface, the superficial layer and the interior.

Fig. 1. Schematic diagram of U71Mn rail

Table 1. Rail material parameters

Attributes	Value	Attributes	Value
Density	7850 kg/m	Elastic modulus	$2.1*10^{11}$ Pa
Thermal conductivity	45W/(m·K)	Poisson's ratio	0.3
Specific heat capacity	460J(kg·K)	Thermal expansion coefficient	$1*10{-}5$

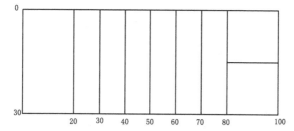

Fig. 2. The distribution position of each crack in U71Mn rail

According to the simulation diagram of U71Mn rail, the material parameters of rail are set, and the simulation model of metal material with defects is constructed by using the distribution position of cracks in U71Mn rail.

2.2 Collect Optical Signals of Pitting Defects in Metal Materials

Camera distortion will affect the accuracy of metal material pitting defect recognition, and the camera calibration can achieve the effect of eliminating distortion. Therefore, before using the camera to collect the image of the phantom, first calibrate it. Camera calibration is actually the process of solving the corresponding relationship between the three-dimensional space position of a point in the camera model and the position of the point in the pixel coordinate system [7–9]. The camera model includes four coordinate systems: world coordinate system, camera coordinate system, image plane coordinate

Table 2. The size of the crack on the imitation body

Numbering	Width (mm)	Depth (mm)
1	0.5	0.5
2	0.5	1.5
3	0.5	1.0
4	0.5	5.5
5	0.5	5.0
6	0.5	5.0
7	0.5	0.5

system and pixel coordinate system, as shown in Fig. 3. The corresponding relations of the four coordinate systems are analyzed below.

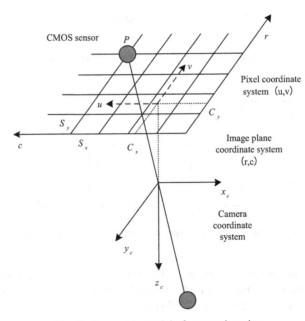

Fig. 3. Geometric model of camera imaging

The transformation relationship between point P_w in the world coordinate system and point P_c in the camera coordinate system is as follows:

$$\begin{bmatrix} x_c \\ y_c \\ z_c \end{bmatrix} = R \begin{bmatrix} x_w \\ y_w \\ z_w \end{bmatrix} + T \qquad (1)$$

Among them, $T = (t_x, t_y, t_z)$ and $R = R(r_\alpha, r_\rho, r_y)$ respectively represent the translation and rotation process when the world coordinate system is converted to the camera coordinate system.

The projection relationship between point P_c and point P in the plane coordinate system of the pitting defect image of metallic materials is:

$$\frac{u}{v} = \frac{f_c}{z_c} \cdot \frac{x_c}{y_c} \tag{2}$$

Where f_c is the main distance of the camera, that is, the distance between the imaging plane and the projection center, and f_c is parallel to the main axis. The line between the point in the world coordinate system and the projection point in the imaging plane originally passes through the optical center of the camera. However, the lens distortion produces a change that can be approximated as radial distortion, so that the corresponding position of P_w in the plane coordinate system of metal material pitting defect image is as follows:

$$\begin{pmatrix} \bar{u} \\ \bar{v} \end{pmatrix} = \frac{2}{1 + \sqrt{1 - 4k(u^2 + v^2)}} \begin{pmatrix} u \\ v \end{pmatrix} \tag{3}$$

In the formula, the parameter k represents the magnitude of radial distortion. If k is a negative number, the state of distortion is barrel distortion; if k is a positive number, the state of distortion is pincushion distortion.

Finally, according to the transformation relationship between $(\bar{u}, \bar{v})$ and pixel coordinate system shown in formula (3), the pixel coordinates corresponding to P_w can be obtained:

$$\begin{pmatrix} r \\ c \end{pmatrix} = \begin{pmatrix} \frac{\bar{v}}{S_y} + C_y \\ \frac{\bar{u}}{S_x} + C_x \end{pmatrix} \tag{4}$$

In formulas (1)–(4), $(t_x, t_x, t_z, r_\alpha, r_\rho, r_y)$ is called the external parameters of the camera, and $(f_c, k, S_x, S_y, C_x, C_y)$ is called the internal parameters of the camera. The process of calibrating the camera is the process of solving these 12 parameters. One tool required for calibration is a calibration board. Commonly used calibration boards include solid circle array patterns and chess array patterns. The size can be selected according to the field of view. In this article, a 50 mm calibration plate with a solid circular array pattern is selected for calibration.

2.3 Fusion and Analysis of Visual Signals of Metal Pitting Defects

The fusion of the visual signals of the pitting defects of metal materials in three different modes can obtain results that cannot be obtained in a single mode, and can also make the results of the single mode detection more accurate and reliable. The photoacoustic and ultrasonic metal material pitting defect images were fused, and complementary and beneficial information were selected from the defect images of the two respectively, and the inaccurate depth detection results in the photoacoustic and ultrasonic longitudinal sections were determined.

Metal material pitting defect image fusion can be divided into pixel level fusion, feature level fusion and decision level fusion according to the order from low to high [10–12]. Pixel level fusion and feature level fusion respectively refer to the fusion according to the corresponding pixels and features of multiple metal material pitting defect images, while decision level fusion is the final decision after classification, recognition and evaluation based on pixel level fusion and feature level fusion. As pixel level metal material pitting defect image fusion directly processes and fuses the data collected by the sensor, retains more original data and provides fine information that the other two fusion methods can not provide. Therefore, this paper studies the pixel level fusion of photoacoustic image and ultrasonic image.

First, visual signal processing must be performed on the image of pitting defects in metal materials. The image of pitting defects in metallic materials can be regarded as a two-dimensional signal, considering that the two-dimensional scale function $\phi(x, y)$ can be separated, namely:

$$\phi(x, y) = \phi(x)\phi(y) \tag{5}$$

Where a is $\phi(x)$ one-dimensional scale function and $\Psi(x)$ is a wavelet function corresponding to $\phi(x)$, i.e.:

$$\Psi(x) = \sum_k h_1(x)\phi(2x - k) \tag{6}$$

Then, the three two-dimensional basic wavelets, $\Psi^{(1)}(x, y) = \phi(x)\Psi(y)$, $\Psi^{(2)}(x, y) = \Psi(x)\phi(y)$, and $\Psi^{(3)}(x, y) = \Psi(x)\Psi(y)$, form a filter bank, which extracts the details of the pitting corrosion defect images of metal materials in different directions and scales. Among them, $\Psi^{(1)}(x, y)$ is used to extract the pitting corrosion defect images of metal materials. For details at low horizontal frequency and high vertical frequency, $\Psi^{(2)}(x, y)$ is used to extract details of metal material pitting defect images at high horizontal frequency and low vertical frequency, $\Psi^{(3)}(x, y)$ is used to extract metal material pitting defect images at high horizontal frequency and high vertical frequency Details under frequency.

For the pitting defect image of source metal material $f(m, n)$, let $C_0(m, n) = f(m, n)$, and mallet algorithm decompose it by wavelet:

$$\begin{cases} C_j(m, n) = \frac{1}{2} \sum\limits_{kj=Z} C_{j-1}(k, l)h_{k-2m}h_{l-2n} \\ d_j^1(m, n) = \frac{1}{2} \sum\limits_{kJeZ} C_{j-1}(k, l)h_{k-2m}g_{i-2n} \\ d_j^2(m, n) = \frac{1}{2} \sum\limits_{k,j=Z} C_{j-1}(k, l)g_{k-2m}h_{i-2n} \\ d_j^3(m, n) = \frac{1}{2} \sum\limits_{k/eZ} C_{j-1}(k, l)g_{k-2m}g_{l-2n} \end{cases} \tag{7}$$

Among them, $C_j(m, n)$ represents the low frequency component, $d_j^1(m, n)$ represents the horizontal edge of the pitting defect image of metal material, $d_j^2(m, n)$ represents the vertical edge of the pitting defect image of metal material, $d_j^3(m, n)$ represents the diagonal edge of the pitting defect image of metal material, and h and g represent filter banks. Corresponding to $\phi(x)$ and $\Psi(x)$ respectively; Z is an integer set, $1 \leq j \leq N$ and N represent the number of decomposition.

After the metal material pitting defect image decomposition is completed, low-frequency components and high-dimensional components with multiple resolutions and features can be obtained. These high-dimensional components are selected according to certain rules. The commonly used fusion rules include: take large value fusion rule, weighted average fusion rule, regional fusion rule, etc.

In this paper, the source metal material pitting defect images a and B are fused into image F. if the fusion rule is used, the mathematical expression is as follows:

$$C(A, B) = \frac{\sum\limits_{m=1}^{M} \sum\limits_{n=1}^{N} (A(m, n) - \bar{A})(B(m, n) - \bar{B})}{\sqrt{\sum\limits_{m=1}^{M} \sum\limits_{n=1}^{N} (A(m, n) - \bar{A})^2 \sum\limits_{m=1}^{M} \sum\limits_{n=1}^{N} (B(m, n) - \bar{B})^2}} \tag{8}$$

In the formula, $\bar{A}$ and $\bar{B}$ represent the average gray value of A and B.

Then define the weights ω_1 and ω_2 of the source metal material pitting defect images A and B, namely:

$$\omega_1 = \frac{1}{2}(1 - |C(A, B)|) \tag{9}$$

$$\omega_2 = 1 - \omega_1 \tag{10}$$

This results in the weighted average fusion rule:

$$F(m, n) = \omega_1 A(m, n) + \omega_2 B(m, n) \tag{11}$$

When the simplest weighted average fusion rule is C(A, B) = 0, take $\omega_1 = \omega_2 = 0.5$.

The region fusion rule considers the variance, energy, gradient and other features of the region in the metal material pitting defect image, and carries out the region weighted fusion according to the matching degree of the features.

Select a specific fusion rule to select the components of each layer obtained by decomposition, and then perform inverse wavelet transformation, as shown in the following formula, to obtain the fusion defect image of the metal material.

$$C_{j-1}(m, n) = \frac{1}{2} \left[\sum_{k/ez} C_j(k, l) h_{m-2k} h_{n-2l} + \sum_{k,j=Z} d_j^1(m, n) h_{m-2k} g_{n-2l} \right] \tag{12}$$

In this paper, the visual signal processing of metal material pitting defect image is carried out, and the details of the image in different directions and scales are extracted The algorithm decomposes the metal material pitting defect image, obtains the low-frequency component and the high-dimensional component with multiple resolution and multiple features. Select the specific fusion rules to select the components of each layer, and then carry out the wavelet inverse transformation to complete the fusion and analysis of the metal material pitting defect visual signal. Next, through the design of metal material pitting defect recognition process, to achieve Identification of pitting defects in existing metal materials.

2.4   Design the Process of Identifying Pitting Defects in Metal Materials

The process of metal material pitting defect identification is shown in Fig. 4.

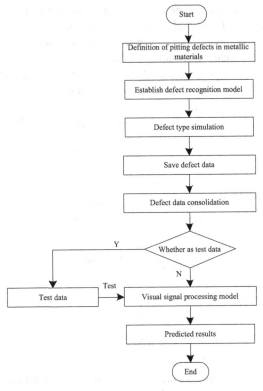

Fig. 4. Process of identifying pitting defects in metallic materials

It can be seen from Fig. 4 that the whole process of metal material pitting defect recognition is based on visual signal processing and recognition platform, which is mainly divided into two parts: visual signal processing training and test data production and application of visual signal processing for recognition, so as to realize the recognition of metal material pitting defect.

3   Experimental Study

In order to verify the effectiveness of the metal pitting defect recognition method based on visual signal processing, the following experiments are designed.

3.1   Test 1 Settings and Results

The basic situation of the first group of experiments is shown in Table 3.

Table 3. The contents of the first group of experiments

Experimental content	Parameter
Material science	Steel
Thickness	8 mm
Identification method	Visual signal processing regression
Types of pitting defects in metallic materials	Hemispherical
Simulation dimension	Three-dimensional
Data type	BY
Radius range of pitting defects in metallic Materials	1 mm–7 mm
Number of training data sets	31
Number of test data sets	3

The test object of the first set of experiments is a steel plate with an area of 460 mm × 46 mm and a thickness of 8 mm. The type of defect is a hemispherical metal material pitting defect, so the length, width and depth of the metal material pitting defect are all equal, and there is only one unknown parameter, that is, the radius of the metal material pitting defect. Therefore, the only parameter to be identified is the radius of pitting defects in metallic materials. The defect radius is between 1 mm and 7 mm, and multiple sets of defects are simulated with a step length of 0.2 mm. So the defect radius is 1 mm, 1.2 mm, 1.4 mm,…, 7 mm, 31 groups in total. Therefore, there are 31 sets of training data. In addition, the visual signal processing regression results of three sets of data are shown in Table 4.

Table 4. Prediction results of the first group of experiments

Simulation defect radius (mm)	Prediction of defect radius (mm)	Identification error
2.1	2.31887	10.04%
2.5	2.43143	2.74%
2.9	2.58893	10.72%

In terms of the amount of training data and test data, the scale of this set of experiments is small, and the types of pitting defects in metal materials are relatively simple. The maximum recognition error is about 10%.

3.2 Setup and Results of Test 2

The basic conditions of the second set of experiments are shown in Table 5.

The test object of the second set of experiments is a steel plate with a size of 460 mm × 460 mm and a thickness of 10 mm. The type of metal material pitting defect is

Table 5. The contents of the second group of experiments

Experimental content	Parameter
Material Science	Steel
Thickness	8 mm
Identification mode	Visual signal processing regression
Number of categories	8 categories
Types of pitting defects in metallic materials	Semiellipsoid
Simulation dimension	Three-dimensional
Data type	BX, BY
Radius range of pitting defects in metallic materials	1 mm–8 mm
Number of training data sets	413
Number of test data sets	32

semi-ellipsoid, so the number of metal material pitting defect parameters is three, the length, width and depth of the defect. The variation range of defect length, width and depth takes an integer value between 1 mm and 8 mm respectively, so that there are 512 groups of metal material pitting defects after permutation and combination. However, the ratio of length, width and depth of pitting corrosion defects in some metal materials is very different. For example, the length, width and depth are respectively 8 mm, 1 mm and 8 mm. Such metal material pitting defects are more like a crack than a corrosion defect. After eliminating defects with a large difference in the ratio of length, width and depth, 445 sets of simulation data were used as training and test data for visual signal processing. Among 445 sets of data, 10 sets are randomly selected as test data, so there are 413 sets of training data and 10 sets of test data. The classification results of pitting defects in metallic materials are shown in Table 6.

Table 6. Prediction results of the second group of experiments

Actual length category	Test length category	Actual width category	Test width category	Actual depth category	Test depth category	Actual depth category	Test depth category
1	2	1	1	3	5	5	5
1	1	3	3	2	2	8	7
1	1	6	7	6	6	6	6
2	2	6	6	4	3	4	3
3	4	2	2	3	4	2	2
4	4	1	2	2	4	7	7

(continued)

Table 6. (*continued*)

Actual length category	Test length category	Actual width category	Test width category	Actual depth category	Test depth category	Actual depth category	Test depth category
5	5	5	5	2	2	2	2
6	5	7	7	7	7	1	1
8	8	4	5	3	2	3	3
8	7	4	4	5	7	7	6

From the experimental results in Table 6, it can be seen that the prediction results of metal material pitting defect recognition obtained by this method are close to the actual results, which proves the effectiveness of the metal material pitting defect recognition method based on visual signal processing.

4 Conclusion

In this paper, a method to identify the pitting defects of metal materials based on visual signal processing is proposed. According to the distribution location of rail cracks, a model of metal materials with defects is constructed. Then, the optical signals of the pitting defects of metal materials are collected and the details of the images in different directions and scales are extracted through the signal processing process. Based on this, the image of metal material pitting defects was decomposed by Mallet algorithm, and specific fusion rules were selected to select each layer component obtained by decomposition. After inverse wavelet transformation, the visual signal fusion and analysis of metal material pitting defects were completed. Experimental results show that the recognition performance of this method is better.

Although the above research results have been achieved in this paper, there are still some deficiencies waiting for improvement, which are mainly reflected in the following aspects: the existing mimics of pitting defects of typical metal materials in the laboratory are few, and it is difficult to obtain through mechanical processing, so it is impossible to obtain rich characteristic parameters of typical defects. In the future, the pitting defect identification system can be used for feature extraction and classification of typical defects, so as to further improve the function of defect recognition.

References

1. Tam, W.C.J., Blanton, R.D.S.: LASIC: layout analysis for systematic IC-defect identification using clustering. IEEE Trans. Comput. Aided Des. Integr. Circuits Syst. **34**(8), 1278–1290 (2015)

2. Zaffuto, B.J., Conley, G.W., Connolly, G.C., et al.: Development of computer-aided radiographic inspection system (II): method of identification and categorization of welded defects. In: Sugita, Y. et al. (eds.) Proceedings of the 10th International Conference on NDE in the Nuclear and Pressure Vessel Industries, Glasgow (Scotland), 11C14 Jun. 1990. 693C699. Edited by M.J. Whittle, J.E. Doherty and K. Iida. ASM International, (1990). Vox Sanguinis, vol. 13, no. 2, pp. 77–87 (2015)

3. Chakaroun, M., Ouladsine, M., Djeziri, M., et al.: Reactive sampling for efficient defect source Identification. IEEE Trans. Semicond. Manuf. 29(2), 104–115 (2017)

4. Sun, J.M., Liu, T., Cheng, X.Z., et al.: Nondestructive detecting metho d for metal material defects based on multimo dal signals[J]. Acta Physica Sinica 16, 223–236 (2016)

5. Liyan, S.: Method of packaging printing defects detection based on machine vision and image processing. Bull. Sci. Technol. 34(10), 105–108 (2018)

6. Yang, C.L.: Micro defects detection in metallic materials based on recurrence analysis of ultrasonic backscattering signal. Opt. Precis. Eng. 27(04), 932–944 (2019)

7. Turkkahraman, D., Alper, O.M., Pehlivanoglu, S., et al.: Analysis of TPO gene in Turkish children with iodide organification defect: identification of a novel mutation. Endocrine 37(1), 124–128 (2010)

8. Liu, S., Li, Z., Zhang, Y., Cheng, X.: Introduction of key problems in long-distance learning and training. Mobile Netw. Appl. 24(1), 1–4 (2019)

9. Shuai, L., Weiling, B., Nianyin, Z., et al.: A fast fractal based compression for MRI images. IEEE Access 7, 62412–62420 (2019)

10. Shuai, L., Dongye, L., Gautam, S., et al.: Overview and methods of correlation filter algorithms in object tracking. Complex Intell. Syst. 3, 1–23 (2020) https://doi.org/10.1007/s40747-020-00161-4

11. Li, X.D., Yin, C.B., Chen, X., et al.: Simulation of infrared thermal wave detection for metal defect recognition hoisting machinery. Constr. Mach. Technol. Manage. 000(003), 58–61 (2019)

12. Dai, X.H., Chen, H.J., Zhu, C.P.: Surface defect detection and realization of metal workpiece based on improved faster RCNN. Surf. Technol. 49(10), 362–371 (2020)

Research on Detection Method of Internal Defects of Metal Materials Based on Computer Vision

Li Zhang[✉] and Ying Zhao

Nanchang Institute of Science and Technology, Nanchang 330108, China

Abstract. In order to improve the accuracy of detecting internal defects of metal materials, a method of detecting internal defects of metal materials is designed based on computer vision. First, computer vision methods are used to collect internal images of metal materials, and then the images are processed and image features are extracted. Finally, accurate detection of internal defects of metal materials was carried out. The experimental results show that, compared with the traditional detection methods, the detection accuracy of the metal material internal defect detection method based on computer vision is high, and the detection time is short, which proves that it has high practical application significance.

Keywords: Computer vision · Metal materials · Internal defect detection · Image feature extraction

1 Introduction

Metal materials generally refer to pure metals or alloys in industrial applications. There are about 70 kinds of pure metals in nature, of which the common ones are iron, copper, aluminum, tin, nickel, gold, silver, lead, zinc, etc. But the alloy often refers to two or more kinds of metals or the combination of metal and non-metal materials and has metal characteristics. At present, a variety of metal materials have become an important material basis for the development of human society. However, due to the influence of the production process, metal materials are prone to internal defects in the manufacturing process. Therefore, it is particularly important to design an effective detection method for internal defects of metal materials.

Computer vision is also often called machine vision. The occurrence and development of this technology has a history of decades. Computer vision is a subject that studies the observation of the surrounding world through image or video data. It mainly uses the image or video taken by the camera as the original data to extract the things that can be observed in the image or video. The problem to be solved by this subject is very similar to the visual perception function of humans observing the world through eyes. Machine vision emphasizes the processing of vision problems with a system composed of machines, while computer vision emphasizes the processing of visual computing problems. The core component is a computer with powerful computing capabilities.

W. Fu et al. (Eds.): ICMTEL 2021, LNICST 387, pp. 27–38, 2021.
https://doi.org/10.1007/978-3-030-82562-1_3

Therefore, this study applied computer vision to metal material internal defect detection process, and designed a metal material internal defect detection method based on computer vision. In this method, the internal images of metal materials are collected by computer vision method, and then the images are processed and the image features are extracted. Finally, the internal defects of metal materials are accurately detected. The experimental results also prove that this method has the advantages of high detection accuracy and detection time.

2 Computer Vision-Based Internal Defect Detection Process of Metal Materials

In the process of metal material internal defect detection based on computer vision, image acquisition technology is used to obtain complete metal material image data, and the image data is associated with metal material information to form a complete metal material defect data record. Then, image processing and pattern recognition technology are used to analyze the image, realize the automatic recognition of the internal defects of metal materials, and record the location information of defects, so as to facilitate the inspection and maintenance of relevant staff [1]. The core part of the system is related technologies and methods in the field of computer vision. The overall process is shown in Fig. 1.

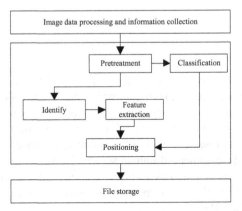

Fig. 1. The internal defect detection process of metal materials based on computer vision

Due to the uneven illumination, occlusion and interference target, the railway image collected in metal materials has poor image quality. Therefore, it is necessary to preprocess the original image to facilitate the subsequent effective image segmentation, feature extraction and recognition [2]. Secondly, in order to automatically identify the state of metal materials through images, it is necessary to extract features that can effectively describe the state of metal materials. There are many methods of image feature extraction. Considering the characteristics of railway fastener itself, the gradient direction histogram feature and local binary mode are selected to describe the metal material image. Finally, according to the known sample features extracted, combined with support vector machine (SVM), the classifier is trained to detect the internal defect state of metal materials.

2.1 Internal Image Processing of Metal Materials

Firstly, the detected image is divided into blocks, and the block size is determined according to the size distribution of the detected object. Firstly, the "block size" must be larger than the largest metal material size in the "image" to ensure the integrity of the detection target in the region containing some blocks; Secondly, after the image is divided into small pieces, it must be rich enough. And the small pieces must contain the metal material in the picture.

Based on the above analysis, the block is set to be square, and the side length is twice the edge of the largest metal material. The block diagram is shown in Fig. 2.

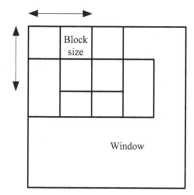

Fig. 2. Block diagram

Then use the back propagation algorithm to pre-train the image, and the cost function formula is as follows:

$$J_d = f + \beta \sum_i w(\rho) \tag{1}$$

In formula (1), J_d is the cost function of a layer of back-propagation network, β is the sparsity cost function, ρ is the activation degree of the training image, $\sum_i w$ is the number of hidden neurons, and f is the expected activation degree of the image. Then, it uses deep learning algorithm to calculate the cost function layer by layer, and carries out unsupervised learning. The process is shown in the following formula:

$$J(w, d) = \frac{q}{m} \sum_f q(x_i, y_i) \tag{2}$$

In formula (2), x_i, y_i represents the training image sample set, $J(w, d)$ represents the hidden layer output parameter, m represents the weight attenuation parameter, q

represents the network layer number, and $\sum\limits_{f} q$ represents the node number of the q layer.

The image is pre-trained through the above process, and the image is processed on this basis.

In the process of image shooting and transmission, due to the influence of various interference factors in the scene, it is easy to lead to the actual image can not meet the needs of viewing, recognition and understanding [3]. The main purpose of image enhancement technology is to purposefully enhance the features of the interested parts of the image according to different needs of people, while suppressing the unnecessary features, and expanding the differences between different objects in the image. Its purpose is to improve the visual effect of the image, improve the clarity, or transform the image into a form more suitable for analysis and processing, and contain as much useful information as possible.

Image enhancement technology is divided into spatial domain processing method and frequency domain processing method according to the different space in the enhancement process. The spatial domain processing method is to directly process the values of the pixels of the collected image, based on the gray-scale mapping transformation, which mainly includes gray-scale correction, image smoothing and image sharpening. The frequency domain processing method is to process the coefficients through a certain transformation, and finally change back to the original space. In order to improve the quality of the original image to facilitate subsequent defect location and recognition, it is necessary to first perform certain enhancement processing on the images collected on the actual railway line.

Based on the analysis of a large number of metal material images, histogram equalization is used to process the original image [4]. Histogram equalization is to transform the original gray distribution of the input image into a gray distribution image with approximately the same number of pixels in each gray level. In the new image obtained by histogram equalization, pixels occupy as many gray levels as possible and are approximately evenly distributed, and the contrast and dynamic range of the image are increased.

The gray distribution of the image is generally represented by a histogram. The histogram describes the number of pixels of each gray level in the image or the frequency of the gray level pixels, and reflects the gray level distribution of the image. The histogram of the image whose gray level is in the range of [0, 1] is a discrete function, and its form is as follows:

$$h(r_k) = n_k \tag{3}$$

In formula (3), r_k represents the gray level of level k, and n_k represents the number of pixels with gray level r_k in the image.

Divide the total number of pixels contained in the image (indicated by n) by the number of pixels in each gray level to get a normalized histogram:

$$h'(r_k) = \frac{n_k}{n} \tag{4}$$

In order to facilitate the analysis of histogram equalization principle, firstly, it is assumed that the gray value range of the image is continuously distributed on the interval

[0, 1]. According to the properties of the probability density function, there are:

$$\int_0^1 p(x)dx = 1 \tag{5}$$

Assuming that the probability density of the image before transformation is $p_r(r)$, the probability density function of the image after transformation is $p_s(s)$, and the transformation function (that is, the gray-scale mapping relationship) is $s = f(r)$, we can get from the probability theory:

$$p_s(s) = p_r(r) \cdot \frac{dr}{ds} \tag{6}$$

For discrete gray values, the corresponding transformation formula is as follows:

$$D_B = f(D_A) = \frac{D_{aax}}{N} \sum_{D_1}^{j=0} n_i \tag{7}$$

In formula (7), n_i represents the number of pixels of the i grayscale; N represents the total number of pixels of the image; f represents the transformation function.

The transform function is a monotone increasing function to ensure that the gray level of the image before and after the transformation will not be reversed. For the original image, the above transformation formula can be used to equalize it, and the original gray level can be mapped to a new gray level, so as to obtain an approximately uniform histogram.

On this basis, image edge detection is carried out. Edge feature is one of the basic features of image, which often contains a lot of useful information. Image edge refers to the discontinuity of image local characteristics, such as the mutation of pixel value and texture structure [5]. Edge exists widely between different objects, which is an important basis for image segmentation. At the same time, the edge is also the symbol of contour and position. In the process of texture feature extraction, shape feature extraction and image understanding and recognition, it is often necessary to detect the edge of the image first. The formula is as follows:

$$S(x, y) = [f(x + n, y) - f(x, y)]^2 \tag{8}$$

In formula (8), $f(x, y)$ is the gray distribution function of the edge image to be detected, and $(x + n, y)$ is the gradient value of the image edge.

Image binarization is a typical threshold segmentation method. The specific processing method is: set an appropriate threshold for an input image with multiple gray levels, and set the gray values of all pixels in the image one by one Comparing with this threshold, pixels larger than this threshold are all set to 1, and pixels smaller than the threshold are set to 0.

Assuming that the gray distribution function of the original image is $f(x, y)$, and the image distribution function after binarization is $g(x, y)$, then:

$$g(x, y) = \begin{cases} 0, f(x, y) < \text{Threshold} \\ 1, \ f(x, y) \geq \text{Threshold} \end{cases} \tag{9}$$

Among them, the threshold is the scale to distinguish the target from the background, and reasonable selection of threshold is the key to achieve satisfactory results of binarization processing. It is required to retain as much useful information as possible and reduce the interference of noise and background [6].

In the process of image binarization, there are usually two strategies for threshold selection. One is the global threshold method, that is, only one threshold is used in the binarization process, which is suitable for the image with obvious distinction between the target and the background, and the histogram presents bimodal characteristics; the other is the local threshold method, which uses different segmentation thresholds for different pixel regions, which belongs to the dynamic adaptive binarization processing method, which is suitable for the background gray change or serious noise in the image The sound quality is poor.

2.2   Feature Extraction of Internal Image of Metal

The first step in automatic image recognition is to extract useful data and information from the image, that is, image features. Through the training process, the computer "understands" these features, so as to achieve the purpose of classifying and identifying the input unknown image. This requires that the features we choose not only describe images well, but also distinguish images belonging to different categories.

Each image contains features that can be distinguished from other types of images, some of which can be intuitively felt by humans, and some of the features need to be obtained by transforming or processing the original image data, such as matrix, Histogram etc. In general, feature extraction should be analyzed by specific issues, and the evaluation criteria are also subjective. In general, the feature extraction process should be relatively easy, and it should be weighed against the feature classification ability. In addition, the extracted features should be insensitive to noise and irrelevant transformations. For example, in the recognition of the license plate number, the shooting angle of each image may be inconsistent. But we are only concerned about the above numbers, so we need to obtain feature descriptors that are not sensitive to geometric distortion and deformation, so as to obtain features that are not subject to rotation or projection distortion.

The local binary mode is an operator used for texture description, which can measure and extract the texture information of local regions in grayscale images [7]. The local binary mode texture unit is shown in Fig. 3.

When using the local binary pattern to extract the texture features of an image, firstly, it is necessary to calculate the binary relationship between the gray value of each pixel in the image and the local neighborhood pixels on the gray level [8]; secondly, the obtained binary relationship is weighted according to certain rules to obtain the local binary pattern; finally, the histogram sequence of multiple regions is used as the binary mode of the whole image, and the calculation is introduced below The mathematical analysis of sub.

For the local texture T of an image, it can be regarded as the joint distribution density of the gray level in the local area of the image

$$T = t\left(g_c, g_0, \cdots, g_{p-1}\right) \tag{10}$$

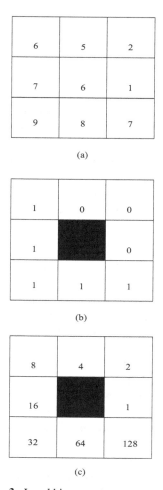

(a)

(b)

(c)

Fig. 3. Local binary pattern texture unit

In formula (10), g_c represents the gray value of the central pixel in the local neighborhood of the image. Without losing the texture information of the local area, subtracting the gray value of the center pixel of the neighborhood from the neighborhood point, the calculation expression is:

$$T = t\big(g_c, g_0 - g_c, \cdots, g_{p-1} - g_c\big) \tag{11}$$

In formula (11), g_c represents the center pixel of the neighborhood.

Performing differential operations on all pixels in the neighborhood can make larger and smaller gray levels uniform (especially under uneven lighting conditions), with uniform brightness invariance, and translation invariance characteristics within the gray range [9]. The difference between the central pixel and the neighboring pixel is independent of the gray value of the central pixel, so the above formula is converted to:

$$T = t(g_c)t\big(g_0 - g_c, \cdots, g_{p-1} - g_c\big) \tag{12}$$

Finally, a coding value is used to represent the local binary pattern of texture units, namely texture characteristics. The correlation coefficient is defined as: 1

$$r_{i,j} = \frac{E[(F_i - F_j)(F_{i2} - F_{j2})]}{\sigma_i \sigma_j} \tag{13}$$

In formula (13), σ_i and σ_j represent the standard deviations of features F and F_j respectively. The closer $r_{i,j}$ and 1, the higher the correlation between the two features.

In addition, feature stability is also an important factor affecting feature selection. Therefore, the following formula is used to measure the stability of the target feature, which is defined as follows:

$$\rho_i = \frac{E[F_{iz}^{(w)z}] - E^2[F_{i2}^{(w)}]}{E[F_i^{(w)2}]} \tag{14}$$

In formula (14), $E[F_{iz}^{(w)z}]$ and $E^2[F_{i2}^{(w)}]$ represent the mean and mean square values of the current characteristic F_i respectively. w represents the label of classification type. The smaller ρ_i is, the more stable the feature is.

The method of thresholding the neighborhood elements with the gray value of the central unit as the threshold can accurately reflect the change characteristics of the gray values of the elements in the neighborhood, and has certain gray invariance and stable output.

Because when the neighborhood of the image rotates, the neighborhood elements will move in the circumferential direction around the center pixel of the unit. When calculating the encoding of the neighborhood, the default will start from the element to the right of the center pixel of the unit as the first element, and then rotate counterclockwise to get other elements in turn, and the corresponding weights will increase in turn. Big. As a result, for the same texture unit, the coded value obtained when the rotation changes occurs often, and the coded value will be different with different rotation angles.

In order to make the local binary pattern be able to describe the element with rotation change effectively, it is necessary to improve the descriptor to make it rotation invariant. The specific processing method is as follows: for the neighborhood unit, a group of coding sequences are obtained according to the original thresholding method, and then the coding sequence is circularly shifted to minimize the corresponding decimal result value, and the minimum value is taken as the coding value of the unit [10]. In this way, no matter how much the rotation angle changes, a coding mode will eventually appear.

2.3 Extraction of Internal Defects of Metallic Materials Based on Computer Vision

On the basis of the above image preprocessing, the edge segmentation line is combined with the image threshold region of interest, and the image is rotated and

$$\text{translated } P(X) = A(X) + b \tag{15}$$

In formula (15), X represents the spatial position of the image pixel, A represents the rotation matrix of the two images, and b represents the translation vector.

Among them, the matrix A needs to meet the constraints:

$$A^t A = I, \det I = 1 \tag{16}$$

In formula (16), A^t represents the rotation value of matrix A and I represents the identity matrix.

After optimizing the spatial transformation, the similarity function is defined to measure the similarity between the image and the reference image, and the similarity measurement function is optimized by continuously adjusting the transformation parameters. The calculation formula is as follows:

$$Z(a, b) = \frac{h(a, b)}{\sum\limits_{i=1} k(a, b)} \tag{17}$$

In formula (17), $h(a, b)$ represents the gray value corresponding to the image, and k represents the image joint similarity coefficient.

Image registration defines a three-dimensional coordinate system. The x axis scans along the image row direction, the y axis scans along the column direction, and the z axis scans along the aspect of layer growth. The expression of the image to be registered is:

$$C = \frac{\left(C_x, C_y, C_z\right)}{\sum\limits_{y} g(x, y, z)} \tag{18}$$

In formula (18), $g(x, y, z)$ represents the gray level of the pixel whose position is (x, y, z) in the image.

On this basis, the position coordinates of the reference image are discretized sufficiently to make the reference image cover the whole style element space to avoid collapse. The expression is as follows:

$$u = \frac{z}{\exp(v/m)} \tag{19}$$

In formula (19), v represents an ordinary image, m represents the content feature of the image, and z represents the spatial position of the style element.

Finally, combined with the background difference method, the possible defects are initially extracted, and then the connected regions are used to extract edge defects based on the area, roundness, and rectangularity. The algorithm flow of edge micro defect extraction is shown in Fig. 4.

In this way, the internal defect detection of metal materials based on computer vision is completed through the above process.

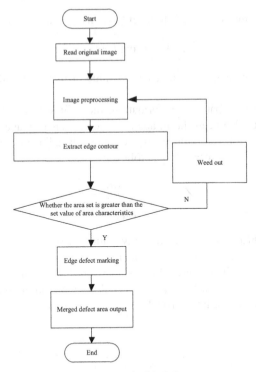

Fig. 4. Process flow of edge defect treatment

3 Experiment

In order to verify the effectiveness of the internal defect detection method of metal materials based on computer vision, experiments are carried out and the traditional internal defect detection method is compared with the method in this paper, and the detection accuracy and detection time of the two methods are compared.

3.1 Comparison of Detection Accuracy

The comparison results of detection accuracy between this method and traditional detection methods are shown in Fig. 5.

According to Fig. 5, compared with the traditional detection methods, the detection accuracy of the metal material internal defects detection method based on computer vision is higher, and the detection accuracy can be controlled above 90%.

3.2 Comparison of Detection Time

The comparison result of the detection time between the traditional detection method and the method in this paper is shown in Fig. 6.

It can be seen from the analysis of Fig. 6 that the detection time curve of the proposed method is below that of the traditional method in many tests, which proves that the

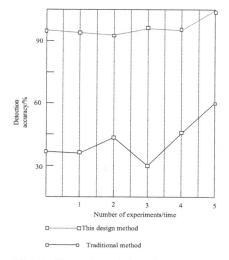

Fig. 5. Comparison of detection accuracy

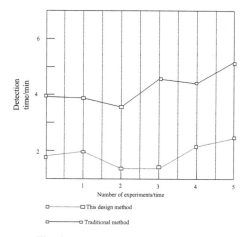

Fig. 6. Comparison of detection time

proposed method consumes less detection time than the traditional method and the detection time is always less than 3 s, thus proving that the proposed method has high timeliness.

4 Conclusion

In this study, an internal defect detection method of metal materials based on computer vision is designed. Firstly, the internal images of metal materials are collected by computer vision method, and then the images are processed and the image features are extracted. Finally, the internal defects of metal materials are accurately detected. In addition, this study also verified the application advantages of this method with high detection accuracy and detection time through experiments. However, due to the limitation of research time, this method still has some shortcomings. To this end, in the follow-up research, will do more in-depth research.

References

1. Haomin, Y., et al.: A coarse-to-fine model for rail surface defect detection. IEEE Trans. Instrum. Meas. **68**(3), 656–666 (2019)
2. Vrana, J., Goldammer, M.: Defect detection mechanisms with induction and conduction thermography: current flow and defect-specific warming. Quant. Infrared Thermography J. **17**(2), 130–151 (2020)
3. Sun, Y., Li, X., Xiao, J.: A cascaded Mura defect detection method based on mean shift and level set algorithm for active-matrix OLED display panel. J. Soc. Inform. Display **27**(1–3), 13–20 (2019)
4. Yao, M.-H., Ma, M., Liu, J.-M.: Defect detection method of magnetic disk image based on improved convolutional neural network. Optoelectron. Lett. **16**(5), 396–400 (2020)
5. He, Z., Wang, H., He, Y., et al.: Joint scanning laser thermography defect detection method for carbon fiber reinforced polymer. IEEE Sens. J. **20**(1), 328–336 (2019)
6. Liu, S., Li, Z., Zhang, Y., Cheng, X.: Introduction of key problems in long-distance learning and training. Mobile Netw. Appl. **24**(1), 1–4 (2018)
7. Shuai, L., Dongye, L., Gautam, S., et al.: Overview and methods of correlation filter algorithms in object tracking. Complex Intell. Syst. **3**, 1–23 (2020) https://doi.org/10.1007/s40747-020-00161-4
8. Lib, C., Gao, G., Liu, Z., et al.: Defect detection for patterned fabric images based on GHOG and low-rank decomposition. IEEE Access **7**(99), 83962–83973 (2019)
9. Shuai, L., Weiling, B., Nianyin, Z., et al.: A fast fractal based compression for MRI images. IEEE Access **7**, 62412–62420 (2019)
10. Wu, Y., Guo, D., Liu, H., et al.: An end-to-end learning method for industrial defect detection. Assem. Autom. **40**(1), 31–39 (2019)

Error Correction Method for Rotating Axis of Large Rotating Machinery Based on Machine Vision

Yu-Shuo Tan[1](✉), Wen-Bin Zhang[2], Jing Wang[3], Han Han[1], and Wei-Ping Cao[4]

[1] Shijiazhuang Posts and Telecommunications Technical College, Shijiazhuang 050021, Hebei, China
ls62322@aliyun.com
[2] Honghe University, Mengzi 661199, China
[3] Shijiazhuang Information Engineering Vocational College, Shijiazhuang 050000, China
[4] West Normal University Physical Culture Institute Chengdu, Nanchong 637099, Sichuan, China

Abstract. The error model of the traditional error correction method has data deviation, which leads to a decline in the ability to identify and separate error data during the error correction process. For this reason, this research proposes a new method of error correction for the rotating shaft of large rotating machinery based on machine vision technology. This method redesigns the shaft error check code and optimizes the shaft error model of large rotating machinery. Then based on the machine vision to detect the shaft error, and realize the reliable correction of the shaft error. The experimental results show that: compared with the traditional method, the recognition similarity coefficient of this method is closer to 1, and the error data separation effect is also superior to the traditional method.

Keywords: Machine vision · Mechanical axis of rotation · Error correction · Error check code

1 Introduction

In the working process of rotating shaft of large rotating machinery, due to the technical errors of manufacturing technology and production process, the rotating effect of rotating shaft may be affected. When this kind of situation occurs, if the detailed and accurate error correction is not carried out, the work efficiency of large rotating machinery will be affected. Therefore, it is one of the effective measures to design an effective error correction method for large rotating machinery to ensure the work efficiency and use safety of large rotating machinery.

Machine vision, also known as computer vision, refers to data measurement and discrimination by machine instead of human eyes. Through the use of machine vision technology, the ability to detect the error data is strengthened, the accuracy of the detection results is improved, and the advanced technical support is provided for the normal operation of the national large-scale rotating machinery.

W. Fu et al. (Eds.): ICMTEL 2021, LNICST 387, pp. 39–50, 2021.
https://doi.org/10.1007/978-3-030-82562-1_4

For this reason, this paper proposes a method of error correction for large rotating machinery based on machine vision. This method redesigns the shaft error check code and optimizes the shaft error model of large rotating machinery. Then, the rotation axis error is detected based on machine vision to realize the reliable correction of the rotation axis error.

2   Error Correction Method for Rotating Shaft of Large Rotating Machinery

2.1   Design Shaft Error Check Code

In the initial stage of error correction of the rotating shaft of large rotating machinery, the shaft error check code is compiled in advance. The design requires that the check code has a shortened basic structure feature, and the check code is used to detect large-scale rotating machinery and basic rotation axis data to obtain the error information flow existing therein. The basic structure of the designed check code is shown in Fig. 1 below.

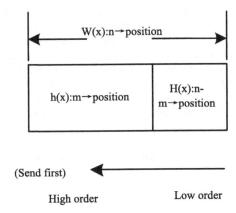

Fig. 1. Basic structure of cyclic redundancy check code

According to the label in Fig. 1, it can be seen that there is a one-to-one correspondence between the m coefficients of $h(x)$ and the m information bits; the $n - m$ coefficients of $H(x)$ correspond to the $n - m$ check bits. From the perspective of channel coding, the entire n bit frame is a codeword, so the $n - m$ parity part is used as the designed check code. Among them, $h(x)$ is a polynomial of degree $(m - 1)$, $H(x)$ is a polynomial of degree $(n - m - 1)$, then $W(X)$ is a polynomial of degree $(m - 1)$, and $k(x)$ is a polynomial of degree $(n - m)$ [1, 2]. Therefore, the cyclic code has a formula at the sending end:

$$W(X) = x^{n-m}h(x) + H(x) \tag{1}$$

In formula (1): $W(X)$ represents the transmission code; $H(x) = \frac{x^{n-m}h(x)}{k(x)}$. If there is no error code in the received code stream, then the received code $H(x)$ should be equal to the transmit code $W(X)$, that is, there is:

$$W(X) = H(x) = x^{n-m}h(x) + H(x) = \varphi(x)k(x) \tag{2}$$

The received code $H(x)$ at this time can be divisible by the generator polynomial $k(x)$. If the received code at this time cannot be divisible by $k(x)$, it means that a code error occurred during the transmission of the shaft data. At this time, the "cyclic" feature of the check code is shown in the cyclic code generator polynomial $k(x)$, and the length of the check bit is $n - m$, which is the embodiment of "redundancy" [3]. Because this code is a cyclic code, it exists:

$$k(x)\mu(x) = x^2 + 1 \tag{3}$$

Here $n - m$ is a factor of n. If $n - m$ is fixed, then parameter n is also fixed. However, in the actual check, the frame length n can be changed continuously, so the cyclic code (n_0, m_0) is shortened to any s bit, and the actual check code is obtained as follows:

$$(n_0 - s, m_0 - s) = (n, m) \tag{4}$$

The shortened check code still has inherent characteristics. Through the analysis and control of the cyclic code, it can be applied to the basic check of the error of the rotating shaft of large rotating machinery [4].

2.2 Setting up Error Model of Rotating Axis of Large Rotating Machinery

Because large-scale rotating machinery is prone to abnormal system operation during the control process, coupled with the influence of basic control hardware and matching errors, it is necessary to establish a rotating axis error model based on the basic structure of large-scale rotating machinery, and meet machine vision inspection according to this model The basic application conditions to obtain the rotation error data.

Suppose the ideal point control position of the rotating shaft of a large rotating machine is $b_1(x_i, y_i)$, and the error point position coordinate is $b_2(x_j, y_j)$, where x_i and x_j represent the abscissa of the point; y_i and y_j represent the ordinate of the point [5]. The relationship between the two points can be expressed by the following formula:

$$\begin{bmatrix} x_a \\ y_a \end{bmatrix} = \left(1 + q_1 d^2 + q_2 d^4\right) \begin{bmatrix} x' \\ y' \end{bmatrix} + \begin{bmatrix} 2\gamma_1 x'y' + \gamma_2\left(d^2 + 2x^2\right) \\ \gamma_1\left(d^2 + 2y^2\right) + 2\gamma_2 x'y' \end{bmatrix} \tag{5}$$

In formula (5): $x' = \frac{x_n - x_{n0}}{\mu_{nx}}$, $y' = \frac{y_n - y_{n0}}{\mu_{ny}}$; where x_{n0} and y_{n0} represent the initial data position coordinates of the ideal point; μ_{nx} and μ_{ny} respectively represent the separation functions of the ideal point coordinates. $d = x'^2 + y'^2$. x' and y' represent the median value of ideal point and error point respectively. $x_a = \frac{x_m - x_{m0}}{\mu_{mx}}$, $y_a = \frac{y_m - y_{m0}}{\mu_{my}}$. Where x_{m0} and y_{m0} are the initial coordinates of the error points; μ_{mx} and μ_{my} are the separation functions of the coordinates of the error points. $x_a \cdot y_a$ is the coordinate value when the correlation strength is a; q_1 and q_2 are the radial error coefficients of the error points; γ_1

and γ_2 are the tangential error coefficients. Due to the error in the relationship processing, an objective function is set up to optimize the influence parameters in the relationship value

$$r = \min \left(\sum_{i=1}^{n} \sum_{j=1}^{m} \left\| \eta_{nij} - \eta \left(A_n, C, Q_i, \eta_{tj} \right) \right\|^2 \right) \tag{6}$$

In formula (6): r represents the objective function; η_{nij} represents the plane coordinates of the j marking point in the i measurement area in the ideal point coordinates; A_n represents the mechanical internal parameter matrix; C represents the degree of error index; Q_i represents the i The external parameter matrix in each area; η_{tj} represents the point function of t at the measurement time. Combining formulas (5) and (6) to set the shaft error model as:

$$_{b_2}^{b_1}T = r(x_a, y_a) \tag{7}$$

In formula (7): $_{b_2}^{b_1}T$ represents the error model under the influence of ideal point and error point [6].

According to the above design, the error parameters of the rotating shaft of large rotating machinery are screened to realize the error detection of machine vision.

2.3 Detection of Shaft Error Based on Machine Vision

The above model is used to obtain the rotation axis error detection feature. According to this feature, the machine vision reverse perception algorithm is used to detect the error. The main detection device is a multilayer perceptron. Using machine vision detection algorithm, the working signal of the rotating shaft is forward divergent and propagated, and the expected value is established. When the signal does not reach the expected value, the signal is defined as an error signal, and the signal is propagated back. Start at the output of the device and spread down layer by layer. Select the initial measurement value of the coefficient, make the sample data input into the sensor $u = (u_0, u_1, \ldots, u_{n-1})$, detect the expected output value of $v = (v_0, v_1, \ldots, v_{n-1})$, and the actual output value of $z = (z_0, z_1, \ldots, z_{n-1})$, adjust the coefficient gradually downward from the layer area where the output terminal is located, and get the adjustment The result is:

$$\phi_{mn}(t+1) = \phi_{mn}(t) + \beta\lambda_n \cdot \delta_m \tag{8}$$

In formula (8): m and n are input layer nodes, ϕ_{mn} is coefficient weight between input layer node m and node n in t period; β is gain term; λ_n is deviation at node n; δ_m is data feature of m node [7]. When n is the output layer node by default, then:

$$\lambda_n = z_n \cdot (1 - z_n) \cdot (v_n - z_n) \tag{9}$$

In formula (9): v_n is the expected output value of node n; z_n is the actual output of node n. When there is a hidden middle layer in the n node, then:

$$\lambda_n = \varepsilon_n \left(1 - \varepsilon_n' \right) \sum_{i=1}^{n} \lambda_u \cdot \alpha_{nu} \tag{10}$$

In formula (10): u represents the number of nodes in the upper layer of node$n$; α_{nu} represents the coefficient convergence parameter under these two nodes. According to the obtained λ_n, the error type of rotation axis is determined, so as to realize the error detection based on machine vision [8].

2.4 Error Correction

Based on the above processing, the error correction process of rotating axis can be deduced as follows:

$$F = G^2\lambda^3 + E_{count} \tag{11}$$

In formula (11): G represents the coefficient matrix; λ represents the error of the measurement point; E_{count} represents the constant term [9]. Continuously transform the error coefficient λ of the above formula, calculate the values of different correction coefficients λ, and obtain the correction model coefficients according to the relationship between the two values, as shown in Table 1:

Table 1. Correction model coefficients

	F1	F2	F3
$\varepsilon 1$	0.344	− 0.128	0.103
$\varepsilon 2$	0.251	− 0.07	0.055
$\varepsilon 3$	0.035	− 0.029	0.266
$\varepsilon 4$	− 0.191	0.248	− 0.047
$\varepsilon 5$	− 0.032	0.066	0.401
$\varepsilon 6$	0.076	− 0.738	− 0.189
$\varepsilon 7$	− 0.029	0.107	0.019
$\varepsilon 8$	− 0.015	0.219	− 0.304
$\varepsilon 9$	− 0.012	− 0.247	− 0.205
$\varepsilon 10$	0.026	0.005	0.033
$\varepsilon 11$	0.087	− 0.463	0.026
$\varepsilon 12$	− 0.266	0.575	− 0.067
$\varepsilon 13$	0.645	− 0.372	0.214
$\varepsilon 14$	− 0.343	0.641	− 0.035
$\varepsilon 15$	− 0.047	0.248	− 0.081

Deal with the coefficients shown in the table above. When the amplitude error exists in the measurement result, calculate the error vector o_r of this part. The calculation formula is as follows:

$$o_r(\lambda, E) = Ga(\lambda, E) \tag{12}$$

In formula (12): G represents the amplitude error matrix, which satisfies the following quantitative relationship:

$$G = diag([c_1, c_2, ..., c_n]^k)$$ (13)

In formula (13): c_n is the amplitude coefficient; when c_1 is 1, the amplitude error square wave is (λ_0, E_0), and the corresponding correction array covariance matrix can be expressed as:

$$R = GR_iG^H + \zeta_{max}c_n$$ (14)

In formula (14): G^H represents the magnitude error matrix coefficient; ζ_{max} represents the corresponding eigenvector; R_i represents the subspace coefficient. Calculate the value of the corresponding eigenvector in the above formula and use this value as the correction amount. The calculation formula is:

$$\zeta_{max} = \frac{G(\varepsilon_0, \eta_0)}{|G^H|^2}$$ (15)

According to the actual work of large-scale rotating machinery, considering the particularity of rotating shaft error, the coefficient in the correction process is constantly changed, and the processing process of the above calculation formula is repeated to obtain the position error correction amount of different rotating axes. So far, with the help of machine vision, the error correction of large-scale rotating machinery's rotating axis is realized [10].

3 Experimental Study

In order to verify the effectiveness of the error correction method of large rotating machinery based on machine vision, this method is compared with two traditional correction methods, and the following experiments are designed. Among them, this method is the experimental group, and two traditional correction methods are control group A and control group B. The experiment takes the error data recognition effect, the signal waveform similarity coefficient of the recognition result and the error data separation effect as the indicators to verify the application performance of different methods.

3.1 Error Data Recognition Test

Based on MATLAB to build an experimental platform, the three test groups used different techniques to identify the rotation errors of large rotating machinery before the calibration started. The results are shown in Fig. 2.

Based on this, according to the similarity evaluation function, the data recognition effect of the three test groups is evaluated. It is known that the data signal will form irregular waveforms under different commands. At the same time, the test environment itself will also bring interference to the experimental results, and the identification waveforms often have timing differences. Therefore, according to the correlation, the signal waveforms of the two test groups are judged to be similar to the real signals. The experiment

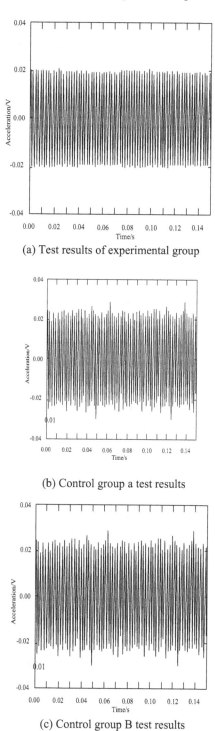

(a) Test results of experimental group

(b) Control group a test results

(c) Control group B test results

Fig. 2. Comparison of error data recognition effect

assumes that the real signal and the identification signal are $x(t)$ and $y(t)$ respectively, and the similarity between the waveforms is measured by the error energy. The error energy is expressed as:

$$\int (x(t) - \omega \cdot y(t))^2 dt \tag{16}$$

In formula (16): ω is the multiple value that makes $\omega \cdot y(t)$ close to $x(t)$. At the same time, it is required to ensure that the error of energy can be minimized when the parameter D is selected:

$$\omega = \frac{\int x(t) \cdot y(t) dt}{\int y(t) \cdot y(t) dt} \tag{17}$$

When the above conditions are met, the error energy is known to be the minimum. Therefore, the correlation coefficient between the real signal and the identification signal is defined as σ_{xy}, and the value of the correlation coefficient can be obtained:

$$\sigma_{xy} = \frac{\int x(t) \cdot y(t) dt}{\sqrt{\int x^2(t) dt \cdot y^2(t) dt}} \tag{18}$$

The result σ_{xy} can be used to describe the waveform similarity between the real signal and the recognition signal. In the process of experimental test, there is a time difference ΔT between the real signal and the recognition signal, so the correlation coefficient of the two signals in ΔT time is obtained by multiplication and integration. When the similarity coefficient is 1, the error energy is 0, which indicates that the correction method has the best recognition effect for the error data; when the similarity coefficient is 0, the result of the correction method is the worst. In 40 tests, the statistical results of error signal waveform similarity coefficient of three test groups are shown in Table 2.

Table 2. Test results of signal waveform similarity coefficient

Test group	Experience group	Control group A	Control group B
Group 1	0.9355	0.8574	0.8781
Group 2	0.9346	0.8585	0.8761
Group 3	0.9351	0.8588	0.8763
Group 4	0.9350	0.8573	0.8777
Group 5	0.9348	0.8575	0.8773
Group 6	0.9346	0.8580	0.8766
Group 7	0.9352	0.8581	0.8771
Group 8	0.9345	0.8575	0.8770
Group 9	0.9347	0.8575	0.8772

(continued)

Table 2. (*continued*)

Test group	Experience group	Control group A	Control group B
Group 10	0.9351	0.8586	0.8765
Group 11	0.9354	0.8577	0.8780
Group 12	0.9347	0.8584	0.8761
Group 13	0.9352	0.8587	0.8760
Group 14	0.9351	0.8577	0.8775
Group 15	0.9345	0.8576	0.8775
Group 16	0.9347	0.8581	0.8767
Group 17	0.9351	0.8581	0.8771
Group 18	0.9348	0.8577	0.8772
Group 19	0.9348	0.8578	0.8777
Group 20	0.9352	0.8589	0.8764
Group 21	0.9355	0.8575	0.8784
Group 22	0.9347	0.8583	0.8768
Group 23	0.9353	0.8585	0.8769
Group 24	0.9350	0.8577	0.8772
Group 25	0.9349	0.8579	0.8771
Group 26	0.9345	0.8582	0.8769
Group 27	0.9352	0.8586	0.8772
Group 28	0.9349	0.8574	0.8774
Group 29	0.9348	0.8577	0.8777
Group 30	0.9351	0.8585	0.8767
Group 31	0.9350	0.8580	0.8771
Group 32	0.9352	0.8742	0.8599
Group 33	0.9350	0.8765	0.8542
Group 34	0.9345	0.8772	0.8540
Group 35	0.9346	0.8763	0.8432
Group 36	0.9352	0.8769	0.8575
Group 37	0.9328	0.8760	0.8543
Group 38	0.9366	0.8785	0.8519
Group 39	0.9347	0.8799	0.8722
Group 40	0.9387	0.8751	0.8658

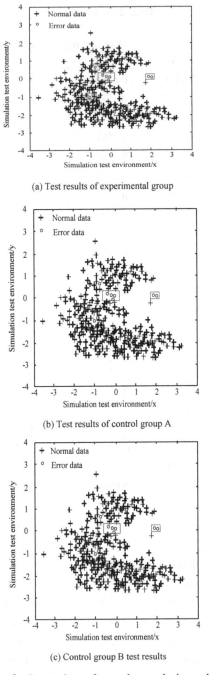

(a) Test results of experimental group

(b) Test results of control group A

(c) Control group B test results

Fig. 3. Comparison of error data analysis results

According to the 40 test results in Table 2, when the error signal is identified by the method in this paper, there is a higher similarity coefficient between the signal waveform and the real signal waveform, and the similarity coefficient value is closer to 1. It can be seen that compared with the control group, this article has a better recognition effect.

3.2 Error Data Separation Effect Test

Three groups of correction methods are loaded into the same test platform respectively, and the detection effect of different correction methods on error data is compared. The simulation test results are shown in Fig. 3.

According to the test results in Fig. 3, the correction method in the experimental group completely separates the rotation error of large rotating machinery from the normal data. However, due to the lack of machine vision, the correction methods of the two control groups failed to completely separate the error data from the normal data, resulting in the error data separation effect can not reach the expected effect. This shows that the error correction method of large rotating machinery based on machine vision designed in this paper can more accurately separate the error data of large rotating machinery, and can lay an effective foundation for error correction.

4 Concluding Remarks

In this study, a method of large rotating machinery rotation axis error correction based on machine vision is designed. Based on the existing research, the technology function of machine vision is fully used to enhance the recognition and separation of large rotating machinery rotation axis error data, so as to effectively improve the correction effect of large rotating machinery rotation axis error. However, due to the difficulty of this method, we should pay attention to the accuracy of the data in the calculation process to ensure that the correction effect is not disturbed by the conventional calculation.

Acknowledgments. Research on Governance of Elderly Sports Health Promotion Sichuan Education Development Research Center CJF20035.

References

1. Shiguang, L.: Glass-bottle defect detection method based on machine vision. Packag. Eng. **39**(03), 183–187 (2018)
2. Erlin, T., Zuhe, L.: Research on position correction method of picking robot—based on wireless sensor network and ultra wide band FM method. J. Agric. Mech. Res. **41**(02), 216–219+224 (2019)
3. Lin, G., Bo, W.: Vision target calibration and error correction simulation at crossroads. Comput. Simul. **35**(11), 141–144+174 (2018)
4. Tao, L., Shibin, Y., Yongjie, R., et al.: Automatic calibration of robot tool center frame robot tool center frames. Opt. Precis. Eng. **27**(03), 661–670 (2019)
5. Bin, L., Guobin, C., Delian, Z.: Fixing error calibration of inertial measurement system in robot. Coal Mine Mach. **39**(01), 41–44 (2018)

6. Li, Z., Zikai, Z., Xiaodong, X.: Research on attitude angle error correction method of inertial gyroscope. Coal Mine Mach. **39**(06), 50–52 (2018)
7. Shuai, L., Dongye, L., Gautam, S., et al.: Overview and methods of correlation filter algorithms in object tracking. Complex Intell. Syst. (3) 2020 https://doi.org/10.1007/s40747-020-00161-4
8. Liu, S., Li, Z., Zhang, Y., Cheng, X.: Introduction of key problems in long-distance learning and training. Mobile Netw. Appl. **24**(1), 1–4 (2019)
9. Shuai, L., Weiling, B., Nianyin, Z., et al.: A fast fractal based compression for MRI images. IEEE Access **7**, 62412–62420 (2019)
10. Feifei, S., Hong, Z., Kaiyu, Z., et al.: Hysteresis prediction and error correction of GMM current transformer. Electr. Mach. Control **22**(07), 85–90 (2018)

Simulation Study on Tensile Mechanical Properties of Graphene Based on Long and Short-Term Memory Neural Network

Li Ang[1](✉) and Wang Hui-jun[2]

[1] Basic Education School, Zhuhai College of Jilin University, Zhuhai 519041, China
liang35789@yeah.net
[2] Xinhua College of Ningxia University, Yinchuan 750021, China

Abstract. The current simulation methods of graphene tensile mechanical properties have not processed the data used in the simulation process, resulting in large errors between the simulation results and the experimental results. For this reason, a graphene tensile mechanics based on long and short-term memory neural networks is proposed. The graphene nanoribbons model was established using Materials Studio software to determine the simulation process of graphene tensile mechanical properties. Use the long and short-term memory neural network to process and store the simulation research data to get the simulation results. Analysis of the simulation results shows that the tensile properties of graphene are affected by the structure of graphene itself, the constituent element atoms, and the distance between atoms, and there will be certain differences in tensile forces in different directions. Three sets of comparative experiments are designed. The experimental results show that the simulation results obtained by the simulation method of graphene tensile mechanical properties in this study are very close to the experimental results, and there is basically no experimental error.

Keyword: Long and short term memory neural network · Graphene · Tensile mechanics · Performance simulation

1 Introduction

Graphene is a two-dimensional periodic honeycomb lattice structure composed of six membered rings of carbon, which is a new low dimensional carbon material [1]. In recent years, due to its unique electrical, thermal, mechanical and magnetic properties, graphene has become one of the hot spots in the field of materials science and condensed matter physics in recent years. The research shows that graphene has extremely excellent mechanical properties and is closely related to the chemical bond and electronic structure between carbon atoms. All of them are composed of the strongest chemical bond α in nature all carbon atoms are bound in the same plane, which makes them have ultra-high strength, stiffness and toughness as well as unique deformation mechanism. Therefore, many scholars have actively studied the mechanical properties of graphene [2, 3]. At

W. Fu et al. (Eds.): ICMTEL 2021, LNICST 387, pp. 51–63, 2021.
https://doi.org/10.1007/978-3-030-82562-1_5

present, domestic and foreign scholars' research on graphene is mainly focused on the preparation, characterization, and physical and chemical properties of graphene. Experimental testing, numerical simulation, and theoretical analysis are mostly used to study the mechanical properties of graphene. The research on its mechanical properties is basically at the initial stage, especially the lack of research on the tensile mechanical properties of graphene, resulting in the tensile properties of graphene, which has not been well applied [4]. At present, there are many researches on using neural network to simulate mechanical properties. However, because long-term and short-term memory neural network improves the long-term dependence problem in RNN, it is usually better than time recurrent neural network and hidden Markov model. Moreover, as a nonlinear model, the network can be used as a complex nonlinear unit to construct a larger deep neural network. Compared with convolution neural network [5] and other methods, it has obvious advantages, so in this study of graphene tensile mechanical properties, long-term and short-term memory neural network is used to minimize the training error and improve the simulation accuracy of graphene tensile mechanical properties.

2   Design of Simulation Method for Tensile Mechanical Properties of Graphene

2.1   Building a Graphene Model

Materials Studio software is used to establish the graphene model. In the materials Studio software, a single-layer square graphene nanobelt model with the size of 122.14 nm * 122.14 nm is established by expanding the unit cell, as shown in Fig. 1.

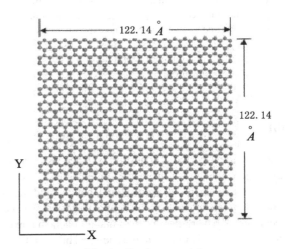

Fig. 1. Graphene model

The graphene nanoribbon model system contains 5800 atoms, the distance between carbon-carbon bonds is 1.42° A, the mass of carbon atoms is 12.0107, and the mass unit is atomic mass unit (1 atomic mass unit = 1.6605402*10^{-27} kg), the density of the polymer is 1.1 g/cm2. According to the study on the tensile mechanical properties of graphene, the required graphene structure is appropriately cut to the edge of the graphene to obtain two different properties of graphene nanoribbons, armchair type and zigzag type, to improve graphene stretching research precision of mechanical properties. Based on the graphene geometric model shown in Fig. 1, the basic geometric properties of the graphene studied in this study can be determined and used as a reference condition for simulating the tensile mechanical properties of graphene.

The graphene model is a honeycomb like two-dimensional crystal composed of single-layer hexagonal cell carbon atoms. The thickness is about 0.335nm, and the length of carbon carbon bond is about 0.142 nm. The final graphene model is square, and the corresponding chiral angles are 0.00°, 5.82°, 10.98°, 15.30°, 19.11°, 24.11°, 25.28°, 27.80° and 30.00° respectively.

2.2 Determine the Simulation Process of Graphene Tensile Mechanical Properties

In the process of studying the tensile mechanical properties of graphene, the graphene model was established and the simulation process of graphene tensile mechanical properties was designed. In the simulation process, the mass of C atom is selected as 12. Control the x direction as a free boundary condition, the y direction as a free boundary condition, and the z direction as a periodic boundary condition. The AIREBO potential function is selected and the long and short-term memory neural network is the default integration algorithm.

Due to the doping of some other elements in graphene materials, it will have a certain impact on the material properties of graphene [6]. However, the radius of silicon atom in graphene is larger than that of carbon atom. The substitution of silicon atom for carbon atom will cause crystal structure distortion, increase the potential energy of graphene, and its stability and mechanical properties will be affected. In order to prevent the whole graphene from being affected too much, the tensile mechanical properties of graphene films with low doping ratio were studied. At this time, the tensile mechanical properties of graphene were simulated as follows:

(1) Simulation of the relaxation characteristics of graphene. Without imposing any external load constraints on the model, the Nose-Hoover thermal bath method is used for temperature adjustment, the control temperature is 0K, the time step is 1fs (Note, $1fs = 10^{-3}ps$), and the entire model is fully unconstrained relaxation.

(2) Tensile simulation of graphene in x direction. The temperature was regulated by Nose-Hoover heat bath method. The temperature was controlled at 0k and the time step was 1FS. The carbon atoms at the left end of the film were fully relaxed, and then the right carbon atoms were loaded with x direction tensile strain. The strain of each step was 0.001. The graphene model was selected to achieve stable relaxation step size. The strain was applied continuously until the graphene film was destroyed.

(3) Tensile simulation of graphene in y direction. The method is the same as that in x direction, but the carbon atoms at the lower end of the film are fixed first, and the tensile strain load in y direction is applied to the upper carbon atoms.

2.3 Simulation Method Based on Short and Long Time Memory Neural Network

Long and short term memory (LSTM) neural network is an improved recurrent neural network (RNN) [7]. The long-term and short-term memory neural network is used to store all the information of the tensile mechanical properties of graphene during the simulation process. The data structure of the memory graphene tensile mechanical properties is shown in Fig. 2.

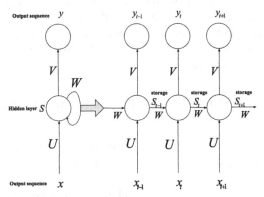

Fig. 2. Data structure diagram of tensile mechanical properties of long and short-term memory neural network memory graphene

In Fig. 2, t represents the long-term and short-term memory neural network, and the time step of storing data, i.e. $t = 1, 2, 3, \cdots$. x_t represents the input in step t, and V, U and W represent the hidden layer position of long and short memory neural network respectively. s_t is the memory unit, which is the state of the t time step of the hidden layer. If the state of the hidden layer W_{x_t} in the previous step is combined with the output U_{x_t} of the current input layer, the calculation formula of s_t is as follows:

$$s_t = f\left(U_{x_t} + W_{x_t} - 1\right) \tag{1}$$

In formula (1), f represents the nonlinear activation function, and y represents the output at the t time step.

According to the long and short-term memory neural network memory graphene tensile mechanical properties data structure diagram shown in Fig. 2, the results of each experiment are directly input into the long and short-term memory neural network architecture diagram, and all the experimental data can be analyzed and sorted, get the simulation result.

2.4 Tensile Mechanical Properties of Simulated Graphene

According to the Mermin-Wagner theory, long-wavelength fluctuations will destroy the long-range order characteristics of the two-dimensional crystal; at the same time, it can be known from the elastic theory that the stability of the two-dimensional film is relatively poor when the effective temperature is greater than 0K, and it is especially prone to bending Phenomenon [8]. Therefore, in the past, scientists believed that "a perfect two-dimensional crystal structure can only exist stably under absolute zero conditions." However, the successful preparation of single-layer graphene broke this argument. Single-layer graphene can exist stably in the external environment of non-absolute zero degrees, which is related to the relaxation characteristics of graphene [9, 10]. Therefore, the study to simulate the tensile mechanical properties of graphene will first analyze the relaxation characteristics of the graphene model established this time, and then analyze the tensile mechanical properties of the graphene in the direction and direction.

2.4.1 Relaxation Properties of Graphene

Based on the experimental process, the graphene model shown in Fig. 1 is treated with unconstrained relaxation, and the total energy change curve of graphene in the relaxation process is obtained, as shown in Fig. 3.

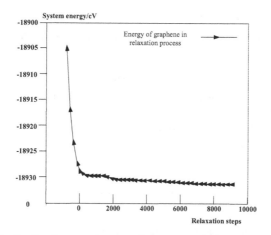

Fig. 3. Graphene total energy change curve during relaxation

It can be seen from Fig. 3 that when the number of simulation steps reaches 1000, the total energy of graphene has basically stabilized. When the number of simulation steps exceeds 2000, the total energy of graphene almost does not change, that is, the total energy of graphene reaches an equilibrium state. Judging from the energy stability, we think that the graphene monolayer is in a relatively stable state.

2.4.2 Stretching Simulation of Graphene in the x Direction

According to the previous section, the full unconstrained relaxation of graphene model is carried out to simulate and analyze the stable process of graphene. The number of relaxation steps for full unconstrained relaxation of graphene model is determined as 1000 steps. The tensile mechanical properties of graphene were simulated under 1000 step relaxation. Based on the above research process, the simulation process of tensile mechanical properties of graphene is determined. For the tensile simulation of graphene in x direction, the experimental results are shown in Fig. 4.

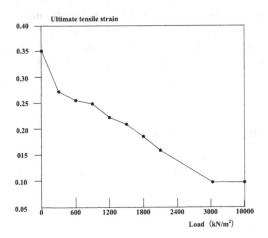

Fig. 4. Tensile simulation of graphene in the x direction

It can be seen from Fig. 4 that when graphene is stretched in the x direction to simulate the tensile mechanical properties of graphene, its initial tensile ultimate strain is 0.35. When the load is increased to 2000 kN/m^2, the tensile strength of graphene is the ultimate strain drops sharply, and the downward trend slows down as the load increases. When the load increases to 3000 kN/m^2, the resulting tensile strain no longer changes, indicating that the graphene film has been stretched under the action of the load. damage. It can be seen that in the x direction, the tensile graphene can withstand a maximum load of 3000 kN/m^2, and the tensile ultimate strain that can be withstood is 0.089.

2.4.3   Stretching Simulation of Graphene in the y Direction

Based on the tensile simulation of x direction, the mechanical properties of y direction tensile simulation were studied. At the same time, the tensile mechanical properties of graphene were simulated under 1000 step relaxation state. Based on the above research process, the simulation process of tensile mechanical properties of graphene is determined. For the tensile simulation of graphene in y direction, the experimental results are shown in Fig. 5.

It can be seen from Fig. 5 that the tensile graphene in the y direction simulates the tensile mechanical properties of graphene. As the load increases, the tensile strain of the graphene continues to decrease. When the load increases to 1800 kN/m^2 When the load reaches 3000 kN/m^2, the tensile strain of graphene has stopped changing and the film ruptures. It can be seen that in the y direction, the tensile graphene can withstand a maximum load of 3000 kN/m^2, and the tensile ultimate strain that can withstand is 0.117.

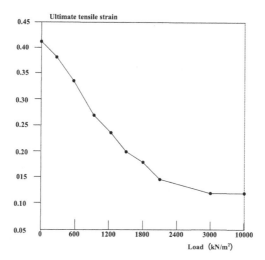

Fig. 5. Tensile simulation of graphene in direction y

2.5 Analysis of Tensile Mechanical Properties of Graphene

In this simulation, the tensile mechanical properties of graphene were studied. The tensile limit strain of graphene was studied by tensile simulation in x direction and y direction respectively. The tensile limit strain of graphene can be obtained under the action of load.

Before the simulation study, graphene was fully unconstrained relaxation to determine the stability of graphene itself and the energy change of graphene itself. According to the experimental results shown in Fig. 3, the relaxation step length of graphene is determined to be 1000 steps. From this, it can be judged that the relaxation results of graphene itself can affect the simulation results of the tensile mechanical properties of graphene. Only according to the relaxation step length of graphene and let the graphene reach an energy stable state can the tensile limit of graphene be obtained.

In the process of simulation, the long-term and short-term memory neural network is used to store and iterate the experimental data and the information before and after the simulation data, so as to determine the validity of the simulation research data. The experimental data shown in Fig. 4 and Fig. 5 are converted into the simulation data table of tensile mechanical properties of graphene, as shown in Table 1.

It can be seen from Table 1 that under this simulation study, the simulation data obtained show that the tensile force of graphene under load has no significant difference in direction x and direction y, but there is a certain difference in the ultimate tensile force that graphene can bear. Under the same load conditions, the young's modulus, tensile strength and ultimate strain of graphene in x direction are higher than those in y direction. It can be inferred that graphene has the phenomenon of non-uniform tensile force, which can bear different degrees of tensile force in different directions.

Since the graphene model used in this study is not perfect graphene, it has a perfect two-dimensional crystal structure, and there is no change in the structure in all directions. Therefore, it is inferred that the tensile strength of graphene is related to the atomic

Table 1. Simulation data of tensile mechanical properties of graphene.

Stretching direction	Load (kN/m^2)	Young's modulus/GPa	Tensile strength/GPa	Ultimate tensile strain
x direction	0	1033.75	200.68	0.409
	300	983.12	190.04	0.380
	600	947.44	170.47	0.336
	900	918.50	138.60	0.271
	1200	907.21	126.38	0.239
	1500	875.23	112.05	0.200
	1800	829.55	104.24	0.178
	2100	786.99	89.38	0.144
	3000	743.48	74.89	0.117
y direction	0	977.05	188.93	0.349
	300	946.13	174.01	0.270
	600	915.84	166.16	0.254
	900	897.73	161.43	0.250
	1200	865.32	142.53	0.220
	1500	837.58	131.09	0.207
	1800	843.70	114.26	0.183
	2100	788.00	97.26	0.156
	3000	732.42	59.57	0.089

distance of the graphene itself, and the amount of matter will also affect the tensile strength of graphene.

In summary, the tensile mechanical properties of graphene will be affected by factors such as its structure, material atoms, and the distance between atoms, and there will be differences in the tensile force that can be withstood in different directions.

3 Experiment and Analysis

In order to verify the simulation method of tensile mechanical properties of graphene, zigzag graphene was selected as the research object of this experiment. Lamps was used as graphene modeling software. ANSYS motion mechanical simulation software was selected as the operation software of the simulation experiment. The simulation method of tensile mechanical properties of graphene in this study was recorded as experimental group A; the two simulation methods of tensile mechanical properties of graphene mentioned in the literature were recorded as group B and group C respectively. The experimental object and the experimental environment were determined. The stress-strain curves and tensile mechanical properties of graphene were compared among the three groups of simulation methods, and the results were in error with the experimental values.

3.1 Experiment Preparation

The sawtooth graphene selected in this experiment uses the lattice command in the LAMMPS modeling software to establish a sawtooth graphene model, as shown in Fig. 6.

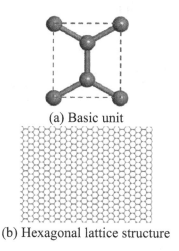

(a) Basic unit

(b) Hexagonal lattice structure

Fig. 6. Sawtooth graphene model

The zigzag graphene model shown in Fig. 6 is a honeycomb 2-D crystal composed of single-layer hexagonal cell carbon atoms. The length of carbon carbon bond is about 0.142 nm, the thickness is 0.335 nm, the number of atoms is 15134, and the size is 19.8839 nm * 19.6800 nm.

According to the experimental objects selected in this experiment, ANSYS motion mechanical simulation software was used to simulate the tensile mechanical properties of serrated graphene model according to three groups of tensile mechanical simulation methods. The experimental environment for its operation is shown in Table 2.

Table 2. Experimental environment.

Lab environment	Configuration	Configuration
Software environment	Drive	Ubuntu 16.04 LTS (64bit)
	Neural network framework	TensorFlow0.12、Keras1.2
Hardware environment	Processor	Intel i7–7700 CPU 3.60 GHz
	RAM	8 GB
	Graphics card model	NVIDIA GeForce GTX 1060
	Graphics card memory	6 GB

According to the experimental parameters set by the selected experimental objects, three groups of graphene tensile mechanical properties simulation methods were used to simulate the selected graphene in this experiment, and the simulation results of the three groups of methods were compared.

3.2　The First Set of Experimental Results

Based on the experimental parameters designed for this experiment, the first set of experiments was carried out. Three sets of mechanical performance simulation methods were used to simulate this experiment respectively. The sawtooth graphene model shown in Fig. 6 was established using the sawtooth graphene to obtain the graphene stress-strain curve. The graphene stress-strain curves simulated by the three sets of simulation methods were compared with the graphene stress-strain curves obtained from experiments, and the simulation results of graphene tensile mechanical properties were obtained, as shown in Fig. 7.

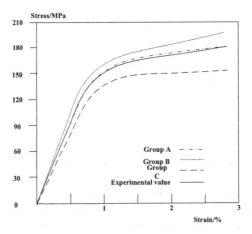

Fig. 7. Comparative analysis of stress-strain curves between simulation and experiment

It can be seen from Fig. 7 that the graphene stress-strain curve obtained in experiment C group is obviously smaller than the experimental value, and there is a gap between the simulated tensile mechanical properties of graphene and the experimental value; the graphene stress obtained in experiment B group is − The strain curve is obviously larger than the experimental value, and there is a gap between the simulated tensile mechanical properties of graphene and the experimental value; experimental group A simulates the tensile mechanical properties of graphene, and the graphene stress-strain curve obtained is very close to the experimental value, and the coincidence rate of experimental results is extremely high. It can be seen that the simulation results of the graphene tensile mechanical properties simulation method studied in this study have extremely high accuracy, which can be used as tensile mechanical properties and stress-strain curve experimental results.

3.3 The Second Group of Experimental Results

On the basis of the first group of experiments, the second group of experiments was carried out. The elastic modulus, tensile strength and ultimate tensile strain of the first group of graphene Tensile Mechanical Properties Simulation and experiment were extracted. Compared with three groups of simulation methods, the numerical simulation results of graphene tensile mechanical properties in the experimental process. The analysis results of tensile mechanical properties of graphene by three groups of simulation methods are judged, as shown in Table 3.

Table 3. Tensile Properties of serrated graphene.

Property method	Experimental value	Group A	Group B	Group C
Elastic model/GPa	174	174	165	155
Tensile strength/GPa	90	87	86	84
Ultimate tensile strain	0.353	0.348	0.335	0.332

It can be seen from Table 3 that the simulated value of the tensile mechanical properties of graphene obtained in the experiment group C differs the most from the experimental value; the gap between the simulated value of the simulated tensile mechanical properties of the graphene in experiment group B and the experimental value Although it is stronger than the experimental group C, there is a large gap between the experimental value; and the tensile mechanical properties of the graphene obtained in the experimental group A are closer to the experimental value, only the difference in tensile strength is 3 GPa and the ultimate tensile strength. The tensile strain, the difference is 0.005, is obviously stronger than the experimental group B and the experimental group C. It can be seen that the tensile mechanical properties of graphene obtained by the simulation method of graphene tensile mechanical properties in this study can be used as experimental results.

Based on the above two groups of experiments, it can be seen that the simulation results obtained by the simulation method of graphene tensile mechanical properties are very close to the experimental results, which can be used as the experimental results.

3.4 Experimental Results of the Third Group

Based on the above experimental, in order to comprehensively compare the comprehensive properties of different methods, the simulation time of graphene tensile mechanical properties was compared, and the results are shown in Table 4.

Analysis of Table 4 shows that the experimental group A graphene tensile mechanical properties of simulation time average of 0.57 s, the experimental group B graphene tensile mechanical properties of simulation time average of 1.59 s, the experimental group C graphene tensile mechanical properties of simulation time average of 1.70 s, compared with the experiment group B and group C, the experimental group A simulation time is shorter, simulation shows the method of graphene the stretch mechanics performance is more efficient.

Table 4. Comparison of simulation time (unit:s)

Number of experiments	Group A	Group B	Group C
1	0.36	1.42	2.01
2	0.56	1.56	1.96
3	0.58	1.78	1.58
4	0.62	1.57	1.63
5	0.66	1.48	1.75
6	0.57	1.63	1.95
7	0.49	1.62	1.47
8	0.63	1.28	1.25
9	0.61	1.57	1.47
10	0.58	1.98	1.96
Average	0.57	1.59	1.70

4 Concluding Remarks

To sum up, the study of graphene tensile mechanical properties simulation method, give full play to the advantages of long-term and long-term memory neural network for data memory and iterative ability, and improve the accuracy of simulation experiment results. However, the simulation method of tensile mechanical properties of graphene in this study did not consider the graphene with different shapes and structures, and the tensile mechanical properties obtained would have certain differences, which would have a certain impact on the research results of tensile mechanical properties of graphene. Therefore, in the future research, it is necessary to further study the simulation method of tensile mechanical properties of graphene, taking into account the shape and structure of graphene itself, so as to ensure the preciseness of simulation results and further improve the simulation accuracy.

Acknowledgments. Teaching Quality and Teaching Reform Project of Guangdong Undergraduate Colleges and Universities: Construction Project of Experiment Demonstration Center (2017002).

References

1. Gao, H., Xu, J.: Numerical study on aerodynamic performance of three-dimensional flapping wing. Comput. Simul. **37**(6), 36–39,151 (2020)
2. Han, Z., Zou, L., Xin, Z., et al.: Molecular dynamics simulation of vital physical properties of epoxy/carbon nanotube composite coatings on DC GIL insulators. Trans. China Electrotech. Soc. **33**(20), 4692–4703, 4721 (2018)
3. Li, J.J., Lu, B.B., Xian, Y.H., et al.: Characterization of nanoporous silver mechanical properties by molecular dynamics simulation. Acta Physica Sinica **67**(5), 226–234 (2018)

4. Liu, S., Lu, M., Li, H., et al.: Prediction of gene expression patterns with generalized linear regression model. Front. Genet. **10**, 120 (2019)
5. Yao, X., Wang, X., Wang, S.H., et al.: A comprehensive survey on convolutional neural network in medical image analysis. Multimedia Tools Appl., 1–45 (2020)
6. Liu, S., Bai, W., Zeng, N., et al.: A fast fractal based compression for MRI images. IEEE Access **7**, 62412–62420 (2019)
7. Huang, S.: Mechanical properties of hydrated calcium silicate simulated by molecular dynamics. Bull. Chin. Ceramic Soc. **37**(5), 1687–1692 (2018)
8. Fu, K., Wang, G., Wang, S., et al.: Simulation and analysis of mechanical properties of bilayered all-ceramic denture. Shandong Sci. **31**(5), 31–37, 88 (2018)
9. Zhang, C., Zhao, X., Fu, X., et al.: Progress in the application of molecular dynamics simulation in the study of physical and chemical properties of propellant components. Chin. J. Explos. Prop. **41**(6), 531–542 (2018)
10. Zheng, C., Cui, Z., Huang, Y.: Simulation of microstructures and mechanical properties of ternary polymer blends. J. Func. Polymers **31**(4), 305–314 (2018)

Design of Distributed Hybrid Pipeline Multimedia Aided Scheduling System

Guang Xie[✉] and Yuxia Pan

School of Information and Intelligence Engineering, University of Sanya, Sanya 572022, Hainan, China

Abstract. The traditional auxiliary scheduling system in the multimedia auxiliary scheduling work, the scheduling scope is very small, resulting in poor scheduling effect. In order to solve this problem, a new distributed hybrid pipelined multimedia assistant scheduling system is designed, and the hardware and software of the system are designed respectively. The hardware part mainly designs the collector, controller and processor. The heater selects the TSDA-523 as the new type to improve the acquisition effect. The controller adopts the LPI controller to realize continuous control. The processor selects the AN176 as the central integrated processor to process a large amount of multimedia data in a short time. The software is composed of information collection, information processing and information dispatching. In order to detect the effect of the system, compared with the traditional system, the results show that the system can achieve large-scale scheduling, and effectively improve the scheduling effect.

Keywords: Distributed · Hybrid pipeline · Multimedia aided · Auxiliary scheduling

1 Introduction

The plant production scheduling and production scheduling should not only consider the production plan of single production line, but also coordinate and arrange the production plan of several different production lines in the workshop, so as to arrange the production order to the appropriate production line, which brings more difficulty and challenge to the production scheduling [1, 2].

After many years of research and development, the scheduling problem of mixed pipelines proposed by Salvador in 1973 has been well solved under various constraints, but the task assignment of multiple mixed pipelines is relatively weak. The distributed hybrid pipeline scheduling problem is developed under the circumstance that the traditional pipeline scheduling is not suitable for the parallelism of the traditional mass production pipeline and the customized pipeline, and is used to coordinate the production conditions of several different pipelines, comprehensively consider the production priority of the production orders in each pipeline, and establish a more scientific, more economical and more executable production planning and production scheduling model

W. Fu et al. (Eds.): ICMTEL 2021, LNICST 387, pp. 64–76, 2021.
https://doi.org/10.1007/978-3-030-82562-1_6

[3]. DHFSP is the synthesis of traditional assembly line scheduling, parallel machine scheduling and planning, and it is the abstract generalization of modern industrial workshop production. To some extent, this method can meet the market demand of multi-category and small-scale customization, so the research of distributed hybrid pipeline has great academic significance and application value [4].

The proposed method only discusses the production scheduling problem with the same process route, and is unable to adapt to the more complex and changeable mixed pipeline production, and is unable to meet the needs of the transformation from mass production to mass customization conducted by the current manufacturing enterprises [5, 6].

In this paper, a distributed hybrid pipeline multi-media assistant scheduling system is designed, which can simulate the scheduling strategy, solve the scheduling problem of the distributed hybrid pipeline, and solve the process matching the actual production, so it has strong availability. In addition, fuzzy adaptive technique is used to automatically adjust the crossover probability and mutation probability, and active detection stop method is used to shorten the computation time and improve the algorithm efficiency. Experimental results show that the system has strong scheduling ability. It is innovation lies in the large-scale scheduling requirements, information collection, information processing and information scheduling three parts of the overall detection system, which can effectively improve the scheduling effect in the process.

2   Hardware Design of Distributed Mixed Pipelined Multimedia Assistant Scheduling System

The hardware structure of the distributed hybrid pipelined multimedia auxiliary scheduling system is complex. The composition diagram is shown in Fig. 1 below:

Looking at Fig. 1, we can see that the hardware of the scheduling system consists of four parts. This paper only designs the collector, controller and processor in Fig. 1.

2.1 Design of Collector

A new type of collector, TSDA-523, is selected. The collector has the advantages of high efficiency, low energy consumption and safe and reliable performance. The collector structure is shown in Fig. 2:

Observation of Fig. 2 can be seen, the collector mainly through the control of a variety of auxiliary information to complete the sub-room control. Ancillary information has a unique design loop that maximizes the use of information. The information analysis system is designed to be integrated, which makes the system very reliable and greatly reduces the difficulty of dispatching [7].

The collector uses the special intelligent processor to solve the big data problem, make it intelligent, and realize automatic running.

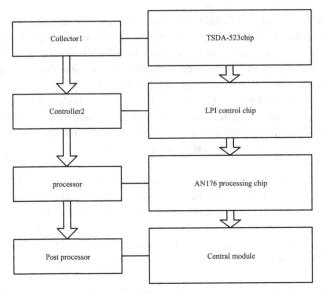

Fig. 1. Hardware structure diagram of distributed mixed pipelined multimedia assistant scheduling system

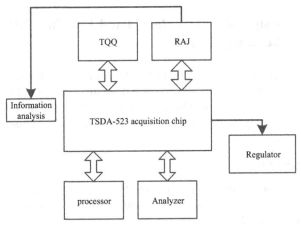

Fig. 2. Collector

2.2 Controller Design

In this paper, LPI controller and switched reluctance motor are used, which has the characteristics of high performance and simple structure and is widely recognized in the market. Switchability refers to the continuous mode of switch when the motor is working. Magnetoresistivity refers to the variable reluctance ability of the reluctance motor, or more accurately, the variable reluctance ability of the doubly salient pole motor. The switched reluctance motor uses the motor's speed control system to replace energy, and its speed control system also includes a controller. Controllers are important for scheduling and provide the energy and control methods required for switched reluctance motors [8].

The controller structure is shown in Fig. 3:

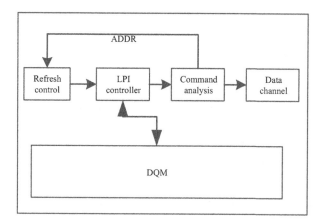

Fig. 3. Controller structure

The controller motor in Fig. 3 is a fully controlled switched reluctance motor. At that time, the technology was not mature enough, the structure was complicated, and the incompatibility and the current interference caused the use of the driving signal. In this paper, the internal structure of SRM controller is optimized and a new structure of SRM controller for ball mill is developed, which solves the problem of complex internal structure of traditional controller and strengthens the use of motor. The left and right layout connects the main circuit of the controller with the control circuit of the electric appliance, and the mounting board and the control interior are provided with upper and lower parts to control the number of rectifier bridges and power devices [9]. It has the advantages of low noise, high output rate, wide range and so on. The outlet mode of the motor controller in the market is single, and needs to match with the new mold, which increases the production capital. The controller circuit diagram is shown in Fig. 4 below:

According to the control circuit diagram in Fig. 4, the controller structure in this paper connects the controller box, capacitor module and power module with 8 connectors, and a cavity is arranged in the controller box. The capacitor module and the power module are connected by a DC bus, which is connected with 3 connectors, and the remaining 5 connectors are connected with the power module. Six connectors are mounted at the front end of the controller housing and two are positioned on the controller side wall. In this paper, a new structure of motor controller is designed and provided, which completely overcomes the problem of single controller output, greatly reduces the cost and reduces the production pressure [10].

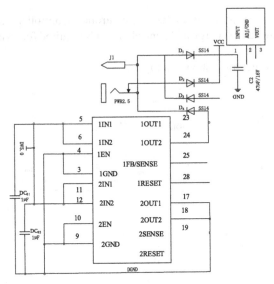

Fig. 4. Controller circuit diagram

2.3 Processor Design

Many different network protocols have been transplanted in the existing embedded system, network transmission is more efficient and reliable than other transmission methods, so this paper chooses to send and receive data by network transmission. Although the embedded processor designed in this paper is the same, the bus can be up to 24, the frequency can reach 50 MHz, and integrated with multi-functional modules. High-performance and ultra-low power consumption are the characteristics of the chip, which can work under various frequencies and support zero-state waiting.

The processor in Fig. 5 interrupts while programming, allocates priorities, handles eight internal and external interrupts, and integrates multiple interfaces with peripherals. The processor is equipped with ROM controller, asynchronous serial port, interrupt pin, timer and other devices, and the production cost is greatly reduced. Processor internals can provide fast unbuffered access, with a dedicated bus Corenuetc connection. Processors are divided into 8/16-bit two, and set the boot mode. Compared with the design structure of this paper, the traditional computer architecture is not compatible with other series processors. The CPU of this paper is AN176, and the depth module of Ethernet driver chip is CS7970B [11–13].

The processor circuit diagram is shown in Fig. 5 below:

As can be seen from Fig. 5, the processor bus consists of a local bus, a peripheral bus, and a device control register bus. XIknx is the foundation for all embedded processors and provides a licensing standard for users. Access to system resources through the peripheral bus and kernel. Fully synchronous bus can be called OPB, which is responsible for bus level functions. Synchronous bus can not be directly connected to the processor core, providing 32-bit separation function. The processor core can access external devices, and the PLV interface can provide 32-bit addresses for instruction data. PLV can support

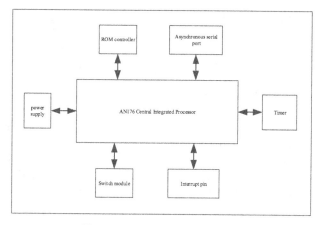

Fig. 5. Processor wiring diagram

the host and slave with multiple bus interfaces, and connect with PLB signal to read and transmit data. PLV host can connect by accessing independent data bus and address bus. The slave computer is connected by separate data line and address line, the bus ownership is obtained by competition, and the host computer can flexibly provide various priorities for the user.

2.4 Network Detection Module

In this paper, the internal network for centralized monitoring operations, to assist the RoF-DAS architecture system for accurate research, for this purpose, select the RH6010 four-channel network detector for this study, and set the network detector as follows (Fig. 6):

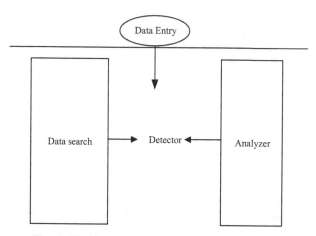

Fig. 6. Working process diagram of network detector

The network detector has aluminum 2U black wire-drawing panel, using Linux system, stable performance, fast running, can use DSP software audio decoding program, high fidelity, ensure the system in the process of running security. Receiving platform instructions and audio signals, supporting platform remote control of volume, supporting the platform to set and manage permissions on the machine and the platform to upgrade the machine remotely. With the function of clock automatic calibration, the platform can broadcast the data to different areas and groups. After getting the related information, it can check and observe the status of the information network, and use the automatic alarm system to warn the abnormal situation.

The internal circuit adopts full SMD process, with more stable performance, built-in four network hardware audio decoding module, support for TCP/IP, UDP, IGMP (multicast) protocol, and can adjust the operation of the system to achieve the setup of the overall network detection module.

2.5 Monitoring Module

After the design and research of the network detection module is realized, the information is monitored, the status and specific flow of the data are grasped, and the judgment and research of the dispatching data are convenient, and the JINSONG wireless remote monitoring camera is selected to monitor and record, and the monitoring camera is constructed as follows (Fig. 7):

Fig. 7. Surveillance camera chart.

The monitoring camera has remote real-time monitoring function. Users can watch remote monitoring video through Internet in real time by using monitoring client software. Monitoring client software can be installed on PCs and Wince mobile phones to facilitate data monitoring operations and reduce the time required for research. The working voltage range is DC9V-100V, and the working current range is 12V/30MA-60MA. The working temperature range is-30 °C–75 °C, and the storage temperature range is-30 °C–80 °C. Can ensure that the system is in a more appropriate environment to work, in the operation process in accordance with the above standards for operation.

3 Software Design of Distributed Mixed Pipelined Multimedia Assistant Scheduling System

After completing the hardware design of the system, the software shall be continuously reformed and studied on the basis of enhancing the performance of hardware components of the system, and the flow chart of software design shall be set up as follows (Fig. 8):

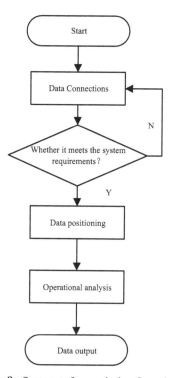

Fig. 8. System software design flow chart

In the above figure, it can be divided into the following steps according to the process of software operation:

Wavelet computing technology is used to connect terminal equipment and cloud computing data center system. Wavelet computing has strong computing ability and can calculate various kinds of information. The wavelet computation process is shown in Fig. 9:

At the same time, the data shall be arranged according to the combination order of the connections, and the data that conform to the system control interval shall be adjusted, and the adjustment equation shall be set for analysis:

$$K = \sqrt{P - A}^{3} \qquad (1)$$

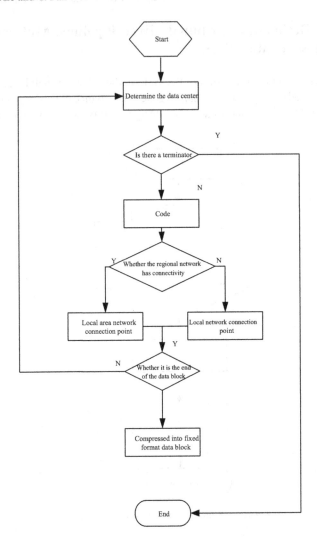

Fig. 9. Wavelet computation flow

In the above expression, K is the adjusted result parameter, P is the system operation interval parameter, and A is the combined order value. After the abovementioned operations, the adjusted data shall be filtered, the filtered data status shall be monitored in real time, and the status data shall be recorded. The setting up of data records is illustrated as follows:

After realizing the data recording operation in the above figure, the filtering data is calibrated to realize the initial judgment operation under the wavelet calculation data.

Under the research environment, the position information of the data is searched by the positioning system, and the scheduling intensity is accurately measured by the wavelet calculation method.

$$F = \frac{G}{N} \cdot \int kt + l \qquad (2)$$

Among them, F represents the dispatch strength research data, G represents the data parameter condition, N represents the research data overall quantity, ft represents the fog computation calibration value, and l represents the data parameter. In the process of measurement, it is necessary to strengthen the control between the cloud user and the terminal system to avoid the information confusion between the user and the terminal. When a contract is signed between the user and the DR implementing agency, the stimulating demand response can be used to establish a model. The contract signed should clearly indicate the amount of user load reduction, compensation and the punishment if the user fails to respond in accordance with the contract. The IBDR response cost refers to the outage loss caused by the reduction of electricity load. The response cost is usually a quadratic function. If the distributed energy storage load of the power system is reduced, the demand-response costing process is as follows:

$$\alpha_{Ij,t} = e_{1,j} \tag{3}$$

Among them, the quadratic coefficient $\alpha_{I,j,t}$ representing the response cost of the excitation load of the node j and the quadratic coefficient $e_{1,j}$ representing the compensation amount received by the node j.

$$\beta_{I,j,t} = e_{2,j} + \rho_P \tag{4}$$

Among them, $\beta_{I,j,t}$ is the primary coefficient representing the response cost of the excitation load of the node, $e_{2,j}$ is the primary coefficient representing the compensation amount of the node j, and the electricity price ρ_P of the corresponding retail end of the power system, which is usually fixed.

According to formulas (3) and (4), it is possible to derive the corresponding cost of demand to reduce the electricity load $P_{I,j,t}$:

$$C_{I,j,t} = \alpha_{I,j,t} P^2_{I,j,t} + \beta_{I,j,t} P_{I,j,t} \tag{5}$$

After the above operation, the system software design is realized and the overall system design research is completed.

4 Experiment and Research

In order to test the scheduling research of the scheduling system in this paper, the simulation operation is carried out in the research experiment scene, and the design effect is compared with that of the traditional scheduling system. Taking the Simulink neural network module of MATLAB software as the simulation analysis tool, 20 groups of historical data of pipeline operation of a certain platform as the simulation data samples, excluding two groups of unavailable data Bureau, and randomly selecting two groups of data in the remaining 18 groups for experiment.

In view of the complexity of the research on RoF-DAS architecture and the difficulty of data manipulation in the research on the degree system, it is necessary to eliminate the experimental environment. The experimental parameters needed in the experiment are as follows (Table 1):

Table 1. Experimental parameters

Project	Data
Node value	20
Operational data rate	25 Mbps
Signal transmission power	0.05W
time interval	100 ms
Simulation experiment time	60 s
Network channel bandwidth	20 MHz

Based on the above experimental parameters, the comparison of vehicle information collection capability between the traditional system and the system studied in this paper is obtained. The experimental diagram is shown in Fig. 10 below:

Due to the use of fog computation, this system can collect a lot of information, distributed RoF-DAS architecture, so that all the information can be saved in the network cloud. During the storage, processing and other operations, the system relies more on local devices than on the server, which relaxes the system's requirements on the server, improves the system's fault tolerance, and enables the system to collect a lot of information in a short time.

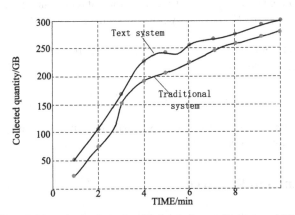

Fig. 10. Experimental results of information-gathering capability

Figure 11 shows the variation of the access time delay rate of time-delay-sensitive information with the amount of data passing through a given number of devices in a system.

In the case of a small number of scheduling, the access time delay rate of the two systems is small, but the access time delay rate of the scheduling system is lower than that of the traditional systems. With the increase of the number of system access time delay rate, the traditional system access time delay rate increases rapidly, because the traditional design algorithm can not meet the needs of a large number of experimental

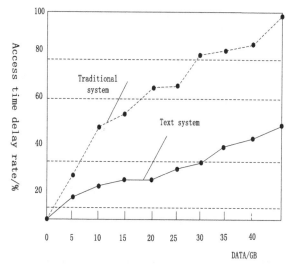

Fig. 11. Comparison chart of simulation experiments.

data through the study, and the contradiction between the more data lead to higher access time delay rate.

To sum up, the design of scheduling system can effectively alleviate the contradictions in the system, reduce the number of interfering factors, and provide a better experimental environment for the study.

5   Summary and Prospect

In this paper, the design of scheduling system is divided into two parts: hardware design and software design. In the process of hardware design, we classify the modules according to the problems of the hardware components, and operate the data according to the corresponding modules, so as to improve the efficiency of system operation and reduce unnecessary time waste. In the process of software design, we use wavelet computing technology and control the data collected to realize the transformation of the system program and realize the design of the whole system.

Compared with the traditional system design, the scheduling system design in this paper can improve the effectiveness of the system to a higher degree, expand the scope of the system data to provide users with more convenient operation services, but still need to continuously strengthen the operation of the system to promote the overall system research to a better state.

References

1. Li, Y., Yang, W., He, P., et al.: Design and management of a distributed hybrid energy system through smart contract and blockchain. Appl. Energy **248**(15), 390–405 (2019)

2. Spencer, A.A.M.S., Luciano, S., Mario, M.: Analysis and design of high-efficiency hybrid high step-up DC-DC converter for distributed PV generation systems. IEEE Trans. Ind. Electron. **66**(5), 3860–3868 (2018)
3. Zhang, L.P., Liu, W., Qi, B.: Innovation design and optimization management of a new drive system for plug-in hybrid electric vehicles. Energy **186**(1), 115823.1–115823.19 (2019)
4. Zkik, K., Hajji, S.E., Orhanou, G.: Design and implementation of a new security plane for hybrid distributed SDNs. J. Commun. **14**(1), 26–32 (2019)
5. Kano, Y., Matsui, N.: Rotor geometry design of saliency-based sensorless controlled distributed-winding IPMSM for hybrid electric vehicles. IEEE Trans. Ind. Appl. **54**(3), 2336–2348 (2018)
6. Kim, H., Kim, S.: Two dimensional cavitation waterhammer model for a reservoir-pipeline-valve system. J. Hydraul. Res. **57**(3), 327–336 (2018)
7. Fu, W., Liu, S., Srivastava, G.: Optimization of big data scheduling in social networks. Entropy **21**(9), 902 (2019)
8. Liu, S., Li, Z., Zhang, Y., et al.: Introduction of key problems in long-distance learning and training. Mobile Netw. Appl. **24**(1), 1–4 (2019)
9. Liu, S., Liu, D., Srivastava, G., et al.: Overview and methods of correlation filter algorithms in object tracking. Complex Intell. Syst. (2020) https://doi.org/10.1007/s40747-020-00161-4
10. Chu, Z., Tian, H., Li, Z., et al.: A High-Performance Design of Generalized Pipeline Cellular Array. IEEE Comput. Archit. Lett. **19**(1), 47–50 (2020)
11. Fu, H., Fu, W.: Research on the influence of multimedia on Chinese teaching in senior high school. World Sci. Res. J. **6**(5), 86–94 (2020)
12. Na, G.: Research on remote control method of English multimedia online teaching system in big data environment. J. Phys. Conf. Ser. **1486**(5), 052010 (8pp) (2020)
13. Jinxia, H.E., Huang, X.: An investigation of pre-service teachers' perceptions and experiences on student-created videos. J. Educ. Multimedia Hypermedia **29**(1), 35–53 (2020)

Intelligent Scheduling of Distributed Displacement Pipeline Based on Hybrid Discrete Drosophila Optimization Algorithm

Pan Yuxia[⊠] and Xie Guang

School of Information and Intelligence Engineering, University of Sanya, Sanya 572022, HaiNan, China
panyuxia12123@yeah.net

Absrtact. In order to solve the problem of long scheduling time and low efficiency of interval number representation scheduling method, a distributed replacement Pipeline Intelligent Scheduling Based on hybrid discrete Drosophila optimization algorithm is proposed. According to the distributed permutation pipeline scheduling problem, the coding method based on operation is adopted to make the algorithm suitable for solving the scheduling problem. The hybrid discrete Drosophila optimization algorithm is used to solve the batch pipeline scheduling problem with the maximum completion time as the goal. In order to balance the local search ability of the algorithm, the evolutionary mechanism is combined with cooperative learning among groups. Build a mathematical model to achieve efficient scheduling in the maximum completion time. The simulation results show that the scheduling time of this method is short, and the overall scheduling efficiency is higher than 80%, which has good scheduling effect.

Keywords: Hybrid discrete Drosophila · Optimization algorithm · Distributed displacement pipeline · Intelligent scheduling

1 Introduction

In the production and operation process of enterprises, there are often various uncertain factors, which lead to the original scheduling plan can not be executed normally. Therefore, the production scheduling problem in uncertain environment has a strong application value, which attracts much attention. Distributed permutation assembly line scheduling problem is widely used in metallurgy, plastics, chemical industry and other industrial production, which has important theoretical research background and practical application value [1, 2]. With the increasingly fierce competition in the market and the diversification of customer demand, multi variety small and medium-sized batch production mode occupies a dominant position [3]. Therefore, the research on batch pipeline scheduling problem has become the focus of academic and engineering circles. Each factory is a permutation flow shop. The processing time of distributed permutation assembly line is usually a definite value, but it is difficult to determine the processing

W. Fu et al. (Eds.): ICMTEL 2021, LNICST 387, pp. 77–90, 2021.
https://doi.org/10.1007/978-3-030-82562-1_7

time accurately in actual production. In the past, interval number was used to represent the uncertainty of process time, and then extended to generate interval number distributed permutation pipeline scheduling problem. When the processing time of an operation was interval number, jobs were allocated to multiple workshops reasonably, and then the scheduling index was optimized by reasonable sequencing [4]. Although the scheduling effect of this method is good, it is affected by the complexity problems such as large-scale, strong coupling and uncertainty, resulting in long scheduling time. Based on this problem, an intelligent scheduling method of distributed displacement pipeline based on hybrid discrete drosophila optimization algorithm is proposed. Drosophila optimization algorithm originated from the simulation of Drosophila foraging behavior, and has been successfully applied to solve mathematical function extremum, automatic picking scheduling problem, etc. its innovation lies in the use of hybrid discrete Drosophila optimization algorithm to solve the batch flow line scheduling problem with the goal of maximum completion time. Through multi operation collaborative search, the effective solution effect is achieved.

2 Distributed Permutation Pipeline Scheduling Problem

Distributed permutation pipeline scheduling is to study the processing process of a certain number $n(n > F)$ of jobs in $\pi = \{\pi(1), \pi(2), \ldots, \pi(n)\}$ number of displacement pipeline F factories with limited buffers. There is a job to be processed in the same factory, and each factory contains m machines. During the processing, the jobs should pass through each machine in turn, and the processing time of each job on each machine is greater than 0. Once the jobs are allocated to After a factory, it can not be assigned to other factories, and all operations of workpieces can only be completed in this factory. In addition, it is agreed that all workpieces are independent and processing can be started at 0:00. In the factory, once the order of the work pieces is determined, it will not change. In the buffer area, the work pieces follow the principle of first in first out. Preemption is not allowed. Once the operation starts, it must be completed and cannot be interrupted. The setting time of the machine and the moving time between operations are ignored [5–9].

In petrochemical production, semiconductor manufacturing and other production processes, the capacity of intermediate storage is often limited, most of which can be modeled as pfssp with buffer. More and more attention has been paid to permutation flow shop scheduling with finite buffers. With the development of globalization, cooperation between factories and annexation between enterprises have been very common, and distributed manufacturing mode is becoming more and more popular [10–15]. As an important part of intelligent factory, intelligent production should coordinate production, scheduling, logistics and management. Production scheduling is an important part of manufacturing industry, and logistics is also an essential link, which directly affects the efficiency and competitiveness of enterprises. In the actual production and transportation, for example, a certain kind of parts in Apple products should be purchased from various suppliers around the world and then transported to the distribution center; Taobao, Jingdong and other major stores order a certain kind of product from all over the world and then transport them to the distribution warehouse [16–20].

3 Local Search Based on Hybrid Discrete Fly Optimization Algorithm

The optimization algorithm of Drosophila mainly includes two parts: olfactory search and visual search. Olfactory search is divergent search, visual search is greedy iteration. The population of flies evolves through continuous iteration of two links. Because of the small control parameters, it is easy to implement.

3.1 Coding and Decoding

The hybrid discrete fly optimization algorithm is used, which is one of the individual representatives in the population $n \times m$. For the scale of the problem $\pi = \{\pi(1), \pi(2), \dots, \pi(n)\}$, the solution is a coding arrangement. For example $\pi = \{\pi(1), \pi(2), \dots, \pi(n)\} = \{3, 5, 4, 1, 2\}$, the first piece 3 is processed, followed by workpiece 5, and so on, and the last one is workpiece 2 [21–25].

One sort decoding is divided into two steps. The first step is to assign all the work pieces to the factory, generate a feasible scheduling scheme in each factory, and the second step is to transport the finished workpiece to the distribution center [26–31]. Here, a sort or solution is called an individual, and a sort in a factory is called a sub individual or individual sub sort. The first distribution rules are designed to arrive at the distribution center, so that the processing order (sub order) of the workpiece in the factory is consistent with that of the individual workpiece. In order to overcome the inconsistency between individual sorting and sub ordering caused by local search, we designed the mapping rule of reverse first arrival to distribution center, which makes probability model learn the information of work-piece sorting in excellent individuals more accurately. In the second stage, after the workpiece processing is completed, according to the weight of the workpiece and the load weight of the transport vehicle, the workpiece is reasonably allocated to the transport vehicle. In order to make the vehicle load as many workpieces as possible, a reasonable vehicle loading rules are designed. Assign the workpiece to each factory in sequence. For the work pieces to be allocated in the sequence, place them at the end of each factory respectively, calculate the completion time of the current factory and assign them to the factory that finished the work piece the earliest.

3.2 Population Initialization

The initial population includes indi_ Num individuals, one of which is determined by the heuristic method neh2_ The other individuals were randomly generated. Neh2_ IM is proposed to improve neh2 by idpfsp, and its steps are shown in Fig. 1.

As can be seen from Fig. 1, all jobs are arranged in descending order according to their total processing time, and the jobs are allocated in order of arrangement. The current jobs to be assigned are assigned to each position of each factory, and the sequence that makes the current minimum is reserved. Select the previous workpiece in the current position and assign it to each position of each factory, and keep the sequence that makes the current minimum. If there is no improved minimum sequence, the next job in the current position is selected and assigned to each position of each factory, and the current

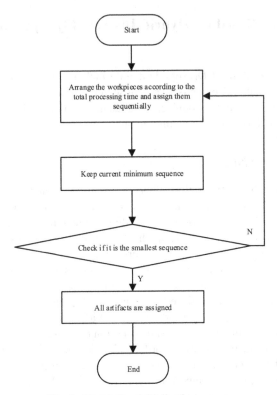

Fig. 1. Population initialization process

minimum sequence is retained until all jobs are assigned. The construction of individuals with good quality and the generation of initial population can guarantee both quality and diversity.

3.3 Sampling to Generate New Species Group

Each individual of the new population is generated by sampling the updated probability distribution model. Generally, roulette or tournament mechanism will be used in sampling, which will waste a lot of time. Half of the population individuals adopt direct sampling method, that is $P(gen + 1)$, the job number on the i position in the individual ranking is directly according to the column with the largest value in each row element $p_i(gen+1) = \{p_{i,1}(gen + 1), p_{i,2}(gen + 1), \ldots, p_{i,n}(gen + 1)\}$ in the probability matrix; the other half of the population individuals use roulette sampling. The process of generating new individual sequences by direct sampling is described as follows:

Step 1: order i = 1;
Step 2: read the i value of row 1 from the probability distribution matrix P(gen + 1)

$$p_i(gen + 1) = \{p_{i,1}(gen + 1), p_{i,2}(gen + 1), \ldots, p_{i,n}(gen + 1)\} \tag{1}$$

Step 3: compare the size of each element $P_i(gen + 1)$ in to find the column where the largest element j is located;

Step 4: set the job number j on the position in the individual sorting as i, and then set the column $P(gen + 1)$ in the probability distribution model j to 0, and $i = i + 1$, then turn to step 2. Until the job number is selected at all positions in the individual sort.

3.4 Dual Mode Local Search Based on Handover Mechanism

In order to enhance the ability of local search, local search based on switching mechanism is designed for the optimal solution and suboptimal solution: if the optimal solution (or sub optimal solution continuous generation search) k_{max} in the population does not improve the performance, the next generation uses the sub optimal solution (or optimal solution) to search.

Local search is divided into two modes: L_{S1} and L_{s2}. L_{S1} uses a variety of local search operations based on the key plant and the factory with the minimum completion time to strengthen the fine search, including F_S_{wap}, $S_{wap}\_F_k$, Insert$\_F_K$, the first three operations are the same as the enhanced search phase in the population coordination stage$\_F_K$ is executed as follows: two non adjacent jobs are randomly selected from the key plant, and then the sequence of jobs between them is reversed, and then the optimal reservation is achieved. The search depth of L_{S1} mode is controlled by parameters.

The steps of L_{s2} mode are as follows:

Step 1: randomly select the workpiece from the key factory and assign it to each position in the key factory, and keep the minimum sequence and position;

Step 2: randomly select the previous job or the next one in the current position of the workpiece, and insert it all the same to keep the smallest sequence.

The search depth ln of L_{s2} mode is controlled by adaptive parameters, and each search ensures that the selected jobs are different. The adaptive parameters ln are as follows:

$$\ln = \lceil \min(jn_{F_k}, 200 \times f/n) \rceil \tag{2}$$

In formula (2), jn_{F_k} denotes the maximum number of workpieces in the factory, n epresents the number of workpieces, f represents the factory, and $\lceil \rceil$ indicates rounding up.

In the process of local search execution, the LS1 search is performed for the individuals to be searched (the first generation adopts the optimal solution). If the individual's performance is improved, the next generation performs L_{s2} search, otherwise the next generation continues to perform L_{S1} search.

4 Design of Intelligent Scheduling Scheme for 3-distributed Permutation Pipeline

Through local search based on hybrid discrete Drosophila optimization algorithm, the parameters needed for intelligent scheduling of distributed displacement pipeline are obtained. All jobs in the distributed displacement pipeline are independent of each other and can be processed at zero time, and the machines are continuously available, that is, without considering the factors such as machine failure; at the same time, a machine can only process one workpiece, and a workpiece will not be processed by multiple machines at the same time; each workpiece can be assigned to any factory, and once the factory allocation is determined, it can not be changed. The sequence of workpieces processed on each machine in the same factory is the same, and the process to be processed for each workpiece is also the same; the time of moving the workpiece on the machine and the setting time of the machine are ignored.

4.1 Optimal Estimation Algorithm

According to the search results, design the optimization estimation process, as shown in Fig. 2.

The overall steps of optimization estimation are as follows:

Step 1: let *genMax* represent the maximum evolution algebra, set the population size *popsize*, buffer size *buffer_size*, learning rate α and the number of good individuals selected to update the probabilistic model N. When executing $FindBestN_{insert}\left(\pi_i^k(gen)\right)$, the continuous cumulative value *Insert_count* of high quality solution is not improved, which is the threshold value *Insert_count* of;

Step 2: initialize.

Let $gen = 0$, $Insert\_count = 0$, initialize the probability matrix $P(0)$ so that the value of each element is $1/n$. The 0 generation individuals $\pi_i(0)$ for $i = 1, \ldots,$ popsize are directly sampled from the initial probability model, and the subsequence of each individual is generated by allocation rules $\pi_i^k(0)$. According to the evaluation value of each individual, the best individual subsequence $\pi_{best}^k(0)$ in the current population is used to update the best individual subsequence π_{gbest}^k in the current population;

Step 3: using the N best previous $\pi(gen)$ individual update matrix $p(gen)$ of the old population, directly sampling the updated probability matrix $p(gen+1)$ to generate the new species group with the size of popsize, and generate the sub ranking of each individual through the allocation rules $\pi_i^k(gen+1)$. According to the evaluation value of each individual subsequence, the best individual subsequence $\pi_{best}^k(gen+1)$ in the population is used to update the individual subsequence with the best history;

Step 4: implement mutation operator based on the best individual subsequence generated $\pi_{best}^k(gen+1)$ by step 3 to generate individual subsequence int*erchange*;

Step 5: $\pi_{best}^k(gen+1)$ map back to individual sorting $\pi_{best}(gen+1)$;

Step 6: if gen < genMax, skip to step 2;

Step 7: output π_{gbest}^k.

4.2 Intelligent Scheduling Model of Distributed Permutation Pipeline

In order to reduce the waiting time of the machine tool, each workpiece is divided into several small batches according to the principle of equal distribution. After the small batch processing of each workpiece is completed, it can be transferred to the next

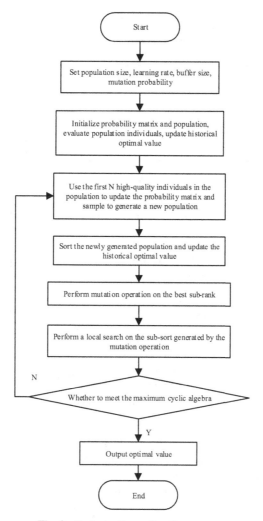

Fig. 2. Optimization estimation process

machine tool for processing, and the processing sequence of all small batches is the same. Suppose that the workpiece is processed in the order of machine tool 1 to, given a process $\pi = (\delta_1, \delta_2, \cdots, \delta_n)$, the workpiece j is divided into s_j small batches, which It_{ij} is the processing time of the small batch j of workpiece on the machine tool i, the completion time ct_{ijk} of the k small batch of the workpiece j on the machine tool i, and the completion time c_j of the workpiece, then the mathematical scaling model j is constructed as shown in Fig. 3.

Based on this model, the scheduling process of distributed permutation pipeline in maximum completion time is designed. Each step of the mathematical model in Fig. 3 represents: the completion time of the first small batch of the first workpiece on the first machine tool I; the completion time of the first small batch of the first workpiece on

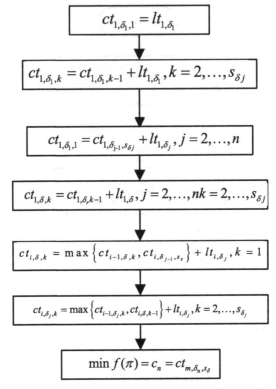

Fig. 3. Scheduling model

the first machine tool; the completion time of the first small batch of the first workpiece on the first machine tool; the completion time of the first small batch of the first job on the first machine tool; the completion time of the first small batch of the first job on the first machine tool; the completion time of the first small batch of the first workpiece on the first machine tool; the completion time of the first small batch of the first workpiece on the first machine; The completion time of the kth small batch of the j-th job on the first machine tool; the completion time of the first small batch of the j-th workpiece on the first machine tool; the completion time of the k-small batch of the j-th job on the i-machine tool; the goal of scheduling is to minimize the maximum completion time. According to the time of each step, the corresponding scheduling steps are completed to achieve efficient scheduling in the maximum completion time.

5   Simulation Experiment

5.1   Experimental Settings

Intel Core i5 processor, which runs on a 3.2 GHz CPU, is programmed in C +. The IDPFSP test suite is obtained by extending the DPFSP standard test suite.There are 12 kinds of combinations in the test set $n \times m$: {(20, 50, 100) × 5}, {(20, 50, 100, 200) × 10},

{(20, 50, 100, 200, 500) × 20}, each of which generates 10 different examples, and then considers 6 kinds of factory numbers, that is f = {2, 3, 4, 5, 6, 7}, all the problems determine the processing time.

5.2 Parameter Settings

Experimental design was used to investigate the influence of parameters on the performance of the algorithm. Ra14_18 was used to test the algorithm. 4 horizontal values were set for each parameter, as shown in Table 1.

Table 1. Parameter level values

Parameter	Level			
	1	2	3	4
Indi_num	100	150	200	250
SN	1	2	3	4
Is	100	150	200	250
kmax	15	20	25	30

According to the orthogonal table, each group of parameter combinations is run independently for 10 times, and the total evaluation of 500000 times is taken as the termination criterion. The average performance of the algorithm is taken as the response value. The results are shown in Table 2.

Table 2. Orthogonal table of parameters

Number	parameter				Response value
	Indi_num	SN	Is	k_{max}	
1	1	1	1	1	660.5
2	1	2	2	2	655.1
3	1	3	3	3	656.3
4	1	4	4	4	658.5
5	2	1	2	3	652.3
6	2	2	1	4	651.7
7	2	3	4	1	654.7
8	2	4	3	2	652.8
9	3	1	3	4	651.0

(*continued*)

Table 2. (*continued*)

Number	parameter				Response value
	Indi_num	SN	Is	k_{max}	
10	3	2	4	3	651.8
11	3	3	1	2	652.0
12	3	4	2	1	655.1
13	4	1	4	2	653.2
14	4	2	3	1	651.0
15	4	3	2	4	651.8
16	4	4	1	3	658.7

The average response value of each parameter at each level is calculated, and then the influence level of parameters on performance is determined. The influence trend of each parameter on performance is shown in Fig. 4.

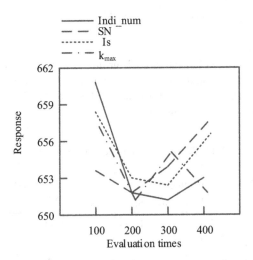

Fig. 4. Trends in the impact of parameters on performance

As shown in Fig. 4, India _ num has a greater impact on performance, followed by SN, Is, and kmax.

5.3 Simulation Results and Analysis

The interval number representation scheduling method and the hybrid discrete Drosophila optimal scheduling method are used to compare the scheduling time and efficiency. The results are shown as follows.

(1) Scheduling time

The scheduling time of different methods is compared and the results are shown in Tables 3 and 4.

Table 3. Interval number represents scheduling time of scheduling method

Scheduling node	1	2	3	4	5	6	7	8	9
1	0	0	0	3	3	4	5	5	5
2	0	0	0	4	3	5	6	6	3
3	0	0	0	5	2	5	5	5	3
4	0	0	0	4	2	4	6	5	4
5	0	0	0	3	2	5	4	6	3
6	0	0	0	4	0	3	3	4	5
7	0	0	0	3	3	4	5	5	3
8	0	0	0	3	2	5	4	4	4
9	0	0	0	4	2	1	4	4	2

Table 4. Scheduling time based on hybrid discrete Drosophila optimization scheduling method

Scheduling node	1	2	3	4	5	6	7	8	9
1	0	0	0	1	2	4	5	5	1
2	0	0	0	3	3	5	6	6	3
3	0	0	0	4	2	5	5	6	3
4	0	0	0	0	2	4	5	5	4
5	0	0	0	0	0	3	4	6	3
6	0	0	0	4	0	3	3	4	5
7	0	0	0	3	3	4	4	5	3
8	0	0	0	1	2	5	3	4	4
9	0	0	0	0	1	1	4	4	1

It can be seen from the above comparison results that the scheduling time of the scheduling method represented by interval number is different from the expected time, while the scheduling method based on hybrid discrete Drosophila is consistent with the expected time, and the error is 0.

(2) Dispatching efficiency

The results of comparative analysis of scheduling efficiency of different methods are shown in Fig. 5.

It can be seen from Fig. 5 that the overall scheduling efficiency of the scheduling method represented by interval number is less than 40%, while the overall scheduling

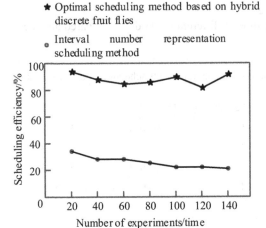

Fig. 5. Comparison results of scheduling efficiency of different methods

efficiency of the scheduling method based on hybrid discrete Drosophila optimization is higher than 80%, which has good scheduling effect.

6   Conclusion

A hybrid discrete Drosophila optimization scheduling algorithm for interval number distribution permutation pipeline problem is proposed. The effectiveness and efficiency of the algorithm are verified by a large number of simulation examples and data analysis. The innovation of the algorithm lies in the combination of improved heuristic rules and random methods to initialize the population, and a multi operation cooperation link based on probability selection mechanism is designed to give full play to the performance of each operator.

Future research work will focus on the extension of other uncertain problems, optimization of other scheduling indicators, design of adaptive algorithm and collaborative optimization of multiple scheduling objectives.

References

1. Liao, Q., Zhang, H., Xu, N., et al.: A MILP model based on flowrate database for detailed scheduling of a multi-product pipeline with multiple pump stations. Comput. Chem. Eng. **117**(2), 63–81 (2018)
2. Asl, N.B., Mirhassani, S.A.: Benders decomposition with integer sub-problem applied to pipeline scheduling problem under flow rate uncertainty. Comput. Chem. Eng. **123**(6), 222–235 (2019)
3. Qin, H., Chen, W., Cao, B., Zeng, M., Li, J., Peng, Y.: DIPS: dual-interface dual-pipeline scheduling for energy-efficient multihop communications in IoT. IEEE Internet Things J. **6**(1), 718–733 (2019). https://doi.org/10.1109/JIOT.2018.2855695

4. Chang, X., Xu, X., Yang, D.: Pipeline scheduling based on constructive interference in strip wireless sensor networks. Comput. Mater. Continua **64**(1), 193–206 (2020)
5. Moradi, S., Mirhassani, S.A., Hooshmand, F.: Efficient decomposition-based algorithm to solve long-term pipeline scheduling problem. Petrol. Sci. **16**(5), 1159–1175 (2019)
6. Amine, A., Mouhoub, M., Ait Mohamed, O., et al.: Optimal Scheduling of Multiproduct Pipeline System Using MILP Continuous Approach. In: IFIP Advances in Information and Communication Technology Computational Intelligence and its Applications, vol. 522 (2018). https://doi.org/10.1007/978-3-319-89743-1(36):411-420
7. Fu, W., Liu, S., Srivastava, G.: Optimization of big data scheduling in social networks. Entropy **21**(9), 902 (2019)
8. Liu, S., Li, Z., Zhang, Y., et al.: Introduction of key problems in long-distance learning and training. Mob. Netw. Appl. **24**(1), 1–4 (2019)
9. Liu, S., Liu, D., Srivastava, G., et al.: Overview and methods of correlation filter algorithms in object tracking. Comp. Intell. Syst. (2020). https://doi.org/10.1007/s40747-020-00161-4
10. Krishnadas, G., Kiprakis, A., Sciubba, E.: A machine learning pipeline for demand response capacity scheduling. Energies **13**(7), 1848 (2020)
11. Qiu, S., Wang, S., Xiao, C., Ge, S.: Assessment of microalgae as a new feeding additive for fruit fly Drosophila melanogaster. Sci. Total Environ. **667**, 455–463 (2019). https://doi.org/10.1016/j.scitotenv.2019.02.414
12. Yang, X., Han, Y., Mu, Y., et al.: Multigenerational effects of cadmium on the lifespan and fertility of Drosophila melanogaster. Chemosphere **245**(Apr), 125533.1-125533.7 (2020)
13. Gärtner, S., Hundertmark, T., Nolte, H., Theofel, I., Eren-Ghiani, Z., Tetzner, C., Duchow, T., Rathke, C., Krüger, M., Renkawitz, R.: Stage-specific testes proteomics of Drosophila melanogaster identifies essential proteins for male fertility. Eur. J. Cell Biol. **98**(2–4), 103–115 (2019). https://doi.org/10.1016/j.ejcb.2019.01.001
14. Hsieh, Fu-Shiung., Guo, Yi-Hong.: A discrete cooperatively coevolving particle swarm optimization algorithm for combinatorial double auctions. Appl. Intell. **49**(11), 3845–3863 (2019). https://doi.org/10.1007/s10489-019-01556-8
15. Lakshman, A.A., et al.: Selection for timing of eclosion results in co-evolution of temperature responsiveness in drosophila melanogaster. J. Biol. Rhyth. **34**(6), 596–609 (2019)
16. Qiu, B., Guo, J., Li, X., et al.: Discrete-time advanced zeroing neurodynamic algorithm applied to future equality-constrained nonlinear optimization with various noises. IEEE Trans. Cybern. (99), 1-14 (2020)
17. Wu, Q., Zhang, R.: Beamforming optimization for wireless network aided by intelligent reflecting surface with discrete phase shifts. IEEE Trans. Commun. **68**(3), 1838–1851 (2020)
18. Shao, Z., Pi, D., Shao, W.: A novel multi-objective discrete water wave optimization for solving multi-objective blocking flow-shop scheduling problem. **165**(FEB.1), 110–131 (2019)
19. Zhang, J., You, K., Basar, T.: Distributed discrete-time optimization in multiagent networks using only sign of relative state. IEEE Trans. Autom. Control **64**(6), 2352–2367 (2019)
20. Teng, Y., Yang, L., Song, X., et al.: An augmented Lagrangian proximal alternating method for sparse discrete optimization problems. Numer. Algor. **83**(3), 833–866 (2020)
21. Li, Y., Yang, W., He, P., et al.: Design and management of a distributed hybrid energy system through smart contract and blockchain. Appl. Energy **248**(15), 390–405 (2019)
22. Spencer, A.A.M.S., Luciano, S., Mario, M.: Analysis and design of high-efficiency hybrid high step-up DC-DC converter for distributed PV generation systems. IEEE Trans. Ind. Electron. (5), 1 (2018)
23. Zhang, L., Liu, W., Qi, B.: Innovation design and optimization management of a new drive system for plug-in hybrid electric vehicles. Energy **186**, 115823.1-115823.19 (2019). https://doi.org/10.1016/j.energy.2019.07.153
24. Zkik, K., Hajji, S.E., Orhanou, G.: Design and implementation of a new security plane for hybrid distributed SDNs. J. Commun. **14**(1), 26–32 (2019)

25. Han, X., Dong, Y., Yue, L., Quanxi, X.: State transition simulated annealing algorithm for discrete-continuous optimization problems. IEEE Access **7**, 44391–44403 (2019). https://doi.org/10.1109/ACCESS.2019.2908961
26. Kamalakis, T., Dogkas, L., Simou, F.: Optimization of a discrete multi-tone visible light communication system using a mixed-integer genetic algorithm. Optics Commun. **485**(1), 126741 (2020)
27. Wang, L., Guohua, W., Gao, L.: Thematic issue on "advanced intelligent scheduling algorithms for smart manufacturing systems." Memetic Comput. **11**(4), 333–334 (2019). https://doi.org/10.1007/s12293-019-00297-y
28. Kamalakis, T., Dogkas, L., Simou, F.: Optimization of a discrete multi-tone visible light communication system using a mixed-integer genetic algorithm. Optics Commun. **485**(8), 126741 (2020)
29. Rui, L., Qin, Y., Li, B., et al.: Context-based intelligent scheduling and knowledge push algorithms for ar-assist communication network maintenance. Comput. Model. Eng. Sci. **118**(2), 291–315 (2019)
30. Bruballa, E., Wong, A., Rexachs, D., et al.: An intelligent scheduling of non-critical patients admission for emergency department. IEEE Access (99), 1 (2019)
31. Yuan, L.: Scheduling analysis of intelligent machining system based on combined weights. IOP Conf. Ser. Mater. Sci. Eng. **493**(1), 12146 (2019)

Research on Grid Planning Method of Distribution Network Based on Artificial Intelligence Technology

Fu Guan-hua[1]([✉]), Chen Da-xing[2], Sun Yang[2], Xia Jia[2], Wang Fei-feng[2], and Zhu Lian-huan[1]

[1] State Grid Hangzhou Xiaoshan Power Supply Company, Hangzhou 311200, China
[2] Zhejiang Zhongxin Power Engineering Construction Co., Ltd., Hangzhou 311200, China

Abstract. In order to improve the reliability of distribution network, a grid planning method of distribution network based on artificial intelligence technology is studied. Firstly, according to the principle of grid division, the planning area is divided into several planning grids reasonably; the existing problems of the existing distribution network are analyzed systematically, and the weak links of the existing distribution network are summarized. According to the current grid structure, load forecasting results and planning objectives of planning grid, the target grid and transition grid of planning grid are determined, and the load forecasting method of distribution network is designed to improve the scientificity of distribution grid division. The experiments show that after the grid planning of the distribution network in a planning area, the target grid of the distribution network is strong, the power supply range is clear, and the power supply reliability is high, which verifies the effectiveness and scientificity of the method.

Keywords: Artificial intelligence · Distribution network · Grid planning · Load forecasting

1 Introduction

With the development of society, power resources have become the main driving force for social development. As an important part of the entire power grid, the distribution network is mainly responsible for providing continuous and stable power supply to end users [1]. Especially with the rapid growth of social power consumption, traditional distribution network planning methods can no longer meet the large-scale medium-voltage distribution network. Under this situation, it is necessary to strengthen the reform of the distribution network to ensure the current power system The reliability and safety of power supply, so the rationality of distribution network planning is directly related to its power supply capacity and power supply quality [2]. The distribution network is an important part of the smart grid. It directly faces the end users and is an important infrastructure serving the people's livelihood. Therefore, the distribution network must be built into a strong, safe, reliable, green, low-carbon, cost-effective, and powerful

W. Fu et al. (Eds.): ICMTEL 2021, LNICST 387, pp. 91–102, 2021.
https://doi.org/10.1007/978-3-030-82562-1_8

resource. First-class distribution network with configuration capability, service guarantee capability and risk resistance capability. In the traditional "top-down" power grid planning, there are many problems, which restrict the quality of power supply. The grid power planning based on power demand and regional regulatory planning can improve the work efficiency and service level of distribution network. This paper mainly takes the grid planning of medium voltage distribution network as the research breakthrough point, and makes a detailed study on the grid planning of power grid, so as to improve the comprehensive benefits of distribution network planning, ensure the reliability and safety of power supply of the whole distribution network, and meet the power demand of power users to the greatest extent.

2 Grid Planning Method of Distribution Network

2.1 Grid Division Principle of Planning Area

In recent years, in order to build a strong distribution network and meet the growing power demand of urban construction and residents, power grid enterprises focus on the development of distribution network, actively connect with government departments, and carry out planning results evaluation [3]. In this context, the "grid" distribution network planning mechanism is proposed, and the partition load forecasting model is constructed to improve the rationality and practicability of the medium voltage distribution network planning. In this process, it is necessary to first determine the zoning principle and count the nature of the partition, so as to lay the foundation for the next step of the zonal load forecasting.

The use of artificial intelligence technology in the grid planning of the distribution network is to divide the area to be planned into several areas according to the classification of the distribution network power supply area, the difference in the nature of the land, and the degree of development. The power supply ranges of these areas are relatively independent and will not overlap, starting from the terminal demand of the power market, meeting the needs of users as the goal and guide, breaking the previous top-down planning method, turning to bottom-up, adopting the planning concept of low voltage first, high voltage, refer to the typical load forecasting model carries out differentiated system load forecasting. Through the optimization and improvement of traditional methods, it is expected to realize the appropriate medium-voltage grid structure in different areas, and extend this idea to the high-voltage distribution network structure and layout. Taking into account communication, power distribution automation and other content, the planning goal is finally completed and balanced with the development of the planned area [4]. The distribution network planning scheme is shown in Fig. 1.

Through practice and calculation, the following problems exist in the urban distribution network planning scheme.

(1) When the power grid is in full operation, the short circuit often occurs in the power system;
(2) The variable capacitance can not meet the supply and demand gradually;
(3) The load of distribution line is too large;
(4) Distribution network construction funds are insufficient.

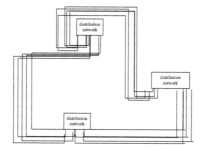

Fig. 1. Traditional distribution network planning scheme

Based on this, it is necessary to clarify the basic expected planning goals when carrying out grid planning. This article mainly uses artificial intelligence technology to determine the scope and content of the plan, determine the base year, level year and saturation year of the plan, and propose relevant planning methods and evaluation standards, and then successively carry out planning for the target area [5]. The structure of regional distribution network is shown in Fig. 2.

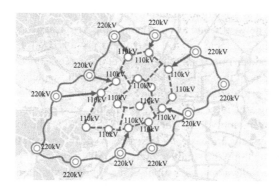

Fig. 2. Regional distribution network structure

In the above process, the use of artificial intelligence technology for grid division, load forecasting and distribution network structure is the core of grid planning. Distribution network structure planning includes three items: substation site selection, power supply range determination, and distribution network line planning [6]. Determine the approximate scope of each power supply area according to the regional scope and administrative level, and make corresponding supplements to the load density requirements of each power supply area according to artificial intelligence technology. There are overlapping parts in each power supply area and should be classified to a higher level power supply area.

The main principles of grid division of planning area are as follows:

Grid division principle of planning area 1: Based on the current situation of medium voltage distribution network, the blocks with different land use properties and development depth are classified according to the regional regulatory detailed planning [7]. At the same time, the load forecasting results of each plot are standardized, and the planning area is subdivided into several grids according to the location of the station source point, the area size of each plot, the load nature, and the conditions of river water area and long-term road planning.

The grid division principle of the planning area 2: The size of each grid should be determined according to the power supply capacity of a set of standard wiring. Each grid should be able to independently undertake the normal power supply tasks in the area, meet the power load demand in the area, and reserve spare capacity to meet the future load growth needs.

The principle of grid division of the planning area 3: The layout of medium and long-term substations should be planned in combination with artificial intelligence technology, and each grid power point should be determined. The selection of power points should meet the principle of proximity.

Principle 4 of grid division in planning area: in principle, the power supply points in each grid shall be from two different substations, and the power supply lines of the same substation shall be from different bus sections.

2.2 Optimization of Grid Generation Method for Distribution Network

Based on the research and analysis of the theory and application of grid planning for domestic distribution networks, and relying on the support of actual engineering projects, an optimization method suitable for grid planning is proposed [8]. Grid is the smallest unit of grid planning and an important foundation for user access, operation management, maintenance management, reliability management, and subsequent project expansion. The usual method of grid division is to divide several small-area plots in a certain sub-region in the planning area into a grid. The plots in the same grid are adjacent and have the same level of power supply area. The nature of the land is, the load density and the power quality requirements are basically the same. Repeat the operation until the entire planning area is divided into the smallest functional unit grid.

According to the relevant power supply area division standards, combined with artificial intelligence technology to determine the planning area power supply category, and use the corresponding technical standards for distribution network construction [9]. On this basis, the grid structure, equipment, operation and other indicators, such as power supply reliability rate RS-3, line power supply radius, insulation rate and other indicators should be taken into account. Combined with the construction and transformation scheme of primary grid structure and equipment, the main indicators of distribution network in the target year of the planning area are proposed. According to the various problems of the current distribution network analysis, combined with the grid division of the planning area, the project scheme is reasonably formulated by using the principle of differentiated planning. Based on the analysis of the current situation and the project schemes in the planning level year, the artificial intelligence technology is used for closed-loop evaluation, and the planning indicators are compared intuitively to verify the planning effect of the grid planning method for distribution network. The optimization of the grid planning process of the distribution network is shown in Fig. 3.

According to the degree of power consumption, the basic grid can be divided into the following three cases:

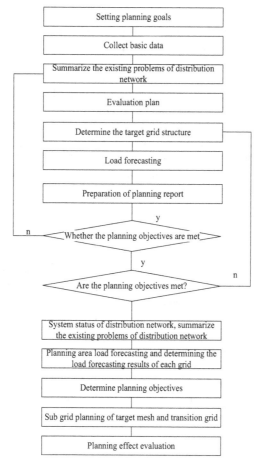

Fig. 3. Optimization of grid planning process for distribution network

The load in the mature grid is concentrated in dense areas such as the city center. This area has been developed to the greatest extent, with high load density and low scalability, and the load has become saturated. Developing grids are generally located in new urban development zones and planned areas. This kind of land has a good room for economic growth and a faster development speed. The load density and power consumption are also increasing year by year following the economic development speed, and the prospective load and increase the space is very clear. Uncertain grids are generally located in the suburbs at a certain distance from the city center. Residents of this kind of plot have limited electricity consumption and low load density. Municipal planning and construction and investment in plant construction are not clear. There is no room for increase in electricity load. After the grid is divided, large-scale adjustments are generally not carried out. In some cases, there is a big gap between the load increase and the expected, and the municipal planning and construction plan has to be adjusted and changed. The divided grid needs to be re-adjusted. The method is as follows:

The load growth in the grid is far more than expected, and it is close to the extreme conditions of the line load, and even overload operation for a long time, the power supply quality and reliability are significantly reduced, which affects the safe operation of the distribution network. At this time, the original grid should be divided into two, three or more sub grids through system analysis according to the distribution of roads and users' electricity in the grid the connection structure of grid structure shall be adjusted accordingly [10]. In this case, if the load growth rate of adjacent grids is also slow, the original grid and adjacent grid can be combined into a new grid. After a period of time, the municipal planning has been adjusted, and the nature of land use in the grid has been determined. In this case, the grid should be re divided, and the load forecast of the target area with reference to the historical experience data, and the number of grid splits can be determined according to the results.

2.3 Distribution Grid Coding

After grid division, each grid needs to be coded. In order to facilitate management, uniform coding rules should be set up, and the grid coding should have good recognition characteristics. The grid coding is composed of grid number and grid features to ensure that the coding of each grid is not repeated. The first item of grid number is the first letter of local city Pinyin, the second item is the first letter of district or county, the third item is the first letter of Pinyin of street or development zone, and the last item is the sequence number of grid. Each item is connected by the character "one". The serial number of grid is numbered according to the sequence rules of left to right (from west to East) and from top to bottom (from south to North). The grid feature code is composed of four items, with a total of five characters. Its representation format is abnnc, the details are shown in Fig. 4.

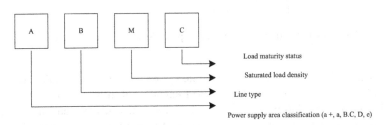

Fig. 4. Composition of grid feature code

The lines in Fig. 1 represent different transmission lines. The first item (A) of the feature code indicates the classification of the grid's power supply area, which occupies one character. According to the DLT5729-2016 guideline, the power supply area can be divided into six types from A+ to E; the second item (B) represents the network the line form in the grid, which occupies one character, is divided into three forms: full cable (A), cable and overhead line combination (B), and full overhead line (C); the third item (nn) represents the saturation load of the grid Density value (unit MW/km^2), occupies two characters, generally rounded to two integers; the fourth item (C) represents the maturity of the load in the grid, occupies one character, and is divided into mature and stable areas (A), basic built-up area (B), under-construction area (C) and uncertain area (D).

In the process of traditional distribution network operation, there are often some problems such as unreasonable distribution of substations, unbalanced load, low capacity utilization efficiency, overlapping of power supply areas, etc., which often lead to the sharp increase of management workload and maintenance difficulty in the later stage, which can not realize fine management. In order to avoid these problems, a hierarchical structure is established for the grid of the distribution network. According to the three voltage levels of high, medium and low, the distribution network is divided into three layers: L1, L2 and L3, as shown in the Fig. 5.

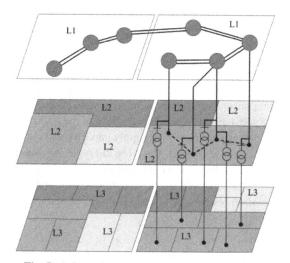

Fig. 5. Schematic diagram of grid layered structure

After the power distribution network is divided into grids, it can ensure that the scope of power supply is extremely clear, so that the large area can be divided into several small areas to ensure the rationality of power supply and distribution, and effectively avoid the phenomenon of cross power supply during the power supply process. In this way, the stability of the power supply in each area can be guaranteed, and the occurrence of short circuits in other phenomena can be avoided. Ensuring power supply from more than two power points in each area can effectively avoid the limitation of power supply from one power point. If only one power point is used for power supply, once a circuit failure occurs, stable power supply in the area cannot be achieved and the distribution network is gridded planning can make the power supply more flexible and improve maintenance efficiency. Grid divides the power distribution into different small areas. When a fault occurs, only one area needs to be repaired. When a power failure occurs, only one area needs to be stopped to avoid large-scale power outages. Affect people's normal life.

According to the concept of grid planning, a bottom-up approach is adopted to carry out layered work on the distribution grid, namely the form of L3 → L2 → L1. The specific process is as follows:

According to the user's reported capacity and the nature of electricity consumption, in order to meet the user's electricity demand as the guide, according to the nature of land use, load nature, plot size, rivers, roads and other physical and geographical boundary conditions, the target area is divided into several grids, each grid has a single basic function. At this time, the grid level is layer L3, and then load system is carried out for the target area. According to the planning objectives, load forecasting is carried out in the planning area, and the existing distribution network situation is evaluated.

According to the load situation and grid division situation of the L3 layer grid, combined with the target area distribution network structure planning, distribution network capacity and physical geographical conditions and other factors, for the purpose of optimal power supply, several power consumption properties are similar and geographically located the adjacently connected L3 layer grids are combined to initially generate L3 layer grids.

According to the combination and division of L2 grid, combined with the urban construction planning scheme of the target area, the power supply scope and power supply capacity of the existing substation, the required new substation capacity is calculated, and the location of the substation is planned according to the grid structure of the target area, so as to meet the corresponding power supply capacity and outgoing line demand. After the L1 network scheme is formed, the L1 grid layout is solidified, According to the relevant grid division and distribution network planning evaluation index, the rationality of the combination scheme of L2 grid generation is comprehensively evaluated. According to the evaluation results, the L2 grid is modified and adjusted to achieve the optimal division scheme.

2.4   Grid Load Forecasting of Distribution Network

The primary content of grid planning is to divide the target planning area into grids with a single function according to the nature of electricity consumption and natural geographical conditions. Different application scenarios adopt different forecasting methods. In the grid planning load forecasting process, not only the total area load must be predicted, but also the growth characteristics and location of the load must be clarified. It has very obvious spatial characteristics. Load forecasting must adopt a spatial load forecasting model that can reflect the distribution of urban power supply areas to ensure that the "grid" load forecasting results have the smallest error. According to the different forecasting time and duration in the future, load forecasting can usually be divided into the following categories, as shown in the Table 1.

According to the current social development trend and the progressive mode of the distribution network, the traditional power distribution method can no longer meet the needs of social development. Therefore, relevant departments and staff must re-examine the reasonable planning of the distribution network, change their ideas, and innovate the way of distribution network planning. Based on this, the load forecasting method of distribution grid planning is analyzed, including:

Table 1. Classification method of load forecasting.

Category	Entry	Characteristic
Time classification	Long term load forecasting	10–30 years
	Medium term load forecasting	5–10 years
	Shorter term load forecasting	1–5 years
	Short term load forecasting	Within 48 h

District load forecasting: the relevant departments and staff should refuse the simplification of the forecasting method, conduct in-depth research and analysis from multiple perspectives, use diversified load forecasting methods to predict the power consumption of each power supply area, and get the average value from it, so as to minimize the prediction error, optimize the distribution mode, and put forward constructive distribution scheme according to the prediction results.

Spatial load forecasting: According to the division of different power supply areas, relevant departments and staff make statistics on the current load status of each block based on the actual situation of regional power distribution. Spatial load forecasting is based on the demand for land parcels, combined with load forecasting models to predict the long-term load situation of the land parcel, formulate a forecasting plan suitable for the long-term development of the land parcel, and further make a reasonable distribution network grid Planning scheme.

Suppose that an L2 level network contains n L3 level grids with single function, l is the maximum load of each L3 level grid, and S is the corresponding land use area of each L3 level grid. Then the load density of each L3 layer grid is as follows:

$$\rho_i = L_i/S_i \tag{1}$$

For the built community, according to the development status of the community and the load density of the typical mature area, set the load density index of each L3 layer grid in the future m year or saturation year as p; for the community under construction, according to empirical data, select the load density index for the future saturation year. Let r be the load weighting coefficient of each L3 layer grid, and k be the load simultaneous rate of each L3 layer grid in the m-th year or saturation year. Then the predicted load of the nth year or saturation year of the L2 grid is

$$P = \sum_{i=1}^{n} r_i k_i \hat{\rho}_i S_i \tag{2}$$

Preprocess the collected information, analyze the processing results, and analyze the relationship between the information output and input components. The specific calculation formula is as follows:

$$f(x_n, y_m) = P \frac{\lambda(x_n, y_m)}{\sqrt{(x_n)(y_m)}} \tag{3}$$

Among them: $\lambda(x_n, y_m)$ represents the covariance between input information x_n and output information y_m; k represents the total amount of information. According to the formula, the normalized calculation formula of input information x_n and output information y_m can be obtained:

$$x'_n = \frac{x_n - x_{min}}{x_{max} - x_{min}}, y'_n = \frac{y_n - y_{min}}{y_{max} - y_{min}} \tag{4}$$

The formula is weighted to obtain the input data vector expression, as shown in the formula:

$$x = \left(f_1(x'_1, y')x'_i, f_2(x'_2, y')x'_{i-1}, ...f_1(x'_j, y')x' \right)^T \tag{5}$$

In the formula: T represents a cycle, and the weighted input information vector can be obtained by this formula. The results of short-term load forecasting are usually used to guide the calculation of generator start-up and shutdown plans, maintenance plans, power distribution and operating costs. Medium- and long-term load forecasting is an important part of power grid planning. The forecast results usually determine the distribution network scale, network structure and investment quota in the target planning area. Medium- and long-term load forecasting is usually coordinated with the municipal planning, which is related to the future economic development speed and scale of the planned target area. Load forecasting is to predict the future electricity consumption situation. Due to various uncertain factors such as weather changes, holidays, emergencies, the accuracy of historical data, municipal planning adjustments, and human factors, the predicted results will have certain errors. In order to reduce the error and improve the accuracy of the forecast, the usual practice is to ensure the completeness and accuracy of the data when collecting historical load data, predict the load of different types and scenarios, and check and correct the forecast results. This improves the accuracy and scientificity of grid planning for the distribution network.

3 Analysis of Experimental Results

Based on the analysis and summary of the current situation of a planned regional power grid, there is still a big gap between the "first-class distribution network" in the connection rate of medium voltage lines, n−1 passing rate of medium voltage lines, average power supply radius of medium voltage lines, insulation rate of medium voltage lines, and power supply reliability rate (RS-3). Written according to the requirements of C++, Microsoft can add multiple functions, including the system throughout the windows program, as well as user interface and file operation. The load forecasting results of a planning area in the target year are shown in the Table 2.

Based on the test results in the above table, it can be seen that in the actual application process, the proposed distribution network grid planning method based on artificial intelligence has relatively high accuracy for regional distribution network load forecasting, which is basically consistent with the target predicted value. Further comparison is made between the current method and the distribution network grid planning error under this method, as shown in Fig. 6.

Table 2. Grid load forecast results of distribution network.

Region	Total load/MW	Target load/MW
Grid 1	6.08	6.10
Grid 2	10.24	10.25
Grid 3	13.46	10.44
Grid 4	17.82	17.80
Grid 5	20.44	20.40
Grid 6	22.45	22.45
Total/considering the simultaneity rate of 0.7	66.35	66.20

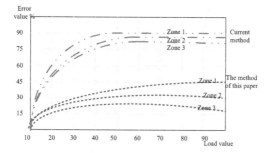

Fig. 6. Comparison test results

Based on the above detection results, it can be seen that the error degree of the grid planning method based on artificial intelligence is relatively low in the practical application process, which proves that the practical application effect of the method is better. Through the grid planning, the main indicators of the distribution network reach the level of "first-class distribution network". The distribution network structure is strong and the power supply reliability is high, which verifies the effectiveness and scientificity of the distribution network grid planning method. In this paper, a grid planning method of distribution network is proposed. The grid planning of the planning area can achieve the following effects.

(1) The power supply range of the medium voltage line of the distribution network is clear.
(2) The target grid and transition grid of the distribution network are strong and reliable.
(3) The main planning indicators of the distribution network can reach the level of "first-class distribution network", and promote the scientific development of the distribution network.
(4) Applying the above method to grid distribution network planning in a certain district of a city, the planning effect is obvious, which verifies the effectiveness and scientificity of the method.

4 Conclusion

With the increase of social production and domestic electricity consumption, power enterprises must carry out grid planning of distribution network to provide power supply quality of distribution network. This requires that in the process of grid planning of medium voltage distribution network, strictly follow its planning principles, and fully combine with the economic development level of distribution grid region, continuously promote the grid planning of medium voltage distribution network, In order to ensure that the power supply of the whole distribution network is more reliable and safe, so as to meet the power demand of power users to the maximum extent.

References

1. Tabrizi, B.H., Rabbani, M.: A graph theoretic-based approach to distribution network planning with routes interaction regarding the fix-charge transportation problem. Int. J. Oper. Res. **38**(1), 112–136 (2020)
2. Huang, Y, Zhuang, X., Liu, H., et al.: Application of power load forecasting in urban distribution network planning based on 3d real scene platform. J. Phys. Conf. Ser. **1549**(5), 052121 (2020)
3. Zhang, L., Tang, W., Liang, J., et al.: Coordinated day-ahead reactive power dispatch in distribution network based on real power forecast errors. IEEE Trans. Power Syst. **31**(3), 2472–2480 (2019)
4. Popovic, Z.N., Kovacki, N.V., Popovic, D.S.: Resilient distribution network planning under the severe windstorms using a risk-based approach. Reliab. Eng. Syst. Saf. **204**(01), 107–114 (2020)
5. Muhammad, M.A., Mokhlis, H., Naidu, K., et al.: Distribution network planning enhancement via network reconfiguration and DG integration using dataset approach and water cycle algorithm. J. Mod. Power Syst. Clean Energy **8**(1), 86–93 (2020)
6. Popovic, Z.N., Knezevic, S.D., Kerleta, V.D.: Network automation planning in distribution networks with distributed generators using a risk-based approach. Electr. Eng. **101**(2), 659–673 (2019)
7. Li, Z., Wu, W., Zhang, B., et al.: Hexagon raster-based method for distribution network planning considering line routes and pole locations. IET Gener. Transm. Distrib. **14**(8), 1420–1429 (2020)
8. Fu, W., Liu, S., Srivastava, G.: Optimization of big data scheduling in social networks. Entropy **21**(9), 902 (2019)
9. Liu, S., Lu, M., Li, H., et al.: Prediction of gene expression patterns with generalized linear regression model. Front. Genet. **10**, 120 (2019)
10. Liu, S., Liu, D., Srivastava, G., Połap, D., Woźniak, M.: Overview and methods of correlation filter algorithms in object tracking. Complex Intell. Syst., 1–23 (2020). https://doi.org/10.1007/s40747-020-00161-4

Intelligent Monitoring Method for Backstage Data Security of Tourism Information Promotion Platform Based on Cloud Computing

Yiqiong Ding[1](✉) and Guozhi Lin[2]

[1] School of Information and Engineering, Sichuan Tourism University, Chengdu 610000, China
[2] Quanzhou Arts and Crafts Vocational College, Quanzhou 362500, China

Abstract. Due to the rapid update of information platform unsafe factors, the monitoring ability and response effect of the monitoring platform of tourism information promotion platform are not high. The monitoring center of the platform is the data acquisition module, and the data acquisition module uses RTL8019AS controller to collect the data transmitted by the nodes and the data of the security status of the nodes. The processing module uses MSP430 processor to monitor the security of the measured data, and connects with the transmission module directly, so as to monitor the error of the processed data and transmit the data. Finally, the experimental results show that the background data security intelligent monitoring method of tourism information promotion platform based on cloud computing has strong monitoring ability and good response.

Keywords: Cloud computing · Tourism · Information promotion · Background monitoring

1 Introduction

In order to avoid the problems of low efficiency and unsafe operation of information monitoring of tourism information promotion platform, and improve the monitoring ability and response effect of the platform, an intelligent data security monitoring method based on cloud computing is proposed [1]. It focuses on the combination of RTL8019AS controller and MSP430 processor to monitor the tested data. The innovation lies in optimizing the error monitoring and data transmission mode of the tested data, reducing the unsafe factors of the information platform, striving for better monitoring ability and response ability, and ensuring the monitoring security of the tourism information promotion platform.

W. Fu et al. (Eds.): ICMTEL 2021, LNICST 387, pp. 103–114, 2021.
https://doi.org/10.1007/978-3-030-82562-1_9

2 Intelligent Monitoring Method for Backstage Data Security of Tourism Information Promotion Platform

2.1 Optimization of Functional Structure of Backstage Intelligent Monitoring Platform for Data Security of Tourism Information Promotion Platform

The monitoring safety monitoring platform of tourism information promotion platform has designed data collection module, processing module and transmission module. The data collection module is the monitoring center of the monitoring safety monitoring platform of the tourism information promotion platform, which is responsible for the collection of monitoring data of the tourism information promotion platform, including node transmission data and monitoring node safety status data [2–5]. In the process of intelligent monitoring of backstage data security of the platform, it is necessary to ensure the real-time monitoring of tourism information promotion platform and prevent the platform effect caused by monitoring data interruption [6–10].

Based on the above factors, the functional structure of the backstage data security intelligent monitoring platform of the tourism information promotion platform is optimized, and the RTL8019AS controller is added to the connection bus between the tourism information promotion platform and the data security intelligent monitoring platform. RTL8019AS controller has the functions of on-demand, monitoring indication and early warning, 16 kB synchronous dynamic random access memory and RTL8019 kernel, which are compatible with all kinds of collection algorithms and external circuits to ensure the real-time monitoring of tourism information promotion platform, so as to realize the high-speed and accurate collection of the data transmitted by nodes and the safe state of nodes. The warning device is equipped with a small LED display, which can emit prominent yellow light in the process of alarming, and display and check the background data parameters of the tourism information promotion platform that have not been successfully collected, so as to facilitate the intervention of platform maintenance personnel until the data collection is successful [10, 11]. The data after acquisition is successfully transferred to synchronous dynamic random access memory. PCI9054 is selected to be responsible for the connection with PC bus and signal monitoring. CPLD is used as the interface to complete the interface conversion between 32bit PCI bus and 8-bit data processing unit FPGA [7–9, 12, 13]. FPGA will write 16-by-8 bit data information into SLM or read the data from CCD into FPGA for decoding after coding. The selected CPLD is a complex programmable logic device CPLDEMP3256AQC20B-10 chip of Altera Company. Based on this, the configuration of the data monitoring platform is optimized, and the specific structure is shown as follows (Fig. 1):

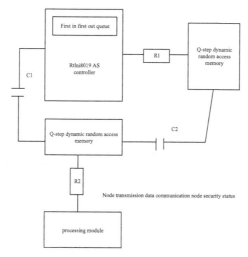

Fig. 1. Data monitoring platform configuration optimization

Using the C/S architecture and the software developed by Power Builder to optimize the functions of the intelligent monitoring platform for the backstage data security of the tourism information promotion platform. Its operating environment is set up to run Oracle and other large databases can be normal professional server, there is enough hard disk space to store monitoring logging. Operating system whichever operating system runs Oracle [14, 15]. Optimize the client environment to properly connect to the database server and have enough space to install the client. The connection bus adopts the first-in, first-out queuing method, and realizes the collection of the data transmitted by the nodes and the safety status data of the monitoring nodes in the monitoring platform of tourism information promotion [16, 17]. In the initial collection of the monitoring platform of tourism information promotion platform, the data collection module transmits the collected data directly to the synchronous RAM of RTL8019AS controller, and sieves the uncollected data. Based on this, the functions of the intelligent monitoring platform for backstage data security of the tourism information promotion platform are standardized as follows (Fig. 2):

Before the SDRAM receives the data, it converts the data transmitted by the node and the security state data of the monitoring node into the data to be tested in a unified format. When the storage capacity of SDRAM reaches one frame, the initial monitoring work is finished immediately. In later monitoring work, the data monitoring module will make prior calls to the data in the SDRAM to improve the monitoring capability of the platform [18–20]. SDRAM inevitably stores the same data in many times, which not only occupies the extra storage space, but also slows down the monitoring efficiency of the platform. To this end, the data monitoring module uses local memory removal to clean up the redundant data. In order to realize the improvement of the structure configuration of the intelligent monitoring platform for tourism information promotion data, the specific structure is shown as follows (Fig. 3):

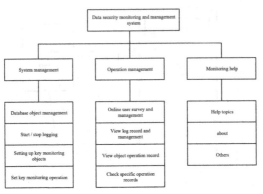

Fig. 2. Functions of backstage data security intelligent monitoring platform of tourism information promotion platform

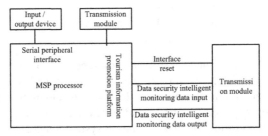

Fig. 3. Structure of intelligent monitoring platform for tourism information promotion data

As shown in the figure, the connection bus based on RTL8019AS controller can not only successfully connect the platform with the tourism information promotion platform, but also connect the data acquisition module with the processing module, and transmit the data to be tested in the data acquisition module to the processing module [21–23]. The external interface of intelligent monitoring platform is the external processing circuit of the data to be tested. Users can choose different processing circuits according to their own needs. The input/output equipment is provided to the platform manager, who can improve the performance of the monitoring platform by controlling the processing flow of the MSP430 processor so as to respond to the updating speed of unsafe factors in the monitoring of the tourism information promotion platform.

2.2 Tourism Information Promotion Platform Background Data Security Intelligent Monitoring Data Collection

Further optimize the methods for collecting the backstage data security intelligent monitoring data of the tourism information promotion platform. The monitoring platform designed for the tourism information promotion platform has data management, monitoring behavior prediction, network management, monitoring management and other functions, all of which are the default basic functions of the platform [24–26]. Based on this, the data collection module of intelligent monitoring for data security is optimized. The functional structure of the module is shown as follows (Fig. 4):

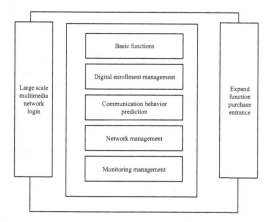

Fig. 4. Data security intelligent monitoring data acquisition module

Monitoring the security of database diagrams Data security intelligence monitoring can be divided into monitoring the connection of users and monitoring the operation of all data objects Data security intelligence monitoring the change of database data and the use of database authority (that is, the use of DML or DDL). Monitoring user connection, every user data security intelligent monitoring connected to the database If you can see its user name, client machine name [27, 28], IP address, running program and other conditions, the data security intelligent monitoring may disconnect the data security intelligent monitoring to prevent illegal access when the DBA deems that the user name, client machine name, IP address or running program is illegal. The DDL and DML rule operations collected from the monitoring were recorded for comparison (Table 1).

Table 1. Operational rules for monitoring data collection

	DDL	DML	GUI	DBA
Real time	High	Secondary	–	Small
Impact on system performance	Small	High	Secondary	Small
Tracking specific objects	–	Small	High	Secondary
System wide monitoring	–	Small	Secondary	High
Accuracy	Small	Secondary	High	Small
Occupied space	Secondary	High	–	Small

The realization of data security intelligent monitoring can provide a reliable and convenient monitoring platform for DBA by providing GUI data security intelligent monitoring for client data security monitoring. According to the different characteristics of the three kinds of monitoring technologies, the intelligent monitoring of data security has realized that the intelligent monitoring of data security can monitor the login user in real time and the operation of database object. However, when there are many objects to be monitored in the database, it is difficult to compile triggers one by one, which will affect the performance of the system. Log analysis can track database changes offline without affecting system performance. Log analysis can monitor specific changes without restoring the entire database. But it cannot get the real-time database change information and data security intelligent monitoring and cannot customize the tracking data items.

The login function of the tourism information promotion platform is the precondition of the basic function of the monitoring platform, that is, the users can use the basic function only when they log in the platform. The function of data management is to manage all the data in the platform by generating reports. Normally, the platform manages the data automatically, but due to the performance limitations of the user terminal, users are also managed manually. The data management feature turns on periodic management reminders for users who choose to manage manually. The function of monitoring behavior prediction can provide users with the security prediction of virtual monitoring behavior of tourism information promotion platform, which can help users better understand which monitoring behaviors will cause monitoring loopholes of tourism information promotion platform by grabbing, filtering and parsing. The network management function inquires and modifies the report forms generated in the data management function, and the user can also inquire the real-time status of the travel information promotion platform. The monitoring management function can query and modify the monitoring data report forms in the data management function, and control the start and stop of the monitoring work of the platform. The monitoring security transmission module of the tourism information promotion platform needs to monitor and transmit the monitoring data (i.e. the processed data to be tested) incorrectly before transmitting the monitoring data to the user terminal, which not only helps to correct the wrong data in the monitoring of the platform, but also provides guarantee for the monitoring security of the platform. The flow chart of intelligent monitoring data transmission, reception and processing is as follows (Fig. 5):

As shown in the figure, when the monitoring platform of tourism information promotion platform monitors the movement of transmitting monitoring data in the processing module, the platform will call the transmission module to intercept and retrieve the data packet. ARP is the address resolution protocol. Each platform monitoring data should contain the corresponding network address, convenient for users to locate the monitoring results. The data with the correct network address is called ARP packet. If the monitoring data transmitted by the platform is an ARP packet, it shall be transmitted directly to the user terminal; if the monitoring data is not an ARP packet, it is necessary to inquire about the parameters of the ARP packet, find out the corresponding network address, input the address into the monitoring data, and form a normal network packet to be transmitted to the user terminal. If the platform is unable to find the network address corresponding

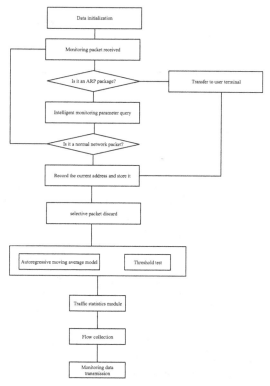

Fig. 5. Intelligent monitoring data transmission, reception and processing flow

to the monitoring data, the monitoring data may be infected by the unsafe data in the monitoring of the tourism information promotion platform, which leads to the loss of some important data and is not effectively monitored by the processing module. Once the current address record of such monitoring data is stored, it is directly discarded. So as to realize the effective monitoring of mass complex tourism information popularization data.

2.3 Realization of Intelligent Data Monitoring of Tourism Promotion Platform

First of all, we need to confirm the application of SaaS Service Data Security Intelligence Monitoring, and then classify the page types in SaaS Service into different categories. Then we use Selenium-driven automatic crawler to monitor the data security in the process of visiting the page to monitor the DOM tree structure of the HTML code after the page is completely rendered, and compute the information needed in the process of constructing the DOM tree. According to the type of the page, different algorithms are used to extract the data part of the page, format the data part, provide the data to the monitor, and transfer the data to the database. The dissemination platform has the following data monitoring methods (Fig. 6):

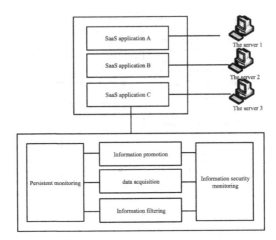

Fig. 6. Popularizing the platform data monitoring data processing method

Classical database security technology Intelligent data security monitoring, such as identity authentication, access control, view, etc., mainly focuses on checking the identity and authority constraints of external users, and intelligent data security monitoring, in order to determine the legality of users or their operations Intelligent data security monitoring identity authentication and access control. Taking prevention as the center of passive security mechanism, data security intelligent monitoring backup recovery restores the data after being invaded and destroyed. Although intrusion monitoring has made great progress, most of these researches are in the network and operating system level and the database itself is a complex structure data security intelligent monitoring data security intelligent monitoring from data storage to data file, table, field to tuple and so on different granularity storage unit. Therefore, the data intelligent monitoring database should have a more active and positive security mechanism to prevent more effective network access to the database to bring endless attacks, based on this platform for tourism data intelligent security monitoring security processing optimization, as follows (Fig. 7).

The concept of database intrusion monitoring has been put forward, which is the same as network intrusion monitoring. Through the intelligent monitoring of the state and activity of the running system, the intelligent monitoring of data security can find out that the intelligent monitoring of intrusion and attempted data security can greatly improve the initiative and automation of database security. Data Security Intelligent Monitoring from the database activity has the activity level Data Security Intelligent Monitoring from the system call layer, the process, the transaction layer, the session layer to the application layer. Moreover, it is very difficult to integrate or exchange the data security intelligent monitoring database with the underlying operating system and network monitoring system. So data security intelligent monitoring database intrusion monitoring cannot go out of the laboratory data security intelligent monitoring to meet today's practical security needs. Database Security Monitoring Data Security Intelligent Monitoring is to use the existing security monitoring technology to monitor the changes of database data and the operations of database users. Data Security Intelligent

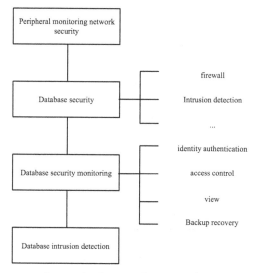

Fig. 7. Data intelligent security monitoring security processing steps optimization of tourism promotion platform

Monitoring can provide a good platform for DBA to actively monitor Data Security Intelligent Monitoring C2 Database Security Intelligent Monitoring to meet the actual security monitoring needs. Furthermore, the data part of HTML format is formatted into normal data format, and the data security intelligent monitoring filters out the useless HTML code data security intelligent monitoring to improve the monitoring accuracy.

3   Analysis of Experimental Results

The monitoring ability and response effect of the monitoring platform of tourism information promotion platform designed in this paper were tested. In order to enhance the persuasiveness of the test results, the sensor security monitoring platform and H235 protocol security monitoring platform are selected to compare with this platform. The purpose of this paper is to test whether the platform can accurately and efficiently monitor the insecurity of the tourism information promotion platform. In the process of testing the monitoring capability of the platform, 5 kinds of unsafe data were given randomly, and 5 unsafe monitoring nodes were placed in the tourism information promotion platform. Using the sensor security monitoring method, H235 protocol security monitoring platform and this method, the monitoring process of the above tourism information promotion platform is monitored for 24 h. The monitoring results of the unsafe data and the monitoring results of the unsafe monitoring nodes are as follows (Table 2):

The above table shows that the sensor safety monitoring method and this method can accurately monitor the unsafe data in the tourism information promotion platform, while the H235 protocol safety monitoring method does not monitor the unsafe data numbered 5. For the monitoring time of the three platforms, the lowest efficiency is sensor safety monitoring, and the highest efficiency is this platform. According to the analysis table,

Table 2. Unsafe monitoring data structure statistics

Unsafe data number	Time consuming (min)		
	Sensor safety monitoring method	H235 protocol security monitoring method	The method of this paper
1	12	10	4
2	14	10	3
3	15	8	3
4	13	8	2
5	16	7	3

the sensor safety monitoring platform and the H235 protocol safety monitoring platform have the phenomenon of missing detection in the monitoring of unsafe nodes in the tourism information promotion platform. For the monitoring time, the H235 protocol security monitoring method has the lowest efficiency and the present method has the highest efficiency. To sum up, the accuracy and efficiency of this method are high, which proves that this method has a good monitoring ability.

The response effect is the foundation of the monitoring platform for tourism information promotion. In the response effect test, the response time of the monitoring data is selected to test the response effect. Response time refers to the time when the platform and the tourism information promotion platform are connected successfully. The smaller and more stable the value is, the better the response effect is. The experiment will control the delay rate of two tourism information promotion platforms with different amount of insecure monitoring data, and use sensor security monitoring platform, H235 protocol security monitoring platform and this platform. First, the three platforms are initialized, and then, under the same conditions, the two tourism information promotion platforms are monitored. The response time of the three platforms is recorded respectively, as shown below (Fig. 8).

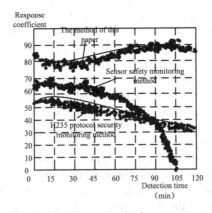

Fig. 8. Data intelligent monitoring response curve

According to the response curve in the graph, the response time curve of H235 protocol security monitoring method and two travel information promotion platforms is the best at the moment of monitoring after the initialization of the platform, but with the lapse of monitoring time, the response time curve of H235 protocol security monitoring method is higher than that of the sensor security monitoring platform and the platform of this paper at the same time, and great fluctuations appear. The response effect of sensor security monitoring method is higher than that of H235 protocol security monitoring method. The response time of this method is short and the fluctuation is not obvious, and the response effect is the best among the three platforms. The results above prove that the background data security intelligent monitoring method of tourism information promotion platform based on cloud computing has better response effect and fully meets the research requirements.

4 Conclusion

Based on the principle of cloud computing, the intelligent monitoring method of background data security of tourism information promotion platform is optimized. The RTL8019AS controller is used to collect the transmission data and security status data of monitoring nodes in the monitoring of tourism information promotion platform, providing the data to be tested in a unified format for the processing module. Safety monitoring of the data to be tested. The experimental results show that the designed platform has strong monitoring ability and good response effect.

References

1. Wang, T., Guomai, S., Zhang, L., et al.: Earthquake response framework on based on campus on multi-source monitoring. J. Cleaner Prod. **238**(20), 117965.1–117965.10 (2019)
2. Xie, K., Chen, Y., Wang, X., et al.: Accurate and fast recovery of network monitoring data with GPU-accelerated tensor completion. IEEE/ACM Trans. Netw. **28**(4), 1–14 (2020)
3. Xiang, C., Li, B.: Research on ship intelligent manufacturing data monitoring and quality control system based on the industrial Internet of Things. Int. J. Adv. Manuf. Technol. **107**(3), 983–992 (2020)
4. Gomez, A., Magno, M., et al.: Precise, energy-efficient data acquisition architecture for radiomonitoring activity using sustainable wireless sensor nodes. IEEE J. Sens. **18**(1), 459–469 (2018)
5. Petersen, H.I., Hillock, P., Milner, S., et al.: Monitoring gas distribution and origin in the Culzean field, UK central north logging, using data sea a from continuous isotope logging, tool and isotube and test samples. J. Petrol. Geol. **42**(4), 435–449 (2019)
6. Khalfallah, C.B., Delatre, E., Ouerchefani, D., et al.: Monitoring vegetation in Southern Tunisia using SPOT-5 (Take5) data: a case of study of the Tozeur. J. Appl. Remote Sens. **12**(4), 1–5 (2018)
7. Fu, W., Liu, S., Srivastava, G.: Optimization of big data scheduling in social networks. Entropy **21**(9), 902 (2019)
8. Liu, S., Li, Z., Zhang, Y., et al.: Introduction of key problems in long-distance learning and training. Mobile Netw. Appl. **24**(1), 1–4 (2019)
9. Liu, S., Liu, D., Srivastava, G., et al.: Overview and methods of correlation filter algorithms in object tracking. Complex Intell. Syst. (2020). https://doi.org/10.1007/s40747-020-00161-4

10. Liu, Y., Sun, R., Jin, S.: A survey on data-driven process monitoring and diagnostic methods for variation in multi-station systems reduction assembly. Assembly Autom. **39**(4), 727–739 (2019)

11. Xin, D., Ji, J., Jing, F., et al.: Efficient fully homomorphic encryption scheme using ring-LWE. J. Phys. Conf. Ser. **1738**(1), 012105 (2021)

12. Wei, T., Qiping, H., Tangzhi, W.: Research on location big data encryption method based on privacy protection. J. Anhui Electr. Eng. Prof. Tech. Coll. **24**(1), 118–122 (2019)

13. Niu, J., Li, X., Gao, J., et al.: Blockchain-based anti-key-leakage key aggregation searchable encryption for IoT. IEEE Internet Things J. **7**(2), 1502–1518 (2020)

14. Zhong, W., Li, Z.: Research on network education system based on learning machine. J. Commun. **39**(1), 135–140 (2018)

15. Yang, W.: Simulation of remote sharing method of database information under architecture of the internet of things. Comput. Simul. **35**(04), 457–461 (2018)

16. Sun, Y., et al.: A comparative study on the security mechanism of open & sharing government date information in China, America and Britain. Libr. Inf. Serv. **62**(21), 5–14 (2018)

17. Jones, L., Credo, J., Parnell, R., et al.: Dissolved uranium and arsenic in unregulated groundwater sources – western Navajo Nation. J. Contemp. Water Res. Educ. **169**(1), 27–43 (2020)

18. Hao, D., Tu, S., Zhang, C.: Experimental study on the effect of moisture content on bituminous coal porosity based on 3D reconstruction of computerized tomography. Nat. Resour. Res. **29**(3), 1657–1673 (2020)

19. Caron, J., Asselin, H., Beaudoin, J.M.: Attitudes and behaviors of mining sector employers towards the Indigenous workforce. Resour. Policy **61**(10), 108–117 (2019)

20. Wang, T., Zhang, H., Gamage, R.P., et al.: The evaluation criteria for rock brittleness based on double-body analysis under uniaxial compression. Geomech. Geophys. Geo-Energy Geo-Resources **6**(3), 1–19 (2020)

21. Hellqvist, M.: Teaching sustainability in geoscience field education at falun mine world heritage site in Sweden. Geoheritage **11**(4), 1785–1798 (2019)

22. Teng, Y., Yang, L., Song, X., et al.: An augmented Lagrangian proximal alternating method for sparse discrete optimization problems. Numer. Algorithms **83**(3), 833–866 (2020)

23. Li, Y., Yang, W., He, P., et al.: Design and management of a distributed hybrid energy system through smart contract and blockchain. Appl. Energy **248**(15), 390–405 (2019)

24. Spencer, A.A.M.S., Luciano, S., Mario, M.: Analysis and design of high-efficiency hybrid high step-up DC-DC converter for distributed PV generation systems. IEEE Trans. Ind. Electron. **66**(5), 3860–3868 (2018)

25. Zhang, L.P., Liu, W., Qi, B.: Innovation design and optimization management of a new drive system for plug-in hybrid electric vehicles. Energy **186**(1), 115823.1–115823.19 (2019)

26. Zkik, K., Hajji, S.E., Orhanou, G.: Sesign and implementation of a new security plane for hybrid distributed SDNs. J. Commun. **14**(1), 26–32 (2019)

27. Han, X., Dong, Y., Yue, L., et al.: State transition simulated annealing algorithm for discrete-continuous optimization problems. IEEE Access **7**(12), 44391–44403 (2019)

28. Kamalakis, T., Dogkas, L., Simou, F.: Optimization of a discrete multi-tone visible light communication system using a mixed-integer genetic algorithm. Optics Commun. **485**(1), 126741 (2020)

Research on Industrial Product Modeling Design Method Based on Deep Learning

Guozhi Lin[1](✉) and Yiqiong Ding[2]

[1] Quanzhou Arts and Crafts Vocational College, Quanzhou 362500, Fujian, China
[2] School of Information and Engineering, Sichuan Tourism University, Chengdu 610000, China

Abstract. In order to use deep learning theory to model the appearance of industrial products, in order to use its advanced technology to improve the efficiency of industrial product modeling design, a deep learning-based industrial product modeling design method is proposed. The ingenious points of appearance design can be found through the deep learning database. The modeling structure of industrial products is analyzed from three aspects of right-angle modeling, bevel modeling and special-shaped modeling, and the projection can be transformed by the calculation method of the model. Reduce the time required for calculation under hardware conditions. In the three-dimensional distribution area m × m of the product, the texture segmentation of the image pixel intensity at the maximum pixel point is carried out to complete the 3D geometric modeling of the industrial product modeling design. The 3D modeling, modeling evaluation and modeling storage operation of the industrial product modeling elements are carried out to realize the industrial product modeling design. The experimental results show that the industrial product modeling design method based on deep learning has better output performance, higher product fidelity and better visualization effect.

Keywords: Deep learning · Industrial products · Modeling design · Modeling structure

1 Introduction

"Industrial design" was born in the process of evolution from "handicraft economy" to "industrial economy". Since the birth of modern design, there have been controversies about the relationship between form and function in design. Affected by large-scale industrialization, the design master Mies' slogan "less is more" was highly respected once it was put forward. From modernism to internationalism, function is always the first element of design. Due to the post-war turmoil and the development of science and technology, postmodernism and pop style, represented by pop style, have gradually become popular and replaced modernism [1, 2]. They pursue the expression of form and pure decoration. Although this trend of formalism is very exploratory, it soon declines because it violates the economic law of industrial production. The new modernism and multiple design styles after that are diversified explorations after the game of form and

W. Fu et al. (Eds.): ICMTEL 2021, LNICST 387, pp. 115–127, 2021.
https://doi.org/10.1007/978-3-030-82562-1_10

function of design. Nowadays, the function and form in industrial design are no longer simply opposites. The harmonious unity of the two is the trend of modern industrial product design. In the process of industrial product design, the conflict arising from the fusion of shape and structure ensures that the product realizes its function, and at the same time, through the shape design, the competitiveness of the product in the market is guaranteed.

In recent years, in addition to being widely used in the field of engineering technology, the research on deep learning has also developed a variety of application versions in other non-technical fields such as teaching. These new studies find that deep learning is very useful in non-technical fields from a certain angle. Product modeling design is an interdisciplinary subject. In addition to the technical field, it also extends to many non-technical fields, such as aesthetics and psychology. This article focuses on and expects to solve the main problems, how deep learning should be applied to effectively solve the technical and non-technical modeling design problems.

In terms of theoretical research, compared with the United States, Russia and other countries, the promotion of deep learning education has penetrated into secondary schools, even primary schools, the gap is indeed obvious. In China, the related courses of deep learning education are only opened in a few colleges and universities, and the practical application defects in the business sector are even greater. In the current research on deep learning [3]. Category is limited to theoretical research and academic discussion. This situation should be paid attention to.

The core content of product design methodology is innovative methods. The theoretical development and methods of modern product design urgently need to apply the theoretical research results of deep learning to the process of product modeling design. It is foreseeable that the only way for enterprise design innovation in my country is the gradual promotion and application of deep learning research results in actual production.

Yan Bao [4] in order to use virtual reality technology to model the appearance of industrial products, so as to facilitate the use of its advanced human-computer interaction technology to improve the efficiency of product modeling design, this paper proposes a method of industrial product modeling design based on virtual reality technology. Firstly, the influencing factors and aesthetic principles of industrial product modeling design are analyzed, and the overall framework of virtual design environment is constructed; then, the stereo vision model is established, and the virtual environment is created by Vega virtual reality development platform; finally, the effect analysis of product modeling in virtual environment is given. By applying virtual technology to product modeling design, product modeling and human-computer interaction effects can be evaluated and improved before product manufacturing, so as to shorten the development cycle and reduce product production costs. In order to effectively improve the efficiency of product modeling design, Li Qiuwen [5] designed an industrial product modeling design system based on improved differential evolution algorithm. Firstly, the process and logical process of product modeling design are analyzed, and then the specific system workflow is given according to the functional structure of requirements. Finally, the improved differential evolution algorithm is proposed and applied to product modeling design. The system software is implemented by. Net development platform. The system running test results show that the system can assist designers to design industrial products and provide a good technical support for further innovation design. Li Jiangyong [6] In order to solve the problem of brand characteristics of product modeling in industrial design, he proposed a product modeling design method based on brand image, and explored the correlation between corporate brand image and product modeling design. Carry out modeling design research with hydraulic excavator as the research object, locate product modeling image according to brand image characteristics, develop product modeling with brand image characteristics, realize sustainable innovation of product modeling design under brand culture, and further enhance product market competition Strength and brand recognition have verified the product modeling design method based on the corporate brand image. Jin Wenkui et al. [7] explored the application of three-dimensional anthropometry technology in the design of wearable products. Methods based on the introduction of the concept of fitness, the new characteristics of the combination of 3D anthropometry technology and wearable product design were analyzed in view of the human body data challenges encountered in the design practice of wearable industrial products, and the product adaptation design strategy based on 3D anthropometry was summarized. Conclusion more detailed data, information and knowledge of human body can be obtained through 3D anthropometry technology, which can improve the adaptability of wearable product design and better explain the user-centered design concept.

Based on the above research background, this paper applies deep learning to industrial product modeling design, analyzes the modeling structure of industrial products through right angle modeling, oblique angle modeling and special-shaped modeling, and transforms the projection through the calculation method of the model. In the three-dimensional distribution area of the product, the image at the largest pixel is processed by texture segmentation, and the 3D geometric model of industrial product modeling design is constructed to realize the industrial product modeling design. The effectiveness of this method is verified by simulation experiments.

2 Modeling Design Method of Industrial Products

2.1 Analyze the Structure of Industrial Products

The appearance modeling of industrial products has a certain purpose. It is restricted by the structure, function, material and technology of industrial products. However, the starting point of the design is to satisfy industrial products in terms of function, and to optimize the design in terms of structure, the rationality and suitability of the design must be fully considered to ensure the balance of the entire shape [8]. Analyze the appearance of industrial products through the deep learning database, and divide the product models into three categories: direct, oblique, and irregular. Through the analysis of various pictures, as shown in Fig. 1.

Through the deep learning database, you can find the ingenious points of appearance design, which can better serve the industrial product styling.

The main purpose of the establishment of deep learning elements is to make the product modeling design meet the requirements of technical beauty. The so-called technical beauty is the product of the integration of science and technology and art. It unifies the

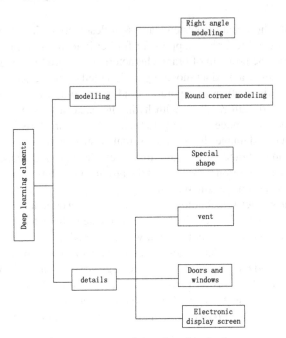

Fig. 1. Structure of deep learning database

law and content of the form through technical means, and achieves a unified aesthetic feeling in the sense. In the future design, the modeling design is analyzed according to the following factors, which is more conducive to the product design.

(1) Functional and structural beauty. Functional beauty reflects the technical rationality of industrial products. Functional beauty is also an aspect that attracts consumers. Its technical quality determines the product's status in consumers' eyes, but it needs to be distinguished between primary and secondary functions; Structure is a system composed of products according to certain principles, and different structures will produce different shapes. Structure, materials and technology are interrelated.

(2) Beautiful workmanship. Material is the basis of realizing product structure, its concrete manifestation is the beauty of texture, to some extent, it is the deepening of technology; technology is the means of product realization, any product want to get the shape of beauty must be implemented through the corresponding process.

(3) Color and standard beauty. The color of the product is dependent on the shape of the product itself. The color can increase the visual power, attractiveness and appeal of the product, and can actively attract people's attention. The beauty of color comes from the harmony and contrast of colors, which changes with the changes of the times; any product should have corresponding specifications, that is, product standardization. The production process of a product requires the cooperation of various disciplines. And the part that can be planned is standardized production.

2.1.1 Analysis of Right Angle Modeling of Industrial Products

In deep learning elements, right-angle modeling is divided into three cases, the first is that all four corners are right angles: the second is the upper right angle, the lower bevel or rounded corners; the third case is the lower right angle, the upper one Bevel or rounded corners [9].

Right angle modeling is widely used in textile machinery design and CNC machine tools. Because of its less change in shape, we need to pay attention to the change and unity in the use of modeling. Right angle modeling gives people a neat aesthetic feeling, but in product design, it is easy to appear that the modeling is too neat, too unified and unchanged, which makes the product modeling appear dull, boring and lack of vividness. In the shape change, when designing a single object, its shape is determined by its structural characteristics. When unifying its shape, the product can be changed appropriately, such as adding decorative lines and chamfering; for serialized products, Because its different product structures and functions determine the different forms of products, resulting in differences in the sense of form, the main task of its appearance design is to use various elements to form a unified set of products under the premise of change. However, it should be noted that the function of the product itself should not be affected by blindly seeking unity, or the processing technology of the product is complex and the cost is high.

The structure, function, industry and other factors of industrial products determine the objective conditions of product modeling. When changing and unifying, the following two principles should be followed [10].

The proportion of segmentation should be coordinated and unified. The proportion relationship between the whole and the part, the part and the part, the part and the detail of the same product should be selected as much as possible, so as to strengthen the interrelation between the various parts. The unity of proportion can strengthen the rationality and make the product design achieve a unified overall effect.

The unity of linear style and color. Regardless of what kind of product is designed, the overall shape of the product is regarded as a whole. The overall contour line and the contour lines between the parts of the product should be roughly the same, and the line type needs to be divided into primary and secondary. The color is unified to form a whole with the line type.

2.1.2 Analysis of Oblique Angle Modeling of Industrial Products

To some extent, the bevel shape is a transformation of the right angle shape. In the case of the right angle shape structure unchanged, in order to break the rules of the shape, the product shape is cut or chamfered. In terms of styling, pay attention to the proportion of the product. The relationship between the overall length, width, and height of the product and the relationship between the whole and the part, and the part and the part. The good ratio is not produced through intuition and estimation, but conforms to the corresponding scientific laws.

In the deep learning elements, the oblique modeling is divided into the upper oblique angle, the lower right angle, the upper right angle, and the four corners are all oblique angles. In recent years, people have less choice for all the corners for right angle modeling, adding the oblique angle and fillet into the line, making the streamline modeling more formal. At the same time, the cultural characteristics of the enterprise and the cognition of the brand should be fully considered in the design. In modeling, overlap, segmentation, moving and adjacency are used to change. In terms of segmentation, large-scale equipment usually adopts digital scale and hierarchical scale. The digital ratio is $1 : \sqrt{2}$ and $1 : \sqrt{3}$. It is a proportional relationship established by integer multiples. Its basic form is a rectangle, which is very helpful for the design of large industrial products; the hierarchical ratio is the connection between the midpoints of each adjacent side of the geometric shape. Therefore, a reduced version under the same form is formed, and a continuous form will appear after multiple repetitions, forming a hierarchical system, which is of great help to product redesign.

2.1.3 Analysis of Abnormal Shape of Industrial Products

The special shape is a form with a large change, and most of it is a large angle chamfer or slope to obtain a change in appearance. Shaped shapes tend to feel unstable, and some shapes with large changes feel bulky. Stability has two basic meanings in terms of product appearance. One is that the weight of the product itself meets the conditions of stability; the other is visual stability, and the appearance of the product pays attention to weight. Not only to meet the actual stability of the product, but also to meet the visual stability. Therefore, in the design, the sense of weight should also be consistent with the actual situation, as well as the integrity of the precision. Not only the structural stability, but also to make the product shape light and have a sense of speed. Large scale equipment are all products of industrial assembly line operation. In the aspect of appearance modeling, the selection of materials should be fully considered under the condition of meeting the modeling rules. The combination of different materials can produce different sense of quantity. Attention should be paid to the stability of the shape when modeling.

In special-shaped product modeling, it is necessary to ensure the balance of the product, so that the product modeling form can form a contrast of different forms on both sides of the fulcrum, such as large and small, sparse and dense, thus forming a kind of static in motion and dynamic in static. The orderly beauty. In the design, we should pay attention to the key points, and form the visual primary and secondary in the treatment of the key points, so as to avoid the constant wandering of the line of sight, thus giving people a feeling of clutter and tediousness. The appropriate use of curves can increase the sense of change in the shape of products, and the curves will give people different feelings in emotion and performance.

Highlighting the key points of product modeling can be seen from four aspects. First, the product form contrast, such as straight lines and curves, simple and complex; second, color contrast, using light colors to set off dark, cool and warm colors; Third, the contrast of materials, such as metal and non-metal, plastic and glass; fourth, the use of line changes and perspective to guide the line of sight to focus on one place.

Through the deep learning database, we can find the ingenious points of appearance modeling design, and analyze the modeling structure of industrial products from three aspects of right angle modeling, oblique angle modeling and special-shaped modeling.

Next, we can process the industrial product modeling through stereo vision to better serve the industrial product modeling.

2.2 Stereo Vision Processing Industrial Product Modeling

Non - uniform rational B - splines (NURBS), which is widely supported in advanced 3D modeling, is used for 3D modeling:

$$P(t) = \frac{\sum_{i=1}^{n} w_i p_i B_{i,k}(t)}{\sum_{i=1}^{n} w_i B_{i,k}(t)} \tag{1}$$

Where: p_i represents the model vertex; w_i represents the weight of the relationship between the vertices; $B_{i,k}(t)$ represents the basis function, the calculation formula is as follows:

$$B_{i,k}(t) = \frac{t - t_i}{t_{i+k-1} - t_i} B_{i,k-1}(t) + \frac{t_{i+k} - t}{t_{i+k} - t_{i+1}} B_{i+1,k-1}(t) \tag{2}$$

During the measurement of industrial products, the angle of view θ can be converted into the projection size of the product through correlation calculation, as shown in Fig. 2.

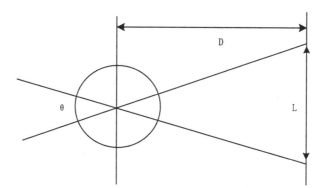

Fig. 2. Definition of viewing angle θ

The view angle θ is defined as follows:

$$\theta = 2 \arctan\left(\frac{L}{2D}\right) \tag{3}$$

In order to generate stereoscopic visual effects in a VR environment, the human body's binocular vision and visual movement perception technology need to be used. The three-dimensional perception of human beings mainly comes from binocular parallax. Therefore, the stereo vision model needs to calculate two pilots separately to generate two monocular views. In the stereo vision model, if the point $I(X_i, Y_i, Z_i)$ on the three-dimensional space object is projected on the Z plane, two points $I_l(X_{sl}, Y_{sl})$ and $I_r(X_{sr}, Y_{sr})$ are generated. There are:

$$X_{sl} = \frac{X_i \times k + \frac{Z_i \times d}{2}}{k - Z_i} \tag{4}$$

$$Y_{sl} = \frac{Y_i \times k}{k - Z_i} \tag{5}$$

$$X_{sr} = \frac{X_i \times k - \frac{Z_i \times d}{2}}{k - Z_i} \tag{6}$$

$$Y_{sr} = \frac{Y_i \times k}{k - Z_i} \tag{7}$$

Since the results of formula (5) and formula (7) are consistent, formula (4) and formula (6) can be expressed as:

$$X_{sl} = \frac{X_i + \frac{d}{2}}{1 - \frac{Z_i}{k}} - \frac{d}{2} \tag{8}$$

$$X_{sr} = \frac{X_i - \frac{d}{2}}{1 - \frac{Z_i}{k}} + \frac{d}{2} \tag{9}$$

Where: d is the distance between the eyes; k is the length between the viewpoint and the projection plane. The time needed for calculation can be reduced under the condition of limited hardware.

2.3 3D Geometric Modeling of Industrial Product Modeling

According to the above-mentioned stereo vision processing of industrial product modeling, the 3D geometric model modeling analysis of industrial product modeling is performed, and the feature rendering and virtual view design of product 3D modeling are performed by combining texture rendering and scene database model construction methods. The product modeling design model development environment based on deep learning designed in this paper is built in 3DStudio MAX and Softimage software environment R_2:

$$g(x, y) = h(x, y) * f(x, y) + \eta(x, y) \tag{10}$$

Where: $h(x, y)$ is the texture rendering disparity function in product design; the symbol * represents convolution. The texture tracking and template grid segmentation methods are used for 3D combined modeling in the product modeling design process, and the vector edge clipping method is used to reconstruct the feature space of 3D product modeling. The feature distribution of the pixel set for model construction is obtained as:

$$g(x, y) = f(x, y) + \eta(x, y) \tag{11}$$

Where $\eta(x, y)$ is the scale to adjust the mesh size. Based on statistical shape model, two-dimensional surface reconstruction in product modeling design is carried out.

$$J = \sum_{k=1}^{n} \sum_{i=1}^{c} u_{ik}^{*m} d(x_k, v_i) + \beta \sum_{k=1}^{n} \sum_{i=1}^{c} u_{ik}^{*m} d(\overline{x}_k, v_i) \tag{12}$$

Connecting the points into polygons, the configuration weight of the output product design design is:

$$w(i, j) = \frac{1}{Z(i)} \exp\left(-\frac{d(i, j)}{h^2}\right) \tag{13}$$

Among them:

$$Z(i) = \sum_{j \in \Omega} \exp\left(-\frac{d(i, j)}{h^2}\right) \tag{14}$$

Combined with the edge pixel decomposition method, the image feature segmentation in the process of product modeling design is carried out.

$$\hat{f}(x, y) = \begin{cases} g(x, y) - 1, & g(x, y) - \hat{f}_{lee}(x, y) \geq t \\ g(x, y) + 1, & g(x, y) - \hat{f}_{Lee}(x, y) < t \\ g(x, y), & \text{else} \end{cases} \tag{15}$$

According to the topological structure information of the image, the image pixels are grouped, and the joint estimated parameter of the volume model reconstruction of the product modeling is obtained as $\hat{f}(x, y)$. According to the smoothing operator in the product modeling image design, the adaptive reconstruction is performed to obtain the scale information of the product 3D geometric modeling Parameter Nl:

$$N_l = \begin{cases} 1, & l = 0, L \\ 2\pi \cdot \frac{D}{2} \cdot \sin \eta / l_{\text{taiangle}}, & l = 1, 2, \cdots, L - 1 \end{cases} \tag{16}$$

In the formula: l triangle $= \pi \cdot D$ 2L represents the wrinkle information of the image, and L is the total length of the designed product edge contour.

In the product's three-dimensional distribution area M $\times$ M, texture segmentation is performed on the image pixel intensity at the maximum pixel point to realize 3D geometric modeling of industrial product design.

2.4 Industrial Product Design Program

At present, the product modeling design methods based on computer-aided design mainly include:

(1) Digital design, which mainly adopts digital modeling technology;
(2) Parallel design, which mainly uses the crossover, reorganization and optimization of the product design process to shorten the product development cycle;

(3) Virtual design. This method mainly uses virtual reality technology for 3D visualization design.

Through the above demand analysis, it can be seen that the industrial product modeling and design system should have the following functions: the generation of parts; the search and matching of the prototype Library of parts; the generation of product design scheme. As shown in Fig. 3.

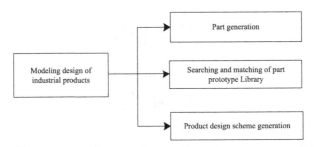

Fig. 3. The functional structure of industrial product modeling design system requirements

This article applies deep learning to product modeling design, and the workflow is shown in Fig. 4.

As can be seen from Fig. 4, in the process of deep learning, 3D modeling, modeling evaluation and modeling storage operations are carried out on the modeling elements of industrial products to realize the modeling design of industrial products.

3 Experimental Analysis

In order to test the performance of this method in the realization of product modeling design and 3D virtual reality simulation, simulation experiments are carried out. The experiment uses Matlab for image algorithm processing in product modeling design, establishes a three-dimensional visual simulation platform for product modeling design on the Vc.net platform, builds a client for visual analysis of product modeling design, and establishes a human-computer interaction interface for visual simulation control. Using Microsoft Visual Studio development components to realize the data collection and information processing of product modeling design, the distribution range of the designed interpolation points is 200 × 300, the pixel level distribution is 400 × 400, and the number of samples collected for the three-dimensional information of product modeling is 2 000, the sample number of discrete product modeling elevation point data is 1024. According to the above-mentioned simulation parameter setting, the product modeling design is carried out. Taking a robot arm product as an example, the original design effect diagram is shown in Fig. 5.

Using the method of this paper to optimize the product design, combined with texture rendering and 3D reconstruction technology, the optimized product modeling design results are shown in Fig. 6.

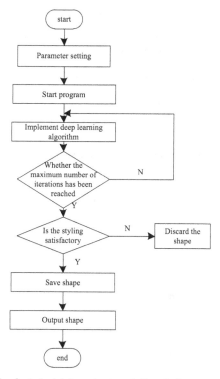

Fig. 4. Industrial product modeling design process

Fig. 5. Original image of product modeling design

Analysis of Fig. 6 shows that the use of this method for product modeling design improves texture rendering and scene performance, and the product has a higher visualization and fidelity. Analyzing the output signal-to-noise ratio of different methods for product modeling design, the results obtained are shown in Fig. 7.

Analysis of Fig. 7 shows that the output signal-to-noise ratio of the product modeling image designed by this method is higher, indicating that the quality is better.

Fig. 6. Optimized product design results

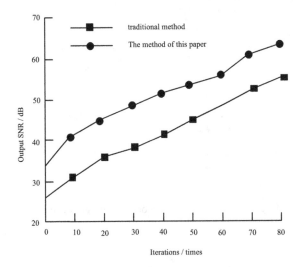

Fig. 7. Output performance comparison

4   Conclusion

This paper proposes a research on the design method of industrial product modeling based on deep learning. The results show that the output performance of this method for product modeling design is better, the fidelity of the designed product is higher, and the visualization effect is better.

References

1. Zhang, L., Yang, Q., Zhang, K., et al.: Research on the integration of industrial design and mechanical product design. IOP Conf. Ser. Mater. Sci. Eng. **772**, 012100 (2020)
2. Parada, L.R., Mayuet, P.F., Gámez, A.J.: Industrial product design: study of FDM technology for the manufacture of thermoformed prototypes. Procedia Manuf. **41**, 587–593 (2019)
3. Liu, B., He, Y.: Analysis of robot case based on product design. Ind. Control Comput. **032**(008), 106–108 (2019)

4. Bao, Y.: Modeling design of industrial products based on virtual reality technology. Mod. Electron. Technol. **42**(03), 184–186 (2019)
5. Li, Q.: The application of evolutionary algorithm in the design of industrial products. Mod. Electron. Technol. **42**(09), 185–187+190 (2019)
6. Watkins, M.A., Higginson, M., Clarke, P.R.: Enhancing graduate employability in product design: a case study exploring approaches taken on a BSc product design course. High. Educ. Skills Work-Based Learn. **8**(1), 80–93 (2018)
7. Jin, W., He, R.: Research on the design of wearable industrial products' shape adaptability based on 3D anthropometry. Packaging Eng. **039**(004), 123–126 (2018)
8. Liu, S., Liu, D., Srivastava, G., Połap, D., Woźniak, M.: Overview and methods of correlation filter algorithms in object tracking. Complex Intell. Syst. 1–23 (2020). https://doi.org/10.1007/s40747-020-00161-4
9. Fu, W., Liu, S., Srivastava, G.: Optimization of big data scheduling in social networks. Entropy **21**(9), 902 (2019)
10. Liu, S., Lu, M., Li, H., et al.: Prediction of gene expression patterns with generalized linear regression model. Front. Genet. **10**, 120 (2019)

A Frequency Conversion Circuit for Piezoelectric Vibrating Energy Harvesting

Xingjun Gao[1], Zijian Li[1], Yongbin Li[1], and Qiang Zhou[2(✉)]

[1] State Grid Dongying Power Supply Company, Dongying, Shandong, China
[2] ShanDong University of Technology, Zibo, China
zhouqiang@sdut.edu.cn

Abstract. More and more piezoelectric power generators are used in the field of energy harvesting in recent years, which are the typical capacitive power sources. The piezoelectric power generator is difficult to achieve maximum power output when it works in a low-frequency energy harvesting system. A frequency conversion management circuit is proposed in this paper, which can achieve the conjugate impedance matching between the power generator and the management circuit. The experiment result shows that the frequency conversion management circuit can obtained 411% more energy compared with traditional management circuit.

Keywords: Vibration energy harvesting · Energy harvesting management circuit · Impedance matching

1 Introduction

With the development of sensor and power electronics technologies, the size of sensors and wireless network nodes become smaller, the power consumption is getting lower, correspondingly. These electronic devices are usually powered by batteries, and used in many applications, such as monitor bird migration, earthquake warning and bridge deformation detecting [1–3]. Because the battery capacity is limited, it is difficult to replace batteries in many applications.

An alternative solution is using the piezoelectric power generator to convert ambient energies into electrical energy. The energy management circuit is the interface circuit between the piezoelectric generator and the electronic load, which is responsible for transferring, storing and releasing the output power of the piezoelectric generator.

A standard energy harvesting management circuit is shown in Fig. 1, which uses a rectifier between the piezoelectric generator and the load R. The structure of the standard management circuit is simple and easy to implement, but the circuit cannot achieve the conjugate impedance matching between the power generator and the management circuit.

A parallel synchronous switch harvesting on inductor (P-SSHI) was first introduced by Guyomar [4]. Experimental results reveal that the P-SSHI management circuit can

W. Fu et al. (Eds.): ICMTEL 2021, LNICST 387, pp. 128–136, 2021.
https://doi.org/10.1007/978-3-030-82562-1_11

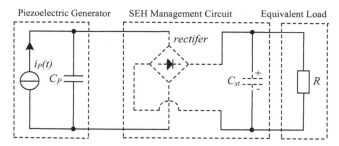

Fig. 1. Standard energy harvesting management circuit

increase the efficiency of energy harvesting by over 800% as compared to the standard energy harvesting management circuit [5–7].

However, when the piezoelectric generator outputs low frequency and weak electrical power, using the P-SSHI circuit to drive a high power load, such as the wireless sensor node, a large storage capacitor (hundreds milli-faradas) is required. Because of the equivalent internal capacitance of the piezoelectric generator is small (nano-faradas), the P-SSHI circuit cannot achieve the impedance matching when using the lager storage capacitor, large amount of energy of the piezoelectric generator is consumed in the internal capacitor.

This paper proposed frequency conversion management circuit for weak low-frequency vibration energy harvesting. This circuit can be achieved impedance matching with the piezoelectric generator at a high resonance frequency.

2 P-SSHI Management Circuit for Energy Harvesting

2.1 Piezoelectric Generator Equivalent Model

Vibration energy in ambient can be converted into electrical energy by the piezoelectric generator, when the external force F perpendicularly acts on the polarization plane of the piezoelectric ceramic, the piezoelectric generator can generate charges Q and output an AC signal, the relationship between Q and F can be expressed as:

$$Q = d_{33}F \tag{1}$$

Where d_{33} is the longitudinal piezoelectric constant. From (1), the piezoelectric generator can be equivalent as a capacitor, the capacitance of the piezoelectric generator can be expressed as:

$$C_p = \frac{\varepsilon_0 \varepsilon_r S}{d} \tag{2}$$

Where ε_0, ε_r, S and d are the vacuum dielectric constant, the relative permittivity, the piezoelectric area and the thickness of the piezoelectric, respectively. From (2), the equivalent capacitance C_p depends on the size and material of the piezoelectric generator. Therefore the equivalent model of the piezoelectric generator is composed of an AC current source parallel with the equivalent capacitor C_p and an equivalent resistor [8, 9]. Normally, the equivalent resistor of the piezoelectric generator can be ignored, and the equivalent internal capacitance is very small (nano-faradas).

2.2 P-SSHI Management Circuit

At present, P-SSHI management circuit is widely used in vibrating energy harvesting, its typical equivalent circuit is shown in Fig. 2. The switch S_1 series connects with the inductor L_1 then parallel with the piezoelectric generator. The AC power can be changed to DC power and restored in the storage capacitor C_{st} by using the P-SSHI circuit.

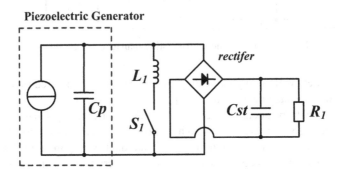

Fig. 2. P-SSHI management circuit.

When the piezoelectric generator outputs low frequency and weak energy in order to drive high power wireless sensor node, a large storage capacitor C_{st} (hundreds milli-faradas) is required in the P-SSHI circuit. In this case, the storage capacitor C_{st} is much larger than the equivalent internal capacitor C_p.

In Fig. 2, the first resonant loop is composed of the internal capacitor C_p and the inductor L_1. The secondary resonant loop is composed of the inductor L_1 and the storage capacitor C_{st}. Because of $C_{st} >> C_p$ and piezoelectric generator outputs low frequency signal, the resonant frequency between the first and secondary resonant loop are different, the impedance matching of this two resonant loops cannot be achieved at the same time. As a result, energy harvesting efficiency is very low, large amount of energy is consumed in the management circuit and there is not enough energy to drive the high power load directly.

3 Frequency Conversion Management Circuit for Vibrating Energy Harvesting

3.1 Principle of Frequency Conversion Management Circuit

The frequency conversion management circuit is shown in Fig. 3, including a matching circuit, a rectifier bridge, an intermediate capacitor and a DC-DC circuit. Most of the time, the piezoelectric generator is in open circuit and the management circuit is not operating. When the management circuit is working, the energy transfers from the piezoelectric generator to the intermediate capacitor C_{int}. The DC-DC circuit can transfer the energy from the intermediate capacitor C_{int} to a large storage capacitor C_{st}. Therefore, the output energy from the piezoelectric generator can be continuously accumulated to the C_{st} in a long period.

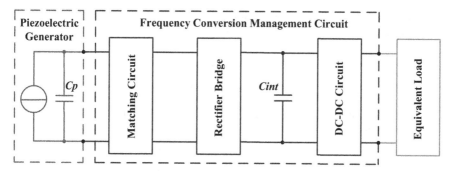

Fig. 3. Management circuit for vibrating energy harvesting.

3.2 First Stage of Energy Transferring

The matching circuit is shown in Fig. 4, which is composed of a bilateral switch K_1 and a transformer. L_p and L_s are the inductance of the primary and secondary coils in the transformer, respectively. M is the mutual inductance of the transformer. R_{In} is equivalent input resistance of the primary resonance circuit. $T_1(t_0 - t_2)$ and $D1$ are the period and duty circle of the switch K_1, respectively. $t_0 - t_1$ and $t_1 - t_2$ are the turn-on time and turn-off time of the switch K_1, respectively.

Most of the time, the piezoelectric generator is in open circuit and the management circuit is not operating. When the piezoelectric generator output voltage reaches maximum, the switch K_1 is closed under the control signal. There is thus the energy transfers from the piezoelectric generator piezoelectric generator to the inductor L_p.

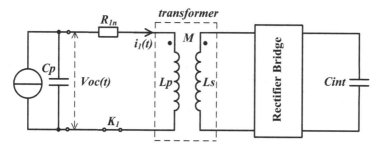

Fig. 4. Matching circuit.

With the piezoelectric generator output voltage reaches maximum, the switch K_1 is closed, the piezoelectric generator is connected to the $C_p - L_p$ resonant circuit. When $t_0 = 0$, the average current $\bar{I}_1$ of the $C_p - L_p$ circuit can be calculated by:

$$\bar{I}_1 = 1/T_1 \int_{t_0}^{t_1} V_{oc(t)} t / L_p dt$$

$$= D_1^2 V_{oc(t)} / 2T_1 \tag{3}$$

$V_{oc}(t)$ is the voltage of the piezoelectric generator. The voltage of the inductor L_p can be expressed as:

$$V_{Lp}(t) = \frac{I_{1P}L_P}{\sqrt{\omega_1^2 + \beta_1^2}} e^{-\beta_1(t-t_0)} \sin[\omega_1(t - t_0) + \alpha] \tag{4}$$

I_{1p} is the maximum current, the damping coefficient is β_1. In the $C_p - L_p$ circuit, the resonant angular frequency is given by

$$\omega_1 = \sqrt{\frac{(L_P - nM)D_1^4T_1^2 - L_P^2C_p}{(L_P - nM)^2D_1^4T_1^2C_p}} \tag{5}$$

3.3 Secondary Stage of Energy Transferring

The $L_s - C_{int}$ resonant circuit is shown in Fig. 5. The R_{2n} is the resistance of the secondary coils in the transformer.

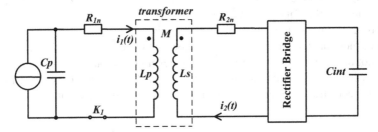

Fig. 5. Energy transfers into the intermediate capacitor.

In the $L_s - C_{int}$ resonant circuit, the output power of the piezoelectric generator transfers from the inductor L_s to the capacitor C_{int} when the voltage reach the break-over voltage of the rectifier bridge.

In the one period time $(t_0 - t_2)$, the voltage of the capacitor L_S can be expressed as:

$$V_{Ls}(t) = \begin{cases} I_{1P}L_Pe^{-\beta_1(t-t_0)} \sin[\omega_1(t - t_0) + \alpha]/n\sqrt{\omega_1^2 + \beta_2^2} & t_0 \leq t \leq t_1 \\ I_{2P}L_Se^{-\beta_2(t-t_1)} \sin[\omega_2(t - t_1) + \gamma]/\sqrt{\omega_2^2 + \beta_2^2} & t_1 \leq t \leq t_2 \end{cases} \tag{6}$$

Where $i_2(t)$ and ω_2 are the current and resonant angular frequency in the $L_s - C_{int}$ resonant circuit, respectively. I_{2P} and β_2 are the maximum current and the damping coefficient of the $L_s - C_{int}$ resonant circuit, respectively.

In order to get the maximum output power from the piezoelectric generator, the resonant frequency in the $C_p - L_p$ resonant circuit is the same as the $L_s - C_{int}$ resonant circuit ($\omega_1 = \omega_2$), the inductance L_p needs to meet the following equation.

$$f_0 = 1/2\pi\sqrt{L_PC_p} \tag{7}$$

According to the Eq. (7), the frequency of the piezoelectric generator output signal is f_0. Normally, the equivalent internal capacitance is very small (nano-faradas), in order to achieve impedance matching, the inductance L_P need to be thousands of Henry, it is very difficult to find and manufacture so large inductance. This problem can be solved by the frequency conversion circuit. Assuming that f_1 and f_2 are the resonant frequency of the $C_p - L_p$ and $L_s - C_{int}$ circuit, respectively,

In one period time of the switch K_1, the voltage across the capacitor L_S exhibits underdamping attenuation oscillation, assuming that f_1 and f_2 are the resonant frequency of the $C_p - L_p$ and $L_s - C_{int}$ circuit, respectively, it can be expressed as:

$$f_1 = f_2 = \sqrt{\frac{(L_P - nM)D_1^4 T_1^2 - L_p^2 C_p}{4\pi^2 (L_P - nM)^2 D_1^4 T_1^2}} \tag{8}$$

From (8), the resonance frequency is related to the duty ratio of the switch K_1, a new high resonant frequency f_1 and f_2 are generated.

The maximum charging power of the intermediate capacitor C_{int} can be expressed as:

$$P_{C_{int}(max)} = \frac{\omega_2^3 C_{int}^3 L_P^2 V_{oc}^4 (1 + e^{-\frac{\beta_2}{\omega_2 \pi}})}{16 T_1^2 [1 + (\frac{\beta_2}{\omega_2})^2]^2} \tag{9}$$

From (9), the maximum charging power $P_{cint(max)}$ can be obtained under the duty cycle $D_{1(opt)}$, expressed as:

$$D_{1(opt)} = \frac{\omega_2 C_{int} L_P}{T_1} \tag{10}$$

3.4 Secondary Stage of Energy Transferring

A buck-boost DC-DC circuit (as show in Fig. 6) is designed in the management circuit, which is composed of a switch K_2, an inductor L_1, a diode Dio and a storage capacitor C_{st}. $i_3(t)$ and R_{3n} are the current and equivalent resistance of the DC-DC circuit, respectively. When the voltage of the capacitor C_{int} reaches $V_{Cint(opt)}$, the switch K_2 turns on, the energy transfers form the C_{int} to the inductor L_1.

The last energy transferring process is transfer the energy stored in the inductor L_1 to the storage capacitor C_{st} as shown in Fig. 7. At this stage, switch K_2 turns off and diode dio turns on.

The harvested energy for a signal period can be expressed as:

$$E_s = \frac{1}{2}\gamma L_1 C_{int}^2 V_{Cint(opt)}^2 \omega_3^2 \tag{11}$$

Where γ is the over efficiency of the DC-DC convert which can be expressed as:

$$\gamma = e^{-\xi_3 \pi} \tag{12}$$

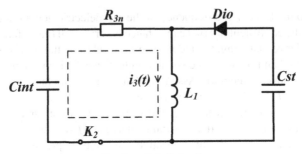

Fig. 6. DC-DC circuit.

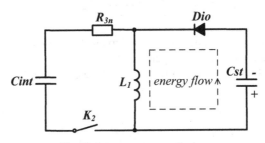

Fig. 7. Last energy transferring.

4 Experiment and Analysis

An experimental platform for energy harvesting is established. The maximum output voltage of the piezoelectric generator is 9 V. Switch K_1 is closed in positive period when the output voltage of the piezoelectric generator reaches maximum. The period of switch K_1 is $T_1 = 44$ ms (46 Hz), the duty cycle of switch K_1 is 9.8%.

The voltage of the inductor L_S is shown in Fig. 8. The frequency of the piezoelectric generator output signal can be transferred from 23 Hz to 2.5 kHz when the switch K_1 closed, thus a new high resonant frequency is generated both in the $C_p - L_p$ resonant circuit and the $L_s - C_{int}$ resonant circuit.

The frequency conversion management circuit is compared with the P-SSHI management circuit. The two management circuits have the same piezoelectric generator. The internal capacitances and frequencies are the same of 50 nF, 23 Hz. The open-circuit voltage is 10 V, and all the storage capacitors have the same capacitance of 0.1 F. In Fig. 9, the voltages across the storage capacitors in the frequency conversion management circuit and the P-SSHI circuit are 1.71 V and 0.29 V respectively.

According to Fig. 9, the harvested energy of the storage capacitor is $C_{st}V_{Cst}^2/2$, hence the frequency conversion management circuit can obtained 411% more energy compared with the P-SSHI circuit. Therefore, the frequency conversion management circuit has higher efficiency of energy harvesting than the P-SSHI management circuit.

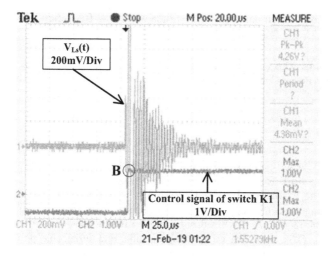

Fig. 8. Voltage waveforms across the intermediate capacitor C_{int}.

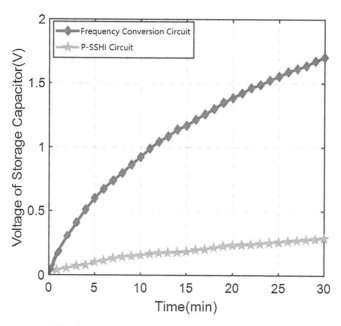

Fig. 9. Charging voltages of the storage capacitor.

5 Conclusion

In this paper, a frequency conversion management circuit has been proposed. A high resonant frequency is produced by using the matching circuit. Therefore, the maximum power can be extracted from the piezoelectric generator and transferred to the storage capacitor. The proposed management circuit also has obvious advantages compared with the P-SSHI circuit, which can be used in other weak low-frequency vibration energy harvesting.

Acknowledgements. This work was supported by Science and Technology Project of State Grid Shandong Electric Power Company (520616190099).

References

1. Chen, M., et al.: A self-powered 3.26-μW 70-m wireless temperature sensor node for power grid monitoring. IEEE Trans. Ind. Electron. **65**(11), 8956–8965 (2018)
2. Gall, O.Z., Meng, C., Bhamra, H., Mei, H., John, S.W.M., Irazoqui, P.P.: A batteryless energy harvesting storage system for implantable medical devices demonstrated in situ. Circuits Syst. Sig. Process. **38**, 1360–1373 (2018). https://doi.org/10.1007/s00034-018-0915-4
3. Chen, J., Kyu, O.S., Noor, N., et al.: Biocompatible and sustainable power supply for self-powered wearable and implantable electronics using III-nitride thin-film-based flexible piezoelectric generator. Nano Energy **57**, 670–679 (2019)
4. Guyomar, D., Badel, A., Lefeuvre, E., Richard, C.: Toward energy harvesting using active materials and conversion improvement by nonlinear processing. IEEE Trans. Ultrason. Ferroelectr. Freq. Control **52**(4), 584–595 (2005)
5. Lu, S.H., Boussaid, F.: A highly efficient P-SSHI rectifier for piezoelectric energy harvesting. IEEE Trans. Power Electron. **30**(10), 5364–5369 (2015)
6. Daniel, S., Joachim, L., Friedrich, H., et al.: A parallel-SSHI rectifier for piezoelectric energy harvesting of periodic and shock excitations. IEEE J. Solid-State Circuits **51**(12), 2867–2879 (2016)
7. Chen, Z.Y., Law, M.K., Mak, P.I.: Fully integrated inductor-less flipping-capacitor rectifier for piezoelectric energy harvesting. IEEE J. Solid-State Circuits **52**(12), 3168–3180 (2017)
8. Liu, L.X., Pang, Y.B., Yuan, W.Z., Zhu, Z.M., Yang, Y.T.: A self-powered piezoelectric energy harvesting interface circuit with efficiencyenhanced P-SSHI rectifier. J. Semicond. **39**(4), 045002.1–045002.11 (2018)
9. Liang, J.R., Liao, W.H.: Improved design and analysis of self-powered synchronized switch interface circuit for piezoelectric energy harvesting systems. IEEE Trans. Power Electron. **59**(4), 1950–1960 (2012)

An Adaptive Optimization Strict Reverse Navigation Algorithm for Ship Fine Alignment Process

Junwei Wang[1,2] , Xiyuan Chen[1,2(✉)] , Xin Shao[1,2] , and Zhen Ma[1,2]

[1] The School of Instrument Science and Engineering, Southeast University, Nanjing 210096, China
chxiyuan@seu.edu.cn
[2] Key Laboratory of Micro-Inertial Instrument and Advanced Navigation Technology of Ministry of Education, Southeast University, Nanjing 210096, China

Abstract. The navigation accuracy of ship work is largely dependent on the initial alignment accuracy of the inertial navigation system. However, azimuth angle alignment cannot be completed rapidly on the sea surface with strong winds and waves, which reduces the work efficiency of ships. Aiming at this problem, an adaptive optimization reverse navigation algorithm is proposed in this paper. Firstly, a reverse navigation method is established to process the original navigation data in reverse time sequence. After multiple forward and reverse navigation calculations in the same time period, the large misalignment angle error is reduced and the filtering convergence speed is improved. Secondly, the adaptive algorithm is introduced to intelligently control the calculation times of forward and backward navigation in different time periods, which can quickly achieve the alignment accuracy and further improve the response speed of the navigation system. Compared with the conventional alignment algorithm, the two horizontal-angle alignment errors and azimuth-angle alignment error of the ship are reduced by 81.15%, 76.44% and 76.58% respectively with the proposed algorithm in the results of the physical experiment.

Keywords: Initial alignment · Misalignment angle error · Reverse navigation algorithm · Adaptive intelligently control

1 Introduction

The initial alignment of the strapdown inertial navigation system is required before the ships enter the working state, and the navigation accuracy of its work depends to a large extent on the initial alignment accuracy of the inertial navigation system [1, 2]. Ships are small in size and light in weight, which will be rocking even in the mooring state by waves. Due to the error drift of the sensors [3, 4], such a large rocking makes the azimuth angle self-alignment unable to be completed rapidly, this situation generally requires the use of alignment methods on moving base to solve [5]. And the combination alignment is the main method in azimuth alignment of moving base [6–8].

W. Fu et al. (Eds.): ICMTEL 2021, LNICST 387, pp. 137–144, 2021.
https://doi.org/10.1007/978-3-030-82562-1_12

The combination alignment has been studied by using the information of strapdown inertial navigation system (SINS) and global navigation satellite system (GNSS) from the level of algorithm, and is extended based on the theory of reverse navigation algorithm. In this regard, some scholars have done lots of work. Yan first proposed a reverse navigation algorithm that relies on computer storage and powerful computing power in 2008 [9]. It used the reverse navigation algorithm to realize the integration of initial alignment and position navigation on moving base, and proved the reliability of the method through practical experiments. Based on the requirement of shortening alignment time, Chang proposed a backtracking method similar to reverse navigation. This method recorded the navigation solution data and applied it to the process of establishing measurement vectors. The author proved that this method can improve the accuracy and robustness of initial alignment in a short time [10].

In this paper, we focus on the ship fine alignment process in the sea with strong winds and wave. An adaptive optimization reverse navigation algorithm is proposed to improve the precision alignment speed under large azimuth misalignment error alignment.

2   Reverse Navigation Algorithm

In the conventional initial alignment method, coarse alignment and fine alignment are a serial process. Fine alignment can only continue the alignment process based on the result of coarse alignment, and the inertial navigation data of coarse alignment cannot be used. In order to accelerate the convergence of the filter, the alignment process hopes to obtain more inertial navigation data. Therefore, it is often necessary to increase the alignment time to obtain more measurement information.

With the continuous development of modern computer technology, its data storage capacity and computing ability have been greatly improved. It is possible to store the sampling data in the whole navigation process. In addition to the normal forward operation, the stored data can also be processed in reverse time order. Then, repeated forward and reverse analysis and calculation of stored data are beneficial to improve navigation accuracy.

The g (geographic) frame is selected as the n (navigation) frame. And considering the forward differential equations of strapdown inertial navigation system are as follows:

$$\dot{C}_b^n = C_b^n \left(\omega_{nb}^b \times \right) = C_b^n \left(\omega_{ib}^b \times \right) - \left[\left(\omega_{ie}^n + \omega_{en}^n \right) \times \right] C_b^n \tag{1}$$

Where $(\omega \times)$ denotes the skew-symmetric matrix of angular rate ω, C_b^n represents the attitude matrix from the b (body) frame to the n frame, $\omega_{nb}^b = \omega_{ib}^b - \omega_{in}^b$ represents the navigation angular rate, ω_{ib}^b represents the gyro output angular rate, $\omega_{ie}^n = \left[0 \ \omega_{ie} \cos L \ \omega_{ie} \sin L \right]^T$ represents the rotation rate of the earth in n frame, $\omega_{en}^n = \left[-\frac{v_N^n}{R_M+h} \ \frac{v_E^n}{R_N+h} \ \frac{v_E^n \tan L}{R_N+h} \right]^T$ represents the transport angular rate.

$$\dot{v}^n = C_b^n f^b - (2\omega_{ie}^n + \omega_{en}^n) \times v^n + g^n \tag{2}$$

where $v^n = \left[v_E \ v_N \ v_U \right]^T$ denotes the velocity in n frame, f^b represents the accelerometer output specific force, $g^n = \left[0 \ 0 \ -g \right]^T$ represents the component of gravitational acceleration in n frame.

$$\dot{L} = \frac{v_N}{R_M + h}, \quad \dot{\lambda} = \frac{v_E \sec L}{R_N + h}, \quad \dot{h} = v_U \tag{3}$$

where L, λ, h denote the latitude, longitude and height respectively, R_M and R_N represent the principal radii of curvature along the meridional section and the principal radii of curvature along the prime-vertical section.

The sampling period of gyroscope and accelerometer is recorded as T_s. Equations (1) to (3) are discretized as follows:

$$C^n_{b,k} = C^n_{b,k-1}(I + T_s \Omega^b_{nb,k}) \tag{4}$$

$$v^n_k = v^n_{k-1} + T_s \left[C^n_{b,k-1} f^b_k - (2\omega^n_{ie,k-1} + \omega^n_{en,k-1}) \times v^n_{k-1} + g^n \right] \tag{5}$$

$$L_k = L_{k-1} + \frac{T_s v^n_{N,k-1}}{R_M + h_{k-1}}, \quad \lambda_k = \lambda_{k-1} + \frac{T_s v^n_{E,k-1} \sec L_{k-1}}{R_N + h_{k-1}}, \quad h_k = h_{k-1} + T_s v^n_{U,k-1} \tag{6}$$

where $k - 1$ and k denote the discrete time points (Fig. 1).

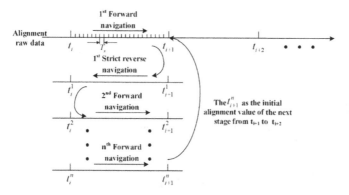

Fig. 1. The process of repeated forward and reverse navigation

The strict process of attitude reverse updating is as follows:

$$C^n_{b,k-1} = C^n_{b,k}\left(I + T_s \breve{\Omega}^b_{nb,k-1}\right) \tag{7}$$

where $\breve{\Omega}^b_{nb,k-1} = -\Omega^b_{nb,k}\left[I + T_s\Omega^b_{nb,k}\right]^{-1}$.

The strict process of velocity reverse updating is as follows:

$$-v^n_{k-1} = -v^n_k + T_s \breve{a}^n_{k-1,k} = -v^n_k + T_s a^n_{k,k-1} = C^n_{b,k-1} f^b_k - \left(2\omega^n_{ie,k-1} + \omega^n_{en,k-1}\right) \times v^n_{k-1} + g^n \tag{8}$$

The strict process of position reverse updating is as follows:

$$L_{k-1} = L_k + \frac{-T_s v_{N,k}^n}{R_M + h_k}, \quad \lambda_{k-1} = \lambda_k + \frac{-T_s v_{E,k}^n \sec L_k}{R_N + h_k}, \quad h_{k-1} = h_k - T_s v_{U,k}^n \quad (9)$$

The symbol '$\leftarrow$' is defined as the representation of the reverse direction, and the symbol m is defined as the navigation terminal time. The parameters in the reverse process are obtained as follows: $\overset{\leftarrow}{C}_{b,m-k}^n = C_{b,k}^n, \; \overset{\leftarrow}{v}_{m-k}^n = -v_k^n, \; \overset{\leftarrow}{L}_{m-k} = L_k, \; \overset{\leftarrow}{\lambda}_{m-k} = \lambda_k, \; \overset{\leftarrow}{h}_{m-k} = h_k, \; \overset{\leftarrow}{f}_{m-k}^n = f_k^n, \; \overset{\leftarrow}{a}_{k-1,k}^n = \overset{\smile}{a}_{k-1,k}^n = a_{k,k-1}^n, \; \overset{\leftarrow}{\omega}_{ie,m-k}^n = -\omega_{ie,k}^n, \; \overset{\leftarrow}{\omega}_{en,m-k}^n = -\omega_{en,k}^n, \; \overset{\leftarrow}{\Omega}_{nb,m-k}^b = \overset{\smile}{\Omega}_{nb,k}^b.$

Further, let $j = m-k+1$. Then the subscript is converted to: $C_{b,k-1}^n = C_{b,m-j}^n = \overset{\leftarrow}{C}_{b,j}^n,$ $C_{b,k}^n = C_{b,m+1-j}^n = \overset{\leftarrow}{C}_{b,j-1}^n, \; \overset{\smile}{\Omega}_{nb,k-1}^b = \overset{\smile}{\Omega}_{nb,m-j}^b = \overset{\leftarrow}{\Omega}_{nb,j}^b.$

Therefore, the new strict process of attitude, velocity and position reverse updating is as follows:

$$\overset{\leftarrow}{C}_{b,j}^n = \overset{\leftarrow}{C}_{b,j-1}^n \left(I + T_s \overset{\leftarrow}{\Omega}_{nb,j}^b \right) \quad (10)$$

$$\overset{\leftarrow}{v}_j^n = \overset{\leftarrow}{v}_{j-1}^n + T_s \overset{\leftarrow}{a}_{j-1,j}^n \quad (11)$$

$$\overset{\leftarrow}{L}_j = \overset{\leftarrow}{L}_{j-1} + \frac{T_s \overset{\leftarrow}{v}_{N,j-1}^n}{R_M + \overset{\leftarrow}{h}_{j-1}}, \quad \overset{\leftarrow}{\lambda}_j = \overset{\leftarrow}{\lambda}_{j-1} + \frac{T_s \overset{\leftarrow}{v}_{E,j-1}^n \sec \overset{\leftarrow}{L}_{j-1}}{R_N + \overset{\leftarrow}{h}_{j-1}}, \quad \overset{\leftarrow}{h}_j = \overset{\leftarrow}{h}_{j-1} + T_s \overset{\leftarrow}{v}_{U,j-1}^n$$

$$(12)$$

After multiple forward and reverse navigation calculations in the same time period, the large misalignment angle error is reduced and the filtering convergence speed is improved without approximation error.

3 Adaptive Optimization Control Process

The staged forward and reverse navigation algorithm with adaptive optimization control process is proposed to adaptively control the calculation times of forward and reverse navigation in different alignment time periods (Fig. 2).

In the initial stage of the optimal estimation fine alignment, the convergence rate of the filter is affected by the rough initial value. Thus, plenty of forward and reverse calculations ought to be required in the initial time period to reduce the initial value error and improve the subsequent convergence speed. After the forward and reverse calculations in this stage are completed, the result is used as the initial value of the next stage, and the forward and reverse navigation calculations are continued, with the alignment process proceeded, the navigation accuracy is improved, and the calculation times of forward and reverse solutions ought to be reduced.

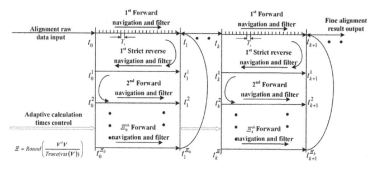

Fig. 2. The staged forward and reverse navigation algorithm with adaptive control process

The kalman filter equations can be written as follows:

$$X_{k|k-1} = \Psi_{k|k-1} X_{k-1} \tag{13}$$

$$P_{k|k-1} = \Psi_{k|k-1} P_{k-1} \Psi_{k|k-1}^T + Q_{k-1} \tag{14}$$

$$K_k = P_{k|k-1} H_k^T \left(H_k P_{k|k-1} H_k^T + R_k \right)^{-1} \tag{15}$$

$$V_k = Z_k - H_k X_{k|k-1} \sim N(0, H_k P_{k|k-1} H_k^T + R_k) \tag{16}$$

$$X_k = X_{k|k-1} + K_k V_k \tag{17}$$

$$P_k = (I - K_k H_k) P_{k|k-1} \tag{18}$$

where X_{k-1} and X_k denote the system state variables at filter time k - 1 and k. Z_k represents the observation variables at filter time k, $\Psi_{k|k-1}$ and H_k represent the state transition matrix and the observation matrix. $P_{k|k-1}$ and P_k represent the error covariance matrix of state prediction $X_{k|k-1}$ and optimal estimation X_k. K_k represents the gain matrix. V_k denotes the innovation matrix. Q_{k-1} and R_k denote the variance matrix of system noise and measurement noise.

In the combination alignment, the innovation matrix V_k reflects the state variable differences between the calculated information of inertial system and the new information of other sensors. Meanwhile, these state variable differences are far bigger than random noise of system and measurement in general. Therefore, the squares sum of the innovation sequence $V_k^T V_k$ indicates the progress in convergence of misalignment angle. The larger the sum of squares of the innovation sequence $V_k^T V_k$, the larger the misalignment angle, and the more calculation times of forward and reverse navigation are required.

Based on the above reason, the innovation matrix V_k ought to be concerned as the key matrix that controls the calculation times of adaptive forward and inverse navigation in the adaptive optimization control process.

$$\varXi_k = Round\left(\frac{V_k^T V_k}{Trace(\text{var}(V_k))}\right) = Round\left(\frac{V_k^T V_k}{Trace(H_k P_{k|k-1} H_k^T + R_k)}\right) \quad (19)$$

where $\varXi_k$ denotes the adaptive calculation times of forward and reverse navigation. The function $Round(\cdot)$ denotes the integer operation. The function $Trace(\cdot)$ denotes the matrix trace operation.

4 Experiment

In order to verify the actual effect of the proposed algorithm, the lake test is experimented and the process of ship fine alignment at mooring condition is analyzed. The experimental equipment is placed as shown in Fig. 3. The micro electro mechanical system - inertial measurement unit (MEMS-IMU) and global navigation satellite system (GNSS) are used as the combination alignment experiment system. Besides, the fiber optic gyroscope - inertial measurement unit (FOG-IMU) is involved in the experiment as the true attitude reference system of the experiment ship due to its excellent precision and stability of angle measurement. The sensor technological parameters are noted in Table 1.

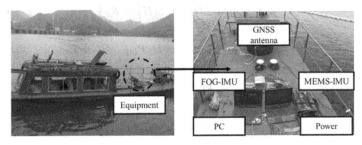

Fig. 3. Lake test setup

Table 1. The sensor technological parameters of experiment device

Sensor		Random bias	Random walk noise	Root mean square error
FOG-IMU	Accelerometer	50 ug	5 ug/Hz$^{1/2}$	-
	Gyroscope	0.01°/h	0.003°/h$^{1/2}$	-
MEMS-IMU	Accelerometer	0.3 mg	35 ug/Hz$^{1/2}$	-
	Gyroscope	1°/h	0.07°/h$^{1/2}$	-
GNSS receiver		-	-	Vel: 0.1 m/s Pos: 1 m

The 100 s experimental navigation data of the ship at mooring state is analyzed. Compared with the real attitude reference system, the alignment error results of the conventional combination alignment method and the proposed alignment method are displayed in Fig. 4. The RMSE of alignment errors of two distinct alignment methods are given in Table 2:

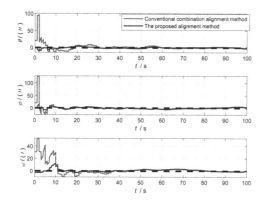

Fig. 4. The alignment errors of different kalman filters in fine alignment process

Table 2. The RMSE of alignment errors of two distinct alignment methods

Alignment errors	Roll $\delta\theta/''$	Pitch $\delta\phi/''$	Yaw $\delta\omega/'$
Conventional combination alignment method	11.0157	13.6242	9.7986
The adaptive optimization strict reverse alignment method	2.0767	3.2092	2.2951

Discussion. It is able to obviously analyzed from Fig. 4 and Table 2 that the convergence speed of the conventional combination alignment method is affected by the rough initial value at the beginning of the ship fine alignment process. The initial inaccurate and oscillating angle value will pollute the ship controller, which needs to be overcome. Unfortunately, it is a great pity that alignment results can achieve higher accuracy only when more inertial navigation data are obtained in fine alignment process. As a result, the ship fine alignment time is too long, which restrains the rapid response ability of the ship.

But in the adaptive optimization strict reverse alignment method, repeated forward and reverse analysis and calculation of stored data are beneficial to improve navigation accuracy. After multiple forward and reverse navigation calculations in the same time period, the large misalignment angle error is reduced, and the filtering convergence speed is improved without approximation error, especially in initial 20 s.

5   Conclusion

The initial alignment is a necessary process for the ship inertial navigation system to work, and the accuracy and time are the two major indicators of the initial alignment.

Alignment in a short period of time cannot achieve high accuracy requirements, and it takes a long time to achieve high navigation accuracy. The reverse navigation algorithm can effectively shorten the initial alignment by repeatedly calculating the sampled data stored for a period of time by means of data storage method. Meanwhile, a staged forward and reverse navigation algorithm with adaptive optimization control process is proposed to adaptively control the calculation times of forward and reverse navigation in different alignment time periods, so that the calculation amount can be controlled on the basis of ensuring the alignment accuracy.

Acknowledgments. This work is supported in part by the National Key Research and Development Project [No. 2017YFC0306303], the National Natural Science Foundation of China [No. 61873064], and also supported the National Defense Advanced Research Foundation [No. 17044141305302].

References

1. Huang, H., Chen, X., Zhang, B., Wang, J.: High accuracy navigation information estimation for inertial system using the multi-model EKF fusing adams explicit formula applied to underwater gliders. ISA Trans. **66**(1), 414–424 (2016)
2. Wang, J., Chen, X., Yang, P.: Adaptive H-infinite kalman filter based on multiple fading factors and its application in unmanned underwater vehicle. ISA Trans. (2020). https://doi.org/10.1016/j.isatra.2020.08.030
3. Narasimhappa, M., Mahindrakar, A., Guizilini, V., Terra, M., Sabat, S.: An improved Sage Husa adaptive robust Kalman Filter for de-noising the MEMS IMU drift signal. In: 2018 Indian Control Conference (ICC), Kanpur, pp. 229–234. IEEE (2018).
4. Xu, Y., Shmaliy, Y., Chen, X., Li, Y., Ma, W.F.: Robust inertial navigation system/ultra wide band integrated indoor quadrotor localization employing adaptive interacting multiple model-unbiased finite impulse response/Kalman filter estimator. Aerosp. Sci. Technol. **98**(1) (2020). https://doi.org/10.1016/j.ast.2020.105683
5. Wang, J., Ma, Z., Chen, X.: Generalized dynamic fuzzy NN model based on multiple fading factors SCKF and its application in integrated navigation. IEEE Sens. J. (2020). https://doi.org/10.1109/JSEN.2020.3022934
6. Wang, Q., Yang, C., Wu, S.: Study on initial alignment under large misalignment angle. J. Inf. Hiding Priv. Prot. **3**(1), 95–108 (2019)
7. Zhang, T., Wang, J., Jin, B., Li, Y.: Application of improved fifth-degree cubature Kalman filter in the nonlinear initial alignment of strapdown inertial navigation system. Rev. Sci. Instrum. **90**(1), 015111 (2019)
8. Ma, Z., Chen, X.: Fiber Bragg gratings sensors for aircraft wing shape measurement: recent applications and technical analysis. Sensors **19**(1), 55 (2018)
9. Yan, G., Yan, W., Xu, D.: On reverse navigation algorithm and its application to SINS gyro-compass in-movement alignment. In: The 27th Chinese Control Conference, Kunming, vol. 5, pp. 724–729. IEEE (2008).
10. Chang, L., Hu, B., Li, A., Qin, F.: Strapdown inertial navigation system alignment based on marginalised unscented Kalman filter. IET Sci. Meas. Technol. **7**(2), 128–138 (2013)

Research on Load Feature Extraction Method of Typical Users Based on Deep Learning

Zhu Lian-huan[1]([✉]), Wei Wei[1], Zhu Wei-yang[2], Ding Can-song[2], Shen Kai[2], and Fu Guan-hua[1]

[1] State Grid Hangzhou Xiaoshan Power Supply Company, Hangzhou 311200, China
[2] Zhejiang Zhongxin Power Engineering Construction Co., Ltd., Hangzhou 311200, China

Abstract. In order to improve the accuracy of typical user load feature extraction, this paper proposes a typical user load feature extraction method based on deep learning. Using k-means algorithm to cluster user load data, select typical user load sample data from the clustering results, and classify user load categories, and implement the extraction of typical user load features based on the classification results combined with deep learning methods. The experimental test results show that the method in this paper has high accuracy in the extraction of typical user load characteristics, high accuracy in load recognition, and good practical application effects.

Keywords: Deep learning · Typical user · Load feature · Feature extraction

1 Introduction

In order to improve the calculation efficiency and extraction accuracy of typical user load extraction, the research on typical user load extraction method is carried out in order to realize the typical user load extraction quickly and accurately. As one of the key technologies of load monitoring for typical users, the function of load extraction is to extract and analyze various power consumption characteristics of residents, businesses and administration by using the load characteristics extracted from load monitoring data [1]. At present, there are many researches on the implementation methods of load extraction of typical users, which mainly use two kinds of methods: mathematical optimization algorithm and pattern extraction algorithm. When using mathematical optimization algorithm to extract load, most of them use differential evolution algorithm and genetic optimization algorithm. Because the mathematical model of typical user load extraction is more complex, the mathematical optimization algorithm is faced with many problems the low efficiency of solving the problem affects the applicability of mathematical optimization algorithm in the typical user load feature extraction method [2]. The commonly used pattern extraction algorithm is supervised learning algorithm. Its working principle is to select the load historical monitoring data in a certain period of time as the training data set, and use the data set to train the algorithm. Finally, the real-time monitoring data of load is extracted according to the training results.

W. Fu et al. (Eds.): ICMTEL 2021, LNICST 387, pp. 145–156, 2021.
https://doi.org/10.1007/978-3-030-82562-1_13

However, these two methods have the problem of low accuracy of typical user load feature extraction, so this paper proposes a typical user load feature extraction method based on deep learning. This paper uses k-means algorithm to cluster user load data, selects typical user load sample data in the clustering results, and divides user load categories. According to the classification results, combined with deep learning method, the typical user load feature extraction is realized, so as to solve the problems existing in traditional methods and improve the accuracy of typical user load feature extraction. I hope this paper can do some research It can lay a solid foundation for the further development of power data analysis.

2   User Load Feature Extraction Method

2.1   Typical User Load Data Clustering

Before clustering with k-means algorithm, data preprocessing is needed: suppose that there are m sample data in the initial data set for deep learning algorithm, and there are k characteristic data attributes in the initial data set, and the $k > 0$ is an integer. In the whole process of data clustering, m sample data are formed into the sum of squares of cluster center distance with characteristic attributes

$$\Delta F = U(j) \sum_{i=1}^{K} \bar{\omega}^* F_i = \sum_{i=1}^{K} \bar{\omega}^* \sum_{j=1}^{m} \alpha_{ij} \left\| A_j - B_i \right\|^2 \tag{1}$$

In the formula: F represents the sum of the squared distance between the cluster centers and the objective function; A_j represents the j data feature attributes, B_i represents the i feature cluster centers, and α_{ij} represents the weight coefficient. In the clustering process, the square of the distance between the cluster centers and the extreme value of the objective function need to be taken. When the k-means algorithm is applied to the extraction of complex power consumption characteristics of users, the original text data must be determined first, and then the cluster centers must be randomly selected. Use the k-means algorithm to find the F value. In the iterative process, as long as the F value keeps changing, it means that the clustering has not reached the optimum. At this time, the cluster center needs to be updated and the iterative process is repeated. The calculation formula for cluster centers is as follows:

$$O_{ij} = \Delta F / \Delta i \left\| A_j - B_i^{i-1} \right\| \tag{2}$$

The above formula mainly calculates the distance between the sample data and the feature clustering center. According to the above formula, the implementation steps are as follows:

1) Take k initial condensation points as the initial centroid;
2) Calculate the distance from the sample data to the feature cluster center;
3) According to the k-means clustering principle, all points are assigned to k feature cluster centers;
4) Calculate the centroid of k feature cluster centers;

5) Repeat steps 2), 3), and 4) until the center of mass no longer needs to be updated;
6) Realize feature recognition.

The power consumption characteristic data is obtained by sampling and processed, and sent to the data processing center to measure the power consumption of the users in combination with the total electricity consumption. With the support of deep learning algorithm, complex power consumption feature extraction is carried out to fill in the missing value of user power consumption, smooth noise data, delete off cluster points, and avoid unreliable data output. For the problem of missing data, the data mean and median can be used for interpolation, and the attribute value closest to the missing sample can be found in the record for interpolation. If the missing value is filled with constant, the data attribute should be analyzed in advance, and the data cleaning should be carried out based on this. In data clustering, we should first improve the data quality and reduce redundant data. Use metadata methods to avoid possible extraction problems in data sets. For data redundancy problems, it is necessary to use correlation analysis to detect whether the data is redundant, and store it in different measurement units, fully consider random variables, and map the original data In a small space, after data compression, it is judged whether the original data can be reconstructed, so as to regulate a large amount of data. Eliminate the noise data in the data, transform continuous attributes into categorical attributes, and divide the data into discrete intervals to analyze the data by clustering.

2.2 User Load Classification

With the development of power grid technology, the situation of users' power consumption becomes more complex, and a large number of power consumption characteristics are generated. Previous load feature extraction methods are affected by noise data, resulting in low extraction accuracy. To solve this problem, a typical user load feature extraction method based on deep learning is proposed [3]. In the deep learning algorithm, the principle of typical user load feature extraction is studied, and the data is cleaned, integrated and pre processed to avoid noise interference. Through the cluster decision-making power consumption feature points, the information gain of power consumption characteristics is obtained, and the complex power consumption characteristics are extracted to provide better and high-quality services for users. Load extraction and decomposition is to extract the components of the total load according to the characteristics of the load work imprint extracted from the measured data, and realize the load decomposition on this basis, including mathematical optimization and mode extraction. Load extraction problem can be described as the following mathematical problems:

$$\Phi = [A_1, A_2, \cdots, A_M] \tag{3}$$

$$A_i = \left[f_{i,1}, f_{i,2}, \cdots, f_{i,n} \right]^T \tag{4}$$

$$B = [F_1, F_2, \ldots, F_n]^T \tag{5}$$

$$X = [x_1, x_2, \cdots, x_M]^T \tag{6}$$

Assuming that the above formula is true, the solution of the following formula is satisfied:

$$\min d(C, B) = d\left(\sum_{i=1}^{M}(x_i A_i), B\right) \tag{7}$$

Among them, Φ is a feature matrix composed of M type electrical equipment, A_i is a feature matrix composed of all the load characteristics of i type electrical equipment, and f_{in} represents the n load feature of i type electrical equipment. B is a feature matrix composed of all the features in the entire electricity use scene, F_n represents the n load feature quantity in the electricity use scene, X is a state matrix composed of the working states of all M types of electrical equipment, and x_i takes 1 to indicate this type of electrical equipment is in the working state. x_i value of 0 means that this type of electrical equipment is off. $d(C, B)$ represents the distance between the possible combination of all load characteristics and the total load. Because the short-term load data of the power dispatching switch is affected by many factors, the data selection is not accurate. In order to solve this problem, it is necessary to select the load data that has a greater impact on it. Time and temperature have the greatest impact on the power load data [4]. In the process of intelligent short-term load forecasting combined with deep learning algorithm, the time and temperature data need to be integrated, and the power load data of a certain period of time can be predicted through the network, and the training sample selection process is shown in the figure (Fig. 1).

It can be seen from the figure that: the initial weight, input each learning sample of current N into the network in turn, calculate the input and output values of each layer, calculate the back propagation error of each layer, and record the number of trained samples M in time. If M is less than N, the learning samples need to be re input into the network to calculate the input and output of each layer; if M is equal to N, the weights of each layer should be corrected according to the weights, and the connection weights of hidden layers should be adjusted. According to the new weight, the error of each layer is recalculated. If the error is less than the set expected value, the training reaches the maximum number of times, and the sample selection is terminated. Otherwise, it returns to the sample input step.

Considering that among independent users, the types of home appliances are limited, the brand models of the same load are relatively fixed, the corresponding waveforms are fixed, and the operating environment and operating habits are relatively stable. Therefore, this article regards each independent user as the basic unit of constructing the feature library, and unlimited categories the classification problem is transformed into a limited category classification problem [5]. In order to ensure that the feature library has universal applicability to most independent users, the classification judgment conditions are set according to the operational characteristics of common loads, so as to transform the unsupervised classification problem into a supervised classification problem of load types. The Bayesian classification model is used to classify the load, the decomposed independent operating load characteristics are used as the posterior knowledge, and the posterior probability is converted into the prior probability of the load category to solve, as shown in the formula.

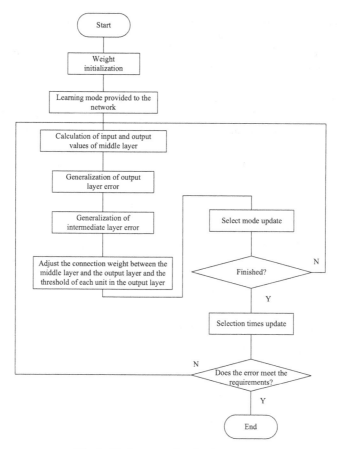

Fig. 1. Feature sample selection process

$$P(\omega_n|F_k) = \frac{P(F_k|\omega_n)P(\omega_n)}{P(F_i)} \quad n = 1, 2, \cdots, N \tag{8}$$

Where: ω_n is the classification of the k independent load signal U_k and I_k; F_k is the extracted unknown load characteristics; N is the total number of electrical appliances in the user; $P(\omega_n)$ is the probability of the occurrence of load category ω_n, $P(F_k|\omega_n)$ is the probability of feature F_k under the condition of known load type; $P(F_k)$ is the probability of switching on and off of load K in the table replaced by F_k after clustering. The prior probability $P(\omega_n)$ is converted to the posterior probability $P(\omega_n|F_k)$ by the obtained stability characteristic F_k, that is, the probability that the load k category belongs to ω_n when F_k is known, and the category with the largest probability is the label of load k, as shown in the formula:

$$L_t = L_k \arg\max P(\omega_n|F_k) \tag{9}$$

Where: L_k is the label of load k. In this way, all the separated independent loads are classified and processed, the unknown loads obtained by successive separations can be labeled and their waveforms, characteristics, and categories are recorded in the feature library to complete the construction of the independent user load feature library. After forming the user's load characteristic database, the data in the database is used to continuously identify the user's independent load waveform after load separation in real time [6]. Since the high-frequency acquisition mode can better retain the integrity of the load waveform, the load identification quick optimization model is further established based on the waveform similarity. The steady-state current of the electrical equipment in normal operation has linear superposition, that is, the collected mixed signal can be estimated by the linear superposition of the current of the N-type electrical equipment. The current mixed current signal can be expressed as:

$$I(t) = L_t \sum_{k=1}^{N} a_i I_k(t) + n(t) \quad k = 1, 2, \cdots, N \tag{10}$$

Where: a_i is the start stop coefficient of load i, $a_i = 0$ is the load I is not opened at time t, and $a_i = w$ is that there are w such loads at the same time. The problem of load identification is transformed into a set of optimal weight coefficients $a_1, a_2, ..., a_n$, which makes the load superimposed current most similar to the real current, so as to determine the mixed load type in the collected current at this time and realize load extraction. The optimal weight coefficient at the current moment is determined by the minimum residual method:

$$\hat{I}_v = I(t) \sum_{i=1}^{N} a_q \hat{I}_q \tag{11}$$

$$\min d = \left\| I_k - \hat{I}_\tau \right\| \tag{12}$$

In the formula: when $a_q = 0$, it means that the corresponding electrical appliance is not turned on, when aq $a_q = 1$, it means that the corresponding electrical appliance is on, and $\hat{I}_q$ is the current of the electrical appliance q stored in the library. The key to load identification is to find the optimal weight coefficient to make the superimposed signal most similar to the real signal at the current moment [7]. The switching operation of an independent load is defined as an electrical event. When the above events occur in the circuit, the most obvious change in the collected data is the current intensity. Therefore, this paper samples the current and voltage according to a certain frequency to detect the event, and records the voltage and current waveforms in the last 2S in the buffer. The current intensity calculation of each cycle current signal can be expressed as follows:

$$i_{\text{vars}} = \min d \sqrt{\sum_{j=1}^{\tau} \frac{i^2(j)}{\tau}} \tag{13}$$

$$\Delta i = i_{\text{RMS}}(T + 1) - i_{\text{vars}}(\eta \tau) \tag{14}$$

In the formula: τ is the number of sampling points in a cycle, $i^2(j)$ is the sampling value of the cycle current; T is the T-th cycle of the current. If the current intensity of one cycle has a sudden change compared with the previous cycle, that is, $\Delta i > \eta$ and η are the thresholds for judging the sudden change of the steady-state current, and it can be considered that a load switching event has occurred. The fundamental phase angle of the steady-state current is determined by the initial phase of the voltage during measurement. Therefore, it is only necessary to ensure that the steady-state current is measured under the same initial phase angle voltage to meet the current superposition. The load current waveform reconstructs the mixed current waveform. Detect the voltage zero-crossing point that shows an upward trend in the corresponding steady-state terminal voltage waveform, and extract the steady-state current waveform I before the electric load k is switched on.

$$\begin{cases} U(j) > 0 \\ U(j-1) < 0 \end{cases} \tag{15}$$

Where: J is the sampling point of current stable period corresponding to the T-1 cycle when the formula is satisfied; U(J) is the steady-state voltage.

2.3 Implementation of Characteristic Extraction of Typical User Load

Deep learning is a method of machine learning based on representation of data. It belongs to the category of machine learning, can be said to be an upgrade on the basis of traditional neural network, about equal to neural network. Its advantage is to use unsupervised or semi supervised feature learning and hierarchical feature extraction algorithm to replace manual feature extraction. Because of its strong learning ability, wide coverage, good adaptability, good portability and other advantages, it is reliable to apply it to typical users' load feature extraction.

Due to the complexity of the data extracted from the user's power load feature, the extraction quality is low due to the interference of external noise in the process of acquisition and transmission. Therefore, it is necessary to preprocess it first, and label the unknown waveform stored in the feature library in this process [8]. Generally, typical user load features are switched on and off for many times, and the extracted load waveform is repetitive. It is not necessary to judge the types of all the extracted waveforms and store them in the feature library in the feature library establishment phase. Therefore, the waveforms extracted by deep learning method are clustered first [9]. In the initial operation stage, the number of load types, load operation modes and the number of modes are unknown. In this paper, the inherent characteristics of load steady-state operation are used for fast clustering. Therefore, the results of load characteristics based on deep learning can be expressed as follows:

$$F_t = \left\{ P_k, Q_k, P_{Ft}, R_{THD,k}, r_k \right\} \tag{16}$$

Where: P_k and Q_k are active and reactive power respectively; P_{Fk} is power factor; R_{THD} and k are current distortion rate; r_k is Pearson coefficient between the current waveform and the constructed standard sine wave, and the peak value and frequency of the standard sine wave are the same as the current waveform. Since the numerical range of different features is different, normalize each feature according to the above formula to get.

$$\bar{\omega}^* = \frac{(\bar{\omega} - \bar{\omega}_{\min})F_t}{O_{ij}(\bar{\omega}_{\max} - \bar{\omega}_{\min})} \tag{17}$$

Where: $\bar{\omega}_{\max}$ and $\bar{\omega}_{\min}$ are the maximum and minimum values of features respectively; $\bar{\omega}$ is the value before and after feature normalization. Single step judgment can not guarantee the accuracy. Therefore, this paper uses the inherent characteristics of the load to pre classify the unknown waveform, narrow the load label range and reduce the burden of subsequent labeling. PFK, RTHD, K and rk are used to divide the load into linear and non-linear. According to the times of detecting such waveform in a short time, it is divided into continuous or intermittent operation. Finally, according to the duration of each switching the change degree is judged as fixed or non fixed operation time load, as shown in the formula:

$$T_{\mathrm{D}} = \bar{\omega}^* \sum_{p=1}^{p} \frac{T_d(p)}{P} \tag{18}$$

$$T_{\mathrm{D}}' \in [T_d(1 - a), T_d(1 + \alpha)] \tag{19}$$

Where: T_d is the average duration of the previous p times of the same load, $T_d(p)$ is the duration of the p-th load; T_{D}' is the duration of the detected load belonging to this type of load; α is the floating factor, if the above formula is satisfied, then This load is a fixed operating time category. Obtain current and voltage sampling data through data acquisition methods such as smart meters, and calculate characteristic values such as overall power and harmonics [10]. The difference feature extraction method is used to obtain the change feature quantity produced by the change of the electrical appliance state at any time, as the data input of the fuzzy clustering; the inter-cluster entropy value of the clustering result is calculated and iterated, and the optimal number of clusters is selected. Finally, calculate the similarity between each type of data and the characteristics of electrical appliances, and select the most similar electrical features as the type of electrical appliances represented by the data. Based on this, the user load feature extraction process is standardized, as shown in the following figure (Fig. 2):

Through the above process, the number and type of electrical appliances can be extracted under the condition that the situation of household appliances is unknown, which can solve the data problems for power consumption behavior analysis and smart home applications. Improve the accuracy of user load feature extraction.

3   Analysis of Results

In order to verify the practical application effect of typical user load feature extraction method based on deep learning, comparative experiments are carried out, and the mathematical optimization algorithm mentioned in the introduction is taken as the traditional method. The subjects of the experiment include residents, commerce, administration, transportation, industry and so on. The sampling current and voltage data are obtained by USB A/D data acquisition card, and the acquisition frequency is 1 kHz. The parameters of the experimental equipment are standardized, as shown in the table below (Table 1).

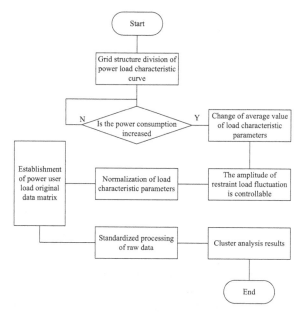

Fig. 2. Flow chart of user load feature extraction

Table 1. Experimental parameter settings.

	Database server	Application server	Client
Number of CPU	5	5	2
Type of CPU	-	-	P43.2G
Memory	16G	16G	512M
Hard disk	2 * 120G	2 * 320G	-
Network card	4 * 1000M	4 * 1000M	100M

During the experiment, one of the equipment was started and stopped randomly for 100 times, and the monitoring time was 10 min. The difference feature extraction method proposed in this paper is used to extract harmonic features as shown in the figure (Fig. 3).

It can be seen that the distribution of active and reactive power features of some electrical equipment is relatively concentrated, which is not conducive to the classification and extraction of clustering algorithms. After harmonic features are used to replace reactive power, the load features are clearly divided into 5 regions, which can be more effectively perform fuzzy clustering extraction. When the active and harmonic features are used, the entropy value between clusters is higher than that of the active and reactive features, and it is optimal when the number of clusters is 5, which is consistent with the actual situation. This shows that the difference feature extraction and fuzzy clustering methods used in this paper can effectively extract load features, and can perform

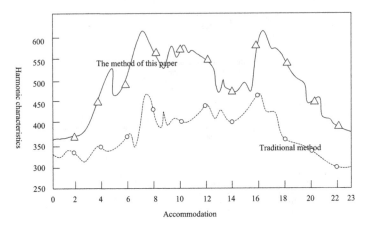

Fig. 3. Harmonic feature extraction results of electrical load

fuzzy clustering based on the inter-cluster entropy when the device type is unknown, and improve the accuracy of load extraction.

The load identification accuracy of typical users such as residents, commerce, administration, transportation and industry is shown in the following table:

Table 2. Correct rate of load identification.

Electrical type	Recognition accuracy/%	
	Traditional method	The method of this paper
Resident	80.0	100.0
Business	73.7	100.0
Administration	80.0	100.0
Traffic	65.4	94.1
Industry	82.0	98.0
Resident	76.2	98.4

It can be seen from Table 2 that the correct rate of load identification of this method is higher. In order to further verify the performance of the method in this paper, high-power home appliances are used to detect load characteristics. Some equipment starts and stops randomly for a total of 200 times, and the monitoring time is 1000 s. The load characteristic data obtained through sampling is normalized. The distribution of power characteristics of a variety of electrical equipment is relatively concentrated, especially the load with lower power, which is not easy to monitor and extract the load. Due to the large harmonic current characteristic value of low-power load, the load characteristic distribution is more scattered, which is more conducive to further fuzzy clustering extraction. Based on this analysis of the test results, the details are as follows:

Table 3. Load identification accuracy of high power household appliances.

Electrical type	Recognition accuracy/%	
	Traditional method	The method of this paper
Resident	75.4	98.4
Business	82.1	100.0
Administration	79.6	100.0
Traffic	80.6	99.2
Industry	81.3	96.5
Resident	85.4	100.0
Resident	77.2	96.4
Business	70.6	100.0
Administration	78.4	100.0
Traffic	79.9	98.9

According to the analysis of Table 3, the extraction accuracy of typical user load feature extraction method based on deep learning has been significantly improved compared with the traditional method.

4   Concluding Remarks

This paper mainly proposes a typical user load feature extraction method based on deep learning. The k-means algorithm is used to cluster the user load data, the typical user load sample data is selected from the clustering results, and the user load categories are divided, and the typical user load characteristics are extracted according to the classification results combined with the deep learning method. Finally, simulation experiments show that the method in this paper can achieve effective and accurate load extraction.

References

1. Angkoon, P., Rami, N.K., Erik, S.: Feature extraction and selection for myoelectric control based on wearable EMG sensors. Sensors 18(5), 1615–1618 (2018)
2. Aliakbary, S., Habibi, J., Movaghar, A.: Feature extraction from degree distribution for comparison and analysis of complex networks. Comput. J. 58(9), 2079–2091 (2018)
3. Christ, M., Braun, N., Neuffer, J., Kempa-Liehr, A.W.: Time series FeatuRe extraction on basis of scalable hypothesis tests (tsfresh – a Python package). Neurocomputing 307, 72–77 (2018). https://doi.org/10.1016/j.neucom.2018.03.067
4. Lijian, Z., Chen, Z., Zuowei, W., et al.: Hierarchical palmprint feature extraction and recognition based on multi-wavelets and complex network. IET Image Proc. 12(6), 985–992 (2018)
5. Taguchi, Y.-H.: Tensor decomposition-based and principal-component-analysis-based unsupervised feature extraction applied to the gene expression and methylation profiles in the brains of social insects with multiple castes. BMC Bioinform. 19(S4), 99 (2018)

6. Woo, J.-H., Kim, C.-W., Bang, T.-K., Lee, S.-H., Lee, K.-S., Choi, J.-Y.: Experimental verification and electromagnetic characteristic analysis of permanent magnet linear oscillating actuator using semi 3D analysis technique with corrected stacking factor. IEEE Trans. Appl. Supercond. **30**(4), 1–5 (2020). https://doi.org/10.1109/TASC.2020.2986737
7. Fu, W., Liu, S., Srivastava, G.: Optimization of big data scheduling in social networks. Entropy **21**(9), 902 (2019)
8. Liu, S., Li, Z., Zhang, Y., et al.: Introduction of key problems in long-distance learning and training. Mob. Netw. Appl. **24**(1), 1–4 (2019)
9. Liu, S., Lu, M., Li, H., et al.: Prediction of gene expression patterns with generalized linear regression model. Front. Genet. **10**, 120 (2019)
10. Takeuchi, K., Matsushita, M., Makino, H., Tsuboi, Y., Amemiya, N.: A novel modeling method for no-load saturation characteristics of synchronous machines using finite element analysis. IEEE Trans. Magn. **57**(2), 1–5 (2021). https://doi.org/10.1109/TMAG.2020.3010859

Enterprise Financial Risk Early Warning System Based on Catastrophe Progression Method

Bo Hou[(✉)] and Chang-song Ma

Mianyang Teachers' College, Mianyang 621000, China
houbo698@yeah.net

Abstract. When acquiring the risk data, the enterprise financial risk early warning system is easily influenced by the noise data, which leads to the early warning error and low warning accuracy. In order to solve this problem, a financial risk early warning system based on catastrophe progression method is designed. S3C2440A microprocessor is used as the core control module in the hardware part. In the software part, the abrupt progression method is used to mine the abnormal running state, calculate the correlation of the financial data of the risk state, and design the risk warning system after setting the residual value of risk warning. Experimental results show that the average response time of the risk early warning system is about 45 ms, and the accuracy is about 94%.

Keywords: Catastrophe series method · Corporate finance · Risk warning · Noise data

1 Introduction

In recent years, the economic environment of our country has been developing towards globalization. The risk factors in the economic environment are increasing day by day. High returns are corresponding to high risks. In the process of pursuing profit maximization, companies will inevitably face the challenges brought by risks. If they fail to actively respond to financial risks in a scientific and effective manner, they will probably fall into the financial crisis or even eventually go bankrupt [1]. In recent years, more and more companies in the capital market "flash in the pan" caused academic and practical areas of attention, began to explore how to keep the smooth state of the company continue to operate. In fact, the company from normal operation to the final bankruptcy will go through a gradual deterioration process. There are many influencing factors, possibly due to the allocation of resources, financing, cash management and many other factors, and these factors are usually significant in the financial performance. Therefore, the establishment of financial early warning system, the use of early warning indicators to help companies discover the financial risks, predicting the company's business potential problems in order to timely deal with, to prevent financial crisis.

© ICST Institute for Computer Sciences, Social Informatics and Telecommunications Engineering 2021
Published by Springer Nature Switzerland AG 2021. All Rights Reserved
W. Fu et al. (Eds.): ICMTEL 2021, LNICST 387, pp. 157–169, 2021.
https://doi.org/10.1007/978-3-030-82562-1_14

As for the financial early-warning, foreign scholars have been leading the research, in contrast, our country's relevant theoretical discussion and practical application are relatively weak, which leads to the lack of reliable theoretical support and model reference for our country's enterprise financial early-warning practice, often copying directly the research results of foreign earlier period, and cannot well adapt to the status quo of our enterprises [2]. At the same time, the traditional financial early-warning system is basically based on the accrual basis of accounting information, and its ability to reveal the actual operation of enterprises is bound to be restricted by the inherent limitations of accounting itself; in addition, the traditional financial early-warning system usually only focuses on the static analysis of cross-sectional data, cannot be very good to reveal the gradual process of crisis deterioration, and too much emphasis on complex mathematical model construction, which increases the difficulty of implementation of enterprises, and affects the actual application effect of financial early-warning research results. Thus, it is urgent to explore the financial early warning system with reliable information foundation, dynamic monitoring, scientific, practical and applicability. Therefore, this paper proposes a financial risk warning system based on catastrophe progression method. Through the design of hardware to support the operation of the system, in the software part, the abrupt progression method is adopted to mine the abnormal operation state, and the correlation of the financial data of the risk state is calculated. According to the set residual value of the risk warning, the dynamic warning of the risk is realized, the timely warning of the financial crisis is realized, the interference of the noise on the risk warning is solved, and the warning result is more accurate.

2   Hardware Design of Enterprise Financial Risk Warning System

2.1   Structure Design of Early Warning Platform

The hardware platform of risk warning system can be designed into four modules, which are microprocessor and memory module, reset and power conversion module, peripheral interface module and sensor signal preprocessing module. The peripheral interface module includes serial interface circuit, JTAG interface circuit, USB interface circuit, buzzer alarm interface circuit, sensor signal preprocessing module.

The early-warning platform uses S3C2440A microprocessor as the core control module, and the periphery includes the storage circuit module, voltage and reset module, peripheral interface module, sensor signal preprocessing module and other hardware platform bottom effects. The actual hardware connection is shown in the following Fig. 1:

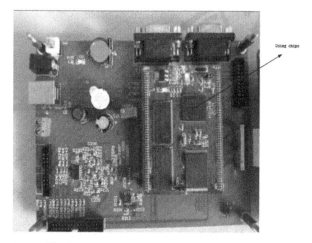

Fig. 1. Platform hardware connection diagram

In the above, under the hardware connection mode, S3C2440A microprocessor and memory circuit is located in the hardware system core board, other functional modules are located in the system bottom board, the core board and the bottom board through two rows of 2 × 50 pin to fix connection [3]. Serial port, JTAG port and USB port are designed on the hardware backplane, and FPC-40 interface is reserved for LCD screen. The connection with LCD screen can be realized through the switching wire. The hardware backplane of the engineering prototype is encapsulated in a box to meet the requirements of sealing. The interface between the power supply and the sensor is based on the original analog interface, which realizes good compatibility with the machine and reduces the cost of the system transformation [4]. The information processing system adopts S3C2440A microprocessor, which is a 16/32 bit Reduced Instruction Set (RISC) microprocessor of Samsung. S3C2440A uses ARM920T as its core, and adopts 0.13 μm CMOS standard macro cell and memory cell. Its low-power, simple and refined and fully static design can meet the requirements of low power and low cost of embedded system. The results of the integrated functions of the settings chip are as follows (Table 1):

Under the integrated functional control as shown in the table above, a risk early warning platform shall be established and the structure of the risk early warning system shall be as follows Fig. 2:

Table 1. Integrated functions of chips

Serial number	Name	Function
1	Address space	8 Bank
2	Simulation debugging	Support for JTAG
3	Real-time clock RTC	Oral calendar function
4	Multiplexed input/output port	130
5	External interrupt port	24
6	UART interface	Channel 3
7	Multi-host IIC bus interface	Channel 1
8	Multiplex ADC	Channel 8
9	Watchdog timer	16 digits
10	PWM timer	Channel 4
11	Internal buffer	4 KB
12	LCD private DMA	Channel 1

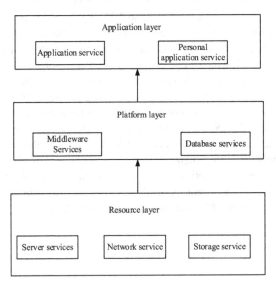

Fig. 2. Risk warning platform structure

Under the structure of the early warning platform shown above, the hardware connection circuit structure is designed.

2.2 Hardware Connection Circuit

In order to improve the accuracy of A/D conversion, ADC uses a separate power circuit, through the circuit filter and shielding measures to remove burr interference from the PCB board. VSSA is a standalone analog power source with a VDDA range of 2.0–3.6 V. The power supply area is: ADC circuit, reset module circuit, RC oscillator and PLL module analog circuit.

ADC works when VDD is greater than 2.4 V. USB works when VDD is greater than 2.7 V. Provides +1.8 V power for processors, memory, and peripherals in run mode, also known as main mode. In this mode, unused clocks on the APB and AHB buses can be turned off to reduce power dissipation. In stop mode, selectively provide a 1.8 V power supply to supply time-sharing power to certain modules, such as registers and SRAMs, to hold the data in them [5]. This mode is also known as the low power mode of the voltage regulator. In standby mode, the power of the processor circuit can be cut off, that is, the output of the regulator is in the high resistance state. The contents of the register and SRAM are all lost except for the backup circuit. This mode, also known as the off mode, is constructed as shown in the following illustration Fig. 3:

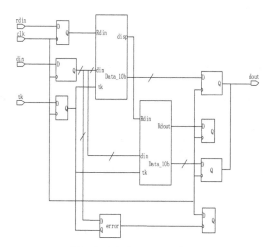

Fig. 3. Mode control circuit

In the regulatory circuit structure shown above, all registers are reset except for the reset flag in the clock-controlled CSR and the spare registers. The low level (external reset) of the S1 pin is associated with the time required, the power supply to the processor, the reset value, etc. [6]. In order to make it fully reset, in the +3.3 V power supply working conditions, reset time can be set to about 20 ms. The reset source will eventually act on the S1 pin and maintain a low level during the reset. The reset entry address is 0 × 00000004. The resulting reset circuit structure is shown in the following Fig. 4:

In the reset circuit structure shown above, the power range for setting the VDD is 2.0–3.6 V. A 3.3 V power supply is usually used to power circuits such as I/O interfaces. Built-in voltage regulator for the CPU core to provide the required 1.8 V high-precision

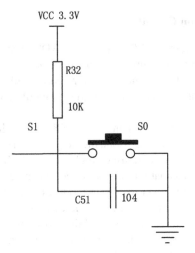

Fig. 4. Reset circuit structure

power. After designing the hardware structure of the early warning system, the software part of the early warning system is designed.

3 Software Design of Enterprise Financial Risk Warning System

3.1 Mining Abnormal Running State by Using Abrupt Progression Method

When diagnosing the running state of a real-time fee control system, the data of abnormal running state of the system shall first be mined and the mining process shown in the following figure shall be followed Fig. 5:

The mining process shown in the figure above, supported by the historical parameters of the operational state of the enterprise financial system, pre-processes the selected data, deletes redundant and inconsistent cleaning data, and unifies the standards for operational state data [7].

The financial system of an enterprise contains a financial system, which defines the relationship between the financial value output and the risk financial value. The expression formula is as follows:

$$P = \frac{1}{2} L_p \left(I^2, R \right) \tag{1}$$

In the above formula, The P represents the output financial data of the enterprise financial system, the L_p represents the data of the risk, the I represents the enterprise profit index, and the R represents the abrupt level parameter. Set the initial value of the cumulative sum in the financial system of the enterprise as 0, and calculate the cumulative sum of each abnormal state data S:

$$S = \sum_{k=1}^{i} \left(x_s - \bar{X} \right), i = 1, 2, 3 \ldots F \tag{2}$$

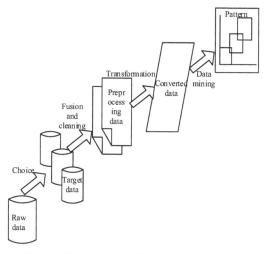

Fig. 5. Mining process for financial anomalies

Using the above formula, the extremum of the state data is calculated:

$$
\begin{cases}
S_{max} = \max_{k=1,2,\ldots F} S \\
S_{min} = \min_{k=1,2,\ldots F} S
\end{cases}
\tag{3}
$$

After calculating the extremes in each abnormal data sample, count the number of abnormal data samples between two extremes in the abnormal data sample, The formula defined as M, confidence λ of the abnormal data at this time is as follows:

$$
\lambda = \frac{M}{T} \times 100\%
\tag{4}
$$

In the above calculation formula, T represents the time series of sliding windows. Set the confidence limit as the warning index [8]. When the confidence limit is exceeded, the financial risk of the enterprise will occur. Based on the abnormal state obtained from the above mining, the relationship between financial data and abnormal state should be established when realizing risk early warning.

3.2 Process for Achieving Early Warning

In order to prevent the weak correlation between the above selected state data and the calculated confidence limits [9], the normal operation state of the error risk warning system and the correlation between the calculated state data, the calculation formula is as follows:

$$
r_i = \frac{\sum_{j=1}^{k} (x_{ij} - \bar{X})(y_j - \bar{y})}{\sqrt{\sum_{j=1}^{k} (x_{ij} - \bar{X})^2} \sqrt{\sum_{j=1}^{k} (y_j - \bar{y})^2}}
\tag{5}
$$

In the above formula, The r_i represents the correlation coefficient of the i state data, x_{ij} represents the i sample value of the j state data, y_j represents the j sample data in the run state, $\bar{y}$ represents the mean value of the state data in the running state. Define the relevance of r_i values in the above calculation formula as follows:

$$\begin{cases} |r_i| = 0 \\ 0.3 \geq |r_i| > 0 \\ 0.6 \geq |r_i| > 0.3 \\ 0.8 \geq |r_i| > 0.6 \\ 1 \geq |r_i| > 0.8 \\ |r_i| = 1 \end{cases} \tag{6}$$

The quantitative relationship of r_i is defined according to the above formula. When the r_i value is 0, there is no correlation between each state data sample. If the absolute value of the r_i is greater than 0 and less than 0.3, there is no correlation. If the absolute value of the r_i is greater than 0.3 and less than 0.6, there is a low correlation. If the absolute value of the r_i is greater than 0.6 and less than 0.8, the running state data shows a significant correlation. When the absolute value of the r_i is greater than 0.8 and less than 1, there is a high correlation. When the absolute value of the r_i is 1, the running data show complete correlation. According to the above definitions, the relationship between the financial data of the enterprise and the running time of the system is obtained, as shown in the following Fig. 6:

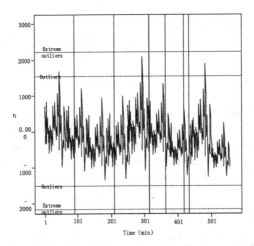

Fig. 6. Abnormal values of the running state of a fee- control system

The residual threshold shall be set up for the abnormal value of the operating conditions as shown in the above figure. When the risk occurs to the financial data of an enterprise, the residual threshold appears and drives the collecting central station in the structure of the early warning system to give early warning [10]. Based on the above research and analysis, the final design of the enterprise financial risk warning system based on catastrophe series method.

4 System Testing

4.1 Build Test Environment

When building a test environment, use a computer with known parameters. The selected computer parameters are shown in the following Table 2:

Table 2. Computer parameters used

Serial number	Name	Parameter
1	Hard disk	128 GB SSD
2	Video card	NVIDIA GT 999M
3	Memory	8 GB DDR1600
4	CPU	Intel core i7-4527QM
5	Optical drive	DVD-E818A4 119

Under the parameters shown in the table above, using Windows CE drivers can be structurally divided into Native Driver and Stream Driver. Local drivers are generally used for built-in, low-level devices, managed by GWES, generally in the system boot is loaded, in the registry also has the corresponding configuration information. The interfaces to implement them are not uniform and the development process is relatively complex. Set the development process for the software as shown below Fig. 7:

Fig. 7. Software development environment

In the software development environment shown in the figure above, after connecting to the CDN server, set up the test environment shown in the Fig. 8:

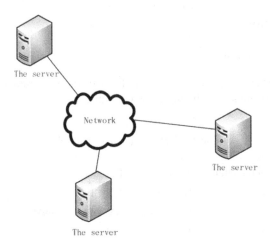

Fig. 8. Test environment built

In the above test environment, we use the traditional risk early warning system, [5] risk early warning system and the designed early warning system to compare the performance of the three types of early warning systems.

4.2 Analysis of Test Results

Based on the above experimental preparation, the selected financial risks of enterprises shall be transformed into data sources and input into the three risk warning systems. When the corrected dimensions and measurements are correct, the risk warning information at the same level shall be cached, and repeated requests for the same risk warning system shall be made 10 times, and the time from the initiation of the requests to the return of the data of the three risk warning systems shall be recorded. The task request time results of the three risk warning systems are as follows Fig. 9:

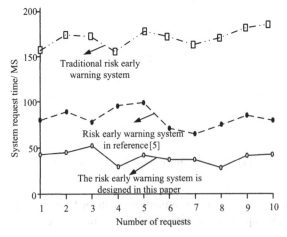

Fig. 9. System task request time

Under the same level of enterprise financial risk information, the task request time of the traditional risk early warning system is the longest, and the average task request time is about 220 ms under ten times of requests. The average task request time of the risk early warning system in [5] is about 180 ms and the request time is relatively short. The average task request time of the financial risk early-warning system designed in this paper is about 90 ms, which greatly corrects the shortcomings of the two existing risk early-warning systems. The average task response time of the risk early warning system is about 45 ms. Compared with the existing risk early warning system, the risk early warning system is the fastest to deal with the financial level data.

Under the aforesaid experimental environment, the financial scale of the enterprise for the past three years shall be determined, and the financial investment scale results shall be as follows (Table 3):

Table 3. Corporate financial risk data set

Project name	2017	2018	2019
Monetary capital	73.36%	73.36%	76.17%
Inventory	0.02%	1.32%	0.01%
Accounts receivable	2.18%	13.98%	1.80%
Prepaid and other receivables	2.18%	5.46%	2.32%
Due from subsidiaries	2.21%	2.46%	12.60%
Investment in other equity instruments	13.98%	5.86%	5.19%
Total current assets	5.84%	2.18%	0.73%
Fixed assets	97.59%	76.4%	1.91%
Long-term equity investments	1.08%	0.01%	25.4%
Deferred income tax assets	0.01%	76.17%	1.15%
Total non-current assets	1.32%	2.41%	2.32%

Under the control of the aforesaid risk data, the three risk early warning systems shall deal with the values shown in the above table, correspond to the names of various items in the above table, and make statistics on the accuracy of the early warning of the three risk early warning systems. The accuracy rate is as follows (Table 4):

According to the results of early warning accuracy shown in the above table, three kinds of financial risk early warning systems show different accuracy results. Based on the numerical changes of all the above-mentioned enterprise risk indicators, the accuracy rate of the traditional risk early warning system is the smallest, about 70%, and the accuracy rate of the risk early warning system in the [5] Document is larger, about 85%. The risk early warning system designed in this paper has the greatest accuracy, the accuracy of the value of 94%.

Table 4. Accuracy of three risk warning systems

Project name	Accuracy/%		
	Traditional risk early warning system	Risk early warning system in literature [5]	Risk warning system designed in this paper
Currency funds	67.6	87.8	93.1
Inventory	73.3	84.2	93.3
Accounts receivable	68.1	87.3	93.2
Advances and other receivables	74.3	80.7	95.8
Due from subsidiaries	66.9	86.8	95.6
Investment in other equity instruments	65.6	83.4	94.1
Total current assets	65.2	87.5	92.9
Fixed assets	74.3	87.9	92.8
Long-term equity investments	72.5	84.5	93.9
Deferred income tax assets	67.4	82.8	92.5
Total non-current assets	67.6	87.8	93.1

Based on the above experimental results, the risk early warning system designed in this paper has the shortest task request time and the largest accuracy rate.

5   Concluding Remarks

Designing an early-warning system of enterprise financial risk based on catastrophe progression method can provide more scientific, reliable and practical early-warning system for enterprises, improve the ability of management, help operators to monitor the financial status and operation of enterprises in real time, explore and construct an early-warning system of enterprise financial risk which is scientific, reliable and practical, and provide theory and method reference for enterprise financial early-warning management.

References

1. Yuqiong, L., Zhenqiang, Z.: Evaluation on the open innovation ability of nuclear power enterprises: based on improved catastrophe progression method. Sci. Technol. Manage. Res. **40**(10), 80–86 (2020)

2. Tedeschi, G., Caccioli, F., Recchioni, M.C.: Taming financial systemic risk: models, instruments and early warning indicators. J. Econ. Interact. Coord. **15**, 1–7 (2020)
3. Lingang, T., Qiyuan, H.: Study on the influencing factors of ecological? Health in small watershed by catastrophe progression method. Yellow River **42**(4), 71–75+80 (2020)
4. Qiu, W.: Enterprise financial risk management platform based on 5G mobile communication and embedded system. Microprocess. Microsyst. **80**, 103594 (2021)
5. Zhu, J.P., Wang, H.C.: Application of unbalanced data classification algorithm in quantitative financial risk management. J. Phys. Conf. Ser. **1648**(4), 042093 (2020)
6. Shang, H., Lu, D., Zhou, Q.: Early warning of enterprise finance risk of big data mining in internet of things based on fuzzy association rules. Neural Comput. Appl. **33**(9), 3901–3909 (2020). https://doi.org/10.1007/s00521-020-05510-5
7. Asadi, M., Mohammadi, A., Bakhshi, A.A.A.: Rating of Iran banking sector based on CAMELS model. J. Financ. Anal. **3**(1), 47–70 (2020)
8. Fu, W., Liu, S., Srivastava, G.: Optimization of big data scheduling in social networks. Entropy **21**(9), 902 (2019)
9. Liu, S., Li, Z., Zhang, Y., et al.: Introduction of key problems in long-distance learning and training. Mobile Netw. Appl. **24**(1), 1–4 (2019)
10. Hao-yi, W., Yu-fang, B., Rui-fang, Z., et al.: Prediction of quality product risk based on extreme learning machine. Comput. Simul. **36**(10), 413–418 (2019)

Research on Transportation Route Planning Method of Regional Logistics Network Based on Transfer Learning

Bo Hou[(✉)] and Chang-song Ma

Mianyang Teachers' College, Mianyang 621000, China
houbo698@yeah.net

Abstract. China is in a period of rapid development of various modes of transportation, comprehensive transportation network is developing and improving rapidly, and the scope of regional logistics network transportation is also expanding. The comprehensive transportation system is the key direction of China's transportation development in the future. It is an important basis for the social and economic development and the improvement of residents' living standards, and is also the main functional element of logistics activities. Therefore, based on transfer learning, this paper designs a transportation path planning method for regional logistics network. Based on the construction of regional logistics network transportation path node and the determination of transportation path objective function, the optimal scheme of regional logistics network transportation path planning is selected. The experimental results show that: compared with the traditional transportation path planning method, this method can reduce the loss of transportation funds and time in logistics network to a greater extent.

Keywords: Regional logistics network · Logistics path planning · Migration learning · Path objective function · Optimal planning

1 Introduction

With the rapid growth of the overall scale and the rapid expansion of infrastructure in China's logistics industry, the problems of unscientific resource allocation and application, and imprecise design of operation process have exposed [1, 2], resulting in the low operation efficiency and high comprehensive cost of the traditional regional logistics network transportation path planning method, and the operation management mechanism and construction theory and method are difficult to meet the needs of the rapid development of the logistics industry [3]. The optimization of regional logistics network transportation path planning is to optimize the design of each link and element of logistics network, so as to improve the efficiency of the whole logistics network system. Therefore, the path optimization problem has its practical economic and academic significance, the effect of regional logistics network route optimization will directly

© ICST Institute for Computer Sciences, Social Informatics and Telecommunications Engineering 2021
Published by Springer Nature Switzerland AG 2021. All Rights Reserved
W. Fu et al. (Eds.): ICMTEL 2021, LNICST 387, pp. 170–179, 2021.
https://doi.org/10.1007/978-3-030-82562-1_15

determine the result of the whole logistics network optimization. Therefore, it is necessary to conduct in-depth research on the transportation route planning of the regional logistics network.

Reference [4] proposes a ship emergency logistics path planning method based on a two-layer ant colony optimization algorithm, establishes a ship emergency logistics path planning model, and then uses particle swarm optimization to quickly find a feasible solution set of ship emergency logistics paths. Take it as the initial information of ants, and finally search for the optimal route of ship emergency logistics based on the initial information, and conduct simulation test of ship emergency logistics route planning. Experimental results show that this method can accurately solve the problem of ship emergency logistics route planning, but the logistics network transportation cost is higher. Reference [5] proposed a port logistics distribution path planning method based on artificial fish swarm algorithm. According to the port logistics distribution path planning framework, the port demand point node expression form was designed, and path planning constraints were set. According to the constraint conditions combined with the VPR mathematical model, the construction of the distribution route planning model is completed. The artificial fish school algorithm is used to simulate the distribution process as a fish school foraging process, and the optimal travel direction and distance are selected to optimize the above-mentioned set path planning model. Experimental results show that this method has the problem of long time loss in logistics network transportation.

Aiming at the problems of traditional methods, a regional logistics network transportation route planning method based on migration learning is proposed. Based on transfer learning, this study explores the transportation path planning method of regional logistics network, optimizes the transportation path by means of data modeling, and focuses on solving the methods of reducing transportation time and cost on each transportation node, and improving the feasibility of the optimal path. From the strategic planning level of "network optimization" and the tactical planning level of "transportation service design", this paper puts forward the optimization theory and method to strengthen the coordination and coordination of regional logistics network transportation and improve the system operation efficiency. The experimental results show that the method in this paper effectively reduces the transportation cost and time of the regional logistics network, and its application performance is significantly better than traditional methods.

2   Design of Transportation Route Planning Method

Logistics network optimization is the design and optimization of all links and elements of the logistics network. Regional logistics route optimization is a key part of the overall optimization of regional logistics. Through specific analysis of the relevant theories and algorithm design of route optimization, the research finds solutions to regional logistics route optimization. The idea and method of the problem. Therefore, in view of the inability to select the optimal route in the traditional transportation route method and solve the high transportation cost, migration learning is used to optimize the transportation route method of the regional logistics network, and the collected data is analyzed by algorithm to realize the transportation route planning method design.

2.1 Construction of Transportation Path Node in Regional Logistics Network

Transfer learning is a machine learning method that uses a model for task development as an initial point and reuses it in another development model. In the computer vision tasks and natural language processing tasks of deep learning, it is a common method to use the pre-trained model as the starting point of the new model. Usually these pre-training models have consumed huge time resources and computing resources when developing neural networks, and transfer learning can transfer the acquired powerful skills to the related modeling process, thereby reducing time and resource consumption. For this reason, based on the transfer learning theory, the data collection process of the transportation route is shown in Fig. 1.

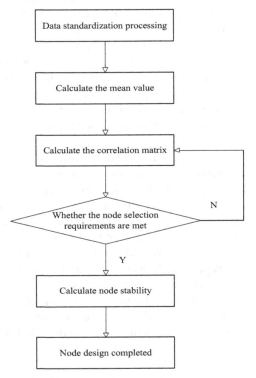

Fig. 1. Transportation path data acquisition process

The construction of logistics nodes in the regional logistics network based on migration learning is to screen multiple logistics nodes in regional logistics. The selection of logistics nodes is the focus of the construction of the entire logistics network. According to the construction ideas and principles, the final regional logistics node is selected by considering the method of transfer learning. The specific process is as follows:

First of all, the internal cause of regional logistics network is the internal structure of logistics network, namely point, line and surface. The essence of the screening of logistics nodes based on internal factors, especially the selection of regional hub logistics nodes, is to analyze, evolve and optimize the regional logistics network structure characteristics, especially in the regional logistics network structure relationship characteristics and regional logistics network optimization model; secondly, in the same region, due to the different economic development level and social and economic conditions of each region Similarly, the status of logistics nodes in regional logistics system is different. It is necessary to comprehensively consider these external factors affecting the selection of logistics node level.

The logistics nodes with different scales, functions, levels, and service scopes selected according to internal and external factors constitute a relatively distinct regional logistics node system. Screen different nodes and determine the specific tasks and scales by determining the layout of each node in the entire regional logistics network.

2.2 Determine the Objective Function of the Transportation Path

Based on the above transfer learning, the transport path planning model is constructed. Let the directed graph $G = (A, B)$ (edge weight $a \geq 0$), divide the node set A in the graph into two groups. The first group is the node set g with the shortest path calculated (there is only one source node in the initial A, i.e. the source point a_0 of the transportation path), and the second group is the node set A whose shortest path has not been determined. The nodes in the A set are moved out to g according to the increasing order of the shortest path length, that is, each shortest path is obtained, the nodes in the shortest path searched are moved from set A to g until all nodes of the graph are added to g, and the algorithm is finished. In the process of iterative operation, always maintain the principle that the shortest path length from source point a_0 to each node in g is not greater than the shortest path length from source point a_0 to any node in A. In addition, each node corresponds to a distance. The distance of the node in g is the shortest path length from j_0 to this node, and the distance of the node in A is only from g to this node. Only the nodes in g are intermediate nodes. The current shortest path length of, the specific application of the following formula to construct the data model:

The objective function considers the cost involved in the completion of the collection task, which is mainly composed of fixed investment cost, transportation cost, storage cost and handling cost [6].

Among them, the fixed investment cost, namely the fixed construction cost, is closely related to the geographical location and economic development level of the alternative nodes. For each node A, a fixed construction cost g_i will be generated, the fixed investment cost is as follows:

$$GT = \sum_{a \in A}^{n} g_a \times z_a \tag{1}$$

In the transportation process of collection, based on the above assumptions, since each node a has a certain damage probability p (the damage probability p conforms to the independent distribution [7]), and any node task with a transportation volume of t_i At the beginning of the execution, it is impossible to know the status of each collection center due to the incomplete information. Therefore, each task sent from the demand point i must pass some different collection centers to meet the demand, so some Additional transportation distances increase transportation costs.

During the transportation of the tasks from demand point i, they will pass through the collection center in turn. If node a_i^1 is not damaged for the first time, then the task is completed and there is no need to visit other node centers. The probability is $(1 - p)$. At this time, the transportation distance from demand point i to node center a_i^1 is d_i. Otherwise, the collection task from demand point i must continue to pass through other node centers in set A in order. From the node center a_i^i to the node center a_i^{i-1}, there will be an additional transportation distance d_i, which will increase the transportation cost. At the same time, it also shows that the node center $\{a_i^1, a_i^2, \ldots, a_i^n\}$ previously visited will be damaged, and the probability of this situation will be p^{i-1}. at this time, the transportation distance from the demand point i to the node center a_i^i is $d_i + \sum_{i=2}^{i} p^{i-1}$, then the total transportation distance can be expressed as follows:

$$D = d_i + \sum_{i=2}^{n} p^{i-1} \times d_{ij} \tag{2}$$

Integrate the above two formulas to obtain the objective function of the transportation route planning result, and use this as the basis for the optimal route selection.

2.3 Selection of Optimal Scheme for Transportation Route Planning of Regional Logistics Network

Using the transportation path planning model constructed above as the basis of this route planning, the paper optimizes the transportation path of regional logistics network by means of transfer learning, and obtains the optimal path. Path planning is carried out from the source node [8, 9], simulation planning is carried out at the next node by using transfer learning, and the above process is repeated to obtain the optimal path.

Initially, let $i = 0$ and g contain only the source node a_0, that is, the distance between $g = \{a_0\}$ and a_0 is 0; A contains other nodes except a_0, that is: $A = \{A - a_0\}$. If node a_i in A has edge r_i, then the weight value between (a_i, a_k) is α (that is, the weight of edge e_i). If node a_k is not the adjacent node of the outgoing edge of node f_i, the weight of (a_i, a_k) is $+\infty$;

Select a node l with the smallest distance d_i from A, remove node l from A and add it to g, let $l = i$; take node a_i as the new intermediate point, update the a_k distance of the remaining nodes in J. If the distance from the source point a_0 to node a_k is shorter than the previous distance (without passing through vertex i), the distance value of node a_k is modified; the modified distance value is the distance of node a_i plus the weight of edge (a_i, a_k). Repeat the above steps until all nodes are included in R, and the path planning is finished.

In this design, part of the path selection operation is designed, and the specific process is as follows: The selection operation is to select individuals with higher fitness values from the population individuals in the previous step to ensure that the genetic algorithm approaches the optimal solution. In the selection operation, the greater the chromosome fitness value [10], the greater the probability of being selected, that is, the better feasible solution individual can get a greater survival probability.

In this design, during the selection operation, the more common roulette mechanism is adopted, the population size is R, the fitness f_i of all individuals is calculated separately, and the sum F_i of the fitness of all individuals is calculated, as shown below:

$$F_i = \sum_{i=1}^{R} f \tag{3}$$

The probability P_i of individual m being selected is calculated as follows:

$$P_i = f_i / F_i \tag{4}$$

Calculate the cumulative probability P_i of each point, then:

$$P_i = \sum_{i=1}^{R} P_n \tag{5}$$

Randomly generate a real number δ in the interval of $[0, 1]$. If $P_1 > \delta$, select individual 1, otherwise select individual q to make $P_{i-1} < \delta \leq P_i$. Repeat the above settings until the optimal route is reached. So far, the design of the regional logistics network transportation route planning method based on transfer learning is completed.

3 Experimental Analysis

In order to verify the feasibility of the regional logistics network transportation route planning method based on transfer learning, the following experiments are designed.

3.1 Experimental Environment Setting

In the experiment, 100 sampling points of different experimental paths are randomly set in the regional logistics network of a city to form a whole set of sampling points. The distribution of some of the sampling points is shown in Fig. 2.

In Fig. 2, each digital node represents the nodes passed by the regional logistics network transportation process. The migration learning-based regional logistics network transportation path planning method and traditional path planning method designed in the article are used to carry out the experimental path samples set above. Transportation planning.

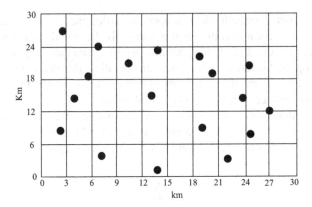

Fig. 2. Sample node setting points of experimental path

3.2 Experimental Process Setting

Under the same road conditions, using the same type of vehicles for regional logistics transportation, the average cost of vehicles per kilometer is 25 yuan, and 10 experiments are carried out. After the completion of the experiment, the cost and time of two different methods of vehicles were compared for statistics. Due to the different transport capacity of the three different transportation routes, in the regional logistics network, the transit capacity of different transport modes of nodes is also different, and the corresponding cost and time consumption of transportation modes among different nodes are generated, as shown in Table 1.

Table 1. Time and cost of unit transfer between different modes of transportation

Cost/yuan (time/h)	Rail transport	Road transport	Waterway transportation
Rail transport	0(0)	6(5.0)	8(10.0)
Road transport	6(5.0)	0(0)	12(15.0)
Waterway transportation	8(10.0)	12(15.0)	0(0)

3.3 Analysis of Results

According to the experimental process set above, the method set in the text and the traditional method data are counted in the form of a table. The specific results are shown in Table 2.

It can be seen intuitively from Table 2 that compared to the traditional path planning method, the regional logistics network transportation path planning method designed in this paper consumes less time and cost.

Table 2. Data analysis of experimental results

Experimental project	The method of this paper		Traditional method 1		Traditional method 2	
	Cost/yuan	Time/h	Cost/yuan	Time/h	Cost/yuan	Time/h
1	5400	5.12	5931	6.13	5400	5.04
2	5369	5.13	6010	6.03	5369	5.13
3	5421	5.02	5946	6.23	5421	5.02
4	5412	5.16	5972	6.07	5931	5.16
5	5389	5.01	5940	6.09	6010	5.24
6	5412	5.01	5945	6.03	5946	5.01
7	5436	5.04	5987	6.13	5931	5.04
8	5378	5.13	5936	6.24	5378	5.13
9	5401	5.18	5899	6.15	5971	5.04
10	5412	5.06	5976	6.07	5412	5.06

The optimal solution of the path calculated by different methods is shown in Fig. 3. It needs to go through the following nodes to make it consume the least resources to complete the transportation between nodes.

Analyzing Fig. 3, it can be seen that the traditional route planning method has the phenomenon of line duplication during the vehicle transportation process, so that it consumes more time and cost and causes a waste of resources. Therefore, the transportation route planning method designed in the article is better than the traditional method. The distribution route diagram designed in this paper conforms to the distribution habits. In a small area, within the limitation of the loading capacity of the logistics vehicle, a logistics vehicle is used for delivery. Considering the overall scope, in a relatively remote area, the use of an electric logistics vehicle for overall distribution to customers in a region has proved that it is reasonable and effective to use migration learning to solve the logistics vehicle distribution path planning problem.

In order to further verify the effectiveness of the method in this paper, considering the various influencing factors in the logistics transportation path, using the stability of the planning method as an experimental indicator, comparing the path stability obtained by different methods of planning, the results are shown in Fig. 4.

The analysis of Fig. 4 shows that the stability coefficient of logistics transportation path under this method is significantly higher than that of traditional methods, which indicates that this method can reduce the influence of interference factors on path planning, thus improving the effectiveness of this method.

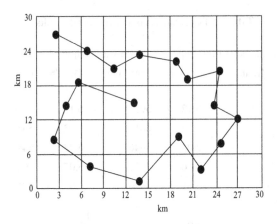

(A) Design method in the text

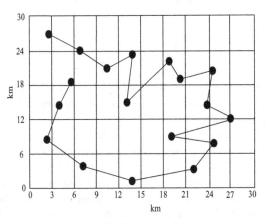

(b) Traditional method 1

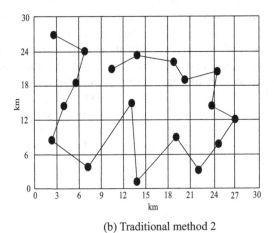

(b) Traditional method 2

Fig. 3. Experimental results of path planning

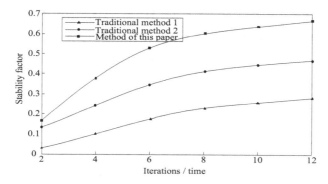

Fig. 4. Comparison of path planning stability

4 Conclusion

In the traditional transportation route selection process, due to the uncontrollability of the road information, the vehicle can not choose the optimal path in the transportation process, which increases the transportation cost to a certain extent. In order to reduce the cost of time and money, regional logistics network transportation adopts transfer learning as the basis of transportation path planning to carry out path planning. Through the above experimental results, we can see that the results of the transportation path planning in this paper are better than the traditional methods. We should vigorously promote the transportation path planning method in the future regional logistics network, so as to better reduce the various costs of regional logistics network transportation and improve economic benefits.

References

1. Xu, W., Zhang, Q., Zou, Y., et al.: Research on transportation path planning for logistics UAV based on improved A* Algorithm. J. East China Jiaotong Univ. **36**(06), 39–46 (2019)
2. Zhang, Q., Weiwei, X., Zhang, H., et al.: Path planning for logistics UAV in complex low-altitude airspace . J. Beijing Univ. Aeronautics Astronautics **46**(07), 1275–1286 (2020)
3. Jie, Z., Hu, H., Sun, Q., et al.: Vehicle path planning based on improved drosophila algorithm. J. Heilongjiang Univ. Sci. Technol. **30**(02),187–192+204 (2020)
4. Zou, J., Yuan, X., Luo, J.: Research on ship emergency logistics path planning based on double-layer ant colony optimization. Ship Sci. Technol. **41**(16), 209–211 (2019)
5. Cui, Y., Liu, M.: Research on port logistics distribution path planning based on artificial fish swarm algorithm. Ship Sci. Technol. **42**(06), 194–196 (2020)
6. Fu, W., Liu, S., Srivastava, G.: Optimization of big data scheduling in social networks. Entropy **21**(9), 902–918 (2019)
7. Liu, S., Liu, D., Srivastava, G., et al.: Overview and methods of correlation filter algorithms in object tracking. Complex Intell. Syst. (2020) (3)
8. Guo, X., Yang, X., Wang, W.: The design of smart car based on segmented combined path planning algorithm. J. Zhongyuan Univ. Technol. **30**(05), 27–30+35 (2019)
9. Xu, L., Huang B., Zhong H.: Time window model and algorithm with AGV system path planning. J. Guangxi Normal Univ. (Natural Science Edition) **37**(03), 1–8 (2019)
10. Zhou, Z., Zhang, M.:The optimal planning method of spatial distribution of urban public service facilities. Comput. Simul. **36**(01), 480–483 (2019)

Simultaneous Localization of Multiple Defects in Software Testing Based on Reinforcement Learning

Jiajuan Fang[1](✉) and Yanjing Lu[2]

[1] Department of Software Engineering, Zhengzhou Technical College, Zhengzhou 450121, China
[2] Zhengzhou Technical College, Zhengzhou, China

Abstract. At present, most software defect localization methods focus on single defect localization, but few on multi-defect localization. Therefore, the multi-defect localization method based on reinforcement learning is proposed. By using genetic algorithm, the candidate distribution population can be transformed into a sort of suspicious value of real program entity, and the location of multiple defects in software testing can be realized simultaneously. Experimental results show that, compared with the average evaluation index of the existing methods, the evaluation index $EXAM_F$ of the proposed method is reduced by 1.19 and $EXAM_L$ reduced by 1.05, which shows that the proposed method has better positioning performance and is suitable for popularization.

Keywords: Reinforcement learning · Software testing · Multiple defects · Positioning · Genetic algorithm

1 Introduction

With the development of computer industry, software has become an indispensable part of modern information society. In order to meet the application requirements of various industries, the scale and complexity of software are increasing [1]. Due to complex requirements, imperfect project management, unreasonable development methods, imperfect development tools, irregular coding and so on, the number of bugs in software is increasing, and accidents are happening constantly. For example, in 1963, an American exploration rocket bound for Mars exploded because of a programmer's error. In the 1991 Gulf War, a Patriot missile killed 28 American soldiers stationed in Saudi Arabia because of a faulty system clock; In 1996, an Ariana rocket exploded due to a software flaw, causing great losses to the country and society; In 2000, a century-old computer software system crashed because of a design flaw, leading to costly software upgrades for all industries. In 2011, a design flaw in signalling equipment led to the July 23 high-speed train crash in Wenzhou. Although software provides people with a better quality of life, the economic loss, social loss and image loss caused by software defects are immeasurable.

© ICST Institute for Computer Sciences, Social Informatics and Telecommunications Engineering 2021
Published by Springer Nature Switzerland AG 2021. All Rights Reserved
W. Fu et al. (Eds.): ICMTEL 2021, LNICST 387, pp. 180–190, 2021.
https://doi.org/10.1007/978-3-030-82562-1_16

In order to guarantee the quality of software, a lot of testing is needed. But if the use case fails, the developer needs to check the code and find the defects. According to a 2002 report by the National Institute of Standards and Technology (NIST), software defects cost the US economy about $59.5 billion (0.6% of GDP) a year, and more than half of the cost of fixing or responding to them is borne by software users, with software developers and vendors paying the rest. In addition, for large software, large defect data makes direct manual inspection difficult. For example, Firefox receives up to 2.5 million software crashes a day, making it extremely difficult to locate defects manually. Therefore, how to use the existing information to quickly locate the defects in the software has become an important issue for researchers.

When the software fails, it needs to locate the software defects, which is one of the most expensive activities in the software development process. Finding an efficient software defect location technology is an important research topic. Testing is an important step in the software development process. Software defect location technology needs to use the information generated from testing for software defect location analysis. At present, most of the software defect location methods mainly focus on the problem of internal defect location under the assumption of single defect, but not enough on the unknown number of defects and system testing. In this paper, making a deep research on these problems, and propose a multi-defect simultaneous localization method for software testing based on reinforcement learning. Augmented learning is one of the paradigms and methodologies of machine learning, which is used to describe and solve the problem of agent maximizing reward or achieving specific goals through learning strategies in interaction with the environment. It hope to enhance the efficiency of bug location in software testing by enhancing the application of learning. It is innovation lies in the introduction of genetic algorithm, which transforms the candidate distribution population into a suspicious value of real program entity, and realizes the simultaneous localization of multiple defects in software testing, so as to enhance the superiority of genetic algorithm and improve the application performance of evaluation index.

2 Research on Simultaneous Location of Multiple Defects in Software Testing

2.1 Simultaneous Location of Multiple Defects Architecture

In order to meet the needs of today's social software, design multi-defect localization architecture for software testing based on reinforcement learning.

Reinforcement learning consists of mobile networks and evaluation networks. Mobile networks are the best thing you can do to your environment at the next moment, based on your current state [2]. For mobile networks, the reinforcement learning algorithm allows its output nodes to be randomly searched. With internal reinforcement signals from the assessment network, the output nodes of the mobile network can efficiently perform random searches and greatly improve the likelihood of selecting good actions, while training the entire mobile network online [3]. Using an auxiliary network to model the environment, the assessment network uses external reinforcement signals for predicting scalar values based on the current state and simulation environment, so that it can predict one-step and multi-step action reinforcement signals currently imposed on the environment by the action network, and can provide advance reinforcement signals to the action network on candidate actions, as well as more rewarding and discouraging information (internal reinforcement signals) to reduce uncertainty and increase learning speed. The reinforcement learning structure is shown in Fig. 1.

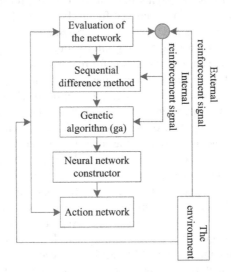

Fig. 1. Diagram of reinforcement learning structure

Based on Fig. 1, strengthen learning to build multiple defects in software testing and locate the architecture simultaneously, as shown in Fig. 2.

As shown in Fig. 2, multi-defect localization in software testing is divided into two stages. The first stage uses genetic algorithms to initialize the multi-defect population; then performs selection, crossover, and mutation operators to generate new individuals and add them to the population. At the same time, the Multi-Ochiai doubtful degree coefficient is used as the fitness value to evaluate the individuals and evolve into a new population. If the termination conditions are met, the final optimal multi-defect population will be obtained. Then enter the second stage, according to the optimal distribution of multiple defects in the program to get the corresponding entity suspicious ranking, the end of the algorithm [4].

2.2 Positioning Basic Block Partition

A basic block is a sequence of statements executed sequentially in a program, in which there is only one entry and one exit. In a method of defect location based on spectrum information, statements in the same basic block have the same coverage information, that is, they have the same degree of suspicion, and in the list of doubts, statements in the same basic block cannot distinguish the priority of the statements being checked [5]. Due to space limitations, this study shows only part of the code, as shown in Table 1.

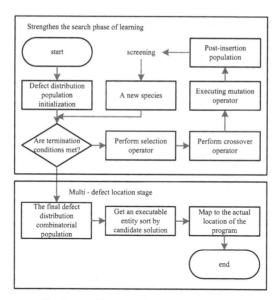

Fig. 2. Simultaneous localization architecture diagram for multiple defects in software testing

Table 1. Code part suspicious degree calculation result table

Code line number	Tarantula	Ochiai	Tarantula*
13	0.667	0.707	0.667
14	0.545	0.375	0.205
15	0.545	0.375	0.205
16	0.769	0.625	0.481

As shown in Table 1, the statements with line numbers 14 and 15 belong to a basic block, and the two lines of code are equally doubtful as calculated using Tarantula, Ochiai, and Tarantula *. Collecting and calculating every statement information in a basic block is a repetitive work, so the basic block is studied as the basic unit of defect location.

In this study, the object of study is mainly C language, C language contains a choice of structure switch and looping mechanism, while, etc., need to extend the definition of the basic block. Locating a basic block is a sequence of statements that, in a high-level language, are executed sequentially and without interruption. As shown in Table 2, the division method of various basic blocks of structure in C language is given.

As shown in Table 2, the execution of the switch (…) select structure statement in the absence of deterministic input data does not determine whether the case was executed or not. Therefore, the switch (…) is divided into one basic block, and each case is divided into one basic block. For the code with nested program statement types, the code in the basic block is further partitioned according to the partitioning rules. If the case 1 in the switch statement contains an if structure statement, the code in location block 2 is divided again according to the partitioning rules, dividing the location block 2 into five basic blocks.

Table 2. C basic block partitioning table

Sequential structure	if	switch	for	while
A...; B...; C...;	If(...) 1 {... 2}	Switch() 1 case1: {... 2}	for(...) 1 {... 2}	while() 1 {... 2}
-	else {... 3}	case2: {... 3}	–	–

In the unit level defect location, dividing the whole code into basic location blocks can effectively merge the repetition information in the coverage matrix, simplify the coverage matrix and reduce the repetition suspicious calculation process. The basic block partition of the find Second function results $\left\{ \begin{array}{l} \{2\}, \{3\}, \{4, 5\}, \{7, 8\}, \{10\}, \{11, 12\}, \{13\}, \\ \{14, 15\}, \{17\}, \{19\}, \{20\}, \{21\}, \{22\}, \{24\} \end{array} \right\}$ in a simplification of the cover matrix of 24×17 to that of 24×14. In addition, the length of chromosome coding can be reduced and the search efficiency can be improved by using ELT to search defect combinations.

2.3 Genetic Algorithm for Searching Optimal Population

Optimizing reinforcement learning algorithm with genetic algorithm, so genetic algorithm is used to search the optimal population and obtain the combination of defects in software testing. This section is divided into four stages, namely, hitting set, chromosome coding, fitness value function and genetic operator, the specific content of each stage as shown below.

Stage One: Hitting Set.

For a set cluster $Z = \{S_1, S_2, \cdots S_n\}$, if the set S_H satisfies $S_1 \cap S_H \neq \emptyset, S_2 \cap S_H \neq \emptyset, \ldots S_n \cap S_H \neq \emptyset$, then the set S_H is said to be the hitting set of the set cluster Z. If S_H any subset of a set is not the hitting set of a set cluster Z, it is the smallest hitting set S_H of the set cluster Z.

For a set $F = \{f_1, f_2, \cdots f_n\}$ of location-based blocks, if all failed test cases F have at least one location-based block f_i in execution, then F is a defect combination. For a program that contains defects, there are multiple combinations of defects $F_{accuracy}$. In all combinations of defects, there is only one combination of defects that contains all defects. This combination of defects is called. Is the accurate solution of defect location, defect location is approximation $F_{accuracy}$.

In a test case, the failed use case overrides the information set cluster $L = \{C_1, C_2, \cdots C_n\}$, where the locating base block C_i representing the i failed use case overrides the information set. Before locating defects, it is necessary to be able to explain all the failure test cases, that is, each failure test case must cover at least one location-based block, so the defect combination is the hitting set of the failure use case coverage F information set. In this study, the failure case overrides the hitting set of information set clusters L as a guess of defect combination. The main step of solving the hitting set of the information set covered by the failed use cases is to form a hitting set by a set, and construct the hitting set for each element in the set; a new set is added to the hitting set, and if the previous hitting set is not the hitting set of the new set, a new element is added to the hitting set, and the new element is an element that belongs to the new set but does not belong to the previous set cluster; until all the failed test case collections are contained in the set cluster. In solving the hitting set, subtract in advance the hitting set consisting of the basic block defining the variable [6]. Because part of the code defined by a variable will be run every time the test case is run, it is not reasonable to guess the defects in the definition of the variable.

Stage Two: Chromosome Coding.

Genetic algorithms represent the distribution of candidate defects as a binary vector:

$$C = \{c_1, c_2, \cdots c_n\} \tag{1}$$

In formula (1), the length n of the binary vector represents the j number of executable entities in the program under test, and the value range of the first position is 0 or 1. At that time $c_j = 1$, it indicates that the j entity of the candidate distribution represented by the vector has defects; at that time $c_j = 0$, it indicates that the j entity of the candidate distribution represented by the vector does not have defects. For example, if $C = \{0, 0, 1, 0, 0, 0, 0, 1, 0\}$ are 9 executable entities in the candidate distribution, it assume that there are defects in the second and seventh entities and no defects in the other entities.

Stage 3: Fitness value function.

The Tarantula and Ochiai formulae for the calculation of the degree of suspicion factor derive the degree of suspicion factor from the calculation of the spectrum information of the test cases and the results of the execution, thereby deriving the degree of suspicion value for each program entity [7]. Then, the ranking list can be obtained by sorting the suspicious values of the program entities from high to low, and the developer can check the program in turn according to the list to find out the specific position of the defects in the software program.

The calculation formulas of Tarantula and Ochiai measure the degree of suspicion of each statement, and this kind of method has a good effect in the case of single defect. However, in the actual process of software debugging, the program under test often contains many defects. Tarantula and Ochiai's list of suspicious rankings can be used as a reference in the case of multiple defects, but because they are not optimized for multiple defects, there are potential problems. The Multi-Ochiai formula used in this study is an improvement on the Ochiai formula for calculating the Ochiai suspicious coefficient [8].

When there are multiple bugs in a program, there is a big difference from the assumption of a single bug program, so the method of this study is based on the following assumption.

Hypothesis 1: The skepticism of a defect distribution is proportional to the number of failed use cases that the distribution can interpret.

Hypothesis 2: The degree of doubt about a defect distribution is inversely proportional to the number of use cases through which the distribution can be interpreted.

Hypothesis 3: Hypothesis 1 accounts for a larger proportion of the set suspicion formula.

In the enhanced learning, using Multi-Ochiai formula to evaluate a candidate defect distribution hypothesis C. The more the candidate distribution can explain, the higher the suspect value is, and the more the candidate distribution is covered by the correct test case, the lower the suspect value is. At the same time, the number of defects included in the candidate distribution assumption is also a consideration index. Under the same coverage condition, the lower the number of defects, the higher the suspicious value. Formula (2) defines the calculation method of the Multi-Ochiai formula for calculating suspicious values:

$$MultiOchiai = \frac{\varphi(c)}{\sqrt{|T_P \times (\varphi(c) + P(c))|}} \tag{2}$$

In Formula (2), $\varphi(c)$ is the ability to interpret a failed test case for a candidate defect distribution is actually the summation of the coincidental numbers of the program entity coverage of the failed test case and the location of the existing defect in the candidate defect distribution; $P(c)$ is the ability of the defect distribution to interpret the correct test case.

Stage 4: Genetic operators.

The selection operator is used to select the individuals that need to be cross-mutated and to determine the number of offspring that will eventually be generated. There are many selection operators in common use. There are random selection operators and roulette selection operators. In general, the higher the fitness value of an individual is, the more likely it is to contain a better gene. Therefore, the roulette selection operator is used in augmented learning to select the operated individual [9]. Roulette selection operator is used to simulate the selection of individuals using the roulette wheel used in gambling, and the fitness value of each individual is converted to the probability of selection in proportion. The whole roulette wheel can be divided into N_p sectors, and the percentage of the area of each individual sector to the total area of the circle shall be calculated by formula (3). In the process of selection, need to set a parameter $GGAP$ to specify the proportion of the selected individuals in the population, so it need to select the $GGAP \times N_p$ number of times to get the individuals. To indicate the $GGAP \times N_p$ number of unselected individuals in the population at the time of the previous selection. N_{nc} To indicate an unselected individual, C_1 is the probability that an individual C will be selected in that selection may be calculated as follows:

$$P(c) = \frac{MultiOchiai(c)}{\sum_{i=1}^{N_{nc}} MultiOchiai(c_i)} \tag{3}$$

The crossover operator acts on the two selected individuals to generate new offspring by gene exchange between them. it chooses shuffle crossover operator to apply to the crossover process of genetic algorithm because of the irregularity of many defects in the program. In the process of crossover, parameters are set P_c to describe the probability of gene exchange between two individuals at a certain location, and shuffle crossover operator allows crossover at all locations.

Because of the limitation of space, the mutation operator and the re-insertion step are not discussed again.

2.4 Identify Multiple Defect Locations

In the stage of determining multiple defect locations, the candidate distribution population obtained by genetic algorithm is transformed into the corresponding ranking of suspicious values of real program entities. First of all, the candidate defect distribution individuals are sorted according to the order from high to low, and the suspect value of the higher individual is, the more likely it is to contain defect location [10–13]. So the final sequencing of program entities will be selected from the candidate distribution in order from the first to the last. If the same candidate distribution contains more than one defect location, the location of these defects will be ranked randomly. For example, the following is a sorted candidate defect distribution population:

$$\left\{ \begin{array}{l} \langle 0, 0, 0, 1, 0, 1, 0, 0, 0, 0 \rangle \\ \langle 0, 1, 0, 1, 0, 0, 0, 0, 0, 0 \rangle \\ \langle 0, 1, 0, 0, 0, 1, 0, 0, 0, 0 \rangle \\ \langle 1, 0, 1, 0, 0, 0, 1, 1, 0, 1 \rangle \\ \langle 1, 0, 0, 0, 1, 0, 0, 1, 1, 0 \rangle \end{array} \right\} \tag{4}$$

From top to bottom, the suspicious value of each candidate distribution decreases in turn, and the defect location in the hypothesis of the candidate distribution nearer to the candidate distribution is more likely to be practical. Therefore, the fourth and sixth program entities of the first candidate distribution have the highest degree of suspicion, and these two program entities are ranked in a random manner, followed by a sequence of program entities selected from the subsequent candidate distribution. The list of the degree of suspicion that can be obtained from this candidate defect distribution is $\langle e4, e6, e2, e1, e8, e3, e7, e10, e5, e9 \rangle$. Because a random strategy is used in the selection of defect distributions with multiple defect assumptions, the ranking of statements by the same candidate distribution population may not be unique.

Through the above process, the simultaneous positioning of multiple defects in software testing is realized, which provides better method support for software application and development.

3 Experiment and Result Analysis

3.1 Evaluation Dataset Preparation

The experimental study used both small-scale and large-scale programs that can be downloaded from the SIR library. Of these, (1) small-scale programs come from seven of the Siemens suites, which have a minimum of 174 lines and a maximum of 539 lines, more than half of which are executable statements. Each program has one correct version and multiple incorrect versions, each of which contains only one defect. These programs are packaged with a minimum of 1052 test cases and a maximum of 5,542 test cases. (2) Large-scale programs from Linux programs are gzip, grep, and sed. These three programs are 6576 lines, 12635 lines and 7125 lines, of which executable statements accounted for about 1/4. But the set of test cases that these programs come with is small, with a minimum of 213 and a maximum of 470.

Some of the bugs in the wrong version of the Siemens program are not executable, which is beyond the scope of the SFL approach and makes it difficult to get accurate results. Therefore, some defects in the experiment need to be reimplanted. It e implanted a single defect in seven of Siemens' programs to perform a single defect evaluation experiment, and in four of them implanted multiple defects to perform multiple defect evaluation experiments. Selecting four programs to implant multiple defects requires that it contain more lines of executable code to implant more combinations of defects. The three Linux source code implants were all in executable lines of code, so combined

Table 3. Schedule of evaluation procedures

Program under test	Multi defect version	Number of test cases
Print_tokens	32	4130
Print_tokens2	34	4115
Replace	45	5542
Schedule	13	2650
Schedule2	15	2710
Tcas	18	1608
Tot_info	48	1052
Gzip	29	213
Grep	15	470
sed	3	360
Program under test	Multi defect version	Number of test cases
Print_tokens	32	4130
Print_tokens2	34	4115
Replace	45	5542
Schedule	13	2650
Schedule2	15	2710
Tcas	18	1608
Tot_info	48	1052
Gzip	29	213
Grep	15	470
sed	3	360

the bugs to produce a batch of two bugs and three bugs, based on a single bug version. Specific information about the evaluation process in the empirical study is shown in Table 3.

3.2 Selection of Evaluation Indicators

In single defect location, an index *EXAM* is usually used to evaluate the validity of the method. The index returns the percentage of all statements that need to be checked before the defect statement is detected. For a given program under test, the smaller the value, the better the effect of defect location is. But in the multi-defect localization, the single defect target is not completely suitable. Therefore, extend the definition to the evaluation of multi-defect localization methods, which mainly includes $EXAM_F$ and $EXAM_L$, which $EXAM_F$ returns the percentage of all statements that need to be checked before the first defect is detected, and $EXAM_L$ returns the percentage of statements that need to be checked before the last defect is detected.

3.3 Analysis of Experimental Results

The evaluation indexes are shown in Table 4.

Table 4. Table of indicators of evaluation

Number of experiments	$EXAM_F$		$EXAM_L$	
	Proposed method	Existing methods	Proposed method	Existing methods
1	1.23	2.56	0.95	1.85
2	0.98	2.00	0.85	1.87
3	0.78	2.01	0.88	1.90
4	0.80	1.98	0.78	2.04
Average value	0.9475	2.1375	0.8650	1.9150

As shown in Table 4, compared with the average evaluation index values of existing methods, the proposed method $EXAM_F$ reduces 1.19 and $EXAM_L$ reduces 1.05, which fully indicates that the proposed method has better positioning performance.

4 Concluding Remarks

Based on Reinforcement Learning, this paper presents a new method of simultaneous defect location in software testing, which greatly reduces the evaluation index $EXAM_F$ and $EXAM_L$, and provides more effective guarantee for software application.

References

1. Qian, H., Tong, H., He, M.Z., et al.: Observation of carrier localization in cubic crystalline Ge2Sb2Te5 by field effect measurement. Sci. Rep. **8**(1), 486 (2018)
2. Hao, Z., Bechtel, H.A., Kneafsey, T., et al.: Cross-scale molecular analysis of chemical heterogeneity in shale rocks. Sci. Rep. **8**(1), 2552 (2018)
3. Lee, S., Lee, J., Ryu, B., et al.: A micromechanics-based analytical solution for the effective thermal conductivity of composites with orthotropic matrices and interfacial thermal resistance. Sci. Rep. **8**(1), 7266 (2018)
4. Ohara, S., Gonçalves dos, J., Angelotti, J.A.F., et al.: A multisystem for multicomponent on a blend of industrial agroeous wastes for the simultaneous manufacturing of industrials for solid-by state. Food. Technol. **38**(1), 131–137 (2018)
5. Naharros, I.O., Cristian, F.B., Zang, J., et al.: The ciliopathy protein TALPID3/KIAA0586 acts upstream of Rab8 activation in zebrafish photoreceptor outer segment formation and maintenance. Rep. **8**(1), 2211 (2018)
6. van den Heuvel, Corina, N.A.M., Das, A.I., De Bitter, T., et al.: Quantification and localization of oncogenic receptor tyrosine kinase variant transcripts using molecular inversion probes. Rep, **8**(1), 7072–7072 (2018)
7. Fu, W., Liu, S., Srivastava, G.: Optimization of big data scheduling in social networks. Entropy **21**(9), 902 (2019)
8. Liu, S., Li, Z., Zhang, Y., et al.: Introduction of key problems in long-distance learning and training. Mob. Networks Appl. **24**(1), 1–4 (2019)
9. Liu, S., Liu, D., Srivastava, G., et al.: Overview and methods of correlation filter algorithms in object tracking. Complex Intell. Syst. (2020). https://doi.org/10.1007/s40747-020-00161-4
10. Kuo, D.H., Abdullah, H., Gultom, N.S., et al.: Ag-decorated mosx laminar-film electrocatalyst made with simple and scalable magnetron sputtering technique for hydrogen evolution: a defect model to explain the enhanced electron transport. ACS Appl. Mater. Interfaces **12**(31), 35011–35021 (2020)
11. Mao, X., Chow, J.K., Tan, P.S., et al.: Domain randomization-enhanced deep learning models for bird detection. Sci. Rep. **11**(1), 639 (2021)
12. Beloborodov, D., Ulanov, A.E., Foerster, J.N., et al.: Reinforcement learning enhanced quantum-inspired algorithm for combinatorial optimization. Mach. Learn. Sci. Technol. **2**(2), 025009 (12pp) (2021)
13. Cai, M., Jiang, Y., Gao, C., Li, H., Yuan, W.: Learning features from enhanced function call graphs for Android malware detection. Neurocomputing **423**(2), 301–307 (2021)

Design of Embedded Network Human Machine Interface Based on VR Technology

Yi Huang[(✉)] and Yubin Wang

Nanchang Business School of Jiangxi Agricultural University, Gongqing 332020, China

Abstract. In order to reduce the number of embedded network control pins in human-computer interface and enhance the reliability of embedded network human-computer interaction interface, a design of embedded network human-computer interaction interface based on virtual reality technology is introduced. In terms of hardware, the controller uses tms320lf28035 DSP chip, and its EVM board is used as the extended digital interface and display module. In terms of software, the keyboard adopts timer interrupt management to save DSP hardware resources and complete human-computer interaction. The circuit meets the requirements of general frequency converter for data input and output display. The serial parallel conversion chip can save hardware resources and provide reference for frequency converter to realize more control functions.

Keywords: VR technology · Embedded · Human-computer interaction · Network interface

1 Introduction

With the development of embedded system and the wide application of FPGA, SOPC based on FPGA is more and more popular with designers because of its flexible design, programmable hardware and software, scalable and tailorable. The MicroBlaze soft core processor embedded in FPGA is configured in the form of IP core [1]. By combining with other peripheral hardware devices, it can quickly complete the design of the whole embedded system, greatly shorten the development time of the system and improve the resource reuse rate. Some scholars have designed the hardware platform of the system development, researched and designed the embedded human-computer interaction interface based on FPGA, and realized the control of the modem through human-computer interaction. The results show that the design of man-machine interface can be realized by FPGA, and the selection and configuration of modem internal modulation mode, code rate and frequency converter parameters can be realized by man-machine interface. Human machine interface is the medium of transferring and exchanging information between human and computer. The rise of embedded system application provides a broader platform for the design of human-machine interface. However, the number of embedded network control pins in the current human-machine interface is large, which

W. Fu et al. (Eds.): ICMTEL 2021, LNICST 387, pp. 191–201, 2021.
https://doi.org/10.1007/978-3-030-82562-1_17

leads to the decline of the reliability of human-machine interaction interface in embedded network [2].

In order to solve the above problems, the network man-machine interface based on VR technology and embedded system is studied. The design of embedded network human-computer interaction interface based on VR technology is realized by CGI program in uClinux operating system on the target circuit board and boa web server which is responsible for processing CGI program. Remote users use Internet browser to input parameters and trigger CGI program on boa web server to process parameter data. Experiments show that using this method and designing a good HTML page, we can quickly design a simple, friendly and user-friendly human-computer interface.

2 Design of Embedded Network Human-Computer Interface

2.1 Configuration of Embedded Network Human-Computer Interface

Embedded system is an application-centric, computer technology-based and software and hardware can be tailored dedicated computer system [3]. Based on the advantages and practical requirements of Qt/Embedded, the human-computer interface of the monitor is designed by Qt/Embedded.

Adopt software and hardware collaborative design, in which, the software part includes uClinux, Boa and CGI program written; the hardware is a self-made Niosi processor development board, mainly composed of FPGA chip EP1C6Q240C8, Ethernet interface chip DM9000A, necessary memory (such as DRASM, FLASH chip) and debugging interface (such as JTAG, RS-232). The interface board based on ARINC429 is composed of five main parts, namely, DSP core system, oscillating clock system, ARINC429 transceiver interface, dual port RAM and logic decoding part. The specific structure diagram is shown in Fig. 1.

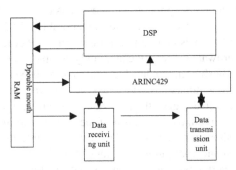

Fig. 1. Configuration structure of human-computer interaction interface in embedded network

As an important core part of the entire interface board, DSP needs to fully consider the real-time performance and data throughput capacity of the system. Therefore, the TMS320LF28035DSP chip is selected as the central processing unit of the system. This chip can provide high performance for the design of the embedded low-level software test platform. Low-consumption processing effect [4]. The login verification design of the embedded low-level software test platform is to verify whether the user's identity is correct by logging in to the verification platform, and whether it can be consistent with the user name and password in the database, which provides protection for the security of the client. Only through identity verification can it be carried out. The main page of the software testing platform. The main reason is that the platform has good confidentiality and security performance. For no registered account, the identity verification design of the test platform is as follows: First, the administrator should design an embedded low-level software test platform based on the ARINC429 interface board Security functions, such as login user name and password, and then assign the set user name and password to different users, and save them in the database server. Finally, in order to realize the safe login of users, encryption algorithms are needed to ensure the storage of user information Safety.

Perform periodic and continuous automatic collection of embedded bottom software data, transfer the collected data to the data processing center through the data transmission center in the test platform, and organize the data that the bottom software needs to run into the database for storage and management Through the display of the operating information of the embedded underlying software, personnel can monitor the operating status of the software in real time [5]. The data query of the embedded low-level software test platform is mainly by querying the specified software running time and type, and receiving the data of the embedded low-level software running through the server, using a table or broken line to show the result of the query, which can be Provide support for the diagnosis of software evaluation data.

2.2 Optimization of Inverter Equipment Based on VR Technology

Modern general frequency converters mostly use diode rectifiers and PWM inverters composed of IGBTs or smart power modules to form AC-DC-AC voltage inverters. The inverter circuit is divided into four parts: rectifier circuit, intermediate DC link, inverter link and control circuit [6]. The main circuit adopts a typical voltage-type AC/DC traffic inverter structure, and the control circuit mainly includes a DSP digital controller, including DSP, drive circuit, detection circuit, protection circuit and auxiliary power circuit. This circuit is composed of inverter and keyboard parallel circuit. Complete data input, parameter setting, data exchange, selection of display information, menu selection, real-time monitoring data viewing and other operations. The software dynamically scans the keyboard and ledVR technology combination to manage key input and data output display. Sensors are the core equipment of wearable devices, the "core" of communication between people and things, the gate of the "perception era", and an important hardware for product functional differentiation.

According to requirements, this design needs to configure and remotely control the modem through the PC, so the Ethernet interface is designed to realize this function [7]. This design uses Wiznet's W5500 chip, which is a full hardware TCP/IP embedded Ethernet controller, which integrates the TCP/IP protocol stack, and the 10/100M Ethernet physical layer and data link layer. It enables users to use the chip to expand network connections in their applications, and provides a simpler Internet connection scheme for embedded systems [8]. W5500 has built-in 32K bytes on-chip buffer for Ethernet packet processing. The full hardware TCP/IP protocol stack supports TCP, UDP, IPv4, ICMP, ARP, IGMP and PPPoE protocols, so this design only needs to pass some Socket programming. Realize Ethernet applications. Users can use 8 hardware sockets for independent communication at the same time. Its main features are as follows:

Because the multi-channel serial communication system has relatively weak signal acquisition and processing capabilities under actual conditions, it is necessary to strengthen the processing of the multi-channel communication conditioning circuit interface, and combine the VR technology to collect and convert information to ensure that it is in digital The communication process effectively performs digital conversion and quickly converts analog communication signals into digital transmission signals [9]. In this way, the influence of noise is avoided and the information is transmitted accurately and at a high speed. The design of the multi-channel serial communication interface circuit based on VR technology can effectively avoid the impact of data transmission delay and information damage caused by software interruption, avoid the problem of data conflicts caused by excessive information during system operation, and improve system operation stability. Combining the above design, design the operation flow of system modules such as priority and trigger conditions of the multi-channel serial communication system [10–13]. XCL bus is a high-performance bus form designed for accessing external memory. MicroBlaze's cache interface directly connects the storage controller and the integrated FSL buffer. It has two types of interfaces, DXCL and IXCL, respectively responsible for data and instruction data transmission. In the design process of VR-based multi-channel serial communication interface, different module loops play different functions during operation. In order to better understand the role of system modules, the specific multi-channel serial communication interface function display module as shown in Fig. 2.

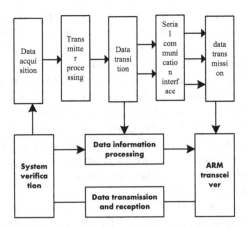

Fig. 2. Multi-channel serial communication interface function module

In order to improve the efficiency of the microprocessor's instruction execution, and to ensure the correct detection of the button value, and to eliminate jitter, only software can be used. Therefore, in the button management, the timer interrupt method is used. The timer interrupt program checks the button at regular intervals. State, and store the return value of the key in the buffer. When the key is detected, a mark about the key is set up. When the key mark is detected in the main program loop, the key is pressed. The timer is about ten milliseconds. The detection interval can effectively filter the jitter of the keys, realize the debouncing of the keyboard, the key value acquisition and the long and short recognition of the key time. The MicroBlaze soft core processor is a powerful 32-bit microprocessor. It uses a configurable RISC streamlined instruction set and optimizes the Xilinx FPGA chip. It is the fastest in the industry's soft processor IP core solutions. Comply with IBM's CoreConnect bus standard, with reusability and compatibility, the most streamlined core only needs about 400 Sfice. In order to cooperate with the software debugging tool based on JTAG, the MicroBlaze soft-core processor introduces a debugging interface, which is usually called a background debugging mode debugger. MDMCXilinxMicroprocessorDebugModule is connected to the JTAG port of Xilinx FPGA, and the MDM core is connected to the debug interface. Multiple MicroBlaze scenes can also be debugged by connecting multiple processes with a single MDM.

In the whole system design, the main function of the software design is to realize the control of the internal modules of the modem through the human-computer interaction interface, and to realize the data communication between the PC and the modem through the Ethernet interface and the DART interface. The main content of the design includes the driver of the keyboard chip, the driver of the LCD module, the configuration program of the inverter, the driver of the Ethernet interface and the driver of the DART interface. In the software design of VR technology display output, the dynamic scanning control of VR technology can make the characters to be displayed by different positioning VR technology. Cache the spatial location point information of the human-computer interaction device, set a strategy within certain conditions to form an input information trajectory, and perform segmentation processing on the trajectory to make it a primitive. Assemble and classify the segmented trajectory, and identify the action behavior input type. According to the different behavior input types, connect the segmented trajectory, analyze the trajectory information according to the human-computer interaction application attribute, and perform surface projection operations on it to form the interaction principle. Language, lay the foundation for the establishment of the information control model of human-computer interaction equipment. The information control model design of human-computer interaction equipment is shown in Fig. 3.

In the human-computer interaction control model shown in Fig. 3, interaction capabilities and execution performance are reflected to facilitate users to understand the interaction process. The description of user goals can complete the description of target interactive tasks, and design buttons and move mouse operators can provide basic operation capabilities for the execution of user goals. Choose the prediction method to decompose the sub-goals and make decisions for the user's goal state. Derive the specific execution method from the control model, use the short-term estimation memory method to analyze the state behavior. Each module loopback structure contains three information transceivers to meet the requirements for accurate processing of multiple complex data loops in time. In the information processing module, the data is configured and

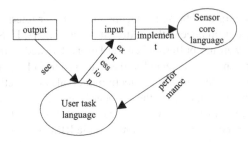

Fig. 3. Information control model of human-computer interactive equipment

compressed and sent to the VR transceiver, and then the big data is detected and stored by the VR transceiver and then sent to the data receiving module. In order to ensure the accuracy of the data, all data must be decompressed in the data verification module, the received data and the generated data are compared and verified, and finally the verified data is encrypted and transmitted to the data receiving end And stored in the designated folder. During the operation of the verification module, once the two data is found to be abnormal, it will immediately send the original primary instructions for deployment, compare the original data to observe, determine the location of the error information and modify it in time. To ensure the accuracy and timeliness of multi-channel serial communication.

2.3 Optimization of Embedded Network Human-Computer Interaction Control Panel

The control panel is selected as the second stage of the embedded network human-computer interaction interface processing. According to the keywords and parameters extracted in the decision-making problem understanding stage, the corresponding decision model is found in the model library and the model with the best correlation is returned., That is, choose a problem solving model that matches the goal of the decision-making problem. This stage is divided into three processes: model type selection, model structure selection and model instance determination. The control panel can provide a man-machine interface for inverter users. There are different function keys and indicator lights on the panel to help users realize functions such as start, stop, steering, parameter setting and real-time information query. The control panel consists of a display screen composed of VR technology, LED indicators and 8 function keys. Its functions include parameter setting and modification, motor control command group, real-time information display, etc. The DSP continuously scans key modules, compares the received key values, and then executes the corresponding function functions stored in the program to achieve the expected execution effect. Based on the hierarchical processing of human-computer interaction space information, surface behaviors and mixed behaviors are uniformly processed in a continuous interaction space. The specific processing flow is shown in Fig. 4.

It can be seen from Fig. 4 that the construction of the hierarchical model is based on the interactive space, corresponding to the input of the air movement form, the surface

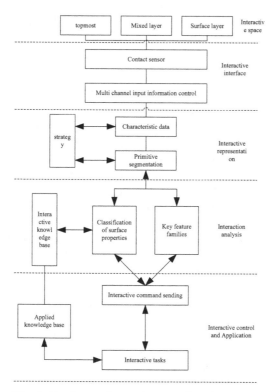

Fig. 4. Continuous interactive space layering process

movement form input, and the multiple device form input respectively. The human-computer interaction device can be responsible for obtaining input perception and output feedback information. Multiple sensors can sense real-time spatial position information of different levels of behavior input. For the same action behavior input, multiple inertial sensors are needed to sense. Therefore, there are only multiple Data can be freely matched only under the condition of inertial sensor sensing, and data can be collected for different levels of spatial gestures under multiple inertial sensors, and then the input position points can be converted. Test according to the functions and variables obtained from the test database, and call according to the architecture of the system. If the position of the function call is the beginning and end of the compilation, then the branch and loop in the statement can be determined as the beginning of the entire compilation. And the end. The driver and application are designed by calling the required API functions. The software design is carried out in the EDK tool, including the keyboard chip driver, the LCD module driver, the inverter configuration program, the Ethernet interface application program and the DART interface driver, etc., based on the hardware, through the driver program to achieve and hardware Communication, through calling the interface to support specific applications, realize the function of human-computer interaction. This model is a low-level physical model that can decompose high-level interaction behaviors, and form low-level physical operation behaviors through re-mapping, which is convenient for predicting the time spent in the execution stage of a low-level interaction task. The data expression is as formula (1) shows:

$$T_e = T_1 + T_2 + T_3 + T_4 + T_5 + T_6 \tag{1}$$

In the formula: T_1 represents button or mouse operation time, T_2 represents state positioning time; T_3 represents reset time; T_4 represents moving action time-consuming; T_5 represents decision time; T_6 represents response time. For the user's execution, it needs to be extracted from various human operating behaviors to ensure that the model outputs characteristic indexes that characterize human operating activities. By analyzing the time of different stages, it can effectively control the information of wearable human-computer interaction devices based on inertial sensors.

The realization process of human-computer interaction is that the DSP calls the corresponding key processing function according to the input information of the key, and then displays it with VR technology according to the display program, thereby displaying the real-time status and fault information of the inverter. When the inverter is powered on, whether it is running or not, the VR technology will display the corresponding information. The interface displays real-time output frequency, real-time current, voltage and fault type prompts. Short press the S6 key to start the inverter operation. Short press S1 to enter the first level menu of the control panel. Long press S1 to return to the upper menu. S3 and S4 are the addition and subtraction of the set value in the corresponding menu respectively. Short press or long press these two keys to increase or decrease the data step by step or to increase or decrease quickly continuously. Press the S2 key to save the corresponding value or parameter; while the inverter is running, press the S5 key to sequentially display the real-time monitoring values of the inverter. When modifying parameters, this key represents the optional parameter modification position. When the inverter is running or malfunctions, press the S7 key, the inverter will decelerate to stop, and the fault can be reset in the fault alarm state; press S8 to indicate that the inverter is switched between forward and reverse; S7 + S6 combination, when running and deceleration stop are pressed at the same time, the inverter will stop freely.

The most important part of the embedded low-level software test platform based on the ARINC429 interface board is the design of a complete set of platform development tools. GNU Tools contains the embedded application system. Its comprehensive source code can provide a tool chain for the embedded environment. The use of this tool can provide tools for the development of code compilation, structural testing and software engineering. The three are combined to form a tool chain, which can meet the independence requirements of the test platform. By using the tool chain, the automatic insertion test function can be added to the compiler. The compilation process is shown in Fig. 5.

It can be seen from Fig. 5 that various source codes can be compiled into assembly codes through the compilation process. Based on this, the effective design of the network human-computer interaction interface is realized to ensure the operation effect of the equipment.

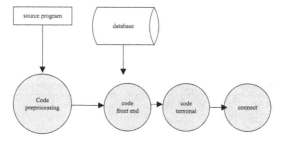

Fig. 5. Compilation process

3   Analysis of Experimental Results

By choosing the method of optimizing and improving the keyboard key circuit, the circuit is optimized. The control panel keyboard is composed of 8 normally open buttons, and the output display adopts four-digit VR technology. In the process of data input and output, serial parallel conversion is adopted, which saves DSP hardware resources. The most concise operation is adopted to realize the expected related functions, and the related data is displayed in the VR technology while realizing the functions. Although only 7 DSP pins are used for input and output display in the design, it can control 6 LED status indicators, detect the input of 8 buttons, 4 bits, 7 segment VR technology and 4 VR technology control bits, which greatly saves The cost of DSP hardware resources. The test platform processing needs to collect user login information, historical data information, real-time data, network information, etc., as shown in Table 1 and Table 2.

Table 1. Information processing rate for traditional interfaces (%)

Serial number	Serial number	Serial number	Serial number	Serial number
1	30.00	45.15	28.55	48.22
2	30.15	46.23	30.15	49.01
3	31.01	45.90	30.38	46.23
4	29.35	46.28	29.35	45.18
5	28.22	47.22	29.13	47.25

Based on the data collected above, the processing rate of the platform designed in this paper is compared with that of the traditional platform. Because the embedded low-level software test platform based on the interface can collect the data in real time, the software can be collected by the database server and the application server processing center. All parts were tested. Data collection can realize offline testing and online testing of the embedded underlying software; for the logical processing of the business and the connection between the database, the collected data can be processed; by transmitting the data, the operating data of the embedded underlying software can be completed

Table 2. Information processing rate for this article interface (%)

Serial number	Serial number	Serial number	Serial number	Serial number
1	80.13	62.15	61.36	82.85
2	79.28	63.24	62.25	79.28
3	78.31	60.98	61.88	78.51
4	77.52	65.13	63.23	76.35
5	77.15	64.14	65.15	76.98

Acquisition, processing, transmission and application on the client side, so using the test platform designed in this paper can improve the processing rate of the platform. In order to verify the performance of the test platform in this article, the frequency of data collection (MB/s) is used as a standard to measure the performance of the traditional test platform and the test platform in this article. The results are shown in Fig. 6.

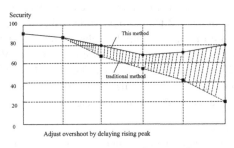

Fig. 6. Comparison of test results

It can be seen from Fig. 6 that the method designed in this paper can continuously collect data in the software and can quickly collect a large amount of software information in a short time. Therefore, at the same time, the collected data is also better than the data collected by the traditional test platform. need more. Practice has proved that the hardware meets the actual application requirements, ensures the working efficiency of the keyboard, saves the hardware port resources of the DSP, and improves the efficiency of the DSP port. The interface design makes the human-computer interaction interface friendly and operable. Realize offline testing and online testing of embedded underlying software through collection, and test each part of the software through the database server and application server processing center. It can complete the logical processing of the business and the connection between the databases, and process the collected data. Regarding the packet loss rate of the test platform in this article, the method designed in this article is obviously more accurate than the traditional method, and at the same time, the data collected is more than that of the traditional test platform. Therefore, the method designed in this article can be used in Save a lot of time in real life and effectively improve test efficiency.

4 Conclusion

The human-computer interaction interface of the monitor is planned with a unified modeling idea, and the state of the module program is decomposed by the finite state machine method. Using VR technology to design the embedded network human-computer interaction interface, research has confirmed that this method has certain reference value.

References

1. Zhang, D., Lei, Y., Shen, Z.: Effect of longitudinal magnetic field on vibration response of double-walled carbon nanotubes embedded in viscoelastic medium. Acta Mech. Solida Sin. **31**(02), 1–20 (2018)
2. Michalakis, K., Aliprantis, J., Caridakis, G.: Visualizing the internet of things: naturalizing human-computer interaction by incorporating AR features. IEEE Consum. Electr. Mag. **7**(3), 64–72 (2018)
3. Hazer-Rau, D., Meudt, S., Daucher, A., et al.: The uulmMAC database—a multimodal affective corpus for affective computing in human-computer interaction. Sensors **20**(8), 2308 (2020)
4. Przybyo, J.: Continuous distant measurement of the user's heart rate in human-computer interaction applications. Sensors **19**(19), 4205–4208 (2019)
5. Liao, Y.F., Chang, Y.H.S., Lin, Y.C., et al.: Formosa speech in the wild corpus for improving Taiwanese Mandarin speech-enabled human-computer interaction. J. Signal Process. Syst. **92**(8), 853–873 (2020)
6. Martins, V.F., Guimaraes, M.D.P.: Star life cycle and games development projects for conducting the human–computer interaction course: a practical experience. Comput. Appl. Eng. Educ. **26**(5), 1539–1551 (2018)
7. Liu, S., Lu, M., Li, H., et al.: Prediction of gene expression patterns with generalized linear regression model. Front. Genet. **10**, 120 (2019)
8. Jyoti, V., Lahiri, U.: Human-computer interaction based joint attention cues: implications on functional and physiological measures for children with autism spectrum disorder. Comput. Hum. Behav. **104**(Mar), 106163.1–106163.14 (2020)
9. El Said, G.R.: The intention to use mobile student portal: a mobile human computer interaction study in a university context in Egypt. Mob. Inf. Syst. **2018**(PT.2), 1512602.1–1512602.8 (2018)
10. Sarzynska, M., Leicht, E.A., Chowell, G., et al.: Null models for community detection in spatially-embedded, temporal networks. J. Complex Netw. **4**(3), 363–406 (2018)
11. Kai, X., Qingshan, D., Lujun, C., et al.: Damage detection of a concrete column subject to blast loads using embedded piezoceramic transducers. Sensors **18**(5), 1377 (2018)
12. Liu, S., Liu, D., Srivastava, G., Połap, D., Woźniak, M.: Overview and methods of correlation filter algorithms in object tracking. Complex Intell. Syst. 1–23 (2020). https://doi.org/10.1007/s40747-020-00161-4
13. Liu, S., Bai, W., Zeng, N., et al.: A fast fractal based compression for MRI images. IEEE Access **7**, 62412–62420 (2019)

Design of Information Security System Based on JSP Technology and Reinforcement Model

Yubin Wang[✉] and Yiping Li

Nanchang Business School of Jiangxi Agricultural University, Gongqing 332020, China

Abstract. Aiming at the security and secrecy of network test question bank, this paper puts forward an information security secrecy system suitable for test question bank. The system has the functions of identification, security enhancement, information encryption and data backup and recovery. Finally, black-box and white-box tests are carried out to test the function and performance of the system, which proves that the system meets the design requirements.

Keywords: JSP technology · Reinforcement model · Test library · Security system

1 Introduction

The security of the test question bank only refers to the protection of the test question bank to prevent the leakage, change or destruction of the test questions due to illegal use. Therefore, schools should pay full attention to the security of the test question bank. Carefully analyze the potential safety hazards and put forward safety requirements of all aspects.

In view of the security and confidentiality of the network examination database, this paper puts forward an information security system suitable for the network examination database. The innovation of this system is to use JSP technology to ensure that the system has the functions of identity recognition, security enhancement, information encryption and data backup and recovery.

2 Design of Information Secrecy System for Test Question Bank

It has become the consensus of the education experts that the examination questions are collected and managed automatically and standardized by using the examination questions database system. The standardization and automation of test questions is beneficial to the improvement of teaching quality and the making of correct decision. Therefore, many colleges and universities have developed and put into use various test question database management systems, which have achieved considerable results and are welcomed by teachers and students. However, the protection undertaken with respect to the security and confidentiality of the system is seriously inadequate [1, 2]. Some managers

W. Fu et al. (Eds.): ICMTEL 2021, LNICST 387, pp. 202–213, 2021.
https://doi.org/10.1007/978-3-030-82562-1_18

lack the awareness of security risks and believe that students are not yet capable of attacking systems. Therefore, we do not pay attention to the improvement of technical skills and the collection of related information. For this reason, this article on the relevant issues for discussion.

2.1 Technologies Related to Test Bank System

2.1.1 JSP Technology

JSP is a technical standard for dynamic web pages. Add Java program snippets and JSP tags to the traditional HTML page files (*.html, *. htm), and have a JSP page (*. jsp). When a Web service encounters a request to access a JSP Web page, it first executes a snippet of the program, and then returns the result in HTML format to the client. The program fragment has the function of operating database, redirecting webpage, sending email and other dynamic webpage. All programs are executed on the server side, and only the results of program execution are transmitted to the client through the network. The requirements for the client side are lower [3].

Characteristics of JSP technology:

Platform adaptability; program execution is efficient; JavaBeans enhancements can be used to save development time; JSP-based applications are easier to maintain and manage;

2.1.2 Database and Related Technologies

A database is the basic framework of an information system, which fundamentally changes the way many companies and individuals work. With the development of database technology for many years, many powerful and easy-to-use database systems have emerged, which enable users to create and apply databases without the knowledge of developing efficient systems. The database platform shall have the online processing capability to support a large number of users, the mass data storage capability, the fast retrieval capability, and the response capability of a large number of concurrent users [4]. The storage and conversion of data between heterogeneous database platforms involves the following technologies:

(1) Data exchange technology
   By using communication network and data exchange technology, the automatic data exchange between computer information systems is realized. Includes Web XML, RDF, SOAP, WSUI, XML, Xquery, and more.
(2) Data linking technology
   The digital campus uses the database management system which is independent of the foreground and the background. The background database management system manages and maintains the database independently. Common data linking techniques are: ADO, ADO. NET, DAO, DB2 Connector, JDBC, ODBC, OLE/DB, etc. [5].
(3) Data storage technology
   In order to realize data sharing, it is necessary to store and transmit data according to certain standards. The commonly used data standard technology includes: EDI,

Namespaces, XLINK, XML and so on; Data transmission technology: XSLT and so on; Data type: DTD and XML Schema and so on.

(4) Data warehouse and data mining

Digital campuses require data unification (such as aggregation and aggregation) from heterogeneous data sources across various application systems to produce high-quality, pure and integrated data. Data warehouse extracts, preprocesses, transforms, integrates, annotates and aggregates the original data and reorganizes them into a semantically consistent data store. The query processing in the data warehouse does not affect the processing on the local data source. The data warehouse supports information processing, provides queries and basic statistical analysis, and reports using cross-tables, charts, or graphs, and enables multidimensional data analysis and OLAP (online analytics processing). Support for data mining, including identifying hidden patterns and associations, discovering new knowledge, constructing analytical models, classifying and predicting, and using visual tools to provide mining results, achieve the reuse of data and information, and enhance the information value of the original data [6]. Such as office systems, JOLAPOLAP, XBRL, etc.

2.1.3 PHP Technology

PHP (Hypertext Preprocessor): Hypertext preprocessor, an easy-to-learn and easy-to-use server-side scripting language, is one of the tools for generating dynamic Web pages. It is a scripting language that embeds HTML files. Most of its syntax is borrowed from C, JAVA, PERL language, and formed its own unique style; the goal is to allow WEB programmers to quickly develop dynamic Web pages. It is one of the hottest scripting languages on the Internet today, and with very little programming knowledge you can build a truly interactive Web site using PHP.

PHP is completely free, with unlimited access to the source code, and you can even add your own features to it. PHP runs on most Unix platforms, GUN/Linux, and Microsoft Windows.

PHP technical features:

In object-oriented programming, PHP provides classes and objects. Web-based programming requires object-oriented programming capabilities, while PHP supports constructors, extraction classes, and so on.

One of the most powerful and notable features of PHP is its support for a wide range of databases. You will find it incredibly simple to write database supported web pages in PHP. PHP and MySQL are the perfect combination right now. Users can also write peripheral functions to access the database indirectly. When users change the database they use, the programmer can easily change the code to accommodate this change.

In terms of adaptability to user platforms, PHP works well on Web servers such as Windows Linux and Unix, and supports general-purpose Web servers such as IIS Apache, allowing users to switch platforms without having to change their PHP code.

Run fast. PHP uses HTML built-in markup technology, and the interpreter itself runs as a module of the Web server, considerably speeding up runtime parsing, while the data submitted from the page form automatically becomes a variable in the program with the same form name, without manual assignment. Tests show that PHP parses four times faster than traditional CGI programs when the Web site is heavily visited, making it ideal for large and medium-sized sites.

2.2 System Requirements Analysis

(1) Because the test questions correspond to specific objects, the system needs to be authenticated before it can be logged in.
(2) The authority of the system is generally divided into two types: administrators and students. Different identities use different permissions and functions.
(3) Administrators shall be responsible for the effective management of examination questions and students, and shall be responsible for the entry, update, modification and classification of examination questions.

2.3 System Architecture

Since the advent of computer technology, computer technology has generally undergone three computing models: the H/TComputer tier architecture (or host-terminal computing model), the Client/Server Computing tier architecture (or client/server computing model), and the Web Computing tier architecture (or Web computing model).

H/T Computer single-layer architecture refers to the architecture mode with the host terminal as the main terminal through which the user can directly use the computer and interact with the application program [7]. However, due to the complexity of mainframe maintenance and the low relative performance, the mainframe -terminal computing model has declined and withdrawn from the stage of history. With the appearance of PC and the maturity of network technology, the computing mode of distributed Client/Server two-tier architecture begins to develop and flourish gradually. Although the resource of PC is limited, the application program can not only utilize the local resource, but also utilize the resource of other computer effectively through network. C/S (Customer and Software Architecture) is widely used in enterprises and other local networks. Running program modules from various servers on the server, such as file servers, database servers, etc., while client programs.

Through access to server-side resources to achieve their own functions. The C/S model is still in use in many sectors, such as banking, postal and other sectors. But because it requires a large number of applications on the client side, is relatively expensive and complex to maintain, it is not suitable for today's Internet networks.

With the further development of network technology, the best way to build a Web application is to make it into a three-tier application, which subtly distinguishes its three components: user interface, computational logic and data storage. The three-tier application structure diagram for this system is shown in Fig. 1.

(1) Data layer
   The data layer is at the bottom of the system. In the item bank system, the data layer mainly includes item bank, examinee information bank, user information bank, paper strategy information, paper bank and other information, they are stored in the database. The database is managed by the SQL Server 2000 database service program, which responds to and provides data services to requests from the logical layer.

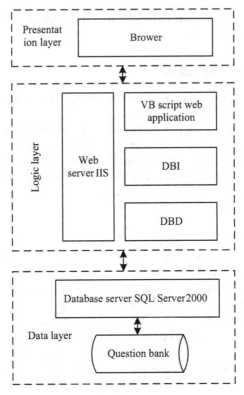

Fig. 1. Three-tier application structure diagram

(2) Logic layer

In the item bank system, the logic layer is mainly composed of Web service programs, which are called by the Web server to respond to the requests of clients (item bank construction members, system administrators, examinees, and invigilators) and serve the clients in accordance with the business rules (or business logic). There are many methods to developing Web program, this system is mainly based on ASP technology programming. Communication with browsers through IIS in ASP programs (output pages and collection parameters): communication with the SQL Server2000 database server through the DBI (Database Interface) module and the DBD (Database Driver) module, making data requests to the database server [8].

(3) Presentation layer

The presentation layer (Web browser) is located on the client side. The user makes a service request to the Web server of the test library system through the Web browser. The Web server authenticates the user and then transmits the desired home page to the client through the HTTP protocol. The client receives the incoming home page and displays it on the Web browser.

While the presentation layer is visible on the client side of the browser, it is essentially hosted on a Web server that sends the page content (often generated through a Web services program) to the browser.

2.4   Functional Module Division

2.4.1   Login Module

Login module includes login page, new user registration page and authentication of password. All users enter the system through this interface, and the system allows the user to perform specific actions based on the privileges previously assigned to the user. Different from the general software, the user login window of this software only allows registered users to log in, whether the new registered users can log in to the management interface can only wait for the examination administrator to review the success. In this system, the user is divided into three levels of authority, namely, the examination administrator, curriculum director, teacher. All users can only log on to the development system after creating and assigning permissions to operate, using a unified logon system that automatically identifies the user by user name and password and allows the user to perform the corresponding operation [9]. The user login module flowchart is shown in Fig. 2.

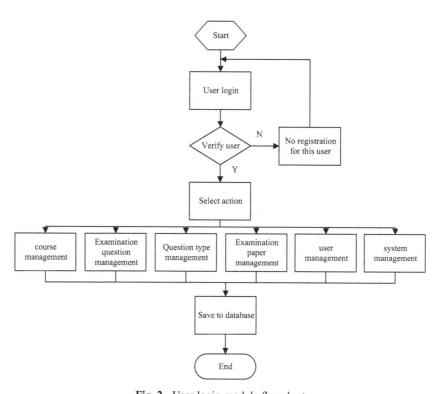

Fig. 2. User login module flowchart

In the login module, except that the examination administrator has the account and password in advance, other users must register as legal users before using the system. After the examination administrator examines the authenticity of their information, they may log into the functional module of the system with corresponding authority. The flowchart shown in Fig. 2 depicts that the user must first enter the login page to access the system. If the verification of the account and password indicates that the user is a registered user, the user may perform the corresponding functions by judging his/her authority; otherwise, the user may not use the system until the registration information is verified through the corresponding prompt information.

2.4.2 DBMS Security Hardening Module

General large database management system such as Oracle, Sybase, SQL Server itself will provide username and password identification, view, access control, audit, stored procedures and other management measures. So we can make full use of these management functions to enhance the security of test database.

First, users can be classified according to the requirements of different access rights. Users will be divided into different roles to manage, usually for the system maintainer role, the role of educational administrators, teachers and students role. Create different logged-in users and passwords under each role. Different role groups and special users are respectively authorized with different granularity and different operations by utilizing the system's flexible privilege control mechanism [10].

Secondly, the view can be used to classify the data conveniently, and the data of the same knowledge points can be used to classify the data of different levels of users in the outer model layer. In addition, by trying to hide the data to be kept secret from the users who have no access right, the security of the test database is improved. View in the establishment of the same time can give the internal data alias, so that the name of the database can be a good object to hide, to further avoid security risks [11, 12].

Third, unnecessary stored procedures should be removed, because some systems of stored procedures can easily be used to elevate permissions or damage. For example: xp _ cmd _ shell is the best shortcut to the operating system, data is left to the operating system's back door, which can be deleted with sp _ dropextendedproc and restored with the sp _ addextendedproc system procedure if needed [13].

Finally, the audit capability provided by the DBMS is another significant security measure that monitors the operations of individual users on the database. Auditing methods are divided into user auditing and system auditing. The audit system of the DBMS records all attempts to access its own database objects and the user name, time, operation code and other information of each operation. System audit is carried out by system administrators, whose audit content is mainly system-level commands and the use of database objects.

2.4.3 Maintenance Module of Question Bank

The maintenance of question bank includes searching, deleting, auditing, modifying and other functions. Question search can be based on the corresponding knowledge points included in the first question, specific search can choose the scope of filter questions, and then according to the time of question entry, difficulty value, the question who, the type of quick sorting to find questions. The deletion function is that the subject experts delete the unqualified questions from the question bank after the preliminary examination or the examination analysis question parameter value modification. The examination function is divided into two circumstances: the examination questions just put into the database need to be checked and audited, and the analysis program needs to be reexamined after the use of the examination questions. The former must be checked by subject experts before it can be used in the examination; the latter, mainly because the difficulty value and differentiation value are so different from the normal value that it needs to be re-checked by statistical analysis program during the use of the question, and if there is indeed an error in the expert inspection, it may be deleted or modified before being used. The function of revision is that subject experts revise the wrong or imperfect test questions. For the convenience of the users, the status of the test questions is represented by an icon, and the interface elements such as the status bar and the prompt bar are used.

2.4.4   Test Database Data Encryption Module

There have been some achievements in the theoretical research and practical application of database encryption. If you can make full use of the shared resources and build up a large database of high quality tests, if that is the case, then proceed.

Encrypting the data items that represent the knowledge content in the test database is redundant. However, we must pay attention to the user name password encryption in the permission control. The identification of a user before entering the system, which determines the legal actions that can be performed in the system. The protection of system password files is the key, and there are many similar approaches.

2.4.5   Test Database Backup and Recovery Module

A backup of a database is the process of copying the database to a dedicated storage device. Backup can be divided into "physical backup" and "logical backup" two types. Physical backup refers to copying database files from one location to another. The files that need to be backed up include data files, archive redo logs, and control files. Logical backup is the use of tools such as EX-PORT to execute SQL statements to read out the data in the database, and then write to other file types. Database recovery refers to restoring the database itself, that is, restoring the database to a correct state or a consistent state after the database is paralyzed and inconsistent. Establishing strict database backup and recovery management mechanism is an effective means to ensure the security of database system in all networks. Database always inevitable system failures, once the system failure, important data is always inevitably destroyed.

In order to prevent the loss or damage of important data, the database administrator should back up the database as soon as possible, so as to maintain the integrity and consistency of the data in case of system failure. Therefore, the data backup module is introduced, that is, the index layer and the criterion layer are analyzed for each data C_i that needs to be backed up, and the corresponding sub index weights are allocated according to the importance of the data. In this case, the input and output of the output layer are described as:

$$S_k = \sum_{j=1}^{m} u_{jk} D_j - \theta_k \tag{1}$$

$$Y_k = \frac{1}{1+e} - S_k \tag{2}$$

Where, u_{jk} is the connection weight of hidden layer neuron j and output layer neuron k, θ_k is the critical value of output node, S_k is the input of the k-th and output nodes, and Y_k is the output of output layer neuron.

In order to ensure that the administrator can use the existing data backup to restore the database to the original state.

2.5 System Testing

The principle of system testing is paramount, and the methodology should be guided by it. The basic principle of software testing is to test the product thoroughly from the user's point of view, find out as many bugs as possible as early as possible, and be responsible for tracking and analyzing the problems in the product, and raise questions and suggestions for improvement. Zero-Bug is an idea, and Good-Enough is the basic principle of testing.

2.5.1 Test Environment

(1) Software environment
    This software can be run in Windows 2000 and all before the Windows NT architecture based on the computer. The test used a Windows XP system.
(2) USB KEY model
    The USB Key used in this paper is ET199, developed by Beijing Jianshi Honesty Technology Co., Ltd.
(3) Computer hardware configuration
    The hardware configuration of the computer used in the test is as follows:
    CPU: Pentium (R) Dual-Core CPU E5400 2.70 GHZ. Memory: 2.72 HZ 2 GB. Hard disk capacity: 320GB.
(4) Environmental infrastructure

After the implementation of the system, this chapter builds the test environment. In this environment, assuming that there are test files on the monitored computer 1 and the monitored computer 2 need to be protected, the protection program of the system is installed on these two hosts. The host computer of employee 1 and the two monitored computers are in the same network segment, and the host computer of user 2 is from 192.168.1 network segment and connected by router and 192.168.3 network segment. Within the 192.168.3 network segment, each host can be connected to each other by a hub or switch. Two monitors are operated on 2, 1, 2, and 3 mainframes respectively to test the function and performance of the system.

2.5.2   System Functional Testing

Functional testing of the system is the most important part of the entire testing process. If the system is not functional, then other aspects of the system will be successful and the technology will not be of interest to customers. Common functional problems can be divided into two categories, one is the customer can not achieve the desired function, the second is to achieve the user does not need the function.

According to the features of the system, the use cases are designed in the following aspects: the test of the operation function of the system interface, the test of the user's permission, the test of the update function and the test of uploading the files. The testing contents of the system mainly include the query function, the document preview function, the data security function and the file sharing function. The functional test of the system is shown in the following aspects as shown in Table 1.

Table 1. System functional test results

Describe	Result
Open the system interface to see if it is friendly	ADOPT
Check whether the interface of the system can be switched correctly	ADOPT
Login test of normal and abnormal users	ADOPT
Different permissions are given to different users	ADOPT
You can input and modify various documents	ADOPT
It provides update and submit functions for document version problems	ADOPT
Query the required documents according to user rights	ADOPT
Parameter setting for specific system	ADOPT
It provides information release and reference function for the system	ADOPT

2.5.3   System Performance Testing

The performance of the system is one of the key factors affecting software product praise, a slightly higher load when the slow snail-like system users will not like. At present, the level of system performance has been considered as an important factor in the quality of software. What we mean by system performance testing is actually a test of the ability of a system to function properly when the system is under heavy load.

In the process of performance testing, not only professional performance testing tools are used to simulate high load, but also practical testing is carried out. The specific situation is as follows: 20 users are added into the system step by step in 20 s, and the maximum number of concurrent users is 2000. The system performance test results are shown in Table 2 below.

Table 2. System performance test results

Test cycle	System throughput (transactions/sec)	Network throughput (bytes/sec)
Single transaction (2)	2. 13	170842
Multiple transactions (1000)	3. 1	219610

Under this high load, the system can run normally for an hour, and then every 10 s to reduce the 10 user operating system can still run normally. Through the performance testing of professional tools and specific cases, the design of the system has fully met the requirements of users.

3   Conclusion

The security and confidentiality system of network test question bank is only an application of information system security and confidentiality. In order to prevent the information system from being threatened by tampering, damaging and stealing, it is necessary to strengthen and utilize the security measures of the database system itself, as well as the comprehensive application of network, system software, hardware, encryption and other technologies as well as moral laws and regulations. Only by improving the managers' awareness of potential safety hazards, can the teaching resources of network test bank play its due role.

References

1. Azeta, A.A., Misra, S., Azeta, V.I., et al.: Determining suitability of speech-enabled examination result management system. Wireless Netw. **25**(6), 3657–3664 (2019)
2. Cheng, Z., Duan, J., Chow, M.Y.: To centralize or to distribute: that is the question: a comparison of advanced microgrid management systems. IEEE Ind. Electron. Mag. **12**(1), 6–24 (2018)
3. Patil, S.P., et al.: Hidden-Markov-model based statistical parametric speech synthesis for Marathi with optimal number of hidden states. Int. J. Speech Technol. **22**(1), 93–98 (2019). https://doi.org/10.1007/s10772-018-09578-2
4. Walsh, J.L., Harris, B.H.L., Denny, P., et al.: Formative student-authored question bank: perceptions, question quality and association with summative performance. Postgrad. Med. J. **94**(1108), 97–103 (2018)
5. Prajapati, U., Rawat, A., Deb, D.: Integrated peripheral security system for different areas based on exchange of specific data rates. Wireless Pers. Commun. **111**(3), 1355–1366 (2020)
6. Sasikaladevi, N., Geetha, K., Venkata Srinivas, K.N.: A multi-tier security system (SAIL) for protecting audio signals from malicious exploits. Int. J. Speech Technol. **21**(3), 1–14 (2018)
7. Fu, W., Liu, S., Srivastava, G.: Optimization of big data scheduling in social networks. Entropy **21**(9), 902 (2019)
8. Liu, S., Li, Z., Zhang, Y., et al.: Introduction of key problems in long-distance learning and training. Mob. Netw. Appl. **24**(1), 1–4 (2019)

9. Liu, S., Liu, D., Srivastava, G., Połap, D., Woźniak, M.: Overview and methods of correlation filter algorithms in object tracking. Complex Intell. Syst. 1–23 (2020). https://doi.org/10. 1007/s40747-020-00161-4

10. Majid, M., Reza, G., Mohsen, G.: Power system security assessment with high wind penetration using the farms models based on their correlation. IET Renew. Power Gener. **12**(8), 893–900 (2018)

11. Song, J., Ouyang, D., Liu, Y., et al.: Improving the accuracy of defect diagnosis by test score based on fault free. Electron. Lett. **56**(16), 845–848 (2020)

12. Qu, H., Wang, Y., Niu, C., et al.: A novel strategy and test of passive shimming for multi-volumes in cylindrical MRI scanner. IEEE Trans. Magn. **56**(2), 1–7 (2020)

13. Huang, S.C., Hsu, C.C., Fu, T.C., et al.: Application of stepper in cardiopulmonary exercise test for patients with hemiplegia. Medicine **99**(28), e21058 (2020)

Sliding Mode Adaptive Control for Sensorless Permanent Magnet Synchronous Motor

Lei Wang[1], Tongwei Liang[2], and Shengjun Wen[3(✉)]

[1] HRG (Shandong) Intelligent Equipment Research Institute, No. 1268 Gongye 4 Road,
Jinan 250000, Shandong, China
wangleisd@hitrobotgroup.com
[2] Department of Electric and Information Engineering, Zhongyuan University of Technology,
No. 41 Zhongyuan Road, Zhengzhou 450007, China
[3] Zhongyuan-Peterburg Aviation College, Zhongyuan University of Technology,
No. 41 Zhongyuan Road, Zhengzhou 450007, China
wsj@zut.edu.cn

Abstract. In this paper, a sliding mode control technology based on sensorless adaptive estimation is proposed for a permanent magnet synchronous motor. Firstly, the motor position and speed is estimated by using an adaptive estimator based on model reference instead of the traditional mechanical sensor, where the stability of the estimating system is ensured by using Popov hyperstability. Then, the sliding mode control is designed to track the rotor position accurately. Finally, the simulation results are given to show the presented scheme, where, the estimation error is less than 1.5% and the tracing error of the rotor speed 0.7% under the sliding mode control scheme.

Keywords: Permanent magnet synchronous motor · Sliding mode control · Adaptive estimation · Sensorless technology

1 Introduction

Permanent magnet synchronous motor (PMSM) is widely used in various complicated working situations due to its high speed, wide speed range, good reliability and excellent control characteristics, especially in high-power AC drive systems. Various sensorless control methods of PMSM with high performance are proposed, inductance method [1], carrier frequency component method [2], high frequency signal injection method [3, 4], which can be applied to low speed control. Most of these methods are considered by analyzing the output response of the motor to suppress the external input signal. The complicated signal processing and analytical algorithm make it difficult to apply these methods to the motor control at a higher speed. Some methods based on the motor back-EMF are suitable for medium speed and high speed control, which include direct calculation method based on the mathematical equations of the motor [5], extended Kalman filter method [6], adaptive observer method [7, 8], sliding mode observer method

© ICST Institute for Computer Sciences, Social Informatics and Telecommunications Engineering 2021
Published by Springer Nature Switzerland AG 2021. All Rights Reserved
W. Fu et al. (Eds.): ICMTEL 2021, LNICST 387, pp. 214–222, 2021.
https://doi.org/10.1007/978-3-030-82562-1_19

[9] and artificial intelligence algorithm [10]. However, for above methods, the estimation accuracy is poor, or there exist complicated calculation problems which need to take up many resources in actual applications.

In this paper, a sliding mode control technology based on sensorless adaptive estimation is proposed for the permanent magnet synchronous motor. The motor position and speed is estimated by using an adaptive estimator based on model reference. And the sliding mode control is designed to ensure the tracking performance accurately.

2   Model of Permanent Magnet Synchronous Motor

The voltage equation of a three-phase permanent magnet synchronous motor can be described as in (1) in the natural coordinate system.

$$
\begin{bmatrix} U_a \\ U_b \\ U_c \end{bmatrix} = \begin{bmatrix} R_1 & 0 & 0 \\ 0 & R_1 & 0 \\ 0 & 0 & R_1 \end{bmatrix} \begin{bmatrix} i_a \\ i_b \\ i_c \end{bmatrix} + \frac{d}{dt} \begin{bmatrix} \psi_a(\theta, i) \\ \psi_b(\theta, i) \\ \psi_c(\theta, i) \end{bmatrix} \tag{1}
$$

Here, U_a, U_b, U_c is the three-phase winding voltage, R_1 is the stator winding resistance; i_a, i_b, i_c is the three-phase winding line current; $\psi_a(\theta, i)$, $\psi_b(\theta, i)$, $\psi_c(\theta, i)$ is the three-phase winding full flux linkage, θ is the space between the rotating coordinate d axis and the three-phase stationary coordinate A axis Electrical angle.

The flux linkage equation for a three-phase winding is:

$$
\begin{bmatrix} \psi_A(\theta, i) \\ \psi_B(\theta, i) \\ \psi_C(\theta, i) \end{bmatrix} = \begin{pmatrix} L_1 & -M_1 & -M_1 \\ -M_1 & L_1 & -M_1 \\ -M_1 & -M_1 & L_1 \end{pmatrix} \bullet \begin{pmatrix} i_a \\ i_b \\ i_c \end{pmatrix} + A \begin{pmatrix} i_a \\ i_b \\ i_c \end{pmatrix} \tag{2}
$$

where

$$
A = \begin{pmatrix} -L_2 \cos 2\theta & M_2 \cos 2(\theta + 30°) & M_2 \cos 2(\theta + 150°) \\ M_2 \cos 2(\theta + 30°) & -L_2 \cos 2(\theta - 120°) & M_2 \cos 2(\theta - 90°) \\ M_2 \cos 2(\theta + 150°) & M_2 \cos 2(\theta - 90°) & -L_2 \cos 2(\theta + 120°) \end{pmatrix}
$$

and L_1 and L_2 are the average and second harmonic amplitude of the phase stator winding self-inductance. M_1 and M_2 are the absolute values of the mutual inductance average and the amplitude of the second harmonic. The electromagnetic torque of a permanent magnet synchronous motor can be expressed as:

$$
T_e = \begin{cases} p \cdot \begin{bmatrix} i_a & i_b & i_c \end{bmatrix} T \cdot \begin{bmatrix} i_a \\ i_b \\ i_c \end{bmatrix} + \frac{p}{\omega} \begin{bmatrix} i_a & i_b & i_c \end{bmatrix} \cdot \begin{bmatrix} E_a \\ E_b \\ E_c \end{bmatrix} \\ \frac{J}{p} \frac{d\omega}{dt} - T_f \end{cases} \tag{3}
$$

where p is the pole pair number of the permanent magnet synchronous motor, ω_e is the motor angular frequency, and E_a, E_b, and E_c are the back electromotive forces generated in the stator winding when the motor rotor rotates. J is the moment of inertia and T_f is the load torque at the shaft end of the motor rotor.

Permanent Magnet Synchronous Motor will be control in two phase d-, q- reference coordinate system through coordinate transformation. In this coordination, the d-axis is the direct-axis, which is related to the rotor flux linkage. The q-axis is quadrature-axis, which is 90° leading d-axis. The PMSM model is shown in Eq. (4).

$$\begin{bmatrix} u_\alpha \\ u_\beta \end{bmatrix} = R \begin{bmatrix} i_\alpha \\ i_\beta \end{bmatrix} + \frac{d}{dt} \begin{bmatrix} \psi_\alpha \\ \psi_\beta \end{bmatrix} \tag{4}$$

We have

$$\begin{bmatrix} \psi_\alpha \\ \psi_\beta \end{bmatrix} = \begin{bmatrix} L + \Delta L \cos 2\theta_r & -\Delta L \sin 2\theta_r \\ -\Delta L \sin 2\theta_r & L - \Delta L \cos 2\theta \end{bmatrix} \begin{bmatrix} i_\alpha \\ i_\beta \end{bmatrix} + \psi_f \begin{bmatrix} \cos \theta_r \\ \sin \theta_r \end{bmatrix}$$

where u_α, u_β i_α i_β ψ_α ψ_β are the stator phase voltage, phase current, and phase total flux linkage, respectively. $L = (L_d + L_q)/2$ is the average inductance; $VL = (L_d - L_q)/2$ is the semi-difference inductance, and θ_r is the rotor position.

3   Adaptive Estimation of the Rotor Speed

The adaptive estimation structure of the rotor speed based on reference model is shown in Fig. 1 for the sensorless permanent magnet synchronous motor. The rotor position is obtained by the adaptive estimation method, and the reference model is selected without the position reference. A reasonable parameter adaptive law is designed to adjust the parameters of the adjustable model and accurately track and estimate the rotation speed.

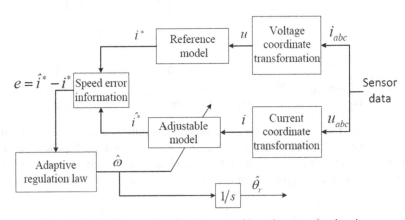

Fig. 1. Block diagram of sensorless control based on speed estimation

Combining the motor mathematical model established by Eqs. (1)–(4), the current equation of the motor in the synchronous rotating coordinate system can be obtained as follows.

$$\begin{cases} \frac{d}{dt} i_d = -\frac{R}{L_d} i_d + \omega \frac{L_q}{L_d} i_q + \frac{1}{L_d} u_d \\ \frac{d}{dt} i_q = -\frac{R}{L_q} i_q - \omega \frac{L_d}{L_q} i_d - \frac{\psi}{L_q} \omega + \frac{1}{L_q} u_q \end{cases} \tag{5}$$

Then, we have the adjustable model equation of the system as follows,

$$\frac{d}{dt}\begin{bmatrix} \hat{i}_d^* \\ \hat{i}_q^* \end{bmatrix} = \begin{bmatrix} -\frac{R}{L_d} & \hat{\omega}\frac{L_q}{L_d} \\ -\hat{\omega}\frac{L_d}{L_q} & -\frac{R}{L_q} \end{bmatrix}\begin{bmatrix} \hat{i}_d^* \\ \hat{i}_q^* \end{bmatrix} + \begin{bmatrix} \frac{1}{L_d}u_d^* \\ \frac{1}{L_q}u_q^* \end{bmatrix} \tag{6}$$

where $\hat{i}_d^* = \hat{i}_d + \frac{\psi}{L_d}, \hat{i}_q^* = \hat{i}_q, u_d^* = u_d + \frac{R_1}{L_d}\psi, u_q^* = u_q$.

Define generalized errors of the currents $e = i^* - \hat{i}^*$, we have

$$\frac{d}{dt}\begin{bmatrix} e_d \\ e_q \end{bmatrix} = \begin{bmatrix} -\frac{R}{L_d} & \omega\frac{L_q}{L_d} \\ -\omega\frac{L_d}{L_q} & -\frac{R}{L_q} \end{bmatrix}\begin{bmatrix} e_d \\ e_q \end{bmatrix} - (\hat{\omega} - \omega)J\begin{bmatrix} \hat{i}_d^* \\ \hat{i}_q^* \end{bmatrix} \tag{7}$$

It can be rewritten as

$$\begin{cases} \frac{d}{dt}e = Ae - W \\ v = C \cdot e \end{cases} \tag{8}$$

where $e_d = \hat{i}_d^* - i_d^*, e_q = \hat{i}_q^* - i_q^*, W = (\hat{\omega} - \omega)J\hat{i}^*, B = \begin{bmatrix} 1 & 0 \\ 0 & 1 \end{bmatrix}, C = I = \begin{bmatrix} 1 & 0 \\ 0 & 1 \end{bmatrix}$,

$J = \begin{bmatrix} 0 & -\frac{L_q}{L_d} \\ \frac{L_d}{L_q} & 0 \end{bmatrix}, A = \begin{bmatrix} -\frac{R}{L_q} & \omega\frac{L_q}{L_d} \\ -\omega\frac{L_d}{L_q} & -\frac{R}{L_q} \end{bmatrix}.$

According to Popov hyperstability [24], to make the system stable, the system (8) shall meet the requirement

$$\eta(0, t') = \int_0^{t'} v^T W \, dt \geq -\gamma_0^2 \ (t' \geq 0, \ \gamma_0 \geq 0)$$

where $W = (\hat{\omega} - \omega)J\hat{i}^*$ satisfies the condition of the positive real.

In order to the above condition, we assume that the parameter adaptive regulation law has the following proportional integral form:

$$\hat{\omega} = \int_0^t F_1(v, t, \tau)d\tau + F_2(v, t) + \hat{\omega}(0) \tag{9}$$

where $\hat{\omega}(0)$ is the angular velocity of the motor at the initial moment, and we have.

$$F_1(v, t, \tau) = k_i e^T J\hat{i}^*, \qquad F_2(v, t) = k_p e^T J\hat{i}^* \tag{10}$$

It can be proved, the above design satisfies the condition of Popov integral inequality. Therefore, the adaptive estimation parameter is convergence. Substitute Eq. (10) into Eq. (9) and the adaptive regulation law of the motor speed can be got

$$\begin{aligned} \hat{\omega} &= \int_0^{t'} k_i e^T J\hat{i}^* d\tau + k_p e^T J\hat{i}^* + \hat{\omega}(0) \\ &= \int_0^{t'} k_i D d\tau + k_p D + \hat{\omega}(0) \end{aligned} \tag{11}$$

where

$$D = e^{T} J \hat{i}^{*} = \frac{L_q}{L_d} i_d \hat{i}_q - \frac{L_d}{L_q} i_q \hat{i}_d + \frac{\psi}{L_d} \frac{L_d}{L_q} \left(\hat{i}_q - i_q \right) + \hat{i}_d \hat{i}_q \left(\frac{L_d}{L_q} - \frac{L_q}{L_d} \right).$$

The estimation position of the rotor can be obtained

$$\hat{\theta}_r = \int_0^t \hat{\omega} dt \tag{12}$$

4 Sliding Mode Control of Permanent Magnet Synchronous Motor

Then, the sliding mode control scheme is considered to track the rotor position accurately along an exponentially approaching rule. The sliding mode control diagram based on speed estimation is shown in Fig. 2.

In this paper, an exponentially approaching rule $\dot{s} = -\varepsilon \, \mathrm{sgn}(s) - qs$, $\varepsilon, q > 0$ is used to design the controller, where we consider $i_q = 0$. In the synchronous rotating coordinate system, the current equation of the motor is

$$\begin{cases} \dfrac{di_q}{dt} = \dfrac{1}{L} \left(u_q - R i_q - p \psi_f \right) \\ \dfrac{d\omega}{dt} = \dfrac{1}{J} \left(\dfrac{3 p \psi_f}{2} i_q - T_L \right) \end{cases} \tag{13}$$

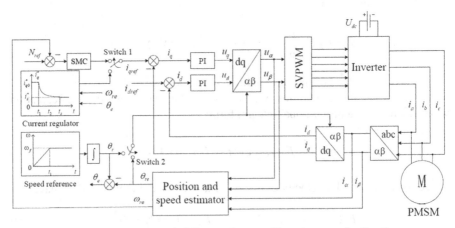

Fig. 2. Block diagram of sliding mode control based on speed estimation

Define the state varies of the motor as

$$\begin{cases} x_1 = \omega_{ref} - \omega \\ x_2 = \dot{x}_1 = -\dot{\omega} \end{cases} \tag{14}$$

where ω_{ref} and ω are the reference speed and real speed of the motor. So, the state equation can be described as

$$\begin{cases} \dot{x}_1 = -\dot{\omega}_m = \frac{1}{J}\left(T_L - \frac{3p\psi_f}{2}i_q\right) \\ \dot{x}_2 = -\ddot{\omega}_m = -\frac{3p\psi_f}{2J}\dot{i}_q \end{cases} \tag{15}$$

Assume that $u = \dot{i}_q$, $H = \frac{3p\psi_f}{2J}$, we have

$$\begin{bmatrix} \dot{x}_1 \\ \dot{x}_2 \end{bmatrix} = \begin{bmatrix} 0 & 1 \\ 0 & 0 \end{bmatrix}\begin{bmatrix} x_1 \\ x_2 \end{bmatrix} + \begin{bmatrix} 0 \\ -H \end{bmatrix}u \tag{16}$$

We design a sliding variable as $s = cx_1 + x_2$, where c is the design parameter and larger than 0. Then, its derivation is

$$\dot{s} = c\dot{x}_1 + \dot{x}_2 = cx_2 + \dot{x}_2 = cx_2 - Hu \tag{17}$$

Ignoring the disturbance estimation error, the equivalent control can be obtained by

$$u = \frac{1}{H}\left[cx_2 + \varepsilon\,\mathrm{sgn}(s) + qs\right] \tag{18}$$

That is, the projection current of the rotating coordinate system is

$$i_q^* = \frac{1}{H}\int_0^t \left[cx_2 + \varepsilon\,\mathrm{sgn}(s) + qs\right]d\tau \tag{19}$$

From the above projection current, we can see that an integral term is included in the design. So that, it can eliminate effectively the chattering phenomenon of the sliding mode control system and reduce the steady-state error of the system. Also, the system is gradually stable under the condition $s\dot{s} = -\varepsilon s\,\mathrm{sgn}(s) - qs^2 < 0$.

5 Simulation Results

In this section, MATLAB Simulink is used to verify the proposed adaptive estimation and sliding mode control scheme. The motor parameters used in the simulation experiment are shown in Table 1.

Table 1. Parameters of PMSM for experiment

Parameters	Value	Parameters	Value
Rated frequency f_n	50 Hz	The rotor ux linkage ψ_f	0.213 wb
Rated power P_w	1 Kw	Stator resistance R	2.878 Ω
Rated speed N_r	1000 r/min	The moment of inertia J	1.94×10^{-3} kg · m^2
Axis inductance L_d, L_q	0.85 mH	Pole pairs p	4

The results of the adaptive estimation are shown in Fig. 3 and Fig. 4, where Fig. 3 shows speed estimation of sensorless motor during load fluctuation and Fig. 4 shows position error of sensorless motor. In order to verify the adaptive performance under the load disturbance, the electromagnetic torque of the motor is transformed from 0 Nm to 2 Nm at 0.2 s and from 2 Nm to 1 Nm at 0.4 s. From the results, we can see that the speed and position can be estimated accurately under the load fluctuation. Also, it shows that the estimation error of the motor position is less than 1.5%.

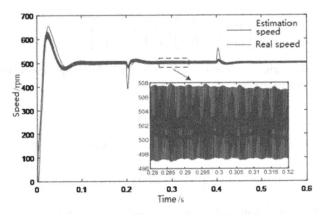

Fig. 3. Real speed and estimation speed.

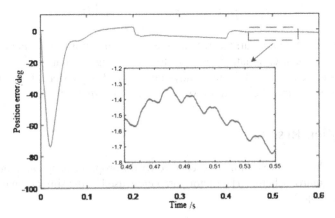

Fig. 4. Position error under adaptive estimation

Figure 5 shows the speed response of sliding mode control during load fluctuation and Fig. 6 shows the speed response of sliding mode control under variable reference input. From Fig. 5, it shows that the robust stability of the system can be ensured when the load torque of the motor is suddenly changed (increase by 0.5 Nm). In Fig. 6, the motor is operated at the rising and falling speed. These results show that the steady-state error of the system is less than 0.9% by using the presented sliding mode control method.

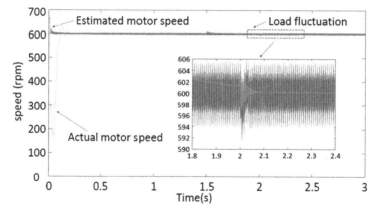

Fig. 5. Speed response with load fluctuation under adaptive estimation

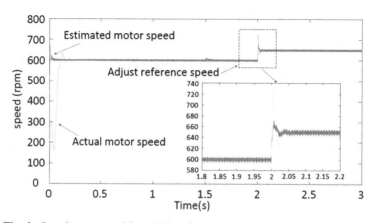

Fig. 6. Speed response with variable reference input under adaptive estimation

6   Conclusion

In this paper, a sliding mode control technology based on sensorless adaptive estimation is proposed for a permanent magnet synchronous motor. Firstly, the motor position and speed is estimated by using an adaptive estimator based on model reference instead of the traditional mechanical sensor, where the stability of the estimating system is ensured by using Popov hyperstability. Then, the sliding mode control is designed to track the rotor position accurately. Finally, the simulation results are given to show the presented scheme, where, the estimation error is less than 1.5% and the tracing error of the rotor speed 0.7% under the sliding mode control scheme.

Acknowledgment. This work was supported in part by the National Natural Science Foundation of China (U1813201, 62073297, 61973157); National Key Research and Development Project of China (2020YFB1712403); Fundamental Research Foundation of Zhongyuan University of Technology (K2020TD005).

References

1. Schmidt, E., Eilenberger, A.: Calculation of position-dependent inductances of a permanent magnet synchronous machine with an external rotor by using voltage-driven finite element analyses. IEEE Trans. Magn. **45**(3), 1788–1791 (2009)
2. Jeong, Y., Lorenz, R.D., Jahns, T.M., Sul, S.: Initial rotor position estimation of an interior permanent-magnet synchronous machine using carrier-frequency injection methods. IEEE Trans. Ind. Appl. **41**(1), 38–45 (2005)
3. Li, Z., Xia, C., Chen, W.: Position sensorless control of brushless DC motor based on line back EMF. J. Electric. Eng. **25**(7), 24–41 (2010)
4. Yuan, L., Hu, B., Wei, K., Chen, W.: The Control Principle and MATLAB Simulation of Modern Permanent Magnet Synchronous Motor. Beijing University of Aeronautics and Astronautics Press, Beijing (2015)
5. Raca, D., Harke, M.C., Lorenz, R.D.: Robust magnet polarity estimation for initialization of PM synchronous machines with near-zero saliency. IEEE Trans. Ind. Appl. **44**(4), 1199–1209 (2008)
6. Wang, G., Yang, R., Yu, Y., et al.: Initial position estimation method for built-in permanent magnet synchronous motor rotor. J. Electric Mach. Control **14**(6), 51–60 (2010)
7. Louis, J.P., Zhu, X.: Synchronous Motor Control. Mechanical Industry Press, Beijing (2016)
8. Wang, Z., Ye, Y.: Self-starting process of permanent magnet synchronous motor without position sensor based on back EMF algorithm. J. Electric Mach. Control **10**(15), 36–41 (2011)
9. Zhaowei, Q., Tingna, S., Yindong, W.: New sliding-mode observer for position senseless control of permanent-magnet synchronous motor. IEEE Trans. Ind. Electron. **60**, 710–741 (2013)
10. Liu, J., Xiao, F., Shen, Y., Mai, Z., Li, C.: A review of the research on position sensorless control technology for permanent magnet synchronous motors. J. Electric. Eng. **16**(32), 76–85 (2010)

An Improved Detection Method of Safety Helmet Wearing Based on CenterNet

Bo Wang[1], Yong Zhang[1], Qinjun Zhao[1(✉)], and Shengjun Shi[2]

[1] School of Electrical Engineering, University of Jinan, Jinan 250022, China
cse_zhaoqj@ujn.edu.cn

[2] Harbin Engineering University Robot Group Co., Ltd., Harbin 150000, China

Abstract. In some factories or construction sites, accidents occur because workers do not wearing safety helmets correctly. In order to reduce the accident rate, an improved detection method of safety helmet wearing based on CenterNet algorithm is proposed. The original IOU method is optimized by combining with GIoU, and debug the training model Res/DLA framework in the training process. At the same time, various parameters are adjusted by experiments. In the safety helmet wearing test task, theoretical analysis and experimental results show that mAP (Mean Average Precision) is up to 42.6%, detection rate is increased to 30.3%. Compared with CenterNet, the detection accuracy and detection rate are slightly improved. The proposed algorithm not only meets the real-time performance of detection task in safety helmet wearing detection but also has higher detection accuracy.

Keywords: Improved detection · Safety helmet · CenterNet

1 Introduction

Helmets recognition systems play a crucial role in the safe production. Through such real-time supervision of the construction operation plant area, it sounds the safety alarm for the workers, and improves the safety awareness of the workers while reducing the occurrence of safety accidents. In the future trend, with the continuous development of the industry and continues to segment demand, helmet identification system will further optimize related functions, leading to a more convenient management for the enterprise.

Domestic and foreign scholars had some research: Girshick and Ren [2] proposed Fast R-CNN and Fast R-CNN respectively, which improved the accuracy and detection speed, and the frame rate reached 5 f/s. In 2015, Redmon J [3] proposed the YOLO detection algorithm, which can detect video at a speed of 45 f/s. Based on YOLO, Redmon also proposed YOLOv2 [4] and YOLOv3 [5]

Supported by the National Key R & D Program of China (2018AAA0101703) and the key research and development project of Shandong province (2019GNC106093).

W. Fu et al. (Eds.): ICMTEL 2021, LNICST 387, pp. 223–231, 2021.
https://doi.org/10.1007/978-3-030-82562-1_20

detection algorithms. In April 2019, Zhou et al. proposed CenterNet: objects as points [6], and proposed a new anchor free algorithm based on key points.

Based on the CenterNet algorithm, this paper optimizes it when it is applied to the safety helmet wearing detection that combining with GIoU to optimize the original IoU method. By adding C detection frame (C detection frame is the smallest rectangular box including detection box and real box) to make up for the defect that IOU's loss is the same when the detection frame and real box do not overlap, we also debug the training model Res/DLA framework in the training process. At the same time, various parameters are adjusted by experiments. To some extent, it eliminates the occurrence of coincidence detection and false detection of non target objects. Experiments show that the improved algorithm based on CenterNet can guarantee the detection rate and improve the detection accuracy.

2   CenterNet Principle

CenterNet takes the target as the centre of BBox when building the model. In the detection, the center point is determined by key point estimation, and other attributes, such as size and position, are regressed.

2.1   Frame

As shown in the Fig. 1.

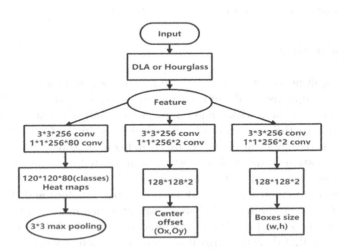

Fig. 1. Flow chart of framework.

2.2 Prediction of Key Point

Set $A \subseteq B^{W*H*3}$ as input image, the goal is to generate a heat map for key point prediction $E \subseteq [0,1]^{\frac{W}{B}*\frac{H}{B}*C}$, the R is the size scaling, and C is the number of feature maps. For the key point c of Ground Truth, its coordinate position is $\theta \in B^2$, after the network processing, the position on the feature map is

$$\tilde{\theta} = \left\lfloor \frac{\theta}{B} \right\rfloor \tag{1}$$

The paper passes the key points of Ground Truth through the Gaussian core

$$E_{d,e,c} = exp(-\frac{(d - \tilde{\theta}_d)^2 + (e - \tilde{\theta}_e)^2}{2\sigma^2\theta}) \tag{2}$$

disperse to $E \subseteq [0,1]^{\frac{W}{B}*\frac{H}{B}*C}$, the loss function is

$$L_k = \frac{1}{N}\sum_{dec}\begin{cases}(1 - \hat{E}_{dec})^\alpha \log(\hat{E}_{dec}) if E_{dec} = 1\\(1 - E_{dec})^\beta(\hat{E}_{dec})^\alpha, otherwise\\\log(1 - \hat{E}_{dec})\end{cases} \tag{3}$$

α and β are set to 2 and 4; N is the number of key points. Without considering $(1 - E_{dec})^\beta$, the new formula is

$$(1 - Z_t)^\alpha * \log Z_t \tag{4}$$

$$Z_t = \begin{cases}\hat{E}_{dec}, if E_{dec} = 1\\1 - \hat{E}_{dec}, otherwise\end{cases} \tag{5}$$

$log Z_t$ is the standard cross-entropy loss function.

And that is adding the prediction of the local offset to each key point $\tilde{T} \subseteq B^{\frac{W}{B}*\frac{H}{B}*2}$.

$$L_{off} = \frac{1}{N}\sum_{\theta}\left|\hat{T}_{\tilde{\theta}} - (\frac{\theta}{B} - \tilde{\theta})\right| \tag{6}$$

2.3 IOU(Intersection over Union)

IoU is what we call cross ratio.

$$IOU = \frac{M \cap N}{M \cup N} \tag{7}$$

(1) It can reflect the effect of the predicted detection frame and the real detection frame;
(2) Scale invariance, that is scale invariant. In regression tasks, IoU is a direct indicator of distance between predict box and ground-truth (Satisfy non-negativity; Identity; Symmetry; Triangle inequality).

Problems (disadvantages) that may occur as a loss function:

(1) If the prediction frame and the detection frame do not intersect, IOU = 0. Moreover, when loss = 0, the gradient can not be returned, resulting in the inability to train;

(2) As shown in the Fig. 2, the IOU of the three cases are equal, but it can be seen that their coincidence degree is not the same. The IOU value can not reflect how the two boxes intersect. The effect is good to bad from left to right.

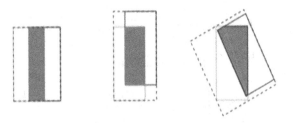

Fig. 2. Chart of comparison.

As shown in the figure above, three boxes with different relative positions have the same IoU = 0.33, but different GIoU = 0.33, 0.24, −0.1. When the alignment direction of the box is better, the value of GIoU is higher.

2.4   Improvement Direction

The regression loss (MSE loss, L1-smooth loss, et al.) optimization of BBox in detection task is not completely equivalent to IOU optimization, and Ln norm is also sensitive to object scale, IOU can not directly optimize the non overlapping part. Therefore, IOU can be directly set as the loss of regression. This method is called GIoU Loss(Generalized Intersection over Union) [7].

$$GIOU = IOU - \frac{P - (M \cup N)}{P} \tag{8}$$

The meaning of the above formula is: firstly, calculate the minimum closure area C of the two boxes (popular understanding: including the area of the smallest box of the prediction box and the real box), and then calculate the IoU, and then calculate the proportion of the closure area that does not belong to the two boxes in the closure area, and finally use IoU to subtract this proportion to get GIoU.

Characteristic:

(1) GIoU as distance, L_{GIoU} = 1-GIoU, which satisfy nonnegativity, identity, symmetry, trigonometric inequality;
(2) Scale invariance;
(3) When two frames overlap wirelessly, IoU = GIoU;
(4) When a and B coincide, GIoU = 1. When the intersection of a and B is very small or there is no intersection, GIoU = −1;
(5) GIoU takes into account non overlapping areas not considered by IoU.

GIoU is used to optimize the original IoU in CenterNet. Finally, the improved CenterNet algorithm is used to test the wearing of safety helmet.

3   Experimental Data Set Making

Data Collection: In this paper uses the same specification but different color helmet wearing pictures collected on the Internet to make the datasets.

Data Filtering: The background image without subject is deleted from the datasets, and the photo of human body wearing safety helmet is needed in the experiment.

Data Marking: In the annotation, we select the target in the image by using lableImg. The interface is shown in Fig. 3.

Fig. 3. Diagram of annotation.

4   Experimental Analysis

As shown in Fig. 4.

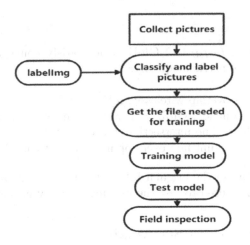

Fig. 4. Chart of experimental flow.

4.1 Experimental Scheme

In this paper, The datasets are divided into five categories: A to E. The classification is shown in Fig. 5.

Fig. 5. Diagram of sample.

4.2 Network Training

The parameters are adjusted according to many experiments, as shown in Table 1.

Table 1. Description of network parameters.

Parameter	Parameter value
Learning rate	1.25e-4
Epoch	140
Batch size	5
NMS	False
$lr_s tep$	[90, 120]
Arch	DLA_{34}
$head_c onv$	256

4.3 Experimental Platform and Network Training

In this paper, the improved CenterNet algorithm is used to test. The improvement point is: the IOU in the original CenterNet algorithm is improved by using the GIoU which calculates the minimum closure region. At the same time, Faster R-CNN in reference [1], RetinaNet in [6], Yolo V3 in reference [5] and CenterNet in reference [7] are used for comparison, the results shown in Table 2.

Table 2. Comparison of experimental results.

Algorithm	mAP(%)	Frame rate recognition
$Faster R - CNN$	42.5	5.3
RetinaNet	30.7	5.3
YOLO v3	31.3	20.2
CenterNet	39.3	28.4
Improved CenterNet	42.6	30.3

4.4 Result Analysis

The experimental results show that although the accuracy rate of improved CenterNet is lower than that of Faster R-CNN, the detection rate ratio is several times of that of Faster R-CNN. Therefore, the improved CenterNet performs better. However, the other methods are not as good as the improved CenterNet algorithm in two aspects. The improved CenterNet algorithm takes into account the detection accuracy and detection rate at the same time, and can complete the safety helmet wearing detection task better.

In addition, in order to feel the detection differences more intuitively between different algorithms, this paper selects some detection images for comparative analysis, in which Fig. 6 is the detection effect of CenterNet algorithm, and Fig. 7 is the detection effect of improved CenterNet algorithm.

Fig. 6. The detection effect of CenterNet algorithm.

Fig. 7. The detection effect of improved CenterNet algorithm.

By observing Fig. 6 and Fig. 7, it can be found that the coincidence frame display and the false recognition of non target objects are solved to a certain extent. Therefore, in this paper that the improved CenterNet algorithm can maintain a high detection rate and meet the requirements of real-time detection for helmet wearing detection and classification tasks.

5   Conclusion

In this paper, an improved method of helmet wearing detection based on CenterNet algorithm is proposed. The safety helmet wearing detection experiment is carried out by using the video taken by mobile phone in the construction site as the data set, which can ensure the high detection accuracy and still have a fast detection speed, and meet the requirements of the accuracy and real-time of the safety helmet wearing detection in the work environment monitoring video basically.

References

1. Tingting Z., Jianwu Z., et al.: A survey of image object detection algorithm based on deep learning. Telecommun. Sci. **36**(7), 92–106 (2020)
2. Girshick, R.: Fast R-CNN. In: IEEE International Conference on Computer Vision, pp. 1440–1448 (2015)

3. Redmon J, Divvala, S., Girshick, R., et al.: You only look once: unified, real-time object detection. In: Proceedings of the IEEE Conference on Computer Vision and Pattern Recognition, pp. 779–788 (2015)
4. Redmon, J., Farhadi, A.: YOLO9000: better, faster, stronger. In: IEEE Conference on Computer Vision and Pattern Recognition, pp. 6517–6525 (2017)
5. Redmon, J., Farhadi, A.: YOLOv3: an incremental improvement. In: IEEE Conference on Computer Vision and Pattern Recognition, pp. 89–95 (2018)
6. Zhou, X.Y, Wang, D., Philipp, K.: Objects as Points. In: Conference on Computer Vision and Pattern Recognition (CVPR) (2019)
7. Rezatofighi, H., Tsoi, N., Gwak, J.Y., et al.: Generalized intersection over union: a metric and a loss for bounding box regression. In: 2019 IEEE/CVF Conference on Computer Vision and Pattern Recognition (CVPR), IEEE (2020)

Information Techniques
for Social/Natural Application

Influence Maximization Based on True Threshold in Social Networks

Wei Hao[1,2], Qianyi Zhan[1,2(✉)], and Yuan Liu[1,2]

[1] School of Artificial Intelligence and Computer Science, Jiangnan University,
Wuxi, China
6201613052@stu.jiangnan.edu.cn
[2] Jiangsu Key Laboratory of Media Design and Software Technology, Wuxi, China
{zhanqianyi,lyuan1800}@jiangnan.edu.cn

Abstract. As E-marketing based on online social networks develops fast, the influence maximization problem draws attention from both academics and industries. This problem focuses on which subset of users should be selected as seed users so that based on the specific information diffusion model, the advertising companies can maximize word-of-mouth effect. Exisiting related work assume there is no cost to choose these seed users, or the cost is given in the problem setting. While in real situation, it is crucial but difficult to elicit users' true attitude over being seeds. Moreover, we notice "threshold" as users' private information in the Linear Threshold model can represent individual's preference. Thus we propose a new model in which users, willing to be seeds, are asked to report their threshold information. The method called TREE is designed to solve this model, especially the payment mechanism should make sure all users tell truth. Experiments on real social network data to verify the effectiveness of TREE.

Keywords: Social networks · Influence maximization · Linear threshold model

1 Introduction

Due to the success of online social networking (OSN) websites in recent years, the trend of using social networks as a marketing tool grows rapidly and spans diverse areas. Based on "word-of-mouth" diffusion process, *viral marketing* has received considerable attention from both field of research and industry. The idea behind viral marketing is using small marketing cost by targeting a set of most influential users in social network to make their aggregated influence reach a large portion of the network. Motivated by this, computer scientists focus on so-called *influence maximization problem*, which is finding such set of initial adopters that maximize the number of users influenced by them eventually.

© ICST Institute for Computer Sciences, Social Informatics and Telecommunications Engineering 2021
Published by Springer Nature Switzerland AG 2021. All Rights Reserved
W. Fu et al. (Eds.): ICMTEL 2021, LNICST 387, pp. 235–247, 2021.
https://doi.org/10.1007/978-3-030-82562-1_21

The influence maximization problem is modeled as an algorithmic problem: given a social network graph $G = (V, E, w)$ and a budget k, where V denotes nodes in the social network, E is the set of directed edge representing the social relationship among nodes, and $w(u, v)$ represents the influence weight of node u on v and $0 \leq w(u, v) \leq 1$. The aim is to select a seed set S of k nodes such that the total influence effect is maximized through propagation.

Domingos and Richardson [11] first studied the problem of influence propagation and identification of influential users. The first systemic study of influence maximization problem was provided by Kempe et al. [3]. They proposed two basic stochastic influence models coming from mathematical sociology, namely, the *Independent Cascade (IC) model* and *Linear Threshold (LT) model*. Kempe et al. proved this problem is NP-hard for both two models, but the objective function of influence spread $\sigma(S)$ is *monotone* and *submodular*. The function is *monotone* if $\sigma(A) \leq \sigma(B)$ when $A \subseteq B$. Moreover it is modular if $\sigma(A \cup v) - \sigma(A) \geq \sigma(B \cup v) - \sigma(B)$ for all $A \subseteq B$ and $v \notin A$. Based on that Kempe et al. [3] proposed discrete optimization methodology and obtained the greedy approximation algorithms which achieved an approximation ratio of $1 - 1/e$.

Each node in both models is active or inactive. In the IC model, the simplest one of dynamic cascade models, an active node u is given a single chance to activate each currently inactive neighbor for example node v; the success probability is $w(u, v)$, which is independently of the history so far. While the linear threshold model is the core of most models based on the use of node-specific thresholds. Each node v holds a threshold θ_v uniformly at random from the interval $[0, 1]$, the node v is activated when the total weight of its active neighbors is no less than its threshold: $\Sigma w(u, v) \geq \theta_v$. The linear threshold model stresses the threshold behavior in propagation of influence, which makes it meets the actual situation better. For example, when enough people recommend a new restaurant or discuss a new book, we may also would like to follow it.

1.1 Related Work

A series of studies have been done to solve the influence maximization problem. The original greedy algorithm with constant-factor approximation was first proposed by Kempe et al. [3]. The Monte-Carol simulations on influence cascade to estimate the spread makes their algorithm not scalable. Leskovec et al. [5] developed an efficient algorithm based on "lazy forward" optimization in selecting new seeds. Experiments show it achieves near-optimal result with 700 times faster than the simple greedy algorithm.

By using properties of the IC model, much algorithms are designed for the IC model specifically. Kimura and Saito [6] proposed a model based on shortest-path. Chen et al. [12] develop a degree discount heuristics for the IC model with same edge probabilities. In [1], maximum influence arborescence (MIA) algorithm is proposed.

In contrast, the research on the LT model is much less. The above heuristic algorithms cannot be applied directly due to special features of the LT model.

To our knowledge, the algorithms in [2] and [4] are state of the art. In [2], Chen et al. observed that computing the spread is NP-hard in general graphs, while it costs linear time on directed acyclic graphs (DAGs). Based on that, they designed LDAG method which principle is similar with MIA in [1]. While [4] proposed an alternative algorithm SIMPATH that computes the spread by exploring simple paths in the neighborhood.

In recent years, a small number of research, as far as we know, only [13] and [9], introduce mechanism design into influence maximization problem. In [13], mechanism was designed to elicit individuals true costs of spreading information. However there is a obvious fault in the proof of budget control, which is the foundation of its other work. [9] designed so-called influencer model and influencer-influencee model to maximize message propagation. In these models, users are asked to report number of their friends, while in most social networks, this kind of information can be automatically and truthfully collected by the application itself.

Much progress has been obtained since the original greedy algorithm, but it still has large development space for research, especially for the LT model. We point out the following drawbacks from the brief summary of current work:

- Almost all the algorithms for the LT model set the nodes' threshold randomly. Moreover, greedy algorithms based on MC simulation assume the information of all nodes' threshold is perfectly known by the system. It is obviously unrealistic because many factors effect the user's threshold. Even to the same user, the value of threshold varies with different subject and different time. And the system will not be easy to get nodes' private information like value of its threshold.
- Traditional work does not take seed users' payment into consideration, instead, the number of seed users is always regarded as marketing budget. It just creates a gap between research and real situation, where budget of an advertising company is more related to how to pay the seed users.
- It is natural that a user with large influence, for example, a celebrity owning large number of followers, will be chosen as a seed node with a higher probability. But in real life, this celebrity may be not willing to spread advertisement information even offered by high payment. However current seed selection methods make decisions regardless of users' will.

1.2 Our Contribution

Our research is just centered around the above three problems.

To the first problem, we notice the necessity of reporting threshold, which is beneficial to both systems and users. Systems can do more accurate advertising according to users' private information, and users can show self preference through this action. Therefore we design a novel model that asks users to report their threshold and selects seed nodes on the basis of it.

To solve the second problem, we not only introduce the payment into the model, but also take incentive compatible condition into account. The payment to the seed nodes is related to their reported threshold, so to maximize the interests of whole system, a truth-telling payment rule is of great importance.

The last problem is a dilemma. But system cannot force users being seeds to maximize the influence. So why not choose seeds from nodes that want to be. In our model, part of nodes are voluntarily to report their threshold and compete for being seeds.

We propose a seed selection algorithm called TREE TREE (Algorithm of Threshold Report and Evaluation for E-marketing) for influence maximization problem, which contains seed selection and seed payment. Experiments show its good performance in practice.

2   Threshold Report Model

The novel model which asks nodes to report their threshold will be proposed in this section. Before detailed description of this model, we first explain the benefit of the system knowing nodes' threshold.

2.1   Behind "Threshold"

Granovetter was among the first to propose models to study the information propagation process through a social network. The LT model is generalized from his seminal paper [8], which laid the foundation of subsequent research on threshold-based model.

In [8], Granovetter pointed when people facing two mutually distinct and exclusive behavior alternatives, they have to make a binary decision. Deciding to do a thing or not to do depends on not only cost and benefit of this action but also many others make which choice.

We now take influence propagation in OSN as an example. When a user sees an advertisement of a skin care product in Twitter, she can forward this message and recommend to her followers or she can do nothing. We assume users are rational, that is, they choose actions to maximize their utility. There exists large individual differences, because for different individuals, cost of spreading the same ad varies and benefit which they expect to derive from the propagation is different too. "Threshold" is the concept to describe such variation among individuals. In this example, a user's "threshold" of spreading advertisement is defined as proportion of identity from her friends. Girls interested in cosmetics and skin care may hold a low threshold: it costs almost nothing for spreading such advertisement and they may even get extra bonus from the company. Some of them, who speak highly of this product after using, will be voluntary to recommend it. Then their threshold is near 0%. On the contrast, a boy who knows little about this will neglect this advertisement quickly even it has drawn much attention from his female friends. In this situation, his threshold is near 100%. Besides, celebrities are group of users who are very cautious about their remarks in OSN. Threshold on advertisement for them is very high, because they have to keep public images and take responsible for their recommend. In this case, large cost of spreading advertisement always plays a more important role than high advertising income.

It is obvious in real situation, threshold varies considerably from person to person on the same object, on the other hand, one person holds different thresholds on variety things. Moreover, even for the same person and object, the value of threshold also changes with time. For example, people's ability of identifying rumors usually improves with age, which means the threshold of believing rumors increases as growing older. According to this diversity and uncertainty of threshold, we collect the users' information rather than make a baseless conjuncture. The above analysis has shown though "threshold" is a notation in the LT model, it measures the attitude of whether taking the same action when others do. In other words, it is a definition independent of the abstract model. Therefore practical applications can still ask users to report their psychological boundaries to the specific things.

2.2   Problem Formulation

After we explain the necessity of reporting threshold, the whole model can be given as following: The social network is represented by a weighted graph $G = (V, E, w)$. Here, V is the set of nodes in the social graph and $E \subseteq V \times V$ denotes the set of directed edges. The influence (weight) function $w : V \times V \rightarrow [0, 1]$ satisfies $\Sigma_{u \in V} w(u, v) \leq 1$. The system select a set of nodes S as initial seeds to spread the information after each node u reporting its threshold θ_u. Each seed node s is paid according to its performance and the threshold which it has reported before, denoted by $p_s = f(S, \theta_s)$. Given a budget B, the model's goal is to find a seed set S that maximizes $\sigma(S)$, which is the number of active nodes after propagation starting from S, in the condition of $\Sigma_{s \in S} p_s \leq B$.

Though this model takes threshold into consideration, this optimization problem is still the well-known NP-hard Max-k-Cover problem. It can also be easily proved that its influence function is monotone and submodular.

3   Proposed Method

To solve this problem, we need two steps: how to select seed nodes and how to pay for these seeds.

3.1   Seed Selection Rules

We first focus on seed selection methods to solve influence maximization problem in OSN. The Algorithm related to threshold, called TREE (Algorithm of **T**hreshold **R**eport and **E**valuation for **E**-marketing) is proposed.

Most existing influence maximization work based on LT model assume users' threshold information is given. While in a large scale social network, collecting threshold information of all users is impossible. But users' willingness of being seeds, which is sidestepped by most research work, shows significant importance. As analysis before, the selected nodes may not want to be seeds for various reasons. A more operable solution is choosing nodes from those intending to be seeds. Therefore we change the model that nodes enter the seed selection voluntarily. If node v wants to be a seed, it will be asked to report its threshold θ_v to the system. Based on it, we design a new sorting rule, which is only related to self threshold.

The threshold represents one user's wish of taking the same action with others. In the case of information propagation, high threshold means the user is not willing to spread this kind of message. It implies the advertising company has to pay more for this user's high cost of spread. Here threshold is also an indication of a node's cost. So this new measurement is the combination of one node's marginal contribution and its threshold. Then the greedy selection uses it sorting: the node selected in each round is the one that has the maximal weighted contribution given the previously chosen nodes. According to this ordering, the ith seed node is:

$$s \in argmax_{v \in N} \gamma_v$$
$$\gamma_v = \frac{\sigma(S_{i-1} \cup v) - \sigma(S_{i-1})}{\theta_v} \tag{1}$$

where S_{i-1} denotes the current seed set of $i-1$ selected nodes. This sorting rule a generalized version that used in greedy algorithm for submodular function maximization [10], and it guarantees constant factor approximation in [7] and [5].

3.2   Payment Rules

We then address the problem of seed nodes' payment, which mainly depends on seeds' performance. In this part, we discuss how different payment rules affect interests of both nodes and system based on the selection rule (1).

A. the Simple Rule. One of widely used payment rules, we call it *the simple rule*, only cares the seeds' marginal contribution. Under this rule, payment of ith seed node v is

$$p_v^{sim} = k \times (\sigma(S_{i-1} \cup v) - \sigma(S_{i-1})) \tag{2}$$

$k > 0$ is constant value related to the budget. It is simple because the payment rule consists with the selection rule, and it means the system can calculate nodes' payment during the process of selection. While due to submodularity of influence spread function, one seed's payment varies with the order added in the seed set.

Another fatal disadvantage of this payment rule is that nodes may misreport its threshold to be seeds. Since all nodes involved hope to be seeds, and whether one node can be selected or not is related to threshold reported by itself, the reality of elicited information can change the result significantly. The following example shown in Fig. 1 abstracted from a simple social network illustrates how false information harms the interests of the system.

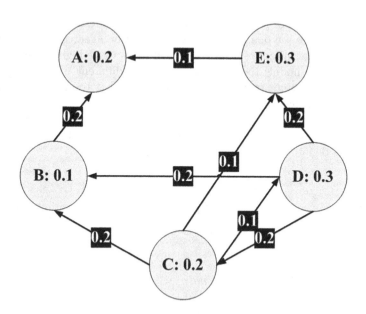

Fig. 1. A simple stylized social network.

In Fig. 1, there are five nodes A-E, and only one seed is needed. The weighted edges of this directed graph denote influence between nodes. True thresholds of nodes' are listed in the circle. It is obvious that node D will be chosen, because $\sigma(D) = 4$, which represents all other nodes can be activated by node D. If we choose node C, after two rounds, node B and A can be activated, thus $\sigma(C) = 2$.

Now all nodes are asked to report its threshold. If the system can collect true threshold information from nodes, then according to the selection rule 1,

$$\gamma_D = \frac{4}{0.3} > \frac{2}{0.2} = \gamma_C$$

So the seed should be node D, and payment is $p_D^{sim} = 4k$ and $p_C^{sim} = 0$. However if node C lies about its threshold as $\theta_C = 0.1$, then

$$\gamma_C = \frac{2}{0.1} > \frac{4}{0.3} = \gamma_D$$

Now node C will be the seed, its payment is $p_C^{sim} = 2k$. Node C increases its income, but this is definitely not the best choice for the system.

B. Mean Payment. In (1), the selection measurement is

$$\gamma_v = \frac{\sigma(S_{i-1} \cup v) - \sigma(S_{i-1})}{\theta_v} \tag{3}$$

which implies the system prefers the node with small threshold. While from the previous analysis, we see one node's threshold may be affected by its influence, in other words, large influence if one node will leads to its higher threshold. On the other side, one node's too low threshold over different messages makes it followers feeling it cannot stand for its position, so that too low threshold will also harm the influence of nodes.

Neither nodes with too low or too high threshold are the best choice of seeds. Therefore payment rules will punish these extreme threshold. Seed node v's payment is denoted by

$$p_v^{mean} = B \times \frac{Con(v)}{\sigma(S)} + \frac{\gamma}{2}(\frac{n-1}{n}(\theta_v - A_v)$$
$$- \sum_{u \in S, u \neq v} \frac{1}{n-2}(\theta_u - A_u)^2) \tag{4}$$

where

$$\Sigma_{v \in S} Con(v) = \sigma(S)$$

$$A_v = \frac{1}{n-1}\Sigma_{u \in S, u \neq v}\theta_u$$

and n is the number of seeds. Variations of the punishment parameter, γ, changes the penalty that is imposed on an individual for deviating from the mean of other seeds' threshold.

Given θu, which $u \in S$ and $u \neq v$, node v reports θv to maximize the income $f(v)$, which equals to

$$f(v) = B \times \frac{Con(v)}{\sigma(S)} + \frac{\gamma}{2}(\frac{n-1}{n}(\theta_v - A_v)$$
$$- \sum_{u \in S, u \neq v} \frac{1}{n-2}(\theta_u - A_u)^2) \tag{5}$$

The first order condition is

$$f'(v) = \frac{1}{n} + \frac{\gamma(n-1)}{n}(\theta_v - A_v) \tag{6}$$

A Nash equilibrium is $\theta_{v\,v=1}^{\,n}$, such that for each node v, θ_v satisfies the above first order condition given $\theta_{u\,u \neq v}$.

Theorem 1. *The Nash equilibrium 6 satisfies the Samuelson Condition.*

Proof. To see this, we simply sum the first order conditions over v, and obtain

$$\sum_{v=1}^{n} f'(v) = 1 + \frac{\gamma(n-1)}{n}(\theta_v - A_v) = 1 \qquad (7)$$

which is the Samuelson efficiency condition.

Theorem 2. *The payment rules balance the budget both on and off the equilibrium path.*

Proof. We sum all seeds' payment, which is

$$\sum_{v=1}^{n} p_v^{mean} = B \sum_{v=1}^{n} \frac{Con(v)}{\sigma(S)} + G \qquad (8)$$

where

$$G = \frac{\gamma(n-1)}{2n} \sum_{v=1}^{n}(\theta_v - A_i)^2 - \sum_{v=1}^{n}\sum_{u \neq v} \frac{1}{n-2}(\theta_u - A_i)^2 \qquad (9)$$

It is trivial to get the calculation result that $G = 0$. And according to

$$\Sigma_{v \in S} Con(v) = \sigma(S)$$

We get

$$\sum_{v=1}^{n} p_v^{mean} = B$$

Actually, the budget balance is achieved by the last term in the payment rule, the squared standard error of the mean of others' information.

4 Experiment

After the introduction of the new algorithm, we are now interested in understanding its behavior in practice, and comparing its performance with other methods.

4.1 Experiment Setup

Some preparation of experiments are listed as following, including network data, other methods used to compare with and threshold setting.

Network Data: We use cit-HepTh, arxiv HEP-TH (high energy physics theory) citation network, as experiment data. This graph is from the e-print arXiv and covers all the citations within a dataset of 27,770 papers with 352,807 edges.

Comparison Algorithms: As discussed above, we transplant TREE into High Degree and Page Rank algorithm. Here we compare information propagation range and runtime of different methods, including Random Selection, High

Degree, Page Rank, TREE on High Degree (High TREE) and TREE on Page Rank (Page TREE).

Threshold Setting: The key factor in LT model is how to set users' threshold, which is beyond this paper's topic. But we observe from realworld dataset that one user's threshold maybe relates to the number of his followers or the number of his following people, which is this node's out degree and in degree in network graph. A node with large out degree always hold a high threshold, because this user will be more cautious about his views and comments than common people. On the hand, a node with large in degree also has a high threshold, and the reason is that they can receive different opinions on the same thing, so the probability of being persuaded easily for him is low. Thus we set three kinds of nodes' threshold: Random Threshold, Out Degree Threshold and In Degree Threshold. Due to $\theta \in [0,1]$, we normalize the node v's out degree and in degree, denoted by:

$$\theta_v^{out} = \frac{out_v - out_{min}}{out_{max} - out_{min}} \tag{10}$$

$$\theta_v^{in} = \frac{in_v - in_{min}}{in_{max} - in_{min}} \tag{11}$$

4.2   Results and Analysis

In the experiments, algorithms' performance lies in the information propagation range and running time. The result is the mean value of 10 times' computation of using one of algorithms in a specific network.

Figure 2 shows different algorithms' performance with three kinds of threshold setting. Naturally, all other algorithms exceed the baseline method, Random Selection. Besides this, the other common conclusion from these three figures is that TREE enlarges the information propagation range in all conditions. It is obvious that using PageTREE (or HighTREE) achieves better results than Page Rank (or High Degree).

We also notice the differences between three figures tell us more information about TREE. Comparing with Random Threshold (shown in (a)) and In Degree Threshold (shown in (c)), TREE in Out Degree Threshold (shown in (b)) does not have evident superiority, especially HighTREE. This is mainly because when node's threshold is close related to its out degree, the two measurements in different algorithms represent the same character of the node. In this situation, the combination of two methods is of lesser significance.

The mean value of algorithms' runtime of selecting 100 seeds is presented in Fig. 3. It is rational that TREE needs more time because it adds another sorting measurement, and more computation is inevitable. However, the time consumption increases slowly. Therefore we think it is still worthy of enlarging the propagation range at the cost of runtime slowdowns.

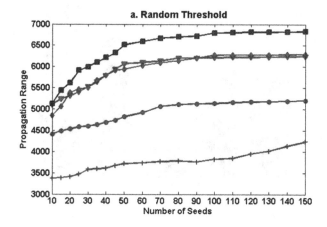

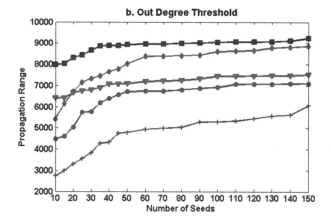

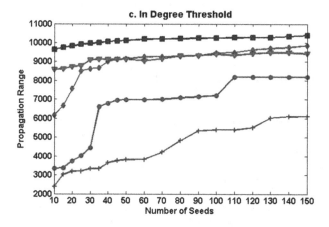

Fig. 2. Propagation range comparison in cit-HepTh.

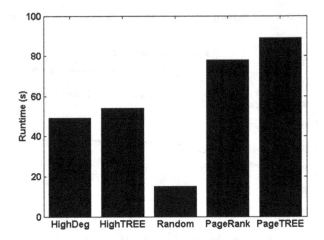

Fig. 3. Runtime comparison in cit-HepTh.

5   Conclusion

In this paper, based on LT model, we propose a new model in which users are voluntarily to report their private information - threshold to be viral marketing seeds. The method, called TREE, is designed to solve this model. Influence maximization problem and mechanism design are involved in the whole process. Experiments verify the good performance of TREE.

Acknowledgement. This work was supported by the National Natural Science Foundation of China (NSFC, project 61902152, 61972182) and the Natural Science Foundation of Jiangsu Province (BK20180600).

References

1. Chen, W., Wang, C., Wang, Y.: Scalable influence maximization for prevalent viral marketing in large-scale social networks. In: Proceedings of the 16th ACM SIGKDD International Conference on Knowledge Discovery and Data Mining, pp. 1029–1038. ACM (2010)
2. Chen, W., Yuan, Y., Zhang, L.: Scalable influence maximization in social networks under the linear threshold model. In: 2010 IEEE 10th International Conference on Data Mining (ICDM), pp. 88–97. IEEE (2010)
3. Kempe, D., Kleinberg, J., Tardos, E.: Maximizing the spread of influence through a social network. In: Proceedings of the 9th ACM SIGKDD International Conference on Knowledge Discovery and Data Mining, pp. 137–146 (2003)
4. Goyal, A., Lu, W., Lakshmanan, L.V.: Simpath: an efficient algorithm for influence maximization under the linear threshold model. In: 2011 IEEE 11th International Conference on Data Mining (ICDM), pp. 211–220. IEEE (2011)
5. Leskovec, J., Krause, A., Guestrin, C.et al.: Cost-effective outbreak detection in networks. In: Proceedings of the 13th ACM SIGKDD International Conference on Knowledge Discovery and Data Mining, pp. 420–429 (2007)

6. Kimura, M., Saito, K.: Tractable models for information diffusion in social networks. In: Fürnkranz, J., Scheffer, T., Spiliopoulou, M. (eds.) PKDD 2006. LNCS (LNAI), vol. 4213, pp. 259–271. Springer, Heidelberg (2006). https://doi.org/10.1007/11871637_27
7. Krause, A., Guestrin, C.: A note on the budgeted maximization of submodular functions (2005)
8. Granovetter, M.: Threshold models of collective behavior. Am. J. Sociolo. **83**(6), 1420–1443 (1978)
9. Mohite, M., Narahari, Y.: Incentive compatible influence maximization in social networks and application to viral marketing. arXiv preprint arXiv:1102.0918 (2011)
10. Nemhauser, G.L., Wolsey, L.A., Fisher, M.L.: An analysis of approximations for maximizing submodular set functions. Math. Program. **14**(1), 265–294 (1978)
11. P. Domingos, M. Richardson: Mining the network value of customers. In: Proceedings of the 7th ACM SIGKDD International Conference on Knowledge Discovery and Data Mining, pp. 57–66 (2001)
12. Chen, W., Wang, Y., Yang, S.: Efficient influence maximization in social networks. In: Proceedings of the 15th ACM SIGKDD International Conference on Knowledge Discovery and Data Mining, pp. 199–208 (2009)
13. Singer,Y.: How to win friends and influence people, truthfully: in-fluence maximization mechanisms for social networks. In: Proceedings of the 5th ACM International Conference on Web Search and Data Mining, pp. 733–742 (2012)

An Exemplar-Based Clustering Model with Loose Constraints in Social Network

Bi Anqi[(✉)] [ID] and Ying Wenhao[ID]

Changshu Institute of Technology, Changshu, Jiangsu, China
anqi_b@cslg.edu.cn

Abstract. Loose constraints have great effects on the study of message passing through social networks. This paper proposes a novel EEM-LC model who joints the pairwise loose constraints existing in social networks and the exemplar-based clustering model together, and also observes the application prospects of this model. Exemplar-based clustering model directly selects cluster centers from actual samples, so the structure and semantics of the comments on social networks would be preserved accordingly. Besides, EEM-LC unifies the two pairwise link constraints by one mathematical definition, and looses the restrictions of strong constraints. Moreover, on the basis of the Bayesian probability framework, EEM-LC implants loose pairwise constraints into its target function. That is to say, enhanced α-expansion move algorithm is capable of optimizing this new model. Experimental results based on several real-world data sets have shown very convincing performance of the proposed EEM-LC model.

Keywords: Loose constraints · Exemplar-based clustering model · Message passing · Social networks

1 Introduction

Sociologists have found that weak ties [8,11,13] have significant effects on the message passing on social network. Weak ties is a more extensive but superficial social cognition of social relationships. Although weak ties are not as straightforward as classical connections, it potentially has extremely fast, low-cost and high efficient propagation efficiency. Artificial intelligence techniques are widely used to study such weak ties. Generally speaking, procedure for artificial intelligence technology to process information on social networks contains 3 steps. Firstly, extract keywords from the comments published on the social networks. Then, analyze these keywords by machine learning models. Thirdly, series the

Supported by the Humanities and Social Sciences Foundation of the Ministry of Education under grant no.18YJCZH229 and the Natural Science Foundation of Jiangsu Province under grant no. BK20161268.

W. Fu et al. (Eds.): ICMTEL 2021, LNICST 387, pp. 248–254, 2021.
https://doi.org/10.1007/978-3-030-82562-1_22

evolution of public opinion. In this paper, we focus on the second step. As there have been many works on incorporating this weak constraints into typical mathematical models in social network processing [1,2,4,5,7,9], including Exemplar-Based Clustering model, Latent Dirichlet Allocation(LDA), Support Vector Machine(SVM) [6], etc. We focus on dealing with this weak constraints start from the exemplar-based clustering framework in this paper.

Unlike strong constraints, the loose constraints are pairwise. Two kinds of this pairwise constraints should be considered, that is must-link(ML) and cannot-link(CL). Clearly, must-link means the linked two samples should be assigned in one cluster, while cannot-link separates these two samples in different clusters. Furthermore by loose, we relax the restriction on sample's constraints. Namely, loose constraint only requires that a sample may have must-link and/or cannot-link, or just have no link.

In summary, in this paper, we derive an extended version of exemplar-based clustering model for loose constraints existing in social networks, called EEM-LC in short. As exemplar-based framework directly selects cluster centers from actual samples, the obtained exemplars would preserve the structure and semantics of keywords naturally. Moreover, EEM-LC also unifies the two pairwise link constraints together, thus we loose the restrictions of the constraints. Obviously, such pattern is more consistent with the broad but superficial nature of weak ties. Besides, Bayesian probability framework is introduced, which can naturally helps us to implant loose pairwise constraints into the exemplar-based clustering model and improve generalization performance of the algorithm. We would deeply discuss the scenario and EEM-LC mechanism in the next sections.

2   Exemplar-Based Clustering Model with Loose Constraints

In this section, we derive a novel exemplar-based clustering model dealing with this pairwise loose constraints exist in social networks. The procedure of this proposed EEM-LC is described in Fig. 1.

Assume $X = \{x_1, x_2, ..., x_N\} \in \mathbb{R}^{N*D}$, N is the total number of D-dimensional data points. E is the output exemplar set, whereas the element $E(i)$ refers to the exemplar for sample x_i. According to the discussion above, we give the mathematical definition of the involved loose pairwise constraints in Eq. (1) below:

$$C(x_i, x_j) = \begin{cases} 1, & x_i \ must-link \ with \ x_j \\ 0, & x_i \ no-link \ with \ x_j \\ -1, & x_i \ cannot-link \ with \ x_j \end{cases} \tag{1}$$

Therefore, for current data x_i, subset $\mathbf{ML}_{x_i} = \{x_j | C(x_i, x_j) = 1\}$ defines all samples must-link with x_i, and subset $\mathbf{CL}_{x_i} = \{x_j | C(x_i, x_j) = -1\}$ defines all samples cannot-link with x_i. So far, start from the theory of machine learning, we have given several definitions related to the loose pairwise constraints. This

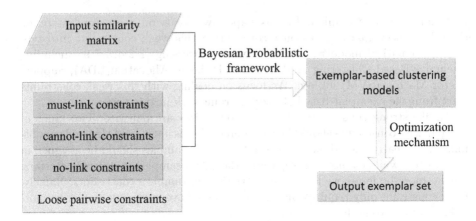

Fig. 1. The procedure of EEM-LC framework. We implant the loose pairwise constraints into the exemplar-based models.

work would naturally helps us to implant loose pairwise constraints into the basic machine learning models.

Theoretically based on the descriptions of exemplar-based clustering model and Bayesian probabilistic framework, the rough target function of EEM-LC equals to Eq. (2).

$$\max_{E} \ln \prod_{i=1}^{N} p(\boldsymbol{x}_i)p(E) \tag{2}$$

where $p(E)$ is the probabilistic information based on the exemplar set, shown in Eq. (3), and $p(\boldsymbol{x}_i)$ represents probability relationship for a single sample which is listed in Eq. (4).

$$p(E) = \frac{1}{\sigma\sqrt{2\pi}} \cdot \exp\left(-\sum_{i=1}^{N}\sum_{j=1}^{N} \theta_{i,j}(E(i), E(j))/2\sigma^2\right) \tag{3}$$

$$p(\boldsymbol{x}_i) = p(\boldsymbol{x}_i, \boldsymbol{x}_{E(i)}) \cdot \prod_{\boldsymbol{x}_j \in \mathbf{ML}_{\boldsymbol{x}_i}} p(\boldsymbol{x}_j, \boldsymbol{x}_{E(j)})p(\boldsymbol{x}_{E(i)}, \boldsymbol{x}_{E(j)}) \cdot \prod_{\boldsymbol{x}_j \in \mathbf{CL}_{\boldsymbol{x}_i}} p(\boldsymbol{x}_j, \boldsymbol{x}_{E(j)})p(\boldsymbol{x}_{E(i)}, \boldsymbol{x}_{E(j)}) \tag{4}$$

Carefully analyze Eq. (4), note that if $\mathbf{ML}_{\boldsymbol{x}_i}$ or $\mathbf{CL}_{\boldsymbol{x}_i}$ is empty, the corresponding value is set to be 1, which means the EEM-LC model is inspective of loose link constraints here. The framework will degrade into classical exemplar-based model EEM in [12]. On the other hand, notations $p(\boldsymbol{x}_i, \boldsymbol{x}_{E(i)})$ and $p(\boldsymbol{x}_{E(i)}, \boldsymbol{x}_{E(j)})$ are defined as Eqs. (5 and 6).

$$p(\boldsymbol{x}_i, \boldsymbol{x}_{E(i)}) = \frac{1}{\sigma\sqrt{2\pi}} \exp(s(\boldsymbol{x}_i, \boldsymbol{x}_{E(i)})/2\sigma^2) \tag{5}$$

$$p(\boldsymbol{x}_{E(i)}, \boldsymbol{x}_{E(j)}) = \frac{1}{\sigma\sqrt{2\pi}} \cdot \exp\left(-\sum_{i=1}^{N}\sum_{j=1}^{N} \eta_{i,j}(E(i), E(j))/2\sigma^2\right) \tag{6}$$

$s(\boldsymbol{x}_i, \boldsymbol{x}_{E(i)})$ is the similarity relationship between $\boldsymbol{x}_i$ and $\boldsymbol{x}_{E(i)}$. Usually we set $s(\boldsymbol{x}_i, \boldsymbol{x}_{E(i)}) = -d(\boldsymbol{x}_i, \boldsymbol{x}_{E(i)})$ where $d(\boldsymbol{x}_i, \boldsymbol{x}_{E(i)})$ is the Euclidean distance between $\boldsymbol{x}_i$ and $\boldsymbol{x}_{E(i)}$.

$\theta_{i,j}(E(i), E(j))$ and $\eta_{i,j}(E(i), E(j))$ in Eqs. (3 and 6)are both set to guarantee the validity of the exemplar set. The definitions are below in Eqs. (7 and 8), where M, L, L' are set to be big here. See [1,12] for detail discussion.

$$\theta_{i,j}(E(i), E(j)) = \begin{cases} M, & E(i) = j, E(j) \neq j, or\, E(j) = i, E(i) \neq j \\ 0, & \text{otherwise} \end{cases} \tag{7}$$

$$\eta_{i,j}(E(i), E(j)) = \begin{cases} L, & E(i) \neq E(j), C(\boldsymbol{x}_i, \boldsymbol{x}_j) = 1 \\ L', & E(i) = E(j), C(\boldsymbol{x}_i, \boldsymbol{x}_j) = -1 \\ 0, & \text{otherwise} \end{cases} \tag{8}$$

Put the definitions of $p(E)$ and $p(\boldsymbol{x}_i)$ in Eqs. (3 and 4) into the rough target function Eq. (2), and after some mathematical simplifications, the final target function becomes

$$\begin{aligned} \min_{E} \; & \sum_{\boldsymbol{x}_i, \boldsymbol{x}_j \in \boldsymbol{X}} d(\boldsymbol{x}_i, \boldsymbol{x}_j) + \sum_{\boldsymbol{x}_i \in \boldsymbol{X}} \sum_{\boldsymbol{x}_j \in \mathbf{ML}_{\boldsymbol{x}_i}} \eta_{i,j}(E(i), E(j)) \\ & + \sum_{\boldsymbol{x}_i \in \boldsymbol{X}} \sum_{\boldsymbol{x}_j \in \mathbf{CL}_{\boldsymbol{x}_i}} \eta_{i,j}(E(i), E(j)) + \sum_{\boldsymbol{x}_i \in \boldsymbol{X}} \sum_{\boldsymbol{x}_j \in \boldsymbol{X}} \theta_{i,j}(E(i), E(j)) \end{aligned} \tag{9}$$

The target function in Eq. (9) can be approximately optimized by α-expansion move algorithm with s-t graph cut [1,10,12]. Hence we utilize the enhanced α-expansion move algorithm to optimize the proposed EEM-LC model. Specifically speaking, the optimization mechanism regards the target function as the energy defined by the Markov random field, thus the energy reduction is introduced to detect the change in the value of the target function. We traverse the possible exemplars, and compare the corresponding values of the reduction in energy. On this basis, we gradually get the minimum energy value, when the current exemplar set is the optimal solution of the target function as well. Besides, the optimization mechanism here also expands the search space for possible exemplars in iteration, that is, sub-optimal exemplar is considered as well. Experiments of correlation algorithms have proved that the trick improves the optimization efficiency of this model.

3 Experimental Analysis

3.1 Setup

Just to be clear, the experiments in this section are implemented in 2010a Matlab on a PC with 64 bit Microsoft Window 10, an Intel(R) Core(TM) i7-4712MQ and 8GB memory. We first utilize Diabetes dataset from UCI Machine Learning Repository[1]. Diabetes dataset has 768 8-dimensional samples, and contains 2 classes. Also to better observe the characteristics of social network, we took "movies" as key word, crawled 1000 comments on Sina Weibo[2] with Python 3.7.3. Then we use the Jieba toolbox for word segmentation, and obtain relevant high-dimensional vector by word2vex toolbox. Finally, PCA is also introduced to reduce the dimension to 20 dimensions, and accordingly establish the dataset called D1 here. Thus, ignore some nonsense words, dataset D1 has 3500 20-dimensional samples. Furthermore, considering that the loose pairwise constraints is extensive and low-cost, for both Diabetes and D1, we randomly assign either must-link or cannot-link constraints to 75% samples.

We compare our model EEM-LC with classical EEM [12] model and AP [3] model, to observe the important role of loose pairwise constraints in the cluster procedure. On the other hand, for Diabetes dataset, true labels for samples are available, so we evaluate the performances of these models by indices RI, which is defined below:

$$RI = \frac{f_{00} + f_{11}}{N(N-1)/2} \tag{10}$$

where f_{00} is the number of data whose cluster is in line with its class, while f_{11} is the number of those data whose cluster is inconsistent with its class. For D1, as true labels are not available, we take the number of clusters as performance indices.

3.2   Results Analysis

Each algorithm is repeatedly executed 10 times, we record the average performance. For the involved 3 models, multiply the median value of similarities by the optimal value in $\{0.01, 0.1, 1, 10, 50, 100\}$, then we get the value of self similarity $d(x_i, x_i)$. Grid search is used to choose parameter for Diabetes dataset. As to D1 dataset, considering that true labels are not available, we set $d(x_i, x_i)$ equals to 10 times of the median value of similarities.

Figure 2 shows the average comparison of EEM, AP and EEM-LC on Diabetes dataset by RI, meanwhile Fig. 3 describes the average number of clusters obtained by the 3 models on D1 dataset. Deeply observing Figs. 2 and 3, we can conclude that when real labels are available, the clustering results of the EEM-LC model are reliable. Though the real labels are absent, EEM-LC still can effectively deal with the information by incorporating with loose pairwise constraints. The performance of EEM-LC is very promising.

In the experiment procedure, we found that compared to both EEM and AP, the EEM-LC model has the longest running time, which is because the model deals with the loose pairwise constraints involved in the sample while processing the input similarity matrix.

---

[1] http://archive.ics.uci.edu/ml/datasets/Diabetes.
[2] http://m.weibo.cn/.

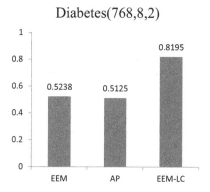

Fig. 2. Comparison of EEM, AP and EEM-LC on Diabetes by *RI*

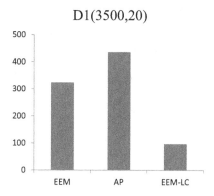

Fig. 3. Average number of clusters obtained by EEM, AP and EEM-LC on D1

4   Conclusion

This paper focuses on incorporating loose pairwise constraints with classical exemplar-based clustering model, and proposes EEM-LC algorithm. Our experimental results have shown promising performance of EEM-LC. In the future, such a model will help us further study the public opinion transmission, event evolution, public opinion monitoring, etc. However, the time complexity of the EEM-LC algorithm needs to be reduced.

References

1. Bi, A., Fulai Chung, S.W.: Bayesian enhanced α-expansion move clustering with loose link constraints. Neurocomputing **194**, 288–300 (2016)
2. Arzeno Natalia M.V.H.: Semi-supervised affinity propagation with soft instance-level constraints. IEEE Trans. Pattern Anal. Mach. Intell. **37**(5), 1041–1052 (2015)
3. Frey, B.J., Dueck, D.: Clustering by passing messages between data points. Science **315**, 972–976 (2017)

4. Blei, D.M., Ng, A., Jordan, M.I.: Latent dirichlet allocation. J. Mach. Learn. Res. **3**, 903–1022 (2003)
5. Bugaychenko, D., Dzuba, A.: Musical recommendations and personalization in a social network (2013). https://doi.org/10.1145/2507157.2507192
6. Cortes, C., Vapnik, V.: Support-vector networks. Mach. Learn. **20**(3), 273–297 (1995)
7. Givoni, I., Frey, B.: Semi-supervised affinity propagation with instance-level constraints. J. Mach. Learn. Res. Proc. Track **5**, 161–168 (2009)
8. Granovetter, M.: The strength of weak ties. Amer. J. Sociol. **78**, 1360–1380 (1973)
9. Luo, D., Huang, H.: Link prediction of multimedia social network via unsupervised face recognition. In: Proceedings of the 17th International Conference on Multimedia 2009, Vancouver, British Columbia, Canada, 19–24 October 2009 (2009)
10. Tappen, M.F., Freeman, W.T.: Comparison of graph cuts with belief propagation for stereo, using identical MRF parameters. In: 9th IEEE International Conference Computer Vision, pp. 900–906 (2003)
11. Weenig, M.W.H.: The strength of weak and strong communication ties in a community information program1. J. Appl. Social Psychol. **23**(20), 1712–1731 (2006)
12. Zheng, Y.,Chang, P.: Clustering based on enhanced -expansion move. IEEE Trans. Knowl. Data Eng. (TKDE) **25** (2013)
13. Zhao, J., Wu, J., Xu, K.: Weak ties: a subtle role in the information diffusion of online social networks. Phys. Rev. E **82**(1), 1–1348 (2010)

Personal Name Disambiguation for Chinese Documents in Online Medium

Chao Fan[1,2]([✉]) [iD] and Yu Li[1,2]

[1] The School of Artificial Intelligence and Computer Science, Jiangnan University,
Wuxi 214122, China
fanchao@jiangnan.edu.cn
[2] Jiangsu Key Laboratory of Media Design and Software Technology, Jiangnan University,
Wuxi 214122, China

Abstract. Disambiguating various people that share the same name is a critical issue for analyzing contents in online medium. This paper develops a framework for dealing with personal names in Chinese dataset. Web pages containing personal name are crawled from the online website and standardized at first. Then documents are parsed with lexical analysis technologies, such as segmentation, part-of-speech tagging, named entity recognition. We extract several groups of words as features, testing different weighting schemes (e.g. Boolean term frequency, absolute term frequency, tf-idf, entropy weights). By conducting the agglomerative clustering, a measure of interdependence within clusters and independence between clusters is proposed for automatically determining the number of clusters. Moreover, a technique that merges noise clusters is utilized to improve the clustering results. Experiments are performed on six groups of Chinese personal names and the final results confirm our proposed approach.

Keywords: Personal name disambiguation · Chinese personal names · Agglomerative clustering

1 Introduction

Personal name disambiguation plays a significant role in analyzing documents on the Internet. When searching a person's name online, we are confused with the problems that the search results often contain web pages of different people with the same name. Therefore, it is necessary to disambiguate names in the retrieved documents by cluster analysis. Furthermore, personal name disambiguation can be applied in the areas such as information collection, information fusion, etc. Exploring the key issue will increase the convenience for the end users and ultimately benefit the content and service providers.

This paper makes an effort to investigate the Chinese personal name disambiguation. Firstly, web pages are crawled from Baidu news via specified personal name keywords. By removing the web page tags, the text body is extracted with a standardized format. Some irrelevant documents are deleted and the rest are manually tagged with labels, which are used for scoring the algorithm. Secondly, we segment all documents with

W. Fu et al. (Eds.): ICMTEL 2021, LNICST 387, pp. 255–264, 2021.
https://doi.org/10.1007/978-3-030-82562-1_23

a segmentation tool, tagging the parts of speech and recognizing the named entities. Six groups of words extracted as features are combined with four weighting models, attempting to reach the best combination for feature selection. Thirdly, an agglomerative clustering algorithm is implemented employing selected features. Further, an indicator is adopted to measure the performance of clustering and the final number of clusters is optimized by removing the noise clusters. The dataset created in this paper is composed of documents with six different Chinese personal names. Each name contains 100 Chinese documents.

The contents can be organized in the following steps. Section 2 introduces related work of personal name disambiguation. Section 3 gives the framework, dataset and evaluation method of this work. Section 4 and 5 display the most important parts of feature generation, clustering approach and experiment results. In Sect. 6, conclusion and future work are discussed.

2 Related Work

The task of personal name disambiguation draws attention from a number of researchers. Li et al. [1] proposed a multi-stage clustering algorithm when the entity knowledge base is provided. Zhao et al. [2] constructed personal ontology and calculated the similarity between ontology and instance built from web pages. Emami [3] extracted semantic information from web pages and exploited a graph-based algorithm to disambiguate personal names. Xiong et al. [4] solved the personal name disambiguation problem based on the sentential semantic structure analysis. Yang et al. [5] presented an algorithm based on ensemble. The method integrates different divisions produced by different clustering algorithms and shows a high accuracy and robustness. Zeng et al. [6] adopted the multi-feature fusion method to disambiguate expert with the same name in the process of building expert database. Shang et al. [7] discussed a disambiguation method based on co-authors and their affiliates. Zhai et al. [8] employed sparse distributed representation to disambiguate English author name. The summary is chosen as disambiguation feature in their research. Yu et al. [9] combined different network embedding methods to eliminate the ambiguity of author names. Pooja et al. [10] identified ambiguous author names applying a graph combination with edge pruning-based approach. Kim et al. [11] introduced a hybrid deep pairwise method by exploiting both structure and global features.

Some variants of this task are also concerned among different scholars. Delgado et al. [12] studied this problem in a multilingual context with real search results. Their method performs better than the translation ways. Khabsa et al. [13] addressed two practical issues: adding constraints and allowing the data to be added partially. These constraints can improve the disambiguation result.

As it is typically completed by an unsupervised method, the previous works concentrate on many aspects such as feature selection, similarity calculation, clustering algorithm, etc. This paper pays attention to traditional personal name ambiguation issue on Chinese dataset and explores both feature selection and clustering algorithm.

3   Overview

3.1   Framework

The framework of Chinese personal name disambiguation proposed in this paper can be depicted in Fig. 1. There are three main modules: corpus building, feature generation and clustering module. Web pages are crawled and standardized into original dataset when building corpus. Features used for clustering can be extracted from corpus via feature generation module. Clustering module applies the hierarchical clustering algorithm to obtain results of cluster analysis.

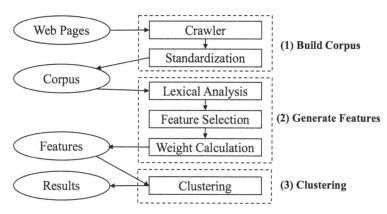

Fig. 1. Framework of Chinese personal name disambiguation

3.2   Dataset

The dataset is constructed in the corpus building module. We crawled Baidu news by keywords of ambiguous personal name. They are in Chinese characters and consist of the following six personal names: 陈卫 (CHEN Wei), 陈坚 (CHEN Jian), 刘伟 (LIU Wei), 刘伟强 (LIU Weiqiang), 李鹏 (LI Peng), 李小鹏 (LI Xiaopeng).

Web pages are parsed by removing the HTML tags at first. Standardization is then done by extracting the text body. Through this step, raw web pages are saved in a text-only format. We checked all documents manually and removed irrelevant ones. Eventually, 100 documents are kept for each personal name. In addition, documents in the dataset are tagged with labels as gold standard for the purpose of scoring the clustering algorithm.

3.3   Evaluation

P-IP score [14] is utilized to evaluate the clustering result of six personal names. The precision of a cluster $P \in P$ for a given category $L \in L$ is given by:

$$Precision(p,\ l) = \frac{|P \cap L|}{|P|} \tag{1}$$

According to the Precision formula, the Purity, Inverse Purity and F-score can be calculated for evaluation.

4 Feature Generation

4.1 Data Preprocessing

The documents in dataset are preprocessed with natural language processing toolkit LTP[1]. Stop words are filtered for texts of documents at the beginning. Then all sentences are segmented into words which are tagged with parts of speech. They are organized as such forms "江南(Jiangnan)/ns 大学(university)/n 校长(president)/n 陈卫(CHEN Wei)/nh …" where character and part of speech are separated with "/". Named entities can also be recognized by LTP with a high accuracy. Named entity often denotes real-world object like a person, an organization, a place and so forth. In this case, "江南大学(Jiangnan University)/Ni 陈卫(CHEN Wei)/Nh" will be identified as named entities. Jiangnan University (江南大学) is a name of organization and CHEN Wei (陈卫) is a Chinese personal name.

Words, parts of speech, and named entities are extracted from corpus at the first step of feature generation, which are prepared for feature selection and weight calculation.

4.2 Feature Selection

Different type of words or named entities can be selected as features. The simplest way is to incorporate all words as features of clustering. In this paper, six groups of features are chosen for testing the performance of hierarchical clustering, which are defined as follows.

Feature 1: all words except for punctuation;
Feature 2: all nouns;
Feature 3: all named entities;
Feature 4: all words with their document frequency (df) $> = 2$;
Feature 5: all nouns with their df $>= 2$;
Feature 6: all named entities with their df $>= 2$.

where document frequency (df) is the number of documents containing a particular term. Since the word with a df of 1 only appears in one document, it cannot distinguish between documents when running clustering. Thus, word with a df of 1 should be neglected even though it appears many times in only one document.

4.3 Feature Weight Calculation

It is necessary to choose the weighting scheme for features, because different words contribute differently to discriminating the documents. Four weight calculation approaches are provided in this paper, which can be elaborated on the following parts.

---

[1] http://ltp.ai.

Boolean Weights. It will be filled with 1 if a document has a word, otherwise it will be 0. It is calculated by formula (2), where f_{ij} is the frequency that word i appears in document j.

$$w_{ij} = \begin{cases} 1 & if \ f_{ij} > 0 \\ 0 & otherwise \end{cases} \tag{2}$$

Frequency Weights. The absolute term frequency f_{ij} counts the frequency of word i contained in document j.

$$w_{ij} = f_{ij} \tag{3}$$

Tf-idf Weights. Term frequency-inverse document frequency (tf-idf) considers both the number of a word in the document and in the corpus. It can be written as the following formula (4).

$$w_{ij} = tf_{ij} * log \frac{N}{n_i} \tag{4}$$

where tf_{ij} is f_{ij} divided by total number of words in the document. N is the total number of documents and n_i is the number of documents with word i.

Entropy Weights. Entropy weights utilize the formula of entropy to reflect the distribution of words in the document, which can be defined as formula (5).

$$w_{ij} = log(tf_{ij} + 1) * \left(1 + \frac{1}{logN} \sum_{j=1}^{N} \frac{tf_{ij}}{n_i} log \left(\frac{tf_{ij}}{n_i} \right) \right) \tag{5}$$

4.4 Experiments of Feature Generation

The experiments combining six groups of features and four weighting schemes are performed for six Chinese personal names in the dataset. The best F-score value is selected from each experiment by testing all thresholds of the hierarchical clustering algorithm. Results of "陈卫 (CHEN Wei)" and "刘伟强 (LIU Weiqiang)" are shown in Figs. 2, 3, 4 and 5. The rest personal names exhibit similar characteristics.

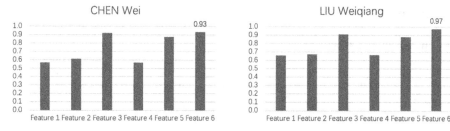

Fig. 2. Results of boolean weights for "CHEN Wei" and "LIU Weiqiang"

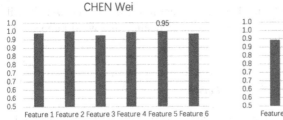

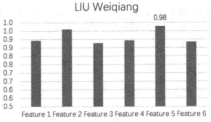

Fig. 3. Results of frequency weights for "CHEN Wei" and "LIU Weiqiang"

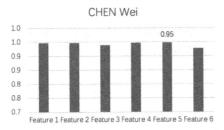

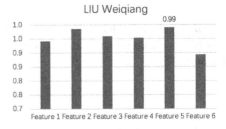

Fig. 4. Results of tf-idf weights for "CHEN Wei" and "LIU Weiqiang"

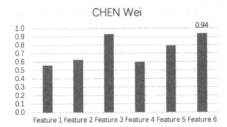

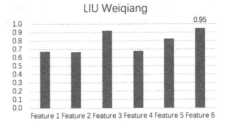

Fig. 5. Results of entropy weights for "CHEN Wei" and "LIU Weiqiang"

According to figures above, feature 6 has a relatively good effect on boolean and entropy weight. In contrast, feature 5 performs well on frequency and tf-idf weight. On average, feature 5 (all nouns with df $>= 2$) and tf-idf weights reach the best performance, so they are selected for cluster analysis.

5   Clustering

5.1   Hierarchical Clustering

An agglomerative hierarchical clustering algorithm is utilized in our personal name disambiguation task. In the first place, each document is reckoned as a single cluster. The similarity (or distance) for each pair of clusters is calculated at each step. Algorithm greedily selects the pair that achieve a greatest similarity and merge two clusters into a bigger one. In this work, the cosine similarity is adopted to measure the similarity between two vectors $x = (x_1, x_2, \ldots, x_n)$ and $y = (y_1, y_2, \ldots, y_n)$. It can be described as the formula (6).

$$sim(x, y) = cos(x, y) = \frac{x \cdot y}{|x| \cdot |y|} = \frac{\sum_{i=1}^{n} x_i \cdot y_i}{\sqrt{\sum_{i=1}^{n} x_i^2 \cdot \sum_{i=1}^{n} y_i^2}} \tag{6}$$

The clustering process is stopped when the similarity between two most similar clusters is smaller than a threshold. In our experiments, the average performance of six personal names achieves the best when the threshold of clustering is set to 0.81.

5.2 Cluster Stopping Measure

Newman devised a modularity Q indicator [15, 16] in community detection, which is used to measure the community structure and identify communities automatically. A high modularity Q denotes dense intra-community links and sparse inter-community links. According to this idea, the number of links can be replaced by the similarity of documents in a hierarchical clustering. Dense intra-community links indicate high intra-cluster similarity, whereas sparse inter-community links suggest low inter-cluster similarity.

Suppose that C_x and C_y are two of the m clusters obtained by clustering algorithm. $sim(x, y)$ is the similarity between document x and document y. The similarity between two clusters can be defined as follows.

$$e_{i, j} = \frac{\sum_{c_x \in C_i} \sum_{c_y \in C_j} sim(x, y)}{\sum_{c_x \in C} \sum_{c_y \in C} sim(x, y)} \quad i, j = 1, 2, \ldots, m \tag{7}$$

The intra-cluster similarity can be represented by $e_{i, i}$ $(i = 1, 2, \ldots, m)$. Hence, the clustering performance measure can be defined by a modularity Q as formula (8).

$$Q = \sum_{i=1}^{m} \left[e_{i, i} - \left(\sum_{j=1}^{m} e_{i, j} \right)^2 \right] \quad i, j = 1, 2, \ldots, m \tag{8}$$

As it measures the quality of clustering results, a high Q value means better performance of clustering. A Q value curve gained in the process of hierarchical clustering for personal name "陈坚 (CHEN Jian)" is drawn in Fig. 6. From the picture, we can find a peak when the number of clusters is 7 and the corresponding Q gains a largest value 0.5428, which represents a best clustering result. Such a Q value will be employed as a cluster stopping measure.

5.3 Noise Cluster Removing

Clustering algorithm using the cluster stopping measure Q can determine the number of clusters automatically for each personal name, which gives a better result than a traditional threshold method. Nevertheless, this algorithm will lead to too many noise clusters with only one document. In this paper, we merge noise clusters into their nearest clusters, which can result in an improvement of clustering performance.

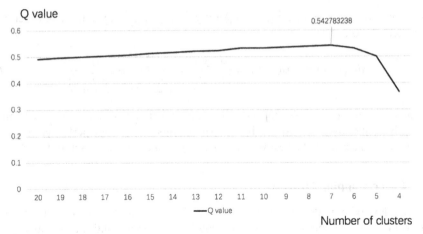

Fig. 6. The Curve of Q value for clustering personal name "CHEN Jian"

5.4 Experimental Result

Experiments are carried out on six groups of personal names for three methods: threshold-based clustering, Q measure-based clustering, and Q measure-based clustering by removing noise clusters. The experimental result for F-score is shown in Fig. 7.

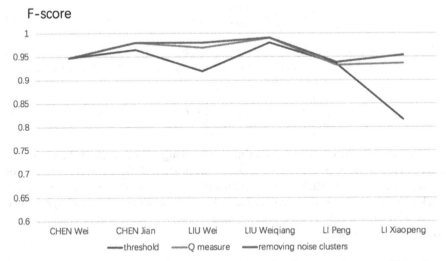

Fig. 7. The F-score of three cluster-stopping algorithm for six personal names. (Color figure online)

As depicted in the Fig. 7, three algorithms achieve the same F-score for personal name "陈卫 (CHEN Wei)". For name "李鹏 (LI Peng)", the threshold-based algorithm performs better than the Q measure-based algorithm, but worse than the algorithm considering noise cluster removing. Q measure-based algorithm by removing the noise clusters outperforms two other algorithms on average (see Red curve in Fig. 7).

Table 1. Result of noise cluster optimization (# represents the number of clusters)

Personal name	Real number of clusters	# for Q-based method	# for optimization method	F-score for Q-based method	F-score for optimization method
CHEN Wei	5	4	4	94.74%	94.74%
CHEN Jian	7	7	7	98.00%	98.00%
LIU Wei	6	9	7	96.91%	97.96%
LIU Weiqiang	5	7	5	98.99%	99.00%
LI Peng	8	13	10	93.18%	93.83%
LI Xiaopeng	3	9	6	93.62%	95.29%

Table 1 displays the result of cluster optimization experiment for Q measure-based algorithm by removing the noise clusters. Even though the results of two clustering algorithms are the same for "CHEN Wei" and "CHEN Jian", the noise cluster optimization approach performs better for the rest groups. Therefore, the Q measure-based algorithm by removing the noise clusters will reduce the number of clusters and eventually improve the effect of clustering algorithm.

6 Conclusions

This paper has proposed a framework to disambiguate personal names in Chinese dataset. The dataset was created by crawling Baidu news with six personal names and removing HTML tags for standardization. A lot of work of lexical analysis has been done, like segmentation, part-of-speech tagging, and named entity recognition. On one hand, different words were extracted as features and six groups of features were selected for clustering. On the other hand, boolean, absolute frequency, tf-idf, and entropy weights were chosen for the weighting scheme. Finally, twenty-four combinations were tested and feature 5 (noun feature with df $>= 2$) plus tf-idf weights achieved the best result.

As for clustering algorithm, we explored the cluster stopping measure by utilizing a Q measure, which can exhibit better performance than threshold-based method. Moreover, noise cluster optimization was done by merging noise clusters into their neighbor clusters with the largest similarity. Experimental results have shown that the final number of noise clusters is reduced and the proposed approach has a better effect on the dataset of six personal names. However, there are some limitations of the Q measure-based method. The algorithm highly depends on the internal similarity across attributes of documents when stopping the clustering. It inclines to cluster with many small groups.

In future, multiple feature generation will be expanded by introducing syntactic information, which is neglected in our research. Furthermore, the method cannot perform well when the lexical analysis fails, so improving the accuracy of early analysis is a direction of future work.

Acknowledgement. This work was supported by the Youth Foundation of Basic Science Research Program of Jiangnan University, 2019 (No. JUSRP11962) and High-level Innovation and Entrepreneurship Talents Introduction Program of Jiangsu Province of China, 2019.

References

1. Li, G., Wang, H.: Chinese named entity recognition and disambiguation based on multi-stage clustering. J. Chin. Inf. Process. **27**(5), 29–34 (2013)
2. Zhao, L., Yan, Z., Liang, H.: Ontology-based personal name disambiguation on the web. In: Proceedings of the 2013 IEEE/WIC/ACM International Joint Conferences on Web Intelligence (WI) and Intelligent Agent Technologies (IAT), vol. 01 (2013)
3. Emami, H.: A graph-based approach to person name disambiguation in web. ACM Trans. Manag. Inf. Syst. **10**(2), 4.1–4.25 (2019)
4. Xiong, L., et al.: Chinese name disambiguation based on analysis of sentential semantic structure. Appl. Res. Comput. **33**(10), 2898–2901 (2016)
5. Yang, Y., Zhou, J., Li, B.: Name disambiguation algorithm based on ensemble. Appl. Res. Comput. **33**(9), 2716–2720 (2016)
6. Zeng, J., et al.: Research on expert disambiguation of same name based on multi-feature fusion. Acta Scientiarum Naturalium Universitatis Pekinensis **56**(4), 607–613 (2020)
7. Shang, Y., et al.: Co-author and afiliate based name disambiguation approach. Comput. Sci. **45**(11), 220–225 (2018)
8. Zhai, X., et al.: Research on English author name disambiguation based on sparse distributed representation. Appl. Res. Comput. **36**(12), 3534–3538 (2019)
9. Yu, C., et al.: Author name disambiguation with network embedding. Data Anal. Knowl. Disc. **4**(2/3), 48–59 (2020)
10. Pooja, K.M., Mondal, S., Chandra, J.: A graph combination with edge pruning-based approach for author name disambiguation. J. Am. Soc. Inf. Sci. **71**(1), 69–83 (2020)
11. Kim, K., Rohatgi, S., Giles, C.L.: Hybrid deep pairwise classification for author name disambiguation. In: Proceedings of the 28th ACM International Conference on Information and Knowledge Management, pp. 2369–2372 (2019)
12. Delgado, D., et al.: Person name disambiguation on the web in a multilingual context. Inf. Sci. **465**, 373–387 (2018)
13. Khabsa, M., Treeratpituk, P., Giles, C.L.: Online person name disambiguation with constraints. In: Proceedings of the 15th ACM/IEEE-CS Joint Conference on Digital Libraries, Knoxville, TN, pp. 37–46 (2015)
14. Hotho, A., Staab, S., Stumme, G.: WordNet improves text document clustering. In: Proceedings of the SIGIR 2003 Semantic Web Workshop, pp. 541–544 (2003)
15. Newman, M.E.J.: Modularity and community structure in networks. Proc. Natl. Acad. Sci. **103**(23), 8577–8582 (2006)
16. Fan, C., Toriumi, F.: High-modularity network generation model based on the muitilayer network. Trans. Jpn. Soc. Artif. Intell. **32**(6), B-H42_1-11 (2017). https://doi.org/10.1527/tjsai.B-H42

Research on Behavior Characteristics of Festival Tourists in Jianye District of Nanjing Based on Big Data

Yueli Ni[✉], Yijuan Ge, and Xiaoling Zhang

Nanjing Institute of Tourism and Hospitality, Nanjing, Jiangsu, China

Abstract. Festival tourism, as a combination of culture and tourism, has multiple economic, social and cultural benefits. It plays an important role in enriching people's cultural life, promoting local economic development and establishing city image. Therefore, it has broad development prospects and research value. This paper collects data from seven key festival activities in Jianye District of Nanjing, including Youth Olympic Art Lantern Festival, may day life season, summer of music, Mochou Lake Garden opening, Xingchao Music Festival, National Day activities and mid autumn festival activities. Based on the big data of tourists, this paper analyzes the characteristics of tourists' behavior, and provides suggestions for the development planning, regulation control and management of festival tourism in Jianye District of Nanjing To provide scientific basis for service and marketing promotion.

Keywords: Big data · Jianye District of Nanjing · Festival and events Tourism · Tourist behavior characteristics

1 Research Background

1.1 Object of Study

Jianye District is the central city of Nanjing, the financial service center of the eastern region of China, and the business and Trade Center, exhibition center, sports center and innovation and Creativity Center of East China. It is an international new district with modern finance, headquarters economy, information service, culture and sports, software research and development, business office and tourism exhibition as its main functions.

Festival tourism, as a form of activity combining culture and tourism, plays an important role in enriching people's cultural life, promoting local economic development and establishing city image. The key festival activities in Jianye District of Nanjing city mainly include Youth Olympic Art Lantern Festival, may day life season, summer of music, Mochou Lake Garden, Xingchao Music Festival, National Day activities and Chinese Music Festival Autumn festival activities, etc. In 2019, Jianye District carried out data monitoring on the above seven key festival activities, so as to better grasp the pulling effect of festival tourism on local image and economy.

W. Fu et al. (Eds.): ICMTEL 2021, LNICST 387, pp. 265–272, 2021.
https://doi.org/10.1007/978-3-030-82562-1_24

1.2 Data Sources

Based on the needs of global tourism development, Jianye District Culture and Tourism Bureau commissioned China Telecom Jiangsu Zhiguan Telecom big data center to establish a smart tourism big data platform. The main data contents include:

Visitor and visitor attributes and origin: according to the mobile phone user registration information, after anonymity and other de privacy processing, obtain the statistical data of age, gender, origin and other attribute information.

The consumption data of UnionPay channel tourists: the Jianye UnionPay POS card terminal swipe card for the consumption of food, accommodation, travel, entertainment and other industries in the whole area of the Jianye area, and the data recorded by WeChat, Alipay and other payment codes are scanned through the UnionPay terminal.

Tourism public resources: combined with Jianye District Culture and Tourism Bureau's own data and telecommunication network and location data, this paper analyzes the spatial distribution of various tourism public resources in Jianye District, such as catering, accommodation, entertainment, scenic spots, travel agencies, public toilets, parking lots, etc.

1.3 The Purpose and Significance of Big Data Monitoring

By monitoring the big data of key festival tourism in Jianye District of Nanjing in 2019 and analyzing the tourist portraits and tourism public opinion of the Lantern Festival, we can effectively improve the ability of collaborative management and public service, and promote the reform of tourism service, tourism marketing, tourism management and tourism innovation. Through the statistics of festival tourism related data, combined with the user's consumption ability, age and other label attributes, the consumption behavior of tourists can be deeply analyzed, the travel rules of tourists can be mined, the orderly travel of tourists can be guided, and the comfort of tourists can be improved. It is helpful for Jianye District government to carry out festival tourism planning, tourism market positioning and marketing, tourism market demand forecasting and monitoring, and big data is conducive to resource allocation in the era of global tourism.

2   Analysis on the Tourist Source of Festival Tourism in Jianye District of Nanjing City

2.1 Analysis of the Tourist Source Areas Outside Jiangsu Province

East China is the main source of tourists. Among the top eight provinces in terms of passenger flow, Shanghai, Anhui, Zhejiang and Shandong rank among them. The passenger flow of four provinces accounts for about 50% of all kinds of festival activities (except the Mid Autumn Festival). East China is the main source of tourists in our region (Fig. 1).

During the Mid Autumn Festival, the tourist sources are scattered. During the Mid Autumn Festival, the top eight provinces accounted for 39.63% of the total passenger flow, and these eight provinces accounted for more than 70% of the total passenger flow in other festival activities. Therefore, in the promotion of tourism activities, we should give full consideration to tourists' love of hometown during the traditional festivals.

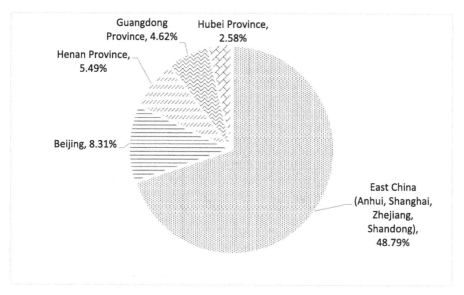

Fig. 1. Proportion of passenger flow outside the province during festival activities (TOP8)

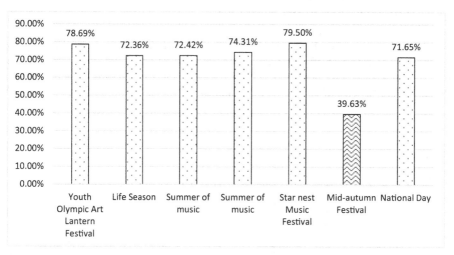

Fig. 2. The proportion of passenger flow outside the province during the Mid Autumn Festival (TOP8)

2.2 Analysis of Tourist Source Areas in Jiangsu Province

Northern Jiangsu is the main cross city tourist in the province. The top cities in Northern Jiangsu are Suqian, Huai'an, Xuzhou and Yancheng, accounting for more than 9% of the total passenger flow. Taizhou, Changzhou and Lianyungang have less passenger flow (Fig. 3).

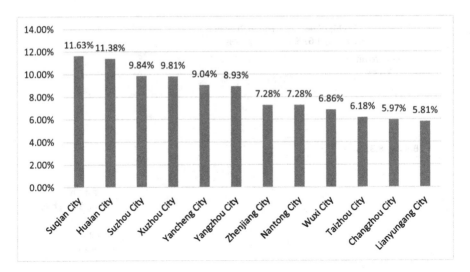

Fig. 3. Proportion of cross city passenger flow in the province during festival activities

3   Analysis on the Population Characteristics of Festival Tourists in Jianye District of Nanjing City

Young customers account for a large proportion. The average proportion of passenger flow in the age group of 45 and below is 58.75%. There are four festival activities in this age group whose proportion exceeds the average. The top three are Xingchao Music Festival (66.83%), Youth Olympic Art Lantern Festival (65.60%) and music summer

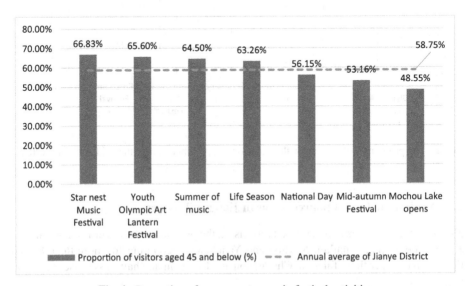

Fig. 4. Proportion of young customers in festival activities

(64.50%). These three festival activities are all related to art, and they are mainly designed for young customers. Among the actual visitors, young visitors accounted for more than 60%, which was in line with the expectation. Among the traditional festivals, such as national day and Mid Autumn Festival, young tourists account for more than 50% of the total, but they are not attractive to young tourists (Fig. 4).

Women accounted for a large proportion of festival activities. In all festival activities, only during the Mid Autumn Festival and the national day, the passenger flow of men is more than that of women. It is opposite to the annual average sex ratio of visitors (51.79% for males, 48.21% for females). Statistics show that women are more enthusiastic about fashion and arts festivals (Fig. 5).

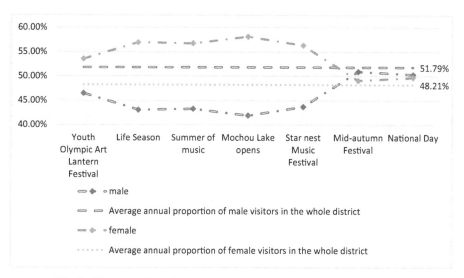

Fig. 5. The proportion of male and female tourists during festival activities

4   Analysis on the Consumption Behavior of Festival Tourists in Jianye District of Nanjing City

The average daily visitors of Jianye District in the whole year is 146800 person times, and there is a certain difference in the average daily visitors of Jianye District during the festival activities. During the Youth Olympic Art Lantern Festival, Jianye District has 191100 visitors per day, ranking first; during the Mid Autumn Festival, Jianye District has 12.62 visitors per day, ranking last; during the Xingchao Music Festival and the Mid Autumn Festival, Jianye District has less visitors per day than the average of the whole year (Fig. 6).

Festival activities have a certain pulling effect on regional consumption. The average daily consumption of the whole region is 54.5401 million yuan, and the corresponding daily average value during festival activities is 55.5234 million yuan. The pulling effect

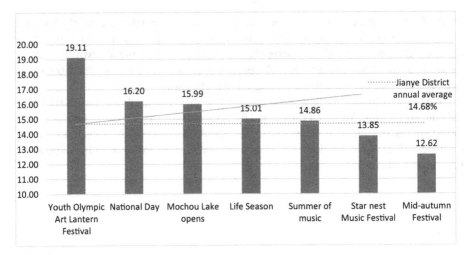

Fig. 6. Average daily visitors during festival activities

is particularly obvious in Xingchao Music Festival (63.1213 million yuan per day), National Day (57.2653 million yuan per day) and music summer (56.2597 million yuan per day) (Fig. 7).

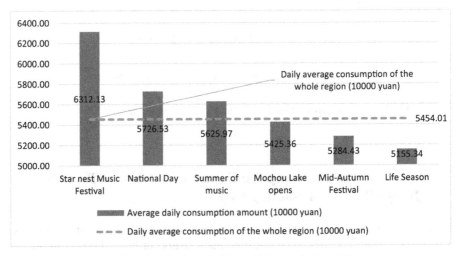

Fig. 7. Consumption of visitors during festival activities

5 Summary

Festival activities significantly promote the passenger flow and consumption. During the Youth Olympic Art Lantern Festival, the daily average number of visitors was 191100, an increase of 30.16% over the annual average number of visitors; during the national day, the daily average number of visitors was 162000, an increase of 10.34%; during the opening of Mochou Lake, the daily average number of visitors was 159900, an increase of 8.95%; during the May Day, the daily average number of visitors was 150100, an increase of 2.28%; during the summer of music, the daily average number of visitors was 148600, an increase of 1.24%.

The daily average consumption of the whole region is 54.5401 million yuan, and the corresponding daily average value during the festival activities is 55.5234 million yuan. The pulling effect is particularly obvious in Xingchao Music Festival (daily average 63.1213 million yuan, increased by 15.74%), National Day (57.2653 million yuan, increased by 5%) and music summer (56.2597 million yuan, increased by 3.15%).

Festival activities boost the overall image of Jianye District. During the festival activities, the proportion of young visitors increased significantly, such as the star nest Music Festival (66.83% of the young visitors under 45 years old), the Youth Olympic Art Lantern Festival (65.60%) and the summer of music (64.50%). These festival activities want to convey the spirit of "Youth and vitality". In the process of holding the event, it successfully attracted a large number of young people, and the young customers accounted for more than 60%, which was in line with the expectation. This has played a positive role in promoting the transmission and expression of the youth and vitality image of science and technology Jianye, humanity Jianye and vitality Jianye.

Acknowledgment. The work is supported by the Philosophy and Social Sciences Project for Colleges and Universities in Jiangsu Province (Nos. 2019SJA2248).

The work is supported by School level project of Nanjing Institute of Tourism & Hospitality (Nos. kyc2019xkt07).

References

1. Peng, Z.: Research on the impact of big data technology on the optimization and upgrading of China's tourism industrial structure. Commercial Econ. Res. **22**, 179–181 (2020)
2. Gege, Z., Di, T., Mu, Z.: A study on the experience of tourists participating in festival activities based on grey correlation -- Taking OCT cultural tourism festival as an example. Tourism Res. **13**(01), 59–72 (2021)
3. Shi, J., Hu, T., Zhang, A.: A study on the difference of cognition and image of intangible cultural heritage from the perspective of subject and object. Green Technol. (05), 173–176+181 (2020)
4. Persson.: The Olympic Games site decision. Tourism Manag. **23**(5), 27–36 (2012)
5. Prentice, A.: Festival as creative destination. Ann. Tour. Res. **30**(1), 7–30 (2013)
6. Crompton, M.: Motives of visitors attending festival events. Ann. Tourism Res. **24**(2), 425–439 (2015)
7. Zhao, X.: Research on the promotion of Xi'an city image by festival activities. Tourism Overv. **19**, 100–102 (2020)
8. Song, C.: On paradigms of geographical research. Prog. Geogr. **35**(1), 1–3 (2016)
9. Yan, S., Liang, L., Suo, Z.: Spatial and temporal distribution characteristics of tourism flow in Luoyang based on big data. Econ. Geogr. **3**(8), 216–224 (2017)
10. Li, C.: The influence of festival activities on city image: a case study of Beijing New Year temple fair. China National Expo **14**, 50–51 (2020)

11. Tao, D.Z., Cui, Z.Y., Bin, L.: Characteristics and path analysis of tourism flow agglomeration and diffusion in Wuhan metropolitan area. Econ. Geography **5**(3),170–175 (2014)
12. Yan, Y., He, W.: Temporal and spatial evolution analysis of domestic tourism flow and quality. Econ. Geogr. **3**(04), 179–185 (2013)
13. Song, T., Guo, S.: Construction and validation of big data statistical model of tourism passenger flow. Stat. Decis. **36**(24), 38–41 (2020)
14. Cheng, C., Shi, P., Song, C.: Geographic big data provides new opportunities for the study of geographic complexity. Acta Geogr. Sin. **73**(8), 1397–1406 (2018)
15. Jin, C., Lu, Y., Fan, L.: Spatial structure of domestic tourist market in Jiangsu Province. Econ. Geogr. **30**(20), 2104–2108 (2010)

Application of GNSS Virtual Reference Station in Poyang Lake Area

Zhigang Wang[1], Hang Guo[1(✉)], Hepeng Wang[1], Min Yu[2(✉)], and Xindong Chen[1]

[1] Nanchang University, Nanchang 330031, China
hguo@ncu.edu.cn

[2] College of Computer Information Engineering, Jiangxi Normal University, Nanchang 330021, China

Abstract. Virtual Reference Station (VRS) is a kind of network RTK technology. For solving the limitations of real-time standard dynamic (RTK) system, a new method for high-precision RTK positioning VRS is proposed. At the same time, aiming at the real-time solution of the ambiguity of VRS network, a new method based on the non-ionospheric combination equation to solve the ambiguity is proposed. The linear interpolation model is used to generate the comprehensive error correction number, and the virtual observation value is proposed. The method was generated and tested in Nanchang University and Poyang Lake area. The test was conducted at different locations around Poyang Lake to assess the accuracy of VRS RTK positioning; the results show that the use of multiple reference station networks increases the coverage of location service areas and enhances robustness over a single reference station system, got higher positioning accuracy. The VRS RTK is positioned in the experimental network with a horizontal accuracy of 1–2 cm and a vertical accuracy AG of 3–5 cm.

Keywords: RTK · VRS · Ambiguity

1 Introduction

RTK (Real-time kinematic) carrier phase difference technology is a differential method for real-time processing of carrier phase observations of two measurement stations. The carrier phase acquired by the base station is sent to the user receiver to perform the difference calculation coordinate. RTK positioning is typically implemented in a single reference station mode. However, the single reference frame lacks data redundancy and must be within 10–15 km of the user, as GPS errors become less spatially correlated over longer baselines, resulting in reduced positioning accuracy [1, 2]. Therefore, in order to achieve high-precision RTK positioning for longer distances, the network RTK method came into being. In order to overcome the limitations of conventional RTK positioning technology and achieve centimeter-level high-precision uniform real-time dynamic positioning in a region, this paper demonstrates a new method for creating VRS positioning VRS, for ambiguity resolution and VRS network in VRS algorithm. The generation of error correction numbers and the generation of VRS virtual observations were studied. The test results of VRS for RTK positioning in different locations of the Poyang Lake network were discussed.

© ICST Institute for Computer Sciences, Social Informatics and Telecommunications Engineering 2021
Published by Springer Nature Switzerland AG 2021. All Rights Reserved
W. Fu et al. (Eds.): ICMTEL 2021, LNICST 387, pp. 273–280, 2021.
https://doi.org/10.1007/978-3-030-82562-1_25

2 Principle of LOAM Algorithm

2.1 VRS Network Full-Circumference Ambiguity Real-Time Solution

11 Real-time and correct fixation of the ambiguity of the whole week is a prerequisite for users to achieve precise positioning.In this paper, the wide lane ambiguity is first solved, and then the L1 ambiguity and the tropospheric zenith delay (RTZD) are estimated by the adaptive Kalman filter using the ionization-free layer observation.

According to the double-difference ionospheric observation ($\nabla\Delta\phi_{77,-60}$), the relationship between the double-difference L1 ambiguity ($\nabla\Delta N_1$) and the double-difference wide ambiguity ($\nabla\Delta N_{1,-1}$), this paper focuses on the modified adaptive Kalman filter for real-time estimation of RTZD. And the double difference L1 ambiguity, the observation equation is:

$$\lambda_{77,-66}\nabla\Delta\phi_{77,-60} = \nabla\Delta\rho + \nabla\Delta N_1\left(17\lambda_{77,-66}\right) + \nabla\Delta N_{1,-1}\left(60\lambda_{77,-66}\right)$$
$$+\nabla\Delta d_{trop} + \varepsilon\left(\nabla\Delta\phi_{77,-60}\right) \tag{1}$$

where: $\nabla\Delta\rho$ is the geometric distance of the double-difference station star, $\varepsilon\left(\nabla\Delta\phi_{77,-60}\right)$ is the phase difference observation noise of the double-difference ionosphere, $\lambda_{77,-66}$ is the combined observation wavelength without ionosphere, and $\nabla\Delta d_{trop}$ is the double-difference tropospheric delay.

First, since the wavelength of the wide-circumference ambiguity is 86.4 cm, it is easy to accurately determine the ambiguity of the whole week. Using the search method or the sequence estimation method, it is possible to determine $\nabla\Delta N_{1,-1}$, in the Eq. (1), The ionospheric ambiguity is determined by the combination of wide lane all-round ambiguity $\nabla\Delta N_{1,-1}$ and L1 full-circumference ambiguity. Since the wide lane ambiguity is first determined, the above relationship is used to obtain L1 full-circumference ambiguity [3]. Using known reference station exact coordinates and wide lane ambiguity, L1 full-circumference ambiguity is only affected by tropospheric delay, multipath interference, and observed noise. The effect of multipath effects can be reduced by selecting an appropriate reference station and using a GPS receiver with multipath mitigation. The challenge therefore is how to mitigate the tropospheric double residual and reduce the observed noise. Since the influence of the troposphere is related to the satellite height angle, introducing a projection function $MF(\cdot)$, the double-difference tropospheric delay can be expressed as the product of the RTZD and the projection function [4]:

$$\nabla\Delta d_{trop}^{xy} = RTZD \cdot \left[MF\left(\varepsilon^x\right) - MF\left(\varepsilon^y\right)\right] \tag{2}$$

where: ε^x and ε^y represent the elevation angle of the satellite x, y, $MF(\cdot) = 1/\sin(\cdot)$, Therefore: (1) can be turned into:

$$\lambda_{77,-66}\nabla\Delta\phi_{77,-60} - \nabla\Delta\rho - \nabla\Delta N_{1,-1}\left(60\lambda_{77,-66}\right)$$
$$= \nabla\Delta N_1\left(17\lambda_{77,-66}\right) + RTZD \cdot \left[MF(\varepsilon^x) - MF(\varepsilon^y)\right] + \varepsilon\left(\nabla\Delta\phi_{77,-60}\right) \tag{3}$$

To estimate the RTZD and the double-difference ambiguity on L1 in real time, an adaptive Kalman filter is used to solve each baseline solution between the primary reference station and other reference stations. The measurement equation and the state equation are:

$$Z_k = H_k X_k + V_k \quad , V_k \sim N(0, R_k) \tag{4}$$

$$X_k = \Phi_{k,k-1} X_{k-1} + W_k \quad , W_k \sim N(0, Q_k) \tag{5}$$

where: V_k is the observed noise, W_k representing the system noise, R_k is the covariance matrix of the observed noise, and the observation vector is:

$$Z_k = \begin{bmatrix} \lambda_{77,-66} \nabla \Delta \phi_{77,-60}^{12} - \nabla \Delta \rho^{12} - \nabla \Delta N_{1,-1}^{12} \cdot (60\lambda_{77,-66}) \\ \lambda_{77,-66} \nabla \Delta \phi_{77,-60}^{13} - \nabla \Delta \rho^{13} - \nabla \Delta N_{1,-1}^{13} \cdot (60\lambda_{77,-66}) \\ \vdots \\ \lambda_{77,-66} \nabla \Delta \phi_{77,-60}^{1n} - \nabla \Delta \rho^{1n} - \nabla \Delta N_{1,-1}^{1n} \cdot (60\lambda_{77,-66}) \end{bmatrix} \tag{6}$$

Among them: superscript 1 represents the reference satellite, and 2 to n represent other satellites. The state vector is defined as:

$$X_k = \begin{bmatrix} RTZD & \nabla \Delta N_1^{12} & \nabla \Delta N_1^{13} & \cdots & \nabla \Delta N_1^{1n} \end{bmatrix}^T \tag{7}$$

And the measurement matrix is:

$$H_k = \begin{bmatrix} MF(\varepsilon^1) - MF(\varepsilon^2) & 17\lambda_{77,-66} & 0 & \cdots & 0 \\ MF(\varepsilon^1) - MF(\varepsilon^3) & 0 & 17\lambda_{77,-66} & \cdots & 0 \\ \vdots & \vdots & \vdots & \ddots & \vdots \\ MF(\varepsilon^1) - MF(\varepsilon^n) & 0 & 0 & \cdots & 17\lambda_{77,-66} \end{bmatrix} \tag{8}$$

where: RTZD is a first-order Gauss-Markov process and assumes that L1 ambiguity is very small white noise. Then define the state transition matrix and the corresponding covariance matrix as:

$$\Phi_{k,k-1} = \begin{bmatrix} e^{-\Delta t/\tau} & 0 & \cdots & 0 \\ 0 & 1 & \cdots & 0 \\ \vdots & \vdots & \ddots & \vdots \\ 0 & 0 & \cdots & 1 \end{bmatrix} \tag{9}$$

$$Q_k = \begin{bmatrix} \frac{\tau}{2}(1 - e^{-2\Delta t/\tau})q & 0 & \cdots & 0 \\ 0 & 1e^{-16} & \cdots & 0 \\ \vdots & \vdots & \ddots & \vdots \\ 0 & 0 & \cdots & 1e^{-16} \end{bmatrix} \tag{10}$$

where: q is the variance of the RTZD process noise at the relevant time τ, which is the sampling interval Δt.

Traditional Kalman filtering requires a priori information, namely noise statistics parameters R_k and Q_k. However, in practice, it is difficult to know the true statistical characteristics of measurement and system noise. Without prior information, it is impossible to do a Kalman filter. Incorrect values will result in inaccurate results and even divergence. On the other hand, the network RTK method usually requires 6 or more satellites to be corrected and no interrupts are allowed [5]. To overcome this problem, the following residual-based adaptive Kalman filter is proposed [6]:

$$X_{k,k-1} = \Phi_{k,k-1} X_{k-1,k-1} \tag{11}$$

$$P_{k,k-1} = \Phi_{k,k-1} P_{k-1,k-1} \Phi_{k,k-1}^T + Q_{k-1} \tag{12}$$

$$J_k = P_{k,k-1} H_k^T (H_k P_{k,k-1} H_k^T + R_{k-1})^{-1} \tag{13}$$

$$X_{k,k} = X_{k,k-1} + J_k (Z_k - H_k X_{k,k-1}) \tag{14}$$

$$P_{k,k} = (I - J_k H_k) P_{k,k-1} \tag{15}$$

$$R_k = C_{v_k} + H_k P_{k,k} H_k^T \tag{16}$$

$$Q_k = J_k C_{v_k} J_k^T \tag{17}$$

among them:

$$C_{v_k} = \frac{1}{N} \sum_{i=i_0}^{k} v_i v_i^T \tag{18}$$

Residual sequence:

$$v_k = Z_k - H_k X_k \tag{19}$$

where $i_0 = k - N + 1$ is the first epoch in the moving window of estimated size N, $X_{k,k-1}$ and $P_{k,k-1}$ are system state prediction values and covariance matrices, respectively, $X_{k,k}$ and $P_{k,k}$ are updated system state prediction values and covariance matrices, J_k represents the gain matrix.

Here, the covariance matrices (R_k and Q_k) of the measurement and system noise are estimated in real time from the previous epoch. With the adaptive Kalman filter recursive formula, the corresponding covariance matrix $P_{k,k}$ can be used to estimate the RTZD sum and the double difference L1 floating point ambiguity. The existing method is then used to perform a double difference L1 integer ambiguity search [7], such as the LAMBDA method. Thus, the L2 full-circumference ambiguity is solved. Details are not included in this article.

2.2   VRS Network Error Correction Number Generation Method

When the spatial correlation error at the baseline of each reference station is determined, the spatial correlation correction at the virtual reference station can be calculated by a specific interpolation algorithm [8, 9]. In this paper, a distance-based linear interpolation algorithm is adopted. The advantage of this real-time method is that it is simple to implement and has high efficiency. By using this method, track deviation and ionospheric delay can be eliminated, and in addition, tropospheric delay, multipath and observed noise can be reduced. In order to apply this method in real time, a modified linear interpolation model with user horizontal coordinates as a parameter is adopted. In the network coverage area, any user station ionospheric correction number can pass through the known coordinates of the reference station and the outline of the subscriber station. The coordinates are interpolated.

When there are at least 3 GPS reference stations around the subscriber station, the interpolation model can be described as follows:

$$
\begin{bmatrix} V_{1,n} \\ V_{2,n} \\ \vdots \\ V_{n-1,n} \end{bmatrix} = \begin{bmatrix} \lambda\nabla\Delta\phi_{1n} - \nabla\Delta\rho_{1n} - \lambda\nabla\Delta N_{1n} \\ \lambda\nabla\Delta\phi_{2n} - \nabla\Delta\rho_{2n} - \lambda\nabla\Delta N_{2n} \\ \vdots \\ \lambda\nabla\Delta\phi_{n-1n} - \nabla\Delta\rho_{n-1n} - \lambda\nabla\Delta N_{n-1n} \end{bmatrix}
$$

$$
= \begin{bmatrix} \Delta X_{1,n} & \Delta Y_{1,n} \\ \Delta X_{2,n} & \Delta Y_{2,n} \\ \vdots & \vdots \\ \Delta X_{n-1,n} & \Delta Y_{n-1,n} \end{bmatrix} \cdot \begin{bmatrix} a \\ b \end{bmatrix} \tag{20}
$$

where $V_{i,n}$ represents the correction of the deviation of the ionosphere; $\Delta X_{i,n}$ and $\Delta Y_{i,n}$ (i = 1, 2,, n−1) represent the plane coordinate difference between the n−1 sub-reference stations and the n-th main station. The parameters a and b are the coefficients of $\Delta X_{i,n}$ and $\Delta Y_{i,n}$. In the case of more than 3 reference stations, the coefficients a and b can be obtained by the least squares method, which is obtained by Eq. (20):

$$
\begin{bmatrix} \hat{a} \\ \hat{b} \end{bmatrix} = (A^T A)^{-1} A^T V \tag{21}
$$

$$
V = \begin{bmatrix} V_{1,n} \\ V_{2,n} \\ \vdots \\ V_{n-1,n} \end{bmatrix} = \begin{bmatrix} \lambda\nabla\Delta\phi_{1n} - \nabla\Delta\rho_{1n} - \lambda\nabla\Delta N_{1n} \\ \lambda\nabla\Delta\phi_{2n} - \nabla\Delta\rho_{2n} - \lambda\nabla\Delta N_{2n} \\ \vdots \\ \lambda\nabla\Delta\phi_{n-1n} - \nabla\Delta\rho_{n-1n} - \lambda\nabla\Delta N_{n-1n} \end{bmatrix} \tag{22}
$$

$$
A = \begin{bmatrix} \Delta X_{1,n} & \Delta Y_{1,n} \\ \Delta X_{2,n} & \Delta Y_{2,n} \\ \vdots & \vdots \\ \Delta X_{n-1,n} & \Delta Y_{n-1,n} \end{bmatrix} \tag{23}
$$

It is assumed that the correction numbers of each sub-reference station to the primary reference station are equal weights of the same precision, and their weight matrix P =

E is taken. The network coverage user station deviation can be interpolated using the following two-dimensional model:

$$Corr_{u,n} = \hat{a} \cdot \Delta X_{u,n} + \hat{b} \cdot \Delta Y_{u,n} \tag{24}$$

$$Corr_{u,n} = \begin{bmatrix} \Delta X_{u,n} & \Delta Y_{u,n} \end{bmatrix} \begin{bmatrix} \hat{a} & \hat{b} \end{bmatrix}^T = \begin{bmatrix} \Delta X_{u,n} & \Delta Y_{u,n} \end{bmatrix} (A^T A)^{-1} A^T V \tag{25}$$

where $Corr_{u,n}$ represents the correction of the ionospheric deviation between the subscriber station and the primary reference station; $\Delta X_{u,n}$ and $\Delta Y_{u,n}$ respectively represent the plane coordinate difference between the subscriber station and the primary reference station.

2.3 VRS Observation Generation

Let x^s be the satellite position vector, x^r is the main reference station position vector, and x^v is the VRS position vector. At epoch time t, the geometric distance between the satellite and the primary reference station receiver is

$$\rho_r^s(t) = \|x^s - x^r\| \tag{26}$$

The geometric distance between the satellite and the VRS is

$$\rho_v^s(t) = \|x^s - x^v\| \tag{27}$$

The geometric correction amount $\Delta \rho^s = \rho_v^s(t) - \rho_r^s(t)$ can be applied to the calculation of satellite s observation data on the primary reference station to the VRS. After applying the geometric correction number to the primary reference station raw data, the data correction number generated according to Sect. 2.2 is used to correct the VRS data, and then the virtual observation value and the reference station coordinates are RTCM encoded and sent to the user station [10, 11], The user station can be decoded to perform differential positioning.

3   VRS/RTK Positioning Performance and Accuracy Analysis

In order to evaluate the basic implementation of the VRS RTK network, Nanchang University GPS observation network project includes four consecutive operation reference stations: Dean (DEAN), Poyang (POYA), Jinxian (JINX), and Duchang (DUCH). Each reference station is equipped. Trimble NetR9 reference station receiver and Zephyr Geodetic 2 antenna. The experiment uses dual-frequency phase observation data from 6:00:00 to 20:00:00 on December 30, 2017. The sampling time is 1S and the satellite cut-off angle is set to 10 degrees. The average baseline of the test network is (96) km. The layout of the system is shown in the figure. Select DEAN as the primary reference station and DUCH as the mobile station.

Fig. 1. Test network of Poyang Lake

The above network correction algorithm is integrated into the self-developed virtual reference station software platform SKY system, and applied to the network experiment of Poyang Lake virtual reference station in Jiangxi Province, as shown in Fig. 1. The results are shown in Fig. 2 and Table 1.

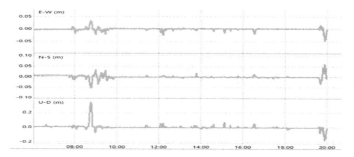

Fig. 2. Distribution of the RTK positioning Result at DUCH

Table 1. Accuracy of Network RTK position

Baseline vector	Network RTK positioning result /mm		
	MEAN	STD	RMS
Eastward	0.4	6.3	6.3
North	13.0	9.0	9.1
Vertical direction	13.0	35.6	35.6

It can be obtained from the RTK experimental results. The linear interpolation method is used to correct the number model. Using a sparse reference station network (3 reference stations with an average baseline length of 96 km), a centimeter-level RTK result of 1–2 cm in the horizontal direction and 3–5 cm in the elevation direction can be achieved.

4 Conclusion

In order to apply the network RTK technology to the medium and long-distance reference station network and achieve centimeter-level high-precision real-time dynamic positioning accuracy, the network correction algorithm model and the VRS observation value model must be established based on the existing error modeling technology. Based on the VRS observation value calculation model, based on the GPS continuous observation network in the Poyang Lake area of Jiangxi Province and the SKY system of the virtual reference station software platform independently developed, the real-time dynamic difference of the VRS centimeter network based on the Internet for the medium and long-distance reference station network over 96km is realized. The positioning service has a horizontal accuracy of 1–2 cm and a vertical accuracy of 3–5 cm in the experimental network. In the future, experiments outside the network and joint positioning of multiple satellites may be carried out.

Acknowledgments. The paper was supported by the projects of the National Natural Science Foundation of China (No. 41764002).

References

1. Hu, G.R., Khoo, H.S., Goh, P.C., et al.: Development and assessment of GPS VRS for RTK positioning. J. Geodesy. **77**(5–6), 292–302 (2003)
2. Chen, H.Y., Rizos, C., Han, S.: From simulation to implementation: low-cost densification of permanent GPS networks in support of geodetic applications. J. Geodesy. **75**(9–10), 515–526 (2001)
3. Sun, H., Cannon, M.E., Melgard, T.E.: Real-time GPS reference network carrier phase ambiguity resolution. In: Proceedings of network Navigation national technical meeting[J].January, San Diego, CA, USA, 25–27 1999, 193–199 (1999)
4. Zhang, J., Lachapelle, G.: Precise estimation of residual tropospheric delays using a regional GPS network for real-time kinematic applications. J. Geodesy. **7**(5–6), 255–266 (2001)
5. Edwards, S.J., Cross, P.A., Barnes, J.B., et al.: A methodology for benchmarking real-time kinematic GPS. Surv. Rev. **35**(273), 163–174 (1999)
6. Hu, G.R., Ou, J.K.: The improved method of adaptive Kalman filter for GPS high kinematic positioning. Acta Geodaetica et Cartographic Sinica **28**(4), 290–294 (1999)
7. Chen, D., Lachapelle, G.: A comparison of the fast and least squares search algorithms for on-the-fly ambiguity resolution. Navigation **42**(2), 371–390 (1995)
8. Wanninger, L.: Improved ambiguity resolution by regional differential modelling of the ionosphere. In: Proceedings 8th International Technical Meeting Satellite Division US Inst Navigation, Palm Springs, CA, pp. 55–62 (1995)
9. Han, S.W., Rizos, C.: GPS network design and error mitigation for real-time continuous array monitoring system. In: Proceedings 9th International Technical Meeting Satellite Division US Institution Navigation, Kansas City, MO, pp. 1827–1836 (1996)
10. Talbot, N.C.: Compact data transmission standard for highprecision GPS. In: Proceedings 9th International Technical Meeting Satellite Division US Institution Navigation, Kansas City, MO, pp. 861–871 (1996)
11. Mervart, L., Weber, G.: Real-time combination of GNSS orbit and clock correction streams using a kalman filter approach. In: Proceedings of International Technical Meeting of the Satellite Division of the Institute of Navigation, pp. 707–711 (2011)

Cruise Tourism Prosperity Index Based on Principal Component Analysis

Fangqing Sheng[1,2], Yang Zhang[1(✉)], Hua Jiang[3], and Gege Ma[1]

[1] Faculty of Hospitality and Tourism Management, Macau University of Science and Technology, Macau 999078, China
yangzhang@must.edu.mo
[2] School of Humanities and Arts, Jiangsu Maritime Institute, Nanjing 211199, Jiangsu, China
[3] School of Hotel Management, Nanjing Institute of Tourism and Hospitality, Nanjing 211199, Jiangsu, China

Abstract. This paper proposes to establish a more robust and flexible framework to formulate the cruise tourism prosperity index (CTPI), which can predict the supply and demand of the cruise industry. However, the use of indicators and cycle selection solves this challenge by incorporating indicators into predictive models. In this paper, CTPI in China from 2010 to 2018 is constructed and evaluated by principal component analysis. Then future development is predicted. Finally, the prediction results show consistency between projected results and actual developments.

Keywords: Cruise tourism prosperity index · Principal component analysis

1 Introduction

The development of the "Belt and Road" development strategy has brought many opportunities to the development of the tourism industry, especially the cruise industry [1]. Port cities have also seized this opportunity to promote port development and accelerate their integration into the "21st Century Maritime Silk Road" [2]. According to the requirements of the National Coastal Cruise Port Layout Plan [3], by 2030, a national port layout will be formed with 2 to 3 cruise home ports as the lead, the departure port as the main body, and the visiting port as the supplement. In 2018, the global economic growth rate has been significantly improved, providing a good foundation for the development of the cruise industry, with nearly 26.9 million passengers taking cruises [4]. The cruise industry is not only a high-growth industry but also a highly volatile industry. The cruise home port economy plays a central and central role in the regional economy and even the world cruise economy [5]. The unhealthy development of the cruise home port economy or large-scale and large fluctuations will have a greater impact on the regional cruise economy [6]. Therefore, it is very important and necessary to use scientific and rigorous methods to analyze, evaluate and calculate the economic operation of my country's cruise home port economy.

© ICST Institute for Computer Sciences, Social Informatics and Telecommunications Engineering 2021
Published by Springer Nature Switzerland AG 2021. All Rights Reserved
W. Fu et al. (Eds.): ICMTEL 2021, LNICST 387, pp. 281–287, 2021.
https://doi.org/10.1007/978-3-030-82562-1_26

Under this background, this paper takes the cruise home port economy as the research object, starting from the construction of the evaluation system of the prosperity index, and exploring the cultivation mechanism of the cruise home port prosperity index.

The organization of this paper is as follows: Sect. 2 explains related research progress, Sect. 3 weight indexes and introduces the principal component analysis method, Sect. 4 describes the data and presents the results of preliminary data analysis. Finally, Sect. 5 examines the findings and draws conclusions.

2 Relate Works

2.1 Economic Measurement Method of Cruise Home Port

From the perspective of qualitative assessment of cruise economy, industrial cluster theory, competitive advantage theory, game theory combined with gray correlation analysis method and SWOT analysis method can be used to analyze the advantages and modes of China's cruise economic development [7]. From the perspective of quantitative measurement of cruise economy, using neural network theory to study the degree of impact of cruise home ports and ports of call on regional economy, it is found that cruise tourism has a greater impact on the economy of home ports. The impact of the local economy is relatively limited. The IMPLAN input-output model prospectively evaluates the impact of the cruise industry on the local economy [8], reflecting that the industry rate of return of the cruise economy is closely related to the complexity of the local economic system. The cruise economic prosperity evaluation index system constructed by Cao Shuang analyzed the prosperity of China's cruise tourism market [9].

For the cruise industry, foreign countries pay more attention to the overall impact of the tourism industry on the region. Most domestic research results are qualitative descriptions. Overall, although scholars have theoretically demonstrated the development value of the cruise economy to the regional economy, and have also proposed a cruise economy prosperity evaluation system, it rarely involves the integration of the cruise economy from a two-dimensional interactive perspective of the "cruise home port-hinterland city" attributes, in-depth exploration of the path and mechanism of the comprehensive effect of various prosperity factors on the cruise home port economy, which makes it difficult for the existing research results to effectively solve the practical problems of cruise home port prosperity evaluation and planning.

2.2 Tourism Industry Prosperity Index

Economic prosperity refers to the overall economic operation and development trend, and is an economic concept used to describe and analyze the degree of economic activity. The prosperity index is a quantitative expression of prosperity. It can not only describe the running status of the economy, indicate the expansion and contraction of the economy, but also predict the future development trend of the economy. Foreign scholars' analysis and research on the tourism industry's prosperity focused on empirical research. Wong predicted the number of international tourists through a business cycle and explained various methods of tourism prediction [10]. On the basis of Wong, Turner introduced indicators such as exchange rate and per capita income of the source country, and used the composite index method to predict the future development of the Australian tourism industry [11]. Regarding the research on the tourism industry prosperity index, domestic scholars mainly focused on: Ni Xiaoning first determined the index weights based on the principal component analysis method, and then used the synthetic index method to calculate the Chinese tourism market prosperity index [12]. Dai Bin used the coefficient of variation method to weight indicators, established a travel agency prosperity index index system, and calculated the Chinese travel agency industry prosperity index [13]. Wang Xinfeng established a tourism boom measurement method and measurement model based on the idea of variable weight [14]. Tang Chengcai established a synthetic model for tourism measurement of heritage sites, and conducted a comparative study of the three tourism heritage sites of Huangshan, Zhangjiajie and Chengde [15].

According to relevant literature research on the tourism industry prosperity index at home and abroad, it can be seen that on the one hand, foreign research on the tourism industry prosperity index should take precedence over my country, and my country's research is based on the experience of foreign research. On the other hand, Chinese scholars have weak research on relevant theories and rich empirical research results, which has laid a good practical foundation for the study of China's tourism prosperity index. However, in the selection of indicators, there are indicators dependent on the domestic research results. Logical confusion; in determining the weights, even if some more complicated evaluation methods are adopted in the evaluation, there is a lack of effective integration of multiple methods.

3 Methodology

3.1 CTPI System

The CTPI (Cruise Tourism Prosperity Index) system explores 3 groups of indicators, i.e., leading coincident and lagging indexes. Leading index refers to peak or valley indicators appearing in advance before economic indicates get to peak or valley, which reflects income and consumption level of the cruise tourist market of the year; coincident indicator is those whose peak or valley time and economic cycle fluctuation is approximately similar to the benchmark time, which indicates the prosperity of the cruise tourist market of the year; lagging indicate is defined as those turning points appear later than the benchmark turning points of economic cycle fluctuations, which reveals the investment heat of the cruise tourist market of the year. Referring to China macro-economic prosperity index developed by National Information Center Economic Prosperity Analysis Research Group, this paper constructs a composite index that consists of leading, coincident and lagging indicators. To demonstrate the tourism prosperity, this paper utilizes consists of leading, coincident and lagging indicators to constructs a composite index.

First, we selected 49 primary indicators from statistical data of cruise tourism development. Then we exclude some relevant indicators by correlation analysis. Finally, we obtained 4 leading indicators, 10 coincident indicators and 3 lagging indicators, as listed in Table 1.

Table 1. The index system and weight of CTPI in China

Classification	Index	Weight
Leading indicator	Home prot city GDP	0.5014
	PGP of local residents in home prot city	0.4986
	Total number of tourists	0.4913
	Economic growth rate	0.5001
Coincident indicator	Total number of cruise ships received	0.4327
	Total number of cruises from home port received	0.4021
	Total number of cruise tourists	0.4123
	Total number of home port cruise tourists	0.4287
	Average consumption of inbound cruise tourists	0.4105
	Average consumption of onbound cruise tourists	0.3964
	Number of cruises in home port	0.3512
	Average tonnage of cruise ships in home ports	0.3796
	Total number of cruise companies	0.3903
	Number of berths at the cruise terminal	0.4489
Lagging indicator	Number of tourists staying overnight in the home port city	0.3758
	Tourists spend the amount in the home port city	0.4920
	Number of people employed onshore in cruise home port	0.4568

3.2 Tourism Prosperity Composite Index

The internationally agreed prosperity indexes associate with Diffusion Index (DI) and Composite Index(CI). DI is a measure of the move in any of the business cycle indicators, showing how many of an indicator components are moving together with the overall indicator index, it lacks essential ability to describe the extent. Hence, CI is used to forecast prosperity index [9]. These steps can be described as follows.

Step 1: Symmetrical Change Rate and Standard of Single Index

Calculating the formula of symmetrical change rate:

$$C_{it} = \frac{d_{it} - d_{it-1}}{(d_{it} + d_{it-1})/2} \times 100 \tag{1}$$

$$A_i = \sum_{t=2}^{N} \frac{|C_{it}|}{N - 1} \tag{2}$$

$$S_{it} = C_{it} - A_i \tag{3}$$

where, C_{it} is the symmetric change rate of the i_{th} indictor in the t_{th} year; d_{it} is the actual indicator value of the i_{th} indictor in the t_{th} year; Ai is ordinal average of C_{it} sequence and

N is the standardized number of period; Sit is the standardized value of the i_{th} indictor's C_{it} in the t_{th} year.

Step 2: Determining weighted average of standardized multi-index symmetric change rate

$$R_t = \sum_{i=1}^{k} S_{it} * \left(\frac{W_i}{\sum_{j=1}^{k} W_j} \right) \tag{4}$$

where, Rt is the value of the composite average symmetrical change rate of the leading indicator or lagging indicator in the t_{th} period; Wi is the weight of the i_{th} indictor, $i = 1$, 2, …, k refers to the number of indicators.

Step 3: Standardizing the average change rate by the synchronization index
   The standardization factor F can be obtained as follows:

$$F = \left[\sum_{t=2}^{N} \frac{|R_t|}{N-1} \right] \Big/ \left[\sum_{t=2}^{N} \frac{|P_t|}{N-1} \right] \tag{5}$$

$$r_t = \frac{R_t}{F} \tag{6}$$

where Pt is the value of the composite average symmetrical change rate of the coincident indicator in the tth period of the time sequence; rt is the average change rate of the synchronic index standardization t = 2, 3…, N refers to the number of period.

Step 4: calculating the CI
   First, calculating the original chain index. with I1 = 100, the calculation formula is:

$$I_t = \frac{I_{t-1} * (200 + r_t)}{200 - r_t} \tag{7}$$

$$CI_t = \frac{I_t}{I_0} \times 100 \tag{8}$$

where, I_0 is the average value of the chosen benchmark year and CI_t is the CI.

4   Result

According to the CI construction method, the statistical software, MATLAB R2018, is employed. The benchmark year is 2010. The cruise tourism prosperity index of three indicators of the tourism industry in China shows a trend of sustained growth on the whole. The cruise tourism prosperity index of the composite indicator rose from 100 in 2010 to 102.15 in 2018, with an annual growth rate of 1.10% (Fig. 1).
   The composite prosperity index of cruise tourism industry pointed out that from 2010 to 2018, the composite prosperity index of China cruise tourism prosperity index of the composite indicator tourism industry had maintained a stable development tendency. Not until 2018 did it drop slightly.

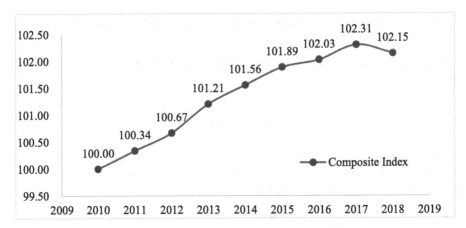

Fig. 1. Composite prosperity index (2010–2018)

In 2006, Costa's "Elan Gona" made its maiden voyage in China, marking the beginning of my country's cruise industry from scratch. For more than ten years, the development of China's cruise industry is second only to that of the United States, and its international market share has increased from 0.5% in 2006 to 9.6%, a nearly 20-fold increase in ten years. The attractive market also attracts the influx of international capital. However, the fierce competition and the slowdown of the industry have brought downhill routes.

The overall decline in the cruise market in 2018 is due to the decline in the capacity of the cruise market in 2018. The slowdown in the growth of the cruise market has already appeared. From the second half of 2017, the cruise market began to show signs of fatigue. Faced with the trough in the Chinese cruise market, some foreign cruise giants have chosen to speed up adjustments or even "flee". In addition to departure, some international cruise companies have chosen to adjust routes to cope with the current fierce market competition.

5   Conclusion

This article takes the cruise home port economy as the research object, starting from the construction of the evaluation system of the prosperity index, and explores the cultivation mechanism of the cruise home port prosperity index. From a theoretical point of view, it is helpful to provide an effective tool for the scientific measurement of the economy of the home port of cruise ships, and to deepen the understanding of the complex changes in the economy of the home port of cruise ships. The concept of the cruise home port prosperity index constructed by this project helps to solve the dilemma that the economic attributes of cruise home ports under the traditional single dimension are difficult to be fully understood. The multi-disciplinary fusion research paradigm is used to construct a cruise home port prosperity evaluation index system to quantify its comprehensive impact and provide a theoretical reference for accurately grasping the complex relationship of cruise home port economic fluctuations. In terms of practical value, it is helpful to provide practical guidance for the economic construction of cruise home ports. The introduction of a prosperity index to monitor the economic operation of the cruise home port is of great significance for verifying and evaluating the effects of the implementation of cruise economic construction. This research will help improve the healthy operation of the cruise home port economy, enrich the construction practices of the cruise home port economy, and cultivate the cultural confidence of China's unique cruise culture.

Acknowledgment. The work is supported by the Philosophy and Social Sciences Project for Colleges and Universities in Jiangsu Province (Nos. 2019SJA0649).

References

1. Su, P., Qi, L.: A study on the globalization strategies of China's cruise tourism market under the "belt and road" initiative. In: Report on the Development of Cruise Industry in China, pp. 171–185. Springer, Singapore (2019). https://doi.org/10.1007/978-981-15-4661-7_9
2. Lam, J., Cullinane, K., Lee, P.T.-W.: The 21st-century Maritime Silk Road: challenges and opportunities for transport management and practice. Transp. Rev. **38**(4), 413–415 (2018). https://doi.org/10.1080/01441647.2018.1453562
3. Ministry of Transport of the People's Republic of China Homepage. http://xxgk.mot.gov.cn/jigou/zhghs/201504/t20150422_2976271.html
4. Wang, H., Shi, J., Mei, J.: Research on the development of the world's cruise industry during 2017–2018: strong demands stimulate the sustainable high growth. In: Report on the Development of Cruise Industry in China, pp. 3–35. Springer, Singapore(2018)
5. Sun, X., Jiao, Y., Tian, P.: Marketing research and revenue optimization for the cruise industry: a concise review. Int. J. Hosp. Manag. **30**(3), 746–755 (2011)
6. Brida, J.G., Pulina, M., Riaño, E., et al.: Cruise passengers in a homeport: amarket analysis. Tour. Geogr. **15**(1), 68–87 (2013)
7. Cai, X., Niu, Y.: Analysis on development potential of China's cruise tourism industry. Prog. Geogr. **29**(10), 1273–1278 (2010)
8. Gabe, T., Lynch, C., McConnon, J., et al.: Economic impact of cruise ship passengers in Bar Harbor. Maine (2003)
9. Wang, H., Ye, X., Cao, S.: Active connection to "the belt and road" initiative to enable the great-leap-forward development of Shanghai cruise economy. In: Wang, H. (ed.) Report on China's Cruise Industry, pp. 77–90. Springer, Singapore (2018). https://doi.org/10.1007/978-981-10-8165-1_3
10. Wong, K.K.F.: The relevance of business cycles in forecasting international tourist arrivals. Tour. Manage. **18**(8), 581–586 (1997)
11. Turner, L., Kulendran, N., Fernando, H.: The use of composite national indicators for tourism forecasting. Tour. Econ. **3**(4), 309–317 (1997)
12. Xiaoning, N., Bin, D.: evaluation and analysis research of composite index on tourist industry of China. J. Beijing Int. Stud. Univ. **11**, 11 (2007)
13. Dai, B., Yan X., Huang, X.: A study on the industry cycle index of China's travel services. Tour. Tribune **9** (2007)
14. Xinfeng, W.: An Empirical Research of China's Tourism Prosperity Index [J]. Statistical Education **11**, 55–60 (2010)
15. Tang, C.C.: Evaluation of the tourism prosperity index and its promotion for heritage sites in China. Resour. Sci **35**, 2344–2351 (2013)

Interactive Evolution Model of Industrial Cluster and Regional Innovation Based on LSTM

Le Tong[1] and Fen Wang[2(✉)]

[1] Wuhan Business University, Wuhan 430050, China
[2] Wuhan Aiwuyou Technology Co. Ltd., Wuhan 430050, China

Abstract. The current evolution model of the interaction between industrial clusters and regional innovation has not measured the interaction factors between industrial clusters and regional innovation, which leads to inaccurate changes in the industrial chain supply and demand, input-output coefficients, and industrial quantities. To this end, this study designed an LSTM-based interaction evolution model of industrial clusters and regional innovation. First, use LSTM to measure the interaction factors between industrial clusters and regional innovation, and form a network structure; according to the measurement results, analyze the factors that exist in the interaction process, so as to establish the interaction evolution model of industrial clusters and regional innovation. Experimental results show that the model in this paper can better describe the supply-demand relationship and input-output coefficient of the industrial chain in the process of interaction between industrial clusters and regional innovation.

Keywords: LSTM · Industrial clusters · Regional innovation · Interactive evolution model

1 Introduction

Industrial clusters have the characteristics of geographic proximity and spatial agglomeration, which enable industrial clusters to develop more economic activities and present a good economic development trend [1]. And with the vigorous development of economic globalization, industrial clusters, as a new form of industrial organization, can rely on its powerful resource allocation function to promote the development of regional economy [2]. At present, on a global scale, industrial clusters have become accelerators that promote regional economic development and national competitiveness, and have become the business card and symbol of their country or region, and have become a ubiquitous organizational form in developed economies [3]. In addition, industrial clusters also provide entrepreneurs with abundant labor, raw materials, and market orders, which effectively reduces the risks and costs of entrepreneurs entering industrial clusters to start businesses, thereby promoting regional innovation.

© ICST Institute for Computer Sciences, Social Informatics and Telecommunications Engineering 2021
Published by Springer Nature Switzerland AG 2021. All Rights Reserved
W. Fu et al. (Eds.): ICMTEL 2021, LNICST 387, pp. 288–297, 2021.
https://doi.org/10.1007/978-3-030-82562-1_27

However, the above process is a long evolutionary process, and not all regional industrial clusters can form a good interactive evolution trend [4]. Therefore, this study uses the chain form of long-term and short-term memory network (LSTM) to deal with and predict the interactive evolution process of industrial clusters and regional innovation, and designs an interactive evolution model of industrial clusters and regional innovation based on LSTM. Firstly, the interactive factors between industrial clusters and regional innovation are measured by LSTM, and the network structure is formed. According to the measurement results, the factors existing in the interactive process are analyzed, and the interactive evolution model of industrial clusters and regional innovation is established. In addition, the model can well describe the supply-demand relationship and input-output coefficient of industrial chain in the process of interaction between industrial cluster and regional innovation.

2 Design of Interactive Evolution Model of Industrial Clusters and Regional Innovation

2.1 Measurement of Interaction Between Industrial Cluster and Regional Innovation Based on LSTM

Based on the analysis of the current interactive evolution of industrial clusters and regional innovation in the introduction, it can be seen that there is a direct causal relationship between industrial clusters and regional innovation interactive evolution, and it is difficult to describe the causality of the interactive evolution process of industrial clusters and regional innovation only through large-scale theories. relationship. Therefore, the interactive evolution model of industrial clusters and regional innovation established in this study will use LSTM to process and predict the causal relationships that exist in the interactive evolution process of industrial clusters and regional innovations, and discover laws from the macroscopic and external environmental connections, thereby completing the industrial Research on the interactive evolution model of clusters and regional innovation.

2.1.1 Degrees

LSTM emphasizes that each actor has a more or less relationship with other actors. According to the structure describing group relations, it studies the influence between industrial clusters and the evolution of regional innovation interaction.

Therefore, a series of regional innovation subjects are assumed to be N and $N = \{1, 2, \cdots, n\}$. If there is a connection between industrial cluster j and regional innovation i, then j is called the "neighbor point" of i; the number of adjacent points of a regional innovation subject N_i is called the "degree" of the point, which is recorded as d_i.

In fact, the "degree" of a regional innovation subject is the number of lines connected to it. If there is a connection between industrial clusters and regional innovation subjects, that is, they are connected by a line, they are called "adjacent." If the degree of an innovative subject is 0, it is called an "isolated point" [5]. At this time, the average value of LSTM points measures the average degree $\bar{d}$ of industrial clusters and regional innovation in a region, and its expression is:

$$\bar{d} = \frac{\sum_{i=l}^{g} d(n_i)}{g} = \frac{2l}{g} \tag{1}$$

In formula (1), g represents the scale of LSTM, that is, the number of interactive evolution between industrial clusters and regional innovation subjects in a region; l is the number of LSTM lines formed between industrial clusters and regional innovation entities.

2.1.2 LSTM Network Density

In addition to the degree parameters obtained by formula (1), we also need to calculate the LSTM density and centrality, so as to obtain the interaction measure between industrial clusters and regional innovation, and infer the causal relationship between industrial clusters and regional innovation.

Taking LSTM density as an index to measure the interaction between industrial clusters and regional innovation can reflect the degree of closeness between industrial clusters and regional innovation subjects in a region. In short, the more connections between fixed scale industrial clusters and regional innovation entities, the greater the LSTM density of industrial clusters and regional innovation.

Therefore, assuming that the LSTM density of industrial clusters and regional innovation in a certain area is 1, then in the LSTM of the region, the industrial clusters and regional innovation entities are connected with industrial clusters and regional innovation entities in other regions; when the LSTM density is 0, It means that the industrial clusters in any region of the network are not connected with the regional innovation subjects. The expression of LSTM network density m is:

$$m = \frac{g * \bar{d}}{g(g-1)} = \frac{2l}{g(g-1)}, m \in [0, 1] \tag{2}$$

According to formula (2), the LSTM density index in the measurement of interaction between industrial clusters and regional innovation can be obtained. At this time, we only need to calculate the LSTM centrality, then we can get the measurement of the interaction between industrial clusters and regional innovation, and analyze the formation and causes of the interactive evolution between industrial clusters and regional innovation.

2.1.3 Centrality

The interactive evolution process of industrial cluster and regional innovation is also the result of artificial promotion [6]. Therefore, there will be power elements, which need to be analyzed from the perspective of network. Therefore, it is divided into local and global dimensions. There are two indexes of local center degree and global center degree.

Calculate the degree index in the measurement of the interaction between industrial clusters and regional innovation based on formula (1), and convert it to obtain a certain regional innovation subject. The expression of the degree centrality index $C_1(i)$ is:

$$C_1(i) = \frac{d_i}{g - 1} \tag{3}$$

When the point degree centrality $C(i) = 0$ in formula (3), the actor is an isolated point; when $C(i) = 1$, it is one of the core points of LSTM and the center point of the evolution of the interaction between industrial clusters and regional innovation, according to formula (3) It can be seen that there is a direct relationship between industrial clusters and regional innovation interaction and evolution.

The intermediate centrality index can express the degree of control over the regional resources during the interaction and evolution of industrial clusters and regional innovation. The intermediate centrality measure expression is:

$$C_{2i} = \sum_{j}^{n} \sum_{k}^{n} b_{jk}(i), j \neq k \neq i, \text{ and } j < k \tag{4}$$

In formula (4), b_{jk} represents the probability that regional innovation subject i is on the geodesic between industrial cluster j and k.

No matter what level (individual, group or organization) the actors in LSTM are at, it is an important goal of network analysis to obtain information about the whole LSTM network through the analysis of actors. At this point, we need to use the concept of near centrality. Therefore, the concept of proximity centrality is: the proximity centrality of a point is the sum of geodesic distances between the point and all other points in the network [7]. Then the expression close to centrality C_{3i}^{-1} is as follows:

$$C_{3i}^{-1} = \sum_{j=1}^{g} d_{ij} \tag{5}$$

In formula (5), d_{ij} represents the geodesic distance between the regional innovation subject i and the industrial cluster j (that is, the number of lines included in the geodesic).

The centrality of LSTM measures the ability of a regional industrial cluster to develop the relationship with regional innovation subjects, and the close to centrality is the regional industrial cluster and regional innovation subject. It depends on the LSTM relationship between the industrial cluster and the regional innovation subject, rather than the direct relationship between the industrial cluster and the regional innovation subject in the neighborhood.

The process shown in formula (1) to (5) above is the measurement of interaction between industrial clusters and regional innovation. According to the measurement index values obtained from formula (1)–formula (5), we can analyze the direct/indirect relationship existing in the interactive evolution process of industrial cluster and regional innovation, and the influence of causality, human factors and asset factors on the interactive evolution process of industrial cluster and regional innovation.

2.2 Establish an Interactive Evolution Model of Industrial Clusters and Regional Innovation

The last section uses LSTM to analyze the influencing factors in the interactive evolution process of industrial cluster and regional innovation by measuring the interaction between industrial cluster and regional innovation. It is found that the interactive evolution process of industrial cluster and regional innovation has certain relationship with the number of people, development space, economy, interactive industrial cluster and regional innovation scale Firstly, the interactive evolution model of industrial cluster and regional innovation is established.

Assuming that the population of this area in year t is $N(t)$, then:

$$N(t) = N_0 e^{r(t-t_0)} \tag{6}$$

In formula (6), N_0 represents the population number under the initial conditions; t_0 represents the initial value of the equation, in this calculation, $t_0 = 0$; r represents the natural growth rate of the population, which is a constant [8].

In the interactive evolution process of industrial cluster and regional innovation, in addition to the influence of population, economic influence is also an important factor in the interactive evolution of industrial cluster and regional innovation

$$\frac{dx}{dt} = R\left(1 - \frac{x}{x_1}\right)x = f(x, R), x(0) = x_0 \tag{7}$$

In formula (7), $x(t)$ represents the amount of economic change produced when the industrial cluster interacts with regional innovation at time t; R represents the economic growth rate generated when the industrial cluster interacts with regional innovation; $\left(1 - \frac{x}{x_1}\right)$ represents the remaining amount when the industrial cluster interacts with regional innovation. The proportion of interactive evolution resources to the total interactive evolution resources.

$\left(1 - \frac{x}{x_1}\right)$ in formula (7) has the following characteristics: if the number of regional innovation individuals tends to zero, then item $\left(1 - \frac{x}{x_1}\right)$ tends to 1, which means that almost all industrial cluster resources are not used, and regional innovation pole is in the best development trend; if x tends to x_1, then $\left(1 - \frac{x}{x_1}\right)$ tends to zero, which means that almost all resources of industrial cluster are utilized, and the growth rate of regional innovation pole will tend to zero; with the development of innovation pole, industry will tend to zero. The cluster resource surplus $\left(1 - \frac{x}{x_1}\right)$ is smaller and smaller, and the growth rate of innovation pole is also slower and slower [9].

If there are relative industrial clusters in a region, and these industrial clusters influence each other, it is assumed that the industrial clusters, regardless of their size, can form a symbiosis and develop together from the perspective of competing for resources. Therefore, assuming that there are two innovation poles, A and B, when they only exist in the regional innovation system, the development and evolution of the innovation poles all follow the Logistic law. At this time, under the influence of industrial clusters of different sizes, the scales of the two innovation poles are denoted as $x_1(t)$ and $x_2(t)$

respectively, and the inherent growth rates of the assets of the two industrial clusters are R_1 and R_2. The maximum increased capacity is denoted as N_1 and N_2 respectively, and for the Innovation Extreme A, there are:

$$\frac{dx}{dt} = R_1 x_1 \left(1 - \frac{x}{N_1}\right) \tag{8}$$

In formula (8), factor $\left(1 - \frac{x}{N_1}\right)$ represents the retarding effect on the growth of its own scale due to the consumption of limited resources of the industrial cluster by the innovation pole A; B $\frac{x}{N_1}$ is the percentage of industrial cluster resources consumed by A. In the model of this study, the total resource of the industrial cluster is set to 1.

When the two innovation poles exist in the same region, as mentioned above, there are three symbiotic relationships between a and B: mutual symbiosis, mutual independence symbiosis, and mutual competition symbiosis. If two innovation poles co-exist with each other, the other will develop better due to the existence of one; if the two innovation poles coexist independently, it is considered that the two innovation poles have no innovation connection in the growth process, and their industrial cluster resources are not in conflict, and the two innovation poles develop separately; if the two innovation poles compete and coexist, one of them consumes a limited industrial cluster Resources have an impact on the growth of the other innovation pole, leading to the decrease of the growth rate of the other innovation pole [10].

Therefore, in view of the above relationship, for innovation pole a $x_1(t)$, the symbiosis coefficient b of innovation pole should be introduced into factor $\left(1 - \frac{x}{N_1}\right)$. The size of the symbiosis coefficient b can indicate the size of the symbiosis effect. Obviously, the symbiotic effect of innovation pole a $x_1(t)$ is directly proportional to the number of innovation pole a x_2 and inversely proportional to N_2. Therefore, under this symbiosis condition, the evolution dynamic equation of innovation polar beetle is as follows:

$$\frac{dx_1}{dt} = R_1 x_1 \left(1 - \frac{x_1}{N_1} - b_1 \frac{x_2}{N_2}\right) = f_1(x_1, x_2) \tag{9}$$

In formula (9), R_1 is the proportional coefficient, b_1 is the symbiosis coefficient of innovation pole B to innovation pole a, and $\frac{x_2}{N_2}$ is the unit number. If the two are symbiotic, then b_1 is negative, and its absolute value indicates the strength of regional innovation and industrial cluster resource symbiosis. If the two innovation poles are symbiotic, then b value is positive, which indicates the degree of competition between them, that is, the consumption intensity of resources of industrial cluster a caused by the existence of b_1; if the two innovation poles coexist independently; if the value of b_1 is 0, then the two innovation poles do not affect each other, and both follow the evolutionary dynamic mode of a single innovation pole.

Therefore, the existence of innovation pole A will inevitably affect the scale growth of innovation pole B. The evolutionary dynamics equation of innovation pole B is:

$$\frac{dx_2}{dt} = R_2 x_2 \left(1 - \frac{x_2}{N_2} - b_2 \frac{x_1}{N_1}\right) = f_2(x_1, x_2) \tag{10}$$

The proportion coefficient b_2 in formula (10) represents the symbiosis coefficient between innovation pole a and innovation pole B, and $b_2 \frac{x_1}{N_1}$ is the consumption percentage of industrial cluster resources of innovation pole B by unit quantity a.

To sum up, it is the interaction evolution model of industrial clusters and regional innovation. According to the model established this time, it is possible to analyze the economic growth trend, population change, impact on the region, Change parameters.

3 Experimental Discussion

In order to verify the application performance of the interactive evolution model of industrial cluster and regional innovation based on LSTM, the following experiments are designed.

In the experiment, the effectiveness of the interactive evolution model of industrial cluster and regional innovation based on LSTM is verified by comparison. The model in this paper is recorded as a model, and the two traditional interactive evolution models are recorded as B model and C model respectively, which are used for complete performance comparison and verification with the model in this paper.

3.1 Experimental Preparation

Select a certain industrial cluster area in a certain province as the experimental verification object. The area has a total area of 13,472 square kilometers and a population of 7.145 million. The mountainous region has a mild climate, diverse landforms, and fertile soil. It is a rich production area for a variety of agricultural and sideline products. The coastline of the coastal land area in this area is 196.5 km long, and the development potential of tidal flats and shallow seas is great. There are many types of mineral resources, large reserves, good quality, concentrated distribution, and easy mining and selection,

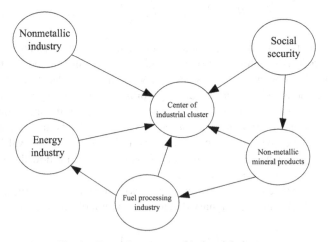

Fig. 1. General structure of industrial clusters

forming major pillar industries such as steel, energy, cement, machinery, chemicals, ceramics, textiles, papermaking, food, and electronics.

In the development process of the region, the above industries belong to industrial clusters with different products. The general structure of the industrial clusters is shown in Fig. 1.

The running environment of the experiment is shown in Table 1.

Table 1. Operating environment of the three groups of models on the computer

Experimental environment	Configuration	Configuration description
Configuration	Hardware framework	RACK
	CPU model	315-2DP
Software environment	Model writing	Matlab
	Operating environment	Windows XP SP3

3.2 The First Group of Experiments

Three sets of models are used to calculate the supply and demand industries and input-output coefficients of the industrial chain in the experimental area, and are compared with the actual calculated coefficients to judge the similarity between the calculated results of the three sets of models and the actual coefficients, so as to compare the analysis effects of different models. The experimental results are shown in Table 2.

Table 2. Supply and demand industries and input-output coefficients of industrial chain

Model	Coefficient of complete consumption	Innovation industry	Coefficient of complete consumption
A model	0.252003	5	0.263984
B model	0.110864	5	0.154844
C model	0.32439	5	0.37132
Actual value	0.253013	5	0.264104

It can be seen from Table 1 that the supply and demand industries and input-output coefficients of the industrial chain evolved from model C are significantly higher than the actual value; the supply and demand industries and input-output coefficients of the industrial chain evolved from model B are significantly lower than the actual value; only the supply and demand industries and input-output coefficients of the industrial chain evolved from model a are very close to the actual value. Therefore, this model can accurately evolve the supply and demand industries and input-output coefficient of the industrial chain.

3.3 The Second Group of Experiments

Perform the second set of experiments on the basis of the first set of experiments. Three sets of models are used to respectively evolve the changes in the number of industries in the process of interaction between industrial clusters and regional innovation, and compare them with actual changes. The comparison results are shown in Fig. 2.

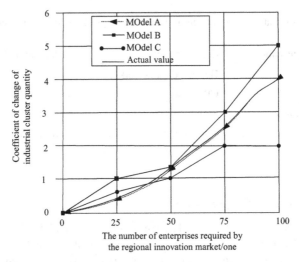

Fig. 2. Comparison of changes in the number of industries

It can be seen from Fig. 2 that the similarity between the quantity change of evolutionary industries obtained by model C and the actual change is the lowest; although the quantity change of evolutionary industries obtained by model B is close to the actual value, there are still large changes; the similarity between the quantity change of evolutionary industries obtained by model a and the actual change is the highest. Therefore, this model can accurately evolve the change of industrial quantity in the process of interaction between industrial clusters and regional innovation.

4   Concluding

This paper designs an interactive evolution model of industrial cluster and regional innovation based on LSTM, which makes full use of the advantages of LSTM to analyze the factors existing in the interactive evolution process of industrial cluster and regional innovation, and effectively reflects the interactive evolution characteristics of industrial cluster and regional innovation. In addition, the model can well describe the supply-demand relationship and input-output coefficient of industrial chain in the process of interaction between industrial cluster and regional innovation. However, this model does not consider the interactive evolution structure and coupling between industrial cluster and regional innovation, which is not comprehensive enough for the interactive evolution process of industrial cluster and regional innovation. Therefore, in the future research, it is necessary to study the interactive evolution model of industrial cluster and regional innovation, and integrate the interactive evolution structure and coupling characteristics of industrial cluster and regional innovation into the evolution model.

Acknowledgments. Hubei Provincial Educational Science Program: "A Research into the Cultivation Model of Practical Personnel in Hubei Provincial Universities from the Perspective of Regional Industry Clusters" (2017GB154).

References

1. Li, W.: Simulation of spatial structure evolution of regional disaster prevention meteorological monitoring information. Comput. Simul. **36**(7), 355–358, 404 (2019)
2. Tian, L., Li, M., Jin, X., et al.: Dynamic tag-based coevolution model for social P2P systems. J. Chin. Comput. Syst. **39**(6), 1250–1254 (2018)
3. Wang, Y., Sun, P., Li, C., et al.: Spatial-temporal evolution features of urban and rural harmonious in northeast China since 2003. Econ. Geogr. **38**(7), 59–66 (2018)
4. Liu, X., Wu, W.: The synergetic evolution mechanism and empirical test of sci-tec-finance and high-tech industry: based on the practice of Guangdong province. J. Guangdong Univ. Finan. Econ. **33**(3), 20–32 (2018)
5. Zheng, L., Hu, L.: Study on symbiotic evolution of energy industry and financial industry in China. J. Xi'an Univ. Finan. Econ. **31**(4), 44–50 (2018)
6. Song, Y., Xue, D., Dai, L., et al.: Spatial pattern of the interaction degree between environmental ethical behavior and environmental quality in China. J. Arid Land Res. Environ. **32**(7), 61–69 (2018)
7. Fu, W., Liu, S., Srivastava, G.: Optimization of big data scheduling in social networks. Entropy **21**(9), 902–918 (2019)
8. Liu, S., Li, Z., Zhang, Y., et al.: Introduction of key problems in long-distance learning and training. Mob. Netw. Appl. **24**(1), 1–4 (2019)
9. Liu, S., Lu, M., Li, H., et al.: Prediction of gene expression patterns with generalized linear regression model. Front. Genet. **10**, 120 (2019)
10. Zhang, Q., Zhang, B., Wang, H.: Study on industrial interaction between construction supervision enterprises and construction enterprises and their regional coupling. J. Civil Eng. Manag. **35**(6), 137–142 (2018)

Design of Hotel Marketing Information Management Model Based on Deep Learning

Lei Tong[1] and Fen Wang[2]([✉])

[1] Wuhan Business University, Wuhan 430050, China
[2] Wuhan Aiwuyou Technology Co. Ltd., Wuhan 430050, China

Abstract. The traditional information management model has poor data transmission efficiency in the process of pushing information services. To solve this problem, this paper designs a hotel marketing information management model based on deep learning. Using Oracle relational database and MVC architecture to build a marketing information database, then use deep learning to extract information features, and classify marketing information of different service categories, connect hotel management and client, and integrate model management functions to provide information services for hotel managers and customers. The experimental results show that the data throughput and transmission rate of the above model are higher than those of the traditional model, and the information transmission efficiency is improved.

Keywords: Deep learning · Hotel marketing · Information management · Information extraction · Marketing information database

1 Introduction

At present, hotel information management is widely used in hotel operations, digitizing and standardizing the hotel's customer service, material movement, transaction processing, cash flow, customer interaction and other business processes, enabling the hotel to manage both internally and externally. Significant changes have taken place in all aspects. Therefore, the research on the hotel marketing information management model has important practical significance [1].

American scholars put forward 4R Theory, using network technology and resources to carry out network relationship marketing through information communication, so as to grasp the two basic strategies of establishing customer files and improving after-sales service network, so as to achieve a larger range of customized marketing. Domestic scholars analyze the theory of "six market model", and think that the relationship marketing of enterprises mainly includes employee relationship marketing strategy, customer relationship marketing strategy, partner relationship marketing strategy, and influencer relationship marketing strategy. Among them, employee relationship marketing strategy is the basis of relationship marketing, customer relationship marketing strategy is the

© ICST Institute for Computer Sciences, Social Informatics and Telecommunications Engineering 2021
Published by Springer Nature Switzerland AG 2021. All Rights Reserved
W. Fu et al. (Eds.): ICMTEL 2021, LNICST 387, pp. 298–310, 2021.
https://doi.org/10.1007/978-3-030-82562-1_28

core and destination of relationship marketing, and then the corresponding marketing strategy is formulated for each related object.

Based on the above points of view, the formulation of relationship marketing strategies should have certain conditions and be carried out step by step. The relationship is maintained and consolidated around the mutually beneficial exchange relationship between related parties, and the use of network information technology to establish customer files and improve file management. On the basis of this theory, this research designs a hotel marketing information management model based on deep learning. The model first uses Oracle relational database and MVC architecture to build marketing information database, then uses deep learning to extract information features, classifies marketing information of different service categories, connects hotel management end and client, and integrates model management functions, so as to provide information services for hotel managers and customers. This study also proves that the model has the advantages of high data throughput and transmission rate through experiments.

2 Design of Hotel Marketing Information Management Model Based on Deep Learning

2.1 Build a Hotel Marketing Information Database

2.1.1 Building Management Model Organizational Structure

Use the classic MVC model and oracle relational database to construct the hotel marketing information database. The full name of the MVC architecture is Model View Controller. This architecture pattern processes business data according to the process, and scientifically divides data input, processing, and display output into three layers, corresponding to the model layer, the view layer and the control layer [2]. The view layer is the interface layer that directly interacts with the user. The model layer is in the application of the B/S architecture. The black box operates the data requested by the user. The user in the view layer cannot know the specific operation, but can only see the data processing result. The control layer is the intermediate interaction layer between the first two. It receives data processing requests from users in the view layer and forwards them to the model layer. After the processing is completed, the data is forwarded back to the view layer. This can isolate users and internal operations. To optimize the safety of the model. The organizational relationship of the scientific planning of the MVC architecture is shown in Fig. 1.

On this basis, J2EE is used to construct a relatively complete application component technology framework, and business information created based on core tasks is migrated to the environment provided by Java, thus simplifying the difficulty of multilevel enterprise development and overcoming many user needs Change, resulting in increased delivery time [3]. This completes the construction of the management model organizational structure.

2.1.2 Building Marketing Information Base

On the basis of the design of the model architecture, the Oracl database is used to build a marketing information database. When managers need to manage a large amount of

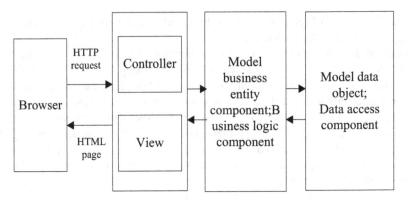

Fig. 1. Organization diagram of model architecture

data, Oracle database can be used. Oracl database is a typical representative of database technology. It has obvious advantages over other databases in many aspects. It is divided into two parts: server and client. When the hotel manager operates the database, he needs to connect to the server and use the database as a local database. When managers use the database for information access, use the database chain to provide support [4].

Oracle database adopts the logic of object relation, which has the characteristics of prudence and authenticity. It not only meets the traditional relational model, but also supports the object mechanism. It can not only solve the table problem, but also meet the other data types provided by various development tools, such as graphics, video, etc., which is helpful for managers to match Oracle database with software products used by hotels. At the same time, Oracle database adds the function of automatic backup and recovery, enhances the operation parallelism of SQL statements, provides practical data partition function, large table, and small block index for information management [5]. The design fields of the information base are shown in Table 1.

Oracle has different server components, storage marketing information can meet the communication of multiple servers, manage the Oracle connection on these servers, and provide users with higher quality images and sound. Oracle database can also manage the text, structured the unstructured data, strengthen the parallel processing function of the database, and divide a query into several subqueries. When managers use computers with multiple CPUs, they can perform operations on different CPUs to improve the business volume of information management and improve the performance of marketing information database.

So far, the construction of hotel marketing information database is completed.

2.2 Classification of Marketing Information Based on Deep Learning

2.2.1 Preprocessing Hotel Marketing Information

This research uses the neural network in deep learning to classify the marketing information in the information database. First, the original marketing information must be pre-processed, including text segmentation and stop-word removal. The words, words and phrases in the information text appear continuously without obvious segmentation

Table 1. Field format of hotel marketing information database

Field name	Data type	Length
User ID	Character type	8
Username	Character type	20
User password	Character type	20
User category	Character type	20
User status	Character type	4
Room ID	Character type	6
Room type	Character type	6
Maximum number of people	Float	6
Room price	Int	8
Discount	Int	8
Discount	Int	4
Check in time	Data	8
End time	Data	8
Registration time	Data	8

marks, and words, as the basic semantic unit, need to express the characteristics of the information text, so the jieba word segmentation tool is used to segment the information text [6]. Then remove the content that has no practical meaning but a higher frequency in the information text. Because these contents cannot represent the text type, they are of no value to the text classification task, but will increase the dimension of the text feature vector and affect the final effect of text classification. This process allows the remaining text information to better express text characteristics.

Based on this, the word vector method is used to represent the text content. Word vector can map every word in the text to a low latitude space, so that each feature word in the text is represented by the same space, instead of using an independent dimension in the vector space model, so that the high-dimensional sparse vector can be transformed into a low-dimensional real number vector [7]. Compared with the traditional information management model, in the mapped low latitude text feature space, the position relationship of different text feature words corresponding to the word vector represents the association of marketing information at the text semantic level, which can provide more abundant text semantic information. Word2vec can be used to train and generate word vectors. It is a tool based on deep learning, which can easily train a large number of corpus, and can efficiently map the feature words in the text in space to form low latitude dense vector.

So far, the preprocessing of hotel marketing information is completed.

2.2.2 Extracting Information Features Based on Deep Learning

Extract text features from the pre-processed marketing information to realize the classified management of marketing information.

Deep learning is a new field in machine learning research. The model essentially has a hidden layer and a perceptual layer. There are nonlinear data processing modules between each layer. The hidden layer and the perceptual layer perform feature learning and feature transformation on information data., Making the data characteristics from low-level to high-level become more and more abstract. Finally, the extraction of data features is completed in a high abstract level, and the essential features of the data are mined, and the essential features of these data are used to realize the classification of marketing information [8]. The basic structure of deep learning classification information is shown in Fig. 2.

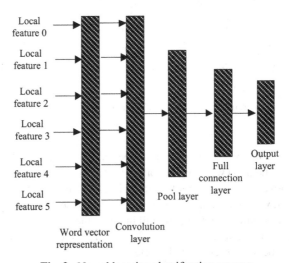

Fig. 2. Neural learning classification process

As shown in Fig. 2, the first half is the input layer, and the middle part is composed of a number of convolutional layers and pooling layers alternately passed, that is, a convolutional layer is connected to a pooling layer, and then a convolutional layer is connected. The half is composed of a fully connected layer and an output layer. The convolutional layer can extract different local features of the input marketing information, and the low-level convolutional layer can extract low-level features of the text, such as words, phrases, phrases, sentences, etc. The high-level convolutional layer can extract high-level features of the text, such as paragraphs and semantics. After the convolutional layer is the pooling layer, the pooling layer can merge semantically similar text features to play the role of secondary feature extraction. After the alternate connection of the convolutional layer and the pooling layer is the fully connected layer, various local text features extracted by the convolutional layer and the pooling layer are summarized and classified, and finally the classified marketing information is obtained through the output layer.

Deep learning can extract higher-level and more abstract text features through the accumulation of convolution layer and pooling layer, which makes the text features have stronger expression ability and more accurately reflect the essential characteristics of the text.

So far, the classification of management information is completed based on deep learning.

2.3 Integrated Hotel Marketing Information

After classifying the information, the association between all kinds of information is established, so that the information can be structured and integrated. The internal and external information stored in the server should be described based on the customer's staying in the hotel, and then the stored information can be dynamically managed by using the attribute characteristics of information resources. On this basis, capture the storage information that needs to be managed and locate it.

Firstly, regular expressions are used to match all the strings of the stored information on the server, and a single string is used to describe the specific matching rules, and the strings generated by different stored information are automatically processed through scripts and meet the syntactic rules [9]. Then use the CSS selector to convert the information string into a CSS style, obtain the specific categories of internal and external information, including information attributes, tags and element combinations, and generate a candidate list for pushing content, and then use XPath to select the data in the CSS style Nodes are used to automatically generate information element nodes through scripts, and then select text nodes and attribute nodes to modify the generated nodes. Then the information element nodes are divided by two writing methods of absolute path and relative path, and XPath is used to define rules, and the information node set is expressed by XPath expression. When capturing dynamic information, it needs to be dynamically acquired from the server side. JavaScript code is executed during the crawling process to realize the rendering of information data, and the behavior of the WeChat client is simulated on the server side to obtain complete dynamic push information. Automatically open the push information through the script, extract the open source browser engine, and directly call the relevant interface of the browser engine, thereby optimizing the rendering parameters of the data node, improving the dynamic data rendering performance, and then extracting the dynamic information node set.

After completing the connection between the management end and the client, the same way is used to wave hands four times. The client sets the field in the packet to 1 as a request to close the connection. After receiving the data packet from the client, the manager will change the connection into a semi closed state, send a fin field to the client actively, and the client will receive the fin field and send the packet again to close the server connection. The integration of information node set and dynamic information node set completes the integration of hotel marketing information.

2.4 Connect Hotel Management and Client

On the basis of marketing information integration, the location of information in information inventory documents is located, and the hotel management end and client are connected. The websocket interface and connection interface are selected as the external call interfaces of the management end and the client respectively. The function modules are shown in Table 2.

Table 2. Hotel management terminal and client calling interface

Block name	Interface name	Interface usage
Connection modular	FrameConnection	Processing information connection related business
	Connection	Processing information connection frame and related services
WebSocket modular	OnFrame	Notify connection to close
	WebSocket	Notify users to receive push messages
	OnBinaryMessage	Notification connection open
	OnControl	Notify users to receive frame level messages
	OnTextMessage	Notify users to receive text messages

As shown in Table 2, websocket interface is used as the general interface between the connection management end and the client. According to the different types of marketing information, the sending and receiving process of the two interfaces to process messages is defined. The server initiates synchronous serial number message and sends connection request to the client by connecting two interfaces by three handshakes and four waves. Then, according to the MPTCP protocol supported by the client, reply the confirmation character to the server, enable the server to open the relevant functions of MPTCP protocol and send the verification information. At this time, the client directly ignores the fields in the message, making the websocket interface and connection interface establish MPTCP connection [10].

On this basis, the validity of the connection subflow is verified. Send a space between the two interfaces to determine whether the MPTCP connection is valid. When the MPTCP connection is valid, the relevant properties of the connection, including domain name and IP address, are obtained. Then the client sends a packet, uses token encryption to verify the relevant attributes of the connection, and establishes a new connection subflow, which is added to the MPTCP connection, and distinguishes the new subflow according to the IP address.

Because the hotel management end and the client side have established multiple connection subflows, the congestion of each connection path is calculated, the optimal transmission path of information push is selected, each MPTCP connection is regarded as multiple TCP connections, and the transmission throughput of different connection paths is obtained on the basis of certain path bandwidth. The throughput requirement Q of information push is as follows:

$$Q = \frac{\beta}{TW}\sqrt{\frac{2}{p}} \tag{1}$$

In Formula (1), T is the round-trip time of the information connection path, W is the throughput ratio of the sub-stream path, p is the packet loss rate of the push path, and β is the weight of the packet loss rate. Use Formula (1) to filter multiple sub-flow paths, remove the connection paths that do not meet the throughput requirement Q, and then conduct an in-depth analysis of the congestion status of the remaining paths to ensure that the connection path has enough intermediate buffers, and use the minimum RTT algorithm to select Appropriate data scheduling strategy. The definition formula of the remaining connection path congestion is:

$$ R = \frac{U}{A} \tag{2} $$

In Formula (2), R is the index to judge the congestion of the connection path, U is the congestion window size of the current path, and A is the number of packets on multiple connection paths that have not been confirmed by the client. The larger the R is, the more congested the path is, and packet loss may occur during the information push process. Using Formula (2), the congestion state of each connection path is compared, and the connection path with minimum R value is selected. The information node set is distributed to the optimal connection path according to the proportion, the data round-trip delay parameters are updated, the data round-trip delay is smoothed, and the smoothing factor is weighted to obtain the shortest information connection delay. So far, the connection between the hotel management end and the client is completed.

2.5 Integrated Model Marketing Information Management Function

After connecting the hotel management terminal and the client terminal, it pushes marketing information to provide customers with information services. On this basis, the service functions are integrated. The core functions of the model include customer information and points management functions, front desk business and shift management functions, online query and reservation functions, guest room configuration management functions, user management functions, reports and background management functions. Among them, customer information management functions are mainly divided into online registration and entry functions, customer identity verification and management functions, account information management functions, grade points and discount management functions; the main business functions of the front desk include customer status inquiry, check-in information registration, Settlement processing, check-out information registration, and shift work also involves the transfer of shift records, abnormal situation reporting information processing; online query provides hotel room status information query, and online reservations, so that customers can query hotel operations without logging in The occupancy status of the room, the reservation status in the future, and the discounted price of the room. During the reservation process, customers log in through their member accounts, and then select the confirmed room number, reservation time and period, and submit the booking application. After receiving the application, the model first determines the reservation conditions. If the reservation application cannot be met, it will automatically feed back to the customer the reservation failure and the reasons; if the reservation conditions are met, the model will remind the front desk staff to confirm by phone. Guest room configuration management mainly includes room number setting and management, room access card or key management, room type and price setting, room goods management; user management includes user account information addition, deletion, information change, account locking, permission setting and change, etc.; the design of background management function module is relatively simple, including report format category setting and report form Sub functions of generating, setting and generating statistical charts.

So far, the integration of marketing information management functions is completed, and the design of hotel marketing information management model based on deep learning is realized.

3 Experiment and Analysis

In order to verify the effectiveness of the hotel marketing information management model based on deep learning, the following comparative experiments are designed. This paper takes the model as experimental group A, two traditional marketing information management models as experimental group B and experimental group C, and completes the performance comparison with this model.

3.1 Experimental Preparation

Select a hotel as the test subject. The hotel receives an average of 7.5 million staying customers annually. Through field surveys and network information collection, the hotel's pricing system is obtained. The specific content is shown in Table 3.

Table 3. Current situation of hotel marketing

Room type	Number of rooms	Sales price (yuan/day)
VIP room	72	5800
View room	160	5900
Deluxe view room	28	5900
Sea view room	56	5999
Deluxe sea view room	95	5999
Poolside room	16	5999
Full sea view room	32	5999
Harbour room	68	5999
Ocean view room	71	5999
Superior sea view room	79	5999

The hotel network topology is shown in Fig. 3.

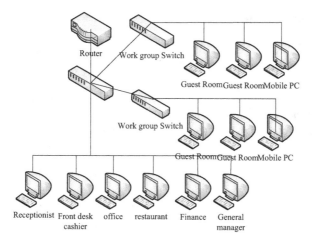

Fig. 3. Hotel network topology

In the hotel network topology shown in Fig. 3, the information management model is deployed. On the basis of the network topology structure, the corresponding web application server, database server and firewall and other hardware equipment are added to provide users with the operation based on Web mode through the internal network and external Internet network.

Three groups of models are used to provide the hotel's information services, and the objects include hotel customers, general hotel staff, hotel senior managers, and model managers. Combining the hotel services, the service functions provided by different models are shown in Fig. 4.

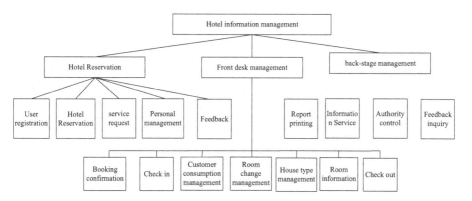

Fig. 4. Functional diagram of marketing information management

3.2   Experimental Results

3.2.1   The First Set of Experimental Results

Push marketing information to service objects. A total of more than 50000 text messages are set, and the login users of the client are 100. Three groups of experiments conduct interactive tests on 100 users. After the test is successful, the service information is pushed in real time. The data throughput of the information push service was compared among the three groups of experiments. The experimental results are shown in Table 4.

Table 4. Comparison results of the first group of experiments

Information push time (s)	Group A data throughput (Mbps)	Group B data throughput (Mbps)	Group C data throughput (Mbps)
10	1.1	1.1	1.1
20	1.3	1.1	1.1
30	1.4	1.2	1.1
40	1.5	1.4	1.2
50	1.7	1.4	1.3
60	1.7	1.5	1.3
70	1.8	1.6	1.4
80	1.9	1.7	1.5
90	2.0	1.8	1.7
100	2.0	1.8	1.7

As shown in Table 4, in different information push time periods, the data throughput of experiment group A is higher than that of experiment Group B and experiment Group C. The data throughput of Group A, Group B, and Group C all reach about 90s. The largest, the maximum throughput of Group A is 2.0 Mbps, and the Experimental Groups B and C Are 1.8 Mbps and 1.7 Mbps respectively. Therefore, compared with the two groups of traditional management models, the maximum throughput of this model is increased by 0.2 Mbps and 0.3 Mbps respectively.

3.2.2   The Second Group of Experimental Results

On the basis of the first group of experiments, the length of the transmitted information data is changed, and the information data generation rate is set to 60 g per second. Test the transmission rate of the three groups of models, and the comparison results are shown in Table 5.

Table 5. Comparison results of the second group of experiments

Data size (byte)	Group A rate (M/s)	Group B rate (M/s)	Group C rate (M/s)
266532	10.26	7.89	6.08
298198	9.82	6.73	6.63
312977	9.53	5.98	5.19
482977	8.72	5.87	6.54
739774	7.89	5.89	6.12
980277	8.03	4.87	4.17
1098739	7.89	4.98	4.02
1378472	6.73	3.27	3.02
1789397	6.34	4.01	3.01
2088872	5.92	3.03	3.24

As shown in Table 5, when the data length is different, the transmission rate of Group A is higher than that of the other two groups, with an average transmission rate of 8.11 m/s, and that of Group B and Group C is 5.25 m/s and 4.80 m/s respectively. Compared with the two traditional models, the transmission rate of Group A is increased by 2.86 m/s and 3.31 m/s respectively. To sum up, the design model in the information service push process, improve the information throughput and transmission rate, information transmission efficiency is higher than the traditional model.

4 Conclusion

This study designs a hotel marketing information management model based on deep learning, which uses deep learning to classify marketing information, improves data throughput and transmission rate, and can effectively provide information services for hotel managers and customers. But there are still some deficiencies in this study, such as the understanding of some specific functions is not in place. In the future research, we will further expand the functions of the hotel, pay attention to the user experience and customer relationship, and improve the user experience of the management model.

Acknowledgments. Hubei Provincial Educational Science Program: "A Research into the Cultivation Model of Practical Personnel in Hubei Provincial Universities from the Perspective of Regional Industry Clusters" (2017GB154).

References

1. Fenglin, W.: Optimal management of marketing channels of edible fungi. Edible Fungi China **39**(7), 244–246 (2020)

2. Yushan, Z.: Exploration on the innovative methods of enterprise marketing management under the background of big data. Value Eng. **39**(21), 24–25 (2020)

3. Liang, L., Ran, W.: Exploration of new models in education services—teaching practice of benchmark course of multi-specialty integration and collaborative innovation technology. J. Beijing Univ. Posts Telecommun. (Soc. Sci. Edn.) **22**(3), 94–100 (2020)

4. Chuqun, G., Weiyu, L., Shoucong, C., et al.: Analysis on the influencing factors of the effect of management under-graduates' graduation practice in Yunnan University of Chinese medicine. China Med. Herald **17**(24), 63–66 (2020)

5. Hong, Z.: Reform of mass entrepreneurship and innovation education for fashion retail and management specialty in higher vocational colleges. Liaoning Higher Vocat. Tech. Inst. J. **22**(6), 84–88 (2020)

6. Rong, Z.: International e-commerce research on recycling marketing of waste and recycled plastics. Synth. Mater. Aging Appl. **49**(4), 150–152+11 (2020)

7. Lin, B., Zhongyuan, Y., Yiming, L., et al.: Power marketing information platform based on data mining and blockchain technology. Inf. Technol. **44**(6), 60–65 (2020)

8. Shuai, L., Glowatz, M., Zappatore, M., et al. (eds.): E-Learning, E-Education, and Online Training. Springer International Publishing, 1–374 (2018). https://doi.org/10.1007/978-3-030-63952-5

9. Shuai, L., Zhaojun, L., Yudong, Z., et al.: Introduction of key problems in long-distance learning and training. Mob. Netw. Appl. **24**(1), 1–4 (2019)

10. Weina, F., Shuai, L., Gautam, S.: Optimization of big data scheduling in social networks. Entropy **21**(9), 902–918 (2019)

Design of Intelligent Dispatching System for Logistics Distribution Vehicles Based on Transfer Learning

Li Yu[✉] and Yuanyuan Guan

College of Finance and Economics, Chongqing Chemical Industry Vocational College, Chongqing 400000, China

Abstract. The traditional logistics vehicle scheduling system can only perform scheduling based on static information, which makes it difficult to change the scheduling decision according to the actual situation, resulting in a high logistics distribution cost and poor timeliness of Veneto. In response to the above problems, this research designs an intelligent dispatching system for logistics distribution vehicles based on migration learning. The hardware part of the system is composed of three modules: GPS satellite positioning module, GPRS wireless communication module and ARM central control module, and then uses migration learning theory to locate the vehicle position. Realize the dispatch of delivery vehicles by establishing a dynamic dispatch model. Through comparative experiments with traditional dispatching systems, it is verified that the system in this paper can effectively reduce the cost of logistics and improve the timeliness of distribution, and has certain practical value.

Keywords: Migration learning · Logistics distribution · Intelligent vehicle scheduling · Vehicle positioning

1 Introduction

With the rapid development of the transportation industry and e-commerce, the development of the logistics and distribution industry tends to be informative, and industry competition is becoming increasingly fierce. The logistics industry is the product of the social and economic development to a certain level. It integrates the warehousing industry, transportation industry and other complex service industries, and is the main component of the national economy. With the improvement of social material living standards, customers have increasingly higher requirements for the timeliness of logistics and distribution. The logistics industry is becoming more and more important in the market economy. To develop the modern logistics industry in a long-term and stable manner, it is necessary to effectively solve the transportation cost problem and optimize the logistics system [1].

Vehicle scheduling problem is the key to optimize the logistics system. In recent years, the vehicle scheduling problem has become a hot topic, which involves many

© ICST Institute for Computer Sciences, Social Informatics and Telecommunications Engineering 2021
Published by Springer Nature Switzerland AG 2021. All Rights Reserved
W. Fu et al. (Eds.): ICMTEL 2021, LNICST 387, pp. 311–320, 2021.
https://doi.org/10.1007/978-3-030-82562-1_29

uncertain factors. In the past, a large number of vehicle scheduling studies are based on static assumptions, that is, all tasks or requirements are known before scheduling decision and route planning. Once the scheduling decision is implemented, all situations will not change. This assumption has become increasingly unrealistic in today's rapid development of e-commerce and logistics. However, there are still few research results for more models and algorithms that are in line with the actual situation, such as vehicle routing problem with multiple time Windows, vehicle routing problem with consideration of road traffic conditions at different time periods, and vehicle routing problem with both requirements of cargo collection and delivery [2]. Therefore, related scholars have also begun to pay attention to the new research direction of dynamic vehicle scheduling.

The core idea of transfer learning is to store and use the knowledge gained in the process of learning tasks in the original field, and apply it to the learning tasks in the new target field, so as to improve the performance effect of the target task [3]. Therefore, according to the above analysis, aiming at the problems of traditional logistics vehicle scheduling system, this paper designs an intelligent vehicle scheduling system based on transfer learning.

2 System Hardware Part Design

The hardware part of the system designed in this paper is mainly to collect the real-time location data of vehicles, so as to adjust the movement path of logistics vehicles in time.

The on-board unit is the hardware part of the whole system, mainly composed of three modules: GPS satellite positioning module, GPRS wireless communication module and ARM9 STM32F101 central control module.

1) GPS satellite positioning module. It is composed of data processing part and antenna, which can receive and analyze GPS satellite message, calculate the longitude and latitude of GPS antenna, carrier movement speed, driving direction and GPS standard time, which are read by the control module and sent back to the server through GPRS module. GPRS technology has the characteristics of real-time, and the maximum transmission rate can reach 171.2 kbit/s [4, 5]. In this paper, the mg323 GSM M2M industrial GPRS communication unit of Huawei Company is selected to realize the transmission of logistics positioning information. Mg323 has four communication bands, supports 8-wire serial port, and the sensitivity of data transmission and reception is less than - 107 dBm. When mg323 carries out GPRS communication, the maximum downlink transmission rate is 85.6 kbps, the maximum uplink transmission rate is 42.8 kbps, and the data transmission protocol is embedded TCP/IP protocol.

2) GPRS wireless communication module. After the connection with the GPRS network is completed, the data exchange between the on-board unit and the server can be realized, the GPS positioning data of the on-board unit and the status information collected by related sensors are packaged and sent to the server, while monitoring and responding to the remote control sent by the monitoring center to the server And scheduling instructions.

The working status of asynchronous transceiver interface of GPRS communication unit is described in Table 1.

3) ARM central control module. The control center of the entire vehicle terminal, on the one hand, completes the extraction, packaging and packaging of GPS satellite positioning data, time synchronization data, and vehicle status data; on the other hand, it controls the communication response, voice call, and data transmission and reception of the GPRS module and the monitoring center. At the same time, it responds to various alarm requests of the on-board unit and executes various instructions of the monitoring center, so that the driver can implement corresponding control of the vehicle in time according to the requirements of the dispatch center and perform vehicle-related scheduling tasks [6].

Table 1. Description of the working status of the asynchronous transceiver interface

Pin	Signal	Describe	Characteristic	Direction
29	UART1_RD	Data sender	DTE receive serial number	DCE—DTE
33	UART1_TD	Data receiver	DTE send serial number	DTE—DCE
38	UART1_RING	Ringing indication	Notify DTE of remote call	DCE—DTE
32	UART1_DTR	Terminal ready	DTE ready	DTE—DCE
34	UART1_RTS	Request to send	Inform DCE to request sending	DTE—DCE
36	UART1_SDR	Data device ready	DCE ready	DCE—DTE
28	UART1_CTS	Clear send	DCE has switched to receive mode	DCE—DTE
24	UART1_DCD	Carrier detection	Data link connected	DCE—DTE

ARM processor controls GPRS module to access mobile GPRS network, and then connects to computer monitoring center through Internet to realize wireless data transmission; GPS module transmits received data to main control chip through serial port for preprocessing; flash memory is used to store debugged application program and embedded uClinux operating system.

On the basis of the above-mentioned system hardware part, the software part of the intelligent dispatching system of logistics distribution vehicles is designed by using the principle of migration learning to complete the system design process and realize the system preset function.

3 System Software Design

3.1 Distribution Vehicle Location Based on Migration Learning

The basis of real-time and accurate scheduling of logistics distribution vehicle intelligent scheduling system is to track the real-time position of the vehicle to be dispatched. Therefore, in addition to using the data transmitted back from the vehicle hardware module, in order to avoid the impact of signal interference on the positioning accuracy, it is also necessary to use the migration learning theory to locate the vehicle license plate, so as to assist the scheduling system.

This article uses transfer learning theory to improve the SSD positioning algorithm. SSD does not need to generate candidate regions during the detection process, so the detection speed has been greatly improved. The SSD algorithm uses the feature maps of different convolutional layers to achieve target detection of different sizes [7]. SSD uses VGG-16 as the basic component of the network to improve and optimize. Using the transfer learning theory, the last two full connection layers of VGG-16 network structure are replaced by the convolution layer. Meanwhile, four convolution layers are added to construct the complete SSD network structure. The feature pyramid of SSD network structure is realized by using the feature graph of six different convolutional layers.

For each feature map, two different 3×3 convolution kernels are used to output the confidence level and regression coordinates. Among them, each default box generates 21 categories of confidence and 4 coordinate values (x, y, w, h). The core idea of the SSD network is to use feature maps of different sizes for convolution calculations to detect target objects of different sizes. Each default box needs to predict the scores of the categories and 4 offsets. Assuming that each feature map cell generates k default box, then for a $m \times n$ size feature map, $m \times n$ feature graph units and $k \times m \times n \times (c + 4)$ output will be generated. Where $k \times m \times n \times c$ is the confidence level of each default box, that is, the probability of the category; $k \times m \times n \times 4$ is the coordinates of each default box after regression. In the training process of transfer learning, a complete picture should be sent to the network and each feature map should be obtained. Then, the default box actually selected should be matched with the real label. If the match is successful, it means that the actual default box contains the desired target, and the default box is positive sample. If the match fails, the default box is negative sample.

SSD network uses feature maps of different layers to detect objects of different sizes. Feature maps of different layers generate default boxes with different scales to cover objects of different shapes and sizes. SSD defines the scale formula of default box as follows [8]:

$$s_k = s_{\min} + \frac{s_{\max} - s_{\min}}{m - 1}(k - 1), k \in [1, m] \tag{1}$$

Among them, m represents the number of feature maps, $s_{\min}$ represents the scale size of the lowest level feature map, and its value is 0.2 by default, and $s_{\max}$ represents the scale size of the highest level feature map, and its value is 0.9 by default. SSD also defines 5 different default frame aspect ratios, as shown in the following formula, the aspect ratio is represented by a_r:

$$a_r = \left\{ 1, 2, 3, \frac{1}{2}, \frac{1}{3} \right\} \tag{2}$$

Thus, the width w_k^a and height h_k^a of each default box can be calculated as follows:

$$\begin{cases} w_k^a = s_k \cdot a_r \\ h_k^a = \dfrac{s_k}{\sqrt{a_r}} \end{cases} \tag{3}$$

After the default frame size is determined, the SSD algorithm is optimized and improved using migration learning technology. In the training process, the loss is composed of two parts: positioning loss and confidence loss. As shown in the following formula [9]:

$$L(x, c, l, g) = \frac{1}{N}\left[L_{conf}(x, c) + \alpha L_{loc}(x, l, g)\right] \tag{4}$$

Where x is the Jaccard coefficient matching the i selection default box with the j real label box of category p. c represents the confidence level, l represents the prediction box, g represents the real label box, N represents the number of matches between the real label box and the actual selected default box, L_{conf} represents the confidence loss, and L_{loc} represents the positioning loss.

By reducing the loss function, the network is trained to obtain the optimal parameters. After using the algorithm to determine the parameters to locate the logistics distribution license plate, a dynamic scheduling model is constructed to realize the scheduling of vehicles.

3.2 Realize the Dynamic Scheduling of Distribution Vehicles

The dynamic vehicle scheduling problem is evolved from the static vehicle scheduling problem, and its main feature is the uncertainty of logistics information. According to the relevant literature on the dynamic vehicle scheduling problem, it can be described as: before optimizing the execution of scheduling, collecting information related to distribution, including customer demand information, cargo distribution information, and dispatching vehicle information, etc., this information is called Is the delivery information. In the process of performing optimal scheduling, the collected distribution information may change over time, and the changed information needs to be optimized and adjusted, instead of using the previous distribution route.

The optimization objective of dynamic vehicle scheduling problem is to minimize the transportation cost or distribution cost. The constraints include the maximum vehicle load constraint, the distribution time constraint and various specified conditions. A customer can only have one vehicle to distribute, and the distribution vehicle starts from the distribution center and must return to the distribution center. The dynamic vehicle scheduling can be regarded as a static vehicle scheduling problem at each time. By calculating the optimal distribution cost at each time, the optimal total distribution cost can be obtained.

The mathematical model of dynamic vehicle scheduling of the entire system is established through the above constraints, and the following variables are defined: t represents the time of the entire distribution network; o represents the distribution center; P represents the key point.

In order to make the driving route arrangement flexible, the number of vehicles required to complete the delivery task at time t can be estimated in advance. The process is as follows:

$$M = \left[\frac{\sum_{i \in W_u(t)} q_i}{Q}\right] + 1 \tag{5}$$

Among them, M is the total number of distribution vehicles that complete all the distribution requirements at time t; [] is the downward rounding of the values in brackets, that is, the integer part; i is the i customer, $W_u(t)$ is the dynamic customer and static customer set of unfinished distribution service at time t; q_i is the cargo demand of the i customer at time t; Q is the maximum load capacity of the distribution vehicle [10].

To establish t mathematical model of the dynamic vehicle scheduling problem at time A, first define two decision variables x_{ijk} and y_{ki}. When the value of x_{ijk} is 1, it means that the vehicle k is driving from point i to point j; otherwise, the value of x_{ijk} is 0. When the value of y_{ki} is 1, it means that the delivery task of point i is completed by vehicle k; otherwise, the value is 0.

Then the objective function of the model is as follows:

$$MinZ = F + \sum_{i,j \in W_{upo}(t)} \sum_{k=1}^{M} c_{ij} x_{ijk} \tag{6}$$

Among them, Z represents the objective function of the model; F is the fixed cost of distribution vehicles; i and j are the i customer and the j customer respectively; $W_{upo}(t)$ is the collection of dynamic customers, all key customer points, static customers who have not completed the distribution service and distribution center at t time; k is the k vehicle; c_{ij} is the transportation cost from customer point i to j.

Constraints of logistics distribution:

$$\sum_{i \in W_u(t)} q_i y_{ki} \leq Q - Q_{jk}(t) \tag{7}$$

$$j \in W_{uo}(t), k = 1, 2, \cdots, M$$

Equation (7) means that the sum of the cargo volume carried by vehicle k is not greater than the maximum load capacity of the vehicle; where $W_u(t)$ represents the set of dynamic customers who put forward new demands at time t and static customers who have not completed the delivery service; $W_{uo}(t)$ represents the distribution center and time t A collection of dynamic customers who propose new requirements and all static customers who have not completed the delivery service; $Q_{jk}(t)$ represents the cumulative weight of the goods after the delivery vehicle departs from customer i at time t ($Q_{0k}(t) = 0$, represents the cumulative weight of the delivery vehicle from the distribution center 0).

After the above model is established, the genetic algorithm is used to solve the model, and the vehicle scheduling scheme is obtained. All the customer points are numbered according to the number a, and these customer points are grouped into chromosomes by natural number coding according to the constraint conditions of the problem. Each gene in the chromosome represents $(1, 2, \cdots, K)$ customer. Since the distribution vehicles need to return to the distribution center after completing the distribution service, the representative distribution center is inserted into these chromosomes to distinguish each sub path.

This paper uses the nearest neighbor search method to create a better initial population of individuals. First, randomly select a customer point as the starting node for the search, find the closest customer node as the suffix node, and then find the closest node to the suffix node as the suffix node, until the demand for these nodes meets the vehicle capacity limit, then a line is formed Sub-path, find the next sub-path in this way, until all customer points are allocated. Then calculate the fitness value of each individual for comparison, select the individual with the largest fitness function value to enter the next-generation mutation, and calculate the population fitness. Select individuals who meet the constraints of the model for mutation processing. Repeat the above steps until the individual fitness function does not change, stop the calculation. The current calculation result is the optimal dispatching plan for the delivery vehicle.

Through the above research on the hardware and software parts of the system, the design of intelligent vehicle scheduling system for logistics distribution based on transfer learning is completed.

4   Test Experiment

In order to test the effectiveness of the intelligent scheduling system for logistics distribution vehicles based on transfer learning designed in this study, the following experiments were designed on the Matlab platform.

4.1   Experiment Design

Contrastive experiments were introduced in this study. Among them, the experimental group is the intelligent logistics distribution vehicle scheduling system based on transfer learning designed in this paper, and the contrast group is the traditional logistics distribution scheduling system. In order to comprehensively verify the performance of the two groups of logistics distribution scheduling systems, the comparative experimental indicators of this experiment are: the cost of logistics distribution under different systems scheduling and the total distance of distribution routes.

This experiment is carried out in the same logistics distribution, and a certain number of customer points are set. The dispatcher uses the scheduling system of the experimental group and the comparison group respectively to dispatch the logistics distribution vehicles. The test contents of the vehicle driving route scheme formulated by the dispatcher are shown in Table 2.

4.2   Experimental Results and Analysis

In the process of the experiment, the realization of the logistics distribution process to determine the cost and its single value, and then the application of different systems after the statistical distribution cost compared with it. The various costs of logistics distribution process and their individual value contents are shown in Table 3.

After applying the experimental group and the comparative group system to logistics vehicle scheduling, the data of logistics distribution cost and total distance of vehicle distribution are shown in Table 4.

According to the analysis of the data in Table 4, the logistics distribution cost and total distribution distance of the experimental group system are lower than those of the control group system. The data in Table 4 shows that there are many distribution paths

Table 2. Test cases of developing vehicle distribution scheme

Numbering	Content	Describe
1	Features	Make a departure plan
2	Specific description	Generating delivery service sequence of vehicles
3	Enter	User demand information, vehicle attribute information, traffic status information
4	Process	Input customer demand information and vehicle resource information
5		Enter traffic information
6		Optimize the delivery route
7	Expected results	If the information is not entered and optimized directly, it will prompt "no relevant information has been entered"; if it is entered, it will be prompted that "no relevant information has been entered" Relevant information and route optimization will generate a vehicle delivery service sequence

Table 3. Cost parameters of logistics distribution

Serial number	Project	Parameter
1	Unit distance freight	50/km
2	Unit freight	$100/m^3$
3	Distribution loss	300/Times
4	Time costs	100/h
5	Distribution staff cost	200/Person times
6	Maximum total distribution	$1000\ m^3$
7	Number distribution centers	2–3
8	Distribution center operating costs	1000/day

that need vehicles to go through repeatedly in the scheduling process of the control group system, which not only increases the total cost of distribution, but also leads to the long distribution distance, which leads to the failure to guarantee the timeliness of distribution.

In summary, it can be seen from the analysis of the above experimental results that the scheduling system based on transfer learning designed in this paper can not only save the logistics distribution cost, but also improve the real-time performance of logistics distribution, with higher practical value.

Table 4. Logistics distribution cost and total distance

Serial number	Experimental group system		Contrast group system	
	Distribution cost/Thousand yuan	Total distance of distribution/Km	Distribution cost/Thousand yuan	Total distance of distribution/Km
1	24.91	38.65	28.63	42.92
2	27.27	29.78	33.62	33.08
3	22.36	26.43	26.57	35.68
4	12.24	18.91	15.65	25.47
5	16.95	17.66	19.28	29.53
6	13.85	14.27	17.31	27.62
7	19.46	20.06	24.08	28.09
8	28.76	41.59	34.53	51.00

5   Conclusion

An important prerequisite for the stable development of the modern logistics industry is to reduce logistics transportation costs, and the key to solving the transportation cost problem in the logistics industry is to optimize the logistics system. The key step in the optimization of the logistics system is the reasonable dispatch of logistics delivery vehicles. By optimizing the dispatch of delivery vehicles, enterprises can reduce transportation costs and improve customer service levels and economic benefits. This paper designs an intelligent dispatching system for logistics distribution vehicles based on transfer learning, and uses transfer learning to effectively improve the reliability and real-time performance of the dispatch system. Through related experiments, it is verified that the system in this paper has practical value.

References

1. Zixuan, L., Xuewen, L.: Research on logistics distribution path optimization based on ant swarm algorithm. J. Chongqing Technol. Bus. (Natural Sciences Edition) **37**(04), 89–94 (2020)
2. Shengjie, Z.: A brief discussion on the logistics distribution vehicle scheduling under industrial interconnection. Logistics Sci-tech **43**(04), 49–52 (2020)
3. Yanrong, Z.: Systematic design of urban logistics distribution scheduling based on ASP. Mod. Electron. Tech. **43**(07), 159–162+168 (2020)
4. Hualong, Y., Liang, Z., Lizhe, J., et al.: Distribution vehicle scheduling problem based on aggregation and prediction of random customer demands. J. Syst. Manage. **28**(05), 917–926 (2019)
5. Yanqiang, X., Jinzhen, L.: Research of express scheduling system based on GIS. Autom. Instrum. **28**(01), 32–35 (2019)
6. Shaoguang, W.: Optimization of logistic scheduling for multi distribution centers under practical constraints. Sci. Technol. Eng. **18**(36), 216–220 (2018)

7. Gonglin, Y., Kuiying, Y., Qixue, L.: Research on vehicle target detection method of aerial images based on transfer learning. Electron. Measur. Technol. **41**(22), 77–81 (2018)
8. Weina, F., Shuai, L., Gautam, S.: Optimization of big data scheduling in social networks. Entropy **21**(9), 902–918 (2019)
9. Shuai, L., Zhaojun, L., Yudong, Z., et al.: Introduction of key problems in long-distance learning and training. Mob. Netw. Appl. **24**(1), 1–4 (2019)
10. Shuai, L., Dongye, L., Gautam, S., et al.: Overview and methods of correlation filter algorithms in object tracking. Complex Intell. Syst. **11**(3), 431–438 (2020)

Design of Supply Chain Resource Distribution Allocation Model Based on Deep Learning

Yuanyuan Guan[✉] and Li Yu

College of Finance and Economics, Chongqing Chemical Industry Vocational College, Chongqing 400000, China

Abstract. With the continuous deepening of economic upgrading and transformation, the scope of the supply chain of SMEs has gradually expanded. At present, in the process of supply chain resource allocation, the supply chain resource distribution allocation model is often used to study it. But the cost control ability of this model is poor. For this reason, this research designs a supply chain resource distribution allocation model based on deep learning. Select the indicators of the supply chain resource distribution allocation model to determine the principle of resource input, risk compensation, maximum utility and comprehensive optimization. Then construct the objective function of supply chain distribution configuration according to the cost and benefit requirements, and then use deep learning technology to obtain the optimal solution of the objective function scheme. By comparing the model in this paper with the traditional model, we can see that the model in this paper has better cost control ability.

Keywords: Deep learning · Resource allocation · Supply chain · Cost control

1 Introduction

With the continuous maturity of macro level supply chain collaboration research, such as collaborative mechanism and collaborative technology, how to guide and manage resource allocation among enterprises from the micro level (i.e. supply chain resource perspective) will become a breakthrough in the bottleneck of supply chain resource allocation [1, 2]. The key to achieve effective resource integration among supply chain members can create greater synergy effect. On the one hand, through the cooperation in material supply, production, distribution, distribution and other links, each member can form the complementary advantages of resources, give full play to their own advantages, enable partners to focus on their areas of expertise, avoid low efficiency and waste caused by decentralized utilization of resources, and realize the efficient utilization of resources of enterprises; On the other hand, by sharing information, both upstream suppliers and downstream distributors can timely and accurately adjust their own resource allocation according to the market information provided by their partners, so as to respond to the market demand and avoid the loss to enterprises caused by information asymmetry in the traditional market. Therefore, the realization of resource collaboration among supply

© ICST Institute for Computer Sciences, Social Informatics and Telecommunications Engineering 2021
Published by Springer Nature Switzerland AG 2021. All Rights Reserved
W. Fu et al. (Eds.): ICMTEL 2021, LNICST 387, pp. 321–332, 2021.
https://doi.org/10.1007/978-3-030-82562-1_30

chain enterprises is of great significance to promote the successful application of supply chain collaboration.

At present, the concept of supply chain competition has been widely circulated in the industry and academia. Scholars at home and abroad have conducted in-depth discussions on the supply chain competition and have achieved certain research results [3]. However, through in-depth analysis of existing research results, this article finds that there are still many issues that need to be further explored in the supply chain resource allocation. In addition, the competition between supply chains will further aggravate the uncertainty in the supply chain system, which makes the supply chain system management more difficult. On the one hand, the dynamics and complexity of the supply chain system often frustrate the efforts of enterprises, and the stable system behavior will reduce the cost of the system. On the other hand, as a complex game problem, supply chain competition often has multiple equilibrium solutions. Therefore, how to refine multiple equilibrium solutions and select stable equilibrium strategies for decision makers is also an important research problem. One of the effective ways to solve this problem is to design an effective distribution allocation model of supply chain resources.

In view of the above background, this study designs a supply chain resource distribution allocation model based on deep learning. By selecting the indicators of the supply chain resource distribution allocation model, the principles of resource input, risk compensation, maximum utility and comprehensive optimization are determined. Then, the objective function of supply chain distribution allocation is constructed according to the requirements of cost and benefit, and the deep learning technology is used The optimal solution of the objective function scheme is obtained to realize the optimal distribution allocation of supply chain resources.

2   Design of Resource Distribution Allocation Model in Supply Chain

In view of the limitations of the current research on supply chain resource allocation, this paper constructs a supply chain resource allocation model with resource allocation and asymmetric supply chain structure, and studies the stability of the game, cooperation strategies between supply chains and effective strategies to deal with interference events. The design process of supply chain resource distribution configuration model is shown in Fig. 1.

This paper studies the problem of income distribution among supply chain partners. First, it analyzes the composition of cooperative benefits in the supply chain and the characteristics and principles of the distribution of benefits; secondly, it focuses on the three main risks that affect the distribution of cooperative benefits in the supply chain: market risk, technology risk, and cooperation risk. A more in-depth analysis was carried out from four perspectives of risk control and distribution, which provided a basis for the realization of risk sharing and avoidance in the income distribution model. Then, it analyzes and compares the income distribution models from the three aspects of the selection of the optimal plan by these models, the comparison between the models and the application of the models.

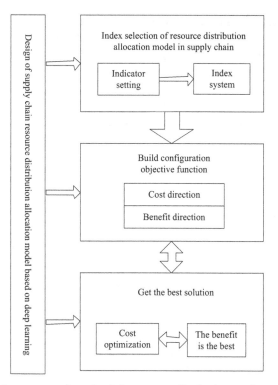

Fig. 1. Design process of supply chain resource distribution configuration model

2.1 Index Selection of Resource Distribution Allocation Model in Supply Chain

There are many principles for resource allocation in the supply chain, but they can be classified into four categories: the principle of resource input, the principle of risk compensation, the principle of maximum utility, and the principle of comprehensive optimization.

Resource allocation based on the principle of performance income: in order to maximize the contribution of enterprises, it is very important to pay and gain in direct proportion - distribution according to work. The input here is not only the input resources mentioned above, but also a lot of investment, such as the completion of multiple tasks in production, design, scientific research and training, and the unknown responsibilities in the supply chain (such as the responsible person of the core enterprise). These data are collectively referred to as contribution $E_i (i = 1, 2, ..., n)$.

$$\frac{v_1}{E_1} = \frac{v_2}{E_2} = ... = \frac{v_n}{E_n} \tag{1}$$

$$v_i = \frac{C_i I_i}{\sum\limits_{i=1}^{n} C_i I_i} V \tag{2}$$

Income distribution based on the principle of risk compensation: First, the determination of risk. Risk refers to an event that is not expected to occur. Therefore, risk U is not only a function of the probability P of the occurrence of a risk event, but also a function of the loss w caused by the risk event, namely:

$$U = f(p, w) = pc \tag{3}$$

As the partner can bear the loss caused by the risk event with all the resources invested, $w = \beta I$, Where β is the risk loss rate. Then according to formula (4), it can be obtained that:

$$U = p\beta I \tag{4}$$

Let $\lambda = pa$, from the above formula, we can get:

$$U = \lambda I \tag{5}$$

Among them, λ is a parameter related to the probability of a risk event and the risk loss rate. It can be obtained by analyzing historical data. Under normal circumstances, the value of λ is between 0.1 and 0.8. Then, the income distribution plan is determined. The income b_i allocated to partner i should be proportional to the risk it bears. Then:

$$\frac{v_1}{U_1} = \frac{v_2}{U_2} = ... = \frac{v_n}{U_n} \tag{6}$$

From Formula (5) and (6), it is concluded that:

$$v_i = \frac{\lambda_i I_i}{\sum\limits_{i=1}^{n} \lambda_i I_i} V \tag{7}$$

Income distribution based on the principle of resource input: the income V_i allocated by partner i should be in direct proportion to its input resource I_i. If the total revenue of the supply chain is V, then:

$$\frac{v_1}{I_1} = \frac{v_2}{I_2} = ... = \frac{v_n}{I_n} \tag{8}$$

However, the role played by each resource in the supply chain is different, so we also have to introduce cost value weight L_i for modification:

$$\frac{v_1}{L_1 I_1} = \frac{v_2}{L_2 I_2} = ... = \frac{v_n}{L_n I_n} \tag{9}$$

Through the above analysis, it can be concluded that:

$$v_i = \frac{L_i I_i}{\sum\limits_{i=1}^{n} L_i I_i} V \tag{10}$$

Income distribution based on the principle of comprehensive optimization. The principle of comprehensive optimization can be said to be a combination of the above three principles. The formulation of the income distribution plan is to scientifically make the partners' income reflect their investment and risks, while maximizing the overall utility and ensuring the stability of the entire supply chain cooperation [4, 5]. Then, based on the principle of comprehensive optimization, the proportions of benefits distributed according to the three single factors are Q_i, T_i, and K_i. When considering the impact of the three factors comprehensively, because the three factors of performance level, risk level and invested resources have different degrees of impact on income distribution, the group center of gravity model is used to determine the total income distribution of the supply chain cooperation. The weights of the three are respectively set as R_q, R_t, R_k, which are obtained through a series of comprehensive evaluation methods, such as expert method, analytic hierarchy process, network analysis method, fuzzy comprehensive evaluation method, gray correlation method, TOPSIS [6], etc.

$$V_i = (R_q Q_i + R_t T_i + R_k K_i) \tag{11}$$

Through the above formula to determine the supply chain resource distribution allocation model indicators, and build the basis of its model.

2.2 Constructing the Objective Function of Deep Learning

On the basis of selecting the indicators of the distribution allocation model of supply chain resources, the deep learning objective function is constructed to lay the foundation for obtaining the optimal distribution model.

Suppose that the whole supply chain is divided into i link. In stage $k - 1$, after a sub supply chain is completed, there are j resources released, waiting for the reallocation of application environment. In order to evaluate the advantages and disadvantages of each resource allocation scheme, the deep learning criterion is to maximize the organizational interests of the whole supply chain. Therefore, the benefit function E_{ij} of the model represents the benefit of allocating j resources to the i sub supply chain; the subject of the benefit function is the measurable organizational value R_i of the project, and the cost P_{ij} of resource allocation is used as the measurement coefficient. In order to simplify the problem and facilitate interpretation, the benefit function $(1 - P_{ij})$ multiplied by R_i is expressed in the formula.

$$R_i = E_{ij} \times (1 - p_{ij}) \tag{12}$$

Assuming that the effective investment ability of worker j in sub-supply chain position i is Y_{ij}, and H is the number of q supply cycles that can be completed when the degree of experience is 1, then the experience distribution value of resource j in supply chain i For $R_i \times E_{ij} \times p_{ij}$, the distribution cost can be expressed as:

$$R_i \times E_{ij} \times p_{ij} \times k = w \tag{13}$$

Where k is the adjustment coefficient, g_{ij} is 0–1 variable, which represents the matching between i supply chain and j resource; $g_{ij} = 0$ is that j resource is not allocated to i

supply chain link; $g_{ij} = 1$ is to allocate j resource to i link. Multiply the benefit function S_{ij} of each allocation scheme by the sum of state variables g_{ij}, the objective function of deep learning can be obtained as follows:

$$\max = \sum_i \sum_j g_{ij} \times S_{ij} \tag{14}$$

The above formula is the objective function formula in this research process, and the corresponding distribution model can be obtained by using this formula.

2.3 Obtain the Optimal Distribution Model

According to the set objective function, more configuration schemes can be obtained. In this design, in order to obtain the optimal result, the selection principle of the optimal scheme is set as follows:

(1) The overall planning level. The standard requires that the order of distribution of sub-supply chains should be consistent with the overall goals of the supply chain, while considering the internal logical relationship of each supply chain [7], mainly including three aspects: the priority of the supply chain should follow the order of supply chain construction; the sub-supply chain The priority should support the priority proposed by the superior supply chain; the priority of the sub-supply chain should conform to the supply chain rules and regulations.

(2) Positive benefit level. The criteria require that projects be prioritized according to the evaluation of supply chain benefits. It mainly includes: the potential benefits of the supply chain should be higher than the cost; the availability of the management information accumulated by the supply chain to the project; and the benefits brought by the supply chain to the people's livelihood and economic operation.

(3) Negative benefit level. The standard requires consideration of the risk of supply chain implementation. In this level, we mainly consider the following factors: the operability of the core technology of the supply chain, the difficulty of the implementation of the supply chain, and the on-time completion rate of the supply chain. According to the above configuration principle, the selection of configuration scheme is set as a multi-objective optimization problem, and its processing flow is shown in Fig. 2.

The project priority is set as multi-attribute problem D, the alternative scheme set is $M = \{m_1, m_2, ..., m_i\}$, $N_{i1} = \{n_{i1}, n_{i2}, ..., n_{ii}\}$ is the attribute set of scheme i, where n_{ii} is the G attribute value of the i scheme and $n_{ij} = n_{ii} \times m_i$ is the i attribute value. The decision matrix of the problem is represented by matrix $V_{m \times n}(m_i)$ [8–10]. The optimal model can be expressed as follows:

$$n'_{ij} = \frac{n_{ii} - n_j^{min}}{n_i^{max} - n_j^{min}} \tag{15}$$

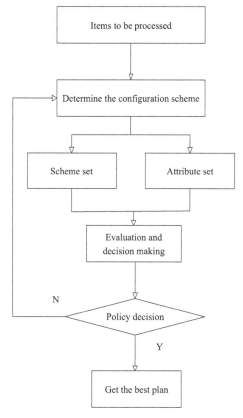

Fig. 2. Scheme selection process

When paying attention to cost in the distribution process, the optimal model can be expressed as:

$$n'_{ij} = \frac{n_j^{\max} - n_{ii}}{n_i^{\max} - n_j^{\min}} \tag{16}$$

Using the above formula, determine the best resource distribution allocation scheme. So far, we have completed the design of the distribution allocation model of supply chain resources based on deep learning.

3 Experimental Demonstration Analysis

3.1 Experimental Environment Setting

In order to verify the practical application effect of the supply chain resource distribution allocation model based on deep learning (the model in this paper) designed above, it is compared with the methods currently in use. The experimental platform parameters are shown in Table 1.

Table 1. Experimental platform parameters

Test environment	Test environment composition	Specific parameters
Experimental server hardware	CPU	Intel
	RAM	8G
	Hard disk	96G
Experimental server software	Operating system	CentOS 6.5 (Linux)
	Development language	Python 2.7
	Web frame	Flask 0.12
	Python analysis environment	Gunicorn + Gevent
	Web performance optimization	Nginx
Database server hardware	RAM	8G
	Hard disk	96G
	CPU	Intel
Database server software	Database	SQL
	Operating system	CentOS 6.5 (Linux)

The above parameters are used to complete the performance comparison between the proposed method and the traditional method. In the process of the experiment, the comparison object is set as two parts: the decline degree of distribution cost and the response time of distribution configuration scheme selection. Through the combination of the two parts, the comprehensive analysis of the use effect of this method is realized. In order to improve the reliability of the experimental results, the experimental environment is set to focus on cost and benefit.

3.2 Preparation of Experimental Data

In this study, a resource distribution allocation model is proposed, and the specific calculations of some empirical examples are supplemented for the theory, which is used to practice the theory and methods. Choose a manufacturing supply chain as a sample of model application. A YD Manufacturing Co., Ltd. is a private enterprise, and it has been showing a good development trend since its establishment. Especially since the company implemented the shareholding system reform, informatization transformation and high-level talent introduction strategy in 2001, the company has transitioned from a family system to a modern management model, and the company has achieved rapid development. Take this enterprise as the experimental object to study the distribution configuration of its supply chain.

3.3 Analysis of Experimental Results

The experimental results of cost reduction effect are shown in Fig. 3.

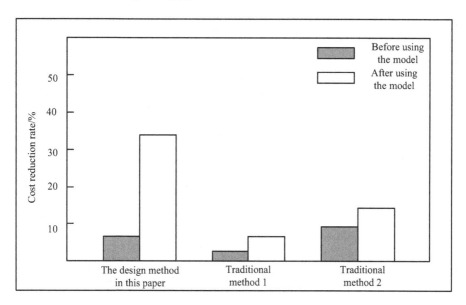

(a) Pay attention to the results of cost experiment

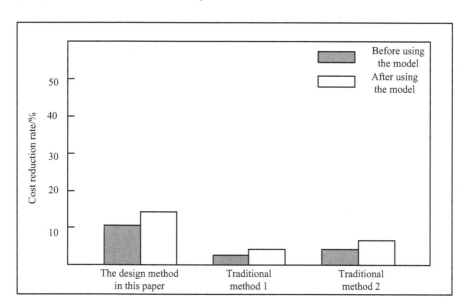

(b) Pay attention to the results of benefit experiment

Fig. 3. Experimental results of cost reduction effects

According to the analysis of Fig. 3, the cost control ability of traditional model 1 and traditional model 2 is low, and the effect of cost reduction is not good. In the process of massive data processing, this situation will have a negative impact on the supply chain

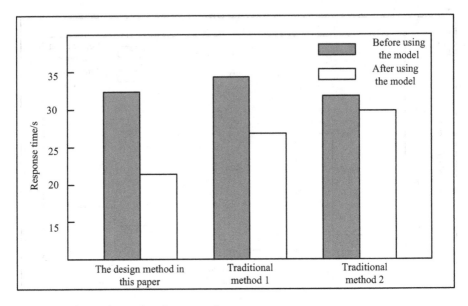

(a) Pay attention to the results of cost experiment

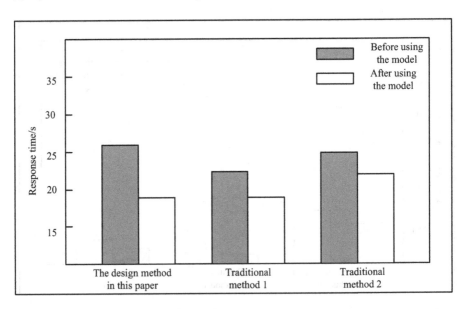

(b) Focus on the results of the benefit experiment

Fig. 4. Response time experiment results

and reduce customer satisfaction. Compared with the two traditional models, the cost control ability of this model is better and will not affect the subsequent calculation.

Under the premise of using the actual problems, the design model can be used to process a variety of supply chains and improve the accuracy of data.

The experimental results of response time are shown in Fig. 4.

It can be seen from Fig. 4 that the use effect of this model is significantly better than that of the traditional model. In the two different environments, the operating state of the model in this paper is obviously relatively stable, and there is no significant fluctuation in the background processing time caused by the change of focus. The traditional model used in this part has the problem of large fluctuation energy. In actual use, fluctuations in response time will have a serious impact on the choice of distribution configuration options. Therefore, it can be determined that the performance of the model in this part of the experiment is better than the traditional model.

4 Conclusion

Based on the self-organization theory and enterprise resource theory, using the methods of synergetics, system dynamics and economic mathematics, this paper focuses on the conceptual framework, mechanism and model of distribution allocation of supply chain resources. According to the requirements of cost and benefit, it constructs the objective function of distribution allocation of supply chain resources, and then uses the deep learning Learning technology obtains the optimal solution of the objective function scheme, so as to realize the optimal distribution allocation of supply chain resources. Through the research on the complex adaptability, dissipative structure, structural model, operation mechanism, evolution process and measurement method of supply chain model, the main conclusions and innovations are as follows: supply chain resource allocation needs reasonable research on risk. In the process of using supply chain model in the future, this part of the content will be mainly studied in order to improve the use effect of the model.

References

1. Jizi, L., Nian, Z., Chunling, L.: Optimization of order-driven production decision making in crowdsourcing supply chain with omnichannel design. Comput. Integr. Manuf. Syst. **25**(05), 1248–1258 (2019)
2. Xuelong, Z., Doudou, W.: An Optimal Design Model of Multi-stage Supply Chain Network With Interval Grey Features. Stat. Dec. **36**(01), 167–171 (2020)
3. Pin, Z., He, X., Fen, L.: The optimal ordering decision under the bargaining power of supply chain partners. J. Ind. Eng. Eng. Manage. **33**(04), 130–135 (2019)
4. Pei, L., Gengjun, G.: P-DEA and Shapley value models based on green supply chain profit distribution. J. Railway Sci. Eng. **15**(09), 2448–2454 (2018)
5. Jiannan, S., Xiaofeng, S.: Operational decision and optimal choice of payment to a supply chain based on wholesale price incentive. Chin. J. Manage. **15**(01), 103–110 (2018)
6. Xiaomei, L., Yangang, F., Jiaxin, S.: Coordination model of telecom supply chain based on network externality. J. Qiqihar Univ. (Nat. Sci. Edn.) **36**(01), 45–50+67 (2020)
7. Nannan, Y., Bogen, D.: Bi-level programming model of port supply chain coordination under revenue sharing contract. J. Shanghai Marit. Univ. **40**(03), 80–86 (2019)

8. Shuai, L., Zhaojun, L., Yudong, Z., et al.: Introduction of key problems in long-distance learning and training. Mob. Netw. Appl. **24**(1), 1–4 (2019)
9. Shuai, L., Mengye, L., Hanshuang, L., et al.: Prediction of gene expression patterns with generalized linear regression model. Front. Genet. (10), 120 (2019)
10. Weina, F., Shuai, L., Gautam, S.: Optimization of big data scheduling in social networks. Entropy **21**(9), 902–918 (2019)

Arabic Question-Answering System Using Search Engine Techniques

Manal Alamir[1], Sadeem Alharth[1], Shahad Alqurashi[1],
and Tahani Alqurashi[2]([✉])

[1] College of Computer and Information Systems, Umm Al Qura University,
Makkah, Saudi Arabia
{s44180009,s44181412,s44180184}@st.uqu.edu.sa
[2] Common First Year Deanship, Umm Al-Qura University, Makkah, Saudi Arabia
tmqurashi@uqu.edu.sa

Abstract. The Arabic language is one of the most widely spoken languages in the world. Many natural language processing experts have tried to understand its linguistic complexity. This makes text processing and its applications difficult, particularly in question-answering systems. Some researchers have unsuccessfully tried to tackle the problem of creating an effective question-answering system. In this paper, we present a question-answering system for a Saudi Arabia labor law dataset. Our system works in three main stages named Data Preparation, Data Preprocessing and Answer Extraction. The main aim of the first two stages is to prepare and preprocess the dataset in order to be in a suitable format for building question-answering system. In the Answer Extraction stage, two text similarity measurements are applied, which is TF-IDF and Cosine. Then, the candidate answers are evaluated and ranked based on their similarity scores and the most relevant answer to the user's query is displayed as a final answer. We evaluated our proposed system by test it using 100 of manually generated user queries and on average we achieved a good results.

Keywords: Arabic natural language processing · Question answering · Search query · Relevant information

1 Introduction

The Internet and related applications have become the main source of information for experts, researchers, students, and the general user [4]. However, these applications contain vast amount of information, and sometimes a query requires a specific answer. The user often must spend excessive time searching the list of retrieved documents or information to find the answer they are looking for. Thus, an application-based search engine would be useful. In addition, most of the documents available for retrieval on the internet are written in English. Many

© ICST Institute for Computer Sciences, Social Informatics and Telecommunications Engineering 2021
Published by Springer Nature Switzerland AG 2021. All Rights Reserved
W. Fu et al. (Eds.): ICMTEL 2021, LNICST 387, pp. 333–343, 2021.
https://doi.org/10.1007/978-3-030-82562-1_31

users need access to papers in other languages, specifically Arabic since a large part of the world's population speak the language [12].

For these reasons, we built a search engine system that caters to Arabic ministries, specifically the System of Labor in the Ministry of Human Resources and Social Development. The System of Labor contains many legal documents and articles concerning many legal details. Government employees and law personnel must currently spend a great deal of time searching the list of retrieved articles or legal documents to find related answers because they are not arranged in a way that makes it easy to obtain information. As we will show in the literature review section, different techniques have been deployed in the creation of question-answering systems. However, free form-based search engines are the most effective means of achieving the objective of the system used here in which the content of a chapter (text) is searched and retrieve back its number and text as an answer to the user. This data was then organized into a free form-based format that can be easily accessed publically. Thus, in this paper, we present a way to organize the data of the System of Labor to be easily retrievable for any user. The rest of this paper illustrates our methodology (Sect. 3) and presents the results that we obtained (Sect. 4).

2   Related Work

There is a difference between a search engine system and a question-answering system. Search engine systems provide query results using databases that have already indexed documents [8]. The typical search engine is not designed to extract specific answers to queries and returns a set of references that may contain the answers; a question-answering system retrieves direct or correct answers to the questions rather than flooding the user with documents or giving general answers [11].

Research in the field of Arabic language processing is very limited, and this is one of the challenges that we faced in the implementation of our project. AlMaayah et al. [5] offered an approach for extracting the synonyms of words in the Qur'an, specifically Juzo Amma. They used the WordNet dataset, which depends on traditional Arabic dictionaries and a collection of techniques, such as frequency and inverse document frequency, cosine similarities, and three measures: precision, recall, and f-measure. Their search performance reached an accuracy of 27%.

Malhas et al. [10] provided (AyaTEC) test set contents 207 questions verse-based on the Holy Qur'an for question answering system. That presented information needs of both skeptical users and inquisitive which covered eleven subject classes of the Holy Qur'an. They made AyaTEC set available to the research society to develop this field further. They proposed many evaluation measures to backing the kind of verse-based answers and questions systems while merging in the evaluation the notion of partial matching of answers. In many instances, the search is incapable to call pertinent verses where it did not use the semantic relation between words in the query.

Recently, Zouaoui et al. [23] introduced an ontology-based semantic search engine as an index and acquired good results in terms of precision and recall measures. The search engine based on a collection of beneficial terms extracted from the Quranic Earab book with grammatical functions that avail as definitions, they concentrate on constructing a new ontology for the Quranic text to use for information retrieval. While, Zeid et al. [21] used graph ontology together with a web search API as an alternate track to get answers and perform the ontology.

Hani et al. [3] used an ontological resource to match their search with semantically similar words. They divided the processing of the query as follows: first they extracted an enhanced query using keywords and then passed those results through an ontological resource to get semantically correlated words. They tested this approach on 50 Arabic questions from the standard set of TREC and CLEF Arabic questions and received a mean reciprocal ratio for retrieving documents of 1.53, which is considered good.

Paolo, et al. [13] used a regular question-answering system that had three modules: a question analysis module, a passage retrieval module, and an answer extraction module. To be able to analyze the question, they implemented their own Arabic Named Entity Recognition system to determine the named entities in the question that will determine the type of answer. They adapted an already implemented system called JIRS for their passage retrieval module. When tested on a dataset of 200 questions, the overall performance of their model was good.

Jaffar et al. [6] provided a query expansion review in Arabic. This was basically divided into three strategies. The first used classical methods of stemming, lemmatization, and word sense disambiguation. The second strategy used a feedback score to find matching results for query enhancement. The third strategy used data extracted from a corpus or external resources such as WordNET.

Dima et al. [19] proposed a system that extracts keywords using word2vec. In their system, the text was first pre-process to word stems. The stems were used to calculate the bag of concepts used to make a linear combination of each word that shows the concepts that define it. Next, the words were catagorized to similar classes to determine synonyms and similar words. They then calculated the different N-gram weights to extract the keywords.

Dima et al. [18] presented a study on the usage of word embeddings in the Arabic language. They showed the effect of the word embeddings used from GLOVE and Skip-gram and CBOW. The study showed that the applications included sentiment analysis and classification of sentiment and that they are applied in measuring semantic-based similarities. The applications also included short-answer grading and information-retrieval applications, such as cosine similarities. The similarity-based applications included plagiarism detection and paraphrasing identification.

Wissam, et al. [20] have tested five web search engines on an information retrieval evaluation for fifty queries chosen randomly essential with the observance of the web-specific estimate requirements. The descriptions of the top ten results and relation they're for all queries were evaluated by independent jurors.

The essence return was that Google perfected roughly all the times better than the other different engines.

Majed, et al. [15] have presented explain and identify the restrictions of the difficulties of Arabic documents retrieving. They approach used three Arabic search engines: Yahoo, Google, and Idrisi. They applied stemming and spelling normalization techniques were not enough techniques requirement significantly develop retrieval, when retrieval by n-grams technique was more efficient for indexing Arabic documents.

Zhong et al. [22] sophisticated approach to retrieve questions pertaining to building regulations. The approach combine deep learning model of Natural Language Processing (NLP) with information retrieval to get specific and fast answers to user's queries about building regulations. They proposed a chatbot System for building regulations question answering.

3   Arabic Question Answering System

Figure 1 shows the architecture of our proposed Arabic Question Answering System. The system consists of three main stages, which are Data Preparation, Data Preprocessing and Answer Extraction. The following subsections explain them in more details:

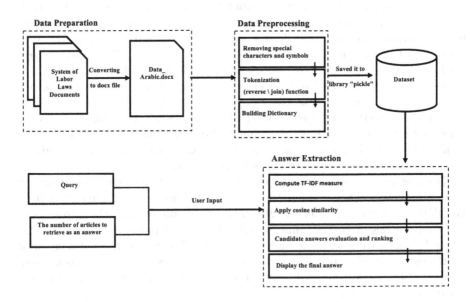

Fig. 1. The Arabic question answering system architecture.

3.1   Data Preparation

For this project, we worked with the labor law dataset available on the website of the Ministry of Human Resources and Social Development in the Kingdom of Saudi Arabia [2]. The dataset contained 245 articles divided into six sections. This type of dataset is known as primary data, which refers to data collected from first-hand experience. Primary data has not yet been published and is more reliable, authentic, and objective.

The data file was originally received in PDF format, and it was converted to a docx file format to facilitate the use of the Python language; unfortunately, when handling Arabic text, Python packages often destroy much of the information. We used docx2txt, which is a pure python-based utility, to read text from Microsoft Word documents or extract images from docx files [1]. Docx2txt also performs a fundamental function of converting data inside the docx files into rows, which enables the mining and programming of data. The next section presents the data preprocessing steps in detail.

3.2   Data Preprocessing

After using the docx2txt library, we were surprised at the amount of preprocessing that the data still needed, as it contained many characters, punctuation marks, and spaces that would have made the query processing difficult; the texts also appeared in reverse, as shown in Fig. 2. Thus, several steps were used to organize the data.

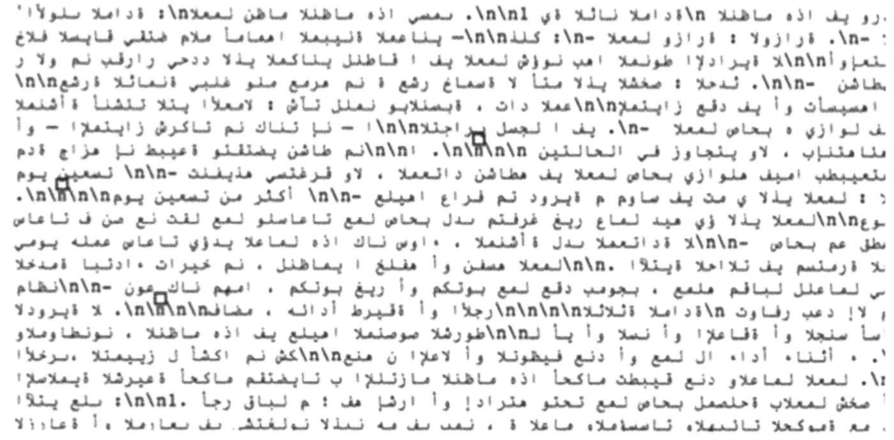

Fig. 2. Outputs before preprocessing stage

First, strip function with separator \n was used to remove specified spaces at the beginning and end of the text; Fig. 2 shows that the text was still in need of further processing.

Next, regular expressions were used to remove any special characters, spaces, punctuations, and English letters, such as $, *, xa0, ...etc. Figure 3 shows the output after this stage.

'، لا زوجي بحاصل لمعلا نا كرتي ملماع لمعي مباسحل صاخلا املك لا زوجي لماعلل نا لمعي مباسحل صاخلا بلوتنو'
'،ةرازو ةيلخادلا طيف فاقيإو لبحرتو ماقيإو تابوقعلا ملع يللاخملا ن مّ نيلماعلا مهباسحل صاخلا ةلامعلا'
'،ةيلاصالا ىف عراوشلا نيدابغلاو نيبيبغتلماو نع لمعلا نيبراملا كلذكو باحصا لمعلا نيلفشغلاو ،لازملا'
'،تستملاو نبر مهيلع فانلاو نيل مهل لكو نم هل رود ىف ةللاخملا قيبطتو تابوقعلا ةرقفلا مهتجب'
'،ةداملا نومرعبلااا'
'.سر ةادقتسا لماعلا ريغ يدوعسلا موسرو ةماقإإا ةصقرو لمعلا اهمهدبجتو امو بترتي ملع ريخأت كلذ نم تامارغ دعم'
'،'و موس ريبخت ةنهملا جورخلاو ةدوعلاو ةركاذتو ةدوع لماعلا ملح منطوم دعم'
'،'ةامتنإ ةللاخلا نيب نيفرطلا'
'،'لمحتي لماعلا فيلاكد متدوع ملح ملاب ىف ةلاح مدع متيحلاس لمعلل وأ اذإ بغر ىف وعلا ةد نود ببس هورشم'
'،'لمحتي بحاص لمعلا موسر لقن خ تامد اعلا لم بدلا بغري ىف لقن دغ متام ميلإ'
'،'مزلي بحاص لمعلا تاقفنب زيهجت نامئج لماعلا هلقنو ملح ةجلا يتلا مرباً اميف دقعلا وأ مدقنسا لماعلا من اه'
'،'ملام نفدي ةقفاومب ميوذ لخاد ةكلمملا لبعيو بحاص لمعلا ىف ةلاح مازلنإ ةسولمسا ا ةماعل تانيمأتلل'

Fig. 3. Outputs after preprocessing

As Fig. 3 shows, the text was in reverse order, so to put it in the correct order, we looped on each word separately and reversed its characters. The output of this stage is shown in Fig. 4.

'،'المادة الحادية وال ثالثون'
'،'بعد العمال السعوديون الذين أسهمد المكانب في نوظيفهم والعمال الذين إسنقدمتنهم نيابة عن أصحاب العمل'
'،'معالا لدى صاحب العمل ويرنبطون به بعالنة عندبا مباشرة'
'،'المادة الثانية والثالئون'
'،'ال يجوز الإسنفدام بفم د العمل إلا بعد موافقة الوزارة'
'،'المادة الثالثة والثالئون'
'،'ال يجوز لغير السعودي أن يمارس عمل وال يجوز أن يسمح له بعزاولته إلا بعد الحصول على رخمة عمل من الوزارة'
'،'وفق النموذج الذي نعده لهذا الغرض ويشنرط لمنح الرخمة ما يأتي'
'،'أن يكون العامل قد دخل البالد بطريقة مشروعة ومصرح له بالعمل'
'أن يكون من ذوي الكفابات المهنية أو المؤهالت الدراسية التي نحناج إليها البالد وال يوجد من أبناء من يعملها أو'
'،'كان العدد العوجود منهم ال يفي بالحاجة وأن يكون من فنة العم ال العاديين التي نحناج إليها البالد'
'،'أن يكون منعانف مع صاحب عمل ونحد مسؤولينه'
'،'وينفمد بكلمة العمل في هذه المادة كل عمل صناعي أو نجاري أو زراعي أو مالي أو غيره وأي خد مة بما في ذلك'
'،'الخدمة المنزلية'
'،'المادة الرابعة والثالئون'

Fig. 4. Final outputs

3.3   Answer Extraction

After preprocessing the data, the user is asked to enter the query into our system, and it should be in the form of asking about the article that is related to specific topic along with the number of articles that he/she wish to retrieve as an answer k.

Then we apply two text similarity measurements to calculate the similarity between each words in the user query and our dataset as follows:

The Term Frequency-Inverse Document Frequency (TF-IDF). Next, we computed the term frequency-inverse document frequency (TF-IDF) for the terms mentioned in our search engine. The idea was to combine the frequency of a term in a context (query) with its relative frequency in the documents overall. According to Salton and Buckley [14], the TF-IDF weighs a term's frequency (TF) and its inverse document frequency (IDF).

To calculate TF, we built the inverted index representation which consists of two basic components: the inverted list and the vocabulary. The inverted list is the reference about the place of that word in the documents set, its frequency, position,... etc. and it is represented by a vector. While, the vocabulary is the one word from the document set. In the index, each word has an inverted list include reference of occurrences of the word in special documents [4, 16].

Then we built the inverted index of our system, in which each word mentioned is connected with the chapter it is mentioned in. Inverted index representation is the main building block for any search engine or information retrieval system and allows for the calculation of the text similarity metrics.

After we calculated TF, we computed the TF-IDF using the following formulas:

$$\text{TF-IDF} = TF(i,j) * IDF(i)$$

$$TF(i,j) = \frac{\text{Frequency of word i in document j}}{\text{Total words in document j}} \tag{1}$$

$$IDF(i) = \log(\frac{\text{Total documents}}{\text{documents with word i}})$$

Cosine Similarity Function. We were then able to compute the similarity functions needed for information retrieval based on the dictionary using the TF-IDF scores for our system. This stage includes two types of computations. First, we summed up the similarities of each word of the query with each document based on the morphology and semantics of the word. We also calculated the length of each of the queries and the length of the chapter's text: this information is needed for the next type of computation, which involves calculating the cosine similarity between the input query from the user and the candidate texts. Since cosine similarity represent the projection of one word vector to another, it was used to measure the whole projection of the word vector (the query) and the text of the chapter in the dataset. The use of this type of similarity proved to be very efficient and useful for our results, which are presented in the next section. After calculation of the similarity metrics with all the chapters available in our data, we ranked the documents in a descending order, and we displayed the k most relevant documents to the whole user's query vector.

4   Experiment Results

In the final stage of this study, we tested the system performance using 100 user queries and calculated both the BLEU [7] and ROUGE [9] as an evaluation measures for each query. BLEU and ROUGE measures were used as they are the most popular methods for testing the performance of machine translation, summarization, and question-answering models. BLEU and ROUGE ranged from 0 to 1, where 0 value indicates a perfect result of the mismatching text, while 1 indicates a perfect result for matched text. ROUGE results contain three symbols: f, p, and r where it refers to f1-score, precision, and recall percentage respectively. Recall simply means how much of the user queries is the model capturing or recovering. In other words, recall (r) means is the number of overlapping words appearing in both model and user queries divided by the number of words in user queries [17]. While precision (p) means is the number of words appearing in both model and user queries divided by the number of words in the model [17]. It is always best to compute both the recall and precision in ROUGE and then report the f1-score [9]. F1-score calculation is done by using the following equation.

$$F - score = \frac{2*p*r}{p+r} \tag{2}$$

However, we used ROUGE measure on unigrams level (ROUGE-1) and biograms level (ROUGE-2). Also, high accuracy was indicated using the BLEU measurement, which indicates a high accuracy when more words match between the result and the entered query. Figures 5 and 6 show some of the user queries tested against the model and their corresponding scores.

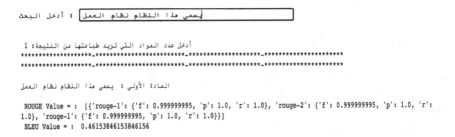

Fig. 5. The result of query that has a high similarity with the text in the dataset.

Figure 5 shows that the highest values of measures ROUGE-1, ROUGE-2 and BLEU are achieved when there is a high percentage of similarity between the user's query and the text in our dataset.

Exactly the contrary in Fig. 6, we believe that these lower values of F, P, and R do not mean mismatching between the user's query and the result, but the number of entered words by the user is much less than the number of result's words. This impacts the scores because the similarity of words is divided by the total number of words in the user's query or results as we have mentioned in P and R laws.

Figure 7 shows the average results of BLEU, ROUGE-1 and ROUGE-2 of the 100 user queries. However, on average our proposed system performance nearly

أدخل البحث : | توظيف المعوقين |

أدخل عدد المواد التي تريد طباعتها من النتيجة: 1

************************ ************************ ************************ ************************
************************ ************************ ************************ ************************

المادة الثامنة والثلاثون : ويحظر على العامل الاشتغال ، ال يجوز لصاحب ا لعمل توظيف العامل في مهنة غير المهنة المدونة
في رخصة عمله ، في غير مهنته قبل انخاذ الإجراءات النظامية لتغيير المهنة

ROUGE Value = : [{'rouge-1': {'f': 0.062499998828125014, 'p': 0.5, 'r': 0.03333333333333333}, 'rouge-2': {'f': 0.0,
'p': 0.0, 'r': 0.0}, 'rouge-1': {'f': 0.0769230755029586, 'p': 0.5, 'r': 0.041666666666666664}}]
BLEU Value = : 0.07547169811320754

Fig. 6. The result of query that has a moderate similarity with the test in the dataset.

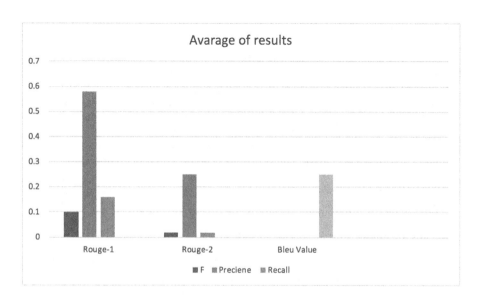

Fig. 7. The average results to evaluate 100 queries.

reached 0.6 using ROUGE-1 (P), and above 0.3 using ROUGE-2 (P) and BLEU
measurements.

In summary, we can say that our system helps people who are familiar with
the words used in the documents of Ministry of Human Resources and Social
Development to get their desired answer in an effective way.

5   Conclusion and Future Work

We implemented an automatic approach for the search engine of the Ministry of
Labor system of the Ministry of Human Resources and Social Development in
the Kingdom of Saudi Arabia. We created a dataset from the original document
from the website of the Ministry of Labor, and we estimated the similarity

between words in a query and each chapter in the document. The more relevant documents were retrieved as an answer to the user. A limitation of the proposed System is that the form of the words in the query must have some similarity as the words in the Ministry of Labor system's dataset to return a high accurate results and this is acceptable at this stage as most user of the Ministry of Labor systems are more familiar with the vocabulary used in its documents.

Future work should include developing a question-answering system that deals with the semantics of words in order to improve the accuracy of a meaning search of a query, creating a dialogue between the user and the system in order to retrieve information more specific to the Ministry of Labor system, and expanding the task for use with more than one system.

References

1. PyPI. https://pypi.org/project/docx2txt/
2. The system of labor, the ministry of human resources and social development, in the kingdom of Saudi Arabia. https://hrsd.gov.sa/ar/policies
3. Al-Chalabi, H., Ray, S., Shaalan, K.: Semantic based query expansion for arabic question answering systems. In: 2015 First International Conference on Arabic Computational Linguistics (ACLing), pp. 127–132. IEEE (2015)
4. Al-Jedady, A.A., Al-Kabi, M.N., Alsmadi, I.M.: Fast arabic query matching for compressed arabic inverted indices. Int. J. Database Theory Appl. 5(4), 81–94 (2012)
5. AlMaayah, M., Sawalha, M., Abushariah, M.A.: Towards an automatic extraction of synonyms for quranic arabic wordnet. Int. J. Speech Technol. 19(2), 177–189 (2016)
6. Atwan, J., Mohd, M.: Arabic query expansion: a review. Asian J. Inf. Technol. 16(10), 754–770 (2017)
7. Callison-Burch, C., Osborne, M., Koehn, P.: Re-evaluation the role of bleu in machine translation research. In: 11th Conference of the European Chapter of the Association for Computational Linguistics (2006)
8. Laurent, D., Séguéla, P., Nègre, S.: Qa better than IR? In: Proceedings of the Workshop on Multilingual Question Answering-MLQA 2006 (2006)
9. Lin, C.Y.: Rouge: a package for automatic evaluation of summaries. In: Text Summarization Branches Out, pp. 74–81 (2004)
10. Malhas, R., Elsayed, T.: Ayatec: building a reusable verse-based test collection for arabic question answering on the holy qur'an. ACM Trans. Asian Low Resour. Lang. Inf. Process. 19, 781–7821 (2020)
11. Mervin, R.: An overview of question answering system. Int. J. Res. Adv. Technol. (IJRATE) 1 (2013)
12. Moukdad, H.: Lost in cyberspace: How do search engines handle arabic queries? In: Proceedings of the Annual Conference of CAIS/Actes du congrès annuel de l'ACSI (2004)
13. Rosso, P., Benajiba, Y., Lyhyaoui, A.: Towards an arabic question answering system (2006)
14. Salton, G., Buckley, C.: Term-weighting approaches in automatic text retrieval. Inf. Process. Manag. 24(5), 513–523 (1988)

15. Sanan, M., Rammal, M., Zreik, K.: Internet arabic search engines studies. In: 2008 3rd International Conference on Information and Communication Technologies: From Theory to Applications, pp. 1–8. IEEE (2008)
16. Scholer, F., Williams, H.E., Yiannis, J., Zobel, J.: Compression of inverted indexes for fast query evaluation. In: Proceedings of the 25th Annual International ACM SIGIR Conference on Research and Development in Information Retrieval, pp. 222–229 (2002)
17. Steinberger, J., Ježek, K.: Evaluation measures for text summarization. Comput. Inf. **28**(2), 251–275 (2012)
18. Suleiman, D., Awajan, A.: Comparative study of word embeddings models and their usage in arabic language applications. In: 2018 International Arab Conference on Information Technology (ACIT), pp. 1–7. IEEE (2018)
19. Suleiman, D., Awajan, A.A., Al Etaiwi, W.: Arabic text keywords extraction using word2vec. In: 2019 2nd International Conference on new Trends in Computing Sciences (ICTCS), pp. 1–7. IEEE (2019)
20. Tawileh, W., et al.: Evaluation of five web search engines in arabic language. In: LWA, pp. 221–228 (2010)
21. Zeid, M.S., Belal, N.A., El-Sonbaty, Y.: Arabic question answering system using graph ontology. In: Silhavy, R., Silhavy, P., Prokopova, Z. (eds.) CoMeSySo 2020. AISC, vol. 1294, pp. 212–224. Springer, Cham (2020). https://doi.org/10.1007/978-3-030-63322-6_17
22. Zhong, B., He, W., Huang, Z., Love, P.E., Tang, J., Luo, H.: A building regulation question answering system: a deep learning methodology. Adv. Eng. Inf. **46**, 101195 (2020)
23. Zouaoui, S., Rezeg, K.: A novel quranic search engine using an ontology-based semantic indexing. Arab. J. Sci. Eng. **46**, 1–22 (2021)

Adaptive Encryption Model of Internet Public Opinion Information Based on Big Data

Yanjing Lu[1]($\boxtimes$) and Jiajuan Fang[2]

[1] Zhengzhou Technical College, Zhengzhou 450121, China
luyanjing23233@yeah.net
[2] Department of Software Engineering, Zhengzhou Technical College, Zhengzhou
450121, China

Abstract. The traditional information encryption model takes advantage of the ergodicity of chaotic system, and processes encryption iteratively for many times. Aiming at the above problems, this paper constructs a big data-based network public opinion information adaptive encryption model. Reptiles are used to collect network public opinion information, and the public opinion information is replaced and diffused. After mining the association rules of public opinion information, the information is encrypted by Logistic mapping, and the encryption model is constructed. Compared with the two traditional encryption models, it is proved that the model has the advantages of good encryption effect, high efficiency and low cost, and can be used widely.

Keywords: Big data · Network public opinion · Adaptive encryption ·
Encryption model · Logistic mapping

1 Introduction

With the rapid popularization of the Internet, the Internet has become one of the main channels for the publication and dissemination of public opinions. At the same time, due to the use and development of various network services, the carriers and content forms of public opinion information also show the characteristics of diversification, including not only traditional e-mail, portal websites, blogs, post bars, forums, but also emerging microblogs, WeChat, etc., and the content of public opinion is not only loaded with news, comments, opinions forwarding, etc., but also various multimedia public opinions, showing great uncontrollability. Government agencies and related research institutions must understand and adhere to public opinion. If Internet public opinion is guided and controlled by lawbreakers, it is likely to endanger social security and stability [1]. However, in the era of big data, the various data generated by the Internet increase in the scale of PB every day, which poses new challenges to the analysis and processing of public opinion information. In addition to mining and distinguishing effective information from network public opinion information, in order to avoid the hidden dangers of social stability, network information security and other problems caused by the leakage of public

W. Fu et al. (Eds.): ICMTEL 2021, LNICST 387, pp. 344–353, 2021.
https://doi.org/10.1007/978-3-030-82562-1_32

opinion information, it is also necessary to adopt effective means to encrypt network public opinion information [2]. The expression forms of public opinion information are various, which can be text, graphics, images, sound, video and so on. Classical DES algorithm, AES algorithm or RSA algorithm is no longer suitable for network information encryption, because these encryption algorithms in the face of large capacity information encryption can not guarantee the encryption effect. The chaotic encryption model based on search mechanism makes use of the ergodicity of chaotic system and controls the number of iterations of chaotic system by the characters of text information. But this encryption model is inefficient and insecure, so it can be cracked by known plaintext attack.

Adaptive technology is a technology that, in the process of processing analytical problems, automatically adjusts the processing method according to the data characteristics of the processed data so as to adapt it to the statistical distribution characteristics of the processed data [3]. Adaptive technology is widely used in many fields such as machinery, manufacture, signal and so on. Therefore, based on the above analysis, this paper will build a big data-based network public opinion information adaptive encryption model, the following is the specific research process. The innovation part is that after mining the association rules of public opinion information, the encryption model of public opinion information is established, and the public opinion information is encrypted by Logistic mapping. Because of the diffusion nature of its association rules, the encryption process of network public opinion information is adaptive, that is, automatic adjustment of parameters, which is also the focus of this paper.

2 Big Data Based Adaptive Network Public Opinion Information Encryption Model

2.1 Internet Public Opinion Information Collection

The crawler completes the crawling task through the Downloader module, the DrawURLer module, and the FilterURLer module in turn, which are iterative, depending on the depth of the crawler site, and after the iteration, executes the DrawTexter module, from and through the following processes:

1) Web crawling: This process is intended to accomplish distributed parallel downloading of HTML text. First, the starting URL of the crawl is stored as a seed in the NEW URL, and then the hash value of the modulus N of the URL domain name (N indicates the number of data nodes in the cluster) is taken. Finally, the seed of the starting URL is distributed to the corresponding node of the starting URL value based on the computed hash value and the different results of the URL to run the subsequent program. During the reduce phase of the crawl process, you can take full advantage of the extensibility of the Big Data platform by assigning downloads to multiple threads at the same time, eventually placing the crawled web file in a file called Pages [4].

2) The process of extracting URL: firstly, the text of the Web page downloaded is parsed in a distributed and parallel manner, and then the original Web page files

of the previous stage are used as input for processing as the extracting URL. The method used to parse this procedure is a regular expression, and the parsed output is then placed in a folder named RAWURL.

3) URL deduplication: This process is run to filter separate URL links, as the extracted new URL may have been used before. To reduce the amount of crawling, the newly resolved URL is compared with the existing URL in the deduplication module to remove the URL that is repeatedly extracted [5].

4) Text extraction: After the iteration of Web page download, URL extraction, and URL deletion, needing to use regular expressions to compute the tag features of all the collected raw HTML to match the various attributes of the specified HTML extraction. Grasping Network Public Opinions by Matching Rule.

After the crawler collects the network public opinion information, the network public opinion information is processed by wavelet transform.

2.2 Public Opinion Information Processing

For the image in the public opinion information, firstly, needing to scramble the plaintext image, so that can change the pixel position of the image without changing the pixel value. The replacement method, also known as permutation transformation, is defined as follows [6]:

A set $A = (a_1, a_2, \cdots, a_n)$ is a finite set, bifurcated from itself as follows:

$$\sigma = \begin{pmatrix} a_1 & a_2 & \cdots & a_n \\ \sigma(a_1) & \sigma(a_2) & \cdots & \sigma(a_n) \end{pmatrix} \tag{1}$$

$$\sigma(a_i) \in A, 1 \leq i \leq n$$

The above bijection process is called permutation in a set A. If $|A| = n$, it is called n meta permutation.

Digital grayscale image is essentially a two-dimensional array of pixel grayscale values, that is, a matrix, if the matrix changes the value of the elements, it becomes another image. The purpose of scrambling is to rearrange the pixels of the original image to produce a new image, that is, to transform the position matrix of the original pixels into that of another permutation [7]. Although the scrambled image looks very different from the original image, the histogram of the image does not change.

In this paper, magic cube transform is used to process public opinion images. Using the rotation of the Rubik's Cube neutron block, the original surface of the Rubik's Cube will be completely disrupted by the idea, so that through the Rubik's Cube transform to achieve image scrambling.

For a matrix $I_{M \times N}$ corresponding to a digital image, the element $i_{l,k}$ of the matrix is the pixel gray value of the position (l, k) in the image, where $l = 1, 2, \cdots, M$, $k = 1, 2, \cdots, N$. The Magic Cube transformation of an image matrix is to rotate the row and column of the matrix. The rotation i_l of the row in the matrix can be seen as a circular movement of the row in a certain direction, and the rotation of the column can be seen as a similar process. The shift sum is obtained by a specific algorithm. When all the rows h_l and h_k columns of the image matrix are rotated once, the new image after the Rubik's cube transformation is obtained, that is $I'_{M \times N}$, the scrambled image $I_{M \times N}$, which has a relationship with the image [8]:

$$I'_{M \times N} = P(I_{M \times N}) \tag{2}$$

P represents the Rubik's Cube transformation. The scrambling transformation can be carried out not only in the space domain but also in the transform domain. Generally speaking, in terms of the complexity of implementation, the scrambling transformation algorithm in spatial domain is relatively simple to implement and requires less computation. By dividing the image into certain size blocks and performing the global scrambling transformation as a unit, the algorithm can achieve better encryption effect in the subsequent encryption process.

Image diffusion can change the pixel gray value itself, and at the same time ensure the algorithm's sensitivity to plaintext. Row scanning is to scan the corresponding matrix element of the image from the upper left corner, and establish the reversible operation relationship between the former pixel value and the latter pixel value by the diffusion function. Through this method, the effect of complete diffusion can be achieved. The diffusion algorithm uses modulo addition, as shown below, to achieve the value transfer function using summation, so that if the value of the previous pixel changes, this change can be passed to the next pixel. The aim of modulus is to control the result within the range of pixel value [9].

$$c_i = (p_i + c_{i-1}) \bmod L \tag{3}$$

Among them, p_i is the current position of the pixel value, c_{i-1} is the previous pixel value of the encrypted output, L representing the image color level, for a gray image, L takes 256. If introduced the sequence generated by chaotic map into the diffusion function, it can get the diffusion encryption function that usually use. Suppose the elements x_i in the chaotic sequence generated by the chaotic map L represent the color level of the image. A sequence s_i of integers generated from a chaotic sequence can be computed as follows:

$$s_i = \left(x_i \times 10^{15}\right) \bmod L \tag{4}$$

The image is divided into several small blocks sequentially, and each pixel value of the ciphertext block is related to all pixel values of the original plaintext block. But scans usually need to be executed several times in a loop, because the diffusion can only be done inside each small block, so it is necessary to adjust the partition of encrypted blocks to achieve the diffusion of the entire plaintext.

2.3 Mining Public Opinion Information Association Rules

The increasing amount of online public opinion information has caused a lot of problems in protecting the security of public opinion data, and there are a lot of association rules between public opinion information. Alien attackers can collect the relevant public opinion information data by obtaining the association rules in the data. Therefore, before encrypting the public opinion data, it need to mine and hide the association rules in the public opinion data.

The data set $I = \{i_1, i_2, \cdots, i_m\}$ of network public opinion information is a collection of public opinion information data items D in the public opinion information data set T. For an item set X in the public opinion information dataset, the association rules between the item set and the public opinion information dataset are $X \rightarrow Y, X \subseteq I, Y \subseteq I, X \cap Y = \phi$.

This paper uses FP-tree frequency set algorithm to mine association rules of public opinion information data [10]. Firstly, the public opinion information database is scanned to record the frequent transactions in the public opinion information data set and its corresponding support. The formula for computing support for frequent transaction items is as follows:

$$\sup(X) = \frac{count(X)}{|D|} \tag{5}$$

In Formula (5), $count(X)$ is the number of transactions containing frequent transaction items in the transaction database corresponding to the network public opinion information data set; x is the total number of frequent transaction items in the transaction database. Create the FP-Tree root node based on the frequency items that are first scanned. If the frequent items do not have the same prefix in FP-Tree, a new branch is added; if the frequent items have the same prefix transaction items, only increase the number of nodes, to construct FP-tree. In FP-Tree, the path is traversed to find the minimum path whose support value is the sum of the support degrees of all nodes in the current path. Then the path of FP-Tree with minimum support is the association rules among the internal transaction items in the data set, that is, the association rules of public opinion data are mined. According to the association rules of public opinion information mined, the network public opinion information is encrypted by Logistic chaotic map.

2.4 Building Encryption Model

In this paper, a typical Logistic map is used as a chaotic system for generating encrypted sequences. The Logistic map is as follows:

$$\begin{cases} x_{n+1} = \mu x_n (1 - x_n) \\ 0 \le \mu \le 4 \\ x_n \in (0, 1) \end{cases} \tag{6}$$

The Logistic map iterates through the following equations:

$$x(t + 1) = rx(t)[1 - x(t)] \tag{7}$$

Among them, t is the synchronization for the iteration time, for any t, $x(t) \in [0, 1]$, r is an adjustable parameter. When parameters $r \in [0, 4]$, you can ensure $x(t)$ that the mapping is always inside $[0, 1]$. The equation exhibits different dynamic r limiting behaviors when different parameters are changed.

The encryption process steps are described below:

Step 1: Treat the encrypted public opinion information plaintext integer wavelet transform.

Step 2: Select the parameters μ and initial value x_0 of the Logistic map, replace it with the Logistic map, get the chaotic sequence, and discard the previous N_0 point, that is $N_0 + 1$, from the $N_0 + M \times N/4$ value to the end.

Step 3: The chaotic sequence obtained in Step 2 is diffused and converted to obtain the public opinion information after encryption and complete the encryption process.

So far, it have completed the research on the construction of adaptive encryption model of network public opinion information based on big data.

3 Experimental Study

Above, the paper studies the big data-based network public opinion information adaptive encryption model, this section will design an experiment to verify the effectiveness and feasibility of the encryption model.

3.1 Experimental Content

In this simulation, it compare the big data-based adaptive encryption model with the traditional search-based encryption model and the homomorphic encryption model, and compare it with the traditional network information encryption model. Through comparative experiments, the paper validates and analyzes the above model of network public opinion information adaptive encryption based on big data. The simulation experiment to run procedures in Visual Studio 2014 as the development environment, using the C + programming language to achieve efficient experimental content.

In the experimental index, the encryption overhead is represented by the authentication throughput before and after encryption coding, and the encryption effect is represented by the correlation between plaintext and ciphertext.

$$r_{xy} = \frac{\text{cov}(x, y)}{\sqrt{D(x) \cdot D(y)}} \tag{8}$$

In the above expression, x is plaintext; y is ciphertext; $\text{cov}(x, y)$ is covariance of plaintext and ciphertext; $D(x)$ is variance of plaintext; $D(y)$ is variance of ciphertext. In the process of experiment, the concrete data of corresponding index is recorded, and the experiment conclusion is obtained after analyzing and processing in MATLAB software. Process and analyze the experimental data, draw the corresponding conclusions, thus completing the simulation experiment preset verification goal.

3.2 Experimental Results

Take the text public opinion information as an example, the encryption effects of the 3 groups of information encryption models are shown in the following Fig. 1.

According to the above analysis, the experimental group encryption model can completely encrypt the text information, while the control group A model and the control

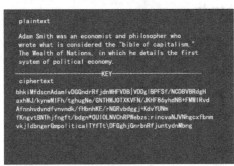

(a) Experimental group model

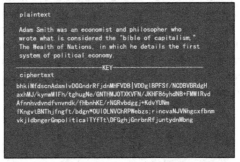

(b) Contrast group model A

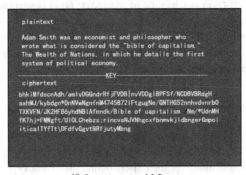

(c) Contrast group model A

(d) Contrast group model B

Fig. 1. Comparison of text encryption

group B model can not encrypt the text completely. Specifically, the encryption effect of the control group A model is better than that of the control group B.

The data of three kinds of network public opinion information encryption models are shown in the following table, and the relationship between the data in the table is analyzed (Table 1).

Table 1. Comparison of experimental data on encryption time consuming and correlation

Experimental data/GB	Experience group		Control group A		Control group B	
	Encryption time/S	Relevance	Encryption time/S	Relevance	Encryption time/S	Relevance
10	1.12	0.0146	1.16	0.0194	1.16	0.0229
20	1.18	0.0161	1.20	0.0199	1.22	0.0251
30	1.15	0.0140	1.19	0.0212	1.18	0.0245
35	1.22	0.0160	1.26	0.0196	1.25	0.0236
40	1.23	0.0162	1.31	0.0205	1.37	0.0253
45	1.24	0.0164	1.35	0.0192	1.43	0.0252
50	1.26	0.0152	1.39	0.0203	1.51	0.0215
55	1.27	0.0155	1.52	0.0201	1.56	0.0222
60	1.26	0.0145	1.68	0.0214	1.73	0.0229
65	1.24	0.0162	1.77	0.0195	1.82	0.0221
70	1.29	0.0151	1.86	0.0207	1.98	0.0244
80	1.28	0.0156	2.01	0.0209	2.24	0.0232

Analysis of the above table shows that when the data is less than 35 GB, the time difference of three encryption models is less than 0.04 s. With the increase of encrypted data, the time of B encryption increased rapidly, but the time of the other two groups increased slightly. When the data amount is less than 50 GB, the difference of encryption time between experimental group and control group A is less than 0.15 s. With the increase of encrypted data, the encrypted time of control group A increased rapidly, which was larger than that of control group B and less than that of experimental group B. The average encryption time of the three encryption models is 1.23 s in the experiment, 1.475 s in the A model and 1.54 s in the B model respectively. Compared with the other two models, the experimental model can reduce encryption time by at least 20% on average. The correlation between plaintext and ciphertext before and after encryption of experimental group is lower than that of the other two groups, which shows that the experimental group has better encryption effect.

Before and after the encryption of the transmission information, the authentication throughput of the public opinion data information in the network is shown in the Fig. 2, and the relationship between curves is analyzed.

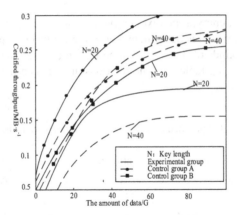

Fig. 2. Comparison of data authentication throughput before and after encryption coding

According to the relationship between the curves in the graph above, the data authentication throughput of the experimental group is faster than that of the other two groups after encrypting different data. Except for the experimental group model, the authentication throughput of the other two groups showed an increasing trend, while the authentication throughput of the experimental group tended to be stable after increasing for a period of time. The higher the authentication throughput is, the greater the encryption overhead of the encryption model is. It can be concluded from the above that the experimental group model can still guarantee a lower encryption overhead when encrypting data.

To sum up, the big data-based network public opinion information adaptive encryption model has the advantages of high encryption efficiency, good encryption effect, low cost, compared with traditional encryption model.

4   Closing Remarks

In order to ensure the security of public opinion information, this paper constructs a big data-based adaptive encryption model of online public opinion information. Compared with the traditional model, the experimental results show that the proposed model has better performance.

References

1. Hamami, F., Dahlan, I.A., Prakosa, S.W., et al.: Implementation face recognition attendance monitoring system for lab surveillance with hash encryption. J. Phys. Conf. Ser. **1641**(1), 012084 (6pp) (2020)
2. Hussain, A., Kiah, M.L.M., Anuar, N.B., et al.: Performance and security challenges digital rights management (DRM) approaches using fog computing for data provenance: a survey. J. Med. Imaging Health Inform. **10**(10), 2404–2420 (2020)
3. Qi, H.: Double encryption method of network privacy information based on dynamic key selection. J. Heilongjiang Univ. Technol. (Compr. Edn.) **20**(03), 89–93 (2020)

4. Chongrui, T., Zhaoxiang, L., Yuxin, L.: Simulation of anonymous privacy protection method based on dynamic data mining. Computer **36**(11), 171–174 233 (2019)
5. Xin, D., Ji, J., Jing, F., et al.: Efficient fully homomorphic encryption scheme using ring-LWE. J. Phys. Conf. Ser. **1738**(1), 012105 (8pp) (2021)
6. Wei, T., Qiping, H., Tangzhi, W.: Research on location big data encryption method based on privacy protection. J. Anhui Electr. Eng. Prof. Tech. Coll. **24**(01), 118–122 (2019)
7. Fu, W., Liu, S., Srivastava, G.: Optimization of big data scheduling in social networks. Entropy **21**(9), 902 (2019)
8. Liu, S., Li, Z., Zhang, Y., et al.: Introduction of key problems in long-distance learning and training. Mob. Netw. Appl. **24**(1), 1–4 (2019)
9. Liu, S., Liu, D., Srivastava, G., et al.: Overview and methods of correlation filter algorithms in object tracking. Complex Intell. Syst. (2020). https://doi.org/10.1007/s40747-020-00161-4
10. Niu, J., Li, X., Gao, J., et al.: Blockchain-based anti-key-leakage key aggregation searchable encryption for IoT. IEEE Internet Things J. **7**(2), 1502–1518 (2020)

Intelligent Classification System of Financial Statistics Information Based on Recurrent Neural Network

Conggang Lv[✉]

Jiangxi Tourism and Commerce Vocational College, Nancang 330039, China

Abstract. The establishment of the information classification system plays a pivotal role in the fiscal information disclosure system. The fiscal statistical information classification is the basis for compiling the fiscal information disclosure catalogue and the prerequisite for the construction of the fiscal information disclosure catalog system. In order to better realize the effective processing of financial information, this research proposes an intelligent classification system for financial statistics information based on recurrent neural networks. First, optimize the system hardware structure and calculate the information security to ensure the accuracy and safety of financial statistics. Finally, it is confirmed by experiments that the intelligent classification system of financial statistics information based on recurrent neural network works better in actual application.

Keywords: Neural network · Financial statistics · Information classification · Information security

1 Introduction

At present, the financial information is basically provided by departments. When it is necessary to search across departments, users must judge which information is related to their own needs and which departments are stored in, which makes the query more difficult [1–3]. Therefore, it is necessary to break the barriers set by departments, put all the information related to something together in the form of theme service, and put the judgment that users need to make before in the financial department as far as possible, so as to improve the efficiency of financial information query. This requires us to consider the standard of classification system to ensure the establishment of a unified and standardized financial information disclosure catalogue system, so as to fundamentally ensure the overall management and macro grasp of financial information disclosure [4, 5].

The promotion of fiscal information disclosure is an inevitable requirement for scientific governance, democratic governance, and governance according to law. It is also an important manifestation of promoting social democracy, improving the social legal system, and building a country under the rule of law. It also makes financial information resources known to the public, fully shared and effective by the society The only way

W. Fu et al. (Eds.): ICMTEL 2021, LNICST 387, pp. 354–367, 2021.
https://doi.org/10.1007/978-3-030-82562-1_33

to use. Many issues are involved in the implementation of fiscal information disclosure, and the research, compilation, and release of the fiscal information disclosure catalog is undoubtedly the foundation and core of the entire fiscal information disclosure work, and it is also a concrete manifestation of the implementation and implementation of the "Regulations." Therefore, the public financial information catalog has become an important part of the public financial information work. Among them, the information classification system and core metadata are the core and foundation of the catalog system.

Recurrent neural network is an effective artificial intelligence algorithm, which has powerful memory function, fast convergence speed and good fitting effect. Therefore, it is applied to this study.

Therefore, this paper intends to discuss the classification system of the public financial information catalogue. It provides the entrance of financial information query and plays an auxiliary and navigational role in user retrieval. With the gradual development of financial information disclosure, the following problems need to be studied and solved: how to break the restriction of financial information, the relationship between the stability requirements of information classification and the change of financial institutions, the continuous improvement of various classification approaches, and the efficiency of information classification.

This paper uses the recurrent neural network to generate independent text information packets, and adjusts the parameters of reinforcement learning while building the framework of generating confrontation network, so as to build the hardware execution environment of recognition system. On this basis, the embedded network framework is built. With the help of EEPROM chip and ld3320 chip circuit, the integration process of network data information identification implementation behavior is supervised, and the software execution environment of the system is built.

2   Design of Intelligent Classification System for Financial Statistics Information

2.1   Hardware Configuration of Intelligent Classification System for Financial Statistics

From the perspective of the development of the Internet, it is easier and more acceptable for people to find information using search engines than to browse through classification levels. However, this method also has shortcomings. In most cases, users do not know the specific name or content of the target file when searching for the required financial information, and users have different information needs. This requires information provision and service departments to describe the characteristics of the information in a multidimensional manner in order to provide users with multiple entries and facilitate users' browsing and inquiries [6–8]. And in information classification, different classification methods can also be used, such as subject classification, organization classification, genre classification, service object classification, etc.

This paper designs and proposes an intelligent classification system of financial statistics information based on recurrent neural network. Firstly, the overall design framework of the system is constructed, and the software function model is constructed according to different levels; finally, the rationality of the system design is analyzed.

The hardware of the recurrent neural network intelligent classification system for financial statistics information is designed based on the principle of recurrent neural network. The recurrent neural network provides a dynamic and easy-scalable way for resources under the network-related service program, and according to the needs of users, Big data is configured in a distributed manner, and based on the SOA component model system, the compatibility of the principle of recurrent neural network is increased, thereby improving the stability of automatic classification and processing of big data.

Cui-techpnxp270 technology processing platform is used as the core content of hardware configuration for intelligent classification of non intrusive information. The platform selects ers2.4 processing chip, pxan-2.4 model as configuration structure, and Intel casxalen embedded microprocessor as the core module, which effectively keeps the main frequency of image processing between 420–462 MHz. In order to better guarantee the performance of intelligent classification of non intrusive load information, pna2.6 microprocessor and Intel speed step dynamic monitoring technology are added to the system. In the process of designing the hardware configuration of the system, considering the universality and long-term characteristics of the intelligent classification of information, we need to consider its compatibility and ensure that the system can be upgraded to pnxa2.4–2.8 level, so as to optimize the core board, motherboard, processor, LCD serial port and other modules. The hardware block diagram of the financial information intelligent classification platform is shown in Fig. 1.

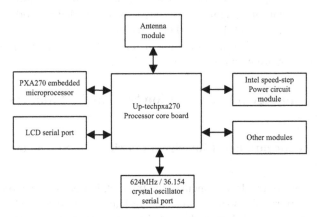

Fig. 1. System hardware block diagram

The design of data collector mainly includes the control chip of titanium network and single chip microcomputer, which transmits the collected data to the big data automatic processor through the interface of recurrent neural network principle. The power supply of the data collector generates 5 V voltage, which is transmitted to the voltage regulator above the MCU through the pin of the MCU, providing 3 V voltage for the work above the MCU [9, 10]. Then the 3 V voltage above the MCU is transmitted to other devices with the remaining 3 V power supply through the pin for its use. After the transmission of information and pin voltage, MCU exchanges information with other microcontrollers. After the circuit adjustment, the network signal based on the principle of recurrent neural network is transmitted to the A/D converter above the MCU by using the pin of p25, and the network signal is converted into data through the A/D converter, so as to realize the acquisition of big data based on the principle of recurrent neural network.

The design requirements of the financial information intelligent classification system are fast information collection and large storage capacity. Based on the design requirements, the data processor is further optimized, and its structure is shown in Fig. 2.

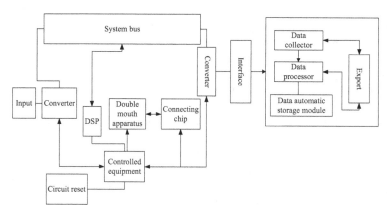

Fig. 2. Data processor architecture

It can be seen from Fig. 2 that the financial data processor mainly includes: bus transmission processor, connected circuit, control device, main control computer, external memory, and circuit reset. Detecting the memory occupancy ratio and CPU occupancy rate, the basic situation of the hardware configuration of related systems such as application servers and databases, and monitoring the operating status of the software platform can guarantee the quality of the system. The system configuration obtained by recording the detection indicators is shown in Table 1.

Table 1. Hardware configuration data of financial information classification

	Database The server	Application The server	Client
Number of CPUs	5	5	2
CPU type	–	–	P43.2G
Memory	16G	16G	512M
Hard disk	2 * 120G	2 * 320G	–
Network card	4 * 1000M	4 * 1000M	100M

Refer to the information in Table 2 and combine the multi-label classification technology to extract the relevant data of the various hardware configurations in the system for comparison and analysis. The system data format can be optimized, and the deviations in the system data can be found in time to properly handle the financial information. In the overall structure of the system, the data input and output are designed based on the trigger device and the acquisition device. The data-triggered main line and the simulated main line jointly construct a data storage area, collect and transmit financial big data to the main control computer, and realize the system design through the data preprocessing module of the simulated main line. The main simulation route of fiscal big data is to transfer the fiscal big data in the classification system to the circular data buffer area through the dispatch of dynamic gain codes, and analyze it.

The design process of financial big data classification system is mainly: the signal flow of buffer and the signal flow transmitted by controller fuse with each other and flow to PCI bus. According to the scheduling of data management and the analysis of evaluator, the data signal is connected through QoS value. Its storage functions include:

(1) Apply the PCI bus to the processor of the external system controller for buffer operation.
(2) The data signal processing chip merges with the external storage space to realize the communication between humans and machines.
(3) Dynamic gain control refers to: the corresponding dynamic gain code is designed through the processor assigned by the computer to stabilize a large amount of data within a certain range.

The data storage module uses C8051F series MCU to complete the data storage. C8051F series of single-chip microcomputer set into a fully mixed SOC chip, its built-in flash memory program has a large storage space. The hardware working principle of C8051F series MCU and at45db80 is shown in Fig. 3.

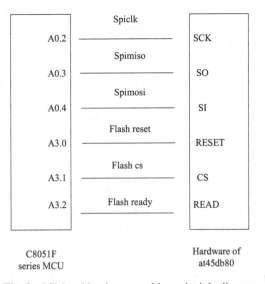

Fig. 3. SCM and hardware working principle diagram

It can be seen from Fig. 3 that the pins P0.2, p0.3 and P0.4 of C8051F series MCU are set as the main signal line of MoSi. Each main line is always connected with the hardware of at45db80 and the signal is output. Connect and reset the chips in the hardware of P3.0, P3.1, p3.2 and at45db80. C8051F series single chip microcomputer uses a one-time data storage with the memory opened instantaneously. The process is: first clear the representation of the serial peripheral interface, and then input bytes into the automatic storage of the data. If the detected serial peripheral interface is composed of at45db80 hardware, then the automatic data storage is finished.

According to the structure of the above-mentioned overall framework, the storage hardware is designed. The hardware modules mainly include: circuit synchronization, circuit reset, trigger device inside the module, circuit program loading, circuit storage interface. The circuit synchronization switch of the financial big data classification system should select a 12-bit sampling data module, and the modulated circuit should be subjected to dynamic gain feedback sampling. The linear dynamics of the classification system of financial big data can fluctuate in the range of −50–50 Bd. According to the characteristics of the Internet of Things environment, the functional module of automatic network interface is adopted, and the feedback dynamic gain module is designed. Based on this, the fiscal data storage sampling circuit diagram is optimized, and the specific structure is shown in Fig. 4.

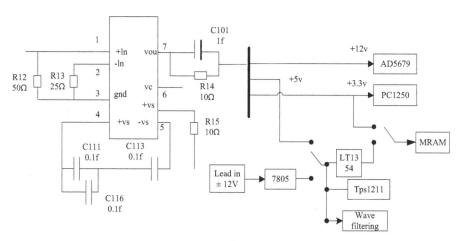

Fig. 4. Sampling circuit diagram of financial data storage

At the port of the clock circuit of the financial big data, the low-pass filter of the AD2014 4-stage switching power supply is placed, so that the output voltage has a certain degree of stability. Through the custom buffer function of the shared port, real-time classification between the host and big data transmission is realized.

The sampling circuit of the clock synchronization system based on financial big data storage can be designed to connect with the external IO device interface. The module of 12 bit sampling data set in the data channel is replaced by 16 bit, the bipolar sample input method of ±15 V is used, and the converter of EOC signal is used to convert tout into cnnst. The converted sequence code is used to realize the storage capacity expansion of financial big data. The external interface of IO device uses the dynamic gain bidirectional channel of ad231 to control the circuit, and connects with the data of 95230a. Through the common power supply of external IO interface power supply and core power supply, the continuous storage of data is realized, so that the output waveform data has certain adaptive performance.

2.2 Optimization of Operating Algorithm of Financial Information Classification System

As we all know, once the financial information classification system is established, it should be relatively stable to facilitate use. With the development and progress of society, the management mode of government departments is constantly changing. Some departments will gradually develop and strengthen their functions, but some departments may gradually weaken or even disappear. At the same time, the merger of financial departments, the change of management scope and the change of document management system will affect the classification of financial information. This will cause difficulties or inconsistencies in the classification of new and old government information, which are the problems that need to be considered in our follow-up research.

In order to better meet the information needs of users, the operation algorithm optimization of the financial information classification system is designed. In the classification system, the most important should be the subject classification, but other classifications also need to be improved. In the description, the recursive neural network was used to label the financial information, such as name, subject, date of creation, genre, etc. Then use the neural network to identify the data and obtain the information of the dynamic control object, so as to solve the nonlinear problem in the traditional algorithm and realize the dynamic adjustment and optimization of the financial information. Figure 5 shows the block diagram of the designed recurrent neural network classification.

Using recurrent neural network method to classify financial information, on the one hand, we need to continue to improve and refine the subject classification, on the other hand, we also need to classify from other ways to facilitate users' search.

Financial information classification is similar to topic based text classification, which is a guided learning process. According to the pre-defined financial information classification system, the financial information classification is automatically determined. Therefore, the classification of financial information can be formally described as: given the class label set $C = \{c_1, c_2, \ldots c_m\}$ and financial information set $D = \{d_1, d_2, \ldots d_n\}$ of financial information, we can learn the relationship model $f : D \times C \rightarrow \{0, 1\}$ from the financial information set to the category set, and determine whether the new financial information f belongs to category c_i according to the relationship model d, that is:

$$f(d, c_i) = \begin{cases} 1 \ d \in c_i \\ 0 \ d \notin c_i \end{cases} \tag{1}$$

Most of the fiscal information classification research is a single label classification problem, at this time, the f function is a one-to-one mapping. There are also a few studies that regard it as a multi-label classification problem, and the corresponding f function is a one-to-many mapping.

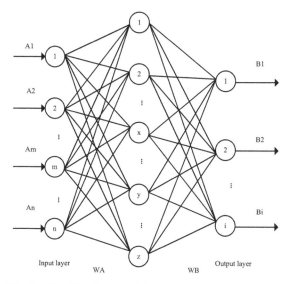

Fig. 5. Classification principle of recurrent neural network

Financial text classification studies the problem of single label classification. C represents all labeled financial information sets, and cdt represents a candidate feature word. If there is no cdt in C', the number of financial information. Before applying likelihood ratio test to feature selection, the following two hypotheses are examined:

$$(H1) : P(d \in C|cdt \in d) = p = P(d \in C|\overline{cdt} \in d) \tag{2}$$

$$(H2): P(d \in C|cdt \in d) = p_1 \neq p_2 = P(d \in C|\overline{cdt} \in d) \tag{3}$$

Assumption H_1 is the formalization of the independence assumption, which means that the appearance of cdt and the appearance of financial information d in financial information d are independent of each other. Hypothesis H_2 is the formalization of the non-independence hypothesis. If the appearance of p_1, p_2, and cdt is related to the appearance of d, then p_1 and p_2 can be calculated using maximum likelihood estimation, which are:

$$p = (f_{11} + f_{21})/(f_{11} + f_{12} + f_{21} + f_{22}) \tag{4}$$

$$p_1 = f_{11}/(f_{11} + f_{12}) \tag{5}$$

$$p_2 = f_{21}/(f_{21} + f_{22}) \tag{6}$$

If it is a Bernoulli event, then all the above hypotheses satisfy binomial distribution

$$b(p, k, n) = \binom{n}{k} p^k (1 - p)^{n-k} f(d, c_i) \tag{7}$$

The logarithm of the likelihood ratio is:

$$\log \lambda = \log \frac{L(H_1)}{L(H_2)}$$

$$= \log \frac{b(p, f_{11}, f_{11} + f_{12}) * b(p, f_{21}, f_{21} + f_{22})}{b(p_1, f_{11}, f_{11} + f_{12}) * b(p_2, f_{21}, f_{21} + f_{22})} \tag{8}$$

λ is only a concrete form of likelihood ratio, while $-2 \log \lambda$ approximates x^2 distribution:

$$-2 \log \lambda = \begin{cases} -2 * lr & p_2 < p_1 \\ 0 & p_2 \geq p_1 \end{cases} \tag{9}$$

Among them:

$$lr = (f_{11} + f_{21}) \log p + (f_{12} + f_{22}) \log(1 - p) - f_{11} \log p_1$$
$$-f_{12} \log(1 - p_1) - f_{21} \log p_2 - f_{22} \log(1 - p_2) \tag{10}$$

The larger the value of $-2 \log \lambda$, the stronger the correlation between cdt and category C, and the better the ability to distinguish categories, the more helpful it is to distinguish C from C'.

$$l_{avg}(cdt) = \sum_{i=1}^{m} \Pr(c_i) * l(cdt, c_i) \tag{11}$$

The detailed process of feature selection algorithm based on LRT is given, which is used to select the feature words with the most classification ability. For each category., and the corresponding corpus each word appearing in it is regarded as C_i candidate feature word cdt, and its likelihood ratio $l(cdt, c_i)$ with category C and is calculated. One of the methods to calculate the final likelihood ratio score of cdt is to calculate the average value:

$$l_{avg}(cdt) = \sum_{i=1}^{m} \Pr(c_i) * l(cdt, c_i) \tag{12}$$

The corresponding feature selection method is referred to as LRTavg in this article. Another way is to find the maximum value.

$$l_{max}(cdt) = \max_{i=1}^{m} \{l(cdt, c_i)\} \tag{13}$$

In many cases, users know what they want when looking for financial information, but sometimes they need to search or query the same kind of information or related information. At this time, the use of retrieval alone can not achieve the best results. In the process of financial information disclosure, it adopts the way of providing subject services according to the classification of service objects (audience), such as dividing the information service objects into citizens, enterprises and foreign citizens, providing specific relevant information for each object, and then clustering according to what they do. Its advantage is that even if the information is not clear, users can browse through the guidance provided by the classification results and quickly find the corresponding information.

2.3   Realization of Intelligent Classification of Financial Statistical Information

In order to ensure the effect of intelligent classification of financial statistical information, it is necessary to establish an information release system and a powerful information retrieval platform, which can ensure the needs of information release and information retrieval. Just like the current Internet, most problems can be solved with search engines. This method is technically easy to implement, consumes less time and energy, and has a lower cost, and the goal can be achieved quickly. Then, how to correctly handle the relationship between the two is not only related to the respective development of information classification and integrated retrieval, but also determines the future trend of my country's fiscal information disclosure work.

Financial project information coding is not only the embodiment of project information classification system, but also the basis of WBS for computer management and PMIS application. The information coding of the project needs to go through a certain process, as shown in Fig. 6.

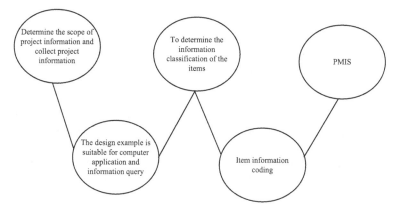

Fig. 6. Optimization of information classification coding process

Financial project information coding includes project structure decomposition and coding, work task decomposition and coding, unit code of project implementation parties, project contract code, design drawing catalogue and coding, design change classification and coding, financial information classification and coding, etc. project decomposition coding and work task coding are the basis of many coding. The description of financial disclosure information can be classified and described through multiple dimensions. Through the following four dimensions: subject classification, genre classification, organization classification and service object classification.

Among them, subject classification: the method of classifying information resources based on their content attributes—themes. Genre classification: that is, the method of classifying information resources based on their external attributes-genres. Institution (department) classification: the method of classifying information resources based on the responsible unit—department or institution. Service object classification: the method of classifying information resources based on the specific groups targeted by the audience.

Specifically applied to the PMIS system, the process and work content of the project coding system are shown in Fig. 7.

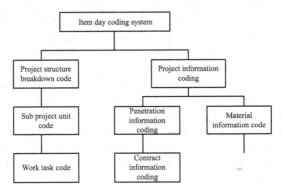

Fig. 7. Classification of abnormal financial information

Project structure coding is the core of the identification system, which enables the information generated in the whole process of project implementation to be linked and classified through the system. All kinds of different information, such as progress information, investment information, capital information, quality information and contract information, can be connected with each other on this basis.

Financial information intelligent classification is the exact opposite of traditional distributed and intrusive information intelligent classification. It has simple hardware configuration and complex analysis software. Analysis software can collect data for complex mathematical analysis and obtain useful information. The system recognizes or estimates the type, operating status and related parameters of each load based on this information. Through the analysis of these data, the system operation law of multi-label classification non-invasive load monitoring can be better studied, so as to realize more intelligent monitoring.

In the process of monitoring data transmission, when the data detected by the non-invasive intelligent classification of information fluctuates up and down within the normal range, the intelligent classification of information automatically defaults to the normal state of the monitored financial data, and no alarm is required. Once the collected characteristic data exceeds the normal range, the information intelligent classification will automatically check the fault area and send an alarm in time, so as to ensure the safety of the system operation. The specific operation flow of the non-invasive intelligent classification of load information is shown in Fig. 8.

When the attributes of a certain dimension of financial disclosure information change, it will not affect the attributes of other dimensions, thus ensuring the stability of the catalog system to the greatest extent. Each category should have at least one corresponding field in the metadata.

In the actual implementation process, the classification methods do not necessarily have to be adopted at the same time, but at least the subject classification must be adopted. After the conditions are mature, other classification methods will be gradually adopted

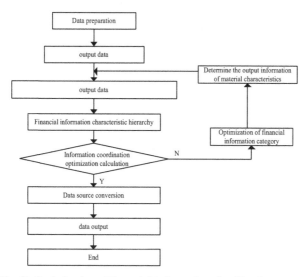

Fig. 8. Optimization of financial information classification process

in order to carry out a more comprehensive and systematic information classification of financial information.

3 Analysis of Results

In order to verify the rationality of the design of the financial statistics information intelligent classification system, this paper takes the data of a financial company as an example. Set the DAC resolution in the controller to 16 bits. Set the power resolution in the amplifier to 15 bits. The system is composed of three computers. The hardware configuration of the system is Intel dual - core 2.6 GHz processor and 16 GB memory size. The experimental parameter settings are shown in Table 2.

Table 2. Experimental parameters

Parameter	Numerical
Number of computers	3 sets
Processor	3.5 GHz
Memory	32 GB
Database	SQL server
Server	Single/double disk array

Based on the above experimental environment, the operation effect of this paper and the traditional system is compared, and the detection results are recorded, as shown in Fig. 9.

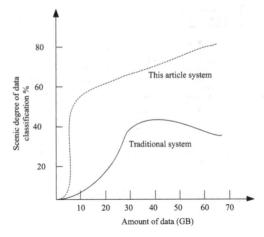

Fig. 9. Comparison test results

As can be seen from Fig. 9, in the actual application process, compared with the traditional system, the financial information classification system designed in this paper has higher accuracy, better processing effect on massive data, and better guarantee the security of financial information processing.

4 Conclusion

In this research, some analysis and discussion of the information classification system in the fiscal information disclosure catalog system are carried out, and an intelligent classification system of fiscal statistics information based on recurrent neural network is proposed. The experimental results prove the effectiveness of the system, which can better assist the implementation and development of the classification and processing of fiscal information in my country.

References

1. Hope, J.: Compare nationwide financial aid statistics with your institution's practices. Success. Regist. **18**(2), 9 (2018)
2. Hope, J.: Compare nationwide financial aid statistics with your institution's practices. Enrollment Manage. Rep. **22**(1), 8 (2018)
3. Alanis, A.Y.: Electricity prices forecasting using artificial neural networks. IEEE Lat. Am. Trans. **16**(1), 105–111 (2018). https://doi.org/10.1109/TLA.2018.8291461
4. Lin, X., et al.: All-optical machine learning using diffractive deep neural networks. Science **361**(6406), 1004–1008 (2018). https://doi.org/10.1126/science.aat8084
5. Zhang, L., Tao, J.: Research on degeneration model of neural network for deep groove ball bearing based on feature fusion. Algorithms **11**(2), 21–22 (2018)
6. Du, B., He, Y., He, Y., et al.: Intelligent classification of silicon photovoltaic cell defects based on eddy current thermography and convolution neural network. IEEE Trans. Ind. Inf. **16**(10), 6242–6251 (2020)

7. Xing, Z., Li, G.: Intelligent classification method of remote sensing image based on big data in spark environment. Int. J. Wirel. Inf. Netw. **26**(3), 183–192 (2019)
8. Liu, S., Lu, M.Y., Li, H.S., et al.: Prediction of gene expression patterns with generalized linear regression model. Front. Genet. **10**, 120 (2019)
9. Fu, W.N., Liu, S., Srivastava, G.: Optimization of big data scheduling in social networks. Entropy **21**(9), 902–918 (2019)
10. Liu, S., Li, Z.J., Zhang, Y.D., et al.: Introduction of key problems in long-distance learning and training. Mob. Netw. Appl. **24**(1), 1–4 (2019)

Design and Implementation of Financial Management Analysis Based on Big Data Platform of Psychiatric Hospital

Meiying Su[(✉)] and Xinlei Chen

Suzhou Guangji Hospital, Suzhou 215000, Jiangsu, China

Abstract. Improve the hospital's core competitiveness such as service level, medical quality, management level and financial indicators through information construction. The improvement of financial management also depends on the development of information technology. Use the construction of a big data platform as an opportunity to realize the informatization of financial management. This article mainly introduces the technical difficulties of data collection and data fusion in the construction of hospital big data platform. It uses ETL data collection tools to collect data, builds the operation data center ODR, and designs the software architecture of the big data platform. And customize the data collection requirements and business realization functions of the big data platform through the characteristics of data requirements in financial management, and also consider data security in the construction of the platform. Use the hospital's big data platform to improve the hospital's clinical, management, and scientific research capabilities.

Keywords: Psychiatric specialty · Big data · Financial management

1 Introduction

The improvement of medical service level is inseparable from medical information construction. With the rapid development of information technology, more and more hospitals are accelerating the implementation of various information construction projects based on the medical information platform HIS system of artificial intelligence, big data analysis and the Internet of Things [1]. To improve the core competitiveness of hospitals such as service level, medical quality, management level, and financial indicators [2, 3]. Informatization can not only improve the efficiency of doctors, but also give doctors more time to serve patients. Improve the hospital's management level and comprehensive development strength, and show the image of a high-tech hospital [4]. The improvement of financial management level also depends on the development and construction of information technology [5].

At present, big data is not only a simple new technology, but also another disruptive technological innovation in the ICT industry after the mobile Internet and cloud computing. It is also an important part of the current national information technology development strategy [6]. To build the big data platform of Guangji Hospital based on

© ICST Institute for Computer Sciences, Social Informatics and Telecommunications Engineering 2021
Published by Springer Nature Switzerland AG 2021. All Rights Reserved
W. Fu et al. (Eds.): ICMTEL 2021, LNICST 387, pp. 368–376, 2021.
https://doi.org/10.1007/978-3-030-82562-1_34

the relevant opinions of the Suzhou Municipal Health Commission's big data platform construction guidance. Use the big data platform to solve and improve the hospital's clinical, management, and scientific research capabilities [5, 7].

With the comprehensive development and deepening of hospital informatization in the past 20 years, hospital business data has exploded, showing the characteristics of big data. In the era of big data, how to obtain as much useful data as possible from big data requires consideration of hospital financial management, and the implementation of decision-making must be closely connected with the hospital's financial management software system [8, 9]. At the same time, it is necessary to combine the actual problems that need to be solved in the development of the current psychiatric hospital [10]. Business-oriented, according to the status quo of the hospital's financial management, such as the hospital's financial management capabilities, revenue and expenditure status, and the actual situation of budget management, grasp the development direction of the hospital's financial management and determine the information requirements of the system [11].

2   Research Status

At present, the characteristics of financial data collection: the diversity of various systems in the hospital, each system is separated, the system is closed, forming an information island [12]. Various systems generate a large amount of data, but the data utilization rate is low, and the degree of sharing is poor. Data collection related to multiple systems is difficult, and there is no unified channel. The reports generated by each system are single and the availability is poor [13].

Problems to be solved in data integration: (1) Multi-source data collection, data comes from almost all business systems, HIS, LIS, PACS, ECG, EEG, emergency, financial systems, etc. [14–16]. (2) Heterogeneous data conversion, the existing business system data dictionary is independent, the data dictionary is inconsistent, data conversion takes up a lot of resources. Such as marital status, judgment of the outcome of illness, etc. (3) The degree of data standardization is low, and the data sources and calculation methods of each business system are different, resulting in inconsistent data. Such as age and admission time are calculated differently [17–19]. (4) Unstructured data, a large amount of freely entered unstructured data, data is not standardized, data utilization rate is low, basically in a state of sleep, unable to play value for hospital management and financial analysis [20, 21].

3   Financial Management Function Requirements

Public welfare is a characteristic of public psychiatric hospitals. The source of funds for hospitals is also the financial balance allocation. Public welfare is a basic principle that must be used in the process of carrying out various medical activities. Hospitals undertake a large number of public functions such as prevention, intervention, rehabilitation, publicity and education of mental and psychological diseases, rather than simply for obtaining more economic benefits. Therefore, in the process of financial management, public psychiatric hospitals should consider how to maximize the use of funds, reduce operating costs as much as possible, and ensure that the benefits they can obtain are always within a reasonable range and will not increase. The burden of patients is of great significance to the sustainable development of the hospital. Specifically, the importance of financial management for public hospitals is mainly reflected in the following aspects: First, the results of financial management can reflect the status of the hospital in terms of operation, capital flow and profitability. And then continue to adjust the management method. Secondly, through financial management, we can better achieve the financial budget goal, that is, to ensure that the financial structure is always scientific, which also helps managers understand the shortcomings and potentials of the hospital in the operating process. And then reasonably allocate resources. Third, through the first-stage results of financial management, a preliminary estimate of subsequent benefits can be made. Fourth, public psychiatric hospitals must not only follow the basic principles of public welfare, but also ensure the rationality of income. This requires cost accounting to be controlled to minimize operating expenses.

4 Platform Outline Design

4.1 System Architecture and Hardware Configuration

The big data integration platform of Guangji Hospital mainly relies on the original physical infrastructure and basic business systems. The server adopts Dell R730 R930 high-end model, 20 servers and 50T storage. Using distributed storage, distributed computing, and Hadoop database, the transmission rate and transportation rate are qualitatively higher than traditional methods. A server resource pool is built for big data computing and big data mining, which provides data security while ensuring data operation speed. And related medical information system (HIS), structured electronic medical record system (EMR), inspection system (LIS), nursing management system (NIS), electrocardiogram, electroencephalogram system (ECG), medical image system (PACS), Office (OA) system has 18 data sources as big data integration platform. Create a set of storage devices through the ODC data storage tool to store the basic business database and the operation process data ODS. Through the above physical architecture and data storage as the underlying framework, a big data integration platform for Guangji Hospital is built (Fig. 1).

4.2 Financial Data Collection and Model Establishment Based on Big Data

(1) Among them, ETL data collection tools are mainly used to extract data from each original data, etc., combined with the his table structure to establish a relatively standard data system, centrally convert, clean and transfer to a standardized data model to form a data set: Patient Master Index (EMPI), Master Data Management (MDM), etc., to solve the problem of reducing repeated statistics and discrepancies in the standards of each system, unify the statistics, and improve the quality of data.

(2) All data generated by clinical activities are extracted, converted, cleaned and transferred to a standardized CDR data model through ETL technology to form a clinical data center CDR, an operation data center ODR, and a scientific research data center RDR. Achieve data sets that are organized by field and are easy to use.

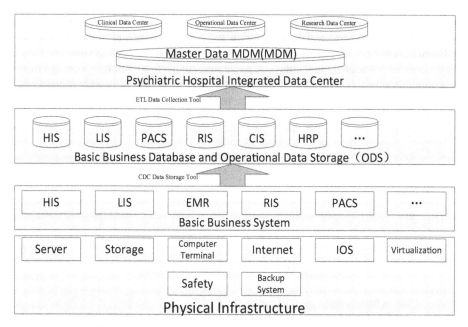

Fig. 1. Data center architecture model of psychiatric hospital

4.3 Data Analysis and Mining

Data analysis is responsible for real-time streaming data processing, non-real-time/offline data processing, supporting structured and unstructured processing, and supporting distributed parallel processing of PB-level data. Therefore, building a healthy data warehouse based on a massively parallel processing architecture, through a number of big data processing technologies such as column storage and coarse-grained indexing, combined with the highly efficient distributed computing mode of the massively parallel processing architecture, completes the support room for analytical applications. In terms of analysis algorithms, it supports machine learning algorithm libraries such as Apache.Mahout and mlib, analyzes big data that is common in business applications, and categorizes and develops them according to different business topics or related entities, comprehensively uses statistics and data mining techniques, and uses multiple To build a feature database, batch processing model database, and real-time processing model database for large-scale data.

4.4 Data Exchange and Sharing

The data exchange and sharing platform must not only meet the data sharing integration function, realize the centralized collection of data, sort and push down, etc., but also need to support the distributed-oriented SOA architecture, and support multiple modes based on Web Service, documents, and DB. More extensive data exchange. Realize the tight coupling within the business and the loose coupling between the businesses, support the unified standards and interface specifications issued by the competent department, and realize the unified and orderly management. Based on the Service Bus (ESB), the core basic service platform and the integration and data exchange and sharing of various application systems are realized internally. Provide external access service interfaces that comply with national standards to achieve interconnection with the existing three-level population health information platform, medical insurance information platform, medical management information platform, and medical and health institutions at all levels. From the perspective of technical architecture, the integrated exchange and sharing platform includes three major parts: management services, operation services, and monitoring services.

5   Business Functions

See (Fig. 2).

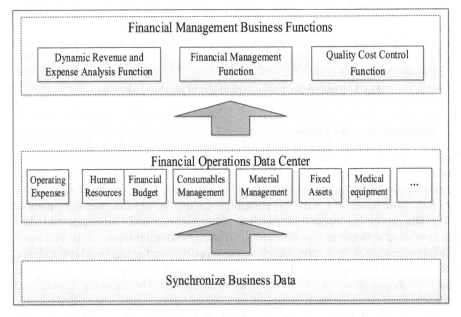

Fig. 2. Schematic diagram of data center financial management functions

5.1   Dynamic Revenue and Expense Analysis Function

The economic benefits generated in public hospitals at regular intervals are usually reflected in the income and expenditure summary table and the corresponding income and expenditure sub-table. The so-called income and expenditure sub-tables are actually the financial statements of the hospital. The accumulated amount and operating results can be directly expressed. The most intuitive is to show the profitability of the hospital during this time interval. In particular, the income and expense statement belongs to the balance sheet, which reflects actual data within a fixed time interval of the hospital, and dynamic information can also be reflected in the income and expense statement. Including the income, cost, and balance of each department, outpatient, and hospitalization within a fixed time interval of the hospital can be displayed. Understand the income and expenditure expense table, in fact, also understand the operation of the hospital for a period of time, the time interval is selected by the manager. The dynamic income and cost analysis function not only supports the reports that can be queried by the existing HIS, but also provides more custom parameter selection and settings to help managers make financial analysis decisions.

5.2 Financial Management Analysis Function

Through financial analysis, managers can further understand the past, present and future development of hospital operations, and analyze problems in hospital operations. And through the corresponding financial indicators to determine business decisions, and use data to make auxiliary decisions. Take effective measures to solve current problems. The financial analysis function can help the hospital administrator to further refine the data and provide the status of the hospital's past and current financial operation indicators. Analyze and list financial indicators for data differences to help analyze problems and indicator fluctuations in hospital operation decisions. And through financial indicators forecast and analysis of operating conditions, early warning. Help managers to take effective measures to solve the operational problems they face and will face. In practical applications, it can be found that the role of financial analysis is mainly to evaluate financial indicators and weigh operating conditions, which is very important for the development of the hospital. It can be said that financial analysis is a very effective way to tap potential, achieve financial management goals and improve work, and is also an important basis for rational decision-making. Based on big data financial management analysis, all information can be displayed in the form of indicators, so that goals and basic values can be set. And set warning thresholds, track financial indicators in hospital operations, and analyze the trend of later revenue growth and cost management.

5.3 Quality Cost Control Function

The smooth implementation of financial management is inseparable from cost management. According to modern management theory, cost management is not only a simple cost reduction, but also its more important role is to optimize management. In the past, the cost management of hospitals was to reduce indicators, which could easily put a lot of pressure on department heads, and even produce opposite emotions. Under the new situation, hospital financial management should focus on improving the quality of medical services and optimizing the cost structure. The idea of cost management should pay more attention to process improvement and adjustment related links, rather than pure low indicators. Through the revenue and expenditure indicators of medical service projects provided by big data, we will strengthen the optimal allocation of resources to a certain extent, reduce costs, and solve public expensive medical problems.

6 Security and Disaster Tolerance Design

The information security design establishes a private cloud platform, and at the same time desensitizes related medical business data to ensure application and data security. The business of each hospital is constructed under the strategy of three-level guarantee standards to meet the data integration security of each system. In the process of system construction, in order to ensure the security of system data and business continuity, the important role of disaster tolerance processing and rapid system recovery is gradually highlighted. According to the "Information System Disaster Recovery Specification", there are six levels of disaster handling. Building fast disaster recovery and recovery processing technology on the software architecture design can quickly restore data switching, which is very important for the financial system.

7 Summary

With the promulgation and implementation of the "National Financial Management Regulations" and the advancement of the general accounting system, the development of modern financial management requires the integration of traditional financial accounting management models into the era of knowledge economy. Taking the opportunity of informatization development and the construction of big data platform to realize the upgrade of financial data analysis, statistics, management and other functions. Update the concept of financial management to meet the needs of hospital managers for science and fine management.

Funding. 2019 Health Finance Research Project (Su Wei Finance Note [2020] No. 9) Research on the Refined Management of Medical Expenses in Tertiary Psychiatric Hospitals Based on DRGs (No. CW201914).

References

1. Jiang, Y.: Network big data mining algorithm based on association rules of computer technology. J. Phys. Conf. Ser. **1574**, 012084 (2020)
2. Rumapea, M., et al.: Evaluation of internal control of payroll system in hospital. In: 2019 International Conference of Computer Science and Information Technology (ICoSNIKOM), p. 4 (2019)
3. Pimenta, D., Souza, J., Caballero, I., Freitas, A.: Toward the measure of credibility of hospital administrative datasets in the context of DRG classification. In: Piattini, M., Rupino da Cunha, P., García Rodríguez de Guzmán, I., Pérez-Castillo, R. (eds.) QUATIC 2019. CCIS, vol. 1010, pp. 289–296. Springer, Cham (2019). https://doi.org/10.1007/978-3-030-29238-6_21
4. Krupička, J.: The relevance of management accounting tools in the public hospital management in the Czech Republic. In: Proceedings of the 32nd International Business Information Management Association Conference, IBIMA 2018 - Vision 2020: Sustainable Economic Development and Application of Innovation Management from Regional expansion to Global Growth, pp. 1583–1593 (2018)
5. Mandal, S., Jha, R.R.: Exploring the importance of collaborative assets to hospital-supplier integration in healthcare supply chains. Int. J. Prod. Res. **56**(7), 2666–2683 (2018)

6. Greenroyd, F.L., Price, A., Demian, P., Hayward, R., Sharma, S.: Modeling and simulating hospital operations in a 3D environment. In: Proceedings - Winter Simulation Conference, 28 June 2017, Winter Simulation Conference, WSC 2017, pp. 2952–2963 (2017)
7. Tsumoto, S., Hirano, S., Kimura, T., Iwata, H.: From hospital Big Data to clinical process: a granular computing approach. In: 2018 IEEE International Conference on Big Data (Big Data), pp. 2669–2678 (2018)
8. Usama, M., Ahmad, B., Wan, J., Hossain, M.S., Alhamid, M.F., Hossain, M.A.: Deep feature learning for disease risk assessment based on convolutional neural network with intra-layer recurrent connection by using hospital big data. IEEE Access 6, 67927–67939 (2018)
9. Kazancigil, M.A.: Innovations in medical apps and the integration of their data into the big data repositories of hospital information systems for improved diagnosis and treatment in healthcare, smart innovation, systems and technologies. In: Human Centred Intelligent Systems - Proceedings of KES-HCIS 2020 Conference, vol. 189, pp. 183–192 (2021)
10. Tao, J.: Application of the Big Data Processing Technology in the Hospital Informatization Construction. In: Hung, J., Yen, N., Chang, J.W. (eds.) Frontier Computing - Theory, Technologies and Applications, FC 2019. Lecture Notes in Electrical Engineering, vol. 551, pp. 1589–1595. Springer, Singapore (2019). https://doi.org/10.1007/978-981-15-3250-4_209
11. Liu, Z., Pu, J.: Analysis and research on intelligent manufacturing medical product design and intelligent hospital system dynamics based on machine learning under big data. Enterprise Information Systems (2019)
12. Santos, R.S., Vaz, T.A., Santos, R.P., de Oliveira, J.M.P.: Big data analytics in a public general hospital. In: Pardalos, P., Conca, P., Giuffrida, G., Nicosia, G. (eds.) Machine Learning, Optimization and Big Data. Second International Workshop, MOD 2016. Revised Selected Papers. LNCS, vol. 10122, pp. 433–441. Springer, Cham (2016). https://doi.org/10.1007/978-3-319-51469-7_38
13. Devika, R., Subramaniyaswamy, V.: A novel model for hospital recommender system using hybrid filtering and big data techniques. In: Proceedings of the International Conference on I-SMAC, I-SMAC 2018, pp. 575–579, 2 July 2018
14. Usugami, J., Walker, R.: Big-data, knowledge capturing and service improvement related to inbound tourism. In: Proceedings of the 20th European Conference on Knowledge Management ECKM 2019, pp. 1061–1068 (2019)
15. Li, D., Ye, Z., Li, L., Wei, X., Qin, B., Li, Y.: Practical data mid-platform design and implementation for medical big data. In: 2019 IEEE 4th Advanced Information Technology, Electronic and Automation Control Conference (IAEAC), pp. 1042–1045 (2019)
16. Devika, R., Subramaniyaswamy, V.: A novel model for hospital recommender system using hybrid filtering and big data techniques. In: 2018 2nd International Conference on I-SMAC, pp. 575–579 (2018)
17. Zhang, C., Ma, R., Sun, S., Li, Y., Wang, Y., Yan, Z.: Optimizing the Electronic Health Records Through Big Data Analytics: A Knowledge-Based View. IEEE Access 7, 136223–1362231 (2019)
18. Nasution, F., Puspitasari, W., Saputra, M.: Automation financial processing in account receivable for integrated hospital system using ERP and quickstart approach. In: Proceedings of the 2020 6th International Conference on Frontiers of Educational Technologies, ICFET 2020, pp. 204–211, 5 June 2020
19. Sirisawat, P., Hasachoo, N., Kaewket, T.: Investigation and prioritization of performance indicators for inventory management in the university hospital. In: 2019 IEEE International Conference on Industrial Engineering and Engineering Management (IEEM), pp. 691–695 (2019)

20. Da Silva Etges, A.P.B., Grenon, V., Felix, E.A., De Souza, J.S., Kliemann Neto, F.J., Polanczyk, C.A.: Proposition of a shared and value-oriented work structure for hospital-based health technology assessment and enterprise risk management processes. Int. J. Technol. Assess. Health Care **35**(3), 195–203 (2019)
21. Canha, M., Loureiro, R., Marques, C.G.: The impact of the introduction of logistics management systems in an organization: a case study in a hospital center. In: 2018 13th Iberian Conference on Information Systems and Technologies (CISTI), p. 4 (2018)

Study of Measurement and Inverse Prediction Methods of Heat Storage Efficiency for the Wood Heating Floor

Guangyue Du[✉]

Shandong Jiaotong University, Jinan 250357, Shandong, China
215050@sdjtu.edu.cn

Abstract. Wood heating floor has been widely used today, but the performance evaluation system still needs to be further improved. The author's team developed the equipment for testing heat storage efficiency of wood floor. The basic principle is to calculate the heat storage efficiency of test samples by temperature field distribution which is measured by the sensor in closed cavity. Based on the study method for the inverse heat transfer problem, this paper proposed an inversion calculation method for the heat storage efficiency of the test sample according to the measured temperature field. BP neural network technique is adopted for the inversion calculation which is a nonlinear problem. Numerical model of the testing cavity is established with CFD software. The temperature field data of a single structure sample under different initial temperature range of 50 °C ~ 130 °C are obtained by simulation (different simulation conditions are divided by interval of 5 °C). After repeated training, a better neural network model is obtained. The average values of the calculation error and the fitting degree of the testing set are $MRE = 0.67\%$, $MAE = 19.68\%$, $MSE = 1.16\%$, $R^2 = 0.97$. It can be seen that, the well trained BP neural network model could predict out the heat storage of different wood floor samples, and provides support for the analysis of heat storage efficiency for wood heating floor.

Keywords: Wood floor · Heat storage performance · Heat transfer inverse problem · Neural network

1 Introduction

The wood heating floor has the advantages of thermal comfort, energy saving, environmental protection, which has been widely used in residential, office and public buildings in recent years [1]. The thermal storage efficiency of floor heating has an important influence on the thermal comfort degree, but there is no equipment and method to detect the thermal storage efficiency of the wood heating floor. The quantification of heat store efficiency for wood heating floor can enrich the evaluation system of different material floors, which is convenient for users to choose, and is also conducive to the promotion and application to wood heating floors. The author's research group has developed the

© ICST Institute for Computer Sciences, Social Informatics and Telecommunications Engineering 2021
Published by Springer Nature Switzerland AG 2021. All Rights Reserved
W. Fu et al. (Eds.): ICMTEL 2021, LNICST 387, pp. 377–387, 2021.
https://doi.org/10.1007/978-3-030-82562-1_35

testing equipment of the floor heat storage efficiency. The purpose of the equipment is to calculate the thermal storage performance of the test sample by the temperature field distribution measured by the temperature sensor inside the cavity. Because the heat transfer process inside the cavity is a composite heat transfer process, including heat conduction, convection and radiation heat transfer, causing the internal heat transfer process is very complex and difficult to quantify. It is difficult to solve this problem by forward heat transfer theory, so it can be transformed into the inverse problem of heat transfer in source seeking. The inverse problem is the relative positive problem, which usually has the characteristic of not being qualitative. Especially in the field of heat transfer, although the theory of forward heat transfer is very mature, but there are still many engineering problems in practical application cannot be solved by forward heat transfer theory, which leads to the research of inverse heat transfer problem in the ascendant. The current research focuses on heat transfer inverse problem include the determination of thermal physical parameters, the inversion of boundary conditions, the identification of heat source terms and the study of various inversion algorithms [2–4]. The inverse problem of heat transfer in source seeking is the identification of heat source item, mainly refers to the process of inversion or solution to the position or intensity of the heat source by collecting the research object's boundary or the internal quantity of the measured point temperature value.

Since most inverse heat transfer problems belong to non-linear problems and artificial neural networks is one of the effective measures to solve non-linear problems. It is a common mathematical method to use neural networks to solve inverse heat transfer problems. Ahamad and Balaji used artificial neural network to invert the intensity of three heat sources inside the ventilation chamber [5]. And the inversion results were verified by experiment and CFD simulation. Tahavvor and Mahmoud used artificial neural network to study the natural convection heat transfer and fluid flow around a cooling horizontal cylinder with constant surface temperature, and established the natural convection correlation of cooling horizontal cylinder [6]. In order to get the best position of the discrete heat source in the interior of the ventilating cavity, Rajeev Reddy and Balaji were studied by two-dimensional numerical simulation with artificial neural network and genetic algorithm [7]. Kumar and Balaji used artificial neural network and principal component analysis method to inverse the boundary heat flow problem of a two-dimensional square cavity with a known wall temperature [8]. Ozgur made a neural network analysis on the natural convection heat transfer problem of horizontal cylinders [9]. The results of network training are in good agreement with the experimental results. Compared with the study of inverse problem of single heat conduction process, the problem of natural convection heat transfer or radiation heat transfer, especially the inversion of the complex heat transfer process is more difficult.

In this paper, problem of testing and calculating the heat storage performance of ground heating floor is studied, that is, the heat transfer inverse problem inside the closed cavity with inner heat source in the field of thermal conduction, and the BP Neural network technique is used to calculate the heat source strength. Firstly, the numerical model of test cavity is established by CFD software, and the temperature field data of single sample structure under different initial temperature are simulated. Then the training set and test set are divided into neural network model, the neural network model is trained and validated. Finally, based on the neural network model, the temperature field data obtained by the test equipment are used to calculate the heat source strength, that is, the thermal storage efficiency of the test sample.

2   Detection device and Data Acquisition

2.1   The Structure of Cavity

As shown in Fig. 1, the testing equipment is divided into upper and lower cavities, the lower cavity is a temperature regulating cavity, where are heating and refrigeration device located. The upper cavity is test cavity, which is an adiabatic closed cavity. There is a channel between the upper and lower cavities that controls the opening and closing, makes both cavities to be connected and isolated. There are 150 temperature sensors evenly distributed inside the test cavity where is divided into six temperature-measuring layers in perpendicular direction, and each of layers has 25 temperature sensors, as shown in Fig. 2. The cavity size, spacing of temperature measurement layer and the test piece size are shown in Table 1.

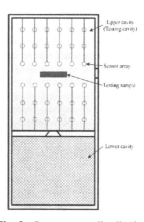

Fig. 1. Detection cavity   **Fig. 2.** Sensor array distribution

2.2   Materials

The laboratory is equipped with more than ten kinds of solid wood flooring of different kinds of materials. This experiment uses the solid wood flooring of four kinds of materials, such as *Betula platyphylla Suk.*, *Ash*, *Southwest birch* and *Eucalyptus*, which are more common in the market.

The wooden floor of different tree species is used in this research. For the convenience of operation, the wooden floor is processed into a test piece having a size of 100 × 60 × 15 mm. In this paper, the *Betula platyphylla Suk., Fraxinus mandshurica Rupr., Betula alnoides Buch. Ham. ex D. Don. and Xylosma racemosum (Sieb. et Zucc.) Miq.* are selected.

Table 1. Size information of the test device

Testing cavity size ($D \times H$)	Vertical spacing of upper cavity (d)	Distance of horizontal concentric circle(c)	Size of samples ($l \times w \times h$)
200×200 mm	20 mm	25 mm	$100 \times 60 \times 15$ mm

The test method is as follows: a wooden floor sample heated to the certain temperature is placed into the center of testing cavity. It is used as an internal heat source to release heat into the cavity space, and the temperature values of each measurement point in the closed space are collected in real time. The collected values are used as the basis data for calculating the heat storage efficiency of the test piece.

In order to obtain the temperature field distribution data of the test sample, the test cavity (Upper cavity) needs to be initialized, that is, the channel between the upper and lower cavity is opened, and the temperature control cavity (Lower cavity) is utilized. The heating and cooling device makes the temperature in the test cavity uniformly constant at 20 °C. Then, the passages between upper and lower cavity is closed, and wood heating floor sample heated to a certain initial temperature is pushed into the test cavity by the pneumatic device through inlet which is opened quickly. The inlet of testing cavity is closed. The before process is completed in a very short time (1.5 s) to reduce initial temperature fluctuations. The sample to be tested and pushing device are shown in Fig. 3.

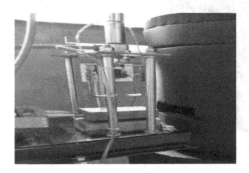

Fig. 3. Sample and push device

2.3 Data Acquisition

Bus type temperature sensors are selected in the test cavity. The controller consists of 12 digital inputs, 4 analog inputs, 9 switches, 2 analog outputs and 1 RS232 serial network communication. It can achieve the functions of collecting, transmitting and saving the temperature sensor array data, and also can realize the operation of terminal actuator, data collect and communication with the host computer.

3 Decomposition of Composite Heat Transfer Process

In order to clearly show the heat transfer relationship between each link in the compound heat transfer process in the test cavity. The test cavity can be simplified to a closed cavity with an internal heat source, as shown in Fig. 4. According to the basic laws of heat transfer, the thermal resistance network diagram of a closed cavity can be listed, as shown in Fig. 5.

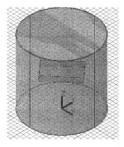
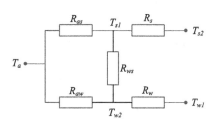

Fig. 4. Detection cavity   **Fig. 5.** Network diagram of thermal resistance

The meanings of the symbols in Fig. 5 are as follows:

T_s-Wall temperature of closed cavity, where, T_{s1}-The temperature of inner wall, T_{s2}-The temperature of outer wall;
T_w-Sample temperature, where, T_{w1}-The temperature inside the sample, T_{w2}-the temperature outside the sample;
T_a-Air temperature;
R_s-Thermal conductivity resistance of wall surface of closed cavity body;
R_w-Heat conduction resistance inside the sample;
R_{as}-Convective heat transfer resistance between air and inner wall surface;
R_{aw}-Convective heat transfer resistance between air and sample wall surface;
R_{ws}-Radiation heat transfers resistance between sample and wall surface of cavity.

According to the above thermal resistance network diagram, we can calculate the heat transfer of each part as shown below:
The heat conductivity of the sample itself:

$$Q_1 = (T_{w2} - T_{w1})/R_w \tag{1}$$

Heat conduction of the wall of the cavity body:

$$Q_5 = (T_{s2} - T_{s1})/R_s \tag{2}$$

Heat transfer between the sample wall surface and the air convection:

$$Q_2 = (T_{w2} - T_a)/R_{aw} \tag{3}$$

Convective heat transfer between the air and the wall of the cavity:

$$Q_3 = (T_{s1} - T_a)/R_{as} \tag{4}$$

Radiant heat transfer between the sample and the wall surface of the cavity:

$$Q_4 = (T_{s1} - T_{w2})/R_{ws} \tag{5}$$

According to the above formulas, if we want to obtain the heat transfer quantity of each part, we can calculate the heat resistance of each link only by calculating the heat resistance value of each link on the premise that the temperature of each link can be measured. Because the wood heating floor is porous medium material whose heat conduction coefficient value is affected by many factors, such as void ratio, moisture content and so on. These parameters are difficult to obtain, which causes its own heat resistance to be difficult to calculate theoretically. The convective heat transfer coefficient is affected by the distribution of air temperature inside the cavity and the size of the cavity, which increases the difficulty of calculating the heat transfer resistance. There are also many factors affecting the radiation heat transfer coefficient, which cannot be directly obtained by general theoretical calculation or measurement.

To summarize, it is not feasible to calculate the heat resistance of each part by the positive heat transfer theory and then to obtain the heat source strength. Therefore, the paper tries to solve the thermal storage performance of the test sample by solving the problem of heat transfer inversion.

4   The Inversion of Sample Regenerative Performance

4.1   Neural Network Model

Neural network BP algorithm has strong nonlinear fitting ability, and can calculate arbitrary nonlinear function with arbitrary accuracy [10]. The network algorithm is divided into two parts: information forward propagation and reverse propagation of error. The basic principle is that the information propagates from the input layer, the hidden layer to the output layer in turn, and then adjusts the weights and thresholds of the neurons in each layer according to the output error until the output results reach the expected value. The number of hidden layers and neurons has great influence on the prediction precision and computational efficiency of BP neural network. If the number of hidden neurons is too small, the computational efficiency can be improved, but the prediction accuracy will be reduced. On the contrary, the excessive number of neurons in the hidden layer will not only reduce the computational efficiency, but also may cause the problem of "excessive fitting" [11]. Therefore, it is necessary to compare the training of different structure models to obtain the best BP neural network model structure.

Because the conventional BP algorithm training speed is slow and also easy to appear the local minimization problem, this paper uses the numerical optimization algorithm Levenberfg Marguardt method. This algorithm calculates the convergence speed fast, and the stability is good, its weight and threshold adjustment formula is as follows:

$$X^{k+1} = X^k + S\left(X^k\right) \tag{6}$$

$$S\left(X^k\right) = \left(H^k + \lambda^k I\right)\nabla f\left(X^k\right) \tag{7}$$

Where $X(k)$ is the weight or threshold value of the time layer k; $H(k)$ is the Haisen matrix of the time layer of k; $f(X(k))$ is the objective function; I is the unit matrix (the same dimension as $H(k)$); $\lambda(k)$ is a positive number, and the program starts running with a larger value, which is gradually reduced to 0.

4.2 Inversion Calculation

Because the wood heating floor belongs to the porous heterogeneous material which is a composite medium composed of solid skeleton and fluid, the void distribution is messy and the internal structure is complex. That cause the heat storage is difficult to be measured directly. In addition, the distribution of temperature field in the closed cavity will be changed by the change of the heat storage in the measured sample. Therefore, the distribution of temperature field can be measured, and then the heat storage of the tested sample can be inversed by neural network. However, the training process of the neural network model needs to know the input and output parameters, that is, the heat storage of the sample and the corresponding temperature field which cannot be realized by the experiment. It is necessary to simulate the temperature field of the samples with known heat storage by means of CFD simulation to obtain the sample training set and test set. Because the model of porous media is difficult to construct in CFD software, but the ideal sample of a single structure does not exist in the reality. So this paper uses Gambit 2.4 of CFD software to modeling and Fluent 6.3 of CFD software to simulate the different heat storage structure of a single sample temperature field. Then the neural network model training optimization, in which the temperature of the test as input, the sample of stored heat as output.

Since the thermal property parameters such as specific heat capacity and density are constant to the single sample of the structure in CFD simulation. According to the heat calculation formula $Q = cm(T_0 - T_1)$ the sample heat storage amount Q and the temperature difference $T_0 - T_1$ are proportional. Letting the temperature $T_1 = 0\ °C$ before the sample is heated; the stored heat quantity Q is proportional to the temperature T_0 after the sample is heated (The initial temperature of the sample in the test chamber). Therefore, the sample initial temperature T_0 can characterize its stored heat quantity Q, and the heat storage performance of different samples can be used as a characterization parameter by the ratio of sample stored heat to sample temperature Q/T_0. The thermal property parameters are difficult to measure because of realistic porous media samples, and the ratio can also be used as the heat storage performance characterization parameter while the sample temperature is known.

1) Training and verification of neural network model.

In this paper, in order to obtain the obvious temperature field change of the air in the cavity, a sample initial temperature is set as a CFD simulation condition at intervals of 5 °C in the range of 50~130 °C under the premise that the sample thermal property parameters are constant and known. The initial temperature is the 50°C/60°C/70°C/80°C/90°C/100°C/110°C/120°C/130°C temperature field distribution data as the training set, the initial temperature is the

55°C/65°C/75°C/85°C/95°C/105°C/115°C/125°C temperature field distribution data as the test set. During the training process of the above neural network model, the temperature field data and the spatial coordinates of the measuring points are taken as the input, and the initial temperature as the output. However, in order to establish the inverse relationship between heat storage and temperature field, it is necessary to convert the initial temperature into heat storage by the heat calculation formula ($Q = cm\Delta t$), and then take the heat storage as the final output of the neural network model.

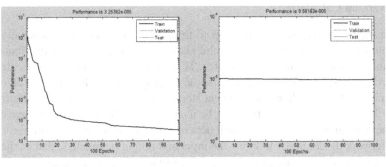

a. The first stage   b. The last stage

Fig. 6. Training curve

In order to avoid the accuracy of the analysis result caused by the large difference of order of magnitude in the inversion calculation, the data should be normalized to make each dimension in the same magnitude. By using the method of deviation standardization, the normalized values are mapped between $[-1, 1]$ or $[0, 1]$. In the process of sample training, the strategy of step-by-step training is used, the total number of training times is 800 times, and 100 times per training is a stage, which stage outputs a weight and a threshold as the initial weight and threshold of the next stage. So the training model can achieve better training effect. As shown in Fig. 6, (a) for the first stage of the training curve; (b) for the last phase of the training curve, visible at the last stage, the performance of the model has stabilized at 10–5 levels, indicating that the model has been convergent.

The average relative error (MRE), the maximum relative error (MAE), the mean square error (MSE) and the fitting R^2 are introduced in this paper for the effective training model parameters, prediction performance of the model, the formulas for calculating the error and fitting degree are as follows:

$$MRE\,(\%\,) = \frac{1}{n}\sum_{i=1}^{n}\frac{|T_{ANN} - T_{CFD}|}{(T_{CFD-\max} - T_{CFD-\min})} \times 100 \tag{8}$$

$$MAE\,(\%\,) = Max(\frac{|T_{ANN} - T_{CFD}|}{T_{CFD-\max} - T_{CFD-\min}}) \times 100 \tag{9}$$

$$MSE\,(\%\,) = \sqrt{\frac{1}{n}\sum_{i=1}^{n}(T_{ANN} - T_{CFD})^2/(T_{CFD-\max} - T_{CFD-\min})} \times 100 \tag{10}$$

$$R^2 = 1 - \frac{\sum_{i=1}^{n} (T_{ANN} - T_{CFD})^2}{\sum_{i=1}^{n} (T_{ANN} - T_{ANN-mean})^2} \tag{11}$$

TANN is the predicted temperature value of the model; TCFD represents the temperature sample extracted from CFD; TANN-mean is the model to predict the average temperature. The Table 2 is the result of the prediction error of the test set. The average relative error $MRE = 0.67\%$, the maximum relative error $MAE = 19.68\%$, the mean square error $MSE = 1.16\%$ and the fitting $R^2 = 0.97$ are shown by averaging the error and fitting degree of the test set. It can be seen that the test set of each error is small; especially MRE and MSE values are around 1%. For most test sets, the R^2 value representing the accuracy of the model approximates 1, which shows the effectiveness of the neural network model.

Table 2. Training output error of the ANN model

Testing set	MRE %	MAE %	MSE %	R^2
55 °C	1.1695	15.5895	1.6775	0.8385
65 °C	0.7386	18.2635	1.2356	0.9905
75 °C	0.6052	19.6989	1.1213	0.9917
85 °C	0.5601	20.3211	1.1062	0.9921
95 °C	0.5321	20.9612	1.0254	0.9915
105 °C	0.5296	21.5012	1.0256	0.9913
115 °C	0.5923	19.3321	1.0451	0.9906
125 °C	0.6429	21.7658	1.0539	0.9913
Average value	0.6713	19.6792	1.1613	0.9722

5   Calculation of Heat Storage Inversion

Based on the trained neural network model, the temperature data and the corresponding coordinate values obtained from the test equipment for the thermal storage performance of wood heating floor can be input to predict the heat storage of the test samples. It is difficult to obtain the thermal physical parameters because of samples are porous heterogeneous materials, but the sample temperature is measurable. Therefore, each sample can be heated to a constant temperature and placed inside the chamber of the ground heating floor heat storage performance tester, then the temperature field distribution data can be measured. The measured temperature field data is used as the input of the neural network model which is trained in the preceding test, and then heat storage of the sample is inversely calculated. In this experiment, the samples of four kinds of floor heating floors of *Betula platyphylla Suk.*, *Fraxinus mandshurica Rupr.*, *Betula alnoides Buch. Ham. ex D. Don* and *Xylosma racemosum (Sieb. et Zucc.) Miq* are tested and retrieved. The results were shown in Table 3.

Table 3. Prediction results of heat storage performance

Testing sample	Initial temperature(T0)	Heat storage(Q)	Heat storage performance J/°C(Q/ T0)
Betula platyphylla Suk.	70	4784	84
Fraxinus mandshurica Rupr.	65	5493	98
Betula alnoides Buch. Ham. ex D. Don.	70	6061	101
Xylosma racemosum (Sieb. et Zucc.) Miq.	75	6792	103

Table 3 is established based on the prediction results of the test sample's heat storage and thermal storage performance gotten from the neural network model in the previous paper. It can be seen that the heat storage performance of the floor samples of four different materials is *Xylosma racemosum (Sieb. et Zucc.) Miq.* > *Betula alnoides Buch. Ham. ex D. Don.* > *Fraxinus mandshurica Rupr.* > *Betula platyphylla Suk.*. Thus, the neural network model established in this paper can effectively calculate the heat storage performance of the floor with different materials.

6 Conclusion

In view of the heat transfer problem in the thermal storage performance testing device of the ground heating floor, this paper calculates the regenerative performance of the sample by using the inverse problem method of the source heat transfer. The inversion is carried out by CFD simulation combined with neural network. Firstly, the corresponding CFD model is established, and the sample training set and test set of neural network are obtained by using the model. After repeated training, the test fitting degree of the neural network model can reach more than 0.97, which fully demonstrates the accuracy and credibility of the model. The prediction results show that the neural network model can be used to calculate the regenerative performance of wood heating floor, and the heat storage performance of different heating floors may be divided effectively, so as to provide theoretical and methodological support for the analysis and identification of the thermal storage performance to wood heating floors of different timber.

References

1. Shen, B.H., Jiang, J., Sun, W.S., et al.: Status review of heating flooring in China. China Wood-Based Panels **11**, 5–8 (2012)
2. Chen, Q.H., Pang, L., Meng, L.M., et al.: A method for calculation of the thermal diffusivity of a solid material based on inverse heat conduction problem analysis. J. Beijing Univ. Chem. Technol. (Natural Science Edition) **41**(5), 76–82 (2014)
3. Han, W.W., Wu, J., Liu, C.L., et al.: Inversion of the third boundary condition on the inner wall of a two-dimensional pipe based on inverse heat conduction problems. J. Mech. Eng. **51**(16), 171–176 (2015)

4. Song, X., Zhang, Y.W., Ma, J.Y.: Inverse heat conduction problem for inner wall temperature fluctuation inversion of high temperature chamber. J. Therm. Sci. Technol. **15**(2), 104–108 (2016)

5. Ahamad, S.I., Balaji, C.: Inverse conjugate mixed convection in a vertical substrate with protruding heat sources: a combined experimental and numerical study. Heat Mass Transf. **52**(6), 1243–1254 (2015)

6. Tahavvor, A.R., Yaghoubi, M.: Natural cooling of horizontal cylinder using artificial neural network (ANN). Int. Commun. Heat Mass Transfer **35**(9), 1196–1203 (2008)

7. Rajeev, R.M., Balaji, C.: Optimization of the location of multiple discrete heat sources in a ventilated cavity using artificial neural networks and genetic algorithm. Int. Commun. Heat Mass Transfer **51**(9–10), 2299–2312 (2008)

8. Kumar, A., Balaji, C.: A principal component analysis and neural network based non-iterative method for inverse conjugate natural convection. Int. Commun. Heat Mass Transfer **53**(21–22), 4684–4695 (2010)

9. Ozgur, A.S., Demir, H., Agra, O.: Application of artificial neural networks for prediction of natural convection from a heated horizontal cylinder. Int. Commun. Heat Mass Transfer **37**(1), 68–73 (2010)

10. Rumelhart, D.E., Hinton, G.E., Williams, R.J.: Learning internal representations by error propagation. Parallel distributed processing: Explorations in macrostructure of cognition. Badford Books, Cambridge (1986)

11. Montana, D.J., Davis, L.: Training feed-forward neutral networks using genetic algorithms. In: Proceeding of the International Joint Conference on Artificial Intelligence, Los Altos, pp. 762–767 (1989)

Apple Classification Based on Information Fusion of Internal and External Qualities

Xue Li, Liyao Ma, Shuhui Bi$^{(\boxtimes)}$, and Tao Shen

School of Electrical Engineering, University of Jinan, Jinan 250002, China
cse_bish@ujn.edu.cn

Abstract. Apple classification plays an important role in improving the sales of apples. Based on both the internal and external qualities of an apple, in this paper, we propose to classify apples by DS theory-based information fusion. Soluble solid content is selected for apple internal quality detection. Making near-infrared spectroscopy nondestructive testing, principal component analysis -Martensitic distance method and multiple Scattering correction are used to preprocess the spectral data collected. Partial least squares prediction model is established with genetic algorithm selecting the wavelength characteristics. The color, shape, diameter and defect of apple are taken as the important indexes of external quality detection, and the sample images are analyzed and studied. The RGB color model and HSI color model commonly used in image processing are introduced. Selecting the median filtering algorithm for image denoising, the prediction model of support vector machine is established. In order to effectively avoid the classification error caused by the traditional hard classification using threshold and to make the detection result more accurate, the analysis of uncertain factors was introduced in the aspect of apple classification, and DS evidence theory was used to fuse the prediction results of internal and external quality.

Keywords: Apple classification · Support vector machine · DS evidence theory · Partial least squares

1 Introduction

Apple is one of the most sold fruits in the world, as well as in China. It not only tastes sweet and sour, but also has a high nutritional value, with a "wisdom fruit" reputation. China has a long history of fruit cultivation and rich variety resources. It is the largest fruit producer in the world. The planting area and total output of orchards rank first in the world [1]. Data released by the Key Agricultural Product Market Information platform of the Ministry of Agriculture shows that the export of apples in China has been increasing gradually since 2010. According to statistics, the world's apple export in 2017 was about 76.21 million tons, of which China's export exceeded 43.43 million tons. As the world's largest apple producer, China accounts for more than 50% of the world's planting area, total output and consumption scale. However, according to the DATA of the United States Department of Agriculture (USDA), in 2017, the world's apple exporters were mainly

W. Fu et al. (Eds.): ICMTEL 2021, LNICST 387, pp. 388–397, 2021.
https://doi.org/10.1007/978-3-030-82562-1_36

European and American countries [2]. The main reason for the fact that the proportion of Apple exports in China is lower than that in Europe and The United States is that China's apples are not classified and packaged in strict accordance with the standards due to outdated post-harvest commercialization processing technology. The post-processing commercialization rate of apples in developed countries is over 90%, while that in China is less than 40% [3, 4]. Therefore, improving the grading level of apples after picking is the key to improving the competitiveness of Chinese apples in the international market. With the improvement of people's living standard, consumers' requirements on fruit are not limited to price, but pay more attention to quality, brand and other aspects. The diversified demands of consumers for apple's appearance, taste, nutrition, function and brand have determined the necessity and urgency of researching postpartum commodity processing technology. Classifying apples according to their appearance and taste not only meets the consumption needs of different groups of people, but also helps to improve the commodity value of apples.

Information fusion combines information from multiple sources, reducing its uncertainty and improving the accuracy of modern intelligent information systems in decision-making, planning and response. Since the 1970s, it has been widely applied in various aspects of military and national economy [5, 6]. DS evidence Theory [7, 8] introduces basic probability assignment and belief function, which can distinguish between "unknown" and "uncertain". The reasoning mechanism of DS theory is simple, and it is close to the thinking habit of human beings, showing its unique advantages [9].

In this paper, DS evidence theory is used to fuse the internal and external qualities of apples. For information fusion, both models for internal and external qualities are established. The final decision is then made with Demspter's rule of combination.

2 Preprocessing of Apple Data

2.1 Physicochemical Analysis of Apple's Internal Quality Data

439 red Fuji apples were selected as the research samples, and 32 sampling modules were scanned at room temperature to collect the near-infrared spectrum of apples. The spectra of different parts of the equator were collected 3 times for each sample, and the average spectrum was calculated as the sample spectrum. Due to the influence of sample background and other factors, noise interference and baseline drift often occur in the NIR spectrum, which greatly affect the accuracy of the model. Therefore, we need to preprocess the spectrum before modeling.

The accuracy of the sample data directly determines the validity of the model architecture. Abnormal parameters will reduce the stability and accuracy of the sample model [10]. Therefore, it is very important to screen out abnormal parameters and store reasonable parameters. Pa-md method is adopted to calculate and eliminate abnormal samples in the original spectrum.

Multiple scatter correction (MSC) is currently the world's one of the most common and most effective means of data processing, can be in the process of spectral measurement optical path difference to a certain extent, the correction, strengthen its detailed information. In this paper, MSC is used to deal with reflected light.

The Savitzky-Golay smoothing filter can improve the spectral smoothness and reduce the noise interference. According to the characteristics of the spectrum, combined with the modeling effect, the window width of 5 time leads to the best processing effect.

The spectral information was pretreated in the early stage, and the noise content was reduced. But the results are still not directly applicable. Further processing is needed to further reduce the redundant information. For this purpose, genetic algorithm (GA) is used to select the optimal characteristic wavelength and take it as the input of partial least squares (PLS) based prediction model.

2.2 Analysis of Apple External Quality Data

Taking Fuji apple as the research object, 439 apple samples were collected for grading processing. The features of each apple were extracted from four aspects including color, fruit shape, fruit diameter and defect, and a 7-dimensional feature vector was constructed for training and testing the grading model. During the processing of Apple's external quality, the images used are taken by CCD industrial camera, and all the collected images are color images.

It is very important to select a suitable color model for color image processing. The RGB color model is easy to understand and has a very good effect in the implementation of hardware devices. The H and S components of the HSI model are in line with the way people perceive colors, and the I component is not reflected in the color information of the image. Therefore, image processing is carried out based on the RGB and HIS color models.

Only when the apple area is completely segmented can the external quality features such as apple color and defects be accurately and efficiently extracted. However, the collected images contain background information as well as apple area [11]. Therefore, the background segmentation method with bimodal threshold of 15 can be used to completely segment the apple region, completely eliminating the interference of the background part and achieving a better effect. In the process of image acquisition and transmission, noise will be generated in the original image under the influence of light source and sensor, etc. Noise is usually random and unpredictable, which is difficult to conduct quantitative analysis [12]. Median filtering algorithm is selected to carry out filtering denoising process. Both color and gray images can retain the original image structure completely, and the filtering effect is the best.

When extracting the external features of apple such as color, shape, diameter and defect, the ratio of red and near-red H values in the apple image was taken as the color index, and the variance of R, G and B components was selected as the color distribution parameter by Fisher's coefficient method. Based on the obtained apple edge, the horizontal and vertical diameters of the apple image are obtained by calculating the minimum enclosing rectangle of the apple, and the shape index is calculated. The pixel diameter and pixel equivalent are obtained by calculating the minimum enclosing circle of an apple image, and the conversion between the actual diameter and the pixel diameter is realized. Since the gray level of the defect area is different from the normal apple area, the common defect area of apple is detected based on the Canny algorithm, and morphological operation and hole filling are introduced into the defect area to segment the defect area, and the ratio of the defect area to the apple area is taken as the defect feature [13, 14].

After extracting the characteristics of apple's external quality, the apple's external quality was graded based on support vector machine.

3   PLS Model for Internal Quality of Apples

PLS is one of the most common methods to construct regression model. It has a good design effect whether it is to analyze a single variable or to deal with multiple different variables at the same time.

The optimal characteristic wavelength selected by genetic algorithm is used as the input of PLS based prediction models. When using PLS to analyze SSC, the collected NIR data and soluble solid content were defined as the main components, and the absorbance and content matrix were used as independent variables. PLS synthesized the external relationship between the spectral matrix X and W. The internal relation between the two is obtained, and then X and W are decomposed into the following forms:

$$X = TP + E \tag{1}$$

$$W = VQ + F \tag{2}$$

$$V = TB \tag{3}$$

$$B = (T^T T)^{-1} T^T W \tag{4}$$

In which T and V are the score matrix of matrix X and W respectively, P and Q are the load matrix of the two matrices respectively, and E and F are the residual matrix of the two.

Finally, according to the formula above, the synthesis matrix B is obtained. B matrix is used to predict the result of the sample to be tested. Collect all kinds of data of test samples, and then decompose them according to formula 1 and 4 to find out the sample concentration W. As shown in Eq. (5).

$$W = tB \tag{5}$$

in which W is the concentration value of the sample to be tested, T is the spectral decomposition score of the samples to be tested.

4   SVM Model for External Quality of Apples

In the mid-1990s, Support Vector Machine (SVM) was proposed by Vapnik et al. [15]. SVM is a dichotomous question, and its main purpose is to maximize two types of sample data by looking for the optimal hyperplane interval. The white dots and the black dots

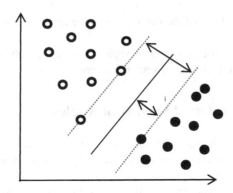

Fig. 1. The classification schematic diagram

in Fig. 1 represent the two types of sample data. The main purpose is to look for a line with the greatest distance between all the characteristic points to divide the two samples. Classification problems using SVM can be divided into linear separable, approximate linear separable and nonlinear separable.

Two linearly separable sample sets are assumed to be in the form

$$D = (Xi, Yi) \tag{6}$$

in which $Xi \in R$, $Yi \in \{-1, +1\}$, $i = 1,2,...,n$.

Therefore, the linear discriminant function can be described as

$$h(x) = \alpha \cdot x + \beta \tag{7}$$

The corresponding segmentation surface equation is shown as

$$\alpha \cdot x + \beta = 0 \tag{8}$$

in which α is normal vector, β is the intercept.

Based on the segmentation surface, the feature space can be divided into positive and negative parts. To correctly classify all samples, the conditions as shown in Eq. (9) should be met:

$$y_i \cdot h(x) - 1 \geq 0, i = 1, 2, \ldots, n \tag{9}$$

The distance from x_i to the hyperplane can be calculated as

$$d = \frac{|h(x)|}{\alpha} = \frac{|\alpha \cdot x + \beta|}{\alpha} \tag{10}$$

Since all the points on the optimal hyperplane satisfy that the molecule is 1, so, the distance between the support vector and the hyperplane is expressed as

$$d = \frac{|\alpha \cdot x + \beta|}{\alpha} = \frac{1}{\alpha} \tag{11}$$

At this point, the classification interval is $\frac{2}{\|\alpha\|}$, If the interval is maximized, it is equivalent to making $\|\alpha\|^2$ the smallest. Therefore, the optimal classification surface can be transformed into

$$\min f(\alpha) = \frac{a^2}{2} \tag{12}$$

Lagrange function is defined as

$$L(\alpha, \beta, c_i) = \frac{\alpha^2}{2} - \sum_{i=1}^{n} c_i[y_i(\alpha \cdot x_i + \beta) - 1] \tag{13}$$

where c_i is Lagrangian multiplier.

Further, in order to calculate the minimum objective function, respectively for α, β partial derivatives and make them are equal to zero, with

$$L(\alpha, \beta, c_i) = \frac{\alpha^2}{2} - \sum_{i=1}^{n} c_i[y_i(\alpha \cdot x_i + \beta) - 1] \tag{14}$$

Therefore, the above problem is transformed into a dual problem of convex quadratic programming optimization, as shown in Eq. (15).

$$\begin{cases} \max \sum_{1}^{n} c_i - \frac{1}{2} \sum_{1}^{n} \sum_{1}^{n} c_i c_j y_i y_j (x_i x_j) \\ \sum_{1}^{n} c_i y_i = 0 \\ c_i \geq 0, i = 1, 2, \ldots, n \end{cases} \tag{15}$$

Assuming c_i^* is the optimal solution, the optimal hyperplane normal vector can be expressed as

$$\alpha^* = \sum_{1}^{n} c_i^* y_i x_i \tag{16}$$

The optimal classification function is

$$f(x) = \text{sgn} \left\{ \sum_{1}^{n} c_i^* y_i (x_i \cdot x) + \beta^* \right\} \tag{17}$$

Nonlinear classification is when the sample data set is indivisible, the input feature vector is mapped to the high-dimensional space and the optimal hyperplane is obtained by selecting the appropriate kernel function.

Assume that A is the input space, B is the high-dimensional feature space, and there is A mapping function (x) from A space to B space. For all real numbers in A space, if there is A function that satisfies the relation

$$k(s, t) = \rho(s) \cdot \rho(t) \tag{18}$$

Then $k(s, t)$ is called the kernel function. Consider the objective function as

$$f(c) = \sum_1^n c_i - \frac{1}{2} \sum_{i=1}^n \sum_{j=1}^n c_i c_j y_i y_j k(s, t) \tag{19}$$

Equation (15) is converted into the form

$$\begin{cases} \max \sum_1^n c_i - \frac{1}{2} \sum_1^n \sum_1^n c_i c_j y_i y_j k(s, t) \\ \sum_1^n c_i y_i = 0 \\ 0 \le c_i, i = 1, 2, \ldots, n \end{cases} \tag{20}$$

If classification or regression is performed directly in a high-dimensional space, there will be problems in determining the form and parameters of the nonlinear mapping function, the dimension of the feature space and etc. The kernel function can effectively solve these problems. Radial basis kernel function is one of the most widely used kernel functions. Compared with polynomial kernel function, it has strong locality and few parameters. As a result, this paper takes RBF as the kernel function of SVM.

The traditional support vector machine (SVM) is a typical two - class classifier. A one-to-many method to construct the multi-classifier is to sort out the samples of a certain category into one group, and the rest samples are classified into another group in the training, so that the samples in k categories can construct k SVMs. When doing this, the unknown samples will be classified into the categories with the maximum classification function value. The brief process of SVM is shown in Fig. 2.

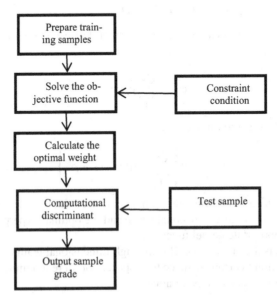

Fig. 2. Flow chart of support vector machine classification processing

5   Apple Classification Fusion Based on DS Evidence Theory

The previous apple classification models both make a hard division of the sample space, which easily leads to misclassification in areas near the decision boundary. In order to reduce the difference of results caused by hard classification, this paper introduces DS theory, which has a strong analysis advantage in dealing with uncertainty.

5.1   Method Description

The DS evidence theory was first proposed by Dempster in 1967 and then extended by Shafer in 1976 [7, 8]. When using belief functions to deal with problems, there is no need to generate accurate probability for each possible outcomes. The basic mass assignments provide a useful way to represent unknown and uncertainty.

Consider the previously discussed internal and external models, each model provide a basic mass assignment m of apple classification, which provides its belief of predicted result. Since each model has its own reliability, each basic mass assignment should be discounted by an evidence discount rate $\alpha \in [0, 1]$ with the following discounting formula

$$m^{\alpha}(U) = (1 - \alpha)m(U) + \alpha \tag{21}$$

$$m^{\alpha}(A) = (1 - \alpha)m(A), \forall A \subset U, A \neq \varphi \tag{22}$$

In which U is the frame of discernment, which contains all the possible outcomes.

Finally, the information fusion of two models is implemented by the combination of evidence. Let m_1 and m_2 be two independent basic probability assignments on 2^U, the fusion results in another basic probability assignment denoted as $m = m_1 \oplus m_2$, which is obtained with Dempster's rule of combination

$$K_1 = \sum_{A_i \cap B_j = \phi} m_1(A_i)m_2(B_j) \tag{23}$$

$$m(C) = \begin{cases} \sum_{A_i \cap B_j = C} m_1(A_i)m_2(B_j), & \phi \neq C \subset U \\ 0, & C = \phi \end{cases} \tag{24}$$

5.2   Realization of Apple Classification Based on DS Evidence Theory

Suppose the Red fuji apples can be classified into three classes A, B and C. We have the frame of discernment $U = \{A, B, C\}$ and corresponding focal elements $F \in 2^U = \{A, B, C, AB, AC, BC, ABC\}$.

The PLS model provides m_1 considering the prediction based on internal quality. Similarly, the SVM model gives m_2 regarding to the external quality. Table 1 shows an example of the basic mass assignments of these two models.

The PLS soluble solid content prediction model and ELM external feature prediction model were combined with Demspter's rule, with the fusion result of

$$m_1 \oplus m_2(A) = 0.88, \quad m_1 \oplus m_2(AB) = 0.09, \quad m_1 \oplus m_2(ABC) = 0.03$$

Table 1. Basic mass assignment table

Prediction model	A	B	C	AB	AC	BC	ABC
PLS model m_1	0.6	0	0	0.3	0	0	0.1
ELM model m_2	0.7	0	0	0	0	0	0.3

From Table 1, it can be seen that these two prediction models provide relatively uncertain results (the basic mass assignment for A are 0.6 and 0.7). Yet when we combine the predictions together, the fusion result becomes much more certain that this apple belongs to class A.

6   Conclusions

In this paper, focused on red Fuji apples, the information fusion model of apple classification is discussed. The spectrum of apple was collected by near-infrared spectroscopy technology and then used for internal quality analysis. After spectral information preprocessing and spectral feature analysis, the prediction model of apple internal quality measurement was established based on PLS. The apple image was collected by machine vision technology and preprocessed with background segmentation and feature extraction. The prediction model of apple external quality was then established based on support vector machine. By using DS evidence theory method, the prediction model of apple internal quality measurement and the prediction model of external quality measurement were fused to improve the accuracy and certainty of Fuji Apple grading prediction model. In future work, more prediction models, as well as the generation approach of basic mass assignment will be considered.

Acknowledgements. This paper was supported by Shandong Provincial Key Research and Development Project (No. 2017GGX10116).

References

1. Zhixia, L., Jiyun, N., Jing, L., et al.: Analysis and suggestions on the development of Apple industry in China. Chin. Fruits **05**, 81–84 (2014)
2. Biao, Z.: Analysis on the annual production, processing and trade status of Apple industry in China in recent 7 years. China Fruit Tree **192**(04), 112–114 (2018)
3. Wu, M., et al.: Research on the status quo and development strategy of post-havest apple industry in China. **34**(10), 17 (2014)
4. Cerutti, A.K., Bruun, S., Donno, D., et al.: Environmental sustainability of traditional foods: the case of ancient apple cultivars in Northern Italy assessed by multifunctional LCA. J. Cleaner Prod. **52**, 245–252 (2013)
5. You, H., Guo-hong, W., Xin, G., et al.: Information Fusion Theory and Application. Electronic Industry Press, Beijing (2010)

6. Sun, B., Cheng, W., Ma, L., Goswami, P.: Anomaly-aware traffic prediction based on automated conditional information fusion. In: 21st International Conference on Information Fusion (FUSION), pp. 2283–2289 (2018)

7. Dempster, A.: Upper and lower probabilities induced by a multivalued mapping. Annals of Math. Stat. **38**(4), 325–339 (1967)

8. Shafer, G.: A Mathematical Theory of Evidence. Princeton University Press, Princeton (1976)

9. Ma, L., Sun, B., Han, C.: Learning decision forest from evidential data: the random training set sampling approach. In: 4th International Conference on Systems and Informatics (ICSAI), pp. 1423–1428 (2017)

10. Lin, H., Zhang, H., Gao, Y., et al.: Hyperspectral identification of desert tree species based on Markov Distance method. Spectrosc. Spectral Anal. **34**(12), 3358–3362 (2014)

11. Wu, Y., Meng, T., Wu, S.: Research progress of image threshold segmentation method in 20 years (1994–2014). Data Acquisit. Process. **30**(1), 1–23 (2015)

12. Li, H., Suen, C.Y.: A novel non-local means image denoising method based on grey theory. Pattern Recogn. **49**, 237–248 (2016)

13. Qiang, L.: Research and Development of Apple Quality Grading Technology Based on Machine Vision. Heilongjiang University, Harbin (2019)

14. Li, S., Li, R., Du, G., Ding, S., Jiang, L., Liu, X.: Nondestructive identification analysis of oats of different brands based on near-infrared spectroscopy and optimized pretreatment. J. Food Saf. Qual. Inspection **10**(24), 8204–8210 (2019)

15. Zhang, H.: Research on multiple classification methods of support vector machine and its application in fund evaluation. Beijing Jiaotong University (2014)

Apple Defect Detection Method Based on Convolutional Neural Network

Zheng Xu, Tao Shen, Shuhui Bi, and Qinjun Zhao[✉]

School of Electrical Engineering, University of Jinan, Jinan 250002, China
`cse_zhaoqj@ujn.edu.cn`

Abstract. The appearance quality of apple is one of the important indicators for consumers to purchase. At present, the classification process of apple is still completed artificially, which not only wastes human resources, but also easily causes subjective misclassification. This paper proposes a convolutional neural network model to classify defective and defect-free apples. Apple images are collected by the smartphone camera, each type of apple has 312 images. The number of apple images is expanded through data enhancement technology, and randomly divided into training set, validation set, and test set according to the ratio of 6:2:2. The final classification accuracy is 99.2%.

Keywords: Deep learning · Convolutional neural network · Classification

1 Introduction

Apple is popular with consumers for its rich nutritive value and luscious taste. It is one of the most common fruits of people's daily life. China is the largest apple-producing country whose apple planting area and output account for more than 50% of the world. From 2003 to 2018, the apple output has maintained a steady growth trend, and reached a peak of 41.39 million tons in 2017 [1]. In addition, China is also the country with the largest export volume of apples in the world. From 1992 to 2017, China's total apple exports increased from 20 million dollars to 1.453 billion dollars, and the total exports increased from 38,300 tons to 1.3284 million tons (Un Comtrade Database, 1992- 2017), the proportion of global apple exports trade rose from 1.40% to 19.21% and 1.91% to 14.40% respectively [2]. However, China is not a powerful apple exporter, and China's apple exports account for 1.83%~3.15% of the total volume merely. While the world's apple exports account for 8.30% of the total output approximately [3].

Supported by Key R&D projects of Shandong Province under grant 2019GNC106093, Shandong Agricultural machinery equipment R&D innovation plan project under grant 2018YF011, Key R&D projects of Shandong Province under grant 2019JZZY021005, Shandong Provincial Key R&D project 2017GGX10116.

W. Fu et al. (Eds.): ICMTEL 2021, LNICST 387, pp. 398–404, 2021.
https://doi.org/10.1007/978-3-030-82562-1_37

The inspection and classification of fruit quality are essential to improve the competitiveness of fruit products. Generally speaking, postpartum treatment of apples is mostly done by manual. So it may lead to some problems which can not meet the production needs, such as low classification accuracy and slow speed because of human subjectivity and visual fatigue. There needs to be a system that can identify whether it is worth based on the quality of two categories of fruit.

In recent years, a lot of researches on the detection and classification of apple have been done by Domestic and foreign scholars. In the work of [4], they extracted characteristic parameters like energy, entropy, and moment of inverse difference, then sent them to the neural network for classifying, the accuracy is 95.5%. The research was conducted by [5] combining with brightness correction technology, segmented the defect candidate areas (defects, fruit stalks, calyx) of apples, then randomly extracted the color, texture, and some other features, obtained 95.7% accuracy using AdaBoost. Subsequent research on the identification of apple defects [6] used Support Vector Machine (SVM), MLP, and K-Nearest Neighbor (KNN) classifier respectively, and SVM is the most accurate method with an accuracy of 92.5%. Most of the above studies include image acquisition, image processing, image features selection, and extraction. It does not only requires a lot of manpower, but the selection and extraction of features are also uncertain and complex. In response to this problem, the convolutional neural network uses the original image as the input, which can effectively learn the features from a large number of images. Thus the convolution neural network can avoid the complex features extraction process. In addition, the characteristic of weight sharing can also greatly decrease the complexity of the network and raise the efficiency of training. A recent study carried out by [7] used a convolutional neural network (CNN) on the dataset of apple images. It took the normal, calyx, fruit stem, and boundary image blocks as positive samples on the one hand, and on the other hand, rotting, scar, insect injury and other defects were made to negative samples, the accuracy is 97.3%. Compared with the above apple defects detection methods, it has a certain improvement in recognition efficiency and accuracy. In this paper, the dataset is expanded by translation, scaling, and rotation first, then sent to a 15-layer convolutional neural network model, and the results show that it can be implemented more accurately and quickly.

2   Image Pre-processing

Red Fuji apple was studied in this paper. The apple images are collected on the white background with the camera of the smartphone at 13MP resolution under the room lighting environment, as shown in Fig. 1. Image preprocessing consists mainly of the following two aspects. Firstly, preserving the part of the apple image that we are interested in through background removal. The second step is to expand the number of sample images through data enhancement to ensure that the network model is fully trained.

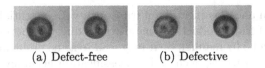

(a) Defect-free   (b) Defective

Fig. 1. The original image captured by the camera

2.1   Background Removal

Choosing an appropriate color space model is critical in background segmentation, which is conducive to fast and accurate segmentation of the target area. Since the HSI color space is approximate to the way of the human eye perceives color, and minimally influenced by light intensity. So this paper converts RGB color space to HSI color space, and the conversion formula is as follows:

$$
\begin{cases}
I = \dfrac{1}{3}(R + G + B) \\
S = 1 - \dfrac{3}{R+G+B}[min(R,G,B)] \\
H = \begin{cases} \theta, & G \geq B \\ 2\pi - \theta, & G < B \end{cases}
\end{cases}
$$

where,

$$
\theta = \arccos\left[\frac{\frac{1}{2}[(R-G)+(R-B)]}{\sqrt{(R-G)^2 + (G-B)(R-B)}}\right].
$$

It is found that the histogram distribution of the S component is double peaks obviously, so we can calculate the threshold value of the S component to segment the image. The specific steps are as follows:

(1) Median filtering of S component;
(2) Otsu algorithm [8] was used for threshold segmentation of S-component images;
(3) The binary image is obtained by the morphological operation;
(4) Multiply the binary image with the original image to remove the background;
(5) Set the image resolution to 100 × 100, as shown in Fig. 2.

(a) Defect-free   (b) Defective

Fig. 2. Apple image with background removed

2.2 Data Enhancement

The deep learning model is complex and requires a sufficient number of samples for training. It's difficult to obtain enough samples due to the constraints of various factors, so the offline expansion of the sample images is carried out in the study. It mainly contains the following methods:

(1) Rotation: Rotate the image randomly to a certain angle;
(2) Shift: Shift the image to a certain range randomly in the horizontal or vertical direction;
(3) Flip: Reverse the image in the horizontal or vertical direction;
(4) Scale: Enlarge or reduce the image according to the specified scale factor;

The images in Fig. 2 are randomly enhanced by the above method, and the expanded images are shown in Fig. 3.

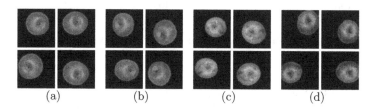

(a)   (b)   (c)   (d)

Fig. 3. Data augmentation of the images in Fig. 2

3 The Convolution Neural Network

The convolutional neural network is a deep learning model or multilayer perceptron similar to the artificial neural network, which is often used to analyze visual images. It mainly consists of the convolution layer, pooling layer, and full connection layer. Also, it includes some auxiliary training modules such as activation function and classifier. Among them, the convolutional layer is the key part of the convolutional neural network. Using local connections and weight sharing to extract features of images can greatly decrease the number of parameters in the neural network. The activation function is a nonlinear mapping to the output of the convolutional layer. The pooling layer is used for decreasing the data dimension, simplifying the complexity of network calculation, and extracting the main features of the image. After then, the full connection layer connects all the features and sends the final value to the classifier.

The convolution neural network model used in this study is shown in Table 1. The input image is an RGB image with a resolution of 100×100, and the features of images are extracted by three convolution layers. The size of kernel/filter used for each convolution layer is 5×5, and 32 filters are used in the first two convolution layers, the third convolution layer uses 64 filters to extract deeper features. The relu activation function is used to nonlinear map the output of convolution layer, and the size of the pooling is 3 × 3. Finally, the extracted features are integrated through the fully connected layers, and then, are sent to the softmax classifier for classification.

Table 1. Summary model with 5 × 5 kernel size

Layers	Type	Activations	Learnables
1	Image Input (RGB)	100 × 100 × 3	–
2	32 Conv.Filter (5 × 5 × 3)	100 × 100 × 32	Weight 5 × 5 × 3 × 32 Bias 1 × 1 × 32
3	Relu	100 × 100 × 32	–
4	Max Pooling (3 × 3)	49 × 49 × 32	–
5	32 Conv.Filter (5 × 5 × 32)	49 × 49 × 32	Weight 5 × 5× 3 × 32 Bias 1 × 1 × 32
6	Relu	49 × 49 × 32	–
7	Max Pooling (3 × 3)	24 × 24 × 32	–
8	64 Conv.Filter (5 × 5 × 32)	24 × 24 × 64	Weight 5 × 5 × 3 × 32 × 64 Bias 1 × 1 × 64
9	Relu	24 × 24 × 64	–
10	Max Pooling (3 × 3)	11 × 11 × 64	–
11	Fully Connected (400)	1 × 1 × 400	Weight 400 × 7744 Bias 400 × 1
12	Relu	1 × 1 × 400	–
13	Fully Connected (2)	1 × 1 × 2	Weight 2 × 400 Bias 2 × 1
14	Softmax	1 × 1 × 2	–
15	Classification Output	–	–

4   Results

In this paper, we divided the expanded dataset into the training set, validation set and test set at the ratio of 6:2:2, which is used to train and test the neural network model respectively, we can see in Table 2.

After many experiments, the parameters were adjusted as follows: MaxEpoch is 40, BatchSize is 128, LearnRate is constant 0.001, the momentum stochastic gradient descent method was used for training. The loss and accuracy of training and validation sets during the experiment are shown in Fig. 4. When the accuracy of the validation set does not change for five consecutive times, we stop training, and the final iteration is 812 times. The losses and accuracies of this model are shown in Table 3, the losses of training and validation sets are 0.0122 and 0.0462 respectively.

Table 2. Dataset

Category	Training set	Validation set	Test set
Defect	1872	624	624
Defect-free	1872	624	624
Total	3744	1248	1248

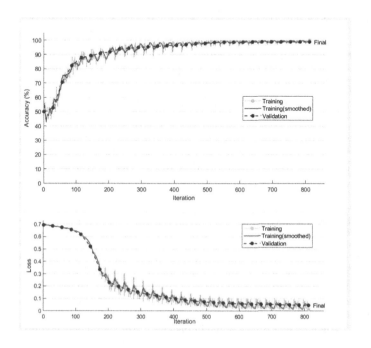

Fig. 4. Loss and accuracy plot from data training and validation

Finally, we test the model and get an accuracy of 99.2%. There are 10 apples were misclassified, including 9 defective apples and 1 defect-free apple, as shown in Table 4.

Table 3. The accuracy and loss of training and validation

	Training	Validation
Amount of data	3744	1248
Loss	0.0122	0.0462
Accuracy	100%	98.96%

Table 4. The result of testing

	Defective	Defect-free
Actual label	624	624
Predict labels	615	623

5   Conclusion

This research studies an apple classification method using the convolutional neural network. The classification process is completed through background removal and image expansion combined with CNN. In the training process, three convolution layers and pooling layers are used to extract the features of the sample images, and the appropriate parameters are adjusted according to the performance of the validation set. We terminate the training when the accuracy of the validation set no longer changes 5 consecutive times, and save the network model at this time. Finally, the reliability of the model is tested and very good results are obtained.

References

1. Yang, J., Meng, X. N., Xin, L.: Analytical report on China's apple market from 2017 to 2019. Deciduous Fruits **51**(5), 5–7 (2019)
2. Su, S.S., Huo, X.X.: Analysis on the changes of structural characteristics of global apple trade network and the transition of China's statue. Issues Agric. Econ. **6**, 99–109 (2020)
3. Zhang, B.: Analysis of China's apple industry's output, processing and trade status in the past 7 years. China Fruit Tree (4), 106–108 (2018)
4. Yu, M., Li, X., Yang, H.C.: Research on apple grading algorithm based on image recognition. Autom. Instrum. **7**, 39–43 (2019)
5. Zhang, B.H.: On-line identification of defect on apples using lightness correction and AdaBoost methods. Trans. Chinese Soc. Agric. Mach. **45**(6), 221–226 (2014)
6. Moallem, P., Serajoddin, A., Pourghassem, H.: Computer vision-based apple grading for golden delicious apples based on surface features. Inf. Process. Agric. **4**(1), 33–40 (2017)
7. Liu, Y., Yang, J.B., Wang, C.X.: Apple defect detection algorithm based on Convolution Neural Network. Electron. Meas. Technol. **40**(3), 108–112 (2017)
8. Otsu, N.: A threshold selection method from gray-level histograms. IEEE Trans. Syst. man Cybern. **9**(1), 62–66 (1979)

Information Fusion and Their Applications

Lidar/IMU Integrated Navigation and Positioning Method

Zhigang Wang[1], Jiehua Liao[1], Hang Guo[1(✉)], and Min Yu[2(✉)]

[1] Nanchang University, Nanchang 330031, China
[2] Jiangxi Normal University, Nanchang 330021, China

Abstract. Aiming at the problem of large positioning accuracy of LiDAR odometry and mapping (LOAM) algorithm, this paper proposes a LOAM algorithm fusion Adaptive Particle Filter (APF) algorithm. Experiments show that the trajectory of the APF algorithm using the LOAM algorithm was half the accuracy of the trajectory using the LOAM algorithm. In order to better verify the accuracy effect, the R-fans 16-line laser radar was used to compare and analyze the test under closed and non-closed routes. The results show that under the closed route, the LOAM algorithm combines the APF algorithm to provide the accurate position trajectory for the car. In the non-closed route, due to the lack of closed-loop constraints, the motion distortion of the car is caused by the accumulation of errors. Through experiments, using the LOAM algorithm to merge the APF algorithm in the non-closed loop could also effectively compensate the motion distortion and filter out the noise, so as to achieve the effect of the trajectory correction, reduce the error with the real trajectory, and improve the positioning accuracy.

Keywords: R-fans 16-line lidar · Closed loop · Non-closed loop · LOAM algorithm · APF algorithm

1 Introduction

With the continuous rise of location-based service (LBS), indoor positioning has become an important direction [1, 2], and accurate positioning trajectories can greatly meet people's positioning needs. Experts at home and abroad have successively proposed improved proximity algorithm [3], dead reckoning algorithm [4], vision-based positioning algorithm [5] and multi-sensor fusion-based positioning algorithm [6–9]. The above method research is relatively deep and extensive, but all have certain limitations and defects. The limitation is that it only conducts positioning research for closed trajectories, and does not involve research on non-closed trajectories. The defect type is manifested in the inefficiency of the improved algorithm of the proximity method, the dead reckoning will cause drift, the vision-based positioning algorithm is too complex, and the positioning algorithm based on multi-sensor fusion is vulnerable to environmental factors. Therefore, the laser radar combined with the logistics trolley is used to form a laser radar trolley system [10], and the accuracy can be in the centimeter level. However,

© ICST Institute for Computer Sciences, Social Informatics and Telecommunications Engineering 2021
Published by Springer Nature Switzerland AG 2021. All Rights Reserved
W. Fu et al. (Eds.): ICMTEL 2021, LNICST 387, pp. 407–413, 2021.
https://doi.org/10.1007/978-3-030-82562-1_38

when solving the trajectory, the LOAM algorithm has no closed-loop constraints, which will produce motion distortion; at the same time, filtering and estimating the state of the variables at the current moment is an iterative process, and the points in the point cloud scanned by the radar are discretized. Ensure that the points of the previous frame of data are still scanned in the next frame. Therefore, an adaptive particle filter algorithm is used to optimize the position and attitude of the laser odometer to estimate the accuracy. The adaptive particle filter algorithm accelerates particle convergence, while taking into account the diversity of particles, using a smaller number of particles to obtain more accurate trajectory results. This paper combines the LOAM algorithm and the APF algorithm to correct the trajectory when calculating the trolley trajectory of closed and semi-closed routes, which can effectively improve the accuracy of trajectory positioning.

2 Principle of LOAM Algorithm

The essence of the LOAM algorithm is a laser odometer. The algorithm divides the SLAM problem into two algorithms that run simultaneously to realize real-time mapping. The main steps of the LOAM algorithm:

1. Extract feature points
2. Find the corresponding point of the feature point
3. Estimation of action

3 Definition of Particle Filter

Adaptive particle filter (APF) algorithm model: The state of the dynamic system is probably distributed to $p(x_0)$. The post-test probability distribution of the target state x_k is $p(x_{0:k}|z_{1:k})$, $\{x_{0:k}^i, w_k^i\}_{i=1}^{N_s}$ is a particle population of the corresponding weight of $\{w_k^i, i = 0, \cdots, N_s\}$, where $x_{0:k} = \{x_j, j = 0, \cdots, k\}$ is the state set of 0 to k.

4 Fusion of LOAM Algorithm and APF Algorithm

4.1 The Initialization

Determine the movement coordinates of the trolley through the calibration of the position, for example, take the number of particles $N = 100$, filter the walking direction of the trolley, set the initial value of the weight to $1/N$, and according to the system setting, the sum of the weight of the particles is 1. Each particle represents the possible motion state of the trolley, that is, the possible position of the trolley.

4.2 State Transition of Particles

Taking into account the continuous transfer of particle states, the position of the trolley is constantly updated over time, and the Bayesian full probability formula is used to estimate its motion model.

$$P(X_{k,i}, X_{k+1,i+1}, U_{(k,k+1)}) \propto P(X_{0,0}|U_{i,0}) \prod_{k=1}^{i} P(X_k|X_{k+1}, U_k, U_{k+1}) \qquad (1)$$

Where: $X_{k,i}$ represents the pose node of the k-the frame lidar at time I, $X_{k+1,i+1}$ represents the pose node of the k-the frame lidar at time I, and $U_{(k,k+1)}$ represents the transfer matrix between two adjacent frames of radar data obtained by the LOAM matching algorithm.

4.3 Particle Update

The APF algorithm approximates the true posterior probability of the system by continuously updating the position and weight of the particle. Through the motion model, the particle continuously updates the position, and at the same time updates the weight value by measuring the model particle.

The feature point screening and matching of the LOAM algorithm and the prior probability density function and posterior probability density function of the particles are combined to obtain an optimized fusion matrix function.

$$f(U) = \min f(\sum_{i=1}^{n} d_{\varepsilon i}(U) + \sum_{j=1}^{m} d_{Hj}(U)) \qquad (2)$$

Where: $d_{\varepsilon i}$ is the distance between the i-th line characteristic point to line ε, d_{Hj} is the distance between the j-th feature point to the surface H.

$d_{\varepsilon i}$ and d_{Hj} are the distance from the $i$tch line feature point to the line and the j-the surface feature point to the surface respectively.

4.4 Re-sampling

The motion state and position of the trolley are estimated by selecting particles with larger weights. Using this distribution, the weight of the first particle:

$$\omega_t^{(i)} = \omega_{t-1}^{(i)} \cdot \eta^{(i)}. \qquad (3)$$

In the formula, the weight is selected by sampling method. If the particle set $\{ x_{0:k}^i \}_{i=1}^{N_s}$ can be obtained by the density function $q(x_{0:k}|z_{1:k})$, the weight is shown in the following formula:

$$w_k^i \propto \frac{p(x_{0:k}^i z_{1:k})}{q(x_{0:k}^i|z_{1:k})} \qquad (4)$$

5 Experiment and Analysis

The experimental equipment uses R-fans16 cable and a laptop equipped with ubuntu system and ROS system. In order to compare the accuracy of positioning, the relevant paths were planned in advance. Four control points including the start point and the end point were set on the fully enclosed path and the semi-closed path respectively, and the precise control points were obtained by using a total station. The location under the coordinates, the experimental equipment is shown in Fig. 1, the experimental routes are respectively selected indoor fully enclosed routes and semi-enclosed routes.

Fig. 1. Experimental equipment diagram

5.1 Fully Enclosed Route Experiment

In a closed indoor environment, a stone is placed every other segment, and the trolley is slowly moving along the closed loop at a speed of 0.5 m/s. The MATLAB simulation results of the two closed-loop experimental trajectories are shown below (Figs. 2 and 3).

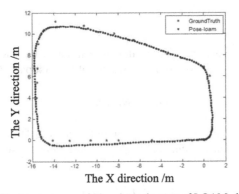

Fig. 2. Real trajectory and blue dot trajectory of LOAM algorithm

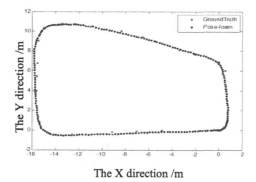

Fig. 3. Real trajectory and blue dot trajectory of LOAM-APF algorithm

Table 1. Trajectory positioning error of a fully enclosed route

Direction error	LOAM	LOAM-APF
X direction error/m	0.07	0.03
Y direction error/m	0.10	0.05

From Table 1, under the closed route, the positioning accuracy of LOAM-APF algorithm in the x direction is improved by 57.1%, and the positioning accuracy in the Y direction is improved by 50%.

5.2 Semi-closed Route Experiment

Four nodes are selected and a semi-enclosed route is planned. The trolley is slowly advancing at a speed of 500 mm/s. The MATLAB simulation results of the semi-circle experimental trajectory are shown in the figure below (Figs. 4, 5 and 6).

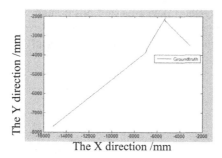

Fig. 4. Real trajectory

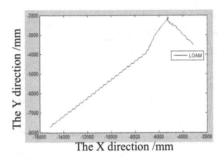

Fig. 5. Motion trajectory of LOAM algorithm

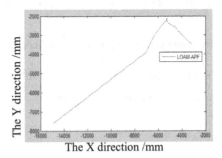

Fig. 6. Motion trajectory of LOAM-APF algorithm

Table 2. Trajectory positioning error of semi-closed route

Error	LOAM	LOAM-APF
Positioning error/mm	56	28
Error respectively/%	0.43	0.22

From Table 2, the standard deviation and positioning error distribution of using the LOAM-APF algorithm in the semi-closed route experiment are reduced by 50% compared to only using the LOAM algorithm, which greatly improves the accuracy of its positioning.

6   Conclusion

As the trajectory of the trolley increases, the trajectory calculated by the LOAM algorithm will fluctuate and deviate from the real trajectory, while the trajectory obtained by the LOAM-APF algorithm will basically not fluctuate. The LOAM-APF algorithm solves the problem of trajectory deviation in closed and semi-closed routes, which has certain practical significance.

Acknowledgments. The paper was supported by the projects of the National Natural Science Foundation of China (No. 41764002).

References

1. Chen, X., Pang, J.: Protecting query privacy in location-based services. GeoInformatica **18**(1), 95–133 (2014)
2. Huang, B., Liu, J., Sun, W., et al.: A Robust indoor positioning method based on Bluetooth Low energy with Separate channel information. Sensors **19**(16), 3487 (2019)
3. Xu, H., Ding, Y., Li, P., et al.: An RFID indoor positioning algorithm based on Bayesian probability and K-nearest neighbor. Sensors **17**(8), 1806 (2017)
4. Sharp, I., Yu, K.: Sensor-based dead-reckoning for indoor positioning. Phys. Commun. **13**(PA), 4–16 (2014)
5. Yang, S., Ma, L., Jia, S., et al.: An improved vision-based indoor positioning method. IEEE Access **8**, 26941–26949 (2020)
6. Ma, M., Song, Q., Gu, Y., et al.: An adaptive zero velocity detection algorithm based on multi-sensor fusion for a pedestrian navigation system. Sensors **18**(10), 3261 (2018)
7. Shi, Y., Zhang, W., Yao, Z., et al.: Design of a hybrid indoor location system based on multi-sensor fusion for robot navigation. Sensors **18**(10), 3581 (2018)
8. Gao, Y., Wang, F., Li, J., et al.: Localization of mobile robot based on multi-sensor fusion. In: 2020 Chinese Control And Decision Conference (CCDC), pp. 4367–4372. IEEE (2020)
9. Li, H.X., Ao, L.H., Guo, H., et al.: Indoor multi-sensor fusion positioning based on federated filtering. Measurement **154**, 107506 (2020)
10. Karam, S., Lehtola, V., Vosselman, G.: Strategies to integrate IMU and LIDAR SLAM for indoor mapping. ISPRS Ann. Photogramm. Remote Sens. Spat. Inf. Sci. **1**, 223–230 (2020)

Indoor Positioning and Navigation Methods Based on Mobile Phone Camera

Min Yu[1], Jiaohao Yu[1], Hailei Li[2], Huixia Li[2], and Hang Guo[2(✉)]

[1] Jiangxi Normal University, Nanchang 330027, China
[2] Nanchang University, Nanchang 330031, China
hguo@ncu.edu.cn

Abstract. The vision technology has been used for the indoor positioning based on a mobile phone camera. In this paper, we studied the 2D positioning method by analyzing the single frame image, obtaining the camera's interior/exterior orientation parameters through the image calibration procedure, and calculating the coordinates with the homography matrix. Further, the mobile phone camera has been used for the indoor navigation. The image data is processed and converted into the mobile phone's moving distance and the attitude by the coordinate transformation method (a four-parameter fitting model), and the trajectory of the mobile phone can be calculated by the visual navigation method. In the first experiment, four points have been selected as the calibration points, and the positioning method has been conducted and analyzed. The experimental results with the software GIANT show that the error is 0.192 m in the area 9.6 m × 3.2 m, which reached a high accuracy of the indoor positioning. In the second experiment, a mobile phone has been moved inside the lab room, image data was collected, the trajectory was calculated with the navigation method proposed, and the mean error of 0.685 m has been obtained. Both results explained that the proposed methods can effectively improve the accuracy and stability of indoor positioning and navigation.

Keywords: Coordinate transformation · Homography matrix · Indoor positioning and navigation · Mobile phone localization

1 Introduction

The previous research shows that 60% of information human acquired is done through eyes. The information is so called visual information. With the continuous development of AI (Artificial Intelligence), people hope to get more and more humanoid products to serve for mankind. Therefore, computer vision arises at the historic moment. In short, computer vision is to install "eyes" on computers to simulate human visual organs. Cameras and other imaging systems are often used to simulate human eyes and provide visual information for computers. At the same time, the computer act as a human brain to process information obtained by imaging systems such as cameras, and then makes the action guidance. According to the number of cameras in the process of collecting image data, they can be divided into monocular vision, binocular vision and multi-vision.

© ICST Institute for Computer Sciences, Social Informatics and Telecommunications Engineering 2021
Published by Springer Nature Switzerland AG 2021. All Rights Reserved
W. Fu et al. (Eds.): ICMTEL 2021, LNICST 387, pp. 414–426, 2021.
https://doi.org/10.1007/978-3-030-82562-1_39

Therefore, positioning techniques include single frame image, double frame image, and multi-frame image method, depending on the number of image frames used.

Mobile phone localization is a method of obtaining external information through a camera. Compared with binocular and multi-visual positioning, the positioning method has the advantages of simple operation and wide applications. This technique does not need to calibrate and optimize the distance between the two cameras in binocular vision, and does not need to consider the problem of large distortion due to the different location of multiple cameras in the visual location. In computer vision, how to solve the location problem under known visual conditions has become an important research field. Mobile phone location technology can be applied to all aspects of production and life, such as target tracking, visual servoing, robot localization, etc. There are also many methods of positioning by vision techniques, such as the localization based on single-frame, double-frame, and multi-frame images. This paper mainly studied the vision localization based on the single-frame image, and the indoor navigation method based on the continue images of the mobile phone camera. The image data is processed and converted into the moving distance and the attitude of the mobile phone by the coordinate transformation (four-parameter fitting model), and the trajectory of the mobile phone can be calculated by the visual navigation method. The proposed methods can effectively improve the accuracy and stability of indoor positioning and navigation. In the future, multi-sensor navigation systems can be implemented by adding other sensors, which can further improve positioning and navigation accuracy.

2   Indoor Positioning Method Based on Single Frame Image

2.1   Visual Localization Based on Single Frame Image

Visual localization based on single-frame image is a method of locating the position information from a single image [1]. Since only one frame is used, the location process is simple, but at the same time, the amount of information contained in one frame is relatively small. Therefore, the artificial marks must be set in the environment that needs to be located. The location parameters of the marks must be known to assist the completion of the positioning process. We can use points, straight lines, and advanced geometry as artificial marks. A straight linear feature is favored by some scholars because of its advantages such as being unobstructed and easy to extract. There is little research on advanced geometric feature for localization at present since the position of geometric features needs to be solved for very complex nonlinear equations, and algorithm has very high complexity. Location algorithm based on the point feature is a classical algorithm in computer vision, and it is also called PnP (Perspective-n-Point) problem. This problem can be solved as: when the pinhole imaging model of the camera is known and the various parameters of the camera have been calibrated, and after the n landmarks of the real environment are acquired, the image coordinates of the n landmarks can be measured, and the coordinate values in the local coordinate system can be calculated by the image coordinates. With the GIANT software, the coordinates of these n landmarks in the local coordinate system can be calculated through the coordinates of the landmarks in the image coordinate system. Four points have been set as the reference points. The location errors can be obtained by comparing the calculated coordinates of the same points with the known reference coordinates.

In this paper, four points were selected as reference points (the local coordinates of the four points in the scene and the image coordinates in the pictures are all known) to calibrate the camera, and to obtain the internal and external orientation parameters as well as the distortion parameters in the camera. By using the geometric correspondence between image points and real locations in the photography, the coordinates of all points on the picture can be used to calculate the coordinates in the local coordinate system by means of the photogrammetry collinear equation. How to match the real locations with the image points is the focus of this paper. The method proposed has the advantages of simple form, convenient calculation and high accuracy.

2.2 Camera Model

The images used in the experiment were obtained by the mobile phone camera. Therefore, we need to study the characteristics and pinhole imaging model of the camera [2].

The pinhole imaging model, also known as the linear camera model, is derived from the principle of pinhole imaging, and is a linearized geometric model. The model does not consider the distortion of the camera, which is the best approximation of the actual camera. The Fig. 1 shows the camera coordinate system (Xc, Yc, Zc) and the world coordinate system (Xw, Yw, Zw), where O is the camera center, O_1 the focal length, and Zc is the optical axis of the camera which is perpendicular to the plane of the image.

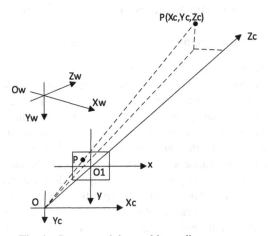

Fig. 1. Camera and the world coordinate systems

Suppose there is a point P in the real world (Fig. 1), and its coordinates in the camera coordinate system are (Xc, Yc, Zc), and the image coordinates of the corresponding points on the image are (x, y), and f is the focal length of the camera. The proportional relation is:

$$\begin{cases} x = \frac{f \cdot X_c}{Z_c} \\ y = \frac{f \cdot Y_c}{Z_c} \end{cases} \tag{1}$$

The above perspective projection relation is represented by the homogeneous coordinates and matrices.

$$
Z_c \begin{bmatrix} x \\ y \\ 1 \end{bmatrix} = \begin{bmatrix} f & 0 & 0 & 0 \\ 0 & f & 0 & 0 \\ 0 & 0 & 1 & 0 \end{bmatrix} \begin{bmatrix} X_c \\ Y_c \\ Z_c \\ 1 \end{bmatrix} = P \begin{bmatrix} X_c \\ Y_c \\ Z_c \\ 1 \end{bmatrix} \tag{2}
$$

Where Z_c is a scale factor also, and P is a perspective projection matrix. The pixel coordinates into the formula can be obtained.

$$
\begin{aligned}
Z_c \begin{bmatrix} u \\ v \\ 1 \end{bmatrix} &= \begin{bmatrix} \frac{1}{dx} & 0 & u_0 \\ 0 & \frac{1}{dy} & v_0 \\ 0 & 0 & 1 \end{bmatrix} \begin{bmatrix} f & 0 & 0 & 0 \\ 0 & f & 0 & 0 \\ 0 & 0 & 1 & 0 \end{bmatrix} \begin{bmatrix} R & T \\ 0^T & 1 \end{bmatrix} \begin{bmatrix} X_w \\ Y_w \\ Z_w \\ 1 \end{bmatrix} \\
&= \begin{bmatrix} a_x & 0 & u_0 & 0 \\ 0 & a_y & v_0 & 0 \\ 0 & 0 & 1 & 0 \end{bmatrix} \begin{bmatrix} R & T \\ 0^T & 1 \end{bmatrix} \begin{bmatrix} X_w \\ Y_w \\ Z_w \\ 1 \end{bmatrix} = M_1 M_2 X_w = M \begin{bmatrix} X_w \\ Y_w \\ Z_w \\ 1 \end{bmatrix}
\end{aligned} \tag{3}
$$

Where the rotation matrix R is the orthogonal unit matrix (3×3) and T is a three-dimensional translation vector, the pixel coordinates are u and v in the pixel coordinate system, the physical scales of each pixel in the direction of the x axis and the y axis are dx, dy, $a_z = f/dx$ is the scaling factor of the u axis, $a_y = f/dy$ is the scaling factor of the v axis, M is the projection matrix, and the M_1 is the directional parameter within the camera. M_2 is the orientation parameter of the camera, and it is determined by the orientation of the camera relative to the local coordinate system. When the camera's internal and external parameters are known, that is, the projection matrix M is known. For any spatial point $P_w(X_w, Y_w, Z_w)$, the coordinates x, y of its image point $p(u, v)$ can be obtained.

2.3 Principle of Image Measurement

According to the principle of the photography, the homography matrix is satisfied between the scene plane and the image plane [3–5]. First, we need to obtain the homography matrix H, and then can calculate the coordinates of all points in the scene plane based on that of the image plane. Suppose that the homography matrix is:

$$
H = \begin{bmatrix} H_{11} & H_{12} & H_{13} \\ H_{21} & H_{22} & H_{23} \\ H_{31} & H_{32} & H_{33} \end{bmatrix} \tag{4}
$$

And

$$
h = (H_{11}, H_{12}, H_{13}, H_{21}, H_{22}, H_{23}, H_{31}, H_{32}, H_{33})^T \tag{5}
$$

$$
x_P' = \left(x_1', y_1', 1 \right)^T \tag{6}
$$

$$X_P = (X_1, Y_1, 1)^T \tag{7}$$

So

$$M_H(X) = \begin{bmatrix} x^T 0^T - X_1 x^T \\ 0^T x^T - Y_1 x^T \end{bmatrix} h = 0 \tag{8}$$

where $x_p^{'} = (x_1^{'}, y_1^{'}, 1)^T$ is the coordinates of any point on the image, and $X_P = (X_1, Y_1, 1)^T$ is the coordinates in the scene. According to the form of the homography matrix, we need the four known points to solve the parameter values in the homography matrix. The basic requirement of the four known points is that the coordinates in the local coordinates and the image coordinates are all known, and these points must have a general position, that is, any three points are not collinear. The locations of these points selected are shown in Fig. 2.

The results of this experiment were obtained by using GIANT software (the copyright belongs to the Mr. Clifford Mugnier of the Louisiana State University, the USA). A similar homography algorithm is used in the GIANT [6–20].

$$\begin{cases} X_w = \frac{a_1 x + a_2 y + a_3}{c_1 x + c_2 y + 1} \\ Y_w = \frac{b_1 x + b_2 y + b_3}{c_1 x + c_2 y + 1} \end{cases} \tag{9}$$

Based on the image plane coordinates of any point w for (x, y), by the homography matrix, one can calculate the coordinates of the point w in the local coordinates (X_w, Y_w).

3 Indoor Navigation Method Based on Monocular Vision

According to the coordinate transformation method, the translation and rotation between two coordinate systems can only be calculated from the three same points on those two coordinate systems, which are non-collinear. The monocular camera can obtain the pixels of the pictures on a two-dimensions pixel coordinate system. Then, the translation and rotation between two continue coordinate systems can be fitted and determined by four parameters. The matrix algorithm is as follows [15–39]:

$$\begin{bmatrix} x_2 \\ y_2 \end{bmatrix} = \begin{bmatrix} \Delta x \\ \Delta y \end{bmatrix} + k \begin{bmatrix} \cos\theta & -\sin\theta \\ \sin\theta & \cos\theta \end{bmatrix} \begin{bmatrix} x_1 \\ y_1 \end{bmatrix} \tag{10}$$

where x_1, y_1 are the pixel coordinates at one time point, x_2, y_2 are the pixel coordinates at next time point, Δx, Δy are the translation components when the mobile phone from the point 1 to the point 2, θ is the rotation between two consecutive coordinate systems, k is the scale factor between them. Set $C = k\cos\theta$, $S = k\sin\theta$, and make the formula (10) expansion, one can get the formulas:

$$\begin{cases} \Delta x + x_1 * C - y_1 * S = x_2 \\ \Delta y + x_1 * S + y_1 * C = y_2 \end{cases} \tag{11}$$

or can be expressed as the following matrix formula:

$$AX = B \tag{12}$$

where $A = \begin{bmatrix} 1 & 0 & x_1 & -y_1 \\ 0 & 1 & y_1 & x_1 \end{bmatrix}$ $X = \begin{bmatrix} \Delta x \\ \Delta y \\ C \\ S \end{bmatrix}$ $B = \begin{bmatrix} x_2 \\ y_2 \end{bmatrix}$

Through the matrix solution, one can obtain the values of the matrix X, and get the translation Δx, Δy, and using C, S can calculate the rotation parameter θ as follows [40–41]:

$$\theta = arcsin \frac{S}{C*sqr\left(1 + \frac{S}{C}^2\right)} \tag{13}$$

4 First Experimental Design and Data Analysis

4.1 Processing of the Feature Points

The horizontal location (two-dimensions) test was conducted inside the building of the institute on the campus as shown in the Fig. 2. The experimental site was in the indoor corridor of the institute building, and the local coordinate system of the corridor was established before the experiment, so that all the coordinates of the points in the corridor can be calculated by the local coordinate system.

Fig. 2. The experiment site with the points on the floor.

The total of 32 points in the place of the experiment are marked as the Fig. 2, including four known points (See the black points for calibrating the coefficients in the homography matrix). Due to the influence of the camera angle, these 32 points cover the length of 9.6 m and the width is 3.2 m area. The selected points are named 0–31 respectively, in and 0–3 points are selected as the known points (the black points) to

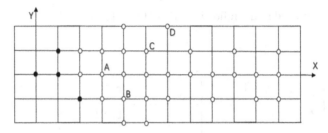

Fig. 3. The point positions in the experiment

solve the homography matrix H. The local coordinates of the remaining 28 points are obtained by the software GIANT, and the coordinates of the points are shown in the hollow points in Fig. 3.

For the purpose of checking the accuracy of the proposed method, several points were selected to calculate and compare the actual coordinates to get their errors (See points A, B, C, and D as the Fig. 3). The maximum error of the four points listed in Table 1 is 0.10 m, and the experimental error was within the allowable range.

Table 1. Comparison of partial point coordinates (Unit: m)

Selected points	Image coordinates (x, y)/pixel	Local coordinates (X, Y)	Calculated coordinates (X, Y)	Point errors (X, Y)
A	(148.24, 0.00)	(2.40, 0.00)	(2.40, 0.00)	(0.00, 0.00)
B	(164.80, −36.50)	(3.20, −0.80)	(3.27, −0.83)	(0.07, −0.03)
C	(175.04, 30.98)	(4.00, 0.80)	(4.06, 0.81)	(0.06, 0.01)
D	(183.28, 54.18)	(4.80, 1.60)	(4.90, 1.64)	(0.10, 0.04)

4.2   Analysis of Experimental Results

The result of experimental data is obtained by GIANT software. In order to show the experimental results more intuitively, Table 2. calculated the absolute error values of some points.

It can be seen from the Table 2. that the error obtained from the point (2.40, 0.00) is (0.00, 0.00), the absolute error obtained from the point (3.20, −0.80) is (0.05, 0.01), and the mean location error $\sqrt{\Delta x^2 + \Delta y^2}$ is 0.192 m in the area of 9.6 m × 3.2 m. From the error values of these points, the position closer to the origin point is very accurate, and with the distance gradually increases the error obtained is increase. The reason is that with the distance from the origin increases the distortion of the camera becomes larger, the sharpness of the image decreases, and the difficulty of finding the target point increases, which leads to an increase in calculation error.

Table 2. Absolute errors (unit: m)

True coordinates (x, y)	Measured coordinates (x, y)	Errors ($\triangle x, \triangle y$)
(2.40, 0.00)	(2.40, 0.00)	(0.00, 0.00)
(3.20, −0.80)	(3.25, −0.81)	(0.05, 0.01)
(4.00, 0.80)	(4.06, 0.81)	(0.06, 0.01)
(4.80, 1.60)	(4.88, 1.64)	(0.08, 0.04)
(5.60, 0.80)	(5.70, 0.83)	(0.10, 0.03)
(6.40, −0.80)	(6.55, −0.83)	(0.15, 0.03)
(7.20, 0.80)	(7.50, 0.83)	(0.30, 0.03)
(8.00, −0.80)	(8.56, −0.85)	(0.56, 0.05)
(8.80, 0.00)	(9.20, 0.05)	(0.40, 0.05)

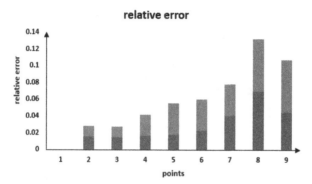

Fig. 4. Relative errors (Unit: m)

Figure 4. is the relative error on the axis X and Y coordinates. The blue color represents the X axis, and the orange represents the Y axis. As can be seen from the figure, the error on both coordinate axes gradually increases with the increase of the distance, and the increase of the two is equivalent.

4.3 Error Analysis and Improvement Measures

With the increasing of the distance from the center of the camera, the accuracy of the point solution decreases. The reasons of reducing the location accuracy are as follows:

Camera distortion is one of the reasons. The experimental basis of this paper is based on the ideal model of camera, pinhole imaging. The imaging system ignores the effect of camera distortion on the image. When the distance from the center of the camera is close, the distortion of the camera is low, and the effect on the image is very small. However, with the distance from the origin is lengthened, the influence of camera distortion on the image increases gradually, which caused positioning errors.

The errors after the initial calibration cannot be eliminated completely. It is more difficult to obtain the location accurately with the software, and the deviation gets larger and larger.

The clarity of the image is reduced, when the distance is closer to the center of the camera, it is very easy to find the location of the points when processing the pictures. However, when the distance becomes longer, it is difficult to find the points, and the recognition degree of fixed-point decreases.

5   Second Experimental Design and Data Analysis

The experiment was performed inside the XIANSU building at the campus Yao lake of Jiangxi Normal University, Nanchang, China. As shown in the Fig. 5, the test area is about 12 m × 13 m, including some sofas, tables, and the office staffs. In the experiment, a mobile phone has been used for conducting the indoor navigation. The trajectory is shown in the red line with the start of a circle and the end of a triangle.

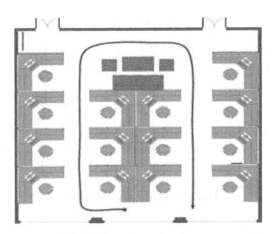

Fig. 5. Experimental trajectory

The Fig. 6 described the mobile phone test results with the green line, which compared with the real trajectory with the red line. The mean error of indoor navigation in the area of 12 m × 13 m is 0.685 m. The feature points are extracted and the processing environment is as shown in the Fig. 7.

Compared to the mobile phone positioning experiment results on the corridor at the section IV, both positioning and navigation results are shown in the Table 3. Through the two experiments, we obtained the valuable experience that a decimeter accuracy of localization and navigation can be reached with the current mobile phone camera and the methods we proposed.

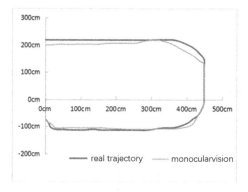

Fig. 6. Comparison of the experimental trajectory

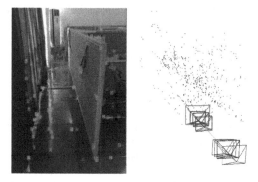

Fig. 7. Monocular visual navigation experiment

Table 3. Mobile phone location errors (unit: m)

Methods	First experiment	Second experiment
Mean errors	0.192	0.685

6 Conclusion

In this paper, the location of any point on the corridor is realized on the basis of the single-frame image. Based on the known camera model and the homography matrix, the location method based on the point feature is adopted. The first experiment proves that the method has high positioning accuracy (the mean error is 0.192 m), but it also has the shortcoming of the positioning precision decline with the distance increasing from the center of the camera. To deal with this deficiency, the reasons for the errors are analyzed, and these errors come from the distortion of the camera due to the single-frame. In the second experiment, the indoor navigation method with the mobile phone used the coordinate transformation, calculated the trajectory, and achieved the accuracy at the level of 0.685 m. In the future, when some other sensors, such as IMU, Lidar, etc., are added to conduct a multi-sensor navigation system the accuracy of positioning and navigation is expected to be improved.

Acknowledgments. The paper was supported by the projects of the National Key R&D Program of China (No. 2016YFB0502204), National Natural Science Foundation of China (No. 41764002), and the corresponding author is Prof. Hang Guo, hguo@ncu.edu.cn.

References

1. Brito, J.H., Angst, R., Köser, K., et al.: Radial Distortion Self-Calibration, Computer Vision and Pattern Recognition, pp. 1368–1375. IEEE, June 2013
2. Bukhari, F., Dailey, M.N.: Automatic radial distortion estimation from a single image. J. Math. Imaging Vis. **45**(1), 1–45 (2013)
3. Fischler, M.A., Bolles, R.C.: Random sample consensus: a paradigm for model fitting with applications to image analysis and automated cartography. Commun. ACM **24**, 381–395 (1981)
4. Fiore, P.D.: Efficient linear solution of exterior orientation. IEEE Trans. Pattern Anal. Mach. Intell. **23**(2), 140–148 (2011)
5. Shi, B., Matsushita, Y., Wei, Y., Xu, C., Tan, P.: Self-calibrating photometric stereo. In: IEEE Conference on computer vision and pattern recognition (CVPR) - San Francisco, CA, USA (2010.06.13-2010.06.18), pp. 1118–1125 (2010)
6. Schweighofer, G., Pinz, A.: Robust pose estimation from a planar target. IEEE Trans. Pattern Anal. Mach. Intell. **28**(12), 2024–2030 (2006)
7. Strobl,K.H., Hirzinger,G.: More accurate pinhole camera calibration with imperfect planar target. IEEE Int. Conf. Comput. Vis. Workshops 1068–1075 (2011)
8. Ma, S.D., Zhang, Z.Y.: Computer Vision-The Theory of Computer and Basis of Algorithm. Science Press, China (1997)
9. Kuthirummal, S., Jawahar, C.V., Narayanan, P.J.: Planar shape recognition across multiple views. Int. Conf. Patt. Recogn. **1**, 456–459 (2002)
10. Kukelova, Z., Pajdla, T.: A minimal solution to radial distortion autocalibration. IEEE Trans. Pattern Anal. Mach. Intell. **33**(12), 2410–2422 (2011)
11. Jain, P.K., Jawahar, C.V.: Homography estimation from planar contours. In: The Third International Symposium on 3D Date Processing Visualization and Transmission, pp. 877–884 (2006)
12. Kanatani, K., Ohta, N., Kanazawa, Y.: Optimal homography computation with a reliability measure. In: IAPR workshop on Machine Vision Applications, pp. 426–429 (1998)
13. Liu, R., Ruan, Z.C., Wei, S.: Algorithm research on monochronous matrix in plane measurement. J. Syst. Simul. **13**(suppl.), 174–176 (2011)
14. Wang, Y.X., Ma, Y., Chen, Q.X.: A method of line matching based on feature points. J. Softw. **7**(7), 1539–1545 (2012)
15. Xu, D., Tan, M., Li, Y.: Robot Vision Measurement and Control. National Defense Industry Press, China (2008)
16. Xu, D., Tan, M., Li, Y.: Visual Measurement and Control for Robots. National Defense Industry Press, China, pp. 35–39 (2011)
17. Liu, R., Wei, S.: Research on plane Measurement method based on Image. M.S. thesis, Elect. Inf. Eng., University of Anhui, Anhui, China (2002)
18. Han, Y.X., Zhang, Z.C., Dai, M.: Monocular vision measurement method for target ranging. Opt. Precis. Eng. **19**(5), 1110–1117 (2011)

19. Hartley, R., Zisserman, A.: Multiple View Geometry in Computer Vision: Camera Models. Cambridge University Press, vol. 30 (9–10), pp. 1865–1872 (2004)
20. Zhang, Y., Liu, Y.: Closed-from solution for circle pose estimation using binocular stereo vision. Electron. Lett. **44**(21), 1246–1247 (2008)
21. Zhang, Q.D., Fan, J.S.: Application and development of satellite navigation and positioning technology in China. J. Navig. Positioning **4**(3), 82–88 (2016)
22. Dwiyasa, F., Lim, M.H.: A survey of problems and approaches in wireless-based indoor positioning. In: International Conference on Indoor Positioning and Indoor Navigation, pp. 1–7. IEEE (2016)
23. Di, K.C., Wan, W.H., Zhao, H.Y., et al.: Progress and applications of visual SLAM. Acta Geodaetica et Cartographica Sinica **47**(6), 770–779 (2018)
24. Li, H.X., Wen, X., Guo, H., et al.: Research into Kinect/Inertial Measurement Units Based on Indoor Robots. Sensors **18**(3), 839 (2018)
25. Chen, X.L.: Research of attitude calculation of single camera visual system. Chin. J. Sci. Instrument **35**(S1), 45–48 (2014)
26. Feng, K.Q., Li, J., Zhang, X.M., et al.: A new quaternion-based Kalman filter for real-time attitude estimation using the two-step geometrically-intuitive correction algorithm. Sensors **17**(9), 2146 (2017)
27. Song, H.H., Yu, G.X., Qu, Y.B.: Monitoring and forecasting system for ship attitude motion based on extended Kalman filtering algorithm. J. Chin. Inertial Technol. **26**(1), 6–12 (2018)
28. Li, J., et al.: High-precision attitude measurement algorithm based on complementary filtering and Kalman filtering. J. Chin. Inertial Technol. **26**(1), 51–55+86 (2018)
29. Mu, X.F., Chen, J., Zhou, Z.X., et al.: accurate initial state estimation in a monocular visual – inertial SLAM system. Sensor **18**(2), 506 (2018)
30. Feng, G., Huang, X.: Observability analysis of navigation system using point-based visual and inertial sensors. Optik – Int. J. Light Electron Opt. **125**(3), 1346–1353 (2014)
31. Guo, H., Li, H., Xiong, J., Yu, M.: Indoor positioning system based on particle swarm optimization algorithm. Measurement **134**, 908–913 (2019)
32. Guo, H., Tian, B.L., Yu, M., Deng, L.K., Wang, H.T.: Improved ambiguity searching method of ultra-short baseline with nonlinear constraint. In: Proceedings of the 2018 International Technical Meeting of the Institute of Navigation, Reston, Virginia, pp. 46–55 (2018)
33. Guo, H., Uradzinski, M.: The usability of MTI IMU sensor data in PDR indoor positioning. In: 2018 25th Saint Petersburg International Conference on Integrated Navigation Systems (ICINS 2018), May 2018
34. Xu, Y., Ahn, C.K., Shmaliy, Y.S., et al.: Adaptive robust INS/UWB-integrated human tracking using UFIR filter bank. Measurement **123**, 1–7 (2018)
35. Xu, Y., Shmaliy, Y.S., Li, Y., Chen, X., Guo, H.: Indoor ins/lidar-based robot localization with improved robustness using cascaded fir filter. IEEE Access **7**(1), 34189–34197 (2019)
36. Xu, Y., Tian, G., Chen, X.: Enhancing INS/UWB integrated position estimation using federated EFIR filtering. IEEE Access **6**, 64461–64469 (2018)
37. Xu, Y., Karimi, H.R., Li, Y.Y., Zhou, F.Y., Bu, L.L.: Real-time accurate pedestrian tracking using EFIR filter bank for tightly coupling recent inertial navigation system and ultra-wideband measurements. Proc. Inst. Mech. Eng. Part I-J. Syst. Control Eng. **232**(4), 464–472 (2018)
38. Xu, Y., Chen, X.: Online cubature Kalman filter Rauch–Tung–Striebel smoothing for indoor inertial navigation system/ultrawideband integrated pedestrian navigation. Proc. Inst. Mech. Eng. Part I-J. Syst. Control Eng. **232**(4), 390–398 (2018)
39. Xu, Y., Shmaliy, Y.S., Li, Y., Chen, X.: UWB-based indoor human localization with time-delayed data using EFIR filtering. IEEE Access **5**(1), 16676–16683 (2017)

40. Uradzinski, M., Guo, H., Mugnier, C.: Checking the accuracy of an inertial-based pedestrian navigation system with a drone. GPS World **28**(6), 58–64 (2017)
41. Uradzinski, M., Guo, H., Liu, X., Yu, M.: Advanced indoor positioning using Zigbee wireless technology. Wireless Pers. Commun. **97**(4), 6509–6518 (2017). https://doi.org/10.1007/s11 277-017-4852-5

PD Controller of a Lower Limb Exoskeleton Robot Based on Sliding Mode RBF Neural Network

Aihui Wang[1]($\boxtimes$), Wei Li[2], and Jun yu[3]

[1] School of Electric and Information Engineering,
Zhongyuan University of Technology, Zhengzhou 450007, China
a.wang@zut.edu.cn
[2] Zhongyuan University of Technology, Zhengzhou 450007, China
2019006091@zut.edu.cn
[3] Zhongyuan-Petersburg Aviation College, Zhongyuan University of Technology,
Zhengzhou 450007, China

Abstract. The lower limb exoskeleton robot (LLER) is a human-robot interaction device that combines human functions and mechanical characteristics. Due to the complexity and strong coupling of human gait, it is difficult for LLER to be worn comfortably and safely for training. In such a scenario, the paper proposes a kind of proportional-derivative(PD) controller of LLER based on sliding mode RBF neural network(SMRBF-nn). In order to verify the effectiveness of the proposed control scheme, pertinent experiments were carried out. The gait data of the subject was collected through the motion capture system. A simulating model was established, different control methods, like conventional SMRBF-nn controller and PD controller based on SMRBF-nn, have been tested on the LLER. The experimental results show that the control strategy proposed in this paper can not only make LLER track the human body's gait trajectory, but also output appropriate torque when there is a disturbance.

Keywords: LLER · PD · SMRBF-nn · Human gait

1 Introduction

Since LLER has been developed, it has shown a genuine advantage in helping patients with lower limb dysfunction to assure rehabilitation training programs and physical movement assistance. In recent years, there have been more and more application scenarios of exoskeleton robots, and their performance has been continuously enhanced, especially assisting human movement and increasing the physical strength of the human muscle [1]. LLER controller plays an

The authors would like to thank the Henan Province Science and Technology R&D projects (182102410056, 202102210097, 202102210135), Young Backbone Teachers in Henan Province (2017GGJS117), and National Natural Science Foundation (62073297, U1813201) for their support of this work.

W. Fu et al. (Eds.): ICMTEL 2021, LNICST 387, pp. 427–436, 2021.
https://doi.org/10.1007/978-3-030-82562-1_40

important role in addressing the issue of Human-computer interaction, controller can quickly and accurately respond to human movement, and improves the fit between the robot and the human body [2]. The collection and analysis of data is the prerequisite to study the whole gait. In this paper, a set of motion capture system is used to collect the gait information of the human body during the movement process. The optical motion capture system is utilized to accurately locate the human gait trajectory in the experimental space [3]. Optical motion capture devices have been applied in many fields. Generally, the dynamic model is optimized on the basis of forward dynamics or reversing dynamics. Forward dynamics directly build muscle and joint models and obtain motion characteristics by optimizing motion equations [4]. In contrast, inverse kinematics regards the motion trajectory as the solution variable and calculates the joint torque according to the motion equation, which can avoid a mass of numerical integration [5]. However, humans' gait movement is extremely complicated, and the complex relationship between energy expenditure, muscle fatigue and joint load must be considered [6]. Therefore, there is no precise formula for the optimization of the dynamic model. Most of the optimization schemes are obtained from specific individuals and lack general adaptability. In order to reduce the error of the model and improve the accuracy of the gait, many researchers have proposed machine learning algorithms and got a good result [7]. For example, employed generalized regression neural network to predict the Fourier coefficient vector of a given gait parameter and lower limb anthropometric data, which is closer to the actual waveform than clinical gait analysis (CGA) data [8]. Radial basis function neural network (RBF-nn) is a nonlinear neural network with a simple structure, which can realize the kinematics controller and inverse dynamics controller, and has good control performance [9].

In this paper, using NoKov optical three-dimensional motion capture system, its gait capture accuracy meets our experimental requirements. This paper employs a control scheme that combines SMRBF-nn with PD to approximate human gait trajectory(as shown Fig. 1). In order to verify the effectiveness of the employed control scheme, we designed a gait capture experiment and MATLAB simulation for normal human. We also compared and evaluated the corresponding simulation results of the employed control scheme.

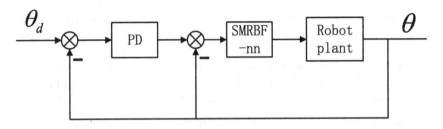

Fig. 1. System flow diagram

2   Laboratory Equipment

2.1   Motion Capture System

The current mainstream gait data acquisition equipment is based on the measurement method of high-speed optical cameras to capture the space trajectory
of the markers. This paper uses NoKov optical motion capture system as shown
in Fig. 2.

The subject's human joints are labeled with mark points, and the motion
capture system will capture the gait trajectory of the subject walking in the
experimental space. The captured gait data needs to be smoothed initially by
the Cortex software, and then the human gait data is derived. Figure 3 depicts
the relationships between joints angles.

2.2   Lower Limb Exoskeleton Robot

LLER realizes the combination of human control and mechanical power, so that
humans have the advantages of mechanical power, speed and endurance and can
better perform the functions of humans and machines. The LLER used in this
paper adopts a flexible bionic design, has four active degrees of freedom and two
passive degrees of freedom, and can be adjusted according to the wearer's body
shape.

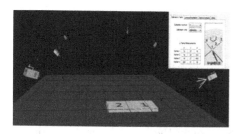

Fig. 2. NoKov optical motion capture
system

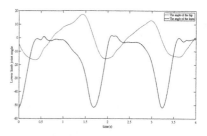

Fig. 3. Joints angle are processed by
inverse kinematics

3   PD Controler Based on SMRBF-nn

3.1   Dynamic Modeling of LLER

Due to the symmetry of the gait motion, the dynamic model of the LLER can
be simply used as a two-link model.

This paper uses a Lagrangian method to establish the exoskeleton dynamics
model.

$$M(\theta)\ddot{\theta} + C(\theta, \dot{\theta})\dot{\theta} + G(\theta) = \tau - \tau_d \tag{1}$$

Where, $M(\theta) \in R^{2\times2}$ is a positive definite inertia matrix, $C(\theta) \in R^{2\times2}$ is the Coriolis force and centrifugal force matrix, $G(\theta) \in R^{2\times1}$ is the gravity matrix, $\tau_d \in R^{2\times1}$ is external disturbances, $\tau=[\tau_h, \tau_k]^T$ are the moments representing the hip joint and knee joint respectively. However, considering the force between the human body and the exoskeleton, the dynamic model expressed in (1) can be rewritten as follows:

$$(M+M_0)\ddot{\theta} + (C + C_0)\dot{\theta} + (G + G_0) = \tau - \tau_d \tag{2}$$

Where, M_0, C_0, G_0 are unknown.

Let's introduce a new variable such that: $x_1 = \theta$ and $x_2 = \dot{\theta}$. So, the dynamic model expressed in (2) can be rewritten as follows:

$$\begin{cases} \dot{x}_1 = x_2 \\ \dot{x}_2 = u(t) - f(t) - g(t) \end{cases} \tag{3}$$

So, $g(t) = M^{-1}C\dot{\theta} + M^{-1}G$, $f(t) = M^{-1}\tau_d + M^{-1}C_0\dot{\theta} + M^{-1}G_0 + M_0\ddot{\theta}$. It is difficult to obtain $f(t)$ due to the indetermination of the dynamic model of the LLER and unknown external disturbances effects. Before explaining the control methodology, the properties and the assumptions that are used in this paper are given as follows:

Property 1. Matrix M is symmetric and positive definite.

Property 2. There exist finite scalars $\eta_i > 0$, $i = 1, 2, 3, 4$. The $\|M\| \le \eta_1$, $\|C\| \le \eta_2$, $\|G\| \le \eta_3$ and $\|\tau_d\| \le \eta_4$ which means all items are bounded [10].

Property 3. The function $f(t)$ is bounded and globally Lipschitz function.

3.2   RBF Neural Network

The RBF neural network has three layers, namely the input layer, the hidden layer and the output layer.

Choose Gaussian function as the activation function of the RBF neural network, $H = [h_1, h_2, \cdots, h_j]^T$. The input of the neural network is x, the coordinate direction of the Gaussian function center point of the is c_j, and the width of the Gaussian function is b_j.

$$h_j = \exp(-\frac{\|x - c_j\|^2}{2b_j^2}) \tag{4}$$

The weight of the RBF neural network is $W = [w_1, w_2, \cdots, w_m]^T$. The output of the RBF neural network can be expressed as:

$$y_m = W^T H = w_1 h_1 + w_2 h_2 + \cdots + w_m h_m \tag{5}$$

The f contains all the information of the lower limb exoskeleton robot model. This article uses the RBF neural network to approximate f.

$$\hat{f} = \widehat{W}^T h$$

The approximation error of the RBF neural network is:

$$\Delta f = f - \hat{f} = \widetilde{W}^T h + \varepsilon \tag{6}$$

Where, ε is a small positive number, $\widetilde{W} = W - \widehat{W}$, $\|W\|_F \leq W_{\max}$.

The input of the RBF neural network is $x = [e, \dot{e}, \theta_d, \dot{\theta}_d, \ddot{\theta}_d]^T$.

3.3 Controller Design

Define tracking error $e = x_d - x_1$. Where, $x_d = [\theta_{dh}, \theta_{dk}]^T$ is the desired joint angle of the robot's hip joint and knee joint.

Close the loop via the PD controller, which is designed as follow:

$$u = \ddot{\theta}_d + f + g + \tau_{PD} \tag{7}$$

Where, $\tau_{PD} = K_P e + K_D \dot{e}$.

Combining Eq. (2) and (7), we can obtain the following equation:

$$\ddot{e} + \tau_{PD} = 0 \tag{8}$$

It is obvious that the poorly known parameters and external disturbances of the plant f is eliminated. The tracking error can be close to zero through a simple zero-pole assignment.

Thus, the PD controller based on SMRBF-nn utilized can be designed as:

$$u = \ddot{\theta}_d + \hat{f} + g + \tau_{PD} \tag{9}$$

Combining Eq. (2) and (9), we can obtain the approximation error of the RBF neural network following equation:

$$\Delta f = f - \hat{f} = \ddot{e} + \tau_{PD} \tag{10}$$

Combining formula (8), we can find that the tracking error may not converge to zero. But the tracking error can be limited in a relatively small bound, namely $|\Delta f| \leq F$ with F a constant positive value.

The τ_{SRRBF} is added to the PD controller based on SMRBF-nn to compensate for the estimation error Δf. Then, the PD controller based on SMRBF-nn is defined as follow:

$$u = \ddot{\theta}_d + \hat{f} + g + \tau_{PD} + \tau_{SMRBF} \tag{11}$$

From Eq. (2), the following closed loop equation can be obtained as:

$$\Delta f = f - \hat{f} = \ddot{e} + \tau_{PD} + \tau_{SMRBF} \tag{12}$$

The sliding mode function is designed as:

$$r = \dot{e} + \lambda e \tag{13}$$

After reaching the sliding mode surface, the tracking error e will gradually approach zero. Its derivative can be calculated as follow:

$$\dot{r} = \ddot{e} + \lambda \dot{e} = \lambda \dot{e} - \tau_{PD} - \tau_{SMRBF} + \Delta f \tag{14}$$

The τ_{SRRBF} can be designed as:

$$\tau_{SRRBF} = \lambda \dot{e} - \tau_{PD} + \eta \, sgn(r) \tag{15}$$

Where, $\eta > 0$. So,

$$\dot{r} = -\eta \, sgn(r) + \Delta f \tag{16}$$

Finally, the design control law becomes:

$$u = \ddot{\theta}_d + \hat{f} + g + \lambda \dot{e} + K_v r - v + \eta \, sgn(r) \tag{17}$$

Where, K_v is a positive definite matrix, $u(t) = M^{-1}\tau$.
The adaptive law of RBF neural network is:

$$\widehat{W} = \gamma h r^T \tag{18}$$

Where, $v = -(\varepsilon + b_d)sgn(r)$ is robust, $\gamma = \gamma^T > 0$, b_d is a positive number.
The Lyapunov function is:

$$V = \frac{1}{2}r^2 + \frac{1}{2}\widetilde{W}^T \gamma^{-1}\widetilde{W} > 0 \tag{19}$$

Its derivative can be expressed as:

$$\dot{V} = r\dot{r} + \widetilde{W}\gamma^{-1}\dot{\widetilde{W}} = \Delta f r - K_v r^2 - \eta|r| + vr + \widetilde{W}\gamma^{-1}\dot{\widetilde{W}} \tag{20}$$

Where,

$$\dot{\widetilde{W}} = -\dot{\widehat{W}} = -\gamma h r^T$$

$$\Delta f r + vr + \widetilde{W}\gamma^{-1}\dot{\widetilde{W}} = -b_d|r|$$

So,

$$\dot{V} = -K_v r^2 - (\eta + b_d)|r| \leq 0 \tag{21}$$

When $\dot{V} \equiv 0$, the $r = 0$, according to the principle of LaSalle invariance, the entire control system is progressively stable.

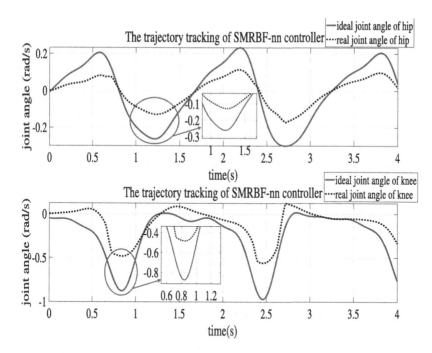

Fig. 4. The joint trajectory tracking state when using the SMRBF neural network controller

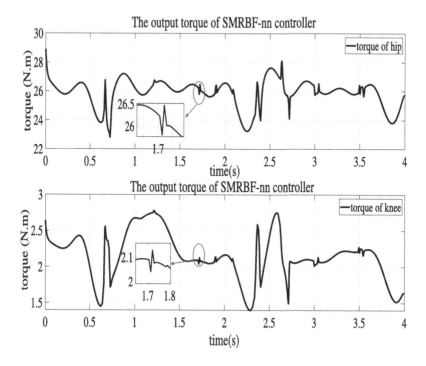

Fig. 5. The joint torque state when using the SMRBF neural network controller

4   Simulation

In order to verify the feasibility of the algorithm, the gait data of a male subject (height 170 cm, weight 66.51 kg) was selected as the reference trajectory. Assuming that the mass of the LLER is evenly distributed, and the initial state is $\theta_0 = [0, 0]^T$. In the design of the controller, the desired joint angles of the hip and knee joints are obtained from the human gait trajectory by the motion capture system.

Designed parameters in the controller is determined as:

$$b_d = 10, \ \gamma = diag(15, 15), \ \lambda = diag(20, 20), \ K_v = diag(30, 30), \ K_P = [50, 50]^T, \ K_D = [0.2, 0.2]^T, \ c = \begin{bmatrix} -1 & -0.9 & -0.7 & -0.3 & 0 & 0.2 & 0.5 & 1 & 1.2 \\ -1 & -0.9 & -0.7 & -0.3 & 0 & 0.2 & 0.5 & 1 & 1.2 \end{bmatrix}.$$

In order to highlight a better contrast, in the simulation experiments, we will use the conventional RBF neural network controller and PD controller based on SMRBF-nn. The simulation results are shown in the Fig. 4 and 5, and the Fig. 6 and 7, respectively.

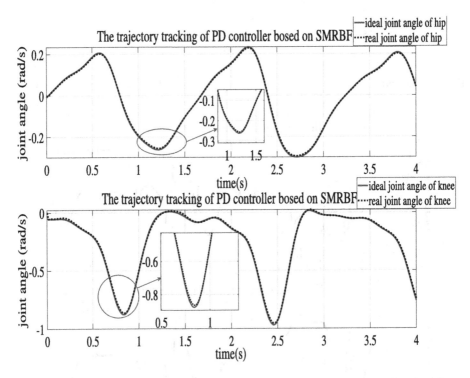

Fig. 6. The joint trajectory tracking state when using the PD controller based on SMRBF-nn

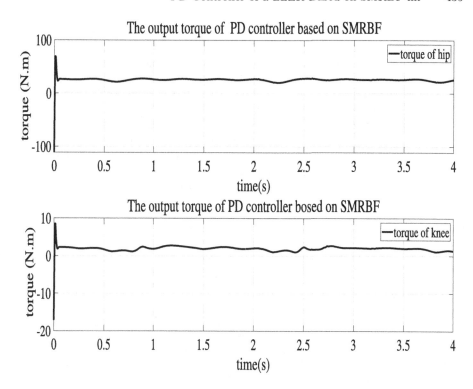

Fig. 7. The joint torque state when using the PD controller based on SMRBF-nn

Experimental results show the tracking of joint angle, tracking error of joint, and the controller output torque. Figure 4 and 6 show the joint trajectory performance for the joint angle of the hip and knee. As could be seen from Fig. 6, the accuracy between ideal joint and the real joint is less than 0.01rad/s. But the accuracy is more than 0.4rad/s for the Fig. 4. It can be seen from the simulation results that the joint angle of the LLER can track the collected normal humans' gait trajectory well, and the tracking error can quickly converge to zero, when employing PD controller based on SMRBF-nn. Furthermore, the conventional SMRBF-nn controler has high-frequency chatter from the Fig. 5. However, the Fig. 7 shows that the output torque is smoother and more in line with the characteristics of human motion. Taking into account that, if the practical application, the PD controller based on SMRBF-nn will be better than just utilize the SMRBF-nn controller.

5   Conclusion

The motion characteristics of LLER are analyzed, and normal human gait data is collected by the motion capture system in this paper. The most important thing is that this paper proposes a PD controller based on the SMRBF-nn. And the controller allows the LLER to follow the normal human gait for rehabilitation training, while ensuring the smooth and supple output torque.

It is verified by MATLAB simulation that the output joint angle of the LLER can quickly track the desired joint angle. Compared with the traditional SMRBF-nn, the control strategy proposed in this paper has smaller joint angle errors, the output torque is smaller and more compliant.

The research also has some shortcomings to be improved. Firstly, only two subjects participated in the experiment, and the results obtained are less generalized. Secondly, LLER cannot change control strategy based on human movement intention. We will recruit more subjects for data collection and introduce EEG and EMG signals to predict human gait in the future.

References

1. Rifa, H., Mohammed, S., Djouani, K.: Toward lower limbs functional rehabilitation through a knee-joint exoskeleton. IEEE Trans. Control Syst. Technol. **25**(2), 712–719 (2016)
2. Ma, Y., Wu, X., Yi, J.: A review on human-exoskeleton coordination towards lower limb robotic exoskeleton systems. Int. J. Rob. Autom. **34**, 431–451 (2019)
3. Guerra-Filho, G.: Optical motion capture: theory and implementation. RITA **12**(2), 61–90 (2005)
4. Chevallereau, C., Aoustin, Y.: Optimal reference trajectories for walking and running of a biped robot. Robotica **19**(5), 557–569 (2001)
5. Feng, S., Xinjilefu, X., Atkeson, C.G.: Robust dynamic walking using online foot step optimization. In: IEEE/RSJ International Conference on Intelligent Robots and Systems (IROS), pp. 5373–5378. IEEE, Daejeon (2016)
6. Li, G., Kawamura, K., Barrance, P.: Prediction of muscle recruitment and its effect on joint reaction forces during knee exercises. Ann. Biomed. Eng. J. Biomed. Eng. Soc. **26**(4), 725–733 (1998)
7. Zhou, Y., Li, Z., Xiao, S.: Auto-conditioned recurrent networks for extended complex human motion synthesis. In: 6th International Conference on Learning Representations, Vancouver (2018)
8. Luu, T.P., Low, K.H., Qu, X.: An individual-specific gait pattern prediction model based on generalized regression neural networks. Gait Posture **39**(1), 443–448 (2014)
9. Rossomando, F.G., Soria, C., Carelli, R.: Autonomous mobile robots navigation using RBF neural compensator. Control Eng. Pract. **19**(3), 215–222 (2011)
10. Aole, S., Elamvazuthi, I., Waghmare, L.: Improved active disturbance rejection control for trajectory tracking control of lower limb robotic rehabilitation exoskeleton. Sensor **20**(13), 3681 (2020)

Verification of Deformation Measurement Method Based on FBG Sensor

Zhen Ma[1,2] , Xiyuan Chen[1,2(✉)] , and Junwei Wang[1,2]

[1] The School of Instrument Science and Engineering, Southeast University,
Nanjing 210096, China
chxiyuan@seu.edu.cn
[2] Key Laboratory of Micro-Inertial Instrument and Advanced Navigation Technology of
Ministry of Education, Southeast University, Nanjing 210096, China

Abstract. Fiber Bragg grating (FBG) sensors are widely used because of their advantages of light weight, corrosion resistance, electromagnetic interference resistance and long life, especially in the field of aerospace. In order to meet the requirements of deformation measurement and structural evaluation of the new generation aircraft, and improve the performance and safety of aircraft, it is of great significance to carry out the research on condition monitoring technology based on FBG sensor in dynamic flight state. In the paper, FBG sensors are applied to the measurement of aircraft wing and the results show that the measurement accuracy of FBG sensor can reach at 1 mm, which has good performance.

Keywords: FBG · Aircraft wing · Measurement

1 Introduction

In recent years, optical fiber measurement technology has been widely used in bridge, dam, tunnel and other large structures [1, 2]. The application of optical fiber measurement technology in the field of aircraft measurement began to be studied in the early 21st century [3–5]. The results show that FBG sensor is very suitable for aircraft strain measurement. On the one hand, FBG sensor has the advantages of small size and light weight. The aircraft structure strain measurement which needs a large number of sensors, the cost of FBG sensor is very cheap. On the other hand, FBG sensor is non-conductive and anti electromagnetic interference, which can be used in noise, corrosion or high-pressure environment. At the same time, due to the multiplicity of optical sensor, FBG sensor can monitor high-density strain distribution in a long distance with only one fiber.

2 Construction of Experimental Platform

FBG sensor can write multiple gratings in one fiber to form a sensing array. As a unique technology of fiber sensor, sensor multiplexing can realize the measurement of distributed field along the fiber laying path. According to the shape and structure characteristics of the real aircraft wing, considering the irregularity of the wing beam section

W. Fu et al. (Eds.): ICMTEL 2021, LNICST 387, pp. 437–441, 2021.
https://doi.org/10.1007/978-3-030-82562-1_41

structure, the two sides of the simulated wing are connected by splicing and fixed on the motion simulation platform with the upper pressure plate. The upper surfaces of both wings are designed to be streamline, which accords with the real wing modal character-istics. The single wing length is 3000 mm, the airfoil length is 2700 mm, the root chord length is 320mm, and the wingtip chord length is 240 mm. Then, the FBG sensor is pasted on the wing surface. The wing structure and FBG sensor installation diagram are shown in Fig. 1. 14 nodes are selected as measurement points on each FBG sensor. The Bragg wavelength of each point is different, and the wavelength range is from 1529 nm to 1584 nm.

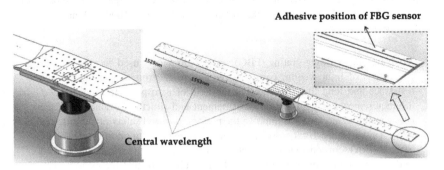

Fig. 1. Wing structure diagram

3   Data Analysis

Due to the asymmetric cross-section of the wing structure, the closer to the root of the wing, the greater the shear force, bending moment and torque on the cross-section are. In the experimental design, the density of FBG sensors is increased at the root of the wing, and four FBG sensor arrays are laid at the root with a spacing of 10 cm. The remaining ten FBG sensor nodes are laid at the far end with a spacing of 20 cm. Two FBGs are installed on the thickest part of the upper and lower surface of the wing. The experimental arrangement is shown in Table 1. The loading method is adopted in the experiment process. The load is continuously applied to one end of the wing to 3 kg. The experimental platform is built as shown in Fig. 2.

Table 1. Measurement experiment scheme

Serial number	Load (kg)	Schedule (s)
1	0	120
2	3	120

Fig. 2. Physical picture of experimental platform

The data acquisition and processing flow of the wing deformation measurement system based on distributed FBG sensor is as follows:

The FBG demodulator is used to collect the wavelength change data of each point on the upper and lower surface, and make difference with the original wavelength of the corresponding point. At the same time, the strain value of the upper and lower surface is obtained by combining the formula, and the difference value of the strain Center of the upper and lower surface is taken as the strain value under the corresponding load.

The strain change data obtained in step (1) is used to fit the relationship between strain and time, as shown in Fig. 3. It can be seen from the figure that as the pressure

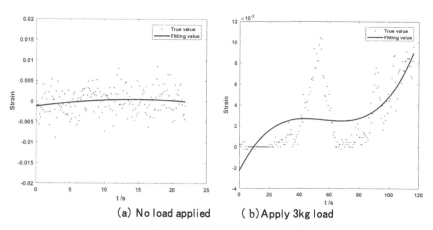

(a) No load applied   (b) Apply 3kg load

Fig. 3. Strain fitting results

increases, the strain is gradually increased, and the closer to the root, the greater the strain.

Combined with the height change data of each point of the wing measured by microm-eter, the change data and height change data are fitted to obtain the relationship between wing shape variable and position, as shown in Fig. 4.

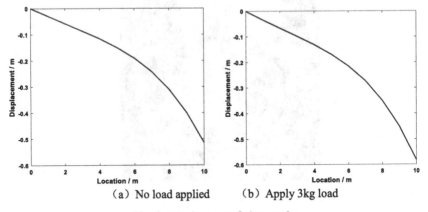

(a) No load applied   (b) Apply 3kg load

Fig. 4. Displacement fitting results

By using the fitting model to calculate the shape of the wing at each time, the paper used finite element analysis to verify the accuracy of the deformation displacement model of the wing measured by FBG sensor. According to the deformation displacement results obtained by FBG sensor measurement and fitting, combined with the deformation displacement of finite element analysis in this section, the fitting error of wing end deformation is shown in Table 2. From the table, it can be seen that the error between the fitting value of deformation model based on FBG sensor and the result of finite element analysis is less than 1mm.

Table 2. Fitting error of wing tip deformation

Load (kg)	Fitting value (mm)	Analysis value (mm)	Difference (mm)
0	77.3845	77.0360	0.3485
3	88.2186	87.6760	0.5426

4   Conclusion

Aiming at the problem of flexible multi baseline deformation measurement modeling, the paper analyzes the influence of aircraft wing mechanical structure and aircraft structure force transfer on flexible baseline structure. Based on structural mechanics, the defor-mation motion law of flexible baseline under interference environment is obtained, and a high-precision deformation modeling method of flexible multi baseline is proposed. Combined with the finite element analysis method, the feasibility and measurement accuracy of the method are verified by experiments, and the maximum error is less than 1 mm.

Acknowledgements. This work was supported by the National Natural Science Foundation of China (No. 61873064 and No. 51375087) and the Scientific Research Foundation of Graduate School of Southeast University (No. YBPY1982).

References

1. Lau, K., Yuan, L., Zhou, L.: Strain monitoring in FRP laminates and concrete beams using FBG sensors. Compos. Struct. **51**, 9–20 (2001)
2. Ma, Z., Chen, X.: Fiber Bragg gratings sensors for aircraft wing shape measurement: recent applications and technical analysis. Sensors **19**(1), 55 (2018). https://doi.org/10.3390/s19 010055
3. Wang, J., Chen, X., Yang, P.: Adaptive H-infinite Kalman filter based on multiple fading factors and its application in unmanned underwater vehicle. ISA Trans. (2020). https://doi.org/ 10.1016/j.isatra.2020.08.030
4. Wang, J., Ma, Z., Chen, X.: Generalized dynamic fuzzy NN model based on multiple fading factors SCKF and its application in integrated navigation. IEEE Sens. J. (2020). https://doi. org/10.1109/JSEN.2020.3022934
5. Yuan, X., Shmaliy, Y.S., Chen, X., Li, Y., Ma, W.: Robust inertial navigation system/ultra wide band integrated indoor quadrotor localization employing adaptive interacting multiple model-unbiased finite impulse response/Kalman filter estimator. Aerosp. Sci. Technol. **98**, 105683 (2020). https://doi.org/10.1016/j.ast.2020.105683

Air Alignment Method of Guided Projectile Based on INS/BDS

Shiqi Li⬤ and Xiyuan Chen(✉) ⬤

School of Instrument Science and Engineering, Southeast University, Nanjing 210096, China
chxiyuan@seu.edu.cn

Abstract. Initial alignment is a prerequisite for the work of INS and integrated navigation system. In order to solve the problem of rapid alignment of guided projectiles under high dynamic conditions, this paper proposes an air coarse alignment method based on kinematics constraints, and compensate for the influence of the earth's rotation. At the same time, this paper increases the pitch and yaw angle measurement information in the fine alignment process, thereby improving the speed and accuracy of air fine alignment. Simulation experiments show that after compensating for the influence of the earth's rotation, the roll angle alignment error is reduced by 1°. Compared with the traditional speed + position six-dimensional measurement fine alignment method, after adding pitch and yaw angle measurement information, The eastward speed error is reduced by 0.044 m/s, the northward speed error is reduced by 0.156 m/s, the sky speed error is reduced by 0.126 m/s, the eastward misalignment angle error is reduced by 2.1°, and the northward misalignment angle error is reduced by 0.7°, and the sky misalignment angle error is reduced by 0.86°.

Keywords: Air alignment · High dynamic · Kinematic constraints · Integrated navigation · Measurement

1 Introduction

Precision strike is the key pursuit of modern warfare. With the rapid development of information technology in the 21st century, the requirements for low-cost conventional ammunition have been guided and informatized to ensure the effectiveness and accuracy of firepower coverage in modern warfare. For guided projectile, the rotating systems can simplify the composition of the control system, reduce the impact of structural asymmetry, and improve the performance. Many countries have conducted in-depth research and application of guided projectile shells with rotating systems [1]. While the rotating systems brings many advantages, it also brings unique problems to the research of guided weapons in rotating systems. The first challenge is the high overload at the moment of launch (not less than 10000 g), and the requirements for high overload resistance are put forward for IMU (Inertial Measurement Unit) components. At the same time, due to the high spin, there are also high requirements for the measurement range of the gyro. Furthermore, the carrier spin will cause complex cone motion, which

W. Fu et al. (Eds.): ICMTEL 2021, LNICST 387, pp. 442–451, 2021.
https://doi.org/10.1007/978-3-030-82562-1_42

brings severe challenges to attitude measurement, especially roll angle measurement, which further affects the reliability and accuracy of navigation and guidance. Finally, due to the particularity of guided projectiles, the cost should also be considered [2–4]. The combination of inertial navigation system (INS) and Beidou global navigation satellite system (BDS) is an effective integrated navigation system, it uses the high-precision positioning information filtering algorithm of the BDS receiver to calibrate and compensate for the accumulated errors of the strapdown system, which improves the navigation accuracy and has been widely used.

Initial alignment is a prerequisite for the normal operation of INS. The accuracy and speed are two indicators for evaluating alignment effects [5]. The traditional initial alignment algorithm takes a long time to align and requires simple linear motion of the carrier [6]. Obviously, it cannot be used for the initial alignment of guided projectiles with weightlessness, high-speed spinning, and high-speed movement. Non-autonomous alignment is different from autonomous alignment. It needs to rely on external auxiliary equipment to provide reference information, such as GNSS (Global Navigation Satellite System), master-sub-inertial navigation transfer alignment system, magnetometer, etc. For guided projectiles, due to their limited size and short flight time, they are obviously not suitable for transfer alignment. On the other hand, due to its high-speed spin characteristics, the acquisition of the roll angle is the focus and difficulty of the current guided projectile alignment technology. The most commonly used method is to install a magnetometer on the projectile [7]. However, the attitude measurement method based on geomagnetic measurement technology has poor anti-interference ability and requires additional sensors [8]. Some scholars solve the problem of attitude calculation from the perspective of non-gyro inertial measurement methods, such as six accelerometers, eight accelerometers [9], but these methods require high accelerometer installation accuracy and angular velocity calculation accuracy, which will cause Real-time issues.

This paper proposes an air alignment method of guided projectile based on INS/BDS. The coarse alignment is completed by the method of rapid air alignment based on kinematics equations, and the influence of the earth's rotation on the coarse alignment is compensated. Then, on the basis of the traditional six-dimensional measurement precision alignment method, the pitch and yaw vector measurement information are added to construct an eight-dimensional measurement, thereby improving the accuracy and speed of the air precision alignment. At the same time, no additional sensors are used, which helps to save costs and control weight.

2   Air Alignment Method of Guided Projectile

2.1   Air Coarse Alignment Algorithm Based on Kinematics Equations

Firstly, the coordinate systems should be defined: Inertial coordinate system $OX_iY_iZ_i$. Navigation coordinate system (ENU) $OX_nY_nZ_n$. Projectile coordinate system $OX_bY_bZ_b$, The Y_b axis is the rotation axis of the guided projectile, the X_b axis is the horizontal axis, and the Z_b axis is the sky axis. Ballistic coordinate system $OX_2Y_2Z_2$, The Y_2 axis is the ballistic pointing axis. The relationship of each coordinate system is shown in Fig. 1. It is stipulated that the yaw angle is $0°$ when pointing north, and it is positive from north to west.

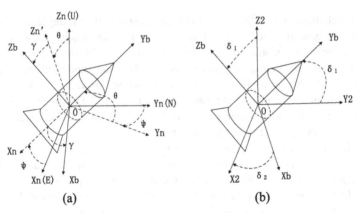

Fig. 1. (a) shows the relationship between navigation coordinate system and projectile coordinate system; (b) shows the relationship between ballistic coordinate system and projectile coordinate system

After the guided projectile is launched and before the satellite receiver is powered on, the guided projectile will be in a complex angular motion state due to the initial disturbance. At this time, the trajectory of the projectile can only be roughly predicted by the ballistic parameters. While the BDS receiver receives the navigation information, according to the component of the velocity measurement value in the navigation coordinate system, the ballistic inclination and the ballistic deflection of the guided projectile can be calculated.

$$\theta_a = \arctan \frac{v_u}{\sqrt{v_e^2 + v_n^2}} \tag{1}$$

$$\psi_2 = -\arctan \frac{v_e}{v_n} \tag{2}$$

v_e, v_n, v_u respectively represent the eastward speed, northward speed, and skyward speed in the satellite navigation results.

According to the theory of external ballistics, the following relationship exists between the projectile coordinate system and the ballistic coordinate system:

$$\psi \approx \psi_2 + \delta_1; \theta \approx \theta_a + \delta_2 \tag{3}$$

At the same time, during the ascent of the guided projectile flight, the angle of attack caused by the initial disturbance will rapidly decay to a small amount in a short time, so the following approximation can be used:

$$\psi \approx \psi_2; \theta \approx \theta_a \tag{4}$$

According to the theory of external ballistics, the kinematic equation of the projectile body rotating around the center of mass is:

$$\begin{cases} \dot{\theta} = \frac{d\theta}{dt} = \omega_{nbz}^b \sin \gamma + \omega_{nbx}^b \cos \gamma \\ \dot{\gamma} = \frac{d\gamma}{dt} = \omega_{nby}^b - (\omega_{nbz}^b \cos \gamma - \omega_{nbx}^b \sin \gamma) \tan \theta \\ \dot{\psi} = \frac{d\psi}{dt} = (\omega_{nbx}^b \sin \gamma - \omega_{nbz}^b \cos \gamma)/\cos \theta \end{cases} \tag{5}$$

In the formula, $\dot{\theta}$, $\dot{\gamma}$, $\dot{\psi}$ represents the pitch rate, roll rate, and yaw rate of the rotating projectile; ω_{nbx}^b, ω_{nby}^b, ω_{nbz}^b respectively represents the sensitive angular rate of the projectile coordinate system relative to the three-axis navigation coordinate system; The first two formulas of (5) can be solved:

$$
\begin{cases}
\sin\gamma = \dfrac{\omega_{nbz}^b\dot{\theta} - \omega_{nbx}^b\dot{\psi}\cos\theta}{\dot{\theta}^2 + (\dot{\psi}\cos\theta)^2} \\[2mm]
\cos\gamma = \dfrac{\omega_{nbx}^b\dot{\theta} + \omega_{nbz}^b\dot{\psi}\cos\theta}{\dot{\theta}^2 + (\dot{\psi}\cos\theta)^2}
\end{cases}
\tag{6}
$$

It can be derived from (6):

$$
\tan\gamma = \frac{\omega_{nbz}^b\dot{\theta} - \omega_{nbx}^b\dot{\psi}\cos\theta}{\omega_{nbx}^b\dot{\theta} + \omega_{nbz}^b\dot{\psi}\cos\theta}
\tag{7}
$$

For a well-designed projectile, the yaw angular rate after launching can be ignored, so (7) can be simplified to:

$$
\tan\gamma \approx \frac{\omega_{nbz}^b}{\omega_{nbx}^b}
\tag{8}
$$

According to the characteristics of the guided projectile in the trajectory of the projectile during the ascent period of flight:

$$
\dot{\theta} \approx \frac{\omega_{nbz}^b}{\sin\gamma} \approx \frac{\omega_{nbx}^b}{\cos\gamma} < 0
\tag{9}
$$

If the definition of the roll angle is $[-180°, 180°]$, the unique solution of the roll angle can be obtained by combining (8) and (9), as shown in Table 1.

Table 1. Roll angle value range judgment table

$\tan\gamma$	ω_{nbz}^b	ω_{nbx}^b	$\sin\gamma$	$\cos\gamma$	Numerical interval	The value of γ
≥ 0	≥ 0	>0	≤ 0	<0	$[-180°, -90°)$	$|\gamma| - 180°$
	≥ 0	$= 0$	$-90°$			
	≤ 0	<0	≥ 0	>0	$[0°, 90°)$	$|\gamma|$
≤ 0	≥ 0	<0	≤ 0	>0	$(-90°, 0°]$	$-|\gamma|$
	<0	$= 0$	$90°$			
	≤ 0	>0	≥ 0	<0	$(-90°, 180°]$	$180° - |\gamma|$

On the other hand, by inertial navigation theory:

$$
\omega_{nb}^b = \omega_{ib}^b - C_n^b\omega_{in}^n
\tag{10}
$$

Among them, ω_{ib}^b is the output value of strapdown gyroscope, and is determined by Eq. (11):

$$\omega_{in}^n = \omega_{ie}^n + \omega_{en}^n = \begin{bmatrix} -\frac{v_n}{R_M} \\ \omega_{ie} \cos L + \frac{v_e}{R_N} \\ \omega_{ie} \sin L + \frac{v_e}{R_N} \tan L \end{bmatrix} \tag{11}$$

v_e, v_n, v_u represents the easterly speed, northerly speed, and celestial speed in the satellite navigation results respectively; ω_{ie} represents the earth's rotation rate, which is a constant value; L is the latitude information in the position; R_M, R_N is the earth's curvature radius.

Expand formula (10) in terms of components:

$$\begin{bmatrix} \omega_{nbx}^b \\ \omega_{nby}^b \\ \omega_{nbz}^b \end{bmatrix} = \begin{bmatrix} \omega_{ibx}^b \\ \omega_{iby}^b \\ \omega_{ibz}^b \end{bmatrix} - C_n^b \begin{bmatrix} \omega_{inx}^n \\ \omega_{iny}^n \\ \omega_{inz}^n \end{bmatrix} \tag{12}$$

Where C_n^b is the attitude transfer matrix. Expand it and calculate it to get:

$$\omega_{nbx}^b = \omega_{ibx}^b - [(\cos \gamma \cos \psi + \sin \gamma \sin \psi \sin \theta)\omega_{inx}^n \\ +(-\cos \gamma \sin \psi + \sin \gamma \cos \psi \sin \theta)\omega_{iny}^n + (-\sin \gamma \cos \theta)\omega_{inz}^n] \tag{13}$$

$$\omega_{nbz}^b = \omega_{ibz}^b - [(\sin \gamma \cos \psi - \cos \gamma \sin \psi \sin \theta)\omega_{inx}^n \\ +(-\sin \gamma \sin \psi - \cos \gamma \cos \psi \sin \theta)\omega_{iny}^n + (\cos \gamma \cos \theta)\omega_{inz}^n] \tag{14}$$

Substituting (13) and (14) into (8), the formula that compensates for the influence of the earth's rotation can be obtained:

$$\sin \gamma \cdot \omega_{ibx}^b = \cos \gamma \cdot \omega_{ibz}^b + M \tag{15}$$

Where:

$$M = \sin \psi \sin \theta \cdot \omega_{inx}^n + \cos \psi \sin \theta \cdot \omega_{iny}^n - \cos \theta \cdot \omega_{inz}^n$$

Equation (15) is the formula for quickly obtaining the compensated roll angle.

Since the roll angle is defined as $[-180°, 180°]$, formula (15) is used in the specific calculation:

If $\omega_{ibx}^b \le 0$: $\sin \gamma \cdot \omega_{ibx}^b = \cos \gamma \cdot \omega_{ibz}^b + M$.

Else if $\omega_{ibx}^b > 0$: $\sin \gamma \cdot \omega_{ibx}^b = \cos \gamma \cdot \omega_{ibz}^b - M$.

After the roll angle is finally calculated, the determination of the roll angle range is consistent with Table 1.

At this time, the attitude angle, speed, and position information required by the coarse alignment of the guided projectile can be obtained.

2.2   Air Fine Alignment Algorithm Added Pitch and Yaw Measurement

Traditional air fine alignment methods mostly use six-dimensional measurement to construct the measurement equation:

$$Z = \begin{bmatrix} r_{GNSS} - r_{INS} \\ v_{GNSS} - v_{INS} \end{bmatrix} = HX + V \tag{16}$$

In the formula, r_{GNSS} represents the three-dimensional position vector output by the GNSS system; r_{INS} represents the three-dimensional position vector output by the INS system; v_{GNSS} represents the three-dimensional velocity vector output by the GNSS, v_{INS} represents the three-dimensional velocity vector output by the INS; $H = \begin{bmatrix} I_{6\times6} & 0_{6\times9} \end{bmatrix}$ is the measurement matrix; V is the quantity Measure noise; Z is the measured value; X is the 15-dimensional state quantity.

Due to the characteristics of fast rotation speed, fast movement speed, and relatively fixed ballistic trajectory of guided projectiles, the yaw and pitch information derived from GNSS speed is considered to construct an eight-dimensional measurement matrix. At the same time, because the fifteen-dimensional state quantity contains the system misalignment angle, not the attitude angle error, it is necessary to build the relationship between the attitude angle error and the system misalignment angle:

$$\begin{bmatrix} \delta\psi \\ \delta\theta \\ \delta\gamma \end{bmatrix} = \begin{bmatrix} -\tan\theta\sin\psi & \tan\theta\cos\psi & -1 \\ -\cos\psi & -\sin\psi & 0 \\ \sin\psi/\cos\theta & -\cos\psi/\cos\theta & 0 \end{bmatrix} \begin{bmatrix} \varphi_E \\ \varphi_N \\ \varphi_U \end{bmatrix} \tag{17}$$

Take the first two rows of the matrix in the above formula:

$$C_{2\times3} = \begin{bmatrix} -\tan\theta\sin\psi & \tan\theta\cos\psi & -1 \\ -\cos\psi & -\sin\psi & 0 \end{bmatrix} \tag{18}$$

Then the new measurement matrix is:

$$H_{8\times15} = \begin{bmatrix} C_{2\times3} & 0_{2\times6} & 0_{2\times6} \\ 0_{6\times3} & I_{6\times6} & 0_{6\times6} \end{bmatrix} \tag{19}$$

On this basis, an 8-dimensional measurement equation can be constructed:

$$Z = \begin{bmatrix} \delta\psi \\ \delta\theta \\ \delta r \\ \delta v \end{bmatrix} = \begin{bmatrix} \psi_{GNSS} - \psi_{INS} \\ \theta_{GNSS} - \theta_{INS} \\ r_{GNSS} - r_{INS} \\ v_{GNSS} - v_{INS} \end{bmatrix} \tag{20}$$

3   Experimental and Comparative Analysis

Firstly, this paper sets the ballistic parameters: the simulation step is 0.001 s, the ballistic duration is 180 s; the initial longitude of the carrier is 114°, the initial latitude of the carrier is 30°, the initial height of the carrier is 5 m; the initial velocity of the carrier is

1500 m/s; The initial roll angle of the carrier is 0°, the initial yaw angle of the carrier is −90° (true north is 0°, and the west by north is positive), and the initial pitch angle of the carrier is 45°; The weight of the shell is 18 kg, and the shell diameter is 0.065 m; The air density is 1.29 kg/m², the air resistance coefficient is 0.0789; the initial roll angular rate is 126 rad/s. Secondly, this paper sets IMU error: 20 deg/h for gyroscope zero offset, 1000 ug/h for accelerometer zero offset, angle random walk 5 deg/sqrt(h), speed random walk 10 ug/sqrt(Hz), and set BDS position error to [5 m, 5 m, 5 m], the speed error is [1 m/s, 1 m/s, 1 m/s].

3.1 Experiment and Comparison of Air Coarse Alignment Methods

In order to verify the air coarse alignment method of guided projectiles based on kinematic equations proposed in this paper, this article first uses the guided projectile trajectory generator to generate ideal gyroscope and accelerometer data. Then this paper adds the corresponding error according to the actual situation. The trajectory parameters of the trajectory generator are used as true values for comparison.

Figure 2 shows the pitch and yaw errors of the guided projectile. It can be seen that the pitch angle error is less than $5*10^{-4}$ rad, and the yaw angle error is less than 10^{-3} rad.

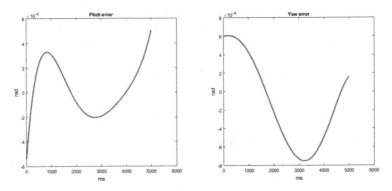

Fig. 2. Pitch and yaw error of coarse alignment

Figure 3(a) shows the alignment error of the roll angle after compensating for the influence of the earth's rotation. Figure 3(b) shows the alignment error of the roll angle when the influence of the earth's rotation is not compensated. It shows that if the effect of the earth's rotation is not compensated, the roll angle alignment result would have a drift of more than 1°.

3.2 Experiment and Comparison of Air Fine Alignment Methods

Figure 4 shows the air fine alignment error of eight-dimensional measurement. The first subfigure shows the east misalignment angle and the north misalignment angle. It can be shown that the east misalignment angle is less than 1.38° and the north misalignment

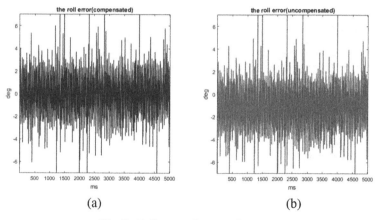

Fig. 3. Roll error of coarse alignment

angle is less than 0.55°. The second subfigure shows the sky misalignment angle is less than 1.4°. In the third subfigure, it can be shown that the speed errors are less than 0.5 m/s. The last subfigure shows the position errors are less than 2 m.

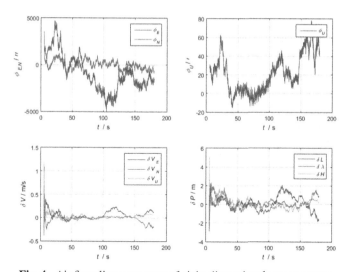

Fig. 4. Air fine alignment error of eight-dimensional measurement

Figure 5 shows the air fine alignment error of six-dimensional measurement. Compared with the Fig. 4, The first subfigure shows that the east misalignment angle can reach 5.56° in maximum and the north misalignment angle can reach 2.78° in maximum which are. The second subfigure shows that the sky misalignment angle can reach 3.33° which is 2 times larger than the sky misalignment angle in Fig. 4. In the third subfigure, it can be shown that the speed errors are less than 1 m/s. The last subfigure shows the position errors are less than 2 m.

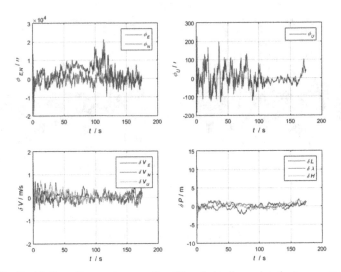

Fig. 5. Air fine alignment error of traditional six-dimensional measurement

Table 2 shows the comparison of the two methods' RMSE error.

Table 2. Comparison table of air fine alignment errors of the two methods

RMSE	Six-dimensional	Eight-dimensional
Eastward position error (m)	0.81	0.66
Northward position error (m)	0.80	0.57
Sky position error (m)	0.6	0.53
Eastward velocity error (m/s)	0.14	0.096
Northward velocity error (m/s)	0.24	0.084
Sky velocity error (m/s)	0.18	0.054
Eastward misalignment angle (°)	2.48	0.38
Northward misalignment angle (°)	0.85	0.14
Sky misalignment angle (°)	1.14	0.28

It can be seen that after adding the pitch and yaw measurement information, The eastward speed error is reduced by 0.044 m/s, the northward speed error is reduced by 0.156 m/s, and the sky speed error is reduced by 0.126 m/s; The eastward misalignment angle error is reduced by 2.1°, the northward misalignment angle error is reduced by 0.7°, and the sky misalignment angle error is reduced by 0.86°.

4   Conclusion

In order to achieve rapid air alignment of guided projectiles, this paper proposes an air coarse alignment algorithm based on kinematics equations and an air fine alignment algorithm which adds pitch and yaw angle measurement information. When the guided projectile receives the BDS signal, it first obtains the speed and position information of the guided projectile at this time, and calculates the yaw angle and pitch angle from the speed information. Then, combined with the above information and the kinematics equation of the guided projectile, the roll angle can be obtained. Simulation experiment shows that the compensated air coarse alignment algorithm reduces the error by 1° compared with the uncompensated algorithm. After finishing the air coarse alignment, on the basis of the traditional six-dimensional measurement information in the air fine alignment method, this paper adds pitch and yaw measurement information. Simulation experiment shows that the speed error and misalignment error of the new air fine alignment are significantly reduced, and the convergence speed is also significantly faster.

References

1. Curry, H.W., Reed, F.J.: Measurement of Magnus effects on a sounding rocket model in a supersonic wind tunnel. In: AIAA, pp. 66–758 (1966)
2. Nicolaides, J.D., Ingram, W.C., Clare, A.T.: An investigation of the non-linear flight dynamics of ordnance weapons. In: AIAA, pp. 69–135 (1970)
3. Zhao, H., Su, Z., Liu, F., Li, C., Li, Q., Liu, N.: Extraction and filter algorithm of roll angular rate for high spinning projectiles. Math. Probl. Eng. **2019**, 1–15 (2019)
4. Zhou, Y., Zhang, X., Xiao, W.: Spinning projectiles angular measurement using crest and trough data of a geomagnetic sensor. Measur. Sci. Technol. **29**(9), 095007 (2018)
5. Wang, Y., Sun, F., Zhang, Y., Liu, H., Min, H.: Central difference particle filter applied to transfer alignment for SINS on missiles. IEEE Trans. Aerosp. Electron. Syst. **48**(1), 375–387 (2012)
6. Meng, W., Xiaqing, T., Xiangyuan, H.: Research on the moving SINS initial alignment method based on strong tracking gauss hermite filter with OD aiding. Piezoelectrics Acoustooptics. **39**(5), 784–789 (2017)
7. Wang, Q., Li, D., Li, R.: Roll estimation for smart munitions using a 3D magnetometer only. In: IEEE International Conference on Unmanned Systems. (ICUS), 27–29 Oct, pp. 214–219 (2017)
8. Li, W., Wang, J.: Effective adaptive Kalman filter for MEMS-IMU/Magnetometers integrated attitude and heading reference systems. J. Navig. **66**, 99–113 (2013)
9. Briend, Y., Chatelet, E., Dufour, R., Legrand, F., Baudin, S.: Identification of real translational and rotational displacements of six-axial shakers with only six measured linear accelerations. Mech. Syst. Sign. Process. **154**, 107584 (2021)

Motion Constraint Aided Underwater Integrated Navigation Method Based on Improved Adaptive Filtering

Siyi Zhang[1] and Xiyuan Chen[2(✉)]

[1] Key Laboratory of Micro-Inertial Instrument and Advanced Navigation Technology Ministry of Education, Southeast University, Nanjing 210096, China
[2] School of Instrument Science and Engineering, Southeast University, Nanjing 210096, China
chxiyuan@seu.edu.cn

Abstract. The underwater environment is complicated. Aiming at the problem of sudden changes in measurement information when the submarine encounters submarine trenches, clusters of fish, and strong maneuvering turns during navigation, this paper introduces centripetal acceleration errors on the basis of traditional motion constraints, which effectively restrict the forward speed of the carrier. Meanwhile, this paper proposed the fault judgment of the measurement information and the optimal estimation of the scale factor to improve the Sage-Husa adaptive filtering. Finally, a simulation experiment is carried out and the results show that the improved algorithm can reduce the computation complexity when the measurement information is correct. What's more, it can also suppress the divergence of the system filter effectively when the measurement information has sudden errors, which proves the robustness and reliability of the system.

Keywords: Motion constraint · Centripetal acceleration · Sage-Husa adaptive filtering · Fault judgment · Scale factor

1 Motion Constraint Model Based on Centripetal Acceleration

1.1 Background

With the development of the technology of underwater vehicles, as reliable detection tools, underwater vehicles have received widespread attention at home and abroad. How to improve the accuracy of underwater navigation has also become the focus of attention of scholars in various fields. However, the underwater environment is complicated. Usually, underwater submarines will glide in sawtooth waves on the bottom of the sea [1]. During the gliding process, if it encounters submarine ditches, clusters of fish or strong maneuvering turns [2]. The measurement information provided by the Doppler will be wrong, and the preset measurement noise matrix will not be able to adapt to the disturbed model, which will affect the accuracy of positioning. Meanwhile, the centripetal acceleration will restrict the speed of the underwater vehicle.

© ICST Institute for Computer Sciences, Social Informatics and Telecommunications Engineering 2021
Published by Springer Nature Switzerland AG 2021. All Rights Reserved
W. Fu et al. (Eds.): ICMTEL 2021, LNICST 387, pp. 452–459, 2021.
https://doi.org/10.1007/978-3-030-82562-1_43

In order to solve the above problems, this paper introduces the centripetal acceleration constraint [3] and the improved Sage-Husa adaptive algorithm [4] to assist inertial/Doppler integrated navigation. When the underwater vehicles encounter submarine trenches, fish schools and strong maneuverability, and the Doppler measurement information is wrong. The centripetal acceleration will be introduced to restrict the speed of the underwater vehicle, and the improved Sage-Husa adaptive filtering algorithm will be adapted to reduce positioning error and improve positioning accuracy.

1.2 Motion Constraint Model

The operating environment of the submarine is usually more than ten meters underwater, and the water flow is relatively gentle. It can be considered that the two directions of the submarine perpendicular to the forward speed are only related to the sea water velocity and assuming that the velocity is 0, the constraint conditions [5] can be obtained as:

$$\begin{cases} v_x^b = 0 \\ v_z^b = 0 \end{cases} \tag{1}$$

Cause any motion of the submarine can be decomposed into two planes perpendicular to the y-axis, as shown in Fig. 1, according to the kinematic formula, we can get:

$$a_{rx} = v_y^b w_{nbz}^b \tag{2}$$

$$a_{rz} = v_y^b w_{nbx}^b \tag{3}$$

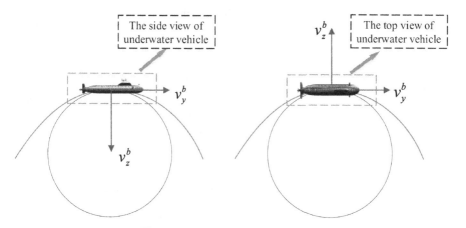

Fig. 1. Motion decomposition diagram

From the inertial device, the formula (4) can be obtained:

$$\begin{cases} a_{rx} = f_x^b + (C_n^b g^n)_1 \\ a_{rz} = -f_z^b + (C_n^b g^n)_3 \\ v_y^b = (C_n^b v^n)_2 \\ w_{nbz}^b = w_{ibz}^b - (C_n^b (w_{ie}^n + w_{en}^n))_3 \\ w_{nbx}^b = w_{ibx}^b - (C_n^b (w_{ie}^n + w_{en}^n))_1 \end{cases} \tag{4}$$

Thus the motion constraint after introducing centripetal acceleration is:

$$\begin{cases} v_x^b = 0 \\ v_z^b = 0 \\ a_{0x} = a_{rx} - v_y^b w_{nbz}^b \\ a_{0z} = a_{rz} - v_z^b w_{nbx}^b \end{cases} \tag{5}$$

The error model is further obtained as follows:

$$\begin{cases} \delta v_x^b = (C_n^b \delta v^n)_1 - (C_n^b \phi^n \times v^n)_1 \\ \delta v_y^b = (C_n^b \delta v^n)_3 - (C_n^b \phi^n \times v^n)_3 \\ \delta a_{0x} = (C_n^b \phi^n \times v^n)_2 \omega_{ibz}^n - (C_n^b \phi^n \times g^n)_1 - (C_n^b \delta v^n)_2 \omega_{ibz}^b + \nabla_x^b - (C_n^b v^n)_2 \varepsilon_z^b \\ \delta a_{0z} = (C_n^b \phi^n \times v^n)_2 \omega_{ibx}^b - (C_n^b \phi^n \times g^n)_3 - (C_n^b \delta v^n)_2 \omega_{ibx}^b - \nabla_z^b - (C_n^b v^n)_2 \varepsilon_x^b \end{cases} \tag{6}$$

where v_x^b, v_y^b, v_z^b are the speed of the submarine in the carrier coordinate system, a_{rx}, a_{rz} are the centripetal acceleration values in the x and z directions under the submarine carrier coordinate system. w_{ibx}^b, w_{ibz}^b are the sensitive angular velocities of the x-axis and z-axis of the inertial device, f_x^b, f_z^b represent the specific force on the x-axis and z-axis of the accelerometer. w_{ie}^n, w_{en}^n are respectively the angular velocity of the earth's rotation and the angular velocity caused by the movement of the carrier.

2 Improved Sage-Husa Adaptive Algorithm

In traditional Kalman filter [6], the measuring prediction error can be expressed as formula (7):

$$\begin{aligned} \tilde{Z}_{k/k-1} &= Z_k - \hat{Z}_{k/k-1} \\ &= H_k \tilde{X}_{k/k-1} + V_k - H_k \hat{X}_{k/k-1} \\ &= H_k \tilde{X}_{k/k-1} + V_k \end{aligned} \tag{7}$$

Find the variance [7] on both sides at the same time to get:

$$E[\tilde{Z}_{k/k-1} \tilde{Z}_{k/k-1}^T] = H_k P_{k/k-1} H_k^T + R_k \tag{8}$$

Using exponential reduction memory weighted average method, we can get:

$$\hat{R}_k = (1 - \beta_k)\hat{R}_{k-1} + \beta_k(\tilde{Z}_{k/k-1} \tilde{Z}_{k/k-1}^T - H_k P_{k/k-1} H_k^T) \tag{9}$$

In traditional Sage-Husa adaptive filtering [8], β_k can be expressed as formula (10):

$$\beta_k = \frac{1-b}{1-b_k} \tag{10}$$

where b is the fading factor, but as the number of filtering k increases, it will approach 0, and the weight of adaptive filtering will approach 1−b and will remain unchanged.

At the same time, the distribution weight of value $\hat{R}_0$ to value $\hat{R}_k$ gradually decays and approaches the constant value 0. The reasons above reduce the adaptive degree of the noise estimator, and the accuracy of filtering will decrease accordingly.

According to the prediction residual method [9], it is possible to artificially judge whether the filtering is divergent. Filtering divergence criterion [10] can be expressed as formula (11):

$$\tilde{Z}_{k/k-1}^T \tilde{Z}_{k/k-1} > \gamma \cdot tr[E(\tilde{Z}_{k/k-1}\tilde{Z}_{k/k-1}^T)] \tag{11}$$

When the above formula is established, it represents the filtering divergence, where γ is the reserve coefficient, when $\gamma = 1$, the strictest convergence criterion will be established. Let $\hat{R}_k$ replace R_k, we can get:

$$\tilde{Z}_{k/k-1}^T \tilde{Z}_{k/k-1} = tr[E(\tilde{Z}_{k/k-1}\tilde{Z}_{k/k-1}^T)]$$
$$= tr(H_k P_{k/k-1} H_k^T + (1 - \beta_k)\hat{R}_{k-1} + \beta_k(\tilde{Z}_{k/k-1}\tilde{Z}_{k/k-1}^T - H_k P_{K/K-1} H_k^T)) \tag{12}$$

From formula (12), β_k can be expressed as follows:

$$\beta_k = \begin{cases} \dfrac{\tilde{Z}_{k/k-1}^T \tilde{Z}_{k/k-1} - tr(H_k P_{k/k-1} H_k^T) - tr(\widehat{R}_{k-1})}{tr(\tilde{Z}_{k/k-1}\tilde{Z}_{k/k-1}^T) - H_k P_{k/k-1} H_k^T) - tr(\widehat{R}_{k-1})} & \tilde{Z}_{k/k-1}^T \tilde{Z}_{k/k-1} > tr[E(\tilde{Z}_{k/k-1}\tilde{Z}_{k/k-1}^T)] \\ 1 & \tilde{Z}_{k/k-1}^T \tilde{Z}_{k/k-1} \le tr[E(\tilde{Z}_{k/k-1}\tilde{Z}_{k/k-1}^T)] \end{cases} \tag{13}$$

3 Simulation Experiment and Comparative Analysis

3.1 Parameter Settings

In order to verify the accuracy of the algorithm, this paper sets up a simulation experiment based on the MATLAB platform, in which the inertial original indicators and the initial navigation parameters are set as follows:

$$\sigma_{\delta r}^2(0) = (1\,\text{m})^2$$

$$\sigma_{\delta v}^2(0) = (0.1\,\text{m/s})^2$$

$$\sigma_{\delta\alpha}^2(0) = \sigma_{\delta\beta}^2(0) = (10'')^2 \quad \sigma_{\delta\gamma}^2(0) = (1')^2$$

Gyro bias stability: $eb = 0.2°/h$
Accelerometer bias stability: $db = 100\,\text{ug}$
Angle random walk: $web = 0.018°/\sqrt{h}$
DVL velocity error: $\sigma_{\delta v_d}^2 = (0.01\,\text{m/s})^2$
DVL deviation angle error: $\sigma_{\delta\Delta}^2 = (1')^2$.
DVL scale factor error: $\sigma_{\delta C}^2 = (0.001)^2$.

3.2 Comparison of Simulation Results

Generally, the submarine often glides in sawtooth waves at the bottom of the water. In order to simulate the navigation state of the submarine, this paper first conducts the trajectory simulation of the submarine, assuming that the initial coordinates of the submarine are [34.246048; 108.909664; 380] and the simulated time is 1029 s. The whole simulation includes different states of motion, such as constant speed, uniform acceleration, uniform deceleration, heading angle change, pitch angle change, and roll angle change.

Combining the above parameters, using the motion constraint aided underwater integrated navigation method based on improved Sage-Husa adaptive filtering proposed in this paper, the velocity error and position error of the submarine are shown in Figs. 2 and 3:

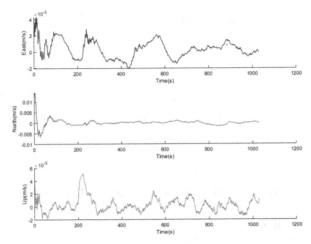

Fig. 2. Velocity errors of the submarine

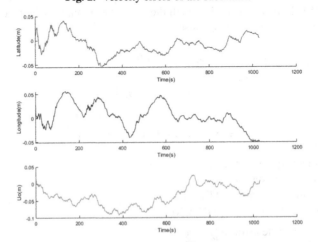

Fig. 3. Position errors of the submarine

Calculate the root mean square errors of the velocity and position errors of the submarine based on the improved algorithm and the traditional Kalman filter method, which are shown in Table 1:

Table 1. Root mean square error

Errors		RMSE	
		Traditional Kalman filter	Motion constrain aided improved Sage-Husa adaptive filtering
Velocity error	East (m/s)	0.0026	1.3907e−04
	North (m/s)	0.0012	3.0682e−04
	Up (m/s)	0.0187	6.9625e−05
Position error	Latitude (°)	1.9037e−07	7.1751e−08
	Longitude (°)	2.0420e−07	1.0497e−08
	Up (m/s)	1.0243	0.0637

It can be seen that the standard Kalman algorithm lacks an understanding of the statistical noise characteristics of the system in the initial stage of the experimental calculation, and the filtering error is relatively large. The improved Sage-Husa adaptive filtering algorithm with additional motion constraints constrains the three-directional speed of the carrier and adapts the measurement noise, which can well suppress the divergence of the combined system error and greatly improve the navigation accuracy of the system.

In order to verify the improved performance of adaptive filtering in the case of filtering divergence, the measurement noise was added ten times from 600 s to 610 s. The final velocity errors and position errors of the submarine are shown in Figs. 4 and 5:

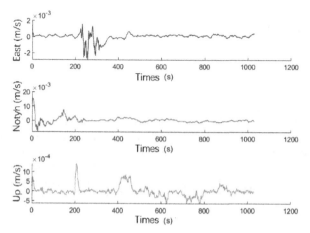

Fig. 4. Velocity errors of the submarine

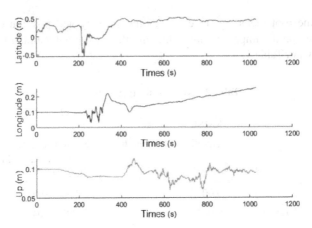

Fig. 5. Position errors of the submarine

Calculate the root mean square errors of the velocity and position of the submarine under the two methods of the traditional Kalman filter and motion constraint aided algorithm based on improved Sage-Husa adaptive filtering, and the results are shown in Table 2:

Table 2. Root mean square errors after adding noise

Errors		RMSE	
		Traditional Kalman filter	Motion constrain aided improved Sage-Husa adaptive filtering
Velocity error	East (m/s)	0.0155	1.2874e−04
	North (m/s)	0.0124	7.4445e−04
	Up (m/s)	0.0103	3.4963e−05
Position error	Latitude (°)	2.5621e−07	4.5233e−08
	Longitude (°)	9.4087e−07	2.4090e−08
	Up (m/s)	3.4723	0.0904

It can be seen from the table that due to the sudden increase of measurement noise and the divergence of the traditional Kalman filter, the trajectory of the submarine cannot be accurately estimated, resulting in the continuous increase of the velocity and position errors of the submarine. But the motion constraint-aided algorithm based on improved Sage-Husa adaptive filtering proposed in this paper can suppress the filtering divergence very well, which has better fault tolerance, and higher accuracy than the traditional Kalman filtering algorithm.

4 Conclusion

The motion constraint-aided adaptive filtering algorithm based on the improved Sage-Husa proposed in this paper is more complete than traditional motion constraints. It can effectively constrain the forward speed of the carrier and avoid the large measurement information caused by strong maneuvering of the carrier, which effectively improves the navigation accuracy of the system. On the basis of the traditional Sage-Husa adaptive filtering, the fault judgment of the measurement information and the optimal estimation of the scale factor are added, which can not only reduce the amount of filtering calculation when the measurement information is correct, but can also reduce the divergence of system filtering when the measurement information has errors, which has better robustness and reliability, and can improve the fault tolerance and navigation accuracy of the entire system.

References

1. Haoqian, H., Xiyuan, C., Caiping, L., et al.: Design and verification of improved Gaussian mixture particle filter for position and attitude estimation of underwater glider. J. Chin. Inertial Technol. **22**(05), 601–605 (2014)
2. Jianhua, C., Daidai, C., Landry, R., Jr., et al.: Research on wavelet singularity detection based fault-tolerant federated filtering algorithm for INS/GPS/DVL integrated navigation system. J. Appl. Math. **2014**, 1–8 (2014)
3. Cao, Y., Fang, S., Xu, X.: Motion control of nonholonomic mobile robot under acceleration constrains. Control Decis. **02**, 193–196 (2006)
4. Wei, W., Yongyuan, Q., Xiaodong, Z., Yachong, Z.: Amelioration of the Sage-Husa algorithm. J. Chin. Inertial Technol. **06**, 678–686 (2012)
5. Chyba, M.: Autonomous underwater vehicles. Ocean Eng. **71**(8), 1–5 (2009)
6. Xu, S., et al.: SINS/CNS/GNSS integrated navigation based on an improved federated sage–husa adaptive filter. Sens. (Switzerland) **19**(17), 1–22 (2019)
7. Akgul, V., Belge, E., Hacioglu, R., et al.: Correlation between INS and GPS based on sea surface vehicle motion. In: 2020 Innovations in Intelligent Systems and Applications Conference (ASYU), Istanbul, pp. 1–5. IEEE (2020)
8. Singh, B., Dahlhaus, D.: Weighted robust Sage-Husa adaptive Kalman filtering for angular velocity estimation. In: 2019 Signal Processing, pp.71–76. Division of Signal Processing and Electronic Systems, Poznan (2019)
9. Zhai, H.-Q., Wang, L.-H.: The robust residual-based adaptive estimation Kalman filter method for strap-down inertial and geomagnetic tightly integrated navigation system. Rev. Sci. Instrum. **91**(10), 1–9 (2020)
10. Cheng, J., Sun, X., Liu, P., Mou, H.: An improved residual chi-square test fault isolation approach in four-gyro SINS. IEEE Access **7**, 174400–174411 (2019). https://doi.org/10.1109/ACCESS.2019.2957103

High-Precision Calibration and Error Estimation of RLG SINS

Yikun Geng[1,2] and Xiyuan Chen[1,2(✉)]

[1] Key Laboratory of Micro-Inertial Instrument and Advanced Navigation Technology Ministry of Education, Southeast University, Nanjing 210096, China
chxiyuan@seu.edu.cn
[2] School of Instrument Science and Engineering, Southeast University, Nanjing 210096, China

Abstract. Since sensor errors limit navigation accuracy in ring laser gyroscope strapdown inertial navigation system (RLG SINS), the calibration of the error parameters is usually a key technology of SINS. This paper mainly studies the error estimation and high-precision calibration of RLG SINS under both static and small-angle swing bases using systematic calibration method. In this paper, firstly, based on the analysis of the error source, the error models of the quartz flexible accelerometers and laser gyroscopes are established. Meanwhile, according to the basic principles of SINS, the error equations of SINS in navigation coordinate system are derived. Then, this paper studies systematic calibration method. In this part, a multi position rotation error excitation method is introduced and a 33-dimensional Kalman filter is designed for the estimation of the error parameters. Finally, the simulation experiments for the error calibration of the inertial sensors under both static and small-angle swing conditions are performed to verify the effectiveness of this systematic calibration method. This method performs well in the simulation experiments and has its value in the online calibration of slight swing conditions, such as ship mooring state and the missile launcher swing state.

Keywords: SINS · Systematic calibration · Error parameter estimation

1 Introduction

The SINS uses three gyroscopes and three accelerometers to measure the angular velocity and acceleration respectively and subsequently calculate the attitude, velocity and position information continuously based on the dead reckoning principle [1]. Therefore, the inertial navigation, a fully autonomous navigation technology, has the characteristic of accumulating positioning errors over time which leads to the result that the error parameter calibration of SINS has great influences on the navigation accuracy. The main calibration methods mainly include discrete calibration and systematic calibration. Among them, systematic calibration establishes the relationship between navigation errors and inertial sensor error parameters, which usually uses navigation errors as the quantitative measurement to estimate the error parameters. This method can calibrate all error parameters simultaneously through the calculation and allows the

© ICST Institute for Computer Sciences, Social Informatics and Telecommunications Engineering 2021
Published by Springer Nature Switzerland AG 2021. All Rights Reserved
W. Fu et al. (Eds.): ICMTEL 2021, LNICST 387, pp. 460–469, 2021.
https://doi.org/10.1007/978-3-030-82562-1_44

accurate attitude of the inertial measurement unit (IMU) unknown, which is therefore also a good online calibration method due to the reduced dependence on the accuracy of the turntable compared to discrete calibration [12–15]. There are lots of studies on self-calibration to establish a proper error model to estimate one or more error parameters of IMU, such as the bias, the scale factor errors, the installation errors and the non-linear errors of gyroscopes and accelerometers. Besides, the designs of error excitation scheme and the observability analysis, the filtering method and signal processing have all been extensively studied worldwide [2–11].

In this essay, a method to perform systematic calibration under both static and small-angle swing bases is developed, which uses the designed multi position rotation scheme to excite the inertial sensor errors, including the bias, the scale factor errors and the misalignments of both two types of the sensors and the quadratic errors of accelerometers. In the simulation experiments, this method performs well under both static and small-angle swing bases, which makes it of certain reference value in the online calibration under the ship mooring state and the missile launcher swing state.

This paper is organized as follows. In Sect. 2, based on the analysis of error source, the error models of the accelerometers and laser gyroscopes are introduced and subsequently the SINS error equations are derived. In Sect. 3, the overall systematic calibration process suitable for both static and small-angle swing bases is introduced firstly and then the multi position rotation error excitation scheme and the Kalman filter used in this article are given. In Sect. 4, the simulation experiments are performed. The results of systematic calibration simulation experiments under both static and small-angle swing bases are given, including the error parameters estimated results and the compensation performance analysis. Section 5 is the conclusion.

2 Error Model

2.1 Sensor Error Model

The inertial sensors of the RLG SINS are composed of three laser gyroscopes and three quartz flexible accelerometers. In the traditional IMU error model, several of the following errors are usually considered, including the bias, the scale factor errors and the misalignments of gyroscopes and accelerometers. In this article, considering the small-angle swing bases, the non-linear errors of the accelerometers may have a great impact on the accuracy of the inertial navigation. Therefore, in order to achieve high-precision calibration under both static and small-angle swing bases, on the basis of the traditional inertial sensor error models, the quadratic errors of accelerometers are added into the accelerometer error model. The formulas of the simplified error model [10] of the gyroscopes and the accelerometers are expressed respectively as follows:

$$
\begin{bmatrix} \varepsilon_x \\ \varepsilon_y \\ \varepsilon_z \end{bmatrix} = \begin{bmatrix} B_{gx} \\ B_{gy} \\ B_{gz} \end{bmatrix} + \left(\begin{bmatrix} K_{gx} & 0 & 0 \\ 0 & K_{gy} & 0 \\ 0 & 0 & K_{gz} \end{bmatrix} + \begin{bmatrix} 0 & M_{gxy} & M_{gxz} \\ M_{gyx} & 0 & M_{gyz} \\ M_{gzx} & M_{gzy} & 0 \end{bmatrix} \right) \begin{bmatrix} \omega_x^b \\ \omega_y^b \\ \omega_z^b \end{bmatrix} \tag{1}
$$

$$\begin{bmatrix} \delta f_x^b \\ \delta f_y^b \\ \delta f_z^b \end{bmatrix} = \begin{bmatrix} B_{ax} \\ B_{ay} \\ B_{az} \end{bmatrix} + \left(\begin{bmatrix} K_{ax} & 0 & 0 \\ 0 & K_{ay} & 0 \\ 0 & 0 & K_{az} \end{bmatrix} + \begin{bmatrix} 0 & M_{axy} & M_{axz} \\ M_{ayx} & 0 & M_{ayz} \\ M_{azx} & M_{azy} & 0 \end{bmatrix} \right) \begin{bmatrix} f_x^b \\ f_y^b \\ f_z^b \end{bmatrix} + \begin{bmatrix} D_{ax} \\ D_{ay} \\ D_{az} \end{bmatrix} \begin{bmatrix} f_x^{b2} \\ f_y^{b2} \\ f_z^{b2} \end{bmatrix}$$

(2)

where ε_i is the total angular velocity error in the i direction of the gyroscopes; ω_i^b is the angular velocity on IMU axes; δf_i^b is the specific force error on IMU axes of the accelerometers; f_i^b is the specific force; f_x^{b2} is the quadratic term of the specific force; B_{gi} and B_{ai} represent the bias of gyroscopes and accelerometers respectively; K_{gi} and K_{ai} are the scale factor errors of gyroscopes and accelerometers respectively; M_{gij} and M_{aij} represent the non-orthogonal installation errors; the IMU axes are defined by the sensitive axes of the accelerometers and therefore $M_{axy}=M_{axz}=M_{ayz}=0$; D_{ai} represents the quadratic error of the accelerometers in the i direction.

Formula (1) uses the sum of the bias of gyroscopes and the product of the measured angular velocities and the error matrix to express the angular velocity errors of gyroscopes. Similarly, formula (2) uses the sum of the bias of accelerometers, the product of the measured specific forces and the first-order error matrix, and the product of the quadratic terms of the specific forces and quadratic error matrix to express the specific force errors of the accelerometers. These two formulas of the inertial sensor model establish the relationship between the inertial sensor errors and the measurement errors of the inertial sensors.

2.2 SINS Error Model

Since there are errors between the ideal navigation coordinate system and the actual navigation coordinate system, in order to reflect the changes of the error angles between these two coordinate systems, the attitude error equations of SINS [11] are derived and established as follows:

$$\begin{cases} \delta\dot{\varphi}_x = -\frac{\delta V_N}{R_e} + \left(\omega_{ie}\sin L + \frac{V_E}{R_e}\tan L \right)\delta\varphi_N - \left(\omega_{ie}\cos L + \frac{V_E}{R_e} \right)\delta\varphi_U + \varepsilon_x^n \\ \delta\dot{\varphi}_y = \frac{\delta V_E}{R_e} - \left(\omega_{ie}\sin L + \frac{V_E}{R_e}\tan L \right)\delta\varphi_E - \frac{V_N}{R_e}\delta\varphi_U + \varepsilon_y^n \\ \delta\dot{\varphi}_z = \frac{\delta V_E}{R_e}\tan L + \left(\omega_{ie}\cos L + \frac{V_E}{R_e} \right)\delta\varphi_E + \frac{V_N}{R_e}\delta\varphi_N + \varepsilon_z^n \end{cases}$$

(3)

where R_e is the radius of the earth; L is the latitude of the IMU; V_I is the speed in navigation coordinate system; ω_{ie} is earth rotation velocity.

Besides, there are also errors between the ideal speeds and the speeds obtained by calculation. The speed error equations of SINS [11] are shown as follows:

$$\begin{cases} \delta\dot{v}_x^n = \frac{V_N}{R_e}\tan L \cdot \delta V_E + \left(2\omega_{ie}\sin L + \frac{V_E}{R_e}\tan L \right)\delta V_N - \left(2\omega_{ie}\cos L + \frac{V_E}{R_e} \right)\delta V_U + g \cdot \delta\varphi_N + \delta f_x^n \\ \delta\dot{v}_y^n = \left(-2\omega_{ie}\sin L + \frac{2V_E}{R_e}\tan L \right)\delta V_E - \frac{V_U}{R_e}\delta V_N - \frac{V_N}{R_e}\delta V_U - g \cdot \delta\varphi_E + \delta f_y^n \\ \delta\dot{v}_z^n = \left(2\omega_{ie}\cos L + \frac{2V_E}{R_e} \right)\delta V_E + \frac{2V_U}{R_e}\delta V_N + \delta f_z^n \end{cases}$$

(4)

The formula (3) and the formula (4) of the SINS error model establish the relationship between the navigation errors and the measurement errors of the inertial sensor. Combining formula (1) and formula (2), the relationship between the navigation errors and the inertial sensor errors is finally established. In this way, navigation errors can be used as the quantitative measurement to estimate the inertial sensor error parameters to perform systematic calibration.

3 Systematic Calibration Method

3.1 Systematic Calibration Process

In order to study the high-precision calibration and error estimation of RLG SINS under both static and small-angle swing bases, the systematic calibration method is used to calibrate the inertial sensor errors by using navigation errors as the quantitative measurement. The systematic calibration process flow chart is shown in Fig. 1. The overall systematic calibration process steps are as follows:

Step 1. Collect the simulated output signals of the IMU which rotates according to the multi position error excitation scheme.

Step 2. Calculate the navigation speed errors in RLG SINS.

Step 3. Input the speed errors as the quantity measurement into the Kalman filter.

Step 4. Continue Kalman filtering until all the collected data are traversed.

Step 5. Feedback the estimated error parameters to compensate the output signals of inertial sensors.

Step 6. Repeat step 2–step 5 until the preset number of iterations is reached.

Step 7. Output the final calibration results of the estimated error parameters.

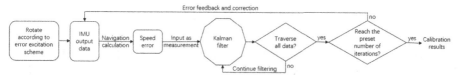

Fig. 1. Systematic calibration process flow chart. Kalman filter is used to estimate the error parameters and the estimation results are used to compensate the original IMU output data.

3.2 Rotation Error Excitation Scheme

Traditional offline calibration methods generally use proper rotation schemes under the static base in the laboratory to excite errors. Traditional online calibration methods, such as [16] and [17], generally design motion paths adapting to the application environment for the IMU by using actions such as straight going at a constant speed, rolling, turning and pitching to complete the excitation of the errors. In this article, however, due to the limitation of the application condition, the movement actions performed by other online calibration methods cannot be realized. Therefore, the rotation error excitation method is used, while the applicability under both static and small-angle swing bases should be taken into consideration in the subsequent simulation experiments.

According to the multi position rotation error excitation method mentioned in reference [8], a trajectory generator is compiled to simulate the rotation of IMU to excite the inertial sensor errors under both static and small-angle swing bases. At the end of the whole process, the IMU has rotated 720° around each axis, and returned to the initial posture, which helps to observe the error parameters. The multi position rotation error excitation scheme is shown in Fig. 2.

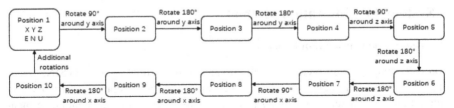

Fig. 2. The multi position rotation error excitation scheme. The rotation speed is 10 °/s. The IMU stays stationary at each position for 10 min to fully stimulate the errors. In the additional rotations, the IMU rotates 90 ° for three times around each of the x, y, and z axes respectively and also stays stationary for a period of time at each position.

3.3 Kalman Filter

In order to separate the calibration error parameters, a suitable Kalman filter needs to be designed. In this article, the Kalman filter uses error model to establish the state equation [8, 15], where Gaussian white noise model is used as the sensor noise model. The system error differential equation is expressed as follows:

$$\dot{X}(t) = F(t)X(t) + G(t)W(t) \tag{5}$$

where $X(t)$ is expressed as follow:

$X(t) = [\delta\varphi_x, \delta\varphi_y, \delta\varphi_z, \delta v_x^n, \delta v_y^n, \delta v_z^n, B_{gx}, B_{gy}, B_{gz}, B_{ax}, B_{ay}, B_{az}, K_{gx}, M_{gyx}, M_{gzx}, M_{gxy}, K_{gy}, M_{gzy}, M_{gxz}, M_{gyz}, K_{gz}, K_{ax}, M_{ayx}, M_{azx}, M_{axy}, K_{ay}, M_{azy}, M_{axz}, M_{ayz}, K_{az}, D_{ax}, D_{ay}, D_{az}]$

In (5), $W(t)$ is the measurement noise of Gaussian white noise model, $W(t) \sim N(0, Q)$ and $W(t) = [\delta\omega \; \delta f]^T$, where gyroscope measurement noise $\delta\omega = [\delta\omega_x \; \delta\omega_y \; \delta\omega_z]^T$; accelerometer measurement noise $\delta f = [\delta f_x \; \delta f_y \; \delta f_z]^T$. $G(t)$ is the system noise output matrix and $G(t) = \begin{bmatrix} -C_b^n & 0_{3\times3} \\ 0_{3\times3} & C_b^n \\ 0_{27\times3} & 0_{27\times3} \end{bmatrix}$. $F(t)$, the system state matrix, is obtained by calculating velocity error equations and attitude error equations and is expressed as follows:

$$F(t) = \begin{bmatrix} -[\omega_{in}^n \times] & F_{12} & -C_b^n & 0_{3\times3} & F_{15} & 0_{3\times9} & 0_{3\times3} \\ [f^n \times] & F_{22} & 0_{3\times3} & C_b^n & 0_{3\times9} & F_{26} & F_{27} \\ 0_{27\times3} & 0_{27\times3} & 0_{27\times3} & 0_{27\times3} & 0_{27\times9} & 0_{27\times9} & 0_{27\times3} \end{bmatrix} \tag{6}$$

where $F_{12} = \begin{bmatrix} 0 & -\frac{1}{R_M+h} & 0 \\ \frac{1}{R_N+h} & 0 & 0 \\ \frac{\tan L}{R_N+h} & 0 & 0 \end{bmatrix}$, $F_{27} = C_b^n \begin{bmatrix} f_x^{b2} & 0 & 0 \\ 0 & f_y^{b2} & 0 \\ 0 & 0 & f_z^{b2} \end{bmatrix}$,

$$F_{22} = \begin{bmatrix} \frac{v_y\tan L - v_z}{R_N+h} & \frac{v_x}{R_N+h} + 2\omega_{ie}\sin L & -\frac{v_x}{R_N+h} - 2\omega_{ie}\cos L \\ \frac{-2v_x\tan L}{R_N+h} 2\omega_{ie}\sin L & -\frac{v_z}{R_M+h} & -\frac{v_y}{R_M+h} \\ \frac{2v_x}{R_N+h} + 2\omega_{ie}\cos L & \frac{2v_y}{R_N+h} & 0 \end{bmatrix},$$

$$F_{26} = \begin{bmatrix} C_b^n \cdot f_x^b & C_b^n \cdot f_y^b & C_b^n \cdot f_z^b \end{bmatrix}, \quad F_{15} = \begin{bmatrix} -C_b^n \cdot \omega_x^b & -C_b^n \cdot \omega_y^b & -C_b^n \cdot \omega_z^b \end{bmatrix}.$$

The observation equation takes velocity errors as the observation and is expressed as follow:

$$Z_v(t) = H_v(t)X(t) + v_v(t) \tag{7}$$

where the observation matrix $H_v(t) = \begin{bmatrix} 0_{3\times3} & I_{3\times3} & 0_{3\times27} \end{bmatrix}$; the system observation noise is of Gaussian white noise model: $v_v(t) \sim N(0, R)$.

4   Calibration Simulation Experiments

In this article, the calibration simulation experiments under both static base and small-angle swing base are performed. The trajectory simulation results of the multi position rotation error excitation scheme under the small-angle swing base are shown in Fig. 3 and the IMU output data can be seen in Fig. 4. The trajectory simulation results show that while the speed on each axis is always 0 m/s, the angles change according to the

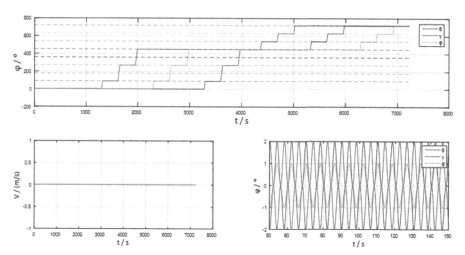

Fig. 3. The trajectory simulation results. The upper figure shows the attitude changes of the trajectory simulation. The bottom-left figure shows the speed changes. The bottom-right figure shows the attitude changes in 50 s–150 s.

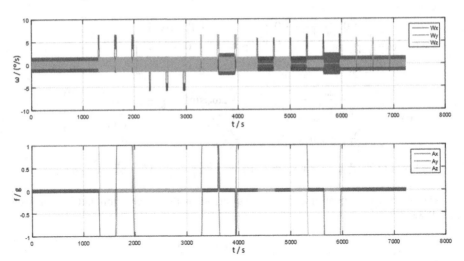

Fig. 4. The simulated IMU output data. The upper figure is the output data of three laser gyroscopes. The bottom figure is the output data of three accelerometers.

Table 1. The comparison of simulation calibration results and preset error parameters.

Parameter	Preset value	Under static base		Under small-angle swing base	
		Estimated value	Relative error (%)	Estimated value	Relative error (%)
B_{gi} (°/h)	0.03	0.029991	−0.0300	0.029995	−0.0167
	0.05	0.049910	−0.1800	0.049968	−0.0640
	0.04	0.039999	−0.0025	0.039994	−0.0150
K_{gi} (ppm)	150	149.967	−0.0220	149.965	−0.0233
	100	100.055	0.0550	100.041	0.0410
	200	199.979	−0.0105	199.980	−0.0100
M_{gij} (″)	50/−50	49.959/−49.965	−0.082/−0.070	49.961/−49.966	−0.078/−0.068
	50/−50	49.957/−49.983	−0.086/−0.034	49.957/−49.985	−0.086/−0.030
	50/−50	49.946/−49.974	−0.108/−0.052	49.945/−49.973	−0.110/−0.054
B_{ai} (ug)	150	149.990	−0.0067	149.993	−0.0047
	100	100.038	0.0380	100.043	0.0430
	200	199.914	−0.0430	199.918	−0.0410
K_{ai} (ppm)	100	100.014	0.014	100.003	0.003
	150	150.018	0.012	150.017	0.011
	200	200.000	0.000	200.007	0.004
M_{aij} (″)	−100	−99.9678	−0.032	−99.9701	−0.030
	100	99.9102	−0.090	99.9113	−0.089
	−100	−99.9532	−0.047	−99.9532	−0.047
D_{ai} (10^{-6} s²/m)	20	19.9978	−0.0110	19.9825	− 0.0875
	15	14.9912	−0.0587	14.9945	− 0.0367
	25	24.9779	− 0.0884	24.9802	− 0.0792

preset multi position rotation error excitation scheme and based on this condition, the small-angle swings are added, of which the periods on each axis are 8 s and, except for the heading angle amplitude of 1°, the amplitudes of the other two are both 2°.

The comparison results between the calibration estimated value and the preset error value under both static and small-angle swing bases using systematic calibration method are shown in Table 1. In Table 1, the results show that the calibration accuracy of each error parameter under these two cases is basically the same. Under both static and small-angle swing bases, the relative errors of the simulation calibration experiment results basically do not exceed ± 0.1%. It can be seen that the systematic calibration method used in this article has a high-precision calibration effect.

The RLG SINS navigation results using this systematic calibration method to compensate the errors are shown in Fig. 5. The calibration and error compensation make the speed errors and the attitude errors not increase significantly with the IMU rotation movement and the increase of time. The navigation errors gradually stabilize during the IMU movement. After the error compensation, the calculation results of the attitudes and the speeds also improve to a certain extent. Therefore, this systematic calibration method has a good compensation performance and is of great significance to the inertial navigation.

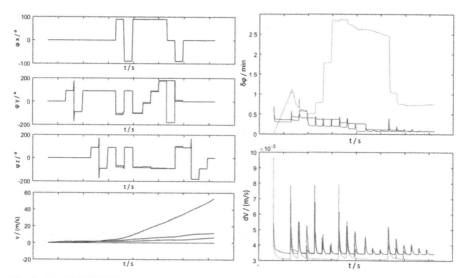

Fig. 5. The RLG SINS navigation results. The first three figures on the left are the navigation results of the attitudes. The fourth figure on the left is the navigation result of the speeds in three axes. In these four pictures, the results after error compensation are red, while the results before correction are blue. Two figures on the right show the changes of the attitude errors and the velocity errors in three axes during filtering process respectively.

5   Conclusion

In this paper, a systematic calibration method for RLG SINS under both static and small-angle swing bases is developed. The calibration simulation experiments are performed under both static and small-angle swing bases. The simulation experiment results show that the calibration accuracy under both of the two cases is basically the same and the relative errors of the simulation calibration experiment results of each error parameter basically do not exceed $\pm$ 0.1%. Besides, the compensation of calibration error parameters also improves the navigation accuracy in the simulation experiments. Therefore, the validity of this high-precision systematic calibration and error estimation method of RLG SINS is verified. This high-precision calibration method not only broadens the environment requirements of calibration, but also has a certain reference value in online calibration applications under the ship mooring state and the missile launcher swing state. In future applications, the requirements for the timeliness of data processing required for online calibration should be emphatically studied.

References

1. Tazartes, D.: An historical perspective on inertial navigation systems. In: 2014 International Symposium on Inertial Sensors and Systems, ISISS. IEEE, Laguna Beach (2014)
2. Nieminen, T., Kangas, J., Suuriniemi, S., et al.: An enhanced multi-position calibration method for consumer-grade inertial measurement units applied and tested. Meas. Sci. Technol. 21(10), 105204 (2010)
3. Gao, P., Li, K., Wang, L., et al.: A self-calibration method for accelerometer nonlinearity errors in triaxis rotational inertial navigation system. IEEE Trans. Instrum. Meas. 66(2), 243–253 (2017)
4. Cai, Q., Yang, G., Song, N., et al.: Online calibration of the geographic-frame-equivalent gyro bias in dual-axis RINS. IEEE Trans. Instrum. Meas. 67(7), 1609–1616 (2018)
5. Li, K., Chen, Y., Wang, L.: Online self-calibration research of single-axis rotational inertial navigation system. Measurement 129, 633–641 (2018)
6. Gao, P., Li, K., Song, T., et al.: An accelerometers-size-effect self-calibration method for triaxis rotational inertial navigation system. IEEE Trans. Industr. Electron. 65(2), 1655–1664 (2018)
7. Glueck, M., Oshinubi, D., Manoli, Y.: Automatic real-time offset calibration of gyroscopes. Microsyst. Technol. 21(2), 429–443 (2014). https://doi.org/10.1007/s00542-014-2115-x
8. Shi, W., Wang, X., Zheng, J., et al.: Multi-position systematic calibration method for RLG-SINS. Infrared Laser Eng. 45(11), 92–99 (2016)
9. Dranitsyna, E.V.: IMU calibration using sins navigation solution: selection of the rate table motion scenario. In: 2017 24th Saint Petersburg International Conference on Integrated Navigation Systems, ICINS, pp. 1–5. IEEE, St. Petersburg (2017)
10. Wang, Q., Wang, L., Qin, W., et al.: Continuous self-calibration path optimization design of inertial platform based on local observability analysis. J. Chin. Inertial Technol. 26(6), 713–720 (2018)
11. Cheng, J., Fang, J., Wu, W., et al.: Integrated calibration method for RLG IMU. J. Chin. Inertial Technol. 4, 445–452 (2014)
12. Jiang, P., Liang, H., Li, H.: Online calibration method of gyro constant drift for low-cost integrated navigator. In: 2019 5th International Conference on Control, Automation and Robotics, ICCAR 2019, pp. 846–850. IEEE (2019)

13. Ma, L., Chen, W., Li, B., et al.: Fast field calibration of MIMU based on the Powell algorithm. Sensors **14**(9), 16062–16081 (2014)
14. Qin, C., Chen, J., Han, Y., et al.: Online calibration method based on dual-axis rotation-modulating laser gyro SINS. In: Proceedings of the 28th Chinese Control and Decision Conference 2016, CCDC, pp. 3311–3315. IEEE, Yinchuan (2016)
15. Jiachong, C., Fei, Y., Ya, Z., et al.: A swing online calibration method of ship-based FOG-IMU. In: 2017 Forum on Cooperative Positioning and Service, CPGPS 2017, pp. 33–38. IEEE (2017)
16. Wang, Z., Shi, Z., Quan, Z.: Online calibration program of SINS for rocket. Infrared Laser Eng. **1**, 266–272 (2015)
17. Wang, H., Shi, Z., Li, G., et al.: Research on simple online calibration scheme of missile SINS. J. Gun Launch Control **39**(4), 6–15 (2018)

Design of an Interactive LiDAR-Vision Integrated Navigation System

Jidong Feng, Wanfeng Ma, Tongqian Liu, and Yuan Xu$^{(\boxtimes)}$ (iD)

School of Electrical Engineering, University of Jinan, Jinan 250022, Shandong, China

Abstract. In order to further improve the accuracy of indoor navigation for mobile robots, this paper introduces the hardware design of a mobile robot combining Light Laser Detection and Ranging (LiDAR) with visual localization system. In this system, the LiDAR-based localization system and visual localization system run in parallel. The LiDAR-based localization system runs on the ROS system for measuring the LiDAR-based position, which helps to solve the deficiencies of low visual navigation frequency.

Visual location makes up for the weakness in short detection range and little data of LiDAR. The pose data obtained by the two methods are filtered by Kalman [1] filter and reweighted fusion to obtain a more accurate position and motion trajectory of the mobile robot. The results from indoor robot movement test show that the mobile robot system integrating visual and LiDAR positioning has an obvious improvement in regard to accuracy compared to other methods.

Keywords: LiDAR · Visual localization system · Mobile robot localization

1 Introduction

Nowadays, with the rapid development of modern society and the maturity of technologies and the needs of better productions and living condition, the application of mobile robots becomes more and more extensive. Compared with human, unmanned mobile robots are more efficient, more convenient and can adapt to various environments such as in many civil engineering fields like medical equipment, warehouse handling, (unmanned) assisted driving, and cleaning, as well as in military fields like remote unmanned combat equipment, replace people in special environments (toxic, nuclear radiation, earthquake-stricken areas [2], outer space, etc.). When mobile robots work becomes more and more complex, the requirements of the results are more and more accurate. In many situations, higher requirements are set for navigation accuracy and anti-interference ability of mobile robots.

Currently, the navigation and positioning of mobile robots in production are mainly using GPS positioning [3]. Developed by a U.S. military project, GPS

© ICST Institute for Computer Sciences, Social Informatics and Telecommunications Engineering 2021
Published by Springer Nature Switzerland AG 2021. All Rights Reserved
W. Fu et al. (Eds.): ICMTEL 2021, LNICST 387, pp. 470–475, 2021.
https://doi.org/10.1007/978-3-030-82562-1_45

has so far built a network of 24 GPS satellites covering 99% of countries and regions on earth. For more than 60 years, the cost of using GPS has been reduced and integrated navigation accuracy has reached millimetre level. These are all advantages of GPS in open/outdoor areas but not in indoor areas especially underground areas. It is due to the influence of buildings and various obstacles which makes it very difficult to receive GPS signals and seriously affects the accuracy of GPS positioning [4].

To solve the problem of indoor GPS positioning, the Lincoln Laboratory at the Massachusetts Institute of the Technology was the first to use LiDAR [5] navigation for indoor mobile robots. By receiving the reflected laser signal, LiDAR can directly scan the position of the surrounding obstacles and terrain to locate itself. One of the most representative usages is laser SLAM [6] technology which has achieved high accuracy in indoor proximity. At present, the development of LiDAR navigation technology has been relatively mature. This method has the advantages of simple structure, long life and high accuracy within short distances. However, limited by a scan line or several scan lines, the laser radar data can not fully restore the surrounding scene information and the details of the scene texture can not be reflected very clearly.

Compared with LiDAR navigation, visual location can acquire more types of information about the surrounding scene. Visual location and navigation obtain image information through monocular, binocular or depth camera, then process the collected image information by computer to obtain the actual position coordinates of the robot. It has the advantages of low cost, wide application range, etc., but the requirements for external environment (ground, light, etc.) are relatively high. At present, a relatively mature solution for visual mileage is the visual SLAM method for image mapping by extracting image features [7]. Usually, visual positioning relies on a single camera to collect data and some feature points cannot be accurately positioned, which affects the accuracy of visual positioning to some extent. When vision SLAM locates complex terrain and broad scene, there will be more image information which requires a high-performance computer to compute. Meanwhile, the computing delay will also greatly affect the timeliness of the entire positioning system.

In the design of a mobile robot positioning system, the single positioning method is often difficult to meet the increasing demand. To adapt to the more complex surrounding environment and enable mobile robots to provide better services [8], LiDAR and binocular cameras are combined to conduct position analysis and to obtain more detailed information about the surrounding environment. In this paper, a hardware design method combining LiDAR and visual positioning is proposed.

The rest of the paper is structured as follows: Sect. 2 proposes the hardware design of each part of the navigation system, Sect. 3 gives the conclusion.

2   Hardware System Design

The hardware part of the whole system consists of six parts: LiDAR navigation module, binocular camera positioning module, mobile robot motor control module, power module, communication module and a host computer. (The relationship among parts is shown in Fig. 1 and the real hardware is shown in Fig. 2)

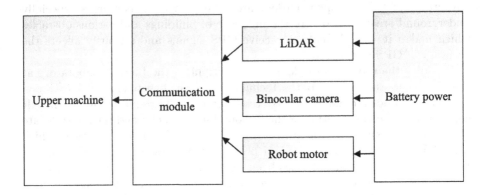

Fig. 1. Design of hardware parts of the mobile robot.

Fig. 2. Mobile robot

2.1 LiDAR System

The LiDAR module is Silan RPLiDARA1 (as shown in Fig. 3). It is a 360-degree laser radar developed by SLAMTEC Company and is able to achieve 360-degree laser scanning within a radius of 12 m. This has met the needs of mobile robot positioning under most indoor conditions. The radar has a normal scanning frequency of 5.5 Hz and can scan up 10 Hz. It can perform up to 8000 ranging operations per second. A1 laser radar uses laser triangulation ranging system. First, light-emitting infrared laser is sent and received after the object reflected laser. Later, its built-in DSP processor calculates the corresponding point of the measured distance and the angle of the object according to each moment received signal. After testing, the positioning accuracy requirement of mobile robot can be satisfied in many different indoor scenes or outdoor scenes with weak light. After the radar is started, the ranging core located at the top of the centre will rotate clockwise under the drive of the motor to scan the surrounding environmental and obtain indoor environmental data of 360°. Then the serial port/USB output the obtained distance information to the host computer for processing.

Fig. 3. RPLiDARA1 LiDAR

2.2 Binocular Camera

The system binocular camera is the Millet camera depth high precision version of d1300-IR-90-color. The camera has a 60FPS frame rate, a 2560*720 resolution for regular images, and a 1280*720 resolution for depth images. The diagonal, horizontal and vertical angles of the images are 103, 90 and 48° respectively. The d1300-IR supports a range of 0.3–4 m from the normal shooting depth. It also supports an infrared mode, which can take infrared images with a detection range of 2.5 m. Compared with the structural light or ToF scheme commonly used in visual cameras, Mi camera innovatively adopts the inertial navigation scheme of Mi binocular structured light (also known as active binocular). The single passive binocular scheme has poor imaging accuracy in the dark and no obvious texture environment, while the small binocular structure photo inertial navigation camera scheme has a good performance. On the other hand, the new scheme can effectively avoid the problem of different cameras interfering with each other and resulting in the deterioration of the collected data. In addition, in order to facilitate visual information acquisition and simplify information processing steps. This camera is built with a chip that can calculate individual depth information, so that depth data can be directly sent to the host computer without an external GPU/CPU, which greatly facilitates the research and design. (MYNT Binocular camera, as shown in Fig. 4)

Fig. 4. MYNT Binocular camera

2.3 Mobile Robot Platform

The experimental platform with LiDAR and binocular cameras is the official ROS Turtlebot2. It is a platform designed to provide an experimental environment for research on different robot projects. Its maximum translational velocity on the horizontal ground is 70 cm/s, and its maximum angular velocity of rotation is 180°/s (when the angular velocity greater than 110°/s, the performance of the gyroscope in the system will be significantly reduced). Mechanical balance on the system is kept by bumpers, cliff sensors, and wheel drop sensors. The flat ground payload is 5 kg. It can travel through the depression with a drop of less than 5 cm, climb the bump, has a battery of 4400 mAh, can operate for more than 2.5 h. The host computer can communicate with the platform through the USB interface or the RX/TX pin of the parallel port. In this experiment, Turtlebot2 can realize horizontal movement and 360° omnidirectional rotation of the mobile robot under indoor conditions and form complex motion trajectory to verify the accuracy and stability of positioning and navigation methods combining LiDAR and vision systems.

3   Conclusion and Future Work

To solve the indoor mobile robot positioning navigation accuracy problem, this paper presents an integrated navigation hardware design that combines LiDAR and visual positioning. The position and pose information of two groups of mobile robots are obtained through two navigation modes, then the host computer fuse the information to calculate accurate positions in real-time. The experimental results show that the design combining LiDAR and visual positioning can greatly improve the accuracy of indoor navigation.

There are some points can be further improved. For example, as more modern machine learning based information fusion methods are emerging and shows great results [6]. Besides, as the information from different systems is not totally trusted, so belief theory can be used to mine deeper information and make decisions [7,8]. We are planning to investigate them in our later work.

References

1. Liu, S.: Research on Lidar Aided Inertial Navigation System. Harbin Engineering University, Harbin (2015)
2. Wei, X.: Research on Robot Positioning/Navigation Technology based on LiDAR Environmental Information Processing. Nanjing University of Science and Technology, Nanjing (2006)
3. Ming, J.: Binocular vision positioning and 2D laser radar mapping of indoor environment based on point-line features. Southwest Jiaotong University, Chengdu (2018)
4. Zhili, L.: Research on local Path Planning Algorithm based on binocular vision and Lidar. University of Electronic Science and Technology, Chengdu (2019)
5. Pengfei, Z.: Research on mobile Platform Positioning integrating Laser and vision. University of Electronic Science and Technology of China, Chengdu (2020)
6. Sun, B., Cheng, W., Ma, L., Goswami, P.: Anomaly-aware traffic prediction based on automated conditional information fusion. In: 21st International Conference on Information Fusion (FUSION), pp. 2283–2289 (2018)
7. Ma, L., Sun, B., Han, C.: Learning decision forest from evidential data: the random training set sampling approach. In: 4th International Conference on Systems and Informatics (ICSAI), pp. 1423–1428 (2017)
8. Ma, L., Sun, B., Han, C.: Training instance random sampling based evidential classification forest algorithms. In: 21st International Conference on Information Fusion (FUSION), pp. 883–888 (2018)

Research on Residential Power Consumption Behavior Based on Typical Load Pattern

Anmeng Mao[✉], Jia Qiao, and Yong Zhang[iD]

School of Electrical Engineering, University of Jinan, Jinan 250022, Shandong, China
cse_zhangy@ujn.edu.cn

Abstract. According to the current analysis of residents' electricity consumption behavior, with the popularization of smart meters, to a certain extent, residents' electricity consumption data can be collected more efficiently and accurately to ensure the accuracy of subsequent electricity consumption behavior analysis. Based on the traditional fuzzy C-means clustering, clustering analysis can be performed on residential electricity consumption behavior. However, due to the large volume of data, more noise points will be generated in traditional clustering analysis, which will affect the clustering results. When studying the electricity consumption behavior of residents, based on a large amount of electricity consumption data, traditional clustering analysis will generate more noise points, which will affect the clustering results. In the study of electricity consumption behavior, the artificial neural network is introduced in the data preprocessing to classify the data. It can be found that the fuzzy C-means clustering combined with the neural network can effectively eliminate the noise points and have a good clustering effect.

Keyword: Data mining · BP neural network · Fuzzy C-means clustering

1 Introduction

Non-intrusive load monitoring analyzes the operating status of various electrical equipment in the tested households through data monitoring of the electrical load port signals of the household users. The correct monitoring of the electrical load of the household users has an impact on the health of the users home. It is of great significance to understand and effectively control energy consumption [1, 2]. The non-intrusive load monitoring power control system is a diversified management data system, which combines communication and computer technology, and incorporates a large amount of data processing and artificial intelligence technology. Using it not only improves the utilization rate of energy consumption, but also ensures the healthy life of household users by monitoring electricity consumption [1].

From the perspective of residential users, through the analysis of electricity consumption data [3], it is possible to monitor whether the electricity consumption behavior of household users is safe, and whether the equipment in the unit family is aging or

© ICST Institute for Computer Sciences, Social Informatics and Telecommunications Engineering 2021
Published by Springer Nature Switzerland AG 2021. All Rights Reserved
W. Fu et al. (Eds.): ICMTEL 2021, LNICST 387, pp. 476–484, 2021.
https://doi.org/10.1007/978-3-030-82562-1_46

damaged, and through the signal data monitoring and analysis of various equipment of household users, it is found Abnormal signals can be processed in time [4, 5]. By observing the electricity consumption behavior status of the monitored households [6, 7], it is possible to observe and record the behavior patterns of the users in the households for long-term monitoring. Once it finds that the user's life status is abnormal, it can promptly feedback to the person in charge of the user's life safety status, thereby ensuring the user's life safety [8, 9].

In terms of power supply demand, through the analysis of user power consumption behavior data, the power system can be more reasonably divided into time periods and power consumption to set electricity prices, and improve the utilization of power system assets [10]. Moreover, peak periods of electricity consumption often occur in different seasons in our country [11]. Through the use of power equipment, the peak period can be consciously avoided and the utilization rate of the power grid can be improved [12, 13].

2 Application of Traditional Fuzzy C-Means Clustering in the Study of Electricity Consumption Section

2.1 Data Collection

In the model analysis, the UK_DALE data set used is an open-access data set from the United Kingdom, which records the household appliance-level electricity consumption of the entire family, with a sampling rate of 16 kHz and a single device at 1/6 Hz. This is the first open-access UK data set at this time resolution. The data set records five houses. The active power consumed by a single device and the apparent power demand of the entire house are recorded every six seconds. After completing the data collection function, the data in this study were mainly concentrated in 48 power load points, and 10 different time points were collected for different load points, and a total of 480 power consumption data were analyzed.

According to the analysis of different power load points at different times, we can find that the data shows a more obvious trend. In Fig. 1, the abscissa represents the user load point, the ordinate represents the power consumption, and the different curves represent the different moments. Electricity consumption can be found to have the same trend over time, so it is universal to analyze and process data.

2.2 Fuzzy C-Means Clustering

Fuzzy C-means clustering divides n vectors ($i = 1,2,...n$) into c fuzzy groups, and finds the clustering center of each group to minimize the value function of the dissimilarity index. The main difference between FCM and HCM is that FCM uses fuzzy division, so that each given data point uses a degree of membership between 0 and 1 to determine the degree to which it belongs to each group.

In FCM the value function (is objective function) is shown in Eq. 1:

$$J(U, C_1, C_2 \cdots C_C) = \sum_{i=1}^{C} J_i = \sum_{i=1}^{C} \sum_{j}^{n} u_{ij}^m d_{ij}^m \tag{1}$$

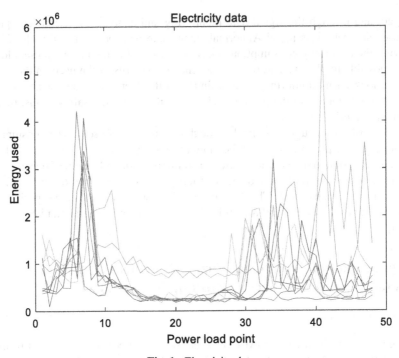

Fig. 1. Electricity data

Here u_{ij} is between 0 and 1, c_i is the cluster center of fuzzy group I, $d_{ij} = \|c_i - x_i\|$ is the Euclidean distance between the $I - th$ cluster center and the J - th data point; and is a weighted index. Calculation of Center c_i:

$$c_i = \frac{\sum\limits_{j=1}^{n} u_{ij}^m x_j}{\sum\limits_{j=1}^{n} u_{ij}^m} \tag{2}$$

Membership calculation:

$$u_{ij} = \frac{1}{\sum\limits_{k=1}^{} (\frac{d_{ij}}{d_{kj}})^{2/m-1}} \tag{3}$$

Perform cluster analysis on the collected electricity consumption data. At the same time, in the case of less electricity consumption data, at present, for analysis, too many classifications will lead to excessive calculations, and classification problems cannot be effectively solved when there are fewer classifications. Divide the data results into 3 categories. In the case of avoiding incomplete classification, effectively analyze the user's electricity consumption behavior. Based on the above analysis and data, the residents' electricity consumption data are awakened by fuzzy C-means clustering. The specific clustering results are as follows (Fig. 2):

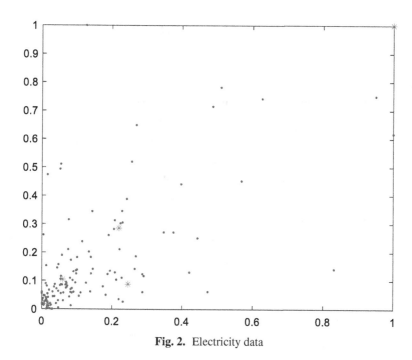

Fig. 2. Electricity data

From the analysis of the clustering results, it can be found that in traditional clustering, there are more noise points and the classification and clustering results are not obvious in combination with the current electricity nodes and loads.

Therefore, artificial neural network is introduced to pro-process the data, and the traditional fuzzy C-means clustering is optimized by combining artificial neural network (BP neural network).

3   Application of Improved Fuzzy C-Means Clustering in the Study of Electricity Consumption

3.1   Data Preprocessing Base on Artificial Neural Network

In the traditional fuzzy C-means clustering, there will be more noise points. that is, for some electricity consumption data, Therefore, data preprocessing is required in this part, combined with artificial neural network (BP neural network) to classify and preprocess the data.

At the first time, from the point of view of node analysis, compare with different collection time points (Fig. 3):

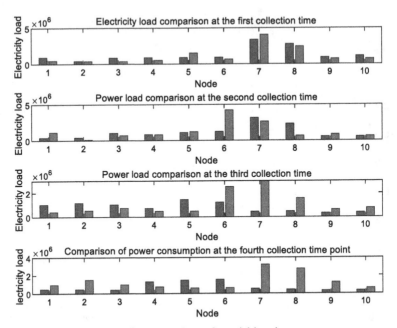

Fig. 3. Comparison of acquisition time

From the above comparison, some node data has a large gap. At the same time, for the node data, due to the particularity of the electricity consumption data, it can be found that the electricity consumption data is relatively large, which will be affected to a certain extent in the subsequent calculation and analysis. Affect the subsequent calculation efficiency and calculation accuracy, so in this step, the power load data is normalized (Fig. 4):

Base on the current data, we will construct a sample database and use the current 480 electricity consumption data for statistics. In order to better calculate the difference between the samples, use the working day data as a and the rest day data as b, and use the following formula to calculate the difference value as an evaluation indicator. Use the formula as follows:

$$u = \frac{|a - b|}{a + b} \tag{4}$$

The calculation result table for 48 nodes through the above formula is as follows: (the previous 10 nodes as an example) (Table 1).

After performing the same processing on 48 nodes, it can be found that the value distribution law of the average index U is as follows (Fig. 5):

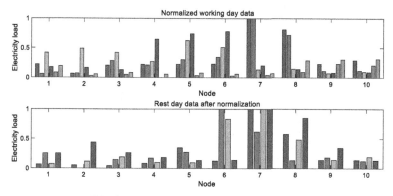

Fig. 4. Time comparison after normalization

Table 1. Data difference value.

Nodes	1st	2nd	3rd	4th	Average
1	0.5485	0.6239	0.7001	0.1771	0.5124
2	0.1235	1	0.6168	0.4534	0.5484
3	0.6483	0.3211	0.3766	0.3352	0.4203
4	0.4549	0.1008	0.4570	0.5614	0.3934
5	0.2155	0.0540	0.7302	0.6907	0.4226
6	0.2918	0.4862	0.2397	0.6943	0.4280
7	1	0.2362	0.7630	0.6638	0.4157
8	0.1678	0.6832	0.5384	0.7173	0.5267
9	0.2403	0.2481	0.3276	0.6166	0.3582
10	0.3498	0.0225	0.3395	0.1853	0.2270

The point data with a small difference between the rest days are subjected to a unified clustering operation, and the nodes greater than 0.5 are clustered separately. Through the above analysis, the sample library is constructed and the BP neural network is trained.

3.2 Improve Fuzzy C-Means Clustering

Perform C-means clustering on the preprocessed data. This part of the data can be found to be divided into three categories, namely: Electricity data is not greatly affected by time, and it is recorded as a; Electricity consumption data is greatly affected by time, and data on working days is recorded as b; The electricity consumption data is greatly affected by time, and the data on the rest day is recorded as c; The data is re-clustered, and the clustering results are as follows (Fig. 6):

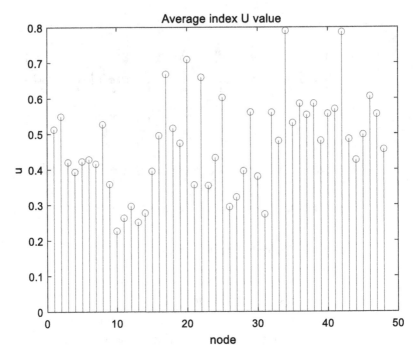

Fig. 5. Average index U

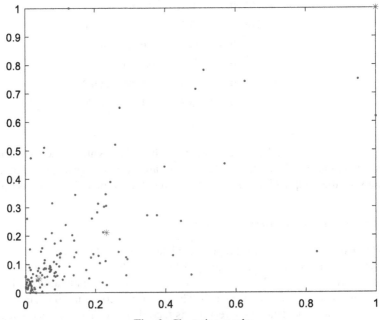

Fig. 6. Clustering results

From the above clustering results, there is a clear gap between the three types of results. At the same time, for the traditional fuzzy C-means clustering, the data clustering effect processed by the BP neural network is better.

4 Conclusion

In the traditional analysis of user electricity consumption behavior, due to the current large amount of data, to a large extent, the increase in the amount of data will greatly increase the noise points in the clustering results, and the large amount of data will the cumulative effect of errors in the clustering center of the clustering results appears everywhere. Therefore, the BP neural network is introduced to analyze the actual situation of data collection and the current electricity consumption, and the data is processed and classified by the BP neural network. Clustering analysis of the data processed by the neural network can find that the noise points and errors in the clustering are largely reduced, which has obvious improvement effects.

Acknowledgment. Funding from the key research and development project of Shandong province (2012CX30302) is gratefully acknowledged.

References

1. Pan, S., et al.: Cluster analysis for occupant-behavior based electricity load patterns in buildings: a case study in Shanghai residences. Build. Simul. **10**(6), 889–898 (2017)
2. Valderrama, J.F.B., Valderrama, D.J.L.B.: Two cluster validity indices for the LAMDA clustering method. Appl. Soft Comput. J. 89, 106102 (2020)
3. Chen, Q., Ma, Y.M.: The research on cloud platform considered privacy household load data processing. Adv. Mater. Res. **1049–1050**, 1929–1933 (2014)
4. Cheng, Q., Min, C., Ciwei, G., Huixing, L., Tugang, S.: Research on the analysis of user's electricity behavior and the application of demand response based on global energy interconnection. In: 2016 China International Conference on Electricity Distribution (CICED) (2016)
5. Jackson, D.B.: System and method for managing energy consumption in a compute environment (2012)
6. Ke, X., Yufeng, X., Wenbin, N., Ting, L.: Analysis of electricity use behavior with clustering method and classification of peak and valley periods (2019)
7. Ozawa, A., Furusato, R., Yoshida, Y.: Determining the relationship between a household's lifestyle and its electricity consumption in Japan by analyzing measured electric load profiles. Energy Build. **119**, 200–210 (2016)
8. Panapakidis, I.P., Alexiadis, M.C., Papagiannis, G.K.: Deriving the optimal number of clusters in the electricity consumer segmentation procedure. In: European Energy Market (2013)
9. Perez, J., Velasquez, J.D., Franco, C.J.: Characterization of the hourly load curve in the colombian electricity market. IEEE Lat. Am. Trans. **13**(12), 3826–3831 (2015)
10. Song, C., Wang, C., Ahuja, N., Zhou, X., Daniel, A.: Optimize datacenter management with multi-tier thermal-intelligent workload placement. In: Thermal Measurement, Modeling and Management Symposium (2015)

11. Tajeuna, E.G., Bouguessa, M., Wang, S.: A network-based approach to enhance electricity load forecasting. In: 2018 IEEE International Conference on Data Mining Workshops (ICDMW) (2018)
12. Trotta, G., Gram-Hanssen, K., Jrgensen, P.L.: Heterogeneity of electricity consumption patterns in vulnerable households. Energies 13 (2020)
13. Yang, Z., Lin, X., Jiang, W., Li, G.: An electricity data cluster analysis method based on saga-fcm algorithm. In: IEEE International Conference on Networking (2017)

A Comparative Study of REST with SOAP

Usman Riaz[⊠], Samir Hussain, and Hemil Patel

University of Leicester, University Road, Leicester LE1 7RH, UK
{UR19,SMH65}@Student.le.ac.uk, HP339@Studen.le.ac.uk

Abstract. Currently most web services obtain REST architectural styles, which were originally founded by Roy Fielding in the year 2000. Alongside the styles, constraints and techniques were also discussed in Roys famous dissertation. In this research paper we will take a look at understanding the techniques used in the REST architecture style, covering the six constraints. Evaluating the testing techniques of REST and finally comparing REST with the SOAP standard. In order to remove the high latency, reduce network traffic and processing delays, which was being caused by SOAP, REST was introduced to overcome all of these issues. Furthermore, 70% of websites use REST architecture as many have found SOAP to be outdated.

Keywords: REST · SOAP · Web-services

1 Introduction

Often REST is considered into two parts: web services and API.

Web services: a service that is offered over the web through standardized web protocols, via the use of data exchange systems, often formatted through XML. The key feature of web services is that your able to write them in various languages, but you are still able to communicate by exchanging data (Cauldwell et al. n.d.).

Application programming interfaces are self-explanatory whereby an interface, programmed with software, can interact with an existing application. Expanding further, an API allows you to build upon information and functionality via a set of functions and procedures. An example of everyday API use would be when logging into a website via your Facebook profile (Kopecký et al. 2008).

There is a key difference between both, web services require a network, compared to API's which can be both on and offline. Web services are not open source meaning the understanding comes through JSON or XML. On the other hand, API's are open source. An interesting aspect of web services is that they are not lightweight and hence often require SOAP to send and receive messages whereas API's are a lightweight architecture (Roy Thomas Fielding 2000).

W. Fu et al. (Eds.): ICMTEL 2021, LNICST 387, pp. 485–491, 2021.
https://doi.org/10.1007/978-3-030-82562-1_47

1.1 Research Gap

In this paper we have studied several research papers spanning from the years 2005 till 2020, this is so that the research gap between these years where rest and soap have evolved is discussed thoroughly and the necessary gaps in research have been filled. REST style is now part of many different social media platforms and this part was intriguing to find out as to how REST has taken over our IoT. Most studies were showing generic research of REST and SOAP, whereas this paper delves into how REST and SOAP relate to everyday circumstances.

2 Representational State Transfer

2.1 What Is Rest?

Representational state transfer (REST), a type of software architecture was developed to ensure the exchange of information between different computer systems. The method builds on existing systems which is one of the reasons why it is popular and is also simplistic in its use. Strict constraints are put in place for the development of web services, these services adapt to the REST architecture which allows for better communication with one another (Battle and Benson 2008).

2.2 The 6 Constraints

The REST architectural style is designed upon these six constraints or design rules. These constraints only define the way data is exchanged between components.

Stateless and Client-Server
There is no restriction between client-server communication to protocol. In the early days of web development, it was needed that the server-side of the web application needed to remember certain details about the user that is using it (Duffy 2015). In REST, the client passes to the server everything that it needs to perform the action and returns to the client with the action complete, this is the complete process. By doing this, when requests get fulfilled, there is no need for the server to remember any of the steps. Systems using REST interact using standard operations on resources, this means that they are not reliant on the implementation of interfaces (Abassi 2015). This makes REST less complex and simplistic as discussed because it removes all server-side state synchronization logic, and the server never loses track of each client in the application as the client sends the necessary information with each request they make. All in all, the client and server application must evolve separately without being dependent on one another (Fig. 1).

Layered System
RESTful allows for the use of layered system architecture. Layered systems consist of layers with different units of functionality. These layers can be added, removed, or modified. The layers only communicate with the layer above or below; the above layers rely on below layers to perform functions. You can deploy the API on server A, store

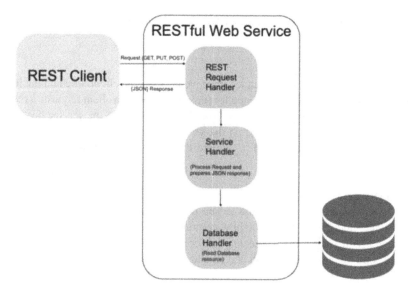

Fig. 1. To show RESTful web Service Architecture (Phppot 2019)

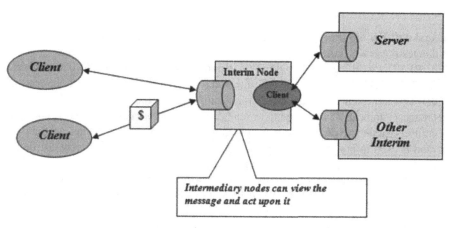

Fig. 2. To show a representation of a layered system (mrbool.com, n.d.).

data on Server B and authenticate requests in Server C. The client cannot talk to the database server directly because it is not the adjacent layer (Abassi 2015) (Fig. 2).

Uniform Interface
The Uniform Interface constraint separates REST from other architecture styles. The uniform constraint decouples the interface, this means that each component can exist and also perform various tasks independently of one another, e.g., being able to read

an article and send emails on the same browser without the need any sort of extension (restfulapi.net, n.d.).

Cacheable
Caching of data will bring performance improvement for the client-side and the load on the server is reduced due to better scope for scalability. When a client requests a resource representation, this request will then go through a cache toward the service hosting that resource. This can either be applied on the server or the client-side, the resources that caching has been applied to need to declare themselves as cacheable (restfulapi.net, n.d.).

Code on Demand
This is an optional constrain in REST. The constraint allows for better flexibility on the client-side and the server decide how certain tasks will be done. The use of code of demand will reduce visibility hence why this constraint is optional. Some examples that influence code on demand are flash and java applets (restfulapi.net, n.d).

3 Testing and Verification Techniques of REST

3.1 HTTP Methods

Several requests are sent to a REST API and verifying responses from it. The purpose of this testing is to record the responses, this is done by sending HTTP requests to see if the REST is working as it should. This is done by using the HTTP request methods, GET, POST, PUT and delete. The GET method is to get information from a server using a URI. This request has no other effect as it is only used for the extraction of data. POST, this request can be used when trying to send data to the server and when trying to create an entity. An example of this action is uploading a file, using HTML forms etc. the PUT method is used to update or replace an existing entity on the server. Lastly, the delete method removes the specified resource given by a URI (W3 schools.com 2019).

A POST writes data to the API, the data can be put into the body of the API request, normally web browser does not allow for data to be put into the body of a request however extensions such as "Postman – REST Client" can be used. An example of using POSTMAN API is being able to send out a tweet over the Twitter API. To send out tweets a form of authentication is required, many big companies use OWASP for authentication. POSTMAN can also be used to run SOAP requests, to do this we first need to get a WSDL sample, it is a web service description language which is used in SOAP. Once WSDL sample has been gained we can take the request URL and run the request using POSTMAN however unlike REST, SOAP is restricted to XML.

3.2 Testing and Verifying

Testing is critical before deployment as during development API testing can reveal issues with your API, server, network and more. The first concern is functional testing, this is to ensure that the API functionals correctly, the main objective is to have no bugs and make sure that implementation is working as expected and as specified in the requirements (Mor 2019). Functional test cases have the same test actions, whether the testing is automated or manual. Some individual actions a test needs to take include, verifying responsive headers, verify correct HTTP status code and basic performance sanity. Apart from testing headers and bodies, every URL should point to an existing location, a broken URL can cause the hypermedia mechanism to fail (Fertig and Braun 2015).

Security testing, the purpose of this is to discover the vulnerabilities of an application and is the first step of the audit process. Security steps include authentication, authorisation, and encryption. There are principles to security testing in RESTful APIs, these can be implemented into a web server. Some tests include incorrect input type must be rejected, an incorrect input size must be rejected, and API must provide the expected output for a given input value (Atlidakis 2018). The next step of security testing is to do some penetrating testing, this is a deliberate attack in a controlled environment and helps with vulnerabilities that may have occurred during the development of web services. A list of vulnerabilities applicable to the application can be listed e.g., exposing a directory traversal attack with resources such as an image. Finally, any unauthorized access that is made during testing can be filed and patched to stop any future intrusions (Fertig and Braun 2015). The final aspect of testing is Fuzz Testing, this where an API is pushed to its limits with vast volumes of requests being sent to it. This technique consists of finding implementation bugs using malformed data injection in an automated fashion (Godefroid, Levin and Molnar, n.d.).

Fuzz testing is a type of testing to see how the API can handle random data which acts as input data, similar to the load testing this type of testing is constructed in order to verify the absolute limit of the API, the random data is used to carry out a crash or uncover negative behavior in the API (Fig. 3).

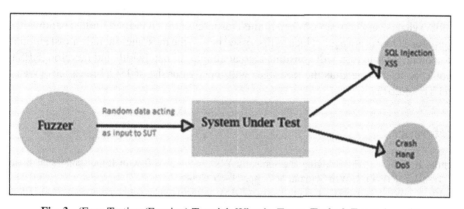

Fig. 3. (Fuzz Testing (Fuzzing) Tutorial: What is, Types, Tools & Example, n.d.)

4   REST Application Compared to SOAP Evaluation

REST is an architecture style, it is more flexible compared to SOAP and does not require processing, on the other hand, the rules in SOAP are important as you cannot achieve any level of standardisation without them. REST seeks to fix the problems with SOAP where soap has been around for some time. SOAP is reliant on XML to provide messaging services and took the place of technologies that were much older and did not work well within the internet (Zur Muehlen et al. 2005). Many developers later discovered that SOAP was complex and hard to use e.g., you need to create the XML structure every time using code to perform simple tasks. Comparing this to REST, web services are reliant on using URL approach and responses do not have to be provided in XML but can use JSON, CSV and RSS. It is easier to parse some forms than others depending on the language being used for the application, this is where REST excels (Soni and Ranga 2019).

A REST API works pretty much normally as a website does, you make a call from a client to a server and you get data back over the HTTP protocol. The best example can be found on Facebook graph API. Searching www.facebook.com/youtube in the google search bar brings up the YouTube page on Facebook. However, if we change the "www" to "graph", the returned result is a response to our API request, a page with JSON formatted data is returned. This is consuming data to API however we can also write data to the API using HTTP request methods. Another example is an application using google translate, this will access google server. It does this through its RESTful API. Words are sent to it according to the language that you have chosen, these words are then returned translated. The list goes on, many services have RESTful interface, including eBay, Flicker, Wikipedia and many more.

In conclusion, SOAP is not able to use REST as it is a protocol compared to REST which is an architectural pattern, however, REST can use SOAP as it is a protocol for web service use. A debate of when to use REST and when to use SOAP when designing a web service is very common. When limited resources are at hand and limited bandwidth, going for SOAP is not a good idea as discussed before the messages include a vast amount of content. This in turn will consume a great amount of bandwidth and therefore REST should be used instead as the messages will mostly consist of JSON messages (Wagh and Thool 2012).

References

Battle, R., Benson, E.: Bridging the semantic Web and Web 2.0 with Representational State Transfer (REST). J. Web Semant. 6(1), pp. 61–69 (2008)

Duffy, S.: What Is REST? | Scott Duffy (2015). https://www.youtube.com/watch?v=LHJk_I SxHHc . Accessed 22 Oct 2020

Roy Thomas Fielding: UNIVERSITY OF CALIFORNIA, IRVINE Architectural Styles and the Design of Network-based Software Architectures (2000). https://www.ics.uci.edu/~fielding/pubs/dissertation/fielding_dissertation.pdf

Abassi, E.: Differentiating Parameters for Selecting Simple Object Access Protocol (SOAP) vs. Representational State Transfer (REST) Based Architecture. [online] researchgate.net (2015). https://www.researchgate.net/publication/280736421. Accessed 22 Oct 2020

Kopecký, J., Gomadam, K., Vitvar, T.: hRESTS: An HTML Microformat for Describing REST-ful Web Services. In: 2008 IEEE/WIC/ACM International Conference on Web Intelligence and Intelligent Agent Technology, Sydney, NSW, 2008, pp. 619–625. https://doi.org/10.1109/WIIAT.2008.379

Mor, R.: REST API Testing Strategy: What Exactly Should You Test? 1 Sisense. [online] Sisense (2019). https://www.sisense.com/en-gb/blog/rest-api-testing-strategy-what-exactly-should-you-test/. Accessed 26 Oct 2020

Fertig, T., Braun, P.: Model-driven Testing of RESTful APIs. https://doi.org/10.1145/2740908.274 3045. http://www.www2015.it/documents/proceedings/companion/p1497.pdf. Accessed 26 Oct 2020

Atlidakis, V., Godefroid, P., Polishchuk, M.: REST-ler: Automatic Intelligent REST API Fuzzing (2018). https://arxiv.org/pdf/1806.09739.pdf. Accessed 26 Oct 2020

Phppot. (n.d.). PHP RESTful Web Service API – Part 1 – Introduction with Step-by-step Example. https://phppot.com/php/php-restful-web-service/. Accessed 26 Oct 2020

Godefroid, P., Levin, M., Molnar, D. (n.d.): Automated Whitebox Fuzz Testing. http://pxzhang.cn/paper/concolic_testing/FuzzTesting.pdf. Accessed 27 Oct 2020

Zur Muehlen, M.V., Nickerson, J., D. Swenson, K.: Developing web services choreography standards—the case of REST vs. SOAP (2005). www.sciencedirect.com. https://d1wqtxts1xzle7.cloudfront.net/. Accessed 28 Oct 2020

Soni, A., Ranga, V.: API Features Individualizing of Web Services: REST and SOAP (2019). www.researchgate.net. https://www.researchgate.net/profile/Virender_Ranga2/public ation/335419384. Accessed 28 Oct 2020

Wagh, K., Thool, R.: A Comparative Study of SOAP Vs REST Web Services Provisioning Techniques for Mobile Host (2012). https://www.researchgate.net/. https://www.researchgate.net/profile/Dr_K_Wagh/publication/264227921. Accessed 10 2020

restfulapi.net. (n.d.). REST Architectural Constraints - REST API Tutorial. https://restfulapi.net/rest-architectural-constraints/#cacheable. Accessed 30 Oct 2020

W3schools.com. HTTP Methods GET vs POST (2019). https://www.w3schools.com/tags/ref_htt pmethods.asp

mrbool.com. (n.d.). REST Architectural Elements and Constraints. http://mrbool.com/rest-archit ectural-elements-and-constraints/29339#:~:text=Data%20Elements. Accessed 31 Oct 2020

Matrix Profile Evolution: An Initial Overview

Bin Sun, Liyao Ma$^{(\boxtimes)}$, Renkang Geng, and Yuan Xu

School of Electrical Engineering, University of Jinan, Jinan 250022, China
cse_maly@ujn.edu.cn

Abstract. Time series data have been investigated for decades in different domains. Recent fast development of wireless networks and cheaper price of small electronic monitoring devices, especially cheap IoT (internet of things) devices start to providing a lot time series data. However, those time series data are mixed with different patterns across lifetime. The patterns should be distinguished so the data can be separated and sent to corresponding process. There are different ways to tackle this challenge, for example by traditional pattern discovery or classification/clustering machine learning algorithms. The matrix profile (MP) method provides a way to handle this problem which can be used individually or together with other methods as an indicator variable or feature. This work aims to take an initial overview of MP method history and evolution from bibliometric aspect.

Keywords: Pattern recognition · Matrix profile · Machine learning · Time series

1 Introduction

Nowadays, with the fast application and deployment of 5G telecommunication technology, internet of things (IoT) devices start to cover bigger daily life domains as well as their enormous volume of data. The data from those devices come with timestamps, thus time series data. IoT data are now much more useful for data analysis in many domains such as positioning [14] and e-health [13]. Equipment and even humans are now monitored by IoT devices and the data are used for different purposes such as incident detection and requirement forecasting.

At the same time, the need of mining those time series to find useful information such as health monitoring and alerting, short-term weather and traffic prediction and so on. However, the time series data from IoT devices are mixed with different patterns across lifetime.

© ICST Institute for Computer Sciences, Social Informatics and Telecommunications Engineering 2021
Published by Springer Nature Switzerland AG 2021. All Rights Reserved
W. Fu et al. (Eds.): ICMTEL 2021, LNICST 387, pp. 492–501, 2021.
https://doi.org/10.1007/978-3-030-82562-1_48

2   Related Papers and Sources

From the work of Keogh E., we select the time-series related ones and their citations in the Web of Knowledge core collection databases. This leads to 4195 documents and more than half of them are journal articles. They are published from 1997 until 2021 from 2065 sources (including journals, books, proceedings etc.) and contributed by 9597 authors. The papers' information is imported into an R library bibliometrix [1] to generate and analyze bibliometrics.

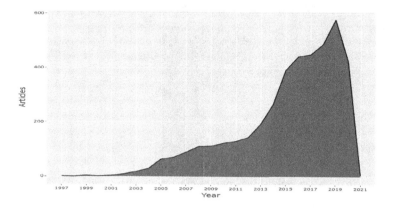

Fig. 1. Annual scientific production

Figure 1 shows that the time-series related research is still climbing a steep hogback even after decades of continuous research. It reflects the fact that the modern life brings more time series which are in more urgent need of fast and effective processing methods.

Figure 2 shows the sources which produce most in our database according to Bradford's Law [10]. Bradford's Law orders sources by publication numbers and then divides and groups sources from top to down and each group has the same amount of publications. In most cases, Bradford's Law follows Pareto distribution.

However, the higher amount does not mean better quality. If we compare with the list of sources ordered by impact (H-index) as shown in Fig. 3, we can see that producing more papers does not mean the papers are in good quality.

The most influencing source is the "Data Mining and Knowledge Discovery" journal which publishes some key papers from Keogh's team. In total, it publishes 76 papers in the collected database including the survey and empirical demonstration regarding time series data mining benchmarks with 391 Web Of Science (WOS) citations (1511 in Google scholar), the SAX algorithm paper "Experiencing SAX: a novel symbolic representation of time series" with 605 WOS citations (1383 in Google scholar), and "Experimental comparison of representation methods and distance measures for time series data" with 376 WOS

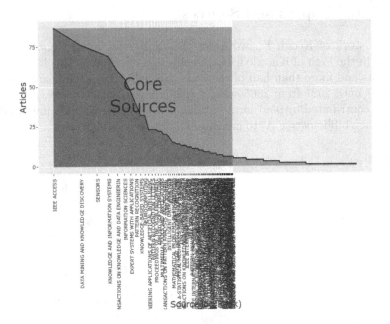

Fig. 2. Most publishing sources clustering with Bradford's law

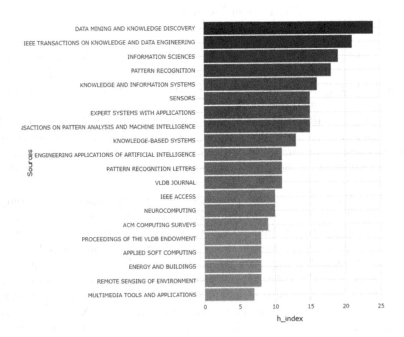

Fig. 3. Source impact (Source H-index)

citations (748 in Google scholar) among many other with more than three-digit citations. The second influencing source is the "IEEE Transactions on Knowledge and Data Engineering" journal. Within our collected database, it publishes four papers with about two hundred WOS citations.

3   Citations and References

Fig. 4. Most cited documents

According to most cited document list (Fig. 4), 4 out of top 10 papers are from Keogh team as follows. The 2nd position is "Clustering of time-series subsequences is meaningless: implications for previous and future research" [6] with 759 citations in WOS. The 4th paper "Experiencing SAX: a novel symbolic representation of time series" [9] has 605 citations. The 9th paper introducs an online algorithm for segmenting time series [5] with 483 citations. The 10th paper is a survey and empirical demonstration which focuses on the need for time series data mining benchmarks [8] with 391 citations.

Other papers come from different affiliations. The top paper is a survey about anomaly detection [2] with more than three thousand citations. The third is a review on time series data mining [3]. The fifth and seventh are overviews about trajectory data mining [15] and urban computing [16] from Microsoft. The sixth is a survey regards vision based gesture recognition [12]. The eighth is a review of novelty detection [11].

From the statistics of references showing in Fig. 5 and Fig. 6, we can see that the top three papers from Keogh team [6,7,9] regarding similarity measurement and fast search are influencing the latter papers most. The reason could be the fact that similarity measurement for time series data is always a hard question and suffers from many difficulties especially the well-known curse of dimensionality.

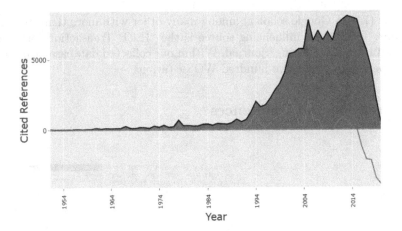

Fig. 5. Reference publication year spectroscopy (RPYS)

Most Cited References

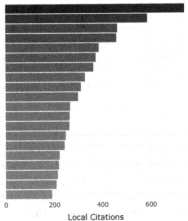

OGH E, 2005, KNOWL INF SYST, V7, P358, DOI 10.10
N J, 2007, DATA MIN KNOWL DISC, V15, P107, DOI 1
H E, 2001, 2001 IEEE INTERNATIONAL CONFERENCE
KOE H, 1978, IEEE T ACOUST SPEECH, V26, P43, DOI
E., 2001, KNOWLEDGE AND INFORMATION SYSTEMS,
)GH E, 2003, DATA MIN KNOWL DISC, V7, P349, DOI
DING H, 2008, PROC VLDB ENDOW, V1, P1542
IG XY, 2013, DATA MIN KNOWL DISC, V26, P275, DOI
BERNDT D.J., 1994, P KDD WORKSH SEATTL, P359
)09, KDD-09: 15TH ACM SIGKDD CONFERENCE ON
TC, 2011, ENG APPL ARTIF INTEL, V24, P164, DOI
TW, 2005, PATTERN RECOGN, V38, P1857, DOI 10.
N KP, 1999, PROC INT CONF DATA, P126, DOI 10.11
ANMANON THANAWIN, 2012, KDD, V2012, P262, DOI
V J., 2003, P 8 ACM SIGMOD WORKS, P2, DOI DOI 10
CHEN Y., 2015, UCR TIME SERIES CLAS
H E, 2005, FIFTH IEEE INTERNATIONAL CONFERENCE
FALOUTSOS C., 1994, SIGMOD RECORD, V23, P419
AL R., 1993, FOUNDATIONS OF DATA ORGANIZATION
IEN L., 2005, P 2005 ACM SIGMOD IN, P491, DOI [10

Fig. 6. Most cited references

The three fields plot is used to show relations among three aspects of collected publications. From the three fields plot by papers, authors and keywords as shown in Fig. 7, we can see the structure of the most important papers, authors and keywords which forms the main research trends and topics. The impact or significance of authors is represented by the amount of relations. We can see that the key authors are Keogh E., Palpanas T., Li H., Anh D. among others.

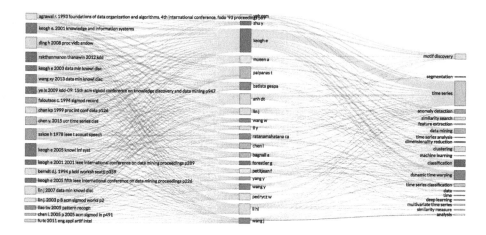

Fig. 7. Three fields plot by papers, authors and keywords

4 Thematic Evolution and Trending Topics

Some more trend details can be seen from the yearly topic frequencies as shown in Fig. 8. It reveals topic trends from WOS keyword-plus. Keyword-plus field from WOS is digested from corresponding paper's title and content. It is a semi-automated and normalized field and it is able to show deeper content and wider variety. In this analysis, we can see that visualization gets continuous attention and is on a peak. Recognition of different types of patterns provides the highest frequency. High frequently mentioned topics.

The thematic evolution of WOS keyword-plus with one cut point after 2016 shows the change of research focus. Classification related problems have been partly solved while models and patterns are now getting more attention and replaces "search". The percentage of focus on time-series has been doubled. The "dynamics" topic is replaced by "variability". The identification (of motif, outliers etc.) gets a bit higher sharing.

The thematic map reveals also the keyword plus field but from another aspect which separate and visualizes trending topics into four different types as shown in Fig. 10 and 11 in four quadrants [4]. The first quadrant contains motor themes with high centrality and high density which constructs the main structure and drives the work of this MP research field. The second quadrant contains niche themes (low centrality, high density) that are well developed but very specialised. The third quadrant contains peripheral themes (low centrality, low density) that are either emerging or declining and are often under developed and marginal. The fourth quadrant contains basic themes (high centrality, low density) which are transversal and general.

From the first thematic map representing keywords until 2016 as shown in Fig. 9, it can be seen that the upper right (first) quadrant with motor themes (high density, high centrality) that presents topics made up of time series, algorithms, and systems. The topics within the lower right (fourth) quadrant with

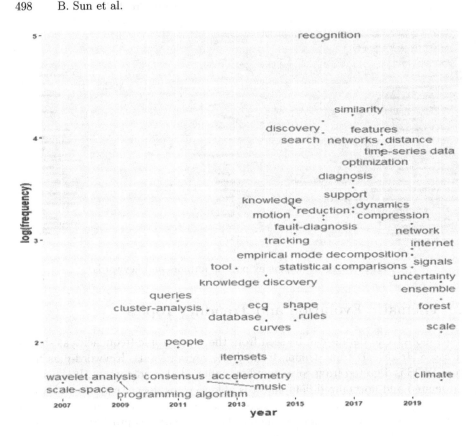

Fig. 8. Topic trend (Frequency)

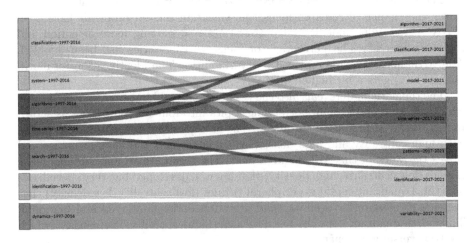

Fig. 9. Thematic evolution

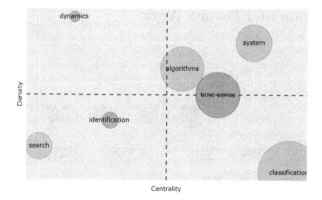

Fig. 10. Thematic map until 2016

basic themes is the classification of time series. Before 2016, dynamics was the one specialized research direction of the upper left quadrant.

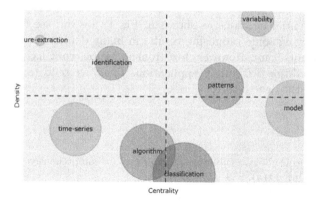

Fig. 11. Thematic map after 2016

However, after 2016, great changes have taken place in the thematic map. Keywords and distribution have produced great changes, the upper right corner appeared variability and patterns. The upper left corner is composed of identification and pure-extraction. The lower left corner contains algorithms of time series. The lower right area mainly consists of classification models, indicating the development of different models for classification is still an important task though it is sliding to the third quadrant.

5   Conclusion and Future Work

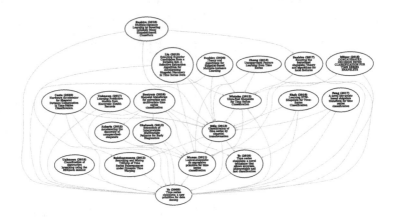

Fig. 12. Citation graph

From the influential citations as shown in Fig. 12 we can see that the matrix profile has showing some promising results in many domains such as computer science and health care. However, few transportation work has been found for urban transportation IoT/AIoT application. Thus, we tend to investigate the related area in the near future.

References

1. Aria, M., Cuccurullo, C.: Bibliometrix: an r-tool for comprehensive science mapping analysis. J. Inf. **11**(4), 959–975 (2017)
2. Chandola, V.: Anomaly Detection for Symbolic Sequences and Time Series Data. Ph.D. thesis, University of Minnesota (2009)
3. Fu, T.C.: A review on time series data mining. Eng. Appl. Artif. Intell. **24**(1), 164–181 (2011)
4. Fusco, F., Marsilio, M., Guglielmetti, C.: Co-production in health policy and management: A comprehensive bibliometric review. BMC Health Serv. Res. **20**(1), 504 (2020)
5. Keogh, E., Chu, S., Hart, D., Pazzani, M.: An online algorithm for segmenting time series. In: Proceedings 2001 IEEE International Conference on Data Mining, pp. 289–296 (November 2001)
6. Keogh, E., Lin, J.: Clustering of time-series subsequences is meaningless: implications for previous and future research. Knowl. Inf. Syst. **8**(2), 154–177 (2005)
7. Keogh, E., Chakrabarti, K., Pazzani, M., Mehrotra, S.: Dimensionality Reduction for Fast Similarity Search in Large Time Series Databases. Knowl. Inf. Syst. **3**(3), 263–286 (2001)
8. Keogh, E., Kasetty, S.: On the need for time series data mining benchmarks: a survey and empirical demonstration. Data Min. Knowl. Disc. **7**(4), 349–371 (2003)

9. Lin, J., Keogh, E., Wei, L., Lonardi, S.: Experiencing SAX: a novel symbolic representation of time series. Data Min. Knowl. Disc. **15**(2), 107–144 (2007)
10. Nisonger, T.E.: The 80/20 rule and core journals. Serials Librarian **55**(1–2), 62–84 (2008)
11. Pimentel, M.A.F., Clifton, D.A., Clifton, L., Tarassenko, L.: A review of novelty detection. Sign. Process. **99**, 215–249 (2014)
12. Rautaray, S.S., Agrawal, A.: Vision based hand gesture recognition for human computer interaction: a survey. Artif. Intell. Rev. **43**(1), 1–54 (2015)
13. Sun, M., et al.: Methods to characterize the real-world use of rollators using inertial sensors–a feasibility study. IEEE Access **7**, 71387–71397 (2019)
14. Xu, Y., Shmaliy, Y.S., Ahn, C.K., Shen, T., Zhuang, Y.: Tightly-coupled integration of INS and UWB using fixed-lag extended UFIR smoothing for quadrotor localization. IEEE Internet Things J. **8**(3), 1716-1727 (2020)
15. Zheng, Y.: Trajectory data mining. ACM Trans. Intell. Syst. Technol. (TIST) **6**(3), 1-41 (2015)
16. Zheng, Y., Capra, L., Wolfson, O., Yang, H.: Urban Computing. ACM Trans. Intell. Syst. Technol. (TIST) **5**(3), 1–55 (2014)

LS-SVM/Federated EKF Based on the Distributed INS/UWB Integrated 2D Localization

Fukun Li[1][iD], Shuhui Bi[1(✉)][iD], Meng Wang[2], Liyao Ma[1][iD], and Bo Zhang[1][iD]

[1] School of Electrical Engineering, University of Jinan, Jinan 250022, China
{lksea2306,zhangboujn}@163.com,
{cse_bish,cse_maly}@ujn.edu.cn
[2] HRG Leapfound Robot Technology (Beijing) Co., Ltd., Beijing, China
wangmeng@hitrobotgroup.com

Abstract. In this paper, a novel distributed integrated 2D localization scheme for fusing the fusing the ultra wide band (UWB)- and inertial navigation system (INS)-derived ranges using least squares-support vector machines (LS-SVM)/federated extended Kalman filter (FEKF) integrated approach is presented. In the proposed scheme, the local filter is capable of fusing UWB- and INS-derived distances, and then, the main filter is employed to fuse the local data fusion filter's outputs and compensate the INS position error. Moreover, for overcoming the outage of the UWB, the LS-SVM is used to assist the FEKF, which can compensate the missing UWB measurement. The test demonstrates that the proposed LS-SVM/FEKF can effectively improve the position accuracy compared with the traditional FEKF.

Keywords: INS/UWB-integrated positioning · Seamless navigation · LS-SVM · Federated EKF

1 Introduction

Nowadays, how to obtain continuous and accurate location information has played an important role on the location based service (LBS) in indoor environment [1,2].

The global positioning system (GPS) positioning accuracy drops rapidly in indoor environment. For avoiding the above problem, many LBS-based localization attempts have been investigated. For instance, radio frequency identification (RFID) based the algorithm of indoor positioning has been considered in [3]. An magnetic field/WiFi integrated indoor localization has been presented in [4]. Moreover, for improving the positioning accuracy of indoor positioning, ultra wide band (UWB)-based methods have been proposed [5]. Meanwhile, the inertial navigation system (INS) has been used to get rid of dependence on additional

© ICST Institute for Computer Sciences, Social Informatics and Telecommunications Engineering 2021
Published by Springer Nature Switzerland AG 2021. All Rights Reserved
W. Fu et al. (Eds.): ICMTEL 2021, LNICST 387, pp. 502–509, 2021.
https://doi.org/10.1007/978-3-030-82562-1_49

equipment [6,7]. However, the INS-based approach is poor in long-term working owing to the cumulative error. As a consequence, the integrated localization strategy has been used in the indoor navigation. For instance, an integrated human tracking fusing INS and UWB measurement has been proposed in [8,9], a weighted least squares-based INS/WiFi system about indoor positioning has been considered in [10]. At the same time, many filtering algorithms have also been considered in [11,12]. In harsh indoor environment, the LBS-based measurement is relatively easy to be outage, which should be also considered in INS-based integrated schemes. Therefore, tightly-coupled integrated model with missing data is not considered.

A novel distributed integrated 2D localization scheme for fusing the UWB's ranges and INS's ranges using LS-SVM/FEKF integrated approach will be considered in this paper. In the remainder of the paper, LS-SVM/FEKF is designed in Sect. 2, a verification is implemented in Sect. 3, and the Sect. 4 presents conclusions.

2   Design of LS-SVM Assisted Federated EKF Filter

At the first place, the distributed tightly-coupled integrated scheme using federated EKF filter will be briefly reviewed.

2.1   The Distributed Integrated Scheme Using the LS-SVM Assisted Federated EKF Filter

The distributed integrated scheme is used in our previous work [2]. Thus, in this subsection, the distributed integrated scheme will be briefly reviewed. Figure 1 demonstrates the distributed integrated scheme. In this model, the UWB reference nodes (RNs) are pre-positioned on known coordinates, inertial measurement unit (IMU) and the UWB blind node (BN) are fixed to a person. Then, the UWB-derived distance between the BN and the RNs $\left(d^{(i)U}, i = 1, 2, \ldots, m\right)$ m is the RNs' number, and INS position $\mathbf{Po}^I$ are employed to input to the LS-SVM assisted federated EKF filter, which will be presented in the next section. Finally, the outputs of the data fusion filter are employed to compensate the INS position error.

2.2   Design of the Federated EKF

In this subsection, the federated EKF filter's state and observation equations based on the distributed integrated scheme will be addressed. The federated EKF includes the local EKF and main EKF, in this model, the local EKF filter is used to estimate the local state of the INS position error, and then, the main EKF integrate the local EKFs' estimations to output the final INS position error estimation of the data fusion filter.

The *ith* local EKF state equation is listed in Eq. (1)–(3).

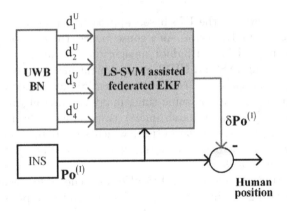

Fig. 1. The distributed integrated scheme.

$$
\underbrace{\begin{bmatrix} \phi_{t|t-1} \\ \delta\mathbf{V}^n_{t|t-1} \\ \delta\mathbf{P}^n_{t|t-1} \\ \nabla^b_{t|t-1} \\ \varepsilon^b_{t|t-1} \end{bmatrix}}_{\mathbf{x}^{(i)}_{t|t-1}} = \underbrace{\begin{bmatrix} \mathbf{I}_{3\times3} & \mathbf{0}_{3\times3} & \mathbf{0}_{3\times3} & \mathbf{0}_{3\times3} & -\mathbf{I}_{3\times3}\mathbf{C}^n_b\Delta T \\ S(\mathbf{f}^n_t)\Delta T & \mathbf{I}_{3\times3} & \mathbf{0}_{3\times3} & \mathbf{I}_{3\times3}\mathbf{C}^n_b\Delta T & \mathbf{0}_{3\times3} \\ \mathbf{0}_{3\times3} & \mathbf{I}_{3\times3}\Delta T & \mathbf{I}_{3\times3} & \mathbf{0}_{3\times3} & \mathbf{0}_{3\times3} \\ \mathbf{0}_{3\times3} & \mathbf{0}_{3\times3} & \mathbf{0}_{3\times3} & \mathbf{I}_{3\times3} & \mathbf{0}_{3\times3} \\ \mathbf{0}_{3\times3} & \mathbf{0}_{3\times3} & \mathbf{0}_{3\times3} & \mathbf{0}_{3\times3} & \mathbf{I}_{3\times3} \end{bmatrix}}_{\mathbf{A}^{(i)}_t} \underbrace{\begin{bmatrix} \phi_{t-1} \\ \delta\mathbf{V}^n_{t-1} \\ \delta\mathbf{P}^n_{t-1} \\ \nabla^b_{t-1} \\ \varepsilon^b_{t-1} \end{bmatrix}}_{\mathbf{x}^{(i)}_{t-1}} + \mathbf{w}^{(i)}_{t-1},
$$

$$
\tag{1}
$$

$$
\mathbf{C}^n_b = \begin{bmatrix} \cos\gamma & 0 & -\sin\gamma \\ 0 & 1 & 0 \\ \sin\gamma & 0 & \cos\gamma \end{bmatrix}\begin{bmatrix} 1 & 0 & 0 \\ 0 & \cos\theta & \sin\theta \\ 0 & -\sin\theta & \cos\theta \end{bmatrix}\begin{bmatrix} \cos\psi & -\sin\psi & 0 \\ \sin\psi & \cos\psi & 0 \\ 0 & 0 & 1 \end{bmatrix}, \tag{2}
$$

$$
S(\mathbf{f}^n_t) = \begin{bmatrix} 0 & f^n_{Ut} & -f^n_{Nt} \\ -f^n_{Ut} & 0 & f^n_{Et} \\ f^n_{Nt} & -f^n_{Et} & 0 \end{bmatrix}. \tag{3}
$$

where the local filter's number is denoted as (i), where the time index t, ϕ_t, $\delta\mathbf{V}^n_t$, and $\delta\mathbf{P}^n_t$ are denoted as the INS's attitude, velocity, and position errors vector respectively, the accelerometer bias and gyroscope drift vectors employ $(\nabla^b_t, \varepsilon^b_t)$, ΔT represents the sample time, $\omega_t \sim N(0, \mathbf{Q})$ is the system noise, $\mathbf{C}^n_b$ is rotation matrix, θ, γ, ψ represent around the X, Y, Z axis of rotation angle, $(f^n_{Ut}, f^n_{Et}, f^n_{Nt})$ is the acceleration up, east and north in the coordinate system.

The ith local EKF's observation equation can be given as Eq. 4.

$$\underbrace{\left[\delta\left(d_t^{(i)}\right)^2\right]}_{\mathbf{Y}_t^{(i)}} = \left[\left(d_t^{I(i)}\right)^2 - \left(d_t^{U(i)}\right)^2\right]$$

$$= \underbrace{\begin{array}{c} 2\left(x_t^I - x_t^{(i)}\right)\delta x_t^{(i)} + 2\left(y_t^I - y_t^{(i)}\right)\delta y_t^{(i)} \\ -\left(\left(\delta x_t^{(i)}\right)^2 + \left(\delta y_t^{(i)}\right)^2\right) \end{array}}_{g\left(\mathbf{X}_{t|t-1}^{(i)}\right)} + \underbrace{\left[\nu_{d_t^{(i)}}\right]}_{\nu_t^{(i)}} \tag{4}$$

where $\left(\delta x_t^{(i)}, \delta y_t^{(i)}\right)$ is the ith local filter's estimation of the 2D INS position errors at time index t, $\left(\delta V x_t^{(i)}, \delta V y_t^{(i)}\right)$ is the ith local filter's estimation of the 2D INS velocity errors at time index t, $\left(x_t^I, y_t^I\right)$ is the 2D INS position at the time index t, $\left(x_t^{(i)}, y_t^{(i)}\right)$ is the 2D position of the ith RN, $\nu_t^{(i)} \sim N\left(0, R^{(i)}\right)$ is the ith local EKF filter's measurement noise at time index t, $\left(d_t^I, d_t^U\right)$ is the distance obtained by INS and UWB respectively. Noted that we employ the data fusion model directly and one can find the detailed deducing in [13].

Nowadays, the centralized filter has been widely used, however, it is poor at the fault detection. The state and observation equations listed in Eqs. (1) and (4) are proposed for the local EKF filter, when the local data fusion filter can provide the local estimation, then the main EKF filter integrates local EKFs' estimations by the following equations ($\mathbf{P}_t$ is the covariance matrix, $\mathbf{X}_t$ is the state vector):

$$\mathbf{P}_t = \left(\left(\mathbf{P}_t^{(1)}\right)^{-1} + \left(\mathbf{P}_t^{(2)}\right)^{-1} + \left(\mathbf{P}_t^{(3)}\right)^{-1} + \ldots + \left(\mathbf{P}_t^{(m)}\right)^{-1}\right)^{-1}, \tag{5}$$

$$\mathbf{X}_t = \mathbf{P}_t \begin{pmatrix} \left(\mathbf{P}_t^{(1)}\right)^{-1}\mathbf{X}_t^{(1)} + \left(\mathbf{P}_t^{(2)}\right)^{-1}\mathbf{X}_t^{(2)} \\ + \left(\mathbf{P}_t^{(3)}\right)^{-1}\mathbf{X}_t^{(3)} + \ldots + \left(\mathbf{P}_t^{(m)}\right)^{-1}\mathbf{X}_t^{(m)} \end{pmatrix}. \tag{6}$$

2.3   Design of the LS-SVM Assisted Federated EKF Filter

In Subsects. 2.1 and 2.2, the distributed integrated scheme using the federated EKF filter (FKF) is investigated. However, it should be emphasized that the distributed integrated scheme's missing data has seldom been considered. In this subsection, we will improve the federated EKF filter by considering the missing the observation vector, which is the main contribution of this work. From the Eq. 4, it can be seen that the observation vector has the following relationship with the 2D INS position error.

$$\mathbf{Y}_t^{(i)} = 2\left(x_t^I - x_t^{(i)}\right)\delta x_t^{(i)} + 2\left(y_t^I - y_t^{(i)}\right)\delta y_t^{(i)} - \left(\left(\delta x_t^{(i)}\right)^2 + \left(\delta y_t^{(i)}\right)^2\right)$$
$$= f\left(\delta x_t^{(i)}, \delta y_t^{(i)}\right) \tag{7}$$

In the INS/UWB-integrated scheme, when the UWB's ranges are not able to be updated, the observation vector is also not be used by the data fusion filter. Aim to overcome this problem, LS-SVM is used to estimate the missing observation vector in this work. It should be pointed out that the proposed seamless schemes are based on the loosely-coupled integrated scheme. This work focuses on the estimation of the missing data based on the distributed tightly-coupled integrated scheme. When the UWB measurement is available, the LS-SVM is applied to build the mapping including the INS position and its error. Once the UWB's range is unavailable, the data fusion filter is unable to continue to work because of the lack of the observation vector. At this time, the proposed LS-SVM/FEKF can work using the predicted missing observation vector of the local EKF provide by the LS-SVM.

Fig. 2. The real test environment.

3   Verification

The performance of the proposed LS-SVM assisted FKF will be investigated in this section, which includes the setting of the real test and the performance comparison of the LS-SVM assisted FKF and FKF.

3.1   Real Test Setup

In this subsection, parameters of the real test will be sketched. The real test scene is shown in Fig. 2. In the test, the INS and UWB measure the target's position in parallel. Here, RoboMaster UWB localization system is employed as the UWB localization system. It includes two kinds of nodes: UWB reference nodes (UWB RNs) and UWB blind node (UWB BN). There are four UWB RNs and one UWB BN. The former is pre-positioned on known coordinates, and the latter is pre-positioned on target. The target is located by the change of the distance between the UWB BN and multiple UWB RNs. By placing the INS on the target carrier, information such as acceleration, direction and attitude can be obtained, and speed and position can be obtained through continuous integration of time. And the reference value is provided by a reference system, which includes the encoder and the compass. The reference velocity is provided by the encoder, and the reference orientation is provided by the compass. The sensors' data is collected by the computer. In the test, we set $\Delta T = 0.02s$.

Comparing with the INS, the UWB's trajectory is stable. The root mean square error (RMSE) of INS in east and north are 19.72 and 9.82 respectively. And the RMSE of UWB in east and north are 0.23 and 0.18. One can note that the UWB's localization approaches to the reference path than INS's localization.

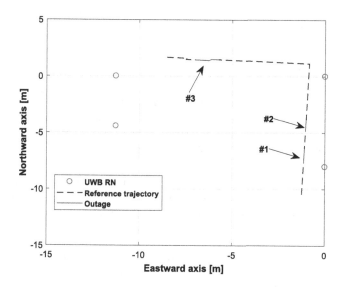

Fig. 3. The simulated outage area (red line). (Color figure online)

3.2   The LS-SVM Assisted FEKF and the FEKF

In this subsection, the performance of the proposed LS-SVM/FEKF will be investigated. In the test, we have created three simulated outage areas, which are shown in Fig. 3. Here, each simulated outage area includes about 50 sample numbers. In these simulated outage area, at least one UWB measurement will be set to be non-updated. If the UWB measurement is unavailable, its logical value is 1, otherwise, its value is 0. It should be emphasized that we do not consider that all the UWB measurements are unavailable in this paper. Once the target in the simulated outage area, the UWB measurement is unable to be updated, the UWB position will be constant. And thus, the measurement error of the data fusion filter will increase.

The RMSEs of the position, in m, produced by the FEKF and LS-SVM/FEKF in #1, #2, and #3 outage area are sketched in Table 1. From the table, we can see that the position RMSEs of the LS-SVM/FEKF are smaller than the position RMSEs of the FEKF. Then we can conclude that, the proposed LS-SVM/FEKF can effectively reduce position error.

Table 1. The RMSEs of position, in m, produced by the FEKF and LS-SVM/FEKF in #1, #2, and #3 outage area.

Method	#1		#2		#3	
	East	North	East	North	East	North
FEKF	0.18	0.71	0.12	0.25	0.36	0.16
LS-SVM/FEKF	0.05	0.13	0.09	0.22	0.29	0.04

4   Conclusion

In this paper, a novel LS-SVM/FEKF for the distributed INS/UWB integrated 2D localization scheme have been investigated to obtain accurate position information. In the proposed scheme, the local data fusion filter is used to fuse the UWB- and INS-derived distances between the UWB RN and the target, and then, the main filter is employed to fuse the local data fusion filter's outputs and compensate the INS position error. Moreover, face the outage of the UWB, the LS-SVM is used to assist FEKF, which can compensate the missing UWB's range. The test results exhibit that the proposed LS-SVM/FEKF can effectively maintain the performance when UWB's range is missing.

Acknowledgment. This work was supported in part by the National Natural Science Foundation of China under Grant 61803175, in part by the Shandong Key R&D Program under Grant 2019GGX104026, Shandong Provincial Natural Science Foundation ZR2020KF027.

References

1. Sung, K., Lee, D., Kim, H.: Indoor pedestrian localization using iBeacon and improved Kalman filter. Sensors **18**(6), 1722 (2018)
2. Xu, Y., Tian, G., Chen, X.: Performance enhancement for INS/UWB integrated indoor tracking using distributed iterated extended Kalman filter. In: Ubiquitous Positioning Indoor Navigation and Location-Based Services, Wuhan, China (2018)
3. Xu, H., Ding, Y., et al.: An RFID indoor positioning algorithm based on Bayesian probability and K-nearest neighbor. Sensors **17**(8), 1806 (2017)

4. Shu, Y., Cheng, B., et al.: Indoor localization using pervasive magnetic field and opportunistic WiFi sensing. IEEE J. Sel. Areas Commun. **33**(7), 1443–1457 (2015)
5. Yu, K., Wen, K., et al.: A novel NLOS mitigation algorithm for UWB localization in harsh indoor environments. IEEE Trans. Veh. Technol. **68**(1), 686–699 (2019)
6. Cao, H., Zhang, Y., et al.: Pole-zero-temperature compensation circuit design and experiment for dual-mass MEMS gyroscope bandwidth expansion. IEEE/ASME Trans. Mechatron. **24**(2), 677–688 (2019)
7. Xu, Y., Shmaliy, Y.S., Ahn, C.K., et al.: Tightly-coupled integration of INS and UWB using fixed-lag extended UFIR smoothing for quadrotor localization. IEEE Internet Things J. **8**(3), 1716–1727 (2018)
8. Woyano, F., Park, S., Lee, S.: A survey of pedestrian dead reckoning technology using multi-sensor fusion for indoor positioning systems. J. Korean Inst. Commun. Sci. **35**(12), 36–45 (2018)
9. Xu, Y., Ahn, C.K., Shmaliy, Y.S., et al.: Adaptive robust INS/UWB-integrated human tracking using UFIR filter bank. Measurement **123**, 1–7 (2018)
10. Chen, J., Ou, G., et al.: An INS/WiFi indoor localization system based on the weighted least squares. Sensors **18**(5), 1458 (2018)
11. Zhao, S., Huang, B.: Trial-and-error or avoiding a guess? Initialization of the Kalman filter. Automatica **121**, 109184 (2020)
12. Zhao, S., Shmaliy, Y.S., Liu, F.: Fast Kalman-like optimal unbiased FIR filtering with applications. IEEE Trans. Signal Process. **64**(9), 2284–2297 (2016)
13. Xu, Y., Chen, X., et al.: Improving tightly-coupled model for indoor pedestrian navigation using foot-mounted IMU and UWB measurements. In: 2016 Instrumentation and Measurement Technology Conference, Taipei, Taiwan (2016)

LiDAR Map Construction Using Improved R-T-S Smoothing Assisted Extended Kalman Filter

Bo Zhang[1], Meng Wang[2], Shuhui Bi[1(✉)], and Fukun Li[1]

[1] School of Electrical Engineering, University of Jinan, Jinan 250022, China
cse_bish@ujn.edu.cn

[2] HRG Leapfound Robot Technology (Beijing) Co., Ltd., Beijing, China
wangmeng@hitrobotgroup.com

Abstract. On account of the low accuracy of boundary point cloud information during map construction of LiDAR used in mobile robots, an data processing scheme based on extended Kalman filter (EKF) and improved R-T-S smoothing and averaging is proposed to obtain accurate point cloud information. The proposed scheme can remove some noise points and make the map boundary more smoother and more accurate. The experimental results show that comparing with the original data, the proposed data processing scheme could reduce the position error of point cloud information effectively.

Keywords: LiDAR · Extended Kalman filter · R-T-S smoothing

1 Introduction

With the continuous improvement of the industrial level, the demand for robots in all walks of life is increasing day by day. A lot of work needs to be done indoors, and when mobile robots are used indoors, constructing accurate environmental information and precise positioning for mobile robots are the main points of autonomous navigation for robots [1–3].

The mobile robot's automatic path planning and automatic obstacle avoidance functions allow the mobile robot to travel safely in an unknown environment, which is inseparable from various sensors, examples include UWB [4], IMU [5], Camera and LiDAR [6]. Among them, the automatic obstacle avoidance technology mainly relies on drawing a point cloud through LiDAR to determine whether there are obstacles in front of the mobile robot [7]. Therefore, the accuracy of the point cloud diagram drawn by the LiDAR is the main factor affecting the automatic obstacle avoidance function.

Kalman filter(KF) is a highly efficient autoregressive filter, which can estimate the system state and reduce noise at the next moment based on the current system state [8,9]. However, the KF must be applied to a linear system conforming to the Gaussian distribution, so when targeting a nonlinear system, an EKF

© ICST Institute for Computer Sciences, Social Informatics and Telecommunications Engineering 2021
Published by Springer Nature Switzerland AG 2021. All Rights Reserved
W. Fu et al. (Eds.): ICMTEL 2021, LNICST 387, pp. 510–517, 2021.
https://doi.org/10.1007/978-3-030-82562-1_50

is required. The EKF is mainly to linearize the nonlinear system through Taylor expansion, and then perform the KF [10,11].

This paper proposes a scheme to process data by using a combination of EKF and R-T-S smoothing to overcome the shortcomings of large errors in a single sensor. The LiDAR data after EKF is then subjected to extended Kalman smoothing. The experimental results verify the effectiveness of this scheme. The rest of the paper is structured as follows: Sect. 2 establishes the motion model and studies the algorithm, Sect. 3 studies the performance of the proposed combined data processing scheme, and Sect. 4 gives the conclusion.

2 Map Construction Based on Extended Kalman Filter and Improved R-T-S Smoothing

The system flow chart is shown in Fig. 1. LiDAR obtains the point cloud information of the surrounding environment and establishes the state equation and observation equation. The data is input into the EKF, and the processed data is obtained through the processing of the EKF. Then input the EKF processed data into improved R-T-S smoothing to smooth the data. Finally, the average value of the improved R-T-S smoothing data is taken to obtain more accurate data.

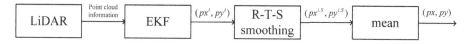

Fig. 1. System flow chart.

2.1 The LiDAR-Based Map Construction Model

The system is composed of LiDAR and observation target is shown in Fig. 2. The LiDAR is located at the origin of the coordinate system, and the observation target is point $P_k(px_k, py_k)$. At the moment k, dis_k is the distance between the LiDAR and the observation point P_k, and φ_k is the angle between the observation point and the X-axis. Then at the moment $k+1$, dis_{k+1} is the distance between the LiDAR and the observation point $P_{k+1}(px_{k+1}, py_{k+1})$, and φ_{k+1} is the angle between the observation point and the X-axis.

Use kinematics equations to describe the state equations of the points in the point cloud graph established by LiDAR is Eqs. 1 and 2. px_k is the position in the north direction, py_k is the position in the east direction, pV_k is the speed, φ_k is the heading angle, dt is the LiDAR obtains the time interval of two adjacent point clouds, ω_k is the system noise at time k and its covariance matrix is Q.

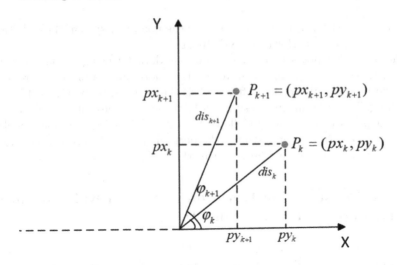

Fig. 2. Dynamic system model.

$$
\underbrace{\begin{bmatrix} px_k \\ py_k \\ pV_k \\ \varphi_k \end{bmatrix}}_{X_k} = \underbrace{\begin{bmatrix} px_{k-1} + dt \cdot pV_{k-1}\sin(\varphi_{k-1}) \\ py_{k-1} + dt \cdot pV_{k-1}\cos(\varphi_{k-1}) \\ pV_{k-1} \\ \varphi_{k-1} \end{bmatrix}}_{f(X_{k-1})} + \omega_k \tag{1}
$$

Observation equations is listed as Eq. 3. h is the mapping of the landmark in the coordinate system, $dis_{j,k}$, $j = 1, 2, ..., i$ is the distance from LiDAR cloud point at time k to landmark j,$(lx^{(j)}, ly^{(j)}), j = 1, 2, ..., i$ is the position of the observation point, and j is the number of landmark. ν_k is the measurement noise.

$$
\underbrace{\begin{bmatrix} dis_{1,k} \\ dis_{2,k} \\ \vdots \\ dis_{i,k} \end{bmatrix}}_{Z_k} = \underbrace{\begin{bmatrix} \sqrt{(px_k - lx^{(1)})^2 + (py_k - ly^{(1)})^2} \\ \sqrt{(px_k - lx^{(2)})^2 + (py_k - ly^{(2)})^2} \\ \vdots \\ \sqrt{(px_k - lx^{(i)})^2 + (py_k - ly^{(i)})^2} \end{bmatrix}}_{h(X_{k-1})} + \nu_k \tag{2}
$$

2.2 Principle of Extended Kalman Filter and R-T-S Smoothing

EKF is linearized on the basis of KF. Starting from the initial time, forward recursively at k time, then recursively from k time forward k times and backward recursive to complete the R-T-S smoothing process. Forward recursion is the EKF process(Eqs. 3 to 9), and backward recursion is the R-T-S smoothing process(Eqs. 9 to 3).

State Prediction

$$\hat{X}_{k|k-1} = f\left(\hat{X}_{k-1}\right) + \omega_k \tag{3}$$

Among them: $\hat{X}_{k|k-1}$ is the predicted value of the system state at time k at $k-1$, $\hat{X}_{k-1}$ is the optimal estimation of the system state at $k-1$, ω_k is the amount of control given by the system.

Covariance Matrix Update

$$P_{k|k-1} = A_k\,P_{k-1}\,A_k^T + Q \tag{4}$$

$$A_k = \frac{\partial f(X_k)}{\partial X_k} \tag{5}$$

Among them: $P_{k|k-1}$ is the covariance matrix corresponding to the state $\hat{X}_{k|k-1}$ to be calculated, A_k is the partial derivative Jacobian matrix of f, and P_{k-1} is The calculated covariance matrix of $\hat{X}_{k-1}$, Q is the covariance matrix of system process noise

Calculate Weight

$$K_k = P_{k|k-1}\,H_k^T\left(H_k\,P_{k|k-1}\,H_k^T + R_k\right)^{-1} \tag{6}$$

$$H_k = \frac{\partial h(X_k)}{\partial X_k} \tag{7}$$

Among them: R_k is the covariance matrix of the system observation noise, H_k is the h partial derivative Jacobian matrix obtained in the previous part, K_k is the Kalman gain, based on the covariance matrix of the system's predicted state and sensor observations, to determine the weight ratio of each in the posterior probability.

Estimate Current State

$$\hat{X}_k = \hat{X}_{k|k-1} + K_k\left(Z_k - h(\hat{X}_{k|k-1})\right) \tag{8}$$

Combine the predicted value $\hat{X}_{k|k-1}$ in the first step and the observation value Z_k of the sensor at the current moment, take the K_k calculated in the third step as the weight, and calculate the weighted sum of the current moment The best estimate $\hat{X}_k$.

Update Covariance

$$P_k = (I - K_k H_k)\,P_{k|k-1} \tag{9}$$

The update of the covariance can not only ensure the accuracy of the covariance at the next moment, but more importantly, because the prior estimate at the next moment comes from the posterior estimate at the previous moment, the algorithm can iterate continuously to achieve self return.

3 Experiment and Discussion

3.1 Experiment Environment

Article conducted an experiment in University of Jinan to verifies the effectiveness of the scheme. The experiment consists of a portable computer, LiDAR and a support. The portable computer and LiDAR are connected by micro USB and USB to serial port module. LiDAR is responsible for collecting the point cloud information of the surrounding environment, and the portable computer is mainly responsible for saving the LiDAR point cloud data and processing the EKF algorithm. LiDAR is located on the support. The schematic diagram is shown in Fig. 3.

The reference position, the LiDAR data and the position after EKF and improved R-T-S smoothing are shows in Fig. 4. In this figure, we can see that the point cloud information after EKF and improved R-T-S smoothing is more accurate than before.

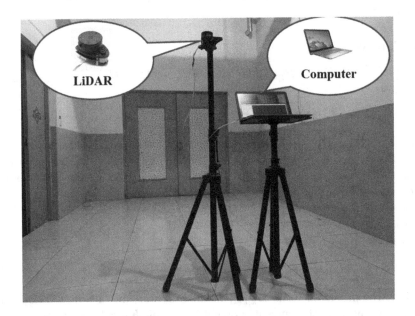

Fig. 3. Test environment.

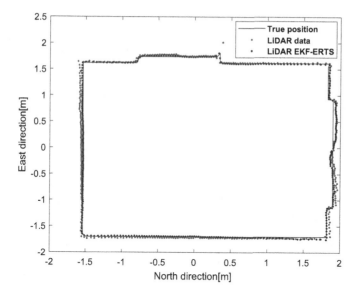

Fig. 4. The reference position, the LiDAR data and the position after EKF and improved R-T-S smoothing.

3.2   Performance of the Scheme

The RMSE calculation is performed on the point cloud data collected by LiDAR and the point cloud data calculated by the EKF, and the results are shown in Table 1. In this table, the data processed by EKF and improved R-T-S smoothing obviously has smaller error than before processing. The root mean square error(RMSE) after EKF and improved R-T-S smoothing of position in north is 0.0166 m and in east is 0.0164 m.

Table 1. RMSE(m) in two directions.

Direction	Before extended Kalman filter	After extended Kalman filtering
East direction	0.0242	0.0164
North direction	0.0247	0.0166
Mean	0.02445	0.0165

The position error in north direction and east direction is shown in Figs. 5 and 6.

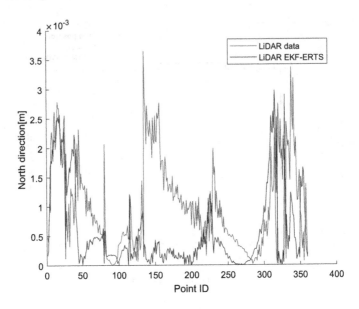

Fig. 5. Position error in north direction.

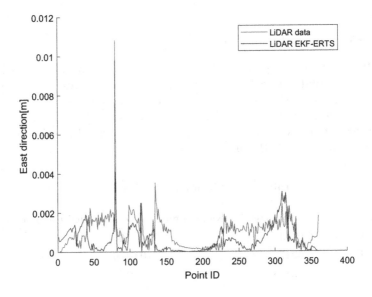

Fig. 6. Position error in east direction.

4   Conclusions

A LiDAR point cloud information graph processing method based on EKF and improved R-T-S smoothing is proposed. In this scheme, the LiDAR point cloud information is processed by using EKF and then the filtered data is smoothed by improved R-T-S smoothing. The experiment verifies the effectiveness of EKF and improved R-T-S smoothing in reducing the position error relative to the original data.

Acknowledgment. This paper was supported by National Natural Science Foundation of China (No. 61803175), Shandong Provincial Natural Science Foundation (No. ZR2018LF01, No. ZR2020KF027), Shandong K&D Program (No. 2019GGX104026).

References

1. Sherwin, T., Easte, M., Chen, A.T., et al.: Robocentric map joining: improving the consistency of EKF-SLAM. Rob. Auton. Syst. **55**(1), 21–29 (2007)
2. Xu, Y., Shmaliy, Y.S., Li, Y., et al.: UWB-based indoor human localization with time-delayed data using EFIR filtering. IEEE Access **5**, 16676–16683 (2017)
3. Song, J., Zhang, W., Wu, X., et al.: Laser-based SLAM automatic parallel parking path planning and tracking for passenger vehicle. IET Intell. Transp. Syst. **13**(10), 1557–1568 (2019)
4. Xu, Y., Ahn, C.K., Shmaliy, Y.S., et al.: Adaptive robust INS/UWB-integrated human tracking using UFIR filter bank. Measurement **123**, 1–7 (2018)
5. Xu, Y., Ahn, C.K., Shmaliy, Y.S., et al.: Tightly-coupled integration of INS and UWB using fixed-lag extended UFIR smoothing for quadrotor localization. IEEE Internet Things J. **8**(3), 1716–1727 (2018)
6. Hutabarat, D., Rivai, M., Purwanto, D., et al.: LiDAR-based obstacle avoidance for the autonomous mobile robot. In: 2019 12th International Conference on Information and Communication Technology and System (ICTS), pp. 197–202. Surabaya (2019)
7. Chelghoum, A., Wang, Q., Wang, K.: Design and simulation of autonomous mobile robots obstacle avoidance system. In: Pan, Z., Cheok, A.D., Müller, W., Zhang, M. (eds.) Transactions on Edutainment XIII. LNCS, vol. 10092, pp. 165–180. Springer, Heidelberg (2017). https://doi.org/10.1007/978-3-662-54395-5_15
8. Zhao, S., Huang, B.: Trial-and-error or avoiding a guess? Initialization of the Kalman filter. Automatica **121**, 109184 (2020)
9. Zhao, S., Shmaliy, Y.S., Liu, F.: Fast Kalman-like optimal unbiased FIR filtering with applications. IEEE Trans. Sig. Process. **64**(9), 2284–2297 (2016)
10. Pengfei, S., Lilan, L., Zenggui, G., et al.: On the target tracking and locating method using EKF algorithm in service robots. Metrol. Meas. Tech. **46**(1), 1–4 (2019)
11. Li, X., Wang, Y., Liu, D.: Research on extended Kalman Filter and particle filter combinational algorithm in UWB and foot-mounted IMU fusion positioning. Mob. Inf. Syst. **4**, 1–17 (2018)

Path Planning Method for Unmanned Surface Vehicle Based on RRT* and DWA

Xiaotian Zhang[ID] and Xiyuan Chen[✉][ID]

School of Instrument Science and Engineering, Southeast University, Nanjing 210096, China
chxiyuan@seu.edu.cn

Abstract. Based on the optimized rapidly-exploring random tree (RRT*) and dynamic window approach (DWA), this paper proposes a method for path planning of unmanned surface vehicle. By inputting the global path generated by RRT* to the local path planner through soft constraints, and combining the obstacle information received by the sensor when the USV is working, the improved DWA is used to obtain a route that can be operated by the USV. The simulation results verify it can effectively avoid dynamic obstacles, ensure the safe navigation of USV in complex environments, and can meet real-time requirements.

Keywords: USV · Path planning · RRT* · DWA · Dynamic obstacle avoidance

1 Introduction

Unmanned surface vehicle (USV) is a type of vehicle carrying multiple types of sensors without manual control. Compared with manned vehicle, USV have the advantages of small dimension, full-time, low-cost, and have strong adaptability to complex water surfaces such as near shores or shallows, especially not suitable for manned vehicle to perform tasks [1]. Equipped with advanced control system, sensor system and communication system, it can perform a variety of high-demand military or conventional tasks.

Path planning is one of the most basic technologies of surface unmanned vehicle. Its purpose is to determine the best trajectory of USV navigation by receiving information from sensors under unmanned conditions, and in the actual driving process of USV. According to the error between the actual position and the preset position, continuously modify the travel route affected by external factors to meet the relevant task requirements. The pros and cons of the path planning algorithm not only determine its level of autonomy, but also a prerequisite for the successful realization of the task. In the process of path planning, the main indicators to be investigated are the total path distance and safety. In addition, the quality of the generated trajectory, such as smoothness and continuity, is also within the scope of investigation [2]. Different from robot or unmanned vehicle path planning, due to the particularity of the working environment of surface unmanned vehicle, the USV is required to successfully complete tasks on the surface

W. Fu et al. (Eds.): ICMTEL 2021, LNICST 387, pp. 518–527, 2021.
https://doi.org/10.1007/978-3-030-82562-1_51

with strong interference such as wind, waves and currents, so it is reliable, real-time and anti-interference ability has also become a factor to be considered in design [3].

The path planning of the USV is a type of robot path planning in a broad sense, so many relatively mature robot path planning methods can be considered for use on the unmanned surface vehicle. Currently, the mainstream path planning algorithms can be divided into three categories: path planning methods based on graph search, methods based on sampling, and methods based on intelligent algorithms. Graph search algorithms are usually based on graphics environment modeling. By mapping real-world environmental information to the graph, the path planning problem is transformed into a mathematical problem for solution. Common graph search algorithms include Dijkstra algorithm [4], A* [5] algorithm, and D* [6] algorithm. These algorithms often have complete solutions, as long as there is a feasible route, these methods can be used within a certain time to search for a route that meets the requirements. However, the cost of this completeness is that the search time is closely related to the complexity of the environment, and the time to obtain a feasible path will increase rapidly with the increase of the map scale and the increase of obstacles in the environment. The path planning of intelligent bionics is inspired by animal behavior in nature and can be used to deal with path planning problems in complex environments. Commonly used methods include ant colony algorithm [7], genetic algorithm, particle swarm optimization algorithm, etc. The advantage is that these algorithms have good robustness, and the speed of path planning has been further improved, but at the same time, premature convergence may occur and fall into Local optimal solution, and parameter settings often need to be adjusted adaptively, which is equivalent to bringing greater computational burden to the path planning algorithm. The sampling-based path planning method mainly uses sampling of the state space to find feasible paths on the basis of sampling. The main advantage of this planning method is that it does not need to model the environment and has high applicability. The sampling-based path planning method represents probabilistic road map (PRM) [8] and Rapidly-exploring Random Tree (RRT). Equally, the problem with this method is that the path search tree is generated by random sampling points. The quality of the route largely depends on the quality of the sampling method.

2 Scheme Design

For unmanned surface vehicle, path planning can be divided into two parts: global path planning and local path planning. Global path planning usually first pre-plans an executable route based on environmental information such as electronic charts. On the basis of global planning, USV obtains surrounding environment information through its own sensor detection device, and then uses the local path planning method to achieve obstacle avoidance. The advantage is that the global path is obtained by taking a long time in advance to plan the global path, which avoids the blindness that may occur during the local obstacle avoidance process, and can effectively reduce the time for the local path planning algorithm. The specific process is shown in Fig. 1.

Global path planning usually requires the establishment of an environmental model that contains the necessary information to ensure the navigation of the ship based on the information of obstacles and dangerous areas in the sea in the electronic chart. Then

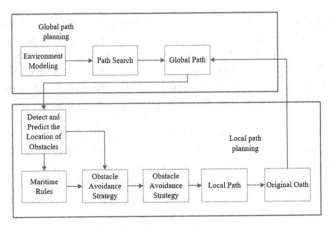

Fig. 1. USV path planning process

find a safe path that can meet various navigation indicators from the established model. Different from global path planning, the local path planning algorithm for USV needs to perceive the information in the surrounding environment in real time based on the multi-type sensors on the vehicle, and dynamically modify the local path according to factors such as distance, wind and waves, to ensure the safe and reliable navigation route.

On the basis of the characteristics of the USV navigation environment, the global path planning method selects the RRT* algorithm. This method is based on incremental search and is particularly suitable for path planning in large spaces. Compared with graph search algorithms like A* or Dijistra, the samples-based RRT* algorithm avoids the limitation that each raster must be searched, and only needs to set the sampling function and step size reasonably according to the size and complexity of the environment, and then global optimal path can be obtained. In the local path planning of the USV, the kinematic parameters must be considered, otherwise the route generated by the planner cannot be actually used on the ship, so the local path planning method chooses the dynamic window approach, which can meet the actual movement of the USV better.

3   RRT*-DWA Algorithm

3.1   RRT Algorithm

It is difficult to solve the problem of path planning when there are nonintegrity constraints or differential constraints. LaValle proposed the RRT algorithm of random sampling in 1998 [10]. He constructed a search tree by using incremental forward sampling, and then searched the tree structure to get the path. The specific process is as follows: after adding the starting position and pose to the random tree, the starting position and pose are directly sampled randomly in the space, the nodes in the whole random tree are traversed, and the nodes nearest to the random position and pose are selected. On the premise of satisfying the constraints, the nodes grow in the direction of the random point with a certain step length until they reach the target region. Starting from the target pose point, the parent node of the current pose point is searched in turn until the starting pose point is returned to obtain the planning path. The algorithm pseudo-code is shown in Table 1:

Table 1. RRT Algorithm.

Algorithm 1: RRT Algorithm

Input: $\mathcal{M}, x_{init}, x_{goal}$
Result: A path Γ from x_{init} to x_{goal}
$\mathcal{T}$.init();
for $i = 1$ *to* n **do**
    $x_{rand} \leftarrow Sample(\mathcal{M})$;
    $x_{near} \leftarrow Near(x_{rand}, \mathcal{T})$;
    $x_{new} \leftarrow Steer(x_{rand}, x_{near}, StepSize)$;
    $E_i \leftarrow Edge(x_{new}, x_{near})$;
    if *CollisionFree($\mathcal{M}, E_i$)* **then**
        $\mathcal{T}.addNode(x_{new})$;
        $\mathcal{T}.addEdge(E_i)$;
    if $x_{new} = x_{goal}$ **then**
        Success();

The input of the algorithm includes map M, initial point x_{init} and target point x_{goal}. The purpose is to get a feasible path from the starting point to the end point. The initial point x_{init} is taken as the root node of the random tree, and the *Sample* function is used for random sampling in the space. The point is marked as x_{rand}. Use the *Near* function to traverse the root node of the current random tree and find the closest point x_{near}, and use the *Steer* function to expand a new child node x_{new} on the line of and in a certain step, as shown in Fig. 2(a). If the connected segment does not collide with the obstacle, add the connected segment as a new child node x_{new} and a new edge to the random expansion tree, as shown in Fig. 2(b); if there is a collision, discard it Reselect this point, as shown in Fig. 2(c). Repeat the above process until reaching or near the goal, as shown in Fig. 2(d), a planned path from to is successfully found; if more than a certain number of expansion nodes have not reached the target area or objectively there is no path from the start to the end. If the path is touched, the plan fails.

The superiority of RRT is fast speed and probabilistic completeness, and the whole state space can be searched in a very short time by means of randomly extending child nodes. However, there are still some defects in the basic RRT algorithm, which cannot be directly applied to the path planning of USV, such as the instability caused by the randomness of node expansion. Since the child nodes of the random tree are generated by random sampling in the state space, different paths are planned each time from the same starting point to the end point in the same map. At the same time, the path cost and the path length are not controllable when the child nodes are extended randomly, the path may be far from the optimal path. The trajectory of RRT is generated by random sampling, and the path composed of random extended node sets is usually dithered and contains many unnecessary folding points. The excessive angle of adjacent child nodes

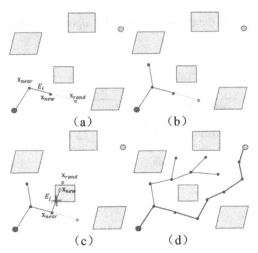

Fig. 2. RRT algorithm example diagram (a) Sampling (b) Extension (c) Collision (d) Results

results in too fast state transition, which cannot be directly applied to the motion planning of USV with non-integrity constraints.

3.2 RRT* Algorithm

Despite the RRT algorithm is a relatively high-efficiency algorithm that can handle path planning problems with non-holonomic constraints, and has great advantages in many aspects, the RRT algorithm does not guarantee that the feasible path obtained is relatively optimized. Therefore, many improvements on the RRT algorithm are also dedicated to solving the problem of path optimization, and the RRT* algorithm is one of them. The main feature of the RRT* algorithm is that it can quickly find the initial path, and then as the sampling points increase, continue to optimize until the target point is found or the maximum number of cycles is reached. The RRT* algorithm is progressively optimized, as the number of iterations increases, the path obtained is more and more optimized, and it is never possible to find the optimal path in a limited time. So in other words, to get a relatively satisfactory optimization path, it takes a certain amount of computing time. Therefore, the convergence time of the RRT* algorithm is a more prominent research problem. But it is undeniable that the cost of the path calculated by the RRT* algorithm is much smaller than that of the RRT.

3.3 Dynamic Window Approach Based on Global Path Planning

The dynamic window approach (DWA) is a local planning method based on velocity sampling [11]. Multiple sets of velocities are sampled in the velocity space, and the trajectory of USV is simulated within a certain period of time. The quality of these tracks are compared according to the preset evaluation function, from which the speed corresponding to the optimal trajectory is selected for execution.

Although the dynamic window approach has good performance in local obstacle avoidance, the path planned in actual operation is prone to lack of purpose. Based on this, this article adds global constraints on the basis of the original DWA, which is to generate RRT* The global route is input into the DWA as a parameter. It can ensure that the route obtained by the planner has good obstacle avoidance performance and will not deviate too much from the original trajectory. According to the limitations and environmental constraints of the USV itself, the sampling space of the speed can be limited within a certain range, as shown in Eqs. (1)–(3).

$$v \in [v_{\min}, v_{\max}], \omega \in [\omega_{\min}, \omega_{\max}] \tag{1}$$

$$v \in [v_c - \dot{v} \cdot dt, v_c + \dot{v} \cdot dt] \tag{2}$$

$$\omega \in [\omega_c - \dot{\omega} \cdot dt, \omega_c + \dot{\omega} \cdot dt] \tag{3}$$

In the formula, v_{min}, v_{max}, ω_{min}, ω_{max} represent the minimum and maximum values of velocity and angular velocity. Respectively, v_c, ω_c represent the current velocity and angular velocity, and $\dot{v}$, $\dot{\omega}$ represent the maximum value of acceleration and angular acceleration.

After sampling multiple sets of velocities, according to the present time window and forward simulation time, the corresponding multiple sets of trajectories are simulated, unsafe trajectories are eliminated from them, and the evaluation functions of other trajectories are calculated. The evaluation function is calculated as formula (4) shown.

$$G = \alpha \cdot hea + \beta \cdot dis + \gamma \cdot vel + \delta \cdot dev \tag{4}$$

Where G is the total evaluation function value. hea is used to evaluate the deviation between the current heading and the direction of the target point. dis is on behalf of the minimum distance between each point on the current trajectory and obstacles. represented as the current speed, to evaluate the degree of deviation between the current trajectory and the trajectory obtained by the global plan. α, β, γ, δ are the weight coefficients of each index respectively. The physical meaning of the average function formed by the four is: in the local planning, the path avoids obstacles and travels toward the target at a faster speed, while reducing the deviation between the path of the local planning and the global planning.

4 Experiment

4.1 Simulation Conditions

To simulate the actual marine environment, the map size is set to 1000 pixels * 1000 pixels, on which six black areas of different sizes and irregular shapes are distributed, which are regarded as obstacles and dangerous areas. The remaining white parts are regarded as feasible space of USV, shown in Fig. 3. The start point is set at (50,50), and the end point is set at (950,950). In this environment, the RRT, RRT*, and DWA algorithms based on RRT* are compared.

The hardware and software parameters of the simulation experiment are shown in Table 2:

Fig. 3. Simulation of the operating environment of USV

Table 2. Simulation software and hardware parameters.

CPU	AMD r7-4800h
RAM	8.00GB
Storage space	500G
OS	Window 10
Simulation platform	MATLAB 2020a

4.2 Comparison of RRT and RRT* Algorithm

According to the RRT algorithm mentioned above, the simulation was carried out on MATLAB platform, and the RRT algorithm was first run. In practical application, the sampling function is the most effective part of this kind of sampling algorithm. A better route can be obtained only by improving the quality of the sampling points obtained by the sampling function.

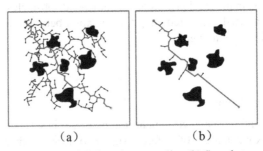

(a)   (b)

Fig. 4. RRT algorithm results (a) Global random sampling (b) Sample towards end point with a 50% probability (Color figure online)

Simulation of RRT algorithm is shown in Fig. 4. Blue represents the spanning tree and red represents the final path.

It can be seen that when the sampling is added with heuristic functions, the efficiency of the search path has a considerable increase. In Fig. 4 (a), 329 nodes are symbiosis, while in Fig. 4 (b), only 128 nodes are generated to complete the search of the path.Therefore, the design of sampling function is often the core part of RRT algorithm.The sampling function should usually be selected according to the complexity of the environment. For more special environments, such as robot mazes, sampling with heuristic values is less explorative than random sampling for the map.

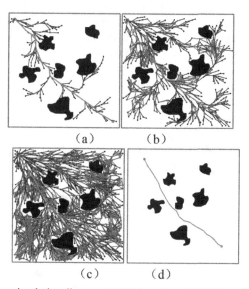

(a)   (b)

(c)   (d)

Fig. 5. RRT* algorithm simulation diagram (a) 200 iterations (b) 500 iterations (c) 1000 iterations (d) final route (Color figure online)

The blue line in the figure represents the route when the new node is generated, the red line represents the updated branch, and the green represents the current optimal route. Figure 5 shows the progressive optimality of the RRT* algorithm. As the number of iterations increases, the number of nodes continues to expand, the distance of the planned path is continuously shortened, and the route is smoother. The comparison between the results of the final RRT* generated path and the average results of multiple RRT algorithms is shown in Table 3. It can be seen that although RRT* takes dozens of times as long as RRT, the path length is shortened by 7.6% and the route is more convenient for actual control.

Table 3. Comparison of RRT and RRT* results.

Algorithm	Nodes	Length/pixel	Time/s
RRT	236	1556. 75114	1.05732
RRT*	1500	1437.32537	56.63981

4.3 RRT*-DWA Algorithm

After RRT* has carried out global planning, the global route is shown in Fig. 5(d). The path information is transmitted to the DWA actuator. As USV runs, it receives obstacle information from the sensor. According to the linear velocity and angular velocity at the time, the planner plans the next velocity and corresponding trajectory.

Introduce two dynamic obstacles in the simulation environment, add two black squares on the basis of the original picture and then perform local path planning. The position of USV at some moments is shown in Fig. 6, and the path obtained by the global plan would collide with obstacles, and local planning can successfully avoid collisions.

Figure 6 (a) to (c) reflect the position of USV at a certain moment in actual operation when there are dynamic obstacles nearby. In the final trajectory, Fig. 6(d), it can be seen that due to the presence of two dynamic obstacles, the red actual route of the USV has shifted from the green global route, and the obstacle has been successfully avoided.

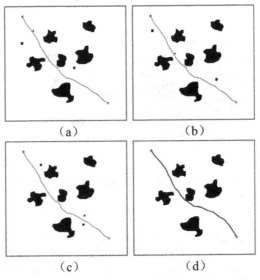

Fig. 6. RRT*-DWA algorithm simulation results (a) t = 20 s (b) t = 40 s (c) t = 60 s (d) final route (Color figure onine)

5   Conclusion

To solve the path planning problem of USV, this paper proposes a dynamic window method based on optimized rapidly-exploring random tree, which is denoted as RRT*-DWA. First, use RRT* to quickly generate an optimal global path, and then DWA algorithm determines the feasible speed sampling space according to the motion parameter constraints of USV, and perform several sets of sampling. According to the evaluation function of the global path, the optimal path is selected to track execution. It is verified by simulation experiments that the USV can effectively avoid dynamic obstacles, and on the basis of ensuring real-time performance, it can ensure the navigation safety of USV in complex environments.

References

1. Wang, N., Jin, X., Er, M.J.: A multilayer path planner for a USV under complex marine environments. Ocean Eng. **184**, 1–10 (2019)
2. Liu, Y., Bucknall, R.: Path planning algorithm for unmanned surface vehicle formations in a practical maritime environment. Ocean Eng. **97**, 126–144 (2015)
3. Singh, Y., Sharma, S., Sutton, R., et al.: A constrained A* approach towards optimal path planning for an unmanned surface vehicle in a maritime environment containing dynamic obstacles and ocean currents. Ocean Eng. **168**(DEC.1), 187–201 (2018)
4. Rhyd, L.: Algorithms for finding shortest paths in networks with vertex transfer penalties. Algorithms **13**(11), 269 (2020)
5. Deci Edward, L., Ryan Richard, M.: Facilitating optimal motivation and psychological well-being across life's domains. Canadian Psychol./Psychologie canadienne **49**(1), 14 (2008)
6. Stentz, A.: Optimal and efficient path planning for partially-known environments. In: IEEE International Conference on Robotics & Automation. IEEE (2002)
7. Dorigo, M., Caro, G.D., Gambardella, L.M.: Ant algorithms for discrete optimization. Artif. Life **5**(2), 137–172 (1999)
8. Boor, V., Overmars, M.H., Stappen, A.F.V.D.: The Gaussian sampling strategy for probabilistic roadmap planners. In: Proceedings 1999 IEEE International Conference on Robotics and Automation (Cat. No.99CH36288C). IEEE (2002)
9. Eberhart, R., Kennedy, J.: A new optimizer using particle swarm theory. In: Mhs95 Sixth International Symposium on Micro Machine & Human Science. IEEE (2002)
10. Karaman, S.: Sampling-based algorithms for optimal motion planning. Int. J. Robot. Res. **30**(7) 846–894 (2011)
11. Fox, D., Burgard, W., Thrun, S.: The dynamic window approach to collision avoidance. IEEE Robot. Autom. Mag. **4**(1), 23–33 (2002)

A Novel Brain-Like Navigation Based on Dynamic Attention with Modified Unet

Yu Zhang[1,2] and Xiyuan Chen[1,2(✉)]

[1] Key Laboratory of Micro-Inertial Instrument and Advanced Navigation Technology, Ministry of Education, Southeast University, Nanjing 210096, China
chxiyuan@seu.edu.cn
[2] School of Instrument Science and Engineering, Southeast University, Nanjing 210096, China

Abstract. In cognitive navigation system, animals show an inborn ability of spatial representations and correct self-positioning errors at every fired cell. Inspired by navigation mechanism of animals, we propose a novel strategy to improve the navigation accuracy of brain-like navigation based on UAV. Firstly, we employs encoder-decoder structure based on Unet to solve semantic segmentation tasks. Unet are able to encoder detailed information of images by constantly pooling and upsampling operations with less training parameters, while it often ignores high-level spatial information. Hence, we propose "dynamic attention with modified Unet" structure, which learns high-level information maintaining less training parameters. Specifically, multi-scale atrous convolutions are adopted in dynamic modules between encoder and decoder to extract features at different resolution. Secondly, the pixels with maximum probability segmentation are extracted, and they will be mapped to satellite map to obtain actual position coordinate of UAV. Finally, positioning errors are corrected at each place cells in the brain-like navigation of UAV. Our results show that proposed segmentation model improve performance by 9.64% compared with conventional Unet, and the positioning accuracy is improved by 90.52%.

Keywords: Semantic segmentation · Dynamic attention · Multi-scale atrous convolution

1 Introduction

With the development of artificial intelligence technology, next-generation navigation devices are endowed with self-correction abilities of positioning to fulfil the demands of applications. The unmanned aerial vehicle (UAV) is an emerging technology where positioning accuracy and robustness are critical for safe guidance and stable control. Conventional UAV navigation system is dominated by the loose-coupled with Inertial Navigation System (INS) and Global Navigation System (GPS). However, UAVs cannot maintain high accuracy because of GPS signal of low quality when flying through complex environments, such as urbans, canyons and electromagnetic interferences, and

© ICST Institute for Computer Sciences, Social Informatics and Telecommunications Engineering 2021
Published by Springer Nature Switzerland AG 2021. All Rights Reserved
W. Fu et al. (Eds.): ICMTEL 2021, LNICST 387, pp. 528–540, 2021.
https://doi.org/10.1007/978-3-030-82562-1_52

the results measured by INS will be divergent over time [1]. Thus, we need to investigate a steady strategy that obtain high position accuracy without relying on traditional measurement devices.

"Place cell" property of hippocampus is found as it have a firing rate when rodent is at a specific place in extensive environment which inspired the proposal of brain-like navigation strategy. Furthermore, there is a phenomenon that mammals such as rats or primates show an inborn ability of spatial representations, and they take advantage of it to implement space navigation [2]. More precisely, once the rodents reach at a specific dot, the cell node on hippocampus will be activated, and the actual position information will be recorded as reference. Also, the path integration of rats can be reset to acquire new information when they are placed in a familiar environment, so that the accuracy of bionic navigation can be remarkably improved by eliminating accumulated errors. Thus, the challenge of this navigation lies in whether it can find correct scenes in "Memory" to match current visual scenes [3].

For one thing, the typical application of scene recognition is on visual navigation. Images captured by camera are used to compare with referenced images to obtain actual navigation information. For another, convolutional neural networks is widely applied in a number of classification tasks, where every image output a predicted single class label. However, we need to focus on localization information in USV-assisted visual navigation. Hence, semantic segmentation with the aim to assign semantic labels to every pixel is proposed. As we all know that several network backbones with Fully Convolutional, U-net modules have shown striking improvements over strategies based on hand-crafted feature extraction [4]. Obviously, these modules have three drawbacks. First, consecutive pooling operations or convolution striding operations may impede dense prediction tasks, even though it allows deep learning model to extract feature representations. Second, we always tend to pay more attention to capture high-level semantic information without fusing low-level feature.

In this work, a novel semantic segmentation network combined with localization extraction is proposed to assist brain-like navigation based on UAV. Firstly, we design upon an elegant architecture, the so-called "U-net", which based on encoder-decoder structure. We modified and extend this architecture that can fuse high-level semantic information and low-level feature effectively with few training images and "dynamic attention" modules. We maintain a large number of feature channels in upsampling process, which allows model to propagate information to higher resolution layers. To improve the response capability of dense space, we add several "dynamic attention" modules consisting of atrous convolutions with different rates between downsampling part and upsampling part, which allows the seamless segmentation of images with different scales. In addition, this special attention module predict the pixels in the border region of the image precisely.

As for the UAV-assisted brain-like navigation system, the location information corresponding to the feature points on segmentation image is extracted and fed back to correct the positioning of INS to improve the navigation accuracy. Furthermore, we endow the positioning errors with 'self-correction' property termed as the navigation error correction (NEC) module so that navigation accuracy can be improved with increasing

familiarity of the flight trajectory. Subsequently, the proposed strategy rectifies positioning errors periodically with low computation cost as the parameters trained in network
is very less, which is critical to meet the requirements of real time analysis.

In summary, our contributions are as follow:

- We propose a novel semantic segmentation network combined with localization
  extraction which employs modified Unet as a backbone.
- Multi-scale dynamic attention modules consisting of atrous convolutions are added
  between encoder-decoder structures, which propagate information to higher resolution
  layers instead of focusing on low-level details. Also, the running time of our proposed
  model will not increase too much.
- Cell models in biological brain-like system are mapped to actual trajectory to assist
  UAV navigation.
- The actual position coordinates corresponding to pixel in segmentation images are
  extracted to assist brain-like navigation.

2 Related Work

With the discovery of the role of grid-like cells, place cells and several brain cognitive
navigation cells, brain navigation technology is investigated widely, which provides a
theoretical basis to study brain-like navigation of UAVs in complex flight environments.

In practice level, a novel brain-like model is inherited from a normal brain-based
device (BBD) which helps understand how rodent cognition and behaviour work [5],
which means that we can build relationship between the spatial mapping property of
entorhinal cortex (EC) and location nodes of the actual UAV trajectory directly. It is
noted that 'place cells' property of hippocampus can be mapped into location nodes in
actual trajectory measured by INS, which can be seen in Fig. 1.

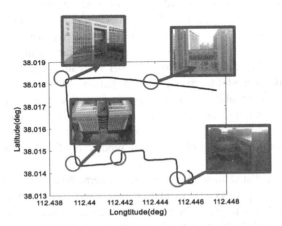

Fig. 1. The schematic diagram of place cells in actual trajectory.

Differ from traditional positioning strategy which applies integrated measurement, we rely on semantic segmentation network combined with localization extraction to finish navigation tasks. It has been proved that the global features or contextual interactions are vital in classifying pixels for semantic segmentation [7]. For semantic segmentation tasks, we consider three challenges. First, consecutive pooling operations or convolution striding operations may impede dense prediction tasks, even though it allows deep learning model to extract feature representations. Second, multi-scale images have to be unified into the same size, as the size of weight matrix in output layer is default. Hence, image pyramid, spatial pyramid pooling and atrous convolution methods is applied to multi-scale inputs to capture context at several ranges [8]. Third, too much parameters is calculated as several consecutive convolution operations, which give a pressure on GPU memory and cannot meet the requirements of real time analysis.

3 Methods

In this section, we discuss the proposed model structure for semantic segmentation. Then, we demonstrate that how the segmented image is used for brain-like navigation with UAVs.

3.1 Cell Model Based on Brain-Like System

We propose a novel strategy for UAV navigation under the scheme of brain-like model, which mainly contains three phases. In the first phase, an intelligent brain-like model is applied it to UAV navigation tasks inspired by rodent navigation mechanism. As we all know, 'place cell' and 'head direction cell' may have a high firing rate when rodents arrive at a particular location. Thus, several location cell nodes can be set in advance. Inputs to the brain-like model come from a camera, and it is used to record flight environment and collect scene images. Then the output from brain-like model goes to semantic segmentation with aim to extract the coordinates of the centroid location of image corresponding to the UAV. In the last phase, we establish a linear error equation based on the time series to model the accumulated errors between two cell nodes. Furthermore, the positioning errors accumulated at current flight can be compensated by the last error calculation, and the error model under the current trajectory is established at the same time to achieve the purpose of correcting the drift error in the next step. We endow the positioning errors with 'self-correction' property termed as the NEC module so that navigation accuracy can be improved with increasing familiarity with the flight trajectory.

3.2 Dynamic Attention Mechanism

The network structure is illustrated in Fig. 2. The whole structure is inherited from classical U-net, which consists of the encoder-decoder benchmark. To be concrete, an encoder module gradually increases receptive field by reducing the size of feature maps with convolution operations, capturing higher semantic information. Meanwhile, a decoder module recovers the spatial information. However, traditional U-net structure focus too much on detailed information by constantly downsampling operations, so that it only captures deeper feature instead of higher spatial information. Hence, we explore the multi-scale atrous convolutions between encoder and decoder during upsampling process, which is denoted as "dynamic attention" module. The encoder module encodes multi-scale spatial information with these dynamic atrous convolutions at multiple scales.

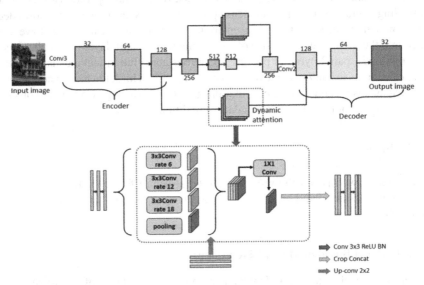

Fig. 2. The structure of proposed segmentation model.

We set the initial feature channels as 32. It comprises of two repeated 3 × 3 convolutions with no-padding, each followed by a rectified linear unit (ReLU) and batch normalization in the encoder process. In addition, 2 × 2 max pooling operations with stride 2 are chosen for downsampling. It is noted that we double the number of feature channels at each downsampling step. Secondly, 2 × 2 convolutions with stride 2 are conducted for upsampling, and the feature channels are halved at each step. Thirdly, features produced by upsampling is concatenated with the corresponding cropped low-level features. Also, the proposed dynamic attention modules are introduced into the copy of features produced by downsamping before cropping. Here, *output_stride* is denote as the ratio of image spatial resolution to output resolution, and we adopt rate = 6, 12, 18 to the copy of features by appling strous convolution correspondingly. In addition, 1 × 1 convolution is added to reduce the feature channels and parameters. By introducing this module, we can extract the features at different resolution. At the final layer, a 1 × 1convolution is used to map each upsampled features to the default number of classes.

3.3 Error Compensation Model

The core module for brain-like navigation with UAV is illustrated in Fig. 3. We construct the semantic segmentation methods under the frame of brain-like system to eliminate the accumulated errors between two place cell nodes. From the Fig. 3 we can see that the place cell is simulated just shown as A, B, C, and D.

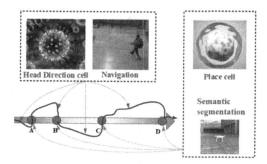

Fig. 3. The structure of the NEC module.

In the actual UAV flight process, due to the drift error of the INS, the error will linearly diverge with time in a short time, so it is necessary to model and analyze the error divergence between two cell nodes. Therefore, the flight trajectory between the two location cell nodes can be approximated as a linear motion for simplify. Then, a linear error equation with time series is established under the scheme of the navigation. The positioning errors at current flight can be compensated by the last flight, and the error model under the current trajectory is established at the same time to achieve the purpose of correcting the drift error in the next step, which can be seen in (1) and (2). In each process of compensating the current trajectory error, it is necessary to adjust the coefficient value of the linear function to achieve self-correction compensation for the error.

$$error(i) = k * (trj_{\text{Ref}}(i) - trj_{\text{INS}}(i)) + b \tag{1}$$

$$trj_{\text{INS}}(i + 1) = error(i) + trj_{\text{INS}}(i) \tag{2}$$

Where $error(i)$ represents flight error function, which can be simplify as linear motion; k, b, represent coefficients of linear function; $trj_{\text{Ref}}(i)$, $trj_{\text{INS}}(i)$ represent the reference and INS trajectory of the i-th flight, respectively; $trj_{\text{INS}}(i + 1)$ represents the INS trajectory of the i + 1-th flight.

Gradually, we endow the positioning errors with 'self-correction' property and navigation accuracy can be improved with increasing familiarity with the flight trajectory, just like the work mechanism of path integrator of rats in brain-like system.

4 Training

In this section, we discuss the training details of our proposed segmentation model. Our implementation is built on Pytorch.

The proposed segmentation model is evaluated on PASCAL VOC2012 semantic segmentation benchmark, which contains 21 classes. It is noted that the origin dataset covers 1464 samples for training, 1449 for validation and 1456 pictures for test, respectively. One background class and 20 object classes is calculated.

Initialization. The features encoded are downsampled by a factor of 2 and then concatenated with the corresponding decoded features. We set initial feature channels as 32 with two repeated 3 × 3 convolutions (no-padding) and a rectified linear unit (ReLU). In addition, 2 × 2 max pooling operation with stride 2 is chosen for downsampling. Also, each modified module on top of basic structure of Unet all includes batch normalization to reconstruct parameters. Basically, we set batch size = 8, and the batch normalization parameters are trained with decay = 0.9997. Accordingly, we set learning rate as simple 0.001 and use a momentum (0.9), which can combine more trained samples to update in the current optimization step.

Dynamic Attention. The core of dynamic attention modules is multi-scale atrous convolutions, which are added between downsamling and upsampling to capture higher spatial information. The characteristic of atrous convolution is that it can modify the filter's field-of-view and control the dense of feature response adaptively. Based on some evaluation discussed in [8], the *output_stride* = 16 sacrifices some accuracy to obtain faster calculation speed compared with *output_stride* = 8 since the inter-mediate feature maps are spatially four times smaller. However, it has been verified that 16 *output_stride* strikes the best trade-off between speed and precision. In addition, the performance when setting *output_stride* = 1 is equal to that without any operations for features. Thus, we set the *output_stride* = 6, 12, 18, and all output of atrous convolution operations are concatenated. Meanwhile, we apply 1 × 1 convolution after concatenation to reduce the number of feature channels (e.g. 512 or 1024), which can make the training easier. We apply 1 × 1 convolution before the finally output to fuse all feature and match the target number of classes. The reason why we call this multi-scale module as "dynamic attention" is that it can be added between encoder and decoder to increase the sensitivity to high-level spatial information and overcome the defect of being only sensitive to detailed features with Unet. Also, the whole training parameters will not increase even adding this module.

5   Experiment Evaluation

To evaluate the proposed semantic segmentation-assisted brain-like navigation, two specific experiment is proceeded for validation.

5.1   Experiment 1

In experiment 1, the trajectory of UAV is shown in Fig. 4 and the start coordinate is 32.0302, 118.8792(deg). The length of the trajectory is approximately 10 km. From the Fig. 4 we can see that four location cell nodes corresponding to specific scenes are marked, which can be used as ground truth. The performance of segmentation can be verified at every location cell node. In order to improve the segmentation accuracy, we modify the training set by adding some specific scene images captured by camera equipped with UAV, and the specific images at each location node are used for validation. In order to verify the effectiveness of proposed model, different flight motions including long straights, turning and sudden accelerations are all performed.

Firstly, we verify the performance of semantic segmentation. The dataset for validation is VOC2012 which has been mentioned before. Figure 5 represents the compared segmentation results on validation set between the proposed multi-scale dynamic attention model with modified Unet network backbone and the conventional Unet. Figure 6 represents visualization results on *val* set with proposed segmentation model.

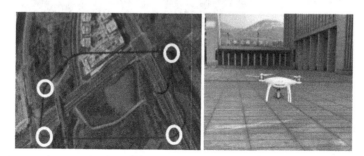

Fig. 4. (1) The trajectory of UAV; (2) The material object of UAV.

The results demonstrate that the detail of images is segmented more comprehensive by applying multi-scale atrous convolution operations. The performance of different models dealing with segemention is shown in Table 1. Unet with 32 employing the proposed multi-scale dynamic attention (multi-scale atrous convolutions), attains the performance of 85.91% on the validation set. We notice that decreasing the initial feature channels of Unet and adding multi-scale atrous convolutions between encoder and decoder inevitably improve the performance by 9.64%. Furthermore, this proposed model performs better than RetNet-101 banckmark with less training parameters. As we all know that conventional Unet is effective to deal with medical images, thanks to atrous convolution, this proposed model also obtains better segmentation results.

Table 1. The results of different segmentation methods. Unet with 32 refers to the initial feature channels of Unet model is 32; Unet with 64 refers to the initial feature channels of Unet mdoel is 64.

Backbone	Dynamic module (multi-scale atrous convolution)	Decoder	mIOU
Unet with 32	✓	✓	85.91%
Unet with 64		✓	77.62%
ResNet-101		✓	84.7%

In order to verify the navigation accuracy with semantic segmentation, we conduct an actual flight experiment. All images captured at each location node during flight are recorded for validation. The experiment system is conducted on a hybrid MEMS-INS/GPS platform, where an Ublox NEO-M8T GPS receiver with a STIM202 and 1521L integrated IMU are connected to a data acquisition module running Windows

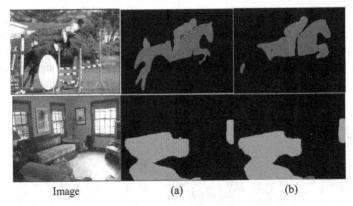

Image   (a)   (b)

Fig. 5. (a) Segmentation performance based on the proposed multi-scale dynamic attention model with modified Unet; (b) Performance based on conventional Unet.

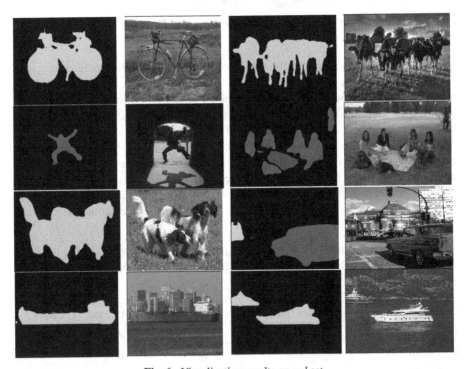

Fig. 6. Visualization results on *val* set.

10 operation system. A NovAtel ProPak6 receiver is used for reference offline. The sampling frequency of INS is set as 200 Hz. The experimental setup is shown in Fig. 7, and specific parameters of sensors are given in Table 2.

As the flying height of the UAV is very high, the proportion of target features in the image will be reduced, which will cause some difficulties in segmentation. Thus, we scale the size of input image proportionally at the expense of resolution. The visualization results at location node are shown in Fig. 8. As we all know that each pixel is categorized as one class with the highest probability output, and each pixel will be masked in the meantime, which makes up the outline of the final target object. Hence, the pixels with maximum probability segmentation are extracted, and the actual location on the map is calculated as the current position coordinate of UAV. Precisely, we select the pixel block corresponding to the maximum probability output as the referenced location, and this location will be mapped to satellite map to obtain actual position coordinate, which also shown in Fig. 8.

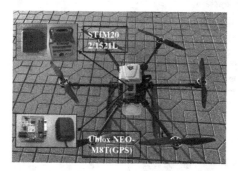

Fig. 7. The experimental setup based on experiment 2.

Table 2. The specific parameters of sensors.

Gyroscope (STIM202)	Bias	0.5°/hr
	Scale factor	200 ppm
	Random walk	0.2°/√hr
Accelerometer (1521L)	Calibration error	0.5–1%
GPS (Ublox NEO-M8T)	Position accuracy	2.5 m
	Velocity accuracy	0.05 m/s
	Time accuracy	60 ns
GPS (NovAtel ProPak6)	Position accuracy	1cm + 1 ppm
	Velocity accuracy	0.03 m/s
	Time accuracy	20 ns

Subsequently, in order to improve positioning accuracy and evaluate the fault-tolerant of UAVs, we verify the performance of proposed NEC module with designed segmentation model. As we discussed before, NEC module corrects accumulated errors by iterative compensation at each flight process. Hence, we conduct three flight experiment, the flight trajectory is shown in Fig. 9(a), flight altitude is 38.4 m, and the flight trajectory of UAV is measured by a NovAtel ProPak6 receiver, which is used for absolute reference.

Fig. 8. The visualization results at location node.

Two-dimensional trajectory corresponding to Fig. 8 is shown in Fig. 9(b), and three place cells are marked in results. The Root Mean Square (RMS) results of position errors are shown in Table 3. From the results shown in Fig. 9(b) we can see that the positioning error can be compensated at current flight after the navigation error was compensated last flight, and the whole trajectory is closer to reference trajectory. From the Table 3 we can see that the RMS errors decrease from 206.44 m to 1.93 m at the third flight, which are improved by 90.52%. Eventually, INS cumulative drift error re-accumulates from 0 after correction at each node by segmentation, so the INS can maintain high accuracy for a certain period of time after correction calculation. Eventually,.

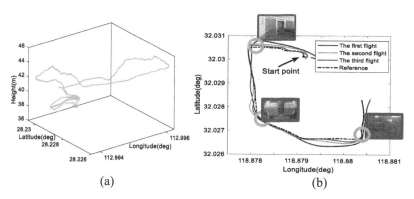

Fig. 9. (a) Flight trajectory; (b) The compensated results at each node with NEC module.

Table 3. The RMS of position errors

NEC module	The RMS of position errors (m)
The first flight	206.44
The second flight	20.36
The third flight	1.93

6 Conclusions

In this work, with the aim to improve brain-like navigation accuracy of UAV, our proposed model "dynamic attention with modified Unet" employs the encoder-decoder where dynamic attention is used to capture rich spatial information without increasing extra much training parameters. Precisely, multi-scale atrous convolutions, as the core of dynamic modules are adopted between encoder and decoder to extract features at different resolution. The pixels with maximum probability segmentation are extracted, and the actual location on the map is calculated as current position coordinate of UAV. Finally, our results show that proposed segmentation model sets a start-of-art performance on VOC2012 datasets compared with conventional Unet, and the final navigation accuracy is improved by NEC module combined with maximum probability of pixel extraction.

References

1. Atia, M.M., Waslander, S.L.: Map-aided adaptive GNSS/IMU sensor fusion scheme for robust urban navigation. Measurement **131**, 615–627 (2019)
2. Huajin, T., Weiwei, H., Aditya, N., Rui, Y.: Cognitive memory and mapping in a brain-like system for robotic navigation. Neural Networks **87**, 27–37 (2017)
3. Shen, C., Liu, X.C., Cao, H.L., Zhou, Y.C.: Brain-Like navigation scheme based on MEMS-INS and place recognition. Appl. Sci. **9**, 1708 (2019)
4. Jiawang, B., Wenyan, L., Yasuyuki, M.: GMS: grid-based motion statistics for fast, ultra-robust feature correspondence. In: IEEE Conference on Computer Vision and Pattern Recognition, pp. 2528–2837 (2017)
5. Krichmar, J.L., Aitz, N.D., Gally, A.J., Edelman, G.M.: Characterizing functional hippocampal pathways in a brain-based device as it solves a spatial memory task. Proc. Natl. Acad. Sci. **102**, 2111–2116 (2004)
6. Weijer, V.D., Gevers, J.T., Gijsenij, A.: Edge-based color constancy. IEEE Trans. Image Process. **16**, 2207–2214 (2007)
7. Ronneberger, O., Fischer, P., Brox, T.: U-Net: convolutional networks for biomedical image segmentation. In: Navab, N., Hornegger, J., Wells, W.M., Frangi, A.F. (eds.) MICCAI 2015. LNCS, vol. 9351, pp. 234–241. Springer, Cham (2015). https://doi.org/10.1007/978-3-319-24574-4_28
8. Chen, L.C., George, P., Florian, S., Hartwig, A.: Rethinking atrous convolution for semantic image segmentation. In: IEEE Conference on Computer Vision and Pattern Recognition (2017)

Feature Extraction of Network Temporal and Spatial Distribution Based on Data Stream Clustering

Hu Rong[1](✉) and Luo Dan[2]

[1] School of Intelligence Technology, Geely University, Chengdu 641402, China
[2] Chengdu College of University of Electronic Science and Technology of China, Chengdu 641402, China

Abstract. Spatio-temporal data contains a lot of knowledge information, including patterns and characteristics, the relationship between data and data and their characteristics, etc. How to extract these characteristics from these spatio-temporal data has become the focus of research. To this end, a method of network spatiotemporal distribution feature extraction based on data stream clustering is studied. This method first analyzes the relevant theories of the clustering algorithm, and then uses the DBSCAN algorithm in the clustering algorithm to extract the characteristics of network temporal and spatial distribution. The results show that: compared with the traditional extraction method, the extraction quality of this method is higher, reaching the goal of this paper.

Keywords: Data stream clustering · Network temporal and spatial distribution · Feature extraction · DBSCAN algorithm

Chinese Library Classification Number: TP231.2 Document Identification Code: A

1 Introduction

With the rapid development of computer network technology, the network has covered all aspects of social life. The contemporary computer network architecture is built on the basis of the tcp/ip protocol. Due to the openness of the tcp/ip protocol, the spread of computer viruses has increasingly become a problem for people, and network security issues are imminent. Information transmission and information interaction in cyberspace use network traffic as the carrier, and traffic data contains a lot of valuable information. Judging the network status by analyzing the network traffic is of great significance to effectively preventing network attacks and maintaining the security of cyberspace. As an important technical support for network situation awareness, abnormal detection of network traffic has received more and more attention in recent years. Abnormal network traffic refers to the network traffic pattern that has a negative impact on the normal use of the network. The abnormal traffic is mainly composed of two reasons, one is

W. Fu et al. (Eds.): ICMTEL 2021, LNICST 387, pp. 541–552, 2021.
https://doi.org/10.1007/978-3-030-82562-1_53

performance reasons, and the other is security reasons. So far, for the anomalies caused by security reasons, the methods of network traffic anomaly detection can be divided into the following four categories: based on statistics, based on clustering, based on information theory, and based on classification. Among them, the basic idea of network traffic classification based on statistics is that the characteristics of traffic generated by different types of applications are different. General traffic characteristics can be divided into two categories, one is network flow characteristics, the other is data packet characteristics, and there are also combinations of the two, that is, the characteristic data that needs to be used are extracted from the original traffic data [1]. For example, Cisco's netflow, Juniper's j-flow, waikato University's maji, cert's network situation awareness research group, yaf, etc.; the behavior-based method uses traffic characteristics to be the behavioral information of host communication, and the basic ideas are different The application produces different behavior patterns. However, this method only extracts the single temporal or spatial characteristics of the network flow, and lacks a comprehensive representation of the temporal and spatial characteristics of the network flow. The original network traffic is composed of a string of bytes in a format specified by the network protocol. Multiple traffic bytes form a data packet, and multiple data packets of the two communicating parties form a network flow. Among them, the data packets are transmitted on the network at the same time as a whole, so the internal traffic bytes do not have too many timing relationships, but the bytes are considered to have a spatial relationship, and the corresponding spatial characteristics can be extracted. However, each data packet in the network stream has a different sending time, which is considered to have a timing relationship, and its corresponding timing characteristics can be extracted. Therefore, spatial characteristics and temporal characteristics are two types of traffic characteristics commonly used in the field of network traffic monitoring.

Based on the above background, the research has been based on the network spatiotemporal distribution feature extraction method based on data stream clustering. The biggest advantage of this method is that there is no need for data annotation, because annotation data is difficult to obtain in practice. Finally, the test proves the effectiveness of the research method.

2   Clustering-Based Feature Extraction of Spatial-Temporal Distribution of Networks

More than 80% of the data in the real world is related to geographic location. Traditional GIS only describes the spatial state characteristics of the research object at a moment, without special processing of temporal characteristics. In reality, spatial data or geospatial data changes with time. Therefore, traditional GIS can only reflect the current or historical state of things at certain moments in history, and cannot connect these states, let alone predict future development trends. Since the existence of objective things is closely related to time, the concept of spatio-temporal data was born.

Different from general data, the definition of spatio-temporal data in this article is a data set that includes temporal characteristics (time dimension) and spatial location characteristics (spatial dimension); at the same time, this type of data also has the comprehensive characteristics of multi-source, massive, and rapid update. Temporal characteristics mean that the state of the data changes with time, and presents a certain law in the time distribution; spatial location characteristics are usually a unified measurement of location through two-dimensional plane coordinates or three-dimensional coordinates, which is measurable, Its distribution also has a certain regularity. In addition, general spatiotemporal data also has scale (resolution) features, multiple heterogeneous features, and multi-dimensional dynamic visualization features. Among them, the scale feature is reflected in the scale change (zooming), the spatial pattern and description details of

GPS data,trajectory

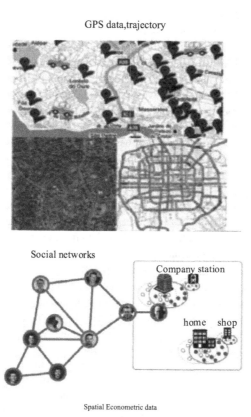

Fig. 1. Multi- source spatiotemporal data sample

different sampling granularities are different; the multi-source heterogeneous feature is reflected in the diversity of data sources and the multi-source heterogeneity of geospatial information (spatial reference Different, different time, different scale, inconsistent semantics); the multi-dimensional dynamic visualization feature refers to the time-varying intelligence data can be fused with three-dimensional geospatial information, and achieve dynamic visualization [2].

There are many types of spatiotemporal data, as shown in Fig. 1. Among them, the most basic and extensive are GPS and trajectory data generated by various mobile devices; when using various software, social networks and online car-hailing orders will also be generated., Driving records and other data. The common feature of these data is that they contain both time and space attributes, and there are multiple influencing factors, such as weather, holidays, and air quality. Due to the influence of many external factors, it is difficult for people to make effective and reasonable judgments through experience when analyzing this type of data. This is different from image processing and machine translation. People can effectively classify images based on their own experience. And complete language translation; but when using spatio-temporal data for analysis and prediction, data mining is more accurate and effective.

2.1 Clustering Algorithm

The technology of cluster analysis is developing rapidly, and certain results have been achieved in some application fields [3]. Such as data mining, psychology and medicine, statistics and pattern analysis, marketing, biology, information retrieval, astronomy, archaeology, geological prospecting and land use, etc.

Clustering mining is an important research direction in the field of data mining. Up to now, there is still no clear academic definition. It can only be simply described as that cluster analysis is based on analyzing and describing objects from a data set and the relationship between them, finding similar objects, and combining these data to form different groups. The similarity within the same data group must be greater than the similarity between the data groups. The important criterion for judging the quality of clustering is that the greater the homogeneity between groups, the greater the homogeneity between groups. Smaller, that is, the larger the gap between groups, the better the quality of clustering [4]. Each object data group can be described by groups or clusters.

The main content of cluster analysis research includes the following five steps:

Pattern representation (including feature extraction or selection): To choose a good representation, it can produce simple and easy-to-understand clusters. The feature selection process is to effectively extract feature subsets, which can improve the quality of clustering.

In the field of data mining, it is necessary to seek a cluster analysis method with high quality and high algorithm efficiency. Therefore, in the application of data mining, the application of cluster analysis algorithm also puts forward some typical requirements for its algorithm, as follows.

(1) The scalability requirements of the algorithm. Many algorithms have very good performance and effects when dealing with small-scale data sets, but when data

mining is performed, when the amount of data increases sharply to level or level, the performance effect must also keep up [5]. Therefore, in data mining, processing large-scale data places high requirements on the high scalability of clustering algorithms.

(2) Whether the algorithm can handle different types of attributes. Some data in data mining are numerical and some are textual, especially the data in this thesis is a semi-structured data format. Therefore, the ability of the algorithm to process different data is required.

(3) Is it possible to find clustering algorithms of arbitrary shapes? Since the shapes of clusters in clusters are diverse, when data mining is performed, an algorithm that can find clusters of arbitrary shapes is required.

(4) Whether the clustering results are interpretable and usable, we expect that the clustering results obtained in data mining are understandable and still usable.

(5) Whether the algorithm has the ability to process high-dimensional data. Today's data is not just simple one-dimensional, two-dimensional, or three-dimensional spatial data. Spatio-temporal data is added to three-dimensional semi-structured spatial data with a time dimension. For this kind of high Dimensional data has very high requirements on clustering algorithms.

(6) Whether the algorithm has the ability to process abnormal noise data in data mining. Most of the data has some outliers or incorrectly recorded data. The clustering algorithm is required to have the ability to deal with abnormal data in this type of data.

(7) Whether the clustering analysis technique and methods under restricted conditions can keep up, and whether there can be good clustering results under such conditions. Since many clustering algorithms will have various restrictions and constraints in practical applications, under these conditions, the clustering algorithm is still required to run with high efficiency and high quality [6].

(8) Whether it is sensitive to the order of data input. In data mining, when the algorithm is required to input the data set in a different order, the result of the algorithm remains the same, or the difference is small.

(9) The dependence of algorithm input parameters on the knowledge domain can be minimized as much as possible. In high-dimensional data mining, such as spatio-temporal data cluster mining, it is difficult to determine the number of clusters that you want to output, and some clustering algorithms

It is sensitive to the project and is prone to problems such as low quality of algorithm output results. This requires an effective clustering algorithm, which can solve this problem well [5].

According to different clustering strategies and different clustering scales, clustering methods can be divided into the following four types: plan-based, hierarchical-based, density-based, and grid-based. The characteristics and common algorithms are shown in Table 1:

The above algorithms are suitable for different application scenarios, some are simple and efficient, and are suitable for noisy data sets; some can find clusters of arbitrary shapes. In general, each type of algorithm has different performances corresponding to different data, mainly from the aspects of scalability, the ability to handle different types

Table 1. Classification of clustering methods

Category	Strategy	Characteristics	Common algorithm
Based on partition	Select a few points as the initial center point, and iterate according to the predetermined heuristic algorithm, until finally reach the target effect of "the points within the class are close enough, and the points between the classes are far enough"	Its advantages are simple and efficient, time complexity, and space complexity are low. The disadvantage is that it is very sensitive to the selection of the first K points; very sensitive to noise and outliers; it cannot solve non-convex data	K-MEANS algorithm K-MEDOIDS algorithm CLARANS algorithm
Based on hierarchy	There are two main types: merged (bottom-up) hierarchical clustering and split (top-down) hierarchical clustering	The interpretability is good, but the time complexity is high, it is difficult to deal with clusters of different sizes, and the wrong decision cannot be corrected	BIRCH algorithm CURE algorithm CHAMELEON algorithm
Based on density	As long as the density of points in a region exceeds a certain threshold, it is added to the clusters close to it	Its advantage is that it is not sensitive to noise; it can find clusters of arbitrary shapes. The disadvantage is that the result of clustering has a great relationship with the parameters	DBSCAN algorithm OPTICS algorithm DENCLUE algorithm
Grid based	The data space is divided into a grid structure with a limited number of cells, and all the processing is based on the cells	The processing speed is very fast, because its speed only depends on the number of units in each dimension in the data space. The disadvantage is that the parameters are sensitive and cannot handle irregularly distributed data	STING algorithm CLIQUE algorithm WAVE-CLUSTER algorithm

of attributes, the discovery of clusters of arbitrary shapes, the ability to handle noise, and the interpretability and usability. It is reasonably selected to enable effective clustering of the data [7, 8].

2.2 DBSCAN - Based Spatiotemporal Feature Extraction

The DBSCAN algorithm in the clustering algorithm is used to extract the characteristics of the temporal and spatial distribution of network data, and the extraction process is shown in Fig. 2.

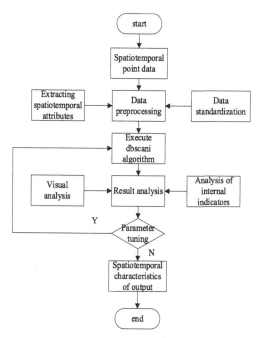

Fig. 2. DBSCAN web spatiotemporal feature extraction process

(1) Data preprocessing

The input data is transformed into the range of [0,1] through linear transformation, thereby turning the dimensional expression into a dimensionless expression, which is convenient for the comparison and weighting of indicators of different units or magnitudes. The calculation method is as follows:

1) Min-Max standardization

Min-Max standardization, also called minimum-maximum standardization, the basic principle is to linearly transform the original data so that the transformed result falls within the interval [0,1]. The Min-Max standardized expression is as follows:

$$x' = \frac{x - \min}{\max - \min} \tag{1}$$

Among them, x' is the normalized data; x is the original data; max is the maximum value of the sample data; min is the minimum value of the sample data [9, 10].

2) Z-score standardization

Z-score standardization, also known as standard deviation normalization, is based on the basic principle of making the processed raw data conform to the standard normal distribution, that is, the mean is 0 and the standard deviation is 1 [11, 12]. The standardized mathematical expression of Z-score is as follows:

$$x' = \frac{x - a}{b} \tag{2}$$

In the formula, a is the mean value of the corresponding characteristic; b is the standard deviation (Table 2).

(2) Execute DBSCAN algorithm

Table 2. DBSCAN algorithm flow

Enter:
D: A data set containing n objects
ε : neighborhood radius parameter
Min Pts: neighborhood density threshold
Output: the temporal and spatial distribution characteristics of the network
Process:
1: Mark all sample objects as unvisited, and set the output cluster set C=empty set
2: While all sample objects contain unvisited object Do
3: Randomly select p' from unvisited objects, mark p as visited
4: There are at least MinPts objects in the ε -adjacent area of If p;
5: Create a new cluster C', add p to C'
6: Let S be p. A collection of objects in a neighborhood;
7: For each point p' Do in For S
8: If p' is unvisited then
9: Mark p' as visited
10: At least MinPts objects in the ε -neighborhood of If p';
11: Add points in the ε -neighborhood of p' to C';
12: End If
13: If p' is not a member of any cluster then
14: Add p to C'
15:End If
16: End If
17: End For
18: Add C'to set C
19: Else marks p as noise
20: End If
21: End While.

3   Simulation Test Analysis

This chapter first builds a test environment for the network spatiotemporal distribution feature extraction method based on data stream clustering proposed in this paper, and then conducts a number of tests on the method, and gives comparative analysis results of system performance in various situations.

3.1   Network Data Acquisition

Construct a node distribution model for network traffic collection in a cloud-based data center to collect network data. The collected network traffic data is a data record of each broadband probe every minute. The record contains the overall data situation within the measuring range of the probe and is collected every minute. Except for the start time and the stop time of each collection, the record also contains the remaining 49 network characteristics, as shown in Table 3. Among them, such as the number of TCP sessions, the average number of packets per TCP session, the number of UCP sessions, the average number of packets per UDP session, and the length of each packet are the characteristic dimensions that we usually focus on when analyzing network traffic anomalies.

Table 3. Network experimental data

Field name	Field meaning	Type of data
ONLINE USERS	Number of users online	numeric(18)
TCP INBPS	Average TCP inflow(bps)	numeric(18)
TCP OUTBPS	Average TCP flow(bps)	numeric(18)
UDP INBPS	Average UDP inflow(bps)	numeric(18)
UDP OUTBPS	Average UDP flow(bps)	numeric(18)
TCP FLOWS	TCP number of meetings	numeric(18)
TCP PEERS	TCP number of meetings	numeric(18)
AVGLEN IN TCPFLOW	Average packet length TCP session (section)	numeric(18)
UDP FLOWS	UDP number of meetings	numeric(18)
UDP PEERS	UDP hosts	numeric(18)
PKTS PER IJDPFLOW	Average number of transactions per UDP session	numeric(18)
AVGLEN IN IJDPFLOW	Average packet length UDP session (section)	numeric(18)
AVGLEN OIJT IJDPFLOW	Average packet length UDP session (section)	numeric(18)

The original data collected by the exploration is arranged in time series, and the collected data is filtered out, which basically covers the data feature dimensions required for network traffic analysis, and the corresponding dimensions are expressed in specific data types and units, making Data changes are more intuitive, and processing is more efficient.

3.2   Testing Tools

Avalanche is an advanced testing tool for 4–7 layer simulation and performance testing in the industry. The Avalanche test solution is used in the test laboratory to realize the authenticity of the network, users and users. The biggest feature of Avalanche is that it can simulate a variety of abnormal conditions, a variety of real user activities, and more than 1 million network connections with different IP addresses, thus well imitating the real network environment.

3.3   Comparison of Clustering Extraction Precision

Contrast and analyze by contour coefficient and extraction accuracy. The former calculation result range is $[-1,1]$, the closer the result is to 1, the better.

Table 4.   Prof coefficients and extraction accuracy

Number of clusters	Methods of this paper		Traditional methods	
	Contour coefficient	Extraction Precision/%	Contour coefficient	Extraction Precision/%
5	0.825	95.36	0.120	83.25
8	0.932	93.12	0.225	85.14
15	0.861	95.20	0.632	85.41
25	0.889	94.12	0.364	86.30
30	0.920	95.66	0.321	84.21

It can be seen from Table 4 that compared with the traditional method, under the application of this method, the contour coefficient is larger, closer to 1, and the extraction accuracy is higher, which proves that this method is more effective.

3.4   Comparison of Clustering Speed

On the basis of the above experiments, we test the speed of extracting the spatiotemporal distribution characteristics of the data flow network of 10 groups of the proposed method and the traditional method respectively to further verify the superiority of the proposed method. The test results are shown in Fig. 3.

As can be seen from Fig. 3, this method can achieve high precision extraction on the basis of short clustering speed, with a maximum of 0.09 bit/ms, which has more advantages than traditional methods.

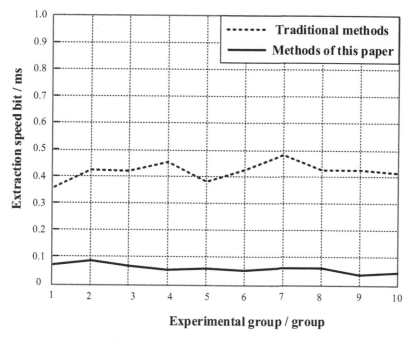

Fig. 3. Comparison of polymeric speed

4   Conclusion

Almost all phenomena in the real world contain three basic characteristics: space, time and attributes. Driven by machine learning, big data analysis, the Internet of Things, and smart cities, spatiotemporal data sources and analysis methods are constantly enriched. At present, spatio-temporal data analysis and mining technologies have important application value in different fields. How to combine spatio-temporal data with other data sources and obtain decisive characteristics through observation and analysis of time and space attributes has important practical significance. For this reason, this paper studies a research on the feature extraction of network temporal and spatial distribution based on data stream clustering. Through this research, the effectiveness of the method is proved.

References

1. Lijian, Z., Chen, Z., Zuowei, W., et al.: Hierarchical palmprint feature extraction and recognition based on multi-wavelets and complex network. IET Image Proc. **12**(6), 985–992 (2018)
2. Yu, X., Wang, R., Liu, B., et al.: Salient feature extraction for hyperspectral image classification. Remote Sensing Letters **10**(6), 553–562 (2019)
3. Liu, S., Liu, D., Srivastava, G., et al.: Overview and methods of correlation filter algorithms in object tracking. Complex Intell. Syst. (2020). https://doi.org/10.1007/s40747-020-00161-4
4. Liu, S., Lu, M., Li, H., et al.: Prediction of gene expression patterns with generalized linear regression model. Front. Genet. **10**, 120 (2019)

5. Zhibin, W., Kaiyi, W., Shouhui, P., et al.: Segmentation of crop disease images with an improved K-means clustering algorithm. Appl. Eng. Agric. **34**(2), 277–289 (2018)
6. Shizhen, Z., Wenfeng, L., Jingjing, C.: A user-adaptive algorithm for activity recognition based on K-means clustering, local outlier factor, and multivariate gaussian distribution. Sensors **18**(6), 1850 (2018)
7. Mansouri, A., Bouhlel, M.S.: Trust in ad hoc networks: a new model based on clustering algorithm. Int. J. Network Secur. **21**(3), 483–493 (2019)
8. Atilgan, C., Nasibov, E.N.: A space efficient minimum spanning tree approach to the fuzzy joint points clustering algorithm. IEEE Trans. Fuzzy Syst. **27**(6), 1317–1322 (2019)
9. Liu, R., Zhao, T., Zhao, X., et al.: Modeling gold nanoparticle radiosensitization using a clustering algorithm to quantitate DNA double-strand breaks with mixed-physics Monte Carlo simulation. Med. Phys. **46**(11), 5314–5325 (2019)
10. Guang, Y., Yewen, C., Amir, E., et al.: SDN-based hierarchical agglomerative clustering algorithm for interference mitigation in ultra-dense small cell networks. ETRI J. **40**(2), 227–236 (2018)
11. Zhang, D., Ge, H., Zhang, T., et al.: New multi-hop clustering algorithm for vehicular ad hoc networks. IEEE Trans. Intell. Transp. Syst. **20**(4), 1517–1530 (2019)
12. Fu, W., Liu, S., Srivastava, G.: Optimization of big data scheduling in social networks. Entropy **21**(9), 902 (2019)

Design of Advance Security Early Warning System for Network Data Based on Artificial Intelligence

Ya-fei Wang[1(✉)] and Wei- na He[2]

[1] Information Engineering College, Pingdingshan University, Pingdingshan 467000, China
wangyafei54512@yeah.net
[2] Pingdingshan University School of Software, Pingdingshan 467000, China

Abstract. At present, the design of network data advance security early warning system warning accuracy rate is low, leading to long warning time, poor stability. Based on artificial intelligence, a new advance security warning system for network data is designed. The hardware of the system is composed of power module, acquisition module, driver module, alarm module and display module. The software program is designed according to the hardware structure of the system. The software program includes integrated control main program, temperature collection program, temperature display program and sound and light alarm program. Experimental results show that the network data advance security early warning system based on artificial intelligence can effectively improve the system early warning accuracy, shorten the warning time and improve stability.

Keywords: Artificial intelligence · Network data · Advanced security · Security early warning · Early warning system

Classification No.: TP277 Literature Identification Code: A

1 Introduction

As the carrier of information, network data automatic identification system has the ability to process information and extract key attributes of information, which facilitates people's lives and ensures the authenticity of information [1]. There are a large number of common signals with nonlinear and non-stationary characteristics in the data signal, and the information contained in the internal time domain and frequency domain must be analyzed by the safety early warning system [2, 3].

Artificial intelligence (AI) technology is a newly emerging technology in recent years. As a branch of computer science, AI includes robot, language recognition, image recognition and switching systems. AI uses the behavior of computer to achieve higher level applications. AI technology is therefore applied in various fields [4].

In order to improve the accuracy and efficiency of the early warning system, this paper designs a new network data advanced security early warning system based on

© ICST Institute for Computer Sciences, Social Informatics and Telecommunications Engineering 2021
Published by Springer Nature Switzerland AG 2021. All Rights Reserved
W. Fu et al. (Eds.): ICMTEL 2021, LNICST 387, pp. 553–565, 2021.
https://doi.org/10.1007/978-3-030-82562-1_54

artificial intelligence. The hardware part consists of five parts: power module, acquisition module, driver module, alarm module and display module. The software program includes Integrated control program, temperature acquisition program, temperature display program and sound light alarm program. The effectiveness of the system is verified by experiments.

2   Hardware Design of Advance Security Early Warning System for Network Data Based on Artificial Intelligence

The hardware of network data advance security warning system based on artificial intelligence is composed of power module, collection module, drive module, alarm module and display module. The structure of AI -based advance security warning hardware for network data is shown in Fig. 1:

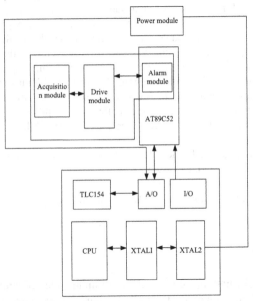

Fig. 1. Hardware structure of network data advanced security early warning system based on Artificial Intelligence

Analysis of Fig. 1 shows that the power module consists of an external AC power supply and an internal battery, both of which work simultaneously to ensure that the system can have continuous power. The stepper motor driver is controlled by the AT89C52 controller and the data acquisition is carried out by the TLC1543 chip.

Single chip microcomputer plays an important role and is the core structure of the advanced safety warning system. Two resistors are added outside the system. When the analog signal is collected by the sensor, the analog signal will be converted into digital signal through the corresponding signal processing circuit. Only the digital signal can be input into the I/O interface of the single chip successfully, and the CPU of the system will scan the four I/O interfaces at regular time. When the I/O interface with high level is found, the system will immediately send out the demand for power failure. The alarm module inside the system is equipped with acoustic alarm. If the submersible pump fails, the acoustic alarm will quickly indicate the type of failure. In order to update and extend the system, a 8255 programmable peripheral parallel I/O interface is added to the peripheral.

2.1 Design of SCM Module

In this paper, the single- chip microcomputer AT89C52 is selected. The single- chip microcomputer is the main control chip of the system, which can realize A/D conversion, data reading, data processing and data output. Compared with the traditional SCM, AT89C52 SCM consumes less power, has higher performance, can realize ISP online programming, and can fully compatible with 51 all sub-series [5]. After the 8-channel analog of A/D conversion is input to ADC0809 chip, the chip will work at the same time with the CPU, choose the appropriate method to interrupt. When the A/D conversion is complete, the conversion signal is sent back to the CPU, which requests an interrupt [6].

2.2 Power Module Design

The control chip AT89C52 is used to control the operation of the whole system, and the crystal circuit and clock circuit are introduced into the power module. The AT89C52 is a CHMOS chip with strong control capability, and the pins are also equipped with XTALI and XTAL2. The reset circuit is programmable X25045 chip, which has the ability to monitor the working state of power supply [7]. The watchdog has the function of timing to meet the requirement of monitoring timing. The power module circuit diagram is shown in Fig. 2:

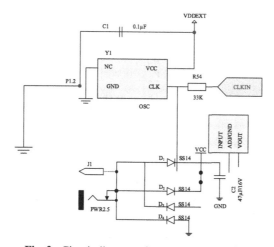

Fig. 2. Circuit diagram of power supply module

Set the working voltage of the intelligent integrated control system studied in this paper to be +5 V. When the +15 V DC voltage is introduced from the outside, the voltage is reduced, and two lithium batteries connected in series are used to charge the system power module. After the charging is completed, the system has a stable voltage. The power module chooses LM317 as the voltage regulator chip. LM317 has a strong series integration capability. While adjusting the system output, it ensures that the output voltage of the system is 2.2 V and the output current is 1.5 A. Compared with other regulators, the operation of LM317 is simpler. Connecting two resistors outside the regulator can set the voltage value. The operation is simple and the operation performance is stable [8].

2.3 Drive Module Design

The motor is also controlled by AT89C52. Three interface signals: pulse signal, offline signal and direction signal are added to the driver. These three signals are responsible for different tasks. The pulse signal is responsible for controlling the working speed of the stepper motor, and the direction signal is responsible for controlling the step. When the stepping motor stops, the off-line signal can ensure that the current of each phase is cut off [9].

The driver module is shown in Fig. 3:

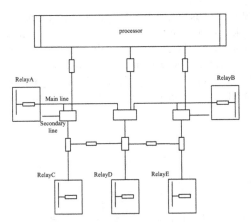

Fig. 3. Driver module

Observing Fig. 3, we can see that the drive module also introduces a double-pole double-throw relay. The double-pole double-throw relay transmits the control signal to the contactor that controls the motor. The normally closed contact in the relay is connected in series with the total number of faults. Once the submersible pump fails, the normally closed contact will be disconnected, and the total fault output circuit will also be disconnected. The setting of the freewheeling diode can well prevent the induced current generated by the relay coil from damaging the circuit components [10–13].

2.4 Sound and Light Alarm Module Design

Different from the traditional module, the alarm module selected in this article is the sound and light alarm module. Use light-emitting diodes and speakers to alarm at the same time. The indicator status lights of the diodes have two colors of red and green. When the submersible pump is in normal working condition, the green light of the system is on; when a fault occurs, the green light of the system is off and the red light is on. At the same time, the corresponding speaker will also emit an alarm sound. The system is equipped with a display, which displays the specific fault type, helping the staff to plan the corresponding solution in a short time.

2.5 Signal Receiver Design

The signal receiver's recognition and analysis speed for sounds in the recognizable range is 200 MHz/s. It can recognize and analyze the signals output by different wave propagation and different frequencies of broadcasting and broadcasting, and can process the received 6 signals in parallel each time. Broadcast audio on non-stop channels.

The special advantage of this type of signal receiver is that after identifying the outside broadcast, it will safely identify the broadcast data and audio to ensure the safety and health of the data. If the requirements are met, the signal receiver will record and backup the broadcast audio store and transmit to the host of the hardware part, and the host performs external transmission. In order to adapt well to the characteristics of broadcasting, the signal receiver opens the corresponding channel five minutes before the start of the broadcast program that can receive the signal, and starts the recording process to ensure the integrity of the broadcast data and prevent loss.

2.6 VS78 Model Host

The VS78 model host is the core part of the hardware area of the automatic broadcast recognition system based on artificial intelligence. The VS78 model host is an inclusive cabinet where the hardware area is placed. The motherboard recommends other hardware devices. The main work is to record the storage of the signal receiver of the hardware part. Perform demodulation and transmission. When the host broadcasts the broadcast audio to the outside, the broadcast recording audio is first encoded and compressed. On the one hand, the size of the broadcast audio is reduced and the operating pressure of the system is reduced. On the other hand, the copyright of the recorded broadcast audio is guaranteed to prevent criminals from carrying out downloads and using the broadcast audio in other unfair industries, bringing bad effects.

The type of the VS78 host is a virtual host. The advantage of the virtual host is to reduce the memory of the system, increase the sensitivity to the broadcast audio signal transmitted by the wireless network, and the virtual host has high variability. In special cases, according to the broadcast audio The special format of the virtual host can change the communication channel for signal reception, which is a manifestation of the high efficiency of automatic broadcast identification. The virtual channel communication direction is shown in Fig. 4:

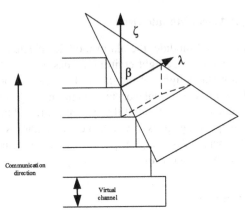

Fig. 4. Virtual channel communication direction

The structural framework of the hardware part the demodulation device is a structural adjustment of the hardware area. Its working principle is to monitor the hardware area equipment in real time, pay attention to the operation of the broadcast automatic identification system hardware area, and if there is a hardware device work processing result If the format and status are abnormal, the equipment is adjusted and the adjustment result is sent to the VS78 model host, and the host sends the final processing result back to the staff in the form of data. Structural framework The demodulation device converts the audio into digital audio signals by scanning the frequency spectrum of various broadcast audio services. If the converted broadcast audio digital signal is not within the normal range, it belongs to abnormal broadcast audio and needs to be demodulated. The demodulation process is to destroy abnormal broadcast audio to prevent other accidents from happening and ensure the normal operation of the automatic broadcast recognition system.

2.7 HI89 Model Chip

This article uses HI89 type chips for the work requirements of the artificial intelligence-based network data advance security early warning system. The chip is the key to system data storage. Therefore, this article chooses a new type of chip produced by the artificial intelligence field. The HI89 type chip is composed of UHF radio waves, wireless identification technology, and a four-channel interface composed of Edifier R2000. Compared with traditional chips, it has higher reading and writing functions. The card reading efficiency is 50 s and can complete 1G broadcast audio recognition. To a certain extent, the speed of automatic broadcast recognition is improved.

In addition, the core program of the HI89 chip is the JR7604 program, which has 4 TNC connectors with a memory of 50 Ω, and has a large memory storage space, which provides the basis for broadcast audio recognition. This chip has ultra-high radio frequency processing function, can run 8 identification channels at the same time, the signal loss of automatic identification is less, and the efficiency is improved. The HI89 type chip does not need the host to send instructions to the incoming system, which reduces the operating procedures of the safety early warning system. HI89 model parameters are shown in Table 1:

Table 1. Model parameters of hi89 chip

Parameter	Numerical value
Working temperature	−40 °C–85 °C
Input forward current	30 mA
Input reverse voltage	10 V
Low level input current	300 μA
High level input current	20 mA
Low level gate voltage	1.0 V
High level gate voltage	VCC
High level delay time	50 ns
Low level delay time	80 ns

The work content of the TI processor of the artificial intelligence-based network data advance safety warning system is mainly to control the core. The processor will sense the operating heat and power consumption of the system in real time. If the internal heat of the system exceeds 70 °C or the thermal power consumption reaches 65 W, then the processor will turn on the cooling function. The processing speed of TI processors is as high as 8GT/s, which meets the operating requirements of the hardware area of network data systems.

3 Software Design of Advanced Security Early Warning System for Network Data Based on Artificial Intelligence

The software program is designed according to the hardware structure of the system. The designed software program includes the integrated control main program, temperature acquisition program, temperature display program and sound and light alarm program. The software flow chart of the network data advanced security early warning system based on artificial intelligence is shown in Fig. 5:

Analyzing the above figure, we can see that the artificial intelligence network data advance safety warning system studied in this article converts the temperature through the look-up table method. The system will automatically set two tables, namely the output voltage-temperature correspondence table and A/D conversion number- Analog voltage correspondence table. After obtaining accurate data information, the data in the table will be recorded in detail in the memory, and the temperature results obtained will be displayed on the LCD. The displayed temperature range is −5–150 °C, and the display accuracy is between ±0.5 °C.

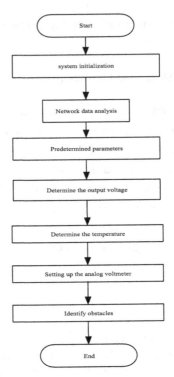

Fig. 5. Flow chart of software main program.

The software detection workflow is shown in Fig. 6:

The content detected by the integrated control system includes motor winding temperature, bearing temperature and motor humidity. If the electric pump in the motor is overloaded or the motor itself has quality problems, it will cause the winding temperature to be too high. When the winding temperature is too high, the motor will automatically sound an alarm. The bearing temperature is too high because the motor is overloaded or the axial force is too large, so the sound and light alarm subroutine and the CPU run at the same time, which can make the software run more flexible. Since the electric power is counted for a long time, once the humidity is too high, leakage may occur, so it is very important to monitor the humidity of the motor. Use I/V to convert the voltage and analyze the reference voltage. If the reference voltage is exceeded, it is necessary the alarm sounds.

4   Experimental Research

In order to further verify the early warning capabilities of the artificial intelligence-based network data advanced security early warning system, a comparative experiment was designed to compare with the traditional early warning system.

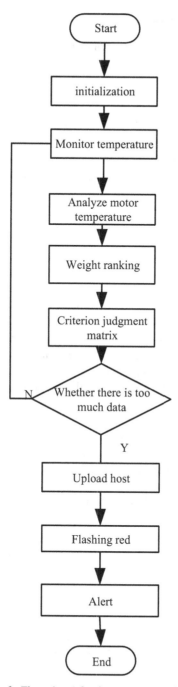

Fig. 6. Flow chart of software early warning

4.1 Experimental Parameters

The selected raw data parameters are shown in Table 2:

Table 2. Experimental data

Experimental project	Specific parameters
Working voltage	5 V
External voltage	15 V
Model of single chip microcomputer	AT89C52
Conversion mode	A/O conversion
Display temperature range	−5–150 °C
Display accuracy	±0.5 °C

4.2 Experimental Process

Experiments are performed according to the above set parameters, and the traditional integrated control system and the artificial intelligence-based network data advanced security early warning system based on this article are selected for integrated control, and the superiority of the control system studied in this article is verified by experimental results.

4.3 Experimental Results and Analysis

The experimental results obtained are shown in Fig. 7.

(1) Accuracy comparison of early warning results

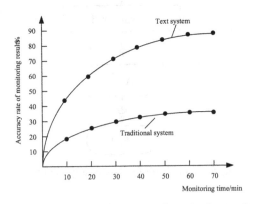

Fig. 7. Comparison of accuracy of monitoring results

Observing Fig. 7 we can see that as the monitoring time increases, the accuracy of the monitoring results of the system in this paper and the accuracy of the monitoring results of the traditional system are increasing, but the accuracy of the early warning system studied in this paper is always higher than that of the traditional early warning system. The circuit of the early warning system studied in this paper can simultaneously monitor the motor winding temperature, bearing temperature, motor humidity and mechanical seal degree, and feed back the monitoring results to the host system. The analog and switch values are closely integrated, which improves the accuracy of the system's early warning (Figs. 8 and 9).

(2) Stability comparison of early warning process

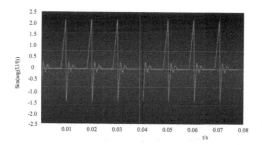

Fig. 8. Process stability of traditional system monitoring

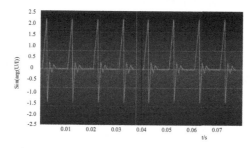

Fig. 9. Stability of monitoring process in this paper

On the whole, the early warning process of the system studied in this article and the traditional early warning control system are relatively stable, but when the early warning time reaches 0.04 s, the traditional early warning system has a fault in the early warning, and the early warning system studied in this article always maintains monitoring in a stable state. It can be seen that the early warning system studied in this paper is more stable.

(3) Comparison of warning time

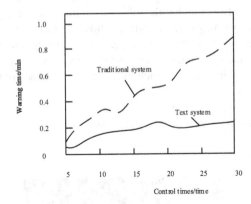

Fig. 10. Comparison results of early warning time

Analyzing Fig. 10, it can be seen that when the number of early warnings is 10 times, the early warning time spent by the traditional system is 0.11 s, and the warning time spent by the system in this paper is 0.08 s; when the number of early warning control times is 20, the warning time spent by the traditional system is 0.47 s, the early warning time spent by the system in this paper is 0.14 s; when the number of warnings is 30 times, the warning time spent by the traditional system is 0.85 s, and the warning time spent by the system in this paper is 0.21 s.

In summary, the overall performance of the early warning system studied in this paper is better than the traditional system. The system studied in this paper is designed with a special signal acquisition circuit and signal conditioning circuit. AT89C52 is very convenient to maintain, and it can monitor analog and switch values in a targeted manner, and control the working status of substation submersible pumps more safely and reliably.

5 Conclusion

The early warning system studied in this paper also introduces fault diagnosis technology, micro-motor technology, sensor technology and intelligent measurement technology, which can not only monitor the operation status of submersible pumps online, but also detect the operation failure of network data in time. Compared with traditional For the early warning system, the system studied in this article has stronger detection capabilities, better monitoring effects, and better realization of safety monitoring. On the whole, the intelligent strength of the system has been strengthened. AT89C52 is low in cost, stable in performance and easy to maintain. Very convenient, rich warning functions greatly reduce the burden of manual work, making the system operation safer and more reliable.

References

1. Rui, N., Lin, Z.: Design of learning quality assessment and early warning system based on artificial intelligence and data analysis. Electron. Des. Eng. **28**(11), 37–41 (2020)
2. Xiaokang, R., Rui, M., Li, Z., et al.: Artificial intelligence-based big data security management platform for dike engineering and its implementation. J. Yangtze River Sci. Res. Inst. **36**(10), 104–110 (2019)
3. Ping, L., Bin, W.: I-based propagation feature mining system for network public opinion big data. Mod. Electron. Tech. **043**(004), 176–179 (2020)
4. Leihua, Z., Hongtai, N., Zhongni, W., et al.: Research on the construction of early warning model of criminals based on big data. Netinfo Secur. **220**(04), 88–95 (2019)
5. Linfeng, Z., Jiancheng, L., Lixin, W.: Early warning technology of oil and gas pipeline based on monitoring data. Press. Vessel Technol. **036**(005), 55–60 (2019)
6. Yabin, L., Xinxiao, Z., Liangjun, M., et al.: Design and research of integrated safety risk early warning platform for hazardous chemicals handling and transportation. J. Safety Sci. Technol. **015**(005), 179–184 (2019)
7. Rong, Y., Benwu, N.: Design of intelligent safety management and control model for hydropower projects based on safety system theory. China Work Saf. Sci. Technol. **015**(009), 147–152 (2019)
8. Chen, Z., Shengrong, Z., Qingwei, M., et al.: Design and implementation of early warning and prompt function of clinical decision support system. Chin. Digital Med. **014**(008), 57–60 (2019)
9. Jiangao, D., Jiayin, Q., Binxing, F., et al.: Research on the governance model of Internet information behavior fusion for national public security. Jiangsu Soc. Sci. **300**(05), 133–145+281 (2018)
10. Wu Qiang, X., Hua, Z.Y., et al.: Mine water disaster smart emergency rescue system and application based on cloud platform. J. China Coal Soc. **43**(10), 5–11 (2018)
11. Liu, S., Liu, D., Srivastava, G., et al.: Overview and methods of correlation filter algorithms in object tracking. Complex Intell. Syst. 2020. https://doi.org/10.1007/s40747-020-00161-4
12. Liu, S., Lu, M., Li, H., et al.: Prediction of gene expression patterns with generalized linear regression model. Front. Genet. **10**, 120 (2019)
13. Fu, W., Liu, S., Srivastava, G.: Optimization of big data scheduling in social networks. Entropy **21**(9), 902 (2019)

Research on Network Information Security Risk Assessment Based on Artificial Intelligence

Ya-fei Wang[1]($\boxtimes$) and Wei-na He[2]

[1] Information Engineering College, Pingdingshan University, Pingdingshan 467000, China
wangyafei54512@yeah.net

[2] Pingdingshan University School of Software, Pingdingshan 467000, China

Abstract. Fault tree analysis and event tree analysis can not analyze the dynamic information, which leads to the long time and precision of network information security risk assessment based on artificial intelligence. Therefore, based on the risk assessment model of artificial intelligence network information security, by obtaining the dynamic index value, establish the evaluation ideal standard, evaluate the dimensionless processing of dynamic index, realize the processing of dynamic information, and then complete the model reasoning. The information security risk assessment process is designed from the perspectives of risk assessment preparation, asset identification, threat identification, vulnerability identification, confirmation of existing security measures and risk calculation. Experimental results show that the method has the advantages of short evaluation time and high accuracy, and plays a guiding role in the security protection of mobile network information transmission.

Keywords: Artificial intelligence · Network information · Security risk · Neural network algorithm · Evaluation

1 Introduction

Information security assessment is an important part of the information security lifecycle and provides security risk analysis reports and recommendations for improvement [1]. Security evaluation of information system refers to the scientific and impartial comprehensive evaluation of the integrity, confidentiality, availability and other security performance of an information system in accordance with relevant technical standards. There is a need for a scientific assessment of the security of information systems, which is one of the core and important issues facing all security-related information systems [2]. At the same time, strengthening the information system security evaluation work is also the objective and urgent need of our information security work [3]. Traditional security analysis methods, such as fault tree analysis and event tree analysis, describe the system statically from the point of view of hardware structure and system function. However, the descriptive ability is still insufficient and highly dependent on the analyst's engineering experience. On this basis, a network information security risk assessment method based

W. Fu et al. (Eds.): ICMTEL 2021, LNICST 387, pp. 566–578, 2021.
https://doi.org/10.1007/978-3-030-82562-1_55

on artificial intelligence is proposed. The risk assessment model of artificial intelligence network information security shall be established, the index system shall be established, the positive and negative ideal assessment standards shall be established according to the index value, and the assessment index shall be subject to dimensionless processing to complete the network information security assessment. Experimental results show that the design method has the advantages of short evaluation time, high evaluation accuracy, and certain application value.

2   Construction of Risk Assessment Model for Network Information Security Based on Artificial Intelligence

Artificial intelligence is a comprehensive subject that integrates many subjects such as information science, technology science and so on. It has high technology and content, and can effectively improve work efficiency [4]. Artificial intelligence technology is the use of computer systems to simulate the structure of the human brain, and then self-analysis, the problems encountered in the independent thinking, planning, can quickly and effectively solve complex problems, because of its high content of evolution, has been widely used in various industries [5].

In the process of risk assessment, the most suitable evaluation method should be selected by the subjective consciousness of the assessors and the intelligent algorithm. Artificial intelligence is of great value in information security risk assessment because it can provide more options and reduce the problem of artificial inaccuracy in information security risk assessment [6]. In addition, the application of artificial intelligence to information security risk assessment can also effectively expand the scalability of the system, which is also helpful to ensure the objectivity of information risk assessment [7].

Using the convolution neural network algorithm of artificial intelligence, a network information security risk assessment model is constructed, and the process is shown in Fig. 1.

The implementation of the algorithm is as follows:

Suppose there are K convolution kernels and N kinds of output layers, then the output layer weight parameter θ is a $X \times Y$ matrix, which can be expressed as a $\theta \in Z^{X \times Y}$. The characteristic of the sample a pool is a K vector, that is, a $f \in Z^K$ Vector. The probability of a sample being assigned to the b category is:

$$P = (b|a, Z) = \frac{e^{(c_y \cdot f + q_y)}}{\sum\limits_{h=1}^{N} e^{(c_y \cdot f + \eta)}} \tag{1}$$

Formula (1): η represents the offset term of the full connecting layer, and the loss function can be obtained by maximizing the likelihood probability:

$$E = -\sum_{y}^{r} \log\left(p\left(u_y | x_y, \theta\right)\right) \tag{2}$$

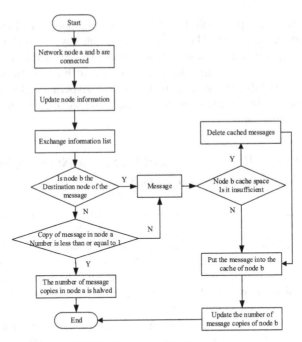

Fig. 1. Implementation process

In formula (2): r is the training data set, u_y represents the y sample real data type. In order to prevent the phenomenon of over-fitting, the structure of convolution layer neurons should be simplified to ensure the weight does not work [8]. After the feature compression processing, the internal state and behavior control of data can be operated freely on the basis of the stable storage space of database. Through the above process, complete the network information security risk assessment model.

3   Model Reasoning

The information security risk assessment model is extended from the static information security risk assessment model, and the reasoning algorithm is also extended from the static assessment model, as shown in Fig. 2.

According to the inference algorithm structure of the network information security risk assessment model, the basic inference process of the artificial intelligence method used in the network risk assessment is described as follows: firstly, the model is initialized with the initial state and conditional probability of the designated network; when a new risk indicator variable information is detected at a certain time, that is, the information update of the various levels of the neural network or the information update of the observation node of the network, the inference of the network model is triggered, and the posterior probability of the network risk is obtained through the inference algorithm, so as to update the probability distribution of the whole network node state, and the updated posterior probability distribution is used as the basis for reasoning at the next

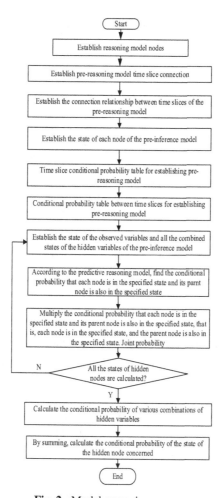

Fig. 2. Model reasoning process

time; and the real-time network risk can be obtained through the continuous input model of the time series observation data, and then the corresponding measures are taken to control the risk in real time [9].

3.1 Indicator Value Acquisition

According to the quantitative contents of the aforesaid security evaluation indicators, the security of network information transmission containing a different host will be tested by means of attack, and then the maximum read permissions, write permissions and service permissions of the host will be obtained, from which the value of each component of the confidentiality of network security, the integrity of network security and the availability of network security will be obtained [10]. In the model of information security risk assessment, the security of information system is determined by the security of assets value, vulnerability and menace, but the security of assets, threat and vulnerability should be considered synthetically. The risk assessment indicator system diagram as shown in Fig. 3 is established.

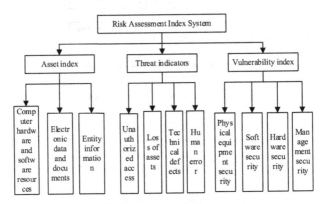

Fig. 3. Risk assessment indicator system

3.2 Establishment of Positive and Negative Criteria for Evaluation

The positive ideal standard of the evaluation index is: $r_0^+ = \{r_0^+(1), r_0^+(2), \cdots, r_0^+(n)\}$, take this standard as the data of the evaluation, and get the best evaluation result of each index; the negative ideal standard of the evaluation index is: $r_0^- = \{r_0^-(1), r_0^-(2), \cdots, r_0^-(n)\}$, take this standard as the data of the evaluation, and get the worst evaluation result of each index. Through the establishment of this standard, we can get the best and worst base points, and compare the distances between different evaluation values.

3.3 Dimensionless Processing of Assessment Indicators

If the r indicator is a benefit indicator, the greater the indicator value, the more beneficial the assessment is:

$$r'(c) = \frac{r(c) - \min\{r_0^+(c), r_0^-(c)\}}{\left|r_0^+(c) - r_0^-(c)\right|} \tag{3}$$

If A is a cost indicator, then the higher the indicator value, the more detrimental the evaluation is:

$$r'(c) = \frac{\max\{r_0^+(c), r_0^-(c)\} - r(c)}{\left|r_0^+(c) - r_0^-(c)\right|} \tag{4}$$

After the dimensionless processing, can be evaluated of the sequence: $r' = (r'(1), r'(2), \cdots, r'(n))$. According to this method, we can deal with the vectors of network security confidentiality, network security integrity and network security availability without dimensionality, and obtain a new evaluation sequence.

3.4 Null Processing

In order to more accurately estimate null values in the new evaluation sequence, a null processing flow is designed as follows:

Step 1: Feature Selection and Data Transformation:

(1) Feature selection, attribute reduction algorithm based on rough set is used to reduce the original data table and get the key attribute set after reduction;

(2) Data conversion, mainly refers to the pretreatment of data to make it an easy-to-use data form. Firstly, the semantic attribute of natural language is numericalized so that it can be easily used for data mining, and then the formula of fuzzy number is used to normalize numerical information to simplify calculation.

Step 2: Artificial Intelligence Clustering:

Clustering is performed using a set of non-empty attributes related to attributes with null values obtained in step 1. Similar data are clustered together, and different data are divided into different clusters. In clustering, considering that the influence weights of different attributes on columns containing nulls are different, the relevant weights are introduced:

$$w = \frac{r^2}{\sum_{k=1}^{m} r_1^2} \tag{5}$$

where m is the number of attributes in the non-null attribute set associated with attributes containing null values, w is the correlation coefficient value of attributes containing null values and the ratio of the sum of the correlation coefficients of all related attributes with attributes containing null values, which reflects the weight of attributes with null values. After the artificial intelligence clustering, the cluster center is obtained.

Step 3: Calculate Impact:

After clustering the data into several clusters, the influence of different independent variables on dependent variables is different for each cluster. Artificial intelligence regression coefficients are used to calculate the influence of different independent variables on dependent variables. Firstly, the fuzzy correlation coefficient is used to express the correlation between attributes, then the independent variable coefficients are determined, and finally the attribute influence degree is obtained.

Among them, the calculation formula of correlation degree is:

$$s_{a,b} = \frac{\sum_{i=1}^{n} (a_i - \overline{a}) \cdot \left(b_i - \overline{b}\right)}{\sqrt{\sum_{i=1}^{n} (a_i - \overline{a})^2 \cdot \sum_{i=1}^{n} \left(b_i - \overline{b}\right)^2}} \tag{6}$$

In formula (6): $\overline{a}$ and $\overline{b}$ represent the sample mean a, b the fuzzy set.

The formula for determining the independent variable coefficient shall be:

$$COD = \pm \frac{r^2}{\sum_{k=1}^{m} r_1^2} \tag{7}$$

Step 4: Estimate Null:
First, the distance between the tuple and each cluster center is calculated, then the tuple in which the null value belongs belongs to the closest class, and the estimated value is obtained by using the null value estimation algorithm.

4 Information Security Risk Assessment Process Design

Information security risk assessment generally includes the following six processes: risk assessment preparation, asset identification, Weili, identification, vulnerability identification, confirmation of existing security measures, risk calculation. The information security risk assessment flow chart is shown in Fig. 4 below.

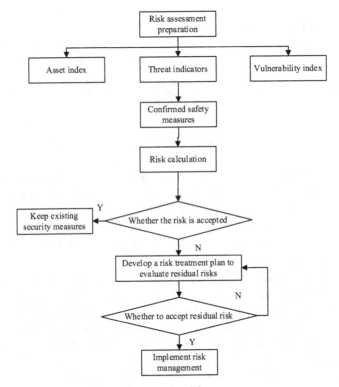

Fig. 4. Information security risk assessment process

4.1 Risk Assessment Reserve

Adequate preparation and planning prior to the information security risk assessment can ensure the controllability of the assessment process and the objectivity of the assessment results. The preparatory work for the risk assessment of information security shall include the following contents: specifying the objectives of the risk assessment, establishing a special assessment team, determining the risk assessment methods and schemes, and obtaining the support of senior managers for the risk assessment work.

4.2 Asset Identification

Assets exist in various forms. In the risk assessment, the three security attributes of assets, confidentiality, usability and integrity, are mainly evaluated. The threat, vulnerability and security measures of assets will affect the security of assets. Therefore, it is necessary to identify the assets. Before the identification of assets, classifying the assets of the information system is conducive to the next step of risk assessment. After the assets are identified, the assets may be assigned by using the importance level, and the assets may be divided into different levels according to the assignment results, so as to determine the scope of important assets and carry out further risk assessment around important assets.

4.3 Threat Identification

When the information assets are weak or the security measures are not in place, the vulnerability will increase the risk of information security. One Weili, may have a Weili for different information assets, and an information asset will face different multiple threats. Direct or indirect threats to important information assets may be identified through sample analysis, log analysis, personnel interviews and other methods of IDS (intrusion detection system).

4.4 Vulnerability Identification

Vulnerability is a general term for the weakness of one or more assets. If it is not exploited and exploited, vulnerability will not in itself cause damage to information assets. Because of the covert nature of vulnerability, the vulnerability of some assets can only be revealed under certain circumstances, which is also the most difficult part of vulnerability identification. Vulnerability identification needs to identify the vulnerabilities that may be exploited, evaluate their severity and assign values.

4.5 Confirmation of Existing Security Measures

Safety measures can be divided into preventive measures and protective measures. It is necessary to confirm the effectiveness of the existing security measures, that is, whether the existing security measures reduce the severity of vulnerability and really resist the threat, and play the role of protecting information assets. Safety measures that are deemed inappropriate shall be cancelled or amended, or replaced by more effective ones, and those that are deemed to be effective shall continue to be maintained.

4.6 Risk Calculation

Scientific algorithms and tools will be adopted to calculate the possibility of security incidents after identifying assets, weili, and vulnerability and confirming the existence of security measures, that is, the information security risk value will be used to determine the information security risk level and handle the risk results according to the risk value, so as to realize the control and treatment of risks and facilitate the formulation of scientific and effective risk treatment plans for the losses caused to the organization.

In this model, the result range of the output is within the [0.1] range, and the qualitative indicators "extremely unsafe, unsafe, safe, very safe" are described respectively, as shown in Table 1.

Table 1. Assessment notes

Rank	Description
Extremely insecure	Network Information Transmission Security Guarantee Ability is Poor and Security Situation is Severe
Insecurity	Network Information Transmission Security Guarantee Ability Is Limited, Existence Security Hidden Trouble
Safety	Network information transmission has certain security guarantee capability and its environment is basically safe
Perfectly safe	The network information transmission has the strong security safeguard ability, the environment is extremely safe

5 Security Simulation Experiment Design

With the help of Packet Tracer software, the paper validates and analyzes the research on network information security risk assessment based on artificial intelligence.By constructing network security simulation topology and configuring network parameters, this paper compares the time and accuracy of network security risk assessment with other methods.

5.1 Simulation Experiment Environment Settings

In the Packet Tracer software, through the configuration of terminal security access to achieve computer network security. Secure access network is realized by binding switch port to terminal address, secure route is realized by OSPF plaintext authentication, packet filtering is realized by configuring standard access list on router.

5.2 Simulation Experiment Network Topology

Based on the principles of OSPF protocol plaintext authentication and encrypted message digest authentication, standard access control list, considering the principle of multi-area OSPF protocol, the topology structure of network security simulation experiment is designed, as shown in Fig. 5.

Following the network topology shown in Fig. 5, the configuration address information is shown in Table 2.

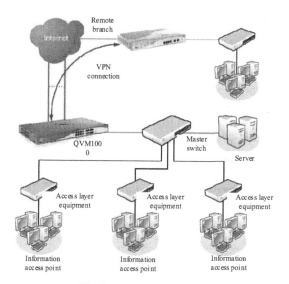

Fig. 5. Network topology

Table 2. IP address information

Network equipment	IP address	Subnet mask	Port rate
P0	192.168.1.2	255.255.255.0	0
P1	192.168.1.3	255.255.255.0	0
P2	192.168.1.4	255.255.255.0	0
P3	192.168.2.2	255.255.255.0	0
Server0	192.168.3.2	255.255.255.0	0

5.3 Experimental Results and Analysis

Based on the above contents, the fault tree analysis method, event tree analysis method and the evaluation time based on artificial intelligence are analyzed.

Table 3. Different method assessment times

Number of assessments/times	Fault tree analysis method	Event tree analysis	Evaluation method based on artificial intelligence
1	62	51	43
5	63	53	46
10	66	58	46
50	70	62	52

As can be seen from Table 3, the maximum assessment time using the fault tree analysis method is 70 s, the maximum assessment time using the event tree analysis method is 62 s, and the maximum assessment time using the AI -based assessment method is 52 s. Thus, the assessment time using the AI method is relatively short.

Fault tree analysis method, event tree analysis method and artificial intelligence - based assessment method are used to analyze the accuracy of the assessment results. The results are shown in Fig. 6.

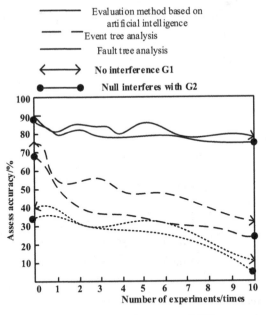

Fig. 6. Comparative analysis of accuracy of different methods

As can be seen from Fig. 6: Under no interference, when the number of experiments is 1, the accuracy of evaluation based on artificial intelligence method is 84%, the accuracy of evaluation based on fault tree analysis method is 55%, and the accuracy of evaluation based on event tree analysis method is 38%; when the number of experiments is 3, the accuracy of evaluation based on artificial intelligence method is 86%, the accuracy of evaluation based on fault tree analysis method is 56%, and the accuracy of evaluation based on event tree analysis method is 32%; when the number of experiments is 5, the accuracy of evaluation based on artificial intelligence method is 87%, the accuracy of evaluation based on fault tree analysis method is 48%, and the accuracy of evaluation based on event tree analysis method is 37%; when the number of experiments is 7, the accuracy of evaluation based on artificial intelligence method is 79%, the accuracy of evaluation based on fault tree analysis method is 45%, and the accuracy of evaluation based on event analysis method is 28%; when the number of experiments is 9, the accuracy of evaluation based on artificial intelligence method is 81%, the accuracy of evaluation based on fault tree analysis method is 40%, and the accuracy of evaluation based on event tree analysis method is 22%.

Under the null interference factor, when the number of experiments is two, the evaluation accuracy based on the artificial intelligence assessment method is 81%, the evaluation accuracy based on the fault tree analysis method is 37%, and the evaluation accuracy based on the event tree analysis method is 33%; when the number of experiments is four, the evaluation accuracy based on the artificial intelligence assessment method is 83%, the evaluation accuracy based on the fault tree analysis method is 36%, and the evaluation accuracy based on the event tree analysis method is 28%; when the number of experiments is six, the evaluation accuracy based on the artificial intelligence assessment method is 80%, the evaluation accuracy based on the fault tree analysis method is 33%, and the evaluation accuracy based on the event tree analysis method is 26%; when the number of experiments is eight, the evaluation accuracy based on the artificial intelligence assessment method is 78%, the evaluation accuracy based on the fault tree analysis method is 35%, and the evaluation accuracy based on the event tree analysis method is 24%; when the number of experiments is ten, the evaluation accuracy based on the artificial intelligence assessment method is 77%, the evaluation accuracy based on the fault tree analysis method is 28%, and the evaluation accuracy based on the event tree analysis method is 7%.

Whether there are disturbing factors or not, the evaluation method based on artificial intelligence is more accurate than fault tree analysis method and event tree analysis method, so it is feasible.

6   Concluding Remarks

Artificial intelligence technology is widely used and plays an important role in the risk assessment of information security. The effective application of Artificial intelligence technology can reduce the incidence of risk, which is indispensable in the daily work. With the continuous progress and development of science and technology, artificial intelligence technology will be seen in the information security risk assessment will have a superior effect.

References

1. Batalla, J.M., Andrukiewicz, E., Gomez, G.P., et al.: Security risk assessment for 5G networks: national perspective. IEEE Wirel. Commun. **27**(4), 16–22 (2020)
2. Huiyu, D., Tao, T., Hongwei, W.: Methods for information security risk assessment of CBTC systems based on two-dimensional structural entropy. J. Autom. **045**(001), 153–162 (2019)
3. Xiong, Z., Hao, G., Xiaoyun, H., et al.: Research on security risk assessment methods for state grid edge computing information system. Comput. Sci. **046**(0z2), 428–432 (2019)
4. Xin, W., Zuoqi, T., Shuo, X.: Information security risk assessment based on fuzzy theory and BRBPNN . Comput. Simul. **036**(011), 184–189 (2019)
5. Liu, S., Liu, D., Srivastava, G., et al.: Overview and methods of correlation filter algorithms in object tracking. Complex & Intelligent Systems (2020). https://doi.org/10.1007/s40747-020-00161-4
6. Ngamboé, M., Berthier, P., Ammari, N., et al.: Risk assessment of cyber-attacks on telemetry-enabled cardiac implantable electronic devices (CIED). Int. J. Inf. Secur., 1–25 (2020)
7. Liu, S., Lu, M., Li, H., et al.: Prediction of gene expression patterns with generalized linear regression model. Front. Genet. **10**, 120 (2019)
8. Mingsong, W., Xinbo, H., Yongcan, Z., Weitao, J.: Risk assessment of cable lines based on AHP . J. Xi'an Univ. Eng. **33**(06), 637–642 (2019)
9. Fu, W., Liu, S., Srivastava, G.: Optimization of big data scheduling in social networks. Entropy **21**(9), 902 (2019)
10. Liao, F., Chen, J., Gan, Z.: Review of research on defense of key information infrastructure driven by artificial intelligence. Comput. Eng. **045**(007), 181–187, 193 (2019)

Research on Normalized Network Information Storage Method Based on Deep Reinforcement Learning

Qiang Wang[1](✉) and Lai-feng Tang[2]

[1] School of Intelligence Technology, Geely University, Chengdu 641402, China
[2] Xinjiang Institute of Technology, Aksu 843100, China

Abstract. This paper makes a deep research on the standardized network information storage method, applies deep reinforcement learning to the standardized network information storage, and proposes a standardized network information storage method based on deep reinforcement learning. Each file to be archived is firstly divided into non-overlapping semantic fragment data blocks according to its information content. Each data block will encrypt its content through hash function, and obtain a signature as its identifier for data archiving. The archived data is divided into task data, resource data and document data. The rack-aware data placement strategy was developed based on the deep reinforcement learning algorithm to improve data reliability, availability and network bandwidth utilization, and the cloud storage model was designed to normalize the network information storage of classified archived data. Experiments show that this method has a high average disk read and write speed and can meet the requirements.

Keywords: Deep reinforcement learning · Normalized network · Information storage · Hash function · Archived data

1 Introduction

Electronic information processing technology and the rapid expansion of digital information resources continue to develop, the continuous development of storage technology and change has been quietly to [1]. Jim Gray, a Turing Prize winner, has pointed out that in an online environment, the amount of data generated every 18 months is roughly equal to the sum of all previous data [2]. For enterprises, data and electronic information have become an important resource for their survival, and play a key role in promoting the sustainable development of enterprises. However, information storage systems will still be inaccessible due to natural disasters or man-made damage, or even face the risk of loss of data. If the disaster causes the loss or damage of important information, the enterprise will not be able to carry out normal business operations, the enterprise and customers will suffer serious economic losses [3]. Global data centres have a disaster probability of approximately 0.2 per cent per year, meaning that 2 out of 1000 data centres have experienced severe data disasters and data loss. After the 911 terrorist attacks, many

W. Fu et al. (Eds.): ICMTEL 2021, LNICST 387, pp. 579–589, 2021.
https://doi.org/10.1007/978-3-030-82562-1_56

enterprises have lost a lot of critical business data because of the lack of disaster-tolerant application, which makes them unable to run their applications normally. According to IDC, 55% of US companies that suffered a system disaster in the 1990s failed immediately because they could no longer operate, 29% went bust within two years, and only about 16% remained open. Studies show that if a company's data and application systems go down for an hour, the company loses $150,000 to $6.45 million. Based on this background, the normalized network information storage method is deeply studied, and a new normalized network information storage method based on DRL is proposed. The innovation of the research method is that deep reinforcement learning goes deep into the standardized network information storage method to meet the use needs to a certain extent.

2   Design of Standardized Network Information Storage Method Based on Deep Reinforcement Learning

2.1   Data Archiving

Each file to be archived is first cut up into discrete chunks of semantic fragment data based on its information content, each chunk encrypts its content through a hash function, and calculates the signature as its identifier [4]. The metadata information for these chunk

Table 1. Main function interface and function description of file segmentation.

Serial number	Interface APIs	Function	Description
1	TagRetrieval	Tags list tagsist = tagRetrieval (File* f, out Data* buo)	Find metadata information for a file
2	FileDriver	Chunk* cp = fileDriver (File* f, Tagsist* t1)	Breaks files into semantic fragments based on their metadata information, and returns a list of pointers to those fragments
3	Check_chunk	Objects op = check chunk (chunk* cp)	Check if semantic fragments should be further divided into objects before being stored
4	ChunkDriver	Object* op = chwikDriver (Chunk*cp)	Divides semantic fragments into data objects as actual units of storage and returns a list of pointers to those objects

fragments is stored in the MDS, which compares the identifiers of the chunk fragments to determine whether there is currently a duplicate data fragment, and the non-duplicate chunk fragments are encapsulated into a fixed-length data object [5]. Sharding of files based on semantic- related information about the files, using a unified file sharding interface to provide standard interfaces for callers [6]. The main function interfaces and functional specifications for file sharding are shown in Table 1.

2.2 Data Typing

The archived data is divided into task-based data, resource-based data and document-based data [7], as shown in Table 2.

Table 2. Data breakdown details.

Serial number	Definition	Give an example	Characteristic
1	Task-based data	Facebook uses Hadoop for log analysis and recommendation systems; Baidu uses Hadoop for log storage and statistics, web page data analysis and mining, etc.; Yahoo! Hadoop will be applied to their own anti- spam system and web search queries	In addition to storage space, task-based data also require nodes to have strong computing power, especially for some large data analysis and processing applications, node computing power is often the performance bottleneck of task execution. The owner of task-based data is usually some enterprise user
2	Resource data	Users will be some commonly used software, hot movies, music, pictures and other data files uploaded to the cloud, through file sharing other users can also browse or download. Or the user uploads the data just for backup purposes. This data is usually stored as a resource to the user, and the operations performed on it are mostly read and write, and generally do not involve large or complex computations	This kind of data storage usually requires data nodes to have better storage space, and safe and reliable, the computing power of the node is not high. In addition, this kind of application is sensitive to data transmission speed and usually requires data nodes to have smaller data access latency and larger data transmission bandwidth

(continued)

Table 2. (*continued*)

Serial number	Definition	Give an example	Characteristic
3	Documental data	Various office files, drawings, program codes and other data related to users' work, study or life	These data are usually private data, confidentiality requirements are relatively high. Security and reliability of data storage are the most important considerations for users

Task-based data is often the source data for some applications, and is stored by the user to provide more valuable data or statistics that the user cares about. Data generated based on applications such as data backup or information sharing is usually resource-based. Documental data refers mainly to some working documents or materials of users.

2.3 Data Copy Placement

Making rack-aware data placement strategies based on deep reinforcement learning algorithms to improve data reliability, availability, and network bandwidth utilization [8]. The first copy of the data block is placed on one node of the local rack, the second copy is placed on another node of the same rack, and the third copy is placed on a node of a different rack. This strategy reduces the transmission of data between racks and shortens the completion time of write operations. Generally, the probability of rack failure is much lower than that of node failure, so the strategy does not affect the security and reliability of the data [9]. At the same time, this strategy reduces the network bandwidth of data transmission because the data copies are only placed on two different racks. However, when using this data placement strategy, the data blocks can not be placed evenly on the various data nodes. Among them, 1/3 of the data blocks exist in a node, 2/3 of the data blocks in a rack, the remaining data blocks are evenly distributed in other racks. This strategy improves the efficiency of write operation without reducing the performance and reliability of data write.

The Chunk module is grouped based on the data queue of the current large-scale network library information data set. If the differentiation vector coefficient k is less than 1 in the current data storage space structure, the current data node is a directional structure. At this time, the structure is set as the key transmission channel and depends on the routing control, then the quantization formula is as follows:

$$K(l) = \frac{M_n(l)}{h_m} \tag{1}$$

In the formula, $K(l)$ is the actual index weight of the current data storage data network transmission channel L; h_m represents the current actual load rate of data storage; $M_n(l)$ is the actual expected load of the current transmission channel; To reflect the quality of the current data transmission channel, the higher the expected value, the better the quality.

According to the actual physical definition of $AVE(l)$, the transmission channel of current data structure may be blocked in some cases. If this part of transmission channel structure is treated as node algebra, its weight will increase. Therefore, the optimization function of distributed data structure is proposed:

$$F_{HJG} = R_j^i \times D_{lj}^i \times K(l) \qquad (2)$$

In the formula, R_j^i represents the effective path distribution rate between the current network transmission channel node i and node j, and D_{lj}^i represents the actual flow element in the current data structure matrix.

2.4 Network Information Storage

Design a cloud storage model to normalize network information storage for classified archived data [10]. The designed cloud storage model can be divided into four main parts by structure: user access layer, data service layer, data management layer and data storage layer, as shown in Fig. 1.

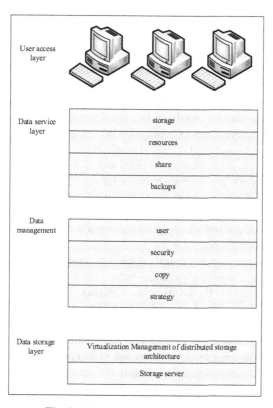

Fig. 1. Cloud storage model designed

The data storage layer is mainly responsible for the actual data storage management of cloud storage model. An excellent cloud storage model can provide users with different types of storage services, and all kinds of data will be uniformly stored in the cloud storage model, forming a huge data storage pool. Traditional data organization based on a single data storage server is not suitable for data storage under network conditions, and it has great limitations in network throughput and storage capacity. However, the data organization based on network architecture needs a huge number of nodes and complex coding algorithm to ensure the reliability of its data. In contrast, the data organization based on multi-storage servers can better meet the needs of online data storage services. When the number of users is large, the distributed data center can provide better data storage services for users [11]. The data storage layer of cloud storage model can connect different types of storage devices to form an organic whole, and realize the centralized and unified management of mass storage data. At the same time, the cloud storage model can monitor the running state of storage devices and dynamically expand storage capacity.

As the name implies, data management is mainly responsible for cloud storage model data management, including data copy strategy, data security access management and other operations. In a cloud storage model architecture, the data management layer provides a common management interface to the upper data services layer [12, 13]. Through user identity management, security access management, data copy management and data distribution policy management, the bottom layer of storage management can be seamlessly connected with the upper layer of storage application, and a large number of heterogeneous storage devices can work together to provide cloud storage users with better storage and management services.

The data service layer is responsible for service matching of user's storage task requests [14, 15]. The data service layer is a flexible part of the cloud storage model, which can provide different business application interfaces and services directly according to the user storage tasks [16, 17]. For example, data storage services, storage space rental services, multi-user data sharing services and data backup services.

The user access layer is the interface between the storage model and the user. Through the User Access Layer, any cloud storage service user can login to the cloud storage platform and use cloud storage service in any place using different network terminal devices according to the standard application interface provided by the cloud storage model [18].

According to the structure and characteristics of cloud storage model, the model can be divided into physical device virtualization, storage node virtualization and storage area network virtualization. By layering the virtualized storage resources, the cloud storage model greatly reduces the complexity of storage management, and makes the model more flexible and scalable. The cloud storage model only needs to add all storage devices to the storage resource pool to create virtual volumes for virtualization of storage resources. The cloud storage model is managed in a centralized manner and does not need to focus on the state of physical devices in the data center.

Using deduplication technology, cloud storage model can optimize the utilization of storage resources, and can save storage space by removing duplicate files or data blocks from storage model; on the other hand, data de-duplication technology can also help cloud storage model reduce data transfer, improve network throughput of storage model, and reduce resource consumption and network resource utilization cost.

3 Experimental Results

3.1 Experimental Design

In order to verify the performance of the designed normalized network information storage method based on deep reinforcement learning, a performance verification experiment was carried out on Hadoop-1.0.0. In the experimental environment, three racks (racks A, B and C) shall be set up, under each rack shall be placed five machine nodes, plus a name node, which is composed of 16 PCs, and the network topology thereof shall be shown in Fig. 2.

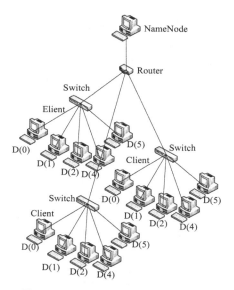

Fig. 2. Experimental network topology.

Among them, the first node D[0] under rack A is the client node, which does not store data, namely there are 14 data nodes in the experimental network cluster. Network communication between nodes uses the TCP/IP protocol, each node has 100M of Ethernet bandwidth. In order to accord with the heterogeneity of cluster environment in cloud storage service, 16 PCs in the cluster are configured to form a heterogeneous experimental environment, which makes the experimental results more authentic. The main configurations of the 17 PCs are shown in Table 3.

The operating system for all machines is Windows xp sp3, and VMware 7.0 is installed on all the machine nodes to emulate the Linux environment. The version of Linux in the virtual machine uses Ubuntu 10.04.

The average disk read and write speeds of the normalized network information storage method based on deep reinforcement learning were tested by HD _ Speed disk

Table 3. Main configurations of 17 PCs.

Group	Cluster node	Processor	Memory	Hard disk
	NameNode	Intel core i5 2.4 GHZ	4 GB	7200 RPM 500 GB
Rack A	Client	AMD P320 2.1 GHZ	2 GB	5400 RPM 320 GB
	D[1]	AMD Athlon64 X2 2.7 GHZ	2 GB	7200 RPM 500 GB
	D[2]	Intel E5200 2.5 GHZ	4 GB	7200 RPM 320 GB
	D[3]	Intel dual core 2 GHZ	1 GB	5400 RPM 320 GB
	D[4]	Intel dual core 1.8 GHZ	2 GB	5400 RPM 320 GB
Rack B	D[0]	Intel dual core 2 GHZ	2 GB	5400 RPM 320 GB
	D[1]	Intel dual core 2.16 GHZ	3 GB	5400 RPM 500 GB
	D[2]	ntel core i5 2.4 GHZ	4 GB	7200 RPM 500 GB
	D[3]	AMD Athlon64 X2 2.7 GHZ	2 GB	7200 RPM 500 GB
	D[4]	AMDLlano APU A6 3.4 GHZ	1 GB	7200 RPM 320 GB
Rack C	D[0]	Intel dual core 1.6 GHZ	1 GB	5400 RPM 320 GB
	D[1]	Intel dual core 2.16 GHZ	2 GB	5400 RPM 320 GB
	D[2]	Intel core i5 2.4 GHZ	4 GB	7200 RPM 500GB
	D[3]	Intel dual core 2.4 GHZ	2 GB	5400 RPM 320 GB
	D[4]	Intel dual core 2 GHZ	1 GB	5400 RPM 320 GB

performance testing tool. The standardized network information storage method based on deep reinforcement learning is proposed as follows:

Step1: Measure the stored information according to the current data information transmission channel, and set the output efficiency value D_j^i of each major source end of the transmission channel to the extreme of the current network traffic demand;

Step2: Update the current network transmission channel;

Step3: Import the updated network transmission channel into the substitute value, and bring in and calculate the current flow at the calculation end;

Step4: Update the source end to resolve the structure rate;

Step5: Standardize the network information storage method according to the structure rate.

3.2 Analysis of Results

When the amount of storage data is small, the experimental data of average disk read and write speed at each node of normalized network information storage method based on deep reinforcement learning is shown in Table 4.

When the storage volume is medium, the experimental data of the average disk read and write speed of each node of the normalized network information storage method based on deep reinforcement learning are shown in Table 5.

Table 4. Experimental data of average disk read and write speed at each node.

Group	Node	Average reading speed (MB/s)	Average write speed (MB/s)
Rack A	D[1]	50.2	40.3
	D[2]	55.6	42.3
	D[3]	54.5	46.1
	D[4]	56.3	41.0
Rack B	D[0]	54.2	46.8
	D[1]	59.3	45.6
	D[2]	54.2	44.5
	D[3]	57.2	49.5
	D[4]	54.0	44.5
Rack C	D[0]	57.2	41.3
	D[1]	58.0	45.3
	D[2]	57.6	48.2
	D[3]	59.3	49.3
	D[4]	57.0	44.2

Table 5. Experimental data of average disk read and write speed at each node.

Group	Node	Average reading speed (MB/s)	Average write speed (MB/s)
Rack A	D[1]	40.2	32.6
	D[2]	42.3	31.5
	D[3]	44.2	37.2
	D[4]	47.2	36.3
Rack B	D[0]	41.3	34.2
	D[1]	45.6	38.0
	D[2]	44.2	36.9
	D[3]	47.0	35.2
	D[4]	42.3	38.0
Rack C	D[0]	45.0	31.2
	D[1]	44.2	35.0
	D[2]	48.9	35.2
	D[3]	45.1	33.2
	D[4]	44.2	30.2

When there is a large amount of storage data, the experimental data of average disk read and write speed at each node of normalized network information storage method based on deep reinforcement learning are shown in Table 6.

Table 6. Experimental data of average disk read and write speed at each node.

Group	Node	Average reading speed (MB/s)	Average write speed (MB/s)
Rack A	D[1]	34.3	20.6
	D[2]	36.9	26.9
	D[3]	35.2	29.6
	D[4]	35.0	29.6
Rack B	D[0]	35.4	28.6
	D[1]	32.6	28.4
	D[2]	31.5	24.5
	D[3]	38.8	28.2
	D[4]	36.4	29.3
Rack C	D[0]	31.5	24.25
	D[1]	37.2	24.6
	D[2]	36.3	29.6
	D[3]	34.2	24.5
	D[4]	38.9	29.9

Experimental results show that the designed normalized network information storage method based on deep reinforcement learning has higher average read and write speed and can meet the use requirements.

4   Conclusions

With the continuous increase in the scale of information, the world created 1234EB of total information in 2011, of which 234EB data is closely related to personal lives of multimedia electronic information, personal information storage data has accounted for 70% of the total size of the digital world. According to IDC, worldwide data storage is growing at an annual rate of 58%. The normalized network information storage method based on deep reinforcement learning realizes high average disk read and write speed, which is of great significance to the normalized storage of network information.

References

1. Blancquaert, L., Everaert, I., Missinne, M., et al.: Effects of histidine and β-alanine supplementation on human muscle carnosine storage. Med. Sci. Sports Exerc. **49**(3), 602–609 (2018)

2. Chen, S., Wang, W., Xu, W., et al.: Plant diversity enhances productivity and soil carbon storage. Proc. Natl. Acad. U S A **115**(16), 4027–4032 (2018)
3. Wang, J., Zhang, W., Li, B., et al.: Effects of Fe Modified Na 2 WO 4 Additive on the Hydrogen Storage Properties of MgH 2. J. Wuhan Univ. Technol.-Mater. Sci. Ed. **34**(5),1030–1036 (2019)
4. Wu, J., Lu, C., Xu, X., et al.: Preparation of Cordierite-mullite Ceramics for Solar Thermal Storage **34**(5), 1062–1070 (2019)
5. Xu, X., Song, J., Wu, J., et al.: Preparation and thermal shock resistance of mullite and corundum Co-bonded SiC ceramics for solar thermal storage. **35**(1), 16–25 (2020)
6. Gentil, D.F.D.O., Ferreira, S.A.D.N., Rebouças, E.R.: Germination of Psidium friedrichsthalianum (O. Berg) Nied. seeds under different temperature and storage conditions. J. Seed Sci. **40**(3), 246–252 (2018)
7. Carvalho, M.L.M.D., Lopes, C.A., Ribeiro, A.M.P., et al.: Could packing and pelleting keep the quality of tobacco seeds during storage? J. Seed **40**(3), 296–303 (2018)
8. Liu, S., Bai, W., Zeng, N., et al.: A fast fractal based compression for MRI images. IEEE Access **7**(99), 62412–62420 (2019)
9. Pero, M., Askari, G., Skra, T., et al.: The change in the color of heat treated vacuum packed broccoli stem and floret during storage: effects of process conditions and modeling by ANN. J. Ence Food Agric. **98**(11), 4151–4159 (2018)
10. Guofang, X., Xinhua, W., Kaihong, W., et al.: Effects of 1-methylcyclopropene on texture properties of Rabbiteye blueberry during long-term storage and simulated transportation. Food. Technol **38**(2), 188–192 (2018)
11. Liu, S., Li, Z., Zhang, Y., et al.: Introduction of key problems in long-distance learning and training. Mobile Networks Appl. **24**(1), 1–4 (2019)
12. Fu, W., Liu, S., Srivastava, G.: Optimization of big data scheduling in social networks. Entropy **21**(9), 902 (2019)
13. Jung, J.T., Lee, J.K., Choi, Y.S., et al.: Effect of rice bran and wheat fibers on microbiological and physicochemical properties of fermented sausages during ripening and storage. Korean. J. Food, Anim. Resour. **38**(2), 302–314 (2018)
14. Ronghui, Y., Shuwei, Y., Yi, X., et al.: NetGO: Improving large-scale protein function prediction with massive network information. Nucleic Acids Res. **1**, 1–9 (2018)
15. Xue, K., Zhou, H., Meng, W., et al.: A Lightweight and Secure group key based handover authentication protocol for the software-defined space information network. IEEE Trans. Wireless Commun. **6**(99), 10–15 (2020)
16. Bai, L., De Cola, T., Yu, Q., et al.: Optimal dynamic multi-resource management in earth observation oriented space information networks. IEEE Wirel. Commun. **26**(2), 8–9 (2019)
17. Guo, S., Zhang, B., Yang, T., et al.: Multitask convolutional neural network with information fusion for bearing fault diagnosis and localization. IEEE Trans. Industr. Electron. **67**(9), 8005–8015 (2020)
18. Ghada, J., Rahim, K., et al.: An adaptive duty-cycle mechanism for energy efficient wireless sensor networks, based on information centric networking design. Wireless Networks **26**(2), 791–805 (2020)

Research on the Method of Eliminating Duplicated Encrypted Data in Cloud Storage Based on Generated Countermeasure Network

Lai-feng Tang[1]($\boxtimes$) and Qiang Wang[2]

[1] Xinjiang Institute of Technology, Aksu 843100, China
[2] School of Intelligence Technology, Geely University, Chengdu 641402, China

Abstract. In order to improve the efficiency of cloud storage and save network communication bandwidth, data De-duplication technology has been widely used. At the same time, data encryption brings new challenges to the De-duplication technology. Therefore, the method of data De-duplication based on cloud storage encryption of generative countermeasure network is proposed to get rid of the constraints of third-party servers. The popularity of user data is divided into two layers. The semantic security of non-popular data is ensured by double-layer encryption. The inner layer is convergence encryption and the outer layer is symmetry encryption. When data popularity changes, the cloud server just needs to remove the outer layer of encryption and store the convergent encryption results. The security analysis of the scheme is given, and the performance of the scheme is discussed by performance analysis and comparison. The simulation results show that the scheme is feasible and efficient.

Keywords: Generative countermeasure network · Cloud storage · Encrypted data · Data deduplication

1   Introduction

In order to protect data privacy, more and more users upload data to cloud server after encrypting. In the information age, the generation of massive data makes data storage a problem. Enterprises and individuals use cloud storage services to store data one after another. When users need to upload large amounts of data, it will cause huge delay, and there is a large amount of data redundancy on a global scale. In response to the current problem, researchers have proposed the data deduplication technology, which reduces data redundancy at the data block level or the file level to improve storage resources and network bandwidth utilization. Using this technology, for the same file, no matter how many users want to upload, if the file already exists in the server, all the file owners link to the file, the customer does not need to upload again.

A cloud storage based on emergent against networks encrypted data to the heavy method, its improved thought is: introducing a random number, ensure timely effectiveness of every file ownership certification process, even if the attacker intercepts ciphertext

W. Fu et al. (Eds.): ICMTEL 2021, LNICST 387, pp. 590–601, 2021.
https://doi.org/10.1007/978-3-030-82562-1_57

hash value, not a random number, also can't calculate the real-time and effective evidence, cannot pass file ownership certification, achieve the purpose of avoid replay attack [1]. The KP algorithm in ML scheme is used to extract the key from the original file instead of using the file itself as the encryption key. Therefore, the generative adversation network scheme not only improves the security, but also greatly reduces the amount of computation in the encryption and decryption process, enabling users to use cloud storage services more convenient and efficient [2]. Therefore, the purpose of this paper is to retain the original features of the scheme, repair the scheme, and make it more safe and efficient.

2 Cloud Storage Encrypted Data De-duplication Method

2.1 Cloud Storage Encryption Data Privacy Optimization

Considering the protection of user privacy information, this paper proposes a generative countermeasure protocol for De-duplication of anonymous encrypted data in a generative countermeasure network, which hides the communication between the network user and the cloud storage server by relying on the anonymous channel technology, and introduces digital certificates to ensure the normal access of data files in a generative countermeasure network [3]. The generative anti-network anonymous De-duplication model is shown in Fig. 1.

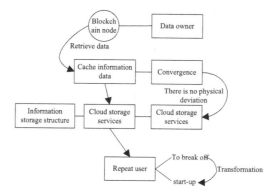

Fig. 1. Cloud storage encrypted data anonymous De-duplication model

Generative counterwork requires fast access to data files when using cloud storage servers against data owners and deduplication users in a network. The cloud storage server is responsible for securely storing user data files and is able to respond correctly to user requests. Trusted intermediaries are intended to enable anonymous channels, and all cloud storage server and user communications are forwarded through Trusted Intermediaries to hide user identity [4]. In order to ensure that the cloud storage server can correctly respond to the user's request for retrieving files, and at the same time can not get any information about the user, it is necessary for users to negotiate with each other to obtain a digital certificate between the generated counterwork network and the cloud storage server, so as to realize the efficient anonymous data file storage.

Asymmetric encryption of a generative counterwork network requires a combination of public and private keys, one for encryption and the other for decryption. Private keys are highly secure, so to be kept, public keys are generally public [5]. Asymmetric encryption is characterized by long time and slow speed of encryption and decryption, so it is only suitable for a very small amount of data encryption. Otherwise, the entire transmission process will be prolonged due to encryption speed. Expression of asymmetric encryption.

Ciphertext:

$$c = Enc_{publicKey} \times m \qquad (1)$$

In the formula, $Enc_{publicKey}$ represents the asymmetric encryption key.
Written:

$$m = Dec_{\text{private key}} \times c \qquad (2)$$

In the formula, $Dec_{\text{private key}}$ means to write the encryption key.
Symmetric key:

$$m_n = Dec_k \times c \qquad (3)$$

In the formula, Dec_k represents symmetric encryption key.
In a generative countermeasure network, two types of attackers are considered:

1) Internal attacker: refers to an opponent within the system, mainly refers to the cloud server. The cloud server is honest and inquisitive, allowing arbitrary access to the user data it stores.
2) "External attacker" refers to an opponent outside the system, mainly refers to an unauthorized user. Access by external adversaries to information about partially uploaded data through eavesdropping on public channels, the main purpose of which is to illegally obtain clear text information about user data stored on cloud servers

Generative countermeasure of encrypted data under the network to re-secure targets as follows:

1) Data privacy: The De-duplication scheme shall ensure the privacy of user data stored on the cloud server, including non-popular data and popular data. The cloud service should not get any clear text information about the user data it stores. Unauthorized users cannot get clear text information about the user data stored on the cloud service.
2) Data integrity: The De-duplication scheme shall ensure the integrity of user data stored on the cloud server. The scheme allows authorized users to verify the data integrity when downloading data.

Anonymous De-duplication schemes include the following steps: proof of full user ownership; encrypted data De-duplication; and user digital certificate negotiation [6]. In order to reduce the redundancy of the data file, the process of judging and proving the ownership of the data file must be carried out in clear text, and the trusted middleman must be introduced to hide the identity information of both sides [7]. At the same time, users can use digital certificates to retrieve files, ensure that only legitimate users can retrieve data, and hide the relationship between users and data. The De-duplication model of anonymous encrypted data is shown in Fig. 2.

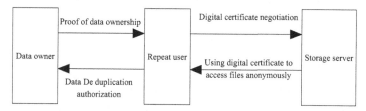

Fig. 2. Anonymous encrypted data De-duplication process

Suppose that the user in the generative countermeasure network encodes and prepro-cesses the data file and encodes the original file with erasure code. The bilinear mapping is used in the scheme. Assuming that the order of the curve filled in the massive data space is M, the S space range of the massive data set can be divided into $2^M \times 2^M$ grids, and each grid has four-dimensional spatial coding

$$M_0 = \left[\log_2 \frac{D_0}{H_1} \right] \tag{4}$$

In the formula: D_0 represents the total amount of data; H_1 represents the storage size of data block. Statistics coding data element information set K', assuming that the total number of data coding blocks is I, if the data block storage size H is greater than the maximum threshold percentage of massive data blocks, then the coding block should be divided into sample set k. Based on the linear filling curve aggregation characteristics of spatial four-dimensional Hilbert code, the massive data coding blocks are decomposed, and the corresponding storage sequence of each coding block H_2 is marked to form the corresponding spatial data partition matrix as follows:

$$F = \begin{vmatrix} H_{2de0} & H_{1a0} & s_0 \\ \cdots & \cdots & \cdots \\ H_{2den} & H_{1an} & s_n \end{vmatrix} \tag{5}$$

In the formula: H_{2den}, H_{1an}, s_n represents the spatial elements of massive data in the generative countermeasure network. According to this element, the corresponding spatial code and the corresponding mass data block storage label after matrix matching are obtained, so as to complete the division of massive data security elements, and optimize the privacy of cloud storage encrypted data according to different types of security elements.

2.2 Improved Solution Security Improvements

In the process of uploading and downloading files, attackers break the data privacy in two ways. Specifically, in file uploads, attackers use hash proof attacks to trick cloud storage servers into downloading private data [8]. In file access, an attacker accesses unauthorized de-reduplicate data. Finally, the loss of shared data blocks in the event of a device failure reduces system availability, meaning that a large number of referenced files are lost and data is unrecoverable. Table 1 shows the main security problems of data De-duplication in cloud storage system.

Table 1. Key security issues for data de-emphasis in cloud storage systems.

Safety objectives	Political attack or problem	Specific implementation
Confidentiality	Brute force attack	Comparison between generating ciphertext well by traversing plaintext set and stealing ciphertext
Privacy	Hash proof attack	Attackers use fingerprints to cheat the server and download private data
	Unauthorized access	An attacker attempts to access private data that does not belong to his/her own rights
Usability	Shared data loss	Device failure results in the loss of shared blocks, aggravating the unavailability of files

Based on Table 1, the security threats faced by internal and external attackers of data De-duplication cloud storage system in Generative countermeasure network are analyzed. In order to protect data confidentiality, users will use their own key to encrypt data and generate different ciphertexts, so duplicate data cannot be found [9]. Convergence encryption CE is used to support the De-duplication of ciphertext, where the key is the data hash value. However, there are brute force attacks on convergent encryption, especially on low entropy files. That is, if the attacker knows that the ciphertext C of the target file D is in a set of known size n, the attacker can recover D from the set S by offline encryption. For each element, D attacker uses convergence encryption to get ciphertext C, and obtains plaintext D data De-duplication compared with $C = C_1$. Cloud storage system is faced with device failure (for example, disk error), which will lead to shared data loss and data unavailability.

1) In the data deduplication cloud storage system, only one duplicate data block is kept, and in case of equipment failure and loss of shared data, multiple files will be unreadable.
2) Devices used in cloud storage systems (e.g. disks) are also at risk of mechanical failure, resulting in loss of data and interruption of system services.

The data de-reencryption method generates a key for each data block, so the key security and clutter degree are typical data de-reencryption key management algorithms.

The following is an introduction and analysis of typical key management methods and their problems, including single-key server, master key management and secret sharing, users losing control over the privacy data in the data de-cloud storage system and data sharing among users, so the problems of unauthorized access in the storage system are more serious. This paper summarizes the research status of three typical methods of data de-re-access control and analyzes their advantages and disadvantages, including proxy re-encryption, attribute encryption and key tree encryption.

Data storage security, i.e., content security, is similar to transmission security, which guarantees the security of all data passing through the network, while content security guarantees the security of the user's data after persistence. If the user's data is stored on the cloud storage side, and how to ensure that the cloud storage side is agnostic to the user's content, users are required to encrypt their data for storage [10]. Combining the high security of asymmetric encryption with the high efficiency of symmetric encryption, users generate symmetric keys to encrypt their own data files symmetrically, and then take symmetric keys as additional properties of data files to be protected by asymmetric encryption with their own public keys [11]. Finally, the symmetric keys of users and the encrypted data files are handed over to the cloud for management. Because the private keys of users are unknown, the cloud cannot decrypt the symmetric keys of users and thus cannot obtain the clear text information of user data files [12, 13]. Based on this, the network De-duplication data backup instructions are standardized, as shown in Table 2.

Table 2. Network redo data backup instruction.

Send De-duplication instruction	Network De-duplication data backup execution
AT*DSO	Send the backup instruction of network De-duplication data to modem and wait for receiving
ATE0	Network De-duplication data backup arrangement, received instruction sequence number
AT XS01	Set the network De-duplication data carrier signal, and modify the signal change parameters
AT*W*DO	Configure the implementation content of De-duplication network data backup, and store all data in the database

On the one hand, the security of data storage in the cloud depends on the encryption of the client to prevent the leakage of data files, on the other hand, it depends on the distributed storage system in the cloud, such as distributed file system and distributed protocol [14, 15]. In order to ensure the integrity of data files, the cloud also needs to do integrity check and necessary redundant backup. In the cloud storage environment, the data transmission efficiency can be improved by increasing the effectiveness control of data link communication. However, in the actual transmission process, the time limit of data link communication is limited, so it is necessary to constantly adjust the data link communication, change the data transmission integrity, and make statistics The communication time limit of fixed information data link t', the real-time transmission time t'_s of fixed information data link and the shortest transmission time of a certain data link with fixed information volume t'_{min}. The relationship among as, t', t'_s and t'_{min} is analyzed, as shown in Table 3.

Table 3. Cloud storage encrypted data reload scheme.

Relationship	De-duplication scheme		
$t'_s < t'$	No control measures to eliminate duplication		
$t'_{min} < t' < t'_s$	Changing the frequency of data transmission	Adjust transmission rate	Take anti-interference measures
$t' < t'_{min}$	Replace data link network		

According to the quantitative content of the above-mentioned security evaluation indexes, the security of different network information transmission is tested to obtain the maximum read, write and service permissions of the host. The vector of network security confidentiality is $A_z = (A_z(c))_n$, the vector of network security integrity is $A_v = (A_v(c))_n$, and the vector of network security availability is $A_t = (A_t(c))_n$. The positive ideal criterion of the evaluation index is: $A_0^+ = \{A_0^+(1), A_0^+(2), \cdots, A_0^+(n)\}$, which is used as the evaluation data to obtain the optimal evaluation results of each index; The negative ideal standard of evaluation index is: $A_0^- = \{A_0^-(1), A_0^-(2), \cdots, A_0^-(n)\}$, take this standard as the evaluation data, and then get the worst evaluation result of each index. Through the establishment of the standard, we can get the best and worst base point, and compare the distance between different evaluation values. Furthermore, the evaluation of data De-duplication security theory is described. The data De-duplication security theory is shown in Table 4.

Table 4. Data de-emphasis security specification.

Level	Explain
Extremely unsafe	The security guarantee ability of De-duplication data transmission is poor, and the security situation is severe
Unsafe	The security guarantee ability of De-duplication data transmission is limited, and there are security risks
Safe	The De-duplication data transmission has certain security guarantee ability, and the environment is basically safe
Very safe	De-duplication data transmission has a strong security capability, and the environment is very safe

Users encrypt their own data files to prevent the cloud storage server from misusing their sensitive data, and must ensure that the cloud storage server cannot get the contents of user files by any means. Users store files in the cloud storage server through anonymous channels and retrieve them through digital certificates. These operations can hide the user's identity information from the cloud storage server. Therefore, even if the cloud storage server and legitimate file owners attack, the encrypted files provided by the cloud storage server cannot provide any additional information. The trusted middleman is the proxy of the proxy reencryption protocol, so the communication information encrypted by the trusted middleman can not get the user file and key information. In this scheme, in order to reduce user information leakage, users need trustworthy intermediaries to hide identity information, and users can't authenticate directly. So trustworthy intermediaries in the system are a more powerful attacker.

2.3 Implementation of Cloud Storage Encrypted Data Deduplication

As one of the participants of the deduplication process, the cloud is mainly responsible for the deduplication of the information communication between the user and the verification service group, and the user's privacy between the user and the data holder can be amicably hidden by such third-party forwarding of the user's information. However, since the public key of the user and the user's information will be accessed by the cloud during the communication process, it may be assumed that the cloud server performs its own tasks according to the agreement, but it may not be reasonable for the cloud to obtain the user's data information through legitimate means based on the information already obtained, which is called "honest but curious". The security concerns require that the communication between users is invisible in the cloud, and the identity authentication of users is carried out by the cloud, and this forwarding mode has hidden man-in-the-middle attack. Convergent encryption is used to ensure the security of the information and the identity of the user based on the data owned by the user and the authenticator.

Data De-duplication can be divided into file level, block level and byte level; generally speaking, the smaller the granularity, the more duplicate data can be found, but the calculation cost is also higher. According to the range, data De-duplication can be divided into local and global De-duplication: local De-duplication can only occur in a single node and part of users, and its calculation and memory costs are less, but the less redundant data is found; global De-duplication can be achieved between multiple nodes and multiple users, which can obtain better compression ratio, but the computational and memory overhead is also higher. According to the time, data De-duplication can be divided into online and offline De-duplication; both online and offline De-duplication can reduce the storage overhead, and online De-duplication occurs before the data is written to the storage device, which may affect the performance of the system. According to the location, data De-duplication can be divided into target end and source side De-duplication. Target side De-duplication is called server side De-duplication, which can only reduce storage overhead. Source side De-duplication is also called client side De-duplication, which can not only reduce the storage cost of client, but also save transmission bandwidth. The data De reordering optimization is shown in Fig. 3.

Generally speaking, block level De-duplication can identify and eliminate more fine-grained redundancy, and the system throughput is high, so block level De-duplication is more widely used in storage systems. Data block is divided into fixed length block and content-based block; secondly, the calculation is to obtain the hash summary of the data block as the identifier; then index query uses the index based on locality and similarity to improve the retrieval speed. Finally, data management mainly includes

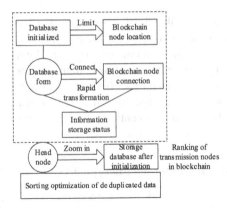

Fig. 3. Data de-sequencing optimization processing steps

container read-write and recovery performance. The storage layer is the bottom layer of cloud storage, which is composed of different storage devices and complex network devices. In addition, there is also a set of storage management system for centralized management, status monitoring, maintenance and upgrading of hardware equipment. In the environment of big data cloud storage, if the output rate of node is equal to the input rate, the output of node i data is determined by $i + 1$. According to the relationship between the input and output of nodes, the transmission control mode of single node is obtained, and the data De-duplication steps are optimized based on the above principles, as shown in Fig. 4.

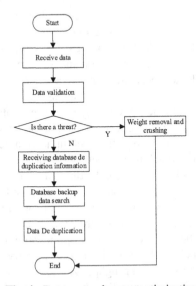

Fig. 4. Data removal restep optimization

In order to save the network bandwidth, this scheme only requires the initial uploader to upload the file data, and the subsequent uploader only needs to verify the file without uploading data. Moreover, this scheme has higher flexibility, if the user has higher security requirements, this scheme can be improved to server-side data deduplication with little cost, and can effectively resist side channel attack.

3 Analysis of Experimental Results

The experimental environment is set up as follows: fix the nodes on the 120 m × 120 m plane, the number of nodes is 80, and the running PC is configured as Pentium (R)4CPU2.40 GHz. The computing operation on the elliptic curve (prime order of the elliptic curve |p|=256bit) is implemented by using the open cryptography library Miracl, and the BLMLE scheme is simulated by using C++ language on the Windows10 operating system, VisualStudio2008, as well as the scheme in this paper. The experimental device's processor is InterCoreTMi5-7200U, the CPU is 2.50 GHz, and the memory is 8 GB. The HASH algorithm uses SHA-256 and the encryption key uses 256bit AES encryption. The experimental parameters are set as shown in Table 5.

Table 5. Experimental parameter settings.

Field	Type	Explain
ID	Short	Host identification
Name	Character string	Host name
Ip	Character string	IP address
YellowAlarm	Short	Warning value

The tests used synthetic and real data sets, respectively. The synthetic data set contains files populated with randomly generated content, and each file is divided into fixed-length data blocks. Fslhomes contains a mirror of the user's home folder, including source code, binaries, documents, and virtual machine images.

Because the label calculation of bl-mle needs to segment the ciphertext block and then perform S-TIMES exponential operation, the efficiency of bl-mle is very low. In the experimental environment, if $p = 256$, it takes $s = (2 \times 1024)/(256/8) = 64$ exponential operations to calculate the tags corresponding to 2 KB data blocks, 128 times for 4 KB blocks, and so on for other sizes.

As can be seen from the Table 6, the label computation overhead of the proposed scheme is much less than that of the BL-MLE scheme. This is because the hash operation is much faster than the exp calculation on the elliptic curve, although this scheme needs two more hash operations. So as the block size increases, the number of exp calculations increases, and the time gap between the two schemes becomes larger. For this project, the number of calculations is fixed, the increase in the size of data blocks will only bring about an increase in AES and hash overhead, and a 16 KB of hash or AES only needs about 1 ms, an exp calculation takes about 20 ms, so the calculation time of this project

Table 6. Computational overhead for generating block labels.

Method	Block size			
	2 KB	4 KB	8 KB	16 KB
BL-MLE method	1406	2496	5609	11154
The method of this paper	46	48	49	52

increases slightly with the increase of data blocks, which proves that this method has a relatively good effect in the actual application process, further compare the accuracy of the application of the two methods, and record, specifically, as shown in Fig. 5.

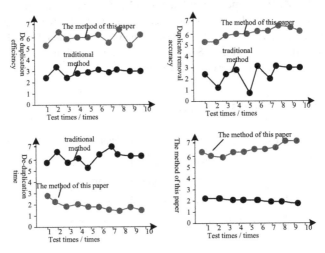

Fig. 5. Data reduplication efficiency comparison

According to the detection results in Fig. 5, the depth and accuracy of cloud storage encryption data De-duplication method based on generative adversary network proposed in this paper are obviously better than traditional methods in the actual application process, and the time consumption is relatively short. Therefore, it is confirmed that the cloud storage encryption data De-duplication method based on generative adversary network fully meets the research requirements.

4   Conclusions

In this paper, some shortcomings of existing cloud storage De-duplication schemes are improved, and a new De-duplication scheme is proposed. Compared with the original scheme, it not only saves the advantages of the original scheme, but also improves the computational efficiency of block label generation in client and block label comparison in cloud storage. At the same time, the file partition method of the new scheme is more flexible. Compared with the traditional scheme, this scheme has obvious advantages in computing efficiency, and is more suitable for the existing cloud storage system.

References

1. Cui, H., Deng, R.H., Li, Y.: Attribute-based cloud storage with secure provenance over encrypted data . Futur. Gener. Comput. Syst. **79**(2), 461–472 (2018)
2. Hu, C.: Calculation of the behavior utility of a network system: conception and principle. Engineering **4**(001), 78–84 (2018)
3. Feng, X., Su, X., Shen, J., et al.: Single space object image denoising and super-resolution reconstructing using deep convolutional networks. Remote Sens. **11**(16), 1910–1915 (2019)
4. Zhu, F.: Dynamic channel allocation method for emergency communication network in vehicle networking. J. Xi'an Polytechnic Univ. **033**(003), 296–301 (2019)
5. Zhang, J., Ou, P.: Privacy-preserving multi-receiver certificateless broadcast encryption scheme with de-duplication. Sensors **19**(15), 3370–3378 (2019)
6. Hochberg, G.K.A., Shepherd, D.A., Marklund, E.G., et al.: Structural principles that enable oligomeric small heat-shock protein paralogs to evolve distinct functions. Ence **359**(6378), 930–935 (2018)
7. Asgari, N., Ayoubi, S., Jafari, A., et al.: Incorporating environmental variables, remote and proximal sensing data for digital soil mapping of USDA soil great groups. Int. J. Remote Sens. **41**(19), 7624–7648 (2020)
8. Liu, S., Bai, W., Zeng, N., et al.: A fast fractal based compression for MRI images. IEEE Access **7**(99), 62412–62420 (2019)
9. Bandi, T., Justin, J., Rinesh, S., et al.: Efficient client-slide deduplication of encrypted data with public auditing cloud storage. Test Eng. Manage. **82**(1), 10425–10430 (2020)
10. Fu, W., Liu, S., Srivastava, G.: Optimization of big data scheduling in social networks. Entropy **21**(9), 902 (2019)
11. Chengetanai, G., Osunmakinde, I.O.: QUACS: routing data packets in ad hoc networks on buffer-constrained load balancing conditions during emergency rescue crisis. Wireless Pers. Commun. **99**(10), 1–31 (2018)
12. Liu, S., Li, Z., Zhang, Y., et al.: Introduction of key problems in long-distance learning and training. Mob. Networks Appl. **24**(1), 1–4 (2019)
13. Inayat-Hussain, S.H., Fukumura, M., Muiz Aziz, A., et al.: Prioritization of reproductive toxicants in unconventional oil and gas operations using a multi-country regulatory data-driven hazard assessment. Environ. Int. **117**(4), 348–358 (2018)
14. Simpson, S.L., et al.: A mixed-modeling framework for analyzing multitask whole-brain network data. Network Neurosci. **3**(2), 307–324 (2019)
15. Ramadhani, E.H., Kabetta, H., Amiruddin, A.: Exploration of the security of free data encryption applications for cloud storage. IOP Conference Series: Materials Science and Engineering **1007**(1), 12–18 (2020)

Author Index

Printed in the United States
by Baker & Taylor Publisher Services